CHRISTOPHER MARLOWE

Volume II

LONDON : HUMPHREY MILFORD
OXFORD UNIVERSITY PRESS

The Tragicall History of
CHRISTOPHER MARLOWE

VOLUME TWO

By *John Bakeless*

CAMBRIDGE · MASSACHUSETTS
HARVARD UNIVERSITY PRESS
1942

PR
2673
B2
V.2

PUBLISHED IN COÖPERATION WITH THE MODERN LANGUAGE ASSOCIATION
OF AMERICA, WITH THE ASSISTANCE OF A GRANT AWARDED BY
THE AMERICAN COUNCIL OF LEARNED SOCIETIES FROM
A FUND PROVIDED BY THE CARNEGIE CORPO-
RATION OF NEW YORK

English

47472

JUN 22 1944

PRINTED AT THE HARVARD UNIVERSITY PRINTING OFFICE
CAMBRIDGE, MASSACHUSETTS, U. S. A.

CONTENTS

VOLUME II

ILLUSTRATIONS

VOLUME II

CHRISTOPHER MARLOWE

EDWARD THE SECOND

Is it not passing braue to be a King?
I *Tamburlaine*, 758

ARLOWE DIED in his immaturity, still an experimenter. In his own plays — in that work which is undoubtedly his own, free from collaboration — he was still shifting uneasily from type to type: the exotic great man in *Tamburlaine*, the aspiring scholar in *Doctor Faustus*, the semi-topical Machiavellian villain in *The Jew of Malta*, English chronicle history in *Edward the Second*. All these, otherwise so diverse, were bound together by the mighty line and even more closely linked by the passionate touch of Marlowe himself, which no man can mistake for any other writer's. But the fiery stylist, the brilliant, powerful craftsman, the most finished technician of the decade was still groping for a firm hold on his art when the assassin's dagger ended everything in that mysterious stabbing affray at Deptford.

Though he was the leading playwright of his day, Marlowe had not yet quite caught his stride. He used a form once — and dropped it. He did not produce a series of classical plays, all in the same style, like Lyly, who preceded him; nor pour out comedy upon comedy, history upon history, tragedy upon tragedy, like his pupil from Stratford, who succeeded him. Nor did he live long enough to go over his earlier handiwork, as Shakespeare did, retouching rough portraiture like Silvia in *Two Gentlemen of Verona* into the deft character painting of Viola in *Twelfth Night*.

Marlowe's reputation rests wholly on the work of his 'prentice hand. He lived to do no other; and what he did, he did almost without models. He was making straight the path — or at least developing a technique — for a greater than himself. Nothing sets the sheer genius of the man so far beyond cavil or dispute as the way in which his plays, one by one, — each in its own separate and unrepeated genre, — are caught up and the formula of each developed by other hands, so that *Tamburlaine* is followed by *Alphonsus of Aragon*, *Doctor Faustus* by *Friar Bacon and Friar Bungay*, while *The Jew of Malta* appears presently as *The Merchant of Venice*.

In *Edward the Second* Marlowe made his only known attempt — except, very doubtfully, as a collaborator with others — to base a play upon English history. Yet the influence of this solitary endeavor appears unmistakably in one after another of Shakespeare's earlier historical plays — most notably of all in *Richard II*.

The play's close-knit unity of structure, unique in Marlowe's writing for the stage, is due to the fact that Marlowe had now learned to carry further the trick that he had introduced in *Tamburlaine* — building his whole play about one central figure, made to seem at once masterfully dominating and humanly appealing. In *Edward the Second* one figure, Young Mortimer, is made masterfully dominating, and another, the weak King Edward, is made humanly appealing. They clash, and to their clash everything else in the play is related. This selection from history of its most human incidents and due subordination of all others gives the play form; and this close-knit structure is instantly copied by other playwrights, not always very skilfully, until it slowly drives out the sprawling, formless chronicle plays of an earlier day, in which event succeeds event with no more relation than exists in beads upon a string.

Edward the Second is so highly finished, its characterization so knowingly wrought, the early exuberance of Marlowe's bombast so rigidly suppressed, that it plainly belongs to the last years of his life, when some six years' experience of the playhouse had taught him his craft.

DATE

All critics are generally agreed that this is the maturest of Marlowe's plays and — except, perhaps, the too frequently tedious *Massacre at Paris* — the latest. The matter of the date is one of the irritating questions, so abundant where Marlowe is concerned, about which there is very little dispute but not much evidence. The first definite ground for assigning a date is found in the *Stationers' Register*, in which, on July 6, 1593, the bookseller, William Jones, enters "A booke. Intituled *The troublesom Reign and Lamentable Death of EDWARD the SECOND, king of England, with the tragicall fall of proud MORTYMER.*" On the other hand, the title page of the quarto of 1594, the earliest that is definitely known to have been published, asserts — in agreement with succeeding quartos — that the play has already been "sondry times publiquely acted in the honorable Cittie of London, By the right honorable the Earle of Pembroke his Seruants." As Elizabethan players did not willingly let their plays get into print until they had grown stale upon the boards, *Edward the Second*, whether first printed in 1593 or 1594, had certainly been written many months before Jones entered it on the *Register*.

It is true that plays were sometimes pirated. In such cases, however, the text was either taken stenographically or a single part was bought from an actor and the gaps filled in. The text of all the quartos of *Edward the Second* is far too good to admit of such an hypothesis.

Marlowe, then, must have been working on the play in 1591 and was very likely still writing the last act during the early months of 1592. Pembroke's company had probably kept the play in production until it would no longer fill the house — a matter of a week or two, for London was a small city and many of the burghers held it a sin to enter a playhouse at all. This would bring us toward the end of 1592. The fact that the title page names Pembroke's Company as the actors is of aid in fixing the date. The company is mentioned in 1575/6 but is not heard of again until December 27, 1592, when it is playing at court.[1] Various authorities date the play between 1590 and 1592, and the more recent authorities tend to place the date of composition either in 1591 or 1592.[2]

[1] John Tucker Murray: *English Dramatic Companies*, I. 59. Supposed allusions to Pembroke's men between 1576 and 1592 seem to have been misinterpreted.

[2] The following dates have been suggested:

1781. Warton: "Written in the year 1590." [*Hist. Eng. Poetry*, III. 348]
1831. Collier: No specific opinion but regards it as late work.
1850. Dyce: Quotes Warton, who "may have made the assertion on sufficient grounds." [I. xxii]
1885. Bullen: "We can hardly assign an earlier date than 1590." [I. xliii]
1899. Ward: "1590-91." [HEDL, I. 347]

TEXT

The existence of four surviving quartos, dated 1594, 1598, 1612, 1622, testifies to steady reading among the discriminating rather than to any great popularity, for a published play, if it caught London's fancy, might run through nine or ten editions.

It is likely, however, that a still earlier edition once existed, brought out by Jones in 1593 as soon as possible after entering his newly acquired manuscript on the *Register*. All that we know of the lost edition is preserved in a manuscript now reposing in the Dyce Collection at the Victoria and Albert Museum. This reproduces a title page dated 1593 and the first seventy lines of text. The manuscript leaves have been inserted in a copy of the 1598 edition, the text of which is easily recognized, in place of the missing title page and first leaf.

The lady who owned the book and who may have inserted the manuscript pages — or caused them to be inserted — has even been thoughtful enough to tell posterity about herself on the reverse of the title page; and thus we know that this is "Mary Clarke her Book and Writting. October the third One Thousand Seven Hundred and Fifty One."

It has been supposed that Mary Clarke herself copied the manuscript found in her book, but examination shows the handwritings to be entirely different. Charlton and Waller are probably right in believing that Mary Clarke's "writting" includes only the lines just quoted, and that "the hand of the copy itself

1902. Albert Probst: "Die genaue Abfassungszeit dieses Dramas ist unbekannt, jedenfalls aber gehört es den letzten Lebensjahren Marlowe's (1564-1593) an." [*Samuel Daniel's "Civil Warres" und Michael Drayton's "Barons Wars*," p. 84]
1904. Ingram: "Marlowe's last work." [p. 114]
1910. Tucker Brooke: "Generally agreed to be the maturest and, with the possible exception of the *Massacre at Paris*, the latest of Marlowe's plays." [*Works*, p. 307]
1922. Tucker Brooke: "The latter part of 1591 and the year 1592." [PMLA 37: 376 (1922)]
1923. Chambers: "Winter of 1592-3 . . . probably." [*Eliz. Stage*, III. 425]
1927. Ellis-Fermor: "Belongs probably to the year 1591, or to the spring of 1591-2." [*Christopher Marlowe*, p. 6]
1931. Robertson: "Penned and staged before *Doctor Faustus*. . . . Since, then, *Faustus* was admittedly played in 1588, *Edward II* presumably also belongs to that year, if not to 1587, in its first form." [*Marlowe*, p. 34]
1933. Charlton and Waller: "*Edward II* (1591) for Pembroke's 1592." [p. 25]
1936. Rupert Taylor: "Cannot have been produced later than 1589." [PMLA, 51: 653 (1936)]

is at least a hundred years earlier in date." [3] The manuscript pages may even have been written toward the end of the sixteenth century. The scribe, who may have been a professional penman, writes an exquisitely careful Italian hand. Certain of his mistakes, notably *este* for *dart*,[4] suggest that he may have been copying from a manuscript in the older English handwriting; but in that case it is hard to account for the name of William Jones as publisher on the title page, which would certainly not have appeared in an original manuscript.

Mary Clarke — was she Miss or Mrs.? — proclaims her ownership clearly enough, but who Mary Clarke may have been or from what edition her copy was made — a matter of much greater importance — there is now no means of learning. It is easy enough to assume that the unknown scribe made a mistake in copying the title page; and that, while filling in a damaged 1598 quarto from another copy of the same edition, he inadvertently wrote a figure 3 for a figure 8. All Marlowe's editors prior to Tucker Brooke either ignore the manuscript entirely, or else fall into this blunder. But, obvious though it is, the hypothesis is untenable. The manuscript cannot be copied from either the 1598, 1612, or 1622 editions, because it varies too markedly from the text they give. It omits, for example, a full half of the subtitle and alters a portion of what it does print. It bears a somewhat closer relation to the 1594 quarto, with which it is in pretty general textual agreement; but even here the agreement is not close enough to warrant any assumption of identity.

In short, we may insult the memory of Mary Clarke by thinking her copyist the most careless that ever existed, and still find it hard to believe that she could possibly crowd fifteen textual variations into seventy lines of manuscript, make 1594 into 1593, and transform "Chri. Marlow" on the 1594 title page into "Chri: Mar:" in the copy. Such an abbreviation of a proper name was common enough among the Elizabethans; it would have been thought odd in the eighteenth century, when Mary Clarke lived; and even if the manuscript itself dates from the latter sixteenth century, there seems to have been no particular reason for the scribe to make such a change.

[3] Charlton and Waller's ed. (1933), p. 4.   [4] Line 41.

It is more reasonable to suppose that there was still another quarto which Jones, who entered the book in the *Stationers' Register* in July, 1593, a month after Marlowe's death — hurried into print to catch the fancy of a public which was still aghast at the suddenness and violence of Marlowe's tragic taking-off. On a forgotten shelf, or hidden in the dusty closet of some English country estate, or, it may be, in some Continental library, a copy may even now be lying.[5]

There is the more reason to hope so, because even the 1594 quarto was lost and had been quite forgotten until Rudolf Genée discovered a copy in the Landesbibliothek at Kassel, about 1876; after which a second copy was found in the municipal library at Zurich. The other three early editions had long been familiar — probably they had never, since they were first printed, quite dropped out of the knowledge of those who care about such things. The quarto of 1622 was printed after a revival of the play, now grown a bit antiquated and distinctly out of fashion, "by the late Queenes Maiesties Servantes at the Red Bull in S. Johns streete." There had at least been interest enough to justify another production.

SOURCES

It is in general pretty well understood where Marlowe found the materials for *Edward the Second.* Though *Fabyan's Chronicle* was at one time regarded as the sole source, it is now admitted by all scholars that *Holinshed's Chronicle* — that well-worked quarry to which so many later Elizabethan dramatists turned for their rough stone — furnished Marlowe with most of the foundation for his play. But Marlowe, following his usual custom, browses about in quest of the fullest possible information from other sources which may afford him a vivid bit of material here and there. Eventually he adopts the mocking ditty of the Scots in their moment of triumph over Edward, from *Fabyan's Chronicle*, and takes the scene in which his jailers subject the captive king to the indignity of being shaved in puddle water from the *Chronicle* of Thomas de la Moor, or More.

Most of this he probably remembered from his student days

5 See Tucker Brooke in MLN, 24: 71–73 (1909); *Magazin f. d. Lit. des Auslandes,* no. 50, p. 723, 9 D 1876.

at Cambridge. Corpus Christi had received a copy of Holinshed as a gift from Henry Clifford, a former fellow; and an inscription on the title page indicates that the gift was made in 1587, the very year of Marlowe's second degree. A manuscript excerpt from De la Moor's *Chronicle*, dealing only with Edward II, was a part of Archbishop Parker's bequest of books,[6] which had been willed to the college only a few years before the lad from Canterbury matriculated. Other possible sources were available to him, but he seems to have made no use of them.

Making allowances for the variations, condensations, and excisions which the dramatist's art demanded and which the public of that day was fully prepared to accept, it is possible to read through Holinshed and find here a paragraph, there a single sentence, upon whose dramatic possibilities Marlowe's quick eye instantly lighted; and then to turn to whole scenes which he has developed from the merest hints in his original. One might think, to be sure, that all this is a mere following of historical facts, which were to be gleaned from any one of a dozen sources, were it not for the appearance in the play of details that are given by Holinshed alone among the chroniclers, as well as telltale reminiscences of Holinshed's phraseology, which, reappearing in the play, point inevitably to his chronicle alone as the undoubted main source.

The dramatist's debt to Holinshed appears at once with the opening scene of the play, where Gaveston, returning from exile, soliloquizes:

> I must haue wanton Poets, pleasant wits,
> Musitians, that with touching of a string
> May draw the pliant king which way I please:
> Musicke and poetrie is his delight,
> Therefore ile haue Italian maskes by night,
> Sweete speeches, comedies, and pleasing showes,
> And in the day when he shall walke abroad,
> Like *Syluan* Nimphes my pages shall be clad.[7]

This is simply a poetic transcript of a passage in Holinshed:

The foresaid Peers, who (as it may be thought, he had sworne to make the king to forget himselfe, and the state, to the which he was called)

---

[6] On the Holinshed, see the MS. list of books numbered 490 in M. R. James's list of the MSS. in the Corpus Christi Library. On De la Moor, see II. 22–23 n.　　[7] I.i. 51–58.

furnished his court with companies of iesters, ruffians, flattering para-
sites, musicians, and other vile and naughtie ribalds, that the king
might spend *both daies and nights* in iesting, plaieng, banketing, and
in such other filthie and dishonorable exercises.[8]

Actually, Marlowe has introduced an anachronism here,
though no contemporary, and few modern, spectators of the
play would detect it. Holinshed is describing the royal revelry
of the fourteenth century; whereas Marlowe, with one eye upon
the groundlings in the pit, who must have been quite as avid
for details of the goings-on in high life as the gum-chewing readers of tabloid newspapers in the twentieth century, quietly inserts descriptions of Her Majesty's Revels as they existed in
his own time.

A few lines further on, Marlowe makes free with his sources
again, this time in order to let his audience see the conflict between his two protagonists — the King and his rebellious subject, Young Mortimer — beginning as early in the play as
possible. Holinshed says that Edward I charged the earls of
Lincoln, Warwick, and Pembroke "to foresee that the aforesaid
Peers returned not againe to England least by his euill example
he might induce his sonne the prince to lewdnesse, as before he
had alreadie doone." This took place while Edward II was still
Prince of Wales, and the episode is therefore not actually presented on the stage. Marlowe, however, makes the fiery Young
Mortimer declare:

> Mine vnckle heere, this Earle, & I my selfe,
> Were sworne to your father at his death,
> That he should nere returne into the realme.[9]

"This earl," whom the actor's gesture would indicate, was
presumably Warwick. None of the other earls whom Holinshed
mentions is on the stage in this scene.

There is another echo of Holinshed in Lancaster's boast to
the King:

> Foure Earldomes haue I besides Lancaster,
> Darbie, Salsburie, Lincolne, Leicester.

[8] Ll. 51–58; Holinshed (ed. 1586), III. 318; (ed. 1807), II. 547.
[9] Ll. 82–84; Holinshed (ed. 1586), III. 320; (ed. 1807), II. 551.

This is nothing more than Holinshed versified, with the order
of the earldoms changed to fit the meter:

> He was possessed of fiue earledomes, Lancaster,
> Lincolne, Salisburie, Leicester, and Derbie.[10]

It is clear that Marlowe is here using Holinshed, and none of
the other chroniclers, for Stow, Walsingham, and Capgrave all
give different lists of the earl's possessions. Comparison with
the other chroniclers presently shows another passage in which
Holinshed's account, again differing from the other chroniclers,
is incorporated in the play. Marlowe's king says to Gaveston:

> I heere create thee Lord high Chamberlaine,
> Cheefe Secretarie to the state and me,
> Earle of Cornewall, king and lord of Man.

This follows Holinshed closely:

For hauing reuoked againe into England his old mate the said Peers
de Gaueston, he receiued him into most high fauour, creating him
earle of Cornewall, and lord of Man, his principall secretarie, and lord
chamberlaine of the realme.[11]

The other chroniclers differ both from Holinshed and from the
play.

The arrest of the Bishop of Coventry is also recounted in the
play almost exactly as in Holinshed, except that the *Chronicle*
says "his lands and tenements were seized to the kings vse, but
his mooueables were giuen to the foresaid Peers," [12] whereas
Marlowe's Edward authorizes the favorite to "take possession
of his house and goods." [13] But at this point Marlowe was probably thinking of *Fabyan's Chronicle*, for where Holinshed says
merely that the Bishop was sent "to prison," Fabyan says
specifically "unto the toure of London." This is echoed by
Marlowe's line: "Tis true, the Bishop is in the tower." [14]

The indignant meeting of the peers contains one unmistakable borrowing from Holinshed, who alone of the chroniclers
mentions the New Temple as the scene. Marlowe repeats this
in dialogue:

[10] Ll. 102–103; Holinshed (ed. 1586), III. 331; (ed. 1807), II. 569.
[11] Ll. 154–156; Holinshed (1586), III. 318; (ed. 1807), II. 547.
[12] Holinshed (ed. 1586), III. 319; (ed. 1807), II. 546–547.
[13] Ll. 202–203.   [14] Line 208.

Warwick.   But say my lord, where shall this meeting bee?
Bishop.   At the new temple.[15]

Holinshed declares that the peers

assembled togither in the parlement time, *at the new temple*, on satur-
daie next before the feast of saint Dunstan, and there ordeined that
the said Peers should abiure the realme, and depart the same on the
morrow after the Natiuitie of saint Iohn Baptist at the furthest, and
not to returne into the same againe at any time then after to come.
To this ordinance the king (although against his will) bicause he saw
himselfe and the realme in danger, gaue his consent.[16]

The king's determination to have revenge, his gifts to the
departing favorite, Gaveston's appointment to be governor of
Ireland, were all probably taken from Holinshed, though they
might easily have been taken from either Fabyan or Stow. The
reasons for which the nobles, in the play, eventually permit
Gaveston's return to England are in the main from Holinshed,
who states them at greater length than most other chroniclers.
After Gaveston's exile, says Holinshed:

The lords perceiuing the kings affection, and that the treasure was
spent as lauishlie as before, thought with themselues that it might be
that the king would both amend his passed trade of life, and that
Peers being restored home, would rather aduise him thereto, than follow
his old maners, considering that it might be well perceiued, that if he
continued in the incouraging of the king to lewdnesse, as in times past
he had doone, he could not thinke but that the lords would be readie
to correct him, as by proofe he had now tried their meanings to be no
lesse. Herevpon to reteine amitie, as was thought on both sides,
Peers by consent of the lords was restored home againe (the king
meeting him at Chester) to his great comfort and reioising for the
time, although the malice of the lords was such, that such ioy lasted
not long.

All this Marlowe somewhat freely interprets into Mortimer's
speech beginning:

> Know you not *Gaueston* hath store of golde,
> Which may in Ireland purchase him such friends,
> As he will front the mightiest of vs all,
> And whereas he shall liue and be beloude,
> Tis hard for vs to worke his ouerthrow. . . .

[15] Ll. 281–282.
[16] Holinshed (ed. 1586), III. 319; (ed. 1807), II. 549.

But were he here, detested as he is,
How easilie might some base slaue be subbornd,
To greet his lordship with a poniard. . . .
Nay more, when he shall know it lies in vs,
To banish him, and then to call him home,
Twill make him vaile the topflag of his pride,
And feare to offend the meanest noble man.[17]

It was a stroke of genius for Marlowe to make the Queen the initiator of Gaveston's recall, thus making her a sympathetic figure to the audience, by demonstrating her wifely forgiveness and her love for King Edward at the beginning of the play, and yet suggesting even thus early the influence which she is beginning to exercise over Young Mortimer. The dramatist's device of having her whisper her arguments to him — not so threadbare then as it has since become — heightens the suggestion of growing intimacy, and saves the necessity of boring the audience with twice hearing of the same arguments, once on the Queen's lips as she persuades Mortimer and again on Mortimer's lips as he reiterates them to the nobles.

The marriage of Gaveston to the Earl of Gloucester's heir, the acquaintance of Baldock and Young Spenser, and Young Spenser's succession to Gaveston as Chamberlain, are all borrowed from Holinshed; but there is a ruthless compression — always a necessity in historical drama — in introducing the Spensers so early in King Edward's reign. Actually, they came much later.

The Queen's effort to mediate between her husband and his rebellious barons:

Sweete husband be content, they all loue you,[18]

harks back to Holinshed's casual observation that "the queene had euer sought to procure peace, loue and concord betwixt the king and his lords." This also justifies Marlowe in making the Queen intercede with the lords on Gaveston's behalf a little earlier in the play.

Gaveston's insolent demeanor toward his persecutors, whom he greets on the stage as "base leaden Earles," finds warrant in Holinshed's observation:

[17] Ll. 555 ff.; Holinshed (ed. 1586), III. 320; (ed. 1807), II. 549–550.
[18] Line 838.

After that the earle of Cornewall was returned into England, he shewed himselfe no changeling . . . but through support of the kings fauour, bare himselfe so high in his doings, which were without all good order, that he seemed to disdaine all the peeres & barons of the realme.[19]

Another passage is even more specific as to the details of Gaveston's behavior toward the lords:

He being nothing at all amended of those his euill manners, rather demeaned himselfe woorse than before he had doone, namelie towards the lords, against whom vsing reprochfull speech, he called the earle of Gloucester bastard, the earle of Lincolne latlie deceased bursten bellie, the earle of Warwike the blacke hound of Arderne, and the earle of Lancaster churle.[20]

It is characteristic of Marlowe that he misses the comic possibilities of these dazzling bits of billingsgate, which would have delighted the far from squeamish taste of his audiences; but perhaps this neglect is partly accounted for by the dramatic necessity he was under of making the King's incredible devotion to his favorite as credible as it could be made, by keeping Gaveston in as sympathetic a light as possible. If this was to be done, Gaveston could hardly be allowed vulgar abuse of distinguished figures in English history.

Old Mortimer's fierce reproach to the King:

> When wert thou in the field with banner spred?
> But once, and then thy souldiers marcht like players,
> With garish robes, not armor, and thy selfe
> Bedaubd with golde, rode laughing at the rest,[21]

is straight from Holinshed, except for the comparison with strolling players, which gives an interesting glimpse of the gay costumes that Elizabethan actors, like their modern fellows, affected. There may have been in Marlowe's mind, also, the picture of Alleyn and his company wandering in the provinces when the plague drove them out of London. The *Chronicle* says that Edward went on this Scottish campaign

with a mightie armie brauelie furnished, and gorgiouslie apparelled, more seemelie for a triumph, than meet to incounter with the cruell enimie in the field.

[19] Holinshed (ed. 1586), III. 320; (ed. 1807), II. 550.
[20] Holinshed (ed. 1586), III. 321; (ed. 1807), II. 551.
[21] Ll. 984–987; Holinshed (1586), III. 321; (ed. 1807), II. 551.

Marlowe has also borrowed, and only slightly altered, the triumphant ditty of the victorious Scots. This is not in Holinshed, but Fabyan gives it as follows:

> Maydens of Englonde, sore maye ye morne,
> For your lemmans ye haue loste at Bannockisborne,
>   With a heue a lowe.
> What wenyth the kynge of Englonde,
> So soone to haue wonne Scotlande
>   With rumbylowe.

This appears in the play, somewhat pruned of its broad Scotch, as:

> Maids of England, sore may you moorne,
> For your lemmons you haue lost at Bannocks borne,
>   With a heaue and a ho.
> What weeneth the king of England,
> So soone to haue woone Scotland,
>   With a rombelow.[22]

There is a telltale verbal echo of Holinshed in the dramatist's account of how Edward, defeated, bids his followers:

> *Take shipping* and away to Scarborough.[23]

The facts differ, however, for Holinshed declares that it was Edward himself who "leauing the queene behind him, *tooke shipping*, and sailed from thence with his dearelie belooued familiar the earle of Cornewall, vnto Scarbourgh."

Holinshed describes the pursuit by the barons in much the same terms as Marlowe, and two more verbal echoes follow almost at once. When the King beseeches his rebellious barons for a last interview with his captured and condemned favorite, he sends word in the play that

> He will but *talke with him* and send him backe,

— a mere variation of Holinshed's statement that Gaveston surrendered "requiring no other condition, but that he might come to the kings presence to *talke with him*." [24]

[22] Holinshed (ed. 1586), III. 322; (ed. 1807), II. 555; Robert Fabyan: *New Chronicles of England and France* (ed. 1811), p. 420; *Edward the Second*, 992–997.
[23] Line 1102; Holinshed (ed. 1586), III. 321; (ed. 1807), II. 551.
[24] Line 1230; Holinshed (ed. 1586), III. 321; (ed. 1807), II. 551.

Making Arundell the bearer of the royal message is Marlowe's own idea, but he draws on Holinshed again for Pembroke's offer:

> I will vpon mine honor vndertake
> To carrie him, and bring him back againe.

Holinshed tells how

The earle of Penbroke persuaded with the barons to grant to the kings desire, vndertaking vpon forfeiture of all that he had, to bring him to the king and backe againe to them, in such state and condition as he receiued him. When the barons had consented to his motion, he tooke the earle of Cornewall with him to bring him where the king laie, and comming to Dedington, left him there in safe keeping with his seruants, whilest he for one night went to visit his wife, lieng *not farre from thence*.[25]

Here is another verbal echo, for in the play Pembroke says to Gaveston:

> My house is *not farre hence*, out of the way
> A little, but our men shall go along.
> We that haue prettie wenches to our wiues,
> Sir, must not come so neare and balke their lips.[26]

The capture and execution of Gaveston reappear in the play precisely as described by Holinshed:

The same night it chanced, that Guie erle of Warwicke came to the verie place where the erle of Cornwall was left, and taking him from his keepers, brought him vnto Warwike, where incontinentlie it was thought best to put him to death.[27]

Marlowe builds up a whole scene upon this paragraph.

It needs no source to justify the dramatist in depicting a furious outburst of wrath by the king, after his favorite had been thus summarily done to death. Marlowe had, nevertheless, full authority in Holinshed, who naïvely observes that:

When the king had knowledge hereof, he was woonderfullie displeased with those lords that had thus put the said earle vnto death, making his vow that he would see his death reuenged.

[25] Line 1250; Holinshed (ed. 1586), III. 321; (ed. 1807), II. 551.
[26] Ll. 1274–1277.
[27] Holinshed (ed. 1586), III. 321; (ed. 1807), II. 551.

This gave Marlowe excuse for a fine bit of bombastic rant in the old style of his *Tamburlaine* days which, as his art matured, he had so nearly left behind. Only occasionally in the later plays do we find such traces of it as King Edward's vow of revenge:

> By earth, the common mother of vs all,
> By heauen, and all the moouing orbes thereof,
> By this right hand, and by my fathers sword,
> And all the honors longing to my crowne,
> I will haue heads, and liues for him as many
> As I haue manors, castels, townes, and towers.
> Tretcherous *Warwicke*, traiterous *Mortimer*:
> If I be Englands king, in lakes of gore
> Your headles trunkes, your bodies will I traile,
> That you may drinke your fill, and quaffe in bloud.[28]

It was just the kind of passage that a robust actor of commanding presence like Alleyn, who had played Tamburlaine with much success, could "get his teeth into." Likely enough, though this is pure conjecture, it was written for that very purpose. Such passages had been a huge success in *Tamburlaine*, and they must still have delighted the groundlings and the less sophisticated of the nobles. Marlowe either inserts this purple passage deliberately or drops back unconsciously into his earlier manner.

There is an obvious reason for the anachronism whereby Marlowe has King Edward instantly adopt the younger Spenser as his new favorite, *vice* Gaveston, deceased, in defiance of the historical fact that neither Spenser was especially close to the King until five or six years after Gaveston was dead. The reason is the time problem, with which a dramatist must always wrestle when he seeks to compress history, which is at shortest a matter of years, into the traffic of the stage, which at its utmost Elizabethan prolixity is a matter of hours.

Marlowe, pondering over the strictly historical material at his disposal, is struck by the fact that two disputes with the barons — both due to the rapid rise of the King's favorites — mark the reign, though otherwise the chronicles are a confused jumble of unrelated events. Here is what he has been seeking —

---

[28] Ll. 1437–1446; Holinshed (ed. 1586), III. 321; (ed. 1807), II. 552.

a mainspring for his play. Discarding all else as irrelevant, he concentrates on Gaveston and the Spensers; and to avoid a yawning gulf of years in the middle of his tragedy, he makes the Spensers the immediate instead of the remote successors of Gaveston. He links them up still more closely by inventing a wholly apocryphal relation between the King's favorites. Gaveston had married the daughter of Gloucester. Marlowe fictitiously declares that Spenser had been Gloucester's servant, and thus brings him more closely into the story.

Except for these liberties with historical fact, the circumstances of the Spensers' rise and Edward's fall are set forth with the same strict adherence to Holinshed's narrative that appears in the earlier part of the play. The younger Spenser's first offense against the nobles is nothing more heinous than worsting them, with royal aid, in a quite commonplace transaction in real estate, an episode which Marlowe versifies thus:

> Because we heare Lord *Bruse* dooth sell his land,
> And that the *Mortimers* are *in hand* withall,
> Thou shalt haue crownes of vs, t'outbid the Barons,
> And *Spenser*, spare them not, but lay it on.

Holinshed, after telling how Bruce offered lands to the Earl of Hereford and the Mortimers, recounts this episode prosaically enough:

At length (as vnhap would) Hugh Spenser the yoonger lord chamberleine, coueting that land . . . found such means through the kings furtherance and helpe, that he went awaie with the purchase, to the great displeasure of the other lords that had beene *in hand* to buie it.[29]

Here, again, Marlowe catches up and echoes a phrase — "in hand" — from his original.

Marlowe treats the King's difficulties with France in much the same way as Holinshed, except that the play names Normandy as the province in dispute because the English king had not done homage for it, while Holinshed names Guienne. The sending of the Queen and the Prince to intercede with the French king is developed from the chronicler's remark that "finallie it was thought good, that the queene shuld go ouer to hir brother the French king"; and that "it was fullie deter-

---

[29] Ll. 1360–1363; Holinshed (ed. 1586), III. 325; (ed. 1807), II. 559.

mined that the kings eldest sonne Edward should go ouer."
But Holinshed makes it clear that the Queen and Prince went
on two separate occasions, not together, as Marlowe has it.[30]
Again he has found it desirable to compress history for dramatic
purposes.

The barons' demand that the King

> . . . remooue
> This *Spenser*, as a putrifying branche,
> That deads the royall vine

is derived from Holinshed's statement:

Their cheefe request was that it might please his highnesse to put from
him the Spensers, whose counsell they knew to be greatlie against his
honour.[31]

Holinshed touches only lightly on the battle of Borough-
bridge, but mentions the defeat of the barons, the capture and
execution of Lancaster, and implies that Mortimer was imprisoned — in all of which Marlowe dutifully follows him.
Holinshed is also authority for Spenser's bribery of the French
nobles, the queen's cold reception at the French court, her
flight to Hainault, Mortimer's escape from the Tower by drug-
ging his jailers, Kent's departure from France, the reward for
the slaying of Mortimer (Marlowe is not specific whether it
is offered for Mortimer dead or alive; Holinshed says clearly
"the head or dead corps"), and the King's departure to Bristol.
In the line, "Come, friends, to Bristow," there is probably an
echo of Holinshed's "the king being come to Bristow."

The tragedy is now approaching its climax in the defeat, capture, and subsequent murder of the King — in all of which Marlowe still clings close to his source. The rebels' creation of
Prince Edward to be Lord Warden of the realm, the capture
and execution of the elder Spenser, and the dispatch of Rice
ap Howell to find the King's hiding place in Wales are all drawn
from the chronicle — even to the reason for choosing Leicester
and Howell for the task. They were, says Holinshed, "to see if
they might find means to apprehend the king by helpe of their
acquaintance in those parts." Marlowe's Mortimer says

---

[30] Ll. 1366–1396; Holinshed (ed. 1586), III. 336; (ed. 1807), II. 577.
[31] Ll. 1470–1472; Holinshed (ed. 1586), III. 326; (ed. 1807), II. 561.

> . . . you *Rice ap Howell,*
> Shall do good seruice to her Maiestie,
> Being of countenance in your countrey here,
> To follow these rebellious runnagates.[32]

The lines which follow soon after,

> But what is he, whome rule and emperie
> Haue not in life or death made miserable?

are a very free rendering of Holinshed's quotation from Polydor
Vergil:

> . . . miser at*que* infœlix est etiam rex,
> Nec quenquam (mihi crede) facit diadema beatum.[33]

Holinshed is also authority for the tempestuous voyage of the
King to Ireland, described a few lines [34] further on. Marlowe
again adheres to his source in the scene depicting the capture
of the King. Holinshed says:

They tooke him in the monasterie of Neith, neere to the castell of
Laturssan, togither with Hugh Spenser the sonne called earle of
Glocester, the lord chancellour Robert de Baldocke, and Simon de
Reading the kings marshall, not caring for other the kings seruants,
whome they suffered to escape.[35]

In both play and chronicle it is Leicester who conveys the King
to Killingworth — so spelled in each — where, says the chronicler, he remained "in custodie of the earle of Leicester."

The scene where King Edward is persuaded to abdicate,
which was to influence Shakespeare's more famous scene in
Richard II,[36] is easily recognized in Holinshed's version, though
Marlowe has somewhat embellished it:

The bishops of Winchester and Lincolne went before, and comming to
Killingworth, associated with them the earle of Leicester, of some
called the earle of Lancaster, that had the king in keeping. And hauing secret conference with the king, they sought to frame his mind,
so as he might be contented to resigne the crowne to his sonne, bearing
him in hand, that if he refused so to doo, the people in respect of the
euill will which they had conceiued against him, would not faile but

---

[32] Ll. 1861–1864; Holinshed (ed. 1586), III. 339; (ed. 1807), II. 583.
[33] Ll. 1881–1882; Holinshed (1586), III. 341; (ed. 1807), II. 585.
[34] Ll. 1900–1902.
[35] Ll. 1913–1966; Holinshed (ed. 1586), III. 339; (ed. 1807), II. 583.
[36] See the present work, II. 242–243.

proceed to the election of some other that should happilie not touch him in linage. . . .

The king being sore troubled to heare such displeasant newes, was brought into a maruelous agonie: but in the end, for the quiet of the realme and doubt of further danger to himselfe, he determined to follow their aduise. . . . He vtterlie renounced his right to the kingdome, and to the whole administration thereof.[37]

On this passage Marlowe bases the abdication scene, in which he displays surprising skill in gaining as much suspense as possible from Edward's indecision and hesitation. Edward refuses to yield, yields, changes his mind, calls back the departing emissaries of his foes, and abdicates in the end — and all this time the Elizabethan audience, which had seen little enough of such dramatic skill on its stage until then, must have been agape.

The relation of Marlowe's version of the abdication to that in the chronicle is apparent throughout, but it emerges most clearly in the lines where the Bishop says:

> . . . it is for Englands good,
> And princely *Edwards* right we craue the crowne.[38]

This corresponds to "the quiet of the realme," and the danger of a new king "that should happilie not touch him in linage."

The various transfers of custody of the royal prisoner are recounted by Holinshed as follows:

But within a while the queene was informed . . . that the erle of Leicester fauoured hir husband too much, . . . wherevpon he was appointed to the keeping of two other lords, Thomas Berkley, and Iohn Matreuers, who . . . conueied him from Killingworth vnto the castell of Berkley. . . . But forsomuch as the lord Berkley vsed him more courteouslie than his aduersaries wished him to doo, he was discharged of that office, and sir Thomas Gourney appointed in his stead, who togither with the lord Matreuers conueied him secretlie . . . from one strong place to another, . . . still remoouing with him in the night season. . . . And so at length they brought him backe againe in secret maner vnto the castell of Berkley.

Numerous passages in the play bear obvious relation to this passage in Holinshed. Edward himself refers to Leicester's kindness as the cause of the first change of jailers:

[37] Ll. 1987–2110; Holinshed (ed. 1586), III. 340–341; (ed. 1807), II. 585.
[38] Ll. 2024–2025.

> Mine enemie hath pitied my estate,
> And thats the cause that I am now remooude.

Mortimer directs Matrevis to

> Remooue him still from place to place by night,
> Till at the last, he come to Killingworth,
> And then from thence to *Bartley* back againe.[39]

Mortimer's suspicions

> That *Edmund* casts to worke his libertie

have historical authority in Holinshed's statement that

there were diuerse of the nobilitie (of whome the earle of Kent was cheefe) began to deuise means by secret conference had togither, how they might restore him to libertie.[40]

The Queen's hypocritical gift (or letter), which she hands to Matrevis with the words,

> Beare him this, as witnesse of my loue,

is also from Holinshed, who says:

The queene would sent vnto him courteous and louing letters with apparell and other such things.[41]

The scene in which the deposed monarch is subjected to the indignity of being shaved with ditch water, however, does not appear in Holinshed. It has hitherto been supposed to come from a passage in Stow's *Chronicle*:

They determined for to shaue as well the hairs of his head, as also of his beard: wherefore, as in their iourny they trauailed by a little water which ranne in a ditch . . . a Barbar comes vnto him with a basen of colde water taken out of the ditch to shaue him withall.[42]

It is quite as probable, however, that this incident is derived from Thomas de la Moor, or de la More, who gives the same facts.[43] Archbishop Parker's bequest of books to the Corpus

---

[39] Ll. 2136–2137, 2203–2205.

[40] Line 2202; cf. l. 2175; Holinshed (ed. 1586), III. 341; (ed. 1807), II. 586.

[41] Ll. 2216; Holinshed (ed. 1586), III. 341; (ed. 1807), II. 586.

[42] By Tzschaschel, Briggs, and Tancock, the principal authorities. The passage appears in Stow's *Chronicle* (1615 ed.), p. 226.

[43] There is some doubt whether De la Moor wrote, or merely caused this to be written. I have retained the name under which Marlowe knew it and by which Stow himself

Christi library — made a few years before Marlowe entered, so that the books were certainly available to him during his student days — contains an "Excerpta ex Thoma de la More de morte Edwardi II. *manu neoterica.*" [44] This excerpt is very brief, however, and does not contain the shaving episode, though it does contain the riddling Latin message. The same bequest also contains the *Historia Brevis, Historia Minor,* and *Ypodigma Neustriae* by the monk of St. Albans, Thomas Walsingham (d. 1422), which likewise describe the reign of Edward II.

As Marlowe could have taken the episode of the shaving either from Stow or from Thomas de la Moor, and as the Parker manuscript might easily have stimulated his interest, it is not unreasonable to regard De la Moor as the source. There are, however, no further similarities; not does he seem to have used any of Thomas Walsingham's books. The fact, however, that they were part of a rather small college library — which Marlowe, as a student, must often have browsed through — makes it exceedingly probable that he at least knew the books. There is no close parallel between them and the play; but they may have aroused his original interest in the subject. This Thomas Walsingham does not appear to have been a relative of Sir Thomas Walsingham, Marlowe's patron.

The passage in Thomas de la Moor's work, from which Marlowe borrowed, runs:

Ingeniati sunt inimici Dei, quomodo Edwardum difformarent, ne foret faciliter notus alicui, unde ipsius cesariem tam capitalem quam barbam radendam constituerunt, venientes provide ad fossam in itinere scaturientem, jusserunt ipsum rasu descendere, cui assidenti super cujusdam talpæ monticulam, pelvem cum aqua frigida de fossa recepta attulit barbitonsor.[45]

The horrible tortures of the King's last days are transcribed from Holinshed with typical Elizabethan gusto. The lines of Matrevis,

refs to it. See Sir E. M. Thompson's edition of the *Chronicon* of Galfridi le Baker, pp. 31, 209; Giles's (1847) ed., p. 85.

[44] Jacobus Nasmyth (ed.), *Catalogus Librorum Manuscriptorum Quos Collegio Corporis Christi . . . Legavit . . . Matthæus Parker,* CCLXXXI.3, p. 319. For Walsingham, see no. CLXXVI.2, p. 258; no. CXCV, p. 27; no. CCXL, p. 302. See also Montague Rhodes James: *Descriptive Catalogue of the Manuscripts in the Library of Corpus Christi College, Cambridge.*

[45] E. M. Thompson's ed., p. 31; J. A. Giles's ed. (1847), p. 91.

Gurney, I wonder the king dies not,
Being in a vault vp to the knees in water,
To which the channels of the castell runne,
From whence a dampe continually ariseth,
That were enough to poison any man. . . .
He hath a body able to endure
More then we can enflict,

are plainly derived from Holinshed's passage:

They lodged the miserable prisoner in a chamber ouer a foule filthie dungeon, full of dead carrion, trusting so to make an end of him, with the abhominable stinch thereof: but he bearing it out stronglie, as a man of a tough nature, continued still in life.[46]

The exact manner of King Edward's eventual murder, as reported by Holinshed, is so horrible that even an Elizabethan dramatist shrank from describing it; and this is odd, for it is hard to see why Marlowe should be so squeamish when we remember his delight in cruelty as displayed in *Tamburlaine* or Shakespeare's willingness to exploit horror in the unspeakable scene of Gloucester's blinding in *King Lear*.

The language of the source is plain enough, however, and the business of the actors on the stage probably supplied whatever brutality does not appear in the poet's lines. The player-murderer's demands for "*a spit*, and let it be *red hote* . . . a *table* and a *fetherbed*," make it seem as if the dramatist were furtively trying to suggest details he dares not name. Holinshed, uncompromisingly brutal, blurts out the truth at which Marlowe's lines only hint, as if he expected his audience to be half familiar with the facts already:

Wherevpon when they sawe that such practises would not serue their turne, they came suddenlie one night into the chamber where he laie in bed fast asleepe, and with heauie *featherbeds* or *a table* (as some write) being cast vpon him, they kept him down and withall put into his fundament an horne, and through the same they thrust vp into his bodie an *hot spit*, . . . the which passing vp into his intrailes, and being rolled to and fro, burnt the same, but so as no appearance of any wound or hurt outwardlie might be once perceiued.[47]

The ambiguous Latin message sent to the slayers, whose meaning reverses itself according to the punctuation,

[46] Ll. 2448–2458; Holinshed (ed. 1586), III. 341; (ed. 1807), II. 586–587.
[47] Ll. 2479–2482; Holinshed (ed. 1586), III. 341; (ed. 1807), II. 587.

THE

troublesome Raigne and
lamentable death of Edward
the second King of England,
with the tragicall fall of proude
Mortimer.

As it was sondry times publiquely
acted in the honorable Cittie of
London, By the right honorable
the Earle of Pembroke his
Seruants.

Written by Chri: Mar: Gent.

troublesome Raigne

Imprinted at London for William Jones
dwelling neere Holborne Conduit at
the Signe of ye Gunne. 1593.

COPY OF THE TITLE PAGE OF THE LOST 1593 *Edward the Second*

Edwardum occidere nolite timere, bonum est
Edwardum occidere nolite, timere bonum est [48]

is from Holinshed, though the Cambridge-trained scholar will
none of the rather halting English translation with which
Holinshed supplements his Latin. Even Matrevis' guilty

I feare mee that this crie will raise the towne

is borrowed from the *Chronicle*, which observes that "his crie
did mooue manie within the castell and towne of Berkley to
compassion" [49] — as well it might.

Having reached his catastrophe, Marlowe hurries the play
to its conclusion, though not before he has let his audience see
justice done on the murderer Lightborne and his instigators,
the two Mortimers, and the Queen — for all of which he has
more or less authority, though it is not always quite explicit,
in Holinshed.

Marlowe's skill as a dramatist is now at its height, even
though in the *Chronicle* he was dealing with especially refractory
material. None of his sources are anything more than hit-or-
miss congeries of facts. The Marlowe of a few years earlier
would have been unable to make the right choice. The Marlowe of these later years sees instantly what material will give
unity, vitality, and sympathetic appeal to his tragedy.

He gives his play unity by grouping events about the King
as a central figure, whom he adroitly makes his audience half
pity, half despise. He displays the fundamental weakness of
Edward's character in his blind devotion to unworthy favorites;
and out of the chaotic mass of material that the chronicles
afforded, seizes upon Gaveston and the Spensers as characters
who will enable him to develop this weakness of the King under
the audience's very eyes, making it lead on, with true tragic in-
evitability, to the hero's downfall — a tragedy that emerges,
according to Aristotle's theory,[50] from fundamental weak-
nesses in his own character.

He gives his play conflict by setting the group of rebellious
barons against their king. He introduces a subtler conflict by

[48] Ll. 2340, 2343 (1586), III. 341; (1807), II. 586.
[49] Line 2562; Holinshed (ed. 1586), III. 341; (1807), II. 587.
[50] *Poetics*, XIII. 5.

making their leader, Young Mortimer, the King's rival for the Queen's love. He gains suspense first by the alternate victories of the rival groups, and also by the long wavering in the Queen's love, so that her surrender to Mortimer, when it comes at last, seems natural and inevitable, and at the same time increases the pathos of the deserted King. The stark black and white of the earlier plays has been replaced by chiaroscuro. Marlowe never dealt more subtly in the lights and shadows of character; and his portrayal of the Queen, abused, hesitant, erring, is his only successful experiment in feminine character.

To do all this, Marlowe had to take large liberties with history. In the play there is scarcely any interval between the fall of the first favorite, Gaveston, and the installation of the Spensers, father and son. Actually, there was a space of ten years. The favorites of the play are of far lower birth than the favorites of history. Marlowe's Edward is made pathetic by his great age; the Edward of history died at forty-three. The young Prince, later Edward III, is made a boy instead of a mere infant. He was not born till five months after Gaveston's death. Baldock and the Spensers are arbitrarily made servants of the former Duke of Cornwall to improve unity. But liberties of this sort with fact were the last things in the world to trouble the Elizabethan literary conscience.[51]

STAGE HISTORY

Little is known of the stage history of *Edward the Second*. The title page of the 1622 edition exists in two states, one of which says that the play was "acted by the late Queenes Maiesties Seruants at the Red Bull in S. Iohns street," while the other agrees with earlier editions in saying that it was "acted by the Earl of Pembroke his seruants." Probably Pembroke's men produced the play some time before July, 1593, when the suppositious 1593 edition was entered in the *Stationers' Register*.[52] Queen Anne's men were playing at the Red Bull between 1604 and 1606 and again in 1617.[53]

Beyond this there is no information except obscure allusions

[51] See McLaughlin's ed., pp. 153–164.
[52] See II. 5.
[53] Chambers: *Eliz. Stage*, II. 420, 447.

in *Henslowe's Diary* [54] to a play called *Mortymer* and another
called *The Spencers*, which Mr. W. W. Greg believes "had some
distant connection with Marlowe's *Edward II*." [55] Henslowe,
however, assigns *The Spencers* to Henry Chettle and "harey
porter." [56] It was probably another play, though it may have
owed a good deal to Marlowe.

There have been a number of modern productions. Mr. William Poel produced it for the Elizabethan Stage Society at Oxford, August 10, 1903, with Granville Barker as Edward.[57] It
was again acted by students of Birkbeck College, London,
in December, 1920.[58] It was twice produced for the Phoenix
Society by Allan Wade, at the Regent Theatre, London, in
November, 1923.[59] The Marlowe Dramatic Society produced
it at Cambridge University in 1926. Members of Christ Church
College, Oxford, produced it in the upper gallery of the library,
February 10 and 11, 1933, under the direction of Mr. John
Izan, of New College, and with the patronage of the Dean of
Christ Church. There was a radio production by the National
Broadcasting Company, November 5, 1939.

There have been at least two European productions. Karel
Hilar directed a highly modernistic performance at Prague in
1922, with stage sets designed by B. Feuerstein.[60] The adaptation of Brecht and Feuchtwanger was produced April, 1924,
by the Münchener Kammerspiele.[61]

INFLUENCE

Though it had less influence than the earlier plays, probably
because the quieter mood of Marlowe's mature period was less
startling to his contemporaries, *Edward the Second* had a direct

[54] Fols. 107*v*, 54, *r* and *v*, 61*r*. *Henslowe's Diary* (ed. Greg), I. 170, 103–105.
[55] *Henslowe's Diary* (ed. Greg), II. 224.
[56] *Ibid.*, I. 103.
[57] London *Times*, August 11, 1903; *Athenaeum*, 7 Mr 1914; Wilhelm Dibelius, in *Nazionalzeitung*, 8 S 1903; Maximilian Dametz in *Jahresbericht v. d. kgl. Staatsschule in Wien*, 54: 4 (1910); Paul Kühl: *Verhältnis von Shaksperes Richard II zu Marlowes Edward II*, p. 44.
[58] *Trans. Connecticut Acad.*, 25: 408 (1922).
[59] I. B., "At the Play," *Manchester Guardian Weekly*, November 23, 1923.
[60] Lawrence Hyde: "In a Prague Café," *Westminster Gazette*, August 30, 1923; "Marlowe in Prague," *Manchester Guardian*, February 17, 1922. See also *Nove Ceske Divadlo* (Prague: Aventinum, 1926) for reproduction of the stage sets.
[61] *Jahrb.*, (OS) 61 (NS) 2: 154–155 (1925).

effect on various works of the succeeding thirty or forty years. George Peele's *Edward I*, Thomas Kyd's *Soliman and Perseda*, Thomas Lodge's *Wounds of Ciuill Warre*, Robert Greene's *Alphonsus of Aragon*, the anonymous *Arden of Feversham, Troublesome Raigne of Iohn King of England, Thomas of Woodstock*, and *Iacke Drums Entertainment* are among the plays that show its influence in greater or less degree. In addition to these, at least four poems show some influence. Michael Drayton's *Barons' Warres*, Richard Barnfield's *Affectionate Shepherd*, and Thomas Middleton's *Wisdom of Solomon Paraphrased* owe something to Marlowe, and there is one doubtful parallel in the *Poems* of William Drummond of Hawthornden. It is interesting to note that for once Marlowe is the borrower — possibly from Greene's *Alphonsus*, certainly from the *Spanish Tragedy*. At least, the line:

> Because he loues me more then all the world [62]

is almost verbatim from the latter.

George Peele: Edward I

George Peele's *Edward I* has a definite relation to Marlowe's *Edward the Second*, but, although several parallels are obvious, it is hard to say which poet is borrower and which is lender. The plays were written at about the same time, and the date of neither is exactly determined. Peele, who borrows from Marlowe elsewhere and who alludes to him by name,[63] in his *Honour of the Garter* (1593), alludes also in this poem to

> . . . that cruel Mortimer
> That plotted Edward's death at Killingworth,
> Edward the Second, father to this king,
> Whose tragic cry even now methinks I hear,
> When graceless wretches murdered him by night.

Mortimer is made more prominent in Marlowe's play than he is in the histories of the period. In the play, the murder is not specifically said to take place "by night," but one of the murderers does carry a light into the dungeon, which would suggest night to a spectator. The cry of the dying King, though

---

[62] *Edward the Second*, 372.
[63] Peele's *Plays and Poems* (Morley's Universal Library, no. 52), pp. 275–276. See also I. 187 of the present work.

mentioned by the chroniclers, is probably taken from the play, since it is especially impressive on the stage. All this suggests Peele's acquaintance with Marlowe's play, whereas there is no evidence that Marlowe ever read Peele's or saw it on the stage.[64]

The verbal parallels are as follows:

> It shall suffice me to enioy your loue,
> Which whiles I haue, I thinke my selfe as great,
> As *Cæsar* riding in the Romaine streete,
> With captiue kings at his triumphant Carre.
>   [*Edward II*, 171–174]
> Not *Cæsar* leading through the streetes of Rome,
> The captiue kings of conquered nations,
> Was in his princely triumphes honoured more,
> Then English *Edward* in this martiall sight.
>   [*Edward I*, sc. 1. 107–110]

> Tis but temporall that thou canst inflict.
>   [*Edward II*, 1550]
> It is but temporall that you can inflict.
>   [*Edward I*, sc. 5. 954]

> These comforts that you giue our wofull queene,
> Binde vs in kindenes all at your commaund.
>   [*Edward II*, 1684–1685]
> This comfort Madam that your grace doth giue
> Binds me in double duety whilst I liue.
>   [*Edward I*, sc. 6. 1165–1166]

> Hence fained weeds, vnfained are my woes.
>   [*Edward II*, 1964]
> Hence faigned weedes, vnfaigned is my griefe.
>   [*Edward I*, sc. 25. 2800]

THOMAS KYD: SOLIMAN AND PERSEDA

Soliman and Perseda, which has been variously claimed for Thomas Kyd and for some unknown imitator of his work,[65]

---

[64] Cf. Briggs's ed., p. 201; Charlton and Waller's ed., p. 8; Tzschaschel, *op. cit.*, p. 33. The Peele references are to the Malone Society Reprint of the 1593 ed.

[65] On the authorship see Fleay: *Biog. Chron.*, II. 26; Gregor Sarrazin: *Thomas Kyd und Sein Kreis*, pp. iv, 2 ff.; Boas: *Works of Thomas Kyd*, p. lxi; J. Schick's review of Sarrazin in [Herrig's] *Archiv f. d. Studium d. neur. Sprach. u. Lit.*, 90: 177 (1893); Robertson: *Did Shakespeare Write Titus Andronicus?* pp. 110, 151, 166; Chambers: *Eliz. Stage*, IV. 46–47.

shows verbal echoes of *Edward the Second*, but no other resemblances. The parallel passages are:

> . . . to equall it receiue my hart.
> [*Edward II*, 162]
> To equall it: receiue my hart to boote.
> [S&P, I. ii. 40]

> And when this fauour *Isabell* forgets,
> Then let her liue abandond and forlorne.
> [*Edward II*, 594–595]
> My gratious Lord, whe[n] Erastus doth forget this fauor,
> Then let him liue abandond and forlorne.
> [S&P, IV. i. 198–199]

> Father, thy face should harbor no deceit.
> [*Edward II*, 1875]
> This face of thine shuld harbour no deceit.
> [S&P, III. i. 72]

> O my starres!
> Why do you lowre vnkindly on a king?
> [*Edward II*, 1929–1930]
> Ah heauens, that hitherto haue smilde on me,
> Why doe you vnkindly lowre on *Solyman*?
> [S&P, V. iv. 82–83]

> I tell thee tis not meet, that one so false
> Should come about the person of a prince.
> [*Edward II*, 2248–2249]
> It is not meete that one so base as thou
> Shouldst come about the person of a King.
> [S&P, I. v. 71–72]

> . . . euen to the utmost verge
> Of *Europe*, or the shore of *Tanaise*.
> [*Edward II*, 1640–1641]
> Euen to the verge of golde abounding Spaine.
> [S&P, I. iii. 59]

> Then come sweete death, and rid me of this greefe.
> [*Edward II*, 2660]
> Come therefore, gentle death, and ease my griefe.
> [S&P, p. 284]

Thomas Lodge: Wounds of Ciuill War

Three of Lodge's plays contain passages closely resembling Marlowe's, but there is some doubt whether Lodge or Marlowe was the borrower. *The Wounds of Ciuill War* has lines that also appear in *Tamburlaine*[66] and in *Edward the Second*. *A Looking-Glass for London* has lines that also appear in *Doctor Faustus*, and *An Alarum against Usurers* (a tract, not a play) has a portrayal of the usurer's remorse that strongly resembles the scene of Faustus' repentance.[67]

Since the dates of these works are not very well established, and since they all belong to pretty much the same period as Marlowe's work, one cannot be dogmatic about the relationship. One is tempted to assert that Marlowe, as the greater poet and stronger personality, probably influenced Lodge; but Mr. N. Burton Paradise takes precisely the opposite view, arguing that Lodge's versification shows little influence by Marlowe, and that Lodge's work came first in point of chronology.[68]

In any case, there are but two sets of parallels:

> Immortall powers, that knowes the painfull cares,
> That waites vpon my poore distressed soule,
> O leuell all your lookes vpon these daring men,
> That wronges their liege and soueraigne, Englands king.
> > [*Edward II*, 2302–2305]

> Immortall powers that know the painefull cares,
> That waight vpon my poor distressed hart,
> O bend your browes and leuill all your lookes
> Of dreadfull awe vpon these daring men.
> > [*Wounds*, p. 55][69]

> Vaild is your pride: me thinkes you hang the heads.
> > [*Edward II*, 1531]

> Twill make him vaile the topflag of his pride.
> > [*Edward II*, 573]

> Disdaines to stoope or vaile his pride to thee.
> > [*Wounds*, p. 8]

[66] See I. 264–265.
[67] Reprint in Shakespeare Society Publications (1853), no. 48.
[68] *Thomas Lodge*, pp. 130 ff., 149.
[69] References are to the Hunterian Club reprint.

Thomas of Woodstock

There is in the British Museum the manuscript of an anonymous and untitled play dealing with Richard II.[70] Never published in Elizabethan times, it was first printed by J. O. Halliwell in 1870 in a limited edition of but eleven copies, one of which is now in the British Museum. It has since been twice reprinted, once by the Deutsche Shakespeare Gesellschaft (1899) and once by the Malone Society.

Since the manuscript has no title, it has been referred to under whatever title pleased the writer dealing with it. Halliwell calls it *A Tragedy of King Richard the Second*. Wolfgang Keller, its German editor, calls it *Richard II. Erster Teil*. Frederick Ives Carpenter described it as "The Anonymous Richard II." The Malone Society calls it *The First Part of the Reign of King Richard the Second or Thomas of Woodstock*. F. S. Boas, in *Shakespeare and the Universities*, calls it *Thomas of Woodstock*, and Tucker Brooke [71] refers to it as "the so-called *Tragedy of Woodstock*."

It exhibits resemblances to *Edward the Second* which go beyond what might be expected from the natural similarities due to similar subjects, and seems also to have some relationship to the Second Part of *Henry VI*. There are numerous verbal parallels with Marlowe.

Woodstock deals with the objection of Richard's nobles to the influence exerted upon the King by his unworthy favorites. The favorite Greene recalls Marlowe's Gaveston, and the timeserving Tressilian recalls Marlowe's timeserver, Baldock. Queen Anne corresponds to Queen Isabella. The love of the royal pair does not, however, waver as in Marlowe's play; but Richard, like Edward, turns a deaf ear to the Queen's pleadings. The play ends in the murder, not of the King, but of his trusty counselor, Thomas of Woodstock. The King is arrested, and his favorites are either made prisoners, driven into exile, or slain.[72]

[70] Egerton MS. 1994, fols. 161–185.

[71] *Trans. Connecticut Acad.*, 25: 380 (1922).

[72] Cf. F. S. Boas: *Shakespeare and the Universities*, chap. VII; Wolfgang Keller: "Richard II. erster Teil," *Jahrb.*, 35: 3–121 (1899); the introduction to the Malone Society reprint (1929); and Frederick Ives Carpenter: "Notes on the Anonymous 'Richard I,' " *Journ. Germ. Philol.*, 3: 138–142 (1900).

In both cases the dramatists are drawing their facts from Holinshed, to whom Marlowe adheres rather more closely than the anonymous dramatist; but the facts chosen are so closely alike that influence of some kind between the plays cannot be doubted. Since *Woodstock* cannot be dated, it is impossible to show that the author imitated Marlowe; but the structural and verbal resemblances establish a fairly satisfactory case for Wolfgang Keller's conclusion "dass es nicht nach Shakespeares Richard II. und nicht vor Heinrich VI. zweiter Teil oder Marlowes Eduard II. entstanden sein kann." [73]

To prove his case, Keller lists some rather farfetched parallels, but the following seem clearly to be drawn from Marlowe: [74]

> *Gaue.* It shall suffice me to enioy your loue,
> Which whiles I haue, I thinke my selfe as great
> As *Cæsar.*
> > [*Edward II*, 171–173]
> Thankes, deerest lord; lett me haue Richards loue,
> And like a rocke vnmoud my state shall stand.
> > [*Woodstock*, II. i. 8]

> > . . . for we haue power,
> And courage to, to be reuengde *at full.*
> > [*Edward II*, 266–267]
> I'le be reuengd *at full* on all ther liues.
> > [*Woodstock*, I. i. 69]

> *Lan.* On that condition Lancaster will graunt.
> *War.* And so will *Penbrooke* and I.
> *Mor.se.* And I.
> > [*Edward II*, 589–591]
> *Yorke. Lanc.* On these conditions, brother, we agree.
> *Arond.* And I.
> *Surry.* And I.   [*Woodstock*, I. i. 190–192]

> The murmuring commons. [*Edward II*, 962]
> The murmoring commons. [*Woodstock*, I. iii. 258]

> I dare not, for the people loue him well.
> > [*Edward II*, 1036]

---

[73] *Jahrb.*, 35: 42 (1899).
[74] References are to Wolfgang Keller's ed., *Jahrb.*, 35: 45–121 (1899). On the resemblances to *Edward the Second*, see pp. 22–27 of Keller's introduction.

I dare not, Greene; for . . .
                    hee's so well beloud.
                         [*Woodstock*, IV. i. 73–74]

As though your highnes were a schoole boy still,
And must be awde and gouernd like a child.
                         [*Edward II*, 1336–1337]
To aw ye like a child.
                         [*Woodstock*, II. i. 12]

TROUBLESOME RAIGNE OF JOHN KING OF ENGLAND

The theme of *The Troublesome Raigne of John King of England* is much like that of *Edward the Second*, so that resemblances are not unnatural. King John's abdication scene is thought to owe something to Edward's. The two plays have similar titles. Verbal parallels are abundant, and, since this play is a Shakespeare source, traces of Marlowe in the Shakespearean *King John* are to be expected. The following parallels [75] are of especial interest:

             . . . a new elected king.
                         [*Edward II*, 2064]
             . . . their new elected King.
                         [TR, pt. II., sc. 2, 80]

             . . . hast pleaded with so good successe.
                         [*Edward II*, 626]
             . . . plead with good successe.
                         [TR, pt. II., sc. 2. 148]

      Fits not the time.
                         [*Edward II*, 1786]
             . . . fit not the season.
                         [TR, pt. II., sc. 2. 105]

             . . . cause of all these iarres.
                         [*Edward II*, 1025]
      Occasion of these vndecided iarres.
                         [TR, pt. I, sc. 2. 95]

[75] References here are to the Praetorius facsimile ed. The parallels with the *Troublesome Raigne of John King of England*, *Faire Em*, and *Alphonsus of Aragon* have been elaborately studied by Professor Rupert Taylor. See PMLA, 51:642–688 (1936), for further material.

Here man, rip vp this panting brest of mine,
And take my heart, in reskew of my friends.
                    [*Edward II*, 1033–1034]
O would she with her hands pull forth my heart,
I could affoord it to appease these broyles.
                    [TR, pt. I, sc. 4. 147–148]

Why should a king be subiect to a priest?
                    [*Edward II*, 392]
. . . so I scorne to be subiect to the greatest
Prelate in the world.
                    [TR, pt. I, sc. 5. 75–76]

Thou proud disturber of thy countries peace.
                    [*Edward II*, 1176]
Proud, and disturber of thy Countreyes peace.
                    [TR, pt. I, sc. 7. 3]
The proud disturber of our state.
                    [*Edward I*, 112]
. . . the proud disturbers of the faith.
                    [MatP, 706]

Anger and wrathfull furie stops my speech.
                    [*Edward II*, 337]
Her passions stop the organ of her voyce.
                    [TR, pt. I, sc. 10. 20]

That from your princely person you remooue
This *Spencer*, as a putrifying branche,
That deads the royall vine.
                    [*Edward II*, 1470–1472]
Sith we haue proynd the more than needfull braunch
That did oppresse the true wel-growing stock.
                    [TR, pt. I, sc. 13. 28–29]

. . . I feele the crowne.
                    [*Edward II*, 2068]
. . . then he may feele the crowne.
                    [TR, pt. I, sc. 13. 210]

. . . our soules are fleeted hence.
                    [*Edward II*, 1972]
Farewell vaine worlde.
                    [*Edward II*, 1557]
My soule doth fleete, worlds vanities farewell.
                    [TR, pt. II, sc. 5. 47]

... life vp this dying hart!
> [*Edward II*, 1910]

... reuiue thy dying heart.
> [TR, Pt. II, sc. 7. 43]

... stay times aduantage.
> [*Edward II*, 1629]

Follow tymes aduantage.
> [TR, pt. II, sc. 7. 47]

... for too long haue I liued.
> [*Edward II*, 2651]

He rather liud too long.
> [TR, pt. II, sc. 8. 85]

MICHAEL DRAYTON: THE BARONS' WARRES

Edward the Second seems to have had more or less influence, perceptible without being very definite, upon Drayton's *Mortimeriados* (1596), later revised as *The Barons' Warres* (1603).[76] Drayton was, of course, thoroughly familiar with Marlowe's work and was probably an acquaintance. His *Endimion and Phoebe* plainly shows the influence of *Hero and Leander*, at least one of his Eglogs alludes to *Tamburlaine*, and his tribute to Marlowe in the Elegy on Henry Reynolds is well-known.[77]

It was natural, therefore, that he should have read *Edward the Second* or seen it performed, and that in dealing with the same subject he should show traces of Marlowe. While the poem on *The Barons' Warres* shows no verbal echoes of *Edward the Second*, the choice of subject matter and the content in general are closer to the play than to the chronicles. Drayton passes rapidly over the first parts of Edward's reign and the troubles due to Gaveston, perhaps because he had already dealt with them in his *Legend of Peirs Gaueston* (1593 or 1594). The first part of Marlowe's play, therefore, exerts no influence on the poem. But Drayton follows Marlowe in treating the love of Queen Isabella and Young Mortimer; where the chronicles gloss over this episode, Drayton is specific, like Marlowe. Both

---

[76] There is some disagreement as to dates, though all dates assigned indicate that Drayton's work is later than Marlowe's. Dates here given are from CHEL, IV. 201–202.

[77] See I. 188.

Drayton and Marlowe indicate that the liaison reaches its climax in France. Both assert that the captive King was placed in Leicester's custody. Both make the Bishop of Winchester protest at Leicester's kindness. Both bring in Matrevis (or, as Drayton calls him, Matrevers) and Gurney, the assassins. Both dwell on these men's ill-treatment of the captive King, and both use the riddling letter. These last three details, however, might have come from the chronicles, and Marlowe and Drayton differ in their death scenes.

Presumably, then, Drayton knew Marlowe's play and was somewhat influenced by it, but he was no slavish copyist. His *Legend of Peirs Gaueston* and his imaginary letters from the Queen to Mortimer and from Mortimer to the Queen, in *Englands Heroicall Epistles* (1597), show no special traces of Marlowe.

RICHARD BARNFIELD: AFFECTIONATE SHEPHERD

The almost forgotten poet, Richard Barnfield (1574-1627), imitates Marlowe frequently.[78] From *Edward the Second*, however, his borrowings are comparatively modest, consisting of but two lines. Marlowe's

> Crownets of pearle about his naked armes

becomes in *The Affectionate Shepherd*

> Crownets of Pearle about thy naked Armes.

A few lines earlier, in Marlowe's play, there appears the line

> And in the day when he shall walke abroad.

In *The Affectionate Shepherd*, a few lines after the passage already quoted, occurs the line

> And when it pleaseth thee to walke abroad.[79]

THOMAS MIDDLETON

There is one echo of *Edward the Second* in Middleton's *Wisdom of Solomon Paraphrased*. This is the passage about the

[78] See I. 269-270, II. 131, 159-160.
[79] *Edward the Second*, 63, 57; *Affectionate Shepherd* (Arber's reprint), pp. 11, 12.

wounded lion, also echoed in *The True Tragedie*.[80] Marlowe's version runs:

> But when the imperiall Lions flesh is gorde,
> He rends and teares it with his wrathfull pawes,
> (And) highly scorning, that the lowly earth
> Should drinke his bloud, mounts vp into the ayre.
>
> *[Edward II, 1997–2000]*

Middleton writes:

> The lion, wounded with a fatal blow,
> Is as impatient as a king in rage;
> Seeing himself in his own bloody show
> Doth rent the harbour of his body's cage;
> Scorning the base-hous'd earth, mounts to the sky,
> To see if heaven can yield him remedy.[81]

There is nothing like this in the apocryphal *Wisdom of Solomon*.

OTHER WORKS

Scattered parallels in various plays show that their authors had been reading *Edward the Second*, or had seen it on the stage. *Iacke Drums Entertainment* and the anonymous Shakespearean source play, *King Leir*,[82] borrow the same line:

> O how a kisse reuiues poore *Isabell*.
> *[Edward II, 630]*
> Oh how a kisse inflames a Louers thought.
> *[Iacke Drum (1601 ed.) C4v]*
> O, how thy words revive my dying soul!
> *[Leir, I. iii. 54]*

There are numerous parallel passages in *Arden of Feversham*, but as this play has itself been erroneously attributed to Marlowe, it is considered in a later chapter on the Marlowe Apocrypha. The anonymous *Faire Em*, one of the Shakespeare apocryphal plays,[83] has two apparent parallels:

[80] See II. 237.
[81] Chapter XVI. 12; Dyce's Middleton, V. 450.
[82] Reference is to the ed. of Sir Sidney Lee (1909).
[83] Reference is to C. F. Tucker Brooke: *Shakespeare Apocrypha*.

My heart is as an anuill vnto sorrow.
[*Edward II*, 609]
The Anuyle whereupon my heart doth be.
[*Faire Em*, I. iv. 2]

Did neuer sorrow go so neere my heart.
[*Edward II*, 603]
How neere this parting goeth to my heart.
[*Faire Em*, II. i. 123]
. . . it would goe verie neere her heart.
[*Faire Em*, IV. iii. 9]

Alphonsus of Aragon [84] shows certain parallels, though if this
play is correctly dated 1588 Marlowe must be the borrower:

Your pardon is quicklie got of *Isabell.*
[*Edward II*, 1032]
. . . thy pardon soon is got.
[*Alphonsus*, I. i, p. 14]

. . . abandond and forlorne.
[*Edward II*, 595]
. . . banish'd and forlorn.
[*Alphonsus*, III. ii, p. 36]

. . . these teares distilling from mine eyes.
[*Edward II*, 2669]
. . . the salt brine tears,
Distilling down poor Fausta's wither'd cheeks.
[*Alphonsus*, V. iii, p. 68]

. . . whiles I haue a sword, a hand, a hart.
[*Edward II*, 719]
This heart, this hand, yea, and this blade.
[*Alphonsus*, III. ii, p. 41]

Drummond of Hawthornden, in his *Poems*, has one seeming
parallel which may be nothing more than common reminiscence
of Virgil:

Inhumaine creatures, nurst with Tigers milke.
[*Edward II*, 2057]
The *Caspian* Tigers with their Milke the fed.
[*Poems*, 2nd ed., 1616, E-1, *r*]

[84] Reference is to Mermaid ed.

This also appears in Marlowe's *Dido* and in his translation of Lucan.[85]

With *Edward the Second* we reach the height of Marlowe's career as a dramatist. Of the two plays that remain, both are inferior and one is known to be only partly his work. He had also written or was soon to write one famous lyric and part of *Hero and Leander*. Beyond that, the rest is silence, or for his reputation's sake had better be silence.

[85] See II. 50.

CHAPTER XI

DIDO, QUEEN OF CARTHAGE

An insolent commaunding louer.
Hero and Leander, I. 409

IDO, *QUEEN OF CARTHAGE,* is one of Marlowe's most interesting plays, not for its literary
merits, which are very slight, but rather as a kind
of index to his mind in his earlier years, and as an
unconscious draft for much of his later work. In it, we seem to
see the youthful Marlowe groping his way through a period of
immaturity toward the greater work that he was to do as his
mind developed and his technical skill increased. This is 'prentice work, perhaps the earliest of Marlowe's plays that has come
down to us, perhaps the first play that he ever wrote.

It is interesting, too, as the only extant play in which he is
definitely known to have had a collaborator.[1] His anonymous
handiwork is undoubtedly present in *Henry VI* and probably in
several other plays, but there such knowledge as we have is
based upon conjecture or textual study.[2] In *Dido,* collaboration
is frankly admitted, and Nashe's name appears upon the title
page.

Nashe's share must have been relatively small, however, for
internal evidence indicates clearly that Marlowe's share is
rather large. Lines that can belong to no one but Christopher
Marlowe appear throughout the play; but interspersed with
them are other passages quite different in tone. These might
conceivably be Marlowe's own work, written while he was still
young and his style unformed, but there is no need to entertain
such an hypothesis. All evidence goes to show that Nashe col-

---

[1] See II. 276–278 for the lost *Maiden's Holiday,* in which John Day is said to have
been collaborator.

[2] Cf. Tucker Brooke's statement: "In no other case can Marlowe be shown to have
collaborated with a fellow dramatist during his London career, unless with Shakespeare
in the Henry VI plays." (*Works,* p. 388.)

laborated with him and that some, at least, of these inferior passages must be from Nashe's pen. The two men were in Cambridge together; they were working in London at the same time; they had every opportunity for association; and contemporaries attributed the play to their collaboration when the quarto of 1594 was published, within a year of Marlowe's death.

Nashe was the younger by three years. He had been in Cambridge from 1582 to 1588, so that he might easily have known Marlowe there. He "forsooke *Cambridge*, being Batchelor of the third yere," [3] about July of 1588, because he had "had a hand in a Show called *Terminus & non terminus*: for which his partener in it was expelled the Colledge." Marlowe was then in the full tide of his early success; and if the two men had really been acquainted at the university, it would have been natural for Nashe to appeal to him for help when he came to London under something of a cloud — as Marlowe himself had come only the year before.

It is probable, then, that if the two collaborated at all, they collaborated either when both were students or immediately after Nashe arrived in London. At least, it is difficult to imagine any friendly collaboration after Nashe published his scornful allusion to "ideot Art-masters, that intrude themselues to our eares as the Alcumists of eloquence, who (mounted on the stage of arrogance) thinke to out-braue better pennes with the swelling bumbast of bragging blanke verse." [4]

The gibe sounds like the petulant outburst of a jealous man who finds an early associate's fame and achievement surpassing his own. But it is by no means certain that this is an allusion to Marlowe at all. Nashe, in his reply to Gabriel Harvey, *Have With You to Saffron-Walden*, insisted: "I neuer abusd *Marloe*, *Greene*, *Chettle* in my life, nor anie of my frends that vsde me like a frend; which both *Marloe* and *Greene* (if they were aliue) vnder their hands would testifie." [5]

---

[3] Gabriel Harvey: *Trimming of Thomas Nashe* in Grosart's Harvey, III. 67–68. See also Fleay: *Biog. Chron.*, II. 124. A passage in Harington's *Apology of Poetry* (1591) suggests that this play was also called *The Cards*. Collier was under the impression that "Marlow and Nash were not acquainted with each other in 1587" (HEDP, III. 138), but there is no longer any reason for this view.

[4] "To the Gentlemen students," McKerrow's Nashe, III. 311 and n.; IV. 445–446.

[5] McKerrow's Nashe, III. 131; Grosart's Nashe, III. 194.

As Mr. Tucker Brooke says, "the conclusion would at first seem almost unavoidable that *Dido* is the product of an old college partnership between two Cambridge contemporaries." [6] There are, however, two facts which have been held to suggest a later association. In the first place, the inclusion of Nashe's name on the title page in 1594 — a time when Marlowe's name was still on all men's lips, and Nashe's reputation was relatively slight — hints at some connection with the play more recent than a half-forgotten university collaboration of eight or ten years before, especially as the title page gives Marlowe's name the larger type and plainly regards Nashe as the less important author. In other words, Nashe is represented as undoubtedly a collaborator but not a very important one. He may merely have revised the play for press.

The other fact which suggests a later date for the collaboration is the alleged existence of an elegy on Marlowe, written by Nashe and affixed to the 1594 quarto of *Dido*. If Nashe wrote an elegy on Marlowe, he was probably associated with him in his later years.

The elegy is mentioned by Bishop Thomas Tanner (1674–1735) and by Thomas Warton the younger (1728–1790), but it does not appear in any of the three known copies of the play.[7] There seems no doubt, however, that it once existed — perhaps in the fourth copy of the 1594 quarto, now lost, which is listed among the books of the early nineteenth-century comedian, William E. Burton.[8]

Tanner says: "Petowius [9] in praefatione ad secundam partem *Herois et Leandri* multa in Marlovii commendationem adfert; hoc etiam facit Tho. Nash in *Carmine elegiaco tragoediae Didonis* praefixo in obitum Christoph. Marlovii, ubi quatuor ejus tragoediarum mentionem facit, nec non et alterius *De duce Guisio*." Warton, perhaps copying this passage, says: "Nashe in his Elegy prefixed to Marlowe's Dido, mentions five of his plays."

This observation stirred Malone's curiosity, and he wrote to

---

[6] *Works*, p. 388.

[7] Tanner: *Bibliotheca Britannico-Hibernica* (1748), p. 512; Warton: *Hist. Eng. Poetry* (1781), III. 435n.

[8] *Bibliotheca dramatica. Catalogue . . . of William E. Burton*, no. 1291, p. 95. Copies in NYPL, Yale, Columbia University, and Grolier Club.

[9] "Petowius" is Henry Petowe. See Chapter XIII.

Warton for further particulars. Warton's reply is recorded in Malone's note affixed to the Bodleian copy and reproduced in the facsimile edition of 1914:

He informed me by letter that a copy of this play was in Osborne's catalogue in the year 1754; that he then saw it in his shop (together with several of Mr Oldys's books that Osborne had purchased), & that the elegy in question "on Marlowe's untimely death" was inserted immediately after the title-page; that it mentioned a play of Marlowe's entitled *The Duke of Guise* and four others; but whether particularly by *name*, he could not recollect. Unluckily he did not purchase this rare piece, & it is now God knows where.

The rare piece, as Mr. Tucker Brooke observes, "is still God knows where." [10] T. Osborne and J. Shipton were booksellers with a shop in Gray's Inn. They issued a catalogue [11] November 11, 1754, but no one [12] has been able to find any reference to *Dido*.

Presumably, however, the elegy did at one time exist. The copy of *Dido* containing it may have been a second edition now lost, or it may, as Mr. Tucker Brooke conjectures, represent merely the existing quarto with "a printed leaf inserted between the title-page and the first page of text." Mr. Brooke further conjectures that "Nashe's elegy reached the publisher after the Quarto had been printed and was simply pasted in in some copies of the edition." [13]

Mr. McKerrow accepts Malone's data as probably authentic. "I think," he says, "there is no reason to doubt that this elegy did actually exist, and fully expect that it will come to light again some day." [14] He also supposes it to have been a single leaf inserted after the title page, though he suggests, as an unlikely possibility, that there may have been two independent editions, one with the elegy and one without, the latter alone surviving.

All this indicates late collaboration. If the bitter comments in "To the Gentlemen Students" really do refer to Marlowe, we must assume that he and Nashe had made up their quarrel

---

[10] Brooke's ed. (1930), p. 122.
[11] Now in the British Museum (128. i. 8. 9).
[12] McKerrow's Nashe, II. 335 n.
[13] *Works*, p. 123.
[14] *Op. cit.*, II. 336.

in the meantime. After all, Marston and Jonson, a few years later, forgot all the bitter things they had said about each other in the "War of the Theatres," and are found peaceably collaborating in *Eastward Hoe* soon after.

Where the evidence is so conflicting, a definite decision is impossible. Dyce considered himself "bound to believe, till some positive evidence be produced to the contrary, that *Dido* was completed for the stage by Nash after the decease of Marlowe."[15] Brooke thinks that though "*Dido* is in its present form mainly the work of Marlowe," the play represents "two stages in that poet's development." In other words, it may be early work of university days, cast aside for some years and then revised with assistance from Nashe.[16] Dyce had already suggested that "Nash's contributions to *Dido* were comparatively small," and had ventured the pertinent reminder that we are hardly "warranted in assigning to the latter poet all the less brilliant passages, since we know that Marlowe, though often soaring to a height which Nash could not have reached, yet frequently sinks to the level of a very ordinary writer."

It was a necessary reminder, for Cunningham, in his edition, suggested practically that. He would have assigned to Nashe all the bad or commonplace passages. Thus, he felt sure Nashe must have written such a line as

> Gentle *Achates*, reach the Tinder boxe

(which is, however, a fair translation of Vergil's "Ac primum silici scintillam excudit Achates") and other dull lines like it.[17] He would assign to Nashe's great collaborator "passages of such genuine vigour and beauty as nobody but the writer of a life of the lesser genius would give to any one but Marlowe."

Fleay had even presumed to cut the play up and divide its parts evenly between the two dramatists:[18]

Marlowe: I, 1a; II, 1, 2; III, 3; IV, 3–4; V, 1–2
Nashe: I, 1b (which should be marked as a new scene); III, 1, 2, 4;
       IV, 1, 2, 5

[15] Ed. 1850, I. xl; ed. 1858, p. xxxvi.
[16] *Works*, p. 389; *Life and Dido*, p. 115.
[17] Line 166; *Aeneid*, I. 173. Collier (HEDP, III. 225) had already made very nearly this suggestion.
[18] *Biog. Chron.*, II. 147.

But this division has very little meaning, because he does not explain the basis of his choices; because collaborating dramatists do not necessarily cut up a play scene by scene, but may work on each scene jointly; and above all because none of the editions of Fleay's day make the scene divisions which he uses.

Knutowski and McKerrow agree with Brooke that *Dido* is mainly Marlowe's. Knutowski, after testing the meter and versification, holds that Nashe's share in the play consists merely of minor alterations and additions.[19] The most recent editor of Nashe, Mr. R. B. McKerrow, says frankly that "the play seems to belong almost entirely to Marlowe" and "seems to throw no light whatever on the rest of Nashe's writings or to be in any way connected with them."[20]

Certain passages are without question Marlowe's. One such is the description of the opening of the wooden horse, which includes the lines:

> And after him a thousand Grecians more,
> In whose sterne faces shin'd the quenchles fire,
> That after burnt the pride of *Asia*.[21]

and Dido's lyric passage which shows the "Passionate Shepherd" music already running in the poet's restless head and appearing in *Dido* as in most of his other work:

> Ile giue thee tackling made of riueld gold,
> Wound on the barkes of odoriferous trees,
> Oares of massie Iuorie full of holes,
> Through which the water shall delight to play.[22]

One of the remarkable things about *Dido*, and probably the best evidence of Marlowe's authorship, is the odd way in which these passages and innumerable others like them foreshadow lines in Marlowe's later plays, among them some of his most famous passages. The Elizabethan writers all echoed themselves and each other to an extent incredible to the modern critic, Shakespeare himself being no exception to the rule. Partly, this was due to a tendency natural to all writers. Partly

[19] Boleslaus Knutowski: *Dido-Drama von Marlowe und Nash*, pp. 30–31.
[20] McKerrow's Nashe, IV. 295.
[21] Ll. 480–483.
[22] *Dido*, 750–753. See II. 157–160.

also, it was due to the fact that the Elizabethan playwrights heard each other's plays in rehearsal and in production so often that lines inevitably stuck in their memories. Sometimes, too, no doubt, the echoes are intentional; and sometimes "gagging" actors may have helped.

Marlowe echoed himself from play to play with the utmost freedom; but the anticipations in *Dido* of passages in later plays are more frequent than ordinary echoes of this sort, and they are of a rather different kind. Sometimes they are mere repetitions of common Elizabethan phrases, like the use of "speake him faire" in *Dido* and *Edward the Second*; [23] or the fourfold re-iteration of "this geare" in *Dido*, *Massacre at Paris*, *Tamburlaine*, and *Edward the Second*.[24]

More frequently, however, the echoing lines are so marked with the stamp of Marlowe's mind that it is impossible to attribute them to any other writer. They sound like first drafts for later and better work in other plays, and are almost invariably less effective than the later versions. It is as if the youthful Marlowe, like so many other young writers, had inspirations and ideas with which he was not yet skilful enough to deal. He did the best he could with his unpracticed hand and later, in the days when he had mastered his craft, remolded them nearer to his heart's desire. All this forms one more argument for placing *Dido* very early among Marlowe's works.

Three of the most striking passages from *Doctor Faustus* are anticipated in *Dido*. One of these is the famous line:

> Sweete *Helen*, make me immortall with a kisse,

which had already appeared in *Dido* as

> And heele make me immortall with a kisse.[25]

The "toplesse Towres" in the same speech of Faustus are very like the "toples hilles" of *Dido*.[26] Again, the passage,

> *Aeneas* may commaund as many Moores,
> As in the Sea are little water drops

---

[23] *Dido*, 1608; *Edward the Second*, 479.
[24] *Dido*, 121; *Massacre*, 822; I *Tamb*. 524; *Edward the Second*, 2487.
[25] *Doctor Faustus*, 1330; *Dido*, 1329.
[26] *Dido*, 1162; *Doctor Faustus*, 1329.

is obviously like Faustus' exclamation in his dying agony:

O soule, be changde into little water drops.[27]

Every literate speaker of English knows these two passages in *Doctor Faustus* for their compelling poignancy and beauty. In *Dido* they are so weak that they are almost unknown. The difference between them is the measure of Marlowe's growth.

Marlowe also uses, in the agonized final soliloquy of Faustus, a quotation from Ovid's *Amores*:

O lente, lente curite noctis equi,[28]

which has an immensely effective irony. Ovid utters it when he is at length in Corinna's arms. It is the lover's plea that dawn may be delayed. Faust utters the words of Ovid's supreme moment of bliss in his own moment of supreme agony, when he wishes the horses of the night to move slowly, because damnation waits him ere the night is over. This is anticipated in *Dido*, where Jove tells Ganymede that to prolong a moment of bliss,

I . . .
Haue oft driuen backe the horses of the night.[29]

The "thousand ships" passage in *Doctor Faustus* is also foreshadowed in *Dido*:

Nor sent a thousand ships vnto the walles.[30]

"Thousand" was a favorite word with Marlowe. He uses it repeatedly in *Tamburlaine*, though with authority from his sources,[31] and repeatedly in *Dido*. It appears in a line there which is echoed word for word in *Hero and Leander*:

Threatning a thousand deaths at euerie glaunce.[32]

For the terrible cry of the Greeks as they sack Troy:

kill, kill they cryed,[33]

[27] *Dido*, 1268–1269; *Doctor Faustus*, 1472.
[28] *Doctor Faustus*, 1428; *Amores*, I. xiii. 40. In the *Elegies* Marlowe translates it, "Stay night and runne not thus."
[29] *Dido*, 26.
[30] *Dido*, 1612; *Doctor Faustus*, 1328.
[31] See I. 216–220.
[32] *Dido*, 526; *Hero and Leander*, I. 382.
[33] *Dido*, 485.

Marlowe has drawn upon accounts of the Massacre of St. Bartholomew's, either because he had already begun work on *The
Massacre at Paris*, or because he was already familiar with the
newsbooks and recent histories which told the story. Thus in
The Massacre we have the line:

> *Tue, tue, tue*, let none escape

and the further passage:

> Guise. *Tue, tue, tue*,
> Let none escape, murder the Hugonets.
> *Anioy*. Kill them, kill them.[34]

In other passages of *Dido*, the parallel with the other plays is
not so close, and yet one can see the young poet experimenting
with favorite words, phrases, or images. Thus, for example:

> His lips an altar, where Ile offer vp
> As many kisses as the Sea hath sands.
>> [*Dido*, 721–722]
> Vpon which Altar I will offer vp
> My daily sacrifice of sighes and teares.
>> [*Jew*, 1213–1214]

> In whose sterne faces shin'd the quenchles fire.
>> [*Dido*, 481]
> Heauens turne it to a blaze of quenchelesse fier.
>> [*Edward II*, 2030]
> The Dyuils there in chaines of quencelesse flame.
>> [II *Tamb.* 2945]
> . . . brands of quenchlesse fire.
>> [II *Tamb.* 3529]

> And wofull *Dido* by these blubbred cheekes.
>> [*Dido*, 1541]
> Their blubbered cheekes. . . .
>> [I *Tamb.* 1802]

> Thy Anchors shall be hewed from Christall Rockes,
> Which if thou lose shall shine aboue the waues.
>> [*Dido*, 754–755]
> Of Christall shining faire the pauement was
>> [H&L, I. 141]

---

[34] *Massacre*, 539, 340–342.

And clad her in a Chrystall liuerie.
                    [*Dido*, 1414]
And cloath it in a christall liuerie.
                    [II *Tamb.* 2573]

When as she meanes to maske the world with clowdes.
                    [*Dido*, 1065]
Muffle your beauties with eternall clowdes.
                    [II *Tamb.* 4398]
And Natures beauty choake with stifeling clouds.
                    [*Jew*, 1095]

And diue into blacke tempests treasurie.
                    [*Dido*, 1064]
And diue into her heart by coloured lookes.
                    [*Dido*, 1126]
Diue to the bottome of *Auernas* poole.
                    [II *Tamb.* 1656]
And Angels diue into the pooles of hell.
                    [II *Tamb.* 4425]

Would, as faire *Troy* was, *Carthage* might be sackt.
                    [*Dido*, 1555]
I wil be *Paris*, and for loue of thee,
Insteede of *Troy* shal *Wertenberge* be sackt.
                    [DF, 1335–1336]

But thou art sprung from *Scythian Caucasus*,
And Tygers of *Hircania* gaue thee sucke.
                    [*Dido*, 1566–1567]
Inhumaine creatures, nurst with Tigers milke.
                    [*Edward II*, 2057]
A brood of barbarous *Tygars* hauing lapt
The bloud of many a heard, whilst with their dams
They kennel'd in *Hircania*, euermore
Wil rage and pray.
                    [*Lucan*, 327–330] [35]
But you are more inhumaine, more inexorable,
O ten times more than Tygers of Arcadia.
                    [*True Tragedy*, 474]
But you are more inhuman, more inexorable
O, ten times more, than tigers of Hyrcania.
                    [III *Henry VI*, I. iv. 154–155]

[35] See II. 39–40.

Aeneas no, although his eyes doe pearce.
[*Dido*, 1007]
His fierie eies are fixt vpon the earth,
As if he now deuis'd some Stratageme:
Or meant to pierce *Auernas* darksome vaults.
[I *Tamb.* 353–355]
Are fixt his piercing instruments of sight.
[I *Tamb.* 468]

That by Characters grauen in thy browes.
[I *Tamb.* 364]
I see my tragedie written in thy browes.
[*Edward II*, 2522]

Not all the world can take thee from mine armes.
[*Dido*, 1267]
Not all the world shall ransom *Baiazeth*.
[I *Tamb.* 1330]

Our hands are not prepar'd to lawles spoyle.
[*Dido*, 260]
That liue by rapine and by lawlesse spoile.
[I *Tamb.* 546]

That erst-while issued from thy watrie loynes.
[*Dido*, 128]
Than all the brats ysprong from *Typhons* loins.
[I *Tamb.* 1207]
Bastardly boy, sprong from some cowards loins.
[II *Tamb.* 2638]
Ah cruel Brat, sprung from a tyrants loines.
[II *Tamb.* 4033]

Whom doe I see, *Ioues* winged messenger?
[*Dido*, 1433]
That *Ioue* shall send his winged Messenger.
[II *Tamb.* 2735]

More then melodious are these words to me.
[*Dido*, 872]
What more then Delian musicke doe I heare?
[*Dido*, 1047]
And speech more pleasant than sweet harmony.
[I *Tamb.* 1219]

I would haue a iewell for mine eare,
And a fine brouch to put in my hat.
[*Dido*, 46–47]
With costlie iewels hanging at their eares,
And shining stones vpon their loftie Crestes.
[I *Tamb.* 152–153]

A Burgonet of steele, and not a Crowne,
A Sword, and not a Scepter fits *Aeneas*.
[*Dido*, 1248–1249]
This compleat armor, and this curtle-axe
Are adiuncts more beseeming *Tamburlaine*.
[I *Tamb.* 238–239]

Aeneas may commaund as many Moores,
As in the Sea are little water drops.
[*Dido*, 1268–1269]
O soule, be changde into little water drops.
[DF, 1472]
As many circumcised Turkes . . .
As hath the Ocean or the Terrene sea
Small drops of water.
[I *Tamb.* 926–929]
Nay could their numbers counteruail the stars
Or euer drisling drops of Aprill showers.
[I *Tamb.* 1402–1403]
In number more than are the drops that fall.
[II *Tamb.* 2728]

Doe thou but smile, and clowdie heauen will cleare.
[*Dido*, 155]
That with thy lookes canst cleare the darkened Sky.
[I *Tamb.* 1220]
Whose chearful looks do cleare the clowdy aire.
[II *Tamb.* 2572]

And teares of pearle, crye stay, *Aeneas*, stay.
[*Dido*, 1202]
Rain'st on the earth resolued pearle in showers.
[I *Tamb.* 1923]

Yet flung I forth, and desperate of my life,
Ran in the thickest throngs.
[*Dido*, 505–506]

But then run desperate through the thickest throngs.
[II *Tamb.* 3329]

What if I sinke his ships? O heele frowne:
Better he frowne, then I should dye for griefe:
I cannot see him frowne, it may not be:
Armies of foes resolu'd to winne this towne . . .
Affright me not, onely *Aeneas* frowne . . .
It is *Aeneas* frowne that ends my daies.
[*Dido*, 1316–1326]
But rathe[r] let the brightsome heauens be dim . . .
Then my faire *Abigal* should frowne on me.
[*Jew*, 1095–1097]

Sent many of their sauadge ghosts to hell.
[*Dido*, 507]
Stab him I say and send him to his freends in hell.
[*Massacre*, 420]
Mounser of *Loraine* sinke away to hell.
[*Massacre*, 1035]
And madnesse send his damned soule to hell.
[I *Tamb.* 2010]
My sword hath sent millions of Turks to hell.
[II *Tamb.* 4291]
Our Turkish swords shal headlong send to hell.
[II *Tamb.* 4348]
No, let the villaine dye, and feele in hell
Iust torments for his trechery.
[*Massacre*, 1187–1188]

Vngentle Queene, is this thy loue to me?
[*Dido*, 670]
Ah *Epernoune*, is this thy loue to me?
[*Massacre*, 1248]

Now bring him backe, and thou shalt be a Queene,
And I will liue a priuate life with him.
[*Dido*, 1605–1606]
And could my crownes reuenew bring him back,
I would freelie giue it to his enemies.
[*Edward II*, 605–606]

And I will either moue the thoughtles flint,
Or drop out both mine eyes in drisling teares.
[*Dido*, 1134–1135]

Or that these teares that drissell from mine eyes,
Had power to mollifie his stonie hart.
                    [*Edward II*, 1116–1117]

If words might moue me I were ouercome.
                    [*Dido*, 1562]
Leister, if gentle words might comfort me,
Thy speeches long agoe had easde my sorrowes.
                    [*Edward II*, 1991–1992]

Whose amorous face like *Pean* sparkles fire.
                    [*Dido*, 1014]
Will sooner sparkle fire then shed a teare.
                    [*Edward II*, 2091]

Forbids all hope to harbour neere our hearts.
                    [*Dido*, 264]
O if thou harborst murther in thy hart.
                    [*Edward II*, 2535]

Depart from *Carthage*, come not in my sight.
                    [*Dido*, 678]
Assure thy selfe thou comst not in my sight.
                    [*Edward II*, 465]

We too will goe a hunting in the woods.
                    [*Dido*, 808]
Come sonne, weele ride a hunting in the parke.
                    [*Edward II*, 2445]

One other passage in *Edward the Second* seems, rather doubtfully, to glance at the first scene of *Dido*:

> For neuer doted *Ioue* on *Ganimed*
> So much as he on cursed *Gaueston*.[36]

Date

While there is fairly general agreement among critics that
Dido is early work, their guesses as to the exact date of composition vary widely. The crudity of the writing, which for once
does not seem due either to rewriting by playhouse hacks or to
printers' clumsiness; the classical theme; the abundance of
Latin quotations; the abnormal frequency of mythological allu-

[36] *Edward the Second*, 476–477.

sions (abnormal even in an age when it was more conventional to use them than it is today, and in a play whose theme necessitated a good many); the close fidelity of the plot to its original in the *Aeneid*; and above all the clever but ineffective turns of phrasing which Marlowe later worked over into some of his greatest passages — all point to very early authorship.

Sir A. W. Ward was the first scholar definitely to pronounce the play "juvenile." The German, Boleslaus Knutowski, in 1905 followed him, describing it as "Marlowe's erste Frucht auf dramatischem Gebiete." [37] He points out that Marlowe here, for the only time, uses an obvious source, lying ready to his hand, which had already been used by other writers, whereas in his later plays the dramatist looks further afield for his materials. He might have strengthened his case, though he does not do so, by adding that in all the other plays Marlowe supplements his main source by careful search for still more material. Knutowski also lays special stress on lapses of taste, which he regards as typical of early work, and points out that feminine endings and substitutions for iambic feet are rare in *Dido*, while they grow steadily more frequent in later plays.

Mr. Tucker Brooke has thrice repeated, at intervals of about ten years, his belief that *Dido* is early work. [38] In his 1910 edition of Marlowe's works, he observed that "the classical story and close dependence on Vergil would naturally point back to the academic period, which seems certainly to have produced the Ovid translations, and which probably inspired the version of Lucan as well." In favor of this view he also pointed out what he regards as the general immaturity of the play's structure — a view which has of later years been questioned [39] — and dwells on the curious foreshadowing of famous lines in later plays.

In 1922 Mr. Brooke wrote: "The most acceptable hypothesis is perhaps that Marlowe wrote the play while still at college, and that Nashe, acting as a (presumably self-appointed) literary executor, revised the manuscript after Marlowe's death."

---

[37] Ward: HEDL (1899), I. 356; Knutowski: *Dido-Drama von Marlowe und Nash,* pp. 31–60.
[38] *Works* (1910), p. 387; PMLA, 37: 368 (1922); Brooke's ed. (1930), p. 115.
[39] See II. 56–57.

In his 1930 edition of the play, he held that "the style is essentially that of Marlowe's earliest period, and is consistent with the idea that *Dido* was composed, at least for the most part, before he left Cambridge" [40] — that is, before the spring of 1587.

Other scholars have in general adhered to this view, though the *Cambridge History of English Literature* describes *Tamburlaine* as "Marlowe's first original work." [41] The biographer, Ingram, regards *Dido* as Marlowe's "unfinished early effort," which was only "nominally" completed by Nashe.[42] Miss Ellis-Fermor assigns "the first draft of *Dido, Queen of Carthage*" to university days, together with the translations of Ovid and Lucan.[43]

On the other hand, the maturity of the stagecraft and the brevity of the speeches have been held to indicate a late date. Colonel Cunningham quotes approvingly Collier's opinion that *Dido* was "written in 1590, although not printed till 1594." [44] Dr. Thomas Matthews Pearce, the most recent investigator, insists that it was "written after 1590" and "as late as 1591 or 1592." [45] This would make *Dido* not only later than *Tamburlaine* and *Doctor Faustus*, but very nearly as late as *Edward the Second*.

Dr. Pearce regards the stagecraft as exceptionally mature for Marlowe. He reasons as follows: There is little effort at localization of scenes in an admittedly early play, like *Tamburlaine*. The First Part might take place anywhere. In the Second Part, the inner stage is probably used for the death scenes of Tamburlaine and Zenocrate, and the walls of Babylon were probably represented by the gallery above. In ten acts, that is the only localization. Otherwise, the play flows endlessly across the stage, unrelated to locale or to properties, the audience being held by the action, the splendor of the verse, the gorgeous costuming. In *Dido*, on the other hand, the rear stage is used re-

[40] PMLA, 37: 368–369 (1922); *Life and Dido*, p. 115.
[41] V. 162.
[42] *Christopher Marlowe and His Associates*, p. 208.
[43] *Christopher Marlowe*, p. 3.
[44] Page xvi.
[45] *Marlowe's "Tragedie of Dido" in Relation to its Latin Source* (Pittsburgh Diss., 1930, MS.), pp. 18, 112–113.

peatedly — for the scene between Jove and Ganymede, where the stage direction of 1594 definitely specifies the inner stage; for the cave scene; and probably for the final scene, where the Queen's funeral pyre is erected. Moreover, the dialogue is closely tied to stage setting and properties. Venus conceals herself with the line

> Here in *this bush* disguised will I stand.[46]

Again she remarks,

> *in this groue*
> Amongst greene brakes Ile lay *Ascanius*.[47]

Juno similarly alludes to

> . . . *these woods*, adioyning to *these walles*.[48]

In all, Mr. Pearce is able to point to twenty-three passages of this sort in which stage sets or properties are closely linked to dialogue.[49]

Finally, the speeches in *Dido* are remarkably short. If we except the 167 lines in which Aeneas describes the sack of Troy, which in itself summarizes 800 lines of the *Aeneid*, the speeches in *Dido* average only four and a half lines. *Tamburlaine*, an early play, averages more than six and a half; *Edward the Second*, a late play, only three. This presumably shows Marlowe advancing toward practical twentieth-century playwriting, with its emphasis on crisply crackling dialogue. But by the severest of practical tests, *Dido* was not a technical advance on *Tamburlaine*. On the stage it was a failure; while *Tamburlaine*, no matter how long its speeches, was a success.

None of Mr. Pearce's evidence for a late date is really very convincing. Allusions to scenery and stage properties may easily have been written in during a late revision. Breaking up long speeches is easy enough and may have been done at the same time. The use of the inner stage is not very frequent at best, and at most means merely that the dramatic material was adapted to it. We are probably safe in regarding *Dido* as a

[46] Line 139.
[47] Ll. 611–612.
[48] Line 898.
[49] *Op. cit.*, pp. 13–17.

play written in Marlowe's earliest years and perhaps revised later.[50]

SOURCE

The source of *Dido* presents no difficulty. The *Aeneid* was the only literary version of the story likely to interest Marlowe; it was known to every university man; texts were easily available. Marlowe invented a few episodes and supplemented Vergil with occasional reminiscences of the *Iliad* and of Ovid's *Amores*, *Fasti*, and *Metamorphoses*. Otherwise the play is simply Vergil's first, second, and fourth books in dramatic form.

[50] Dates have been assigned as follows:

1781. Thomas Warton: "Completed and published by his friend Thomas Nashe, in 1594." [*Hist. Eng. Poetry* (ed. 1781), III. 435; (ed. 1824), IV. 262]

1831. Collier: "Apparently written previous to 1590." [HEDP, III. 221]

1870. Cunningham: "In Mr. Collier's opinion, . . . written in 1590." [P. xvi]

1887. Ellis: "Probably an early work of Marlowe's, so far as it is his at all, and it must have been elaborated and considerably enlarged by Nash in a manner that is sometimes a caricature, perhaps not quite unconsciously, of Marlowe's manner." [Mermaid ed., p. xliii]

1891. Fleay: "Collaboration . . . early work written at Cambridge before either author left the University." [*Biog. Chron.*, II. 147]

1899. Ward: "Juvenile work, very probably composed before he left Cambridge. . . . It seems most likely that this unfinished juvenile work was completed by Nashe not long before its publication." [HEDL, I. 356–357]

1904. Ingram: "His alliterative skill is much displayed, making it probable that *Dido* was an unfinished early effort." [*Christopher Marlowe and His Associates*, p. 208]

1905. Knutowski: "Marlowe's erste Frucht auf dramatischem Gebiete und wahrscheinlich schon während seiner Studienjahre (1581–87) in Cambridge geschrieben worden." [*Dido-Drama von Marlowe und Nash*, p. 60]

1910. Brooke: "Probably sketched in its earliest form before Marlowe left Cambridge. . . . Yet it seems pretty clear that the extant text of *Dido* dates from a later period." [*Works*, p. 387]

1914. Ingram: "Evidently an early production of Marlowe's, thrown aside through some unknown circumstances, and never completed." [*Marlowe & His Poetry*, p. 131]

1922. Brooke: "The most acceptable hypothesis is perhaps that Marlowe wrote the play while still at college, and that Nashe . . . revised the manuscript after Marlowe's death." [PMLA, 37: 368–369]

1927. Ellis-Fermor: "Literary work of his last years at Cambridge." [*Christopher Marlowe*, p. 3]

1930. Brooke: "The style is essentially that of Marlowe's earliest period." [*Dido*, p. 115]

1930. Pearce: "The maturity of technique in the play, supported further by the study of plot and characterization, offers convincing testimony for a date later than 1587." [*Univ. of Pittsburgh Bulletin*, 27: 142]

1931. Robertson: "If we could be at all sure that Nashe . . . had not to his own ends modified the versification, . . . we should be led to reckon that play the first item in Marlowe's surviving work." [*Marlowe*, p. 37]

1936. Taylor: "Some form of *Dido* was known in 1590." [PMLA, 51: 660 (1936)]

Most of the borrowings from Ovid and Homer appear in the first act and are mere allusions or bits of phrasing. Thus Jupiter's allusion to

> . . . this earth threatning haire,
> That shaken thrise makes Natures buildings quake

is simple translation of

> Terrificam capitis concussit terque, quarterque
> Caesariem, cum qua terram, mare, sidera movit,

which in turn may owe something to the *Iliad*:

> ἀμβρόσιαι δ' ἄρα χαῖται ἐπερρώσαντο ἄνακτος
> κρατὸς ἀπ' ἀθανάτοιο, μέγαν δ' ἐλέλιξεν Ὄλυμπον.[51]

When in the same scene Venus pleads on behalf of Aeneas:

> For my sake pitie him *Oceanus*,
> That erst-while issued from thy watrie loynes,
> And had my being from thy bubling froth,

she is recalling Ovid's

> . . . aliqua et mihi gratia ponto est,
> Si tamen in dio quondam concreta profundo
> Spuma fui.[52]

And when a little later the goddess, pitying her exiled and ship-wrecked son, exclaims:

> See what strange arts necessitie findes out,

she is again echoing the *Metamorphoses*:

> . . . grande doloris
> Ingenium est, miserisque venit sollertia rebus.[53]

Marlowe's allusion to "Helen's brother" — that is, either Castor or Pollux — might have come either from the *Fasti*, from Lucian, whom Marlowe quotes in *Doctor Faustus*, or from the *Iliad*, where there is an allusion to Helen's relationship to the Twins.[54] The phrase "*Iunos* bird" for a peacock is an echo of Marlowe's own translation of *Ovid's Elegies* (the *Amores*):

[51] *Dido*, 10–11; *Metamorphoses*, I. 179 ff.; *Iliad*, A. 529–530.
[52] Ll. 127–129; *Metamorphoses*, IV. 536 ff.
[53] Line 169; *Metamorphoses*, VI. 574 ff.
[54] Line 17; *Fasti*, V. 699–730; Lucian's *Dialogue of the Gods*, XVI; *Iliad*, C. 237.

There *Iunoes* bird displayes his gorgious feather.[55]

In general, Marlowe adheres with surprising fidelity to the text of the *Aeneid*. Something over one third of his lines are direct translation or very close paraphrase.[56] He frequently translates entire passages and sometimes even quotes the Latin untranslated. He makes only such omissions and expansions as are required by the change from the extended epic to the compressed dramatic form.

Perhaps Marlowe was thinking of Aristotle's observation in the *Poetics* that

Epic has a special advantage which enables the length to be increased, because in tragedy it is not possible to represent several parts of the story as going on simultaneously, but only to show what is on the stage, that part of the story which the actors are performing.[57]

Whether he knew this passage or not, Marlowe at least acts on its principle, notably when he compresses the eight hundred lines of Vergil's second book to a single speech. The second book of the *Aeneid* is a mere monologue, offering no opportunity for action on the stage.

Vergil's casual allusion to the Ganymede story is expanded in the first scene of *Dido*.[58] The detail is apparently original with Marlowe and seems to have been intended as a kind of prologue. The rest of the scene, from the point where Venus intercedes for Aeneas, comes from Vergil. The expansion of the role of Iarbas as a rival to Aeneas is an effort to introduce the element of conflict essential in drama. In the *Aeneid*, Iarbas actually appears but once, though he is mentioned in two other passages. In the fourth book he offers sacrifice to Jove to secure favor against Aeneas. In the first book Anna mentions him as a suitor of Dido's, and later Dido herself alludes to the possibility of her marriage to him.[59] In the *Aeneid* he is a Numidian prince, who may become either Dido's lover or her foe. He

---

[55] Line 34; *Elegies*, II. vi. 55.
[56] Thomas Matthews Pearce: *Marlowe's "Tragedy of Dido" in Relation to Its Latin Source* (Pittsburgh Diss., 1930, MS.), p. 6. Cf. Knutowski's appendix, McKerrow, IV. 294–30.
[57] *Poetics*, XXIV. 6.
[58] Ll. 1–49.
[59] *Aeneid*, IV. 196; I. 36, 326.

learns of Aeneas only when Fama, or Rumor, flies out to him from Dido's court.

In the play Iarbas appears nine times. He is a kind of master of ceremonies at Dido's court, and he wishes to marry her. He greets the shipwrecked Aeneas with an offer of welcome at the court of Dido, "my Queene." He gradually becomes hostile through jealousy, especially after seeing Dido and Aeneas emerge from the cave; and he eventually gets rid of his rival by helping on his flight from Carthage. These episodes, his relations with Anna, his last appeal to Dido, and his death at her feet are all added by the dramatist.

The episode in which Cupid is substituted for Ascanius is expanded in the dramatic version because of the opportunity it gives the boy actors. Indeed, this episode provides one reason for supposing that the play was originally written for a children's company. Though this material is in general from Vergil, several of these scenes have no specific Vergilian prototype whatever.

Marlowe takes over from the *Aeneid* the appearances of Hermes, whom he also calls Mercury. In the epic Hermes first appears to Aeneas in reality and then later in a vision. In the drama he appears first as a vision and later as a reality. Aeneas, influenced by the vision, determines to leave Carthage but is persuaded by Dido to remain. Then Hermes appears physically before the hero, who reaches his final decision and departs.[60] The change heightens the suspense, which is more necessary on the stage than in an epic recital; and adds to the dramatic effect by having Aeneas and his men obey the command of Jove's messenger while actually building the city. The deaths of Anna and Iarbas, with which Marlowe closes his play, do not appear in the *Aeneid*, but they are in the general vein of Elizabethan stage convention.

The most striking changes are those which Marlowe makes in the character and achievements of Aeneas. In the *Aeneid* he is always "pius Aeneas." Marlowe uses the adjective but once, and depicts the Trojan hero as a rash Elizabethan of exagger-

---

[60] Mr. R. B. McKerrow in his Nashe (II. 387, 300) mistakenly supposes that Hermes appears but once in the *Aeneid* and that either Marlowe or Nashe invented the second appearance.

ated energy. Marlowe's Aeneas tells how he rushed alone against the Greeks; [61] Vergil's is accompanied by a band of warriors. Marlowe's Aeneas fights his way boldly out of the city; Vergil's, like a prudent commander, moves cautiously in the shadows. Marlowe's Aeneas claims to have carried Anchises on his back, Iulus in his arms, while leading Creusa by the hand; Vergil's Aeneas carries only Anchises. As a final touch, Marlowe makes Aeneas leap into the sea in a vain effort to save Polyxena. Vergil describes the building of the city by the Carthaginians; Marlowe's hero, in about the same language, sets out to build it himself.

Many of the most famous lines in the *Aeneid* are literally translated in the play. To quote all of them would be to transcribe a large part of it, [62] but the following examples are sufficient to show Marlowe's method:

> . . . famam qui terminet astris.
> > [*Aeneid*, I. 287]
> No bounds but heauen shall bound his Emperie.
> > [*Dido*, 100]

> Et vera incessu patuit dea.
> > [*Aeneid*, I. 405]
> I know her by the mouings of her feete.
> > [*Dido*, 241]

> . . . cur dextrae iungere dextram
> Non datur?
> > [*Aeneid*, I. 408–409]
> Why talke we not together hand in hand?
> > [*Dido*, 245]

> Succedunt tecto, et flammas ad culmina iactant.
> > [*Aeneid*, II. 478]
> With balles of wilde fire in their murdering pawes.
> > [*Dido*, 512]

> Parce metu, Cytherea: manent immota tuorum
> Fata tibi; cernes urbem et promissa Lavini
> Moenia.
> > [*Aeneid*, I. 257–259]

[61] Ll. 505 ff.
[62] Thomas Matthews Pearce, *op. cit.*, pp. 115–134, provides a line-by-line table of Marlowe's borrowings from bk. II of the *Aeneid*.

Content thee *Cytherea* in thy care,
Since thy *Aeneas* wandring fate is firme,
Whose wearie lims shall shortly make repose
In those faire walles I promist him of yore.
                                    [*Dido*, 82–85]

The play shows no relationship to the various translations of
Vergil that had been made in Marlowe's time or earlier. The
poet naturally went straight to the Latin text, with which he
had been familiar from boyhood.[63] Neither does Marlowe appear
to have used the earlier plays on the same subject, several of
which already existed. Warton [64] mentions an "interlude of
Dido and Eneas at Chester." Anthony à Wood [65] records that
John Ritwise, or Rightwise, master of St. Paul's School, London, had "made the *Tragedy of Dido* out of Virgil; and acted
the same with the scholars of his school before cardinal Wolsey,
with great applause." Queen Elizabeth saw "a Tragedie named
'Dido,' in hexametre verse, without anie chorus," when she
visited Cambridge in 1564, the year of Marlowe's birth. It was
the work of one Edward Haliwell. In 1583, while Marlowe was
at Cambridge, still another *Dido* was performed in Latin at
Christ Church Hall, Oxford. The author was Dr. William
Gager.[66]

There had also been two Italian plays on *Didone*, one by
Ludovico Dolce (1508–1568/9) and one by Giambattista Gi-
raldi Cinthio (1504–1573), which was posthumously printed in
1583. In France, Étienne Jodelle (1532–1573) had written a
Didon (1552).

None of these plays, however, shows any closer resemblance
to Marlowe's play than might be anticipated from the identical
source and similar theme. It is doubtful whether Marlowe had
ever heard of any of them, though Mr. Tucker Brooke hazards
the conjecture that either Haliwell's or Gager's play "may have
offered the original suggestion." [67]

[63] Cf. Thomas Matthews Pearce, *op. cit.*, p. 6.
[64] *Hist. English Poetry* (ed. 1781), III. 435n; (ed. 1824), IV. 262n.
[65] *Athenae Oxonienses* (ed. 1813), I. 35; Warton, *loc. cit.*
[66] Bodleian Library, Rawlinson MS. B. 274; John Nichols: *Progresses and Public
Processions of Queen Elizabeth* (1823), I. 186; *Athenae Oxonienses* (ed. 1813), I. 35n; Dyce
(ed. 1858), p. xxxvii n.
[67] *Works* (1910), p. 390.

It is possible, however, that there were other plays on Dido, now lost, from which Marlowe gleaned more than a mere suggestion. The two entries in *Henslowe's Diary* suggest the existence of such plays, though it is entirely possible that Henslowe is alluding to Marlowe's *Dido*. Occasional references to a lost play called *Aeneas' Revenge* also suggest a possible model for Marlowe.

STAGE HISTORY

Dido seems to have been pretty generally recognized as a dramatic and literary failure from the start. Only one edition appeared, and there is no really satisfactory record of any stage performance, except the assertion on the title page that it was played by the Children of Her Majesty's Chapel. *Henslowe's Diary* mentions several productions of a play that may have been the Marlowe-Nashe *Dido*; but these entries may, as Sir Edmund K. Chambers thinks, refer to some other play.[68]

On January 3, 1597/8, Henslowe records the expenditure of twenty-nine shillings "ageanste the playe of dido & enevs." [69] Five days later he records, "Lent vnto the company when they fyrst played dido at nyght the some of thirtishillynges wch wasse the 8 of Jenewary 1597 [i.e., 1597/8]." As this was three years after the publication of *Dido*, the play must have been a revival. M. de la Boderie, the French ambassador, saw a tragedy of Aeneas and Dido at an entertainment given by the Earl of Arundel for the court of James I.[70] This was probably the last production of *Dido* ever given. There is no record of any modern production.

Mr. Tucker Brooke points out that the Chapel Children were playing at Norwich and Ipswich, not far from Cambridge, in May, 1587, while Marlowe was still technically in residence, and suggests that they may then have secured the manuscript from the budding playwright, produced it at once in the provinces, and brought it to London later.[71] If this is the case, *Dido* was the first of Marlowe's plays to grace the boards. It has also been suggested that the Children produced the Marlowe-Nashe

---

[68] *Elizabethan Stage*, III. 427.
[69] *Henslowe's Diary*, fol. 44r; Greg's ed., I. 83.
[70] T. S. Graves in MLR, 9: 525–526 (1914). See *Ambassades*, II. 263–264.
[71] *Life and Dido*, p. 116n.

Dido before the Queen at Croydon in 1591, but this seems doubtful.[72]

INFLUENCE

Although Marlowe himself so frequently reworks lines from *Dido* in other plays, his contemporaries and successors seem to have paid almost no attention to the play. In Nashe's *Summers Last Will and Testament* one passage appears to parallel a line in *Dido*, as is natural in view of his collaboration. In *Dido* appears the line:

> *Vulcan* shall daunce to make thee laughing sport.

In Nashe's book is the passage: "To make the gods merry, the cœlestiall clowne *Vulcan* tun'de his polt foote to the measures of *Apolloes* Lute, and daunst a limping Gallyard in *Ioues* starrie hall." [73] Both, however, may be mere reminiscences of the *Iliad*.

Equally natural, if Thomas Kyd is the author, are similarities in the *Spanish Tragedy* and *Soliman and Perseda*, which may date from Kyd's early association with Marlowe.

There is marked resemblance between the scene in *The Spanish Tragedy* in which Isabella undertakes to destroy the tree on which her lover has been hanged, and Dido's destruction of the tackle and oars of Aeneas' fleet. Isabella exclaims

> And as I curse this tree from further fruit.

Dido exclaims

> O cursed tree.[74]

Iarbas, with his hopeless attachment to Dido, is very like Basilisco, with his fatal attachment to Perseda in *Soliman and Perseda*. Both Kyd and Marlowe employ the device of a rag dipped in blood, which turns up later in *The True Tragedie*, a play that has been attributed to Marlowe.[75]

Among the verbal parallels, the following are very close:

[72] Chambers: *Eliz. Stage*, III. 427.
[73] *Dido*, 32; McKerrow's Nashe, III. 294.
[74] *Spanish Tragedy*, IV. ii. 35; *Dido*, 1345.
[75] See II. 221–241.

Whose memorie like pale deaths stony mace.
[*Dido*, 410]
Could win pale Death from his usurpèd right.
[ST, I. iv. 39]
Pale, dim, cruel death.   [ST, IV. iv. 106]
Death which the poets
Faine to be pale and meager.
[S&P, V. iii. 63–64]
And now pale Death.   [S&P, V. iv. 152]

Sent many of their sauadge ghosts to hell.[76]
[*Dido*, 505–506]
Then stab the slaues, and send their soules to hell.
[S&P, III. v. 10]
Myself should send their hateful souls to hell.
[ST, IV. i. 28]

And I alas, was forst to let her lye.
[*Dido*, 574]
No, let her lie, a prey to ravening birds.
[S&P, V. iii. 55]

Aeneas, O *Aeneas*, quench these flames.
[*Dido*, 1018]
I may asswage, but neuer quench loues fire.
[S&P, IV. i. 261]

Weare the emperiall Crowne of *Libia*. . . .
O how a Crowne becomes *Aeneas* head!
[*Dido*, 1240–1244]
Perseda for my sake weare this crowne.
Now is she fairer than she was before.
[S&P, IV. i. 187–188]

How now *Aeneas*, sad, what meanes these dumpes?
[*Dido*, 1470]
Why, how now, Erastus, alwaies in thy dumpes?
[S&P, IV. i. 25]

It is especially interesting to find in *Soliman and Perseda*[77]
a passage alluding to "Venus milke white Doves." Not only
does this parallel "those milke white Doues" of Venus in

---

[76] See II. 53.   [77] IV. i. 71.

Dido,[78] but it employs Marlowe's favorite adjective of color, which he uses over and over throughout his whole career.

There are several rather faint parallels between *Dido* and the *Troublesome Raigne of John, King of England*, which was published in 1591.[79] The closest of these are

> O dull conceipted *Dido*.
> > [*Dido*, 716]
> Ah dull conceited peazant.
> > [TR, Pt. I, sc. 13, 264]

> Breake ope their brazen doores.
> > [*Dido*, 62]
> Break their brazen gates.
> > [TR, Pt. I, sc. 2, 91]

Before copies of Marlowe's play had been discovered, early Elizabethan scholars suspected that the passage recited by the player king in *Hamlet* [80] came from *Dido*. After copies had been found and it was possible to compare the two plays, it was seen that this could not be true; but there remained certain similarities which suggested that though Shakespeare did not actually quote *Dido*, he quite possibly had it in mind. In both scenes, Priam falls, not from the blow of a sword, but from the wind of the blow:

> Which he disdaining whiskt his sword about,
> And with the wind thereof the King fell downe.
> > [*Dido*, 548–549]
> But with the whiff and wind of his fell sword
> The unnerved father falls.
> > [*Hamlet*, II. ii. 494–495]
> . . . The captive Grecian falls,
> Even in the fan and wind of your fair sword.
> > [*Troilus and Cressida*, V. iii. 40–41]

> So leaning on his sword he stood stone still,
> Viewing the fire wherewith rich *Ilion* burnt.
> > [*Dido*, 558–559]

[78] Line 615. Thomas Matthews Pearce, *loc. cit.*, carries the parallels even further.
[79] See Rupert Taylor in PMLA, 51: 660 (1936), for further examples.
[80] II. ii. See Edward Capell: "*Notes and Various Readings to Shakespeare* (ed. 1783), I. 134–135.

So, as a painted tyrant, Pyrrhus stood
And like a neutral to his will and matter,
Did nothing.
[*Hamlet*, II. ii. 502–504]

In both plays the harness of Pyrrhus drips blood and his eyes are specially mentioned. The "mincing" of Priam's limbs in *Hamlet* is rather like the slashing of his body "from the nauell to the throat" [81] in Marlowe's play. Shakespeare may have recalled this rather awkward sword stroke when in *Macbeth* that heroic soldier unseams a foeman "from the nave to the chaps." [82]

Again, we have in *Dido*,

Yong infants swimming in their parents bloud,
Headles carkasses piled vp in heapes,
Virgins halfe dead dragged by their golden haire, [83]

all of which is very like the "blood of fathers, mothers, daughters, sons," in *Hamlet*. [84]

Like the play in *Hamlet*, *Dido* "pleas'd not the million," and Shakespeare exaggerates very slightly in saying that "it was never acted; or, if it was, not above once" — though *Dido* can scarcely be called "an excellent play, well digested in the scenes, set down with as much modesty as cunning." All in all, the player's speech in *Hamlet* sounds strangely as if Master Shakespeare were recalling, rather vaguely, the unsuccessful play of a great rival.

[81] Line 550.
[82] I. ii. 22.
[83] Ll. 488–490.
[84] II. ii. 480.

CHAPTER XII

THE MASSACRE AT PARIS

Inhumaine creatures, nurst with Tigers milke.
Edward the Second, 2057

NO JUDGMENT, however charitable, can set down *The Massacre at Paris* as anything but one of Marlowe's failures. It is, if anything, a worse play than *Dido,* which at least foreshadows Marlowe's greater work, still to come, and has many passages that are genuinely fine in themselves. *The Massacre* is almost destitute of poetry, and relies for its stage effects on the most sensational kind of Elizabethan blood and bombast. In judging *Dido,* Marlowe's idolaters can always attempt to save their poet's reputation by attributing the worst passages to Nashe; but in dealing with *The Massacre,* even this resource is denied them.

AUTHORSHIP

No real doubt exists as to Marlowe's authorship of *The Massacre at Paris.* The first edition, an octavo instead of the usual quarto, bears the words: "Written by Chriſtopher Marlow." This, though undated, probably appeared before 1600, and thus carries the attribution of authorship very close to Marlowe's death. No one, however, is inclined to date the edition within his lifetime,[1] and the title page seems to be the earliest allusion to the play as Marlowe's work.

Though early writers make no reference to the presence of another pen, a number of more recent scholars have attempted to show either that Marlowe had collaboration in writing *The Massacre at Paris* or that he left it to be completed by another hand. There is, however, no real reason for setting up such a theory, which has been attempted mainly as a means of accounting for the confusion of the existing text.

[1] "The publication has been conjecturally ascribed to various years between 1594 and 1600." — Tucker Brooke: *Works* (1910), p. 441.

The plain fact seems to be that the play is a botched-up job, tossed off by the dramatist in a careless or hasty mood and still further mangled in a printer's surreptitious transcript of a stage production.[2] The best evidence of this is that, bad though the play is, lines wholly typical of Marlowe occur throughout. Tucker Brooke points particularly to the closing lines as markedly characteristic:

> And then I vow for to reuenge his death,
> As Rome and all those popish Prelates there,
> Shall curse the time that ere *Nauarre* was King,
> And rulde in France by *Henries* fatall death.[3]

These, he says, are "as convincing in their swing and melody as the poet's autograph." But many other lines scattered through the piece are equally typical. Notable among these are the last speeches of the dying King Henry, one of which even contains two lines (italicized here) that are practically identical with two in *Edward the Second* — a repetition of his own work wholly habitual with Marlowe:

> Tell her for all this that I hope to liue,
> Which if I doe, the Papall Monarck goes
> To wrack and antechristian kingdome falles.
> These bloudy hands shall teare his triple Crowne,
> And fire accursed Rome about his eares.
> *Ile fire his crased buildings and inforse*
> *The papall towers to kisse the holy earth.*[4]

Other lines are clearly in the mood of *Tamburlaine*, notably Dumaine's speech:

> O wordes of power to kill a thousand men.
> Come let vs away and leauy men,
> Tis warre that must asswage this tyrantes pride.[5]

No one familiar with Marlowe's style will fail to recognize as his the long soliloquy by the Duke of Guise,[6] with its curious suggestion of *The Jew of Malta* and of *Doctor Faustus* com-

---

[2] "There is nothing to indicate collaboration or methodical revision." Brooke, *loc. cit.*
[3] *Op. cit.*, p. 442; ll. 1260–1263.
[4] *Edward the Second*, 396–397; *Massacre*, 1209–1215.
[5] *Massacre*, 1138–1140.
[6] *Massacre*, 91–166; the quotation is ll. 97–104.

mingled. It is difficult to imagine anything more completely like Marlowe's verse than the Guise's lines:

> What glory is there in a common good,
> That hanges for euery peasant to atchiue?
> That like I best that flyes beyond my reach.
> Set me to scale the high Peramides,
> And thereon set the Diadem of Fraunce.
> Ile either rend it with my nayles to naught,
> Or mount the top with my aspiring winges,
> Although my downfall be the deepest hell.[7]

The Machiavellian influence is also as clear here as it is in the prologue to *The Jew of Malta*, which contains a reference to "the Guise." [8] But it is idle to multiply instances proving what nobody doubts to begin with.

DATE

The date of *The Massacre at Paris* offers a far more difficult problem. There is very little positive external evidence and, since there is only a badly mangled text as basis, equally little internal evidence. The title page of the only edition is undated, and — to make matters worse — the book was never entered in the *Stationers' Register* at all.

A convenient *terminus a quo* is provided by the death of Henri III, King of France, with which the play closes. This is an integral part of the dramatic structure which cannot be regarded as an interpolation. The King died August 2, 1589, when Marlowe's brief professional career had well begun, and this was, presumably, the event that fixed his attention on his subject, which is not really the Massacre of St. Bartholomew's, but rather the dramatic conflict between the Duke of Guise and Henry of Navarre. Henslowe, evidently recognizing this, habitually refers to the play — if he really refers to the same play — as "The Guise," employing his usual fantastic array of variant spellings.

An equally definite *terminus ad quem* is provided by the first production of "the tragedy of the gvyes," which *Henslowe's Diary* marks as "ne" on January 30, 1593/4. But this is ex-

[7] Ll. 97–104.
[8] See I. 347–354.

actly six months after Marlowe's death, which — collaboration excluded — is a still more definite *terminus ad quem*. Henslowe's takings at this performance were the highest of the season, £3 14*s.*, which strongly suggests a new play.⁹

Other contemporary allusions are of doubtful value in dating. The allusion to the death of Pope Sixtus V, who died on August 27, 1590,

> . . . whet thy sword on *Sextus* bones,
> That it may keenly slice the Catholicks,¹⁰

might easily have been interpolated, as might also the allusion to the Spanish Armada:

> Did he not cause the King of Spaines huge fleete
> To threaten England and to menace me?¹¹

The confused and shapeless structure of the play may indicate the author's inexperience, which would make this an early play; but it more probably indicates mere haste and carelessness, which would permit us to give *The Massacre* a later date. There is a sureness of touch in the finer passages which is not apparent in such obviously early work as *Dido*. The clear relation to *The Jew of Malta* is important chiefly as showing what was in the poet's mind while writing — a keen interest in the Machiavellian hero as a type and in the Duke of Guise as an individual. This presumably indicates that the two plays were written close together.

In that case, a date somewhere between 1590 and 1593 would pretty well agree with the known facts. It is at least safe to say that *The Massacre at Paris* dates from the latter part of Marlowe's career. Beyond that, it is not wise to be dogmatic.¹²

⁹ Greg's ed., I. 15; Collier's ed., p. 30.
¹⁰ Ll. 1250–1251.
¹¹ Ll. 1045–1046.
¹² The following dates have been suggested:

1831. Collier: "Produced soon after 1588." [HEDP, III. 132]
1850. Dyce: "Composed after August 2nd, 1589, when Henry the Third, with whose death it terminates, expired." [I. xxiii]
1885. Bullen: "One of Marlowe's latest works." [I. xlvi]
1910. Brooke: "One of the latest of Marlowe's dramatic works." [p. 440]
1922. Brooke: "1590 or 1591." [PMLA, 37: 378]
1927. Ellis-Fermor: "The relative order is then, first, *The Jew of Malta*; second, *The Massacre*; third and fourth, *The Contention* and *The True Tragedy.* . . . The

It is especially dangerous to attach undue importance to the murder of Henri III as a means of fixing the date. *The Massacre at Paris* is not a topical or "news" play like *Arden of Feversham*, *A Warning for Fair Women*, or *A Yorkshire Tragedy*. No single event is the center of the action. Otherwise, Marlowe's play has points of resemblance to the news plays, since it deals with relatively recent sensations in the news, and takes a definite "editorial" attitude on a political question, like Middleton's *Game at Chesse*. The authors of such plays were often willing to go back over a period of years to find sensational "news" on which to build a play. Even *Arden of Feversham* and *A Yorkshire Tragedy* are based on crimes some years in the past. Marlowe, too, may have been willing to write of the murder of Henri III long after it happened, going back some years for a still-remembered horror, which, like the other writers of news plays, he exploits in a manner closely akin to that of the modern sensational press.

Source

Although no single satisfactory source has ever been made out for *The Massacre at Paris*, the general provenience of Marlowe's material is not in the least doubt, when one understands the journalistic methods of the sixteenth century and the interests of the reading public they were meant to satisfy. The newspaper and magazine had not yet arisen, since the conditions necessary to periodical publishing — swift and relatively uncensored dispersal of news, a fairly large reading public, and a postal organization capable of distributing editions to scattered subscribers — did not exist. Nevertheless, the fundamental human craving to know the news and to hear comment on it was as strong then as it is now; and the place of the modern newspaper was taken by the broadside ballad, by the newssheet or broadside in prose, by the newsbook, also called a "re-

---

group as a whole cannot well have been begun before the end of 1588." [*Christopher Marlowe*, p. 5]

1929. Greg: "Between the summer of 1590 and the end of 1592." [Reprint, p. vi]

1931. H. S. Bennett: "Between the summer of 1590 and some time in 1592 (probably late that year)." [p. 170]

1931. Robertson: "Probably earlier than the date 1592–3, commonly assigned to it." [*Marlowe*, p. 42]

1936. Rupert Taylor: "Produced early in 1590." [PMLA, 51: 653 (1936)]

lation," which as the idea of periodical publication developed gradually grew into the "coranto," running on from number to number.

In the beginning there was no idea of serial production. Ambitious printers simply brought out their broadsides or newsbooks whenever the events of the day were startling enough to sell off an edition. Newspaper work was, in other words, a perpetual series of extra editions and nothing else.

Usually, readers of the sixteenth century retained their interest in a striking event long after it had occurred; but in some cases publication of the news was extremely prompt.[13] Thus, in the *Stationers' Register* for September 25, 1590, we find entry of "The true newes from Ffraunce broughte by the laste post the 23th [*sic*] of September 1590."[14] Two days after the news had been received the entry is made in the *Register*, and by that time the presses were probably already working.

Corresponding to the modern magazine were miscellanies published as books — like *The Foreste*, which was so important as source material for *Tamburlaine* — and individual pamphlets dealing with public questions, often fiercely propagandist and at best usually halfway between dispassionate news reporting and distinctly partisan editorial comment. Together with these, there were also numerous books on public affairs, much like their modern congeners, except for a partisanship more ferocious than is common today. All these were under a strict government censorship, which did not wholly end in England until the middle of the nineteenth century. The censorship, however, gave the news writers a relatively free hand in dealing with foreign affairs, and as a result events on the Continent occupy a disproportionate share of space in the early newsbooks.

The sensational and dramatic events of the French religious wars were obviously good copy for the newsmongers and equally certain to provide material for the propagandist writers. It is not surprising, therefore, to find that the surviving pamphlet literature of the time is copious and that from it we can reconstruct Marlowe's play piecemeal. It has never been possible to discover any one individual source from which the play was

[13] See I. 335–336 for the use of similar sources for *The Jew of Malta*.
[14] Arber's reprint, II. 563.

exclusively taken; but this is not surprising. Marlowe habitually used several sources, and *The Massacre at Paris* deals with
events scattered over about a quarter of a century and likely to
be treated in many pamphlets. There is every reason to suppose
that he made free use of the abundant printed newsbooks and
contemporary histories dealing with the massacre and the events
that followed it.

Publication of these began on the Continent earlier than in
England, and it was for a time customary to import English
editions printed abroad. Even earlier than this, Latin newsbooks were common, apparently because the learned language
gave the printers a public everywhere and consequently a wider
sale. These Latin newsbooks probably circulated in England
from the beginning of the sixteenth century. Though evidence
is lacking, it is hard to imagine that the English were completely
indifferent to news of the meeting of Henry VIII and Francis I
at the Field of the Cloth of Gold in 1519. Presumably they read
the Latin account published in Paris in 1520 as *Campi, Convivii
atque ludorum antagonisticorum ordo, modus atque descriptio*.
After 1555 the importation of foreign newsbooks is known to
have developed rapidly, favored by the technical imperfections
of English printing.[15]

In some such way Marlowe's materials for *The Massacre at
Paris* unquestionably reached him. Since we know that he used
a variety of sources in *Tamburlaine*, *The Jew of Malta*, and to
some degree in *Edward the Second*, there is every reason to suppose that in *The Massacre at Paris* he may have drawn largely
on a number of pamphlets, on current gossip of the time, and
even on secret governmental sources of information. In that
case, the lack of a single source is not surprising: There never
was any.

Marlowe probably used various histories by Jean de Serres
for the events of the Massacre of St. Bartholomew's itself and
the events immediately preceding it. He probably relied on
contemporary newsbooks for the murder of the Duke of Guise
and the murder of Henri III, events which fell within the dramatist's working years in the theatre. In using the newsbooks as
sources here, he unconsciously established a precedent which

[15] Cf. Matthias A. Shaaber: *Some Forerunners of the Newspaper in England*, pp. 9–10.

Thomas Middleton followed when he, too, used them as sources for *A Game at Chesse*.

We know that these books were abundant; for, says de Serres, with all a scholar's disdain for the mere journalist, after the Guise had been murdered, "There was no foolish Poet nor Ballet-singer within *Parris*, that deuised not one couple of songs touching this action." Worse still, "there was no Printer, that set not his Presse on work with discourses made touching his death." [16] The Massacre of St. Bartholomew's was, of course, an even greater sensation. "Bokes are extant on both parts," says the anonymous author of *A true and plaine report of the Furious outrages of Fraunce*.[17] Pamphlets reporting the massacre abounded in France. One appeared in Poland, where the future Henri III of France then reigned; and a special account was drawn up by Camillo Capilupi, the Pope's secretary.

The propagandist motive behind these accounts is obvious enough; but the French government also made clandestine efforts, in which the propaganda was concealed, to mitigate the adverse effect of the slaughter on public opinion. The story that the massacre merely anticipated a Protestant rising is, of course, familiar. Private representations were made to the English ambassador, who was none other than Sir Francis Walsingham, relative of Marlowe's patron. According to a seventeenth-century account published in London:

They took another course to stop the Queen of *Englands* resentments, who, besides the common Cause of Religion, had a particular esteem for the Admiral, for they shewed a Memorial, which he had given the King to perswade the War of *Flanders*, to *Walsingham* (the ever renowned Secretary of State) then her Ambassador in France.[18]

There is also record of a private letter from Charles IX to Bertrand Salignac de la Mothe Fénelon, his ambassador in London:

Monsieur de La Mothe, je vous envoye une douzaine de livres d'une espistre faicte par Carpentier [i.e., the "Lettre de Pierre Charpentier"], que je desire qui soit secrètement publiée et faicte courir de

---

[16] *First Booke of the historie of the last troubles of France*, p. 202, wrongly numbered 184. (Bound with *Historical Collection* in NYPL.)

[17] Matthias A. Shaaber, *op. cit.*, pp. 179n, 237.

[18] *Relation of the Barbarous and Bloody Massacre* (London, 1678), p. 39. Copy in NYPL.

main en main, sans que l'on saiche que cella vienne de vous ny de moy; mais que l'on dye et croye qu'elle a esté imprimée en Allemaigne. Je vous y en envoyerai, d'icy à quelque temps, qui seront en françois, dont il faudra que faciés de mesme. Charles.[19]

It would be difficult to imagine a more frankly cynical statement of the methods and objects of a modern propagandist.

Other news reports, doubtless quite as tendencious, must have reached England; but the *Stationers' Register* for these years is unfortunately given over largely to the business affairs of the Most Worshipful Company of Stationers and not to the usual lists of newly licensed books. In any case, Marlowe — a child of six or seven at the time of the massacre — would hardly have used newsbooks for any but the later events of the play, which fell within his active years. He probably used histories for the early part of his drama. The actual newsbooks that he used have so far defied identification and may well have perished, since nothing printed disappears more readily than an old newspaper.

For the massacre itself, Marlowe may have in part relied on the accounts of Francis Walsingham, either directly, or at second hand from the lips of his relative, Thomas Walsingham, the dramatist's patron. Francis Walsingham, not yet a knight, had been English ambassador in Paris at the time of the massacre. By order of the French government, his embassy in the Faubourg-Saint-Germain was protected by troops while the slaughter was in progress, though the diplomat's safety was probably due in the main to the embassy's remoteness from the scene of the worst bloodshed. The youthful Philip Sidney was a guest in the embassy at this time, and many English Protestants sought refuge there, any one of whom [20] Marlowe may have known in later years. Walsingham's official dispatches at this time are very guarded, as if he feared they might be intercepted, and his official account of the massacre was entrusted to the messenger's memory.

Marlowe may also have discussed the massacre with Raleigh,

[19] *Correspondance diplomatique de Bertrand Salignac de La Mothe Fénelon*, VII. 402.
[20] Cf. article "Walsingham, Francis," in DNB, XX. 690; Strype: *Annals*, II. i. 225 ff.; Conyers Read: *Sir Francis Walsingham*, I. 220–222; Walsingham to Smith, August 27, 1572, in Dudley Digges: *The Compleat Ambassador*, p. 238; Walsingham to Burghley, September 3, 1572, *Cal. State Papers, Foreign, Elizabeth, 1572–1574*, no. 549.

who had himself fought in the French wars and was a friend of the murdered Admiral Coligny.

Though these possible sources of Marlowe's information have been oddly overlooked, they deserve consideration. Marlowe's relationship to the Walsingham family is well known, and it is inconceivable that Sir Francis, after living through an experience like the Massacre of St. Bartholomew's, should not in after life discuss it with his family and friends.

The Walsinghams may also have provided Marlowe's information about the scandals relating to the Duc d'Espernon and the Duchesse de Guise. Most of the newsbooks only hint at these — it was hardly safe to spread scandal about the King's favorite or about a duchess. But a diplomat would have been well-informed on all such matters and might easily have passed the scandals on to a dramatist who was also a government secret agent.

There were further sources of information in Canterbury itself, during Marlowe's lifetime. When the poet was a boy of nine or ten, French and Flemish refugees began to arrive in the city, where they settled, either joining the local churches or worshipping in that Huguenot congregation which to this day holds weekly services in the cathedral.[21] They must have told the story of St. Bartholomew's over and over again, until the Kentish folk knew it by heart.

There was a further link between Canterbury and the French religious wars. Odet de Coligny, Cardinal de Chastillon, a brother of the murdered Admiral Coligny, also took refuge in Canterbury in 1568, and died there in 1571, said to have been poisoned. His body was laid in the cathedral in a plain coffin, waiting to be taken back to France. It lies there still, for France did not in the least want her cardinal back and has not asked for him these three hundred years.

These childhood impressions may not be source material; but they certainly did nothing to lessen Marlowe's interest in the subject.[22]

The materials with which *The Massacre at Paris* deals cover

[21] Dorothy Gardiner: *Literary Tradition of Canterbury*, p. 19. Huguenot names abound in the Register of Holy Cross, Westgate.
[22] Boas: *Christopher Marlowe*, p. 154, questions this view.

a period of seventeen years, beginning with the marriage of Henry of Navarre to Margaret of Valois, and ending with the stabbing of Henri III which cleared Navarre's way to the throne, as Henri IV. The important scenes are the marriage; the poisoning of the Old Queen of Navarre with perfumed gloves; the wounding of Admiral Coligny; the council held by Catherine de' Medici before the massacre; the massacre itself, including the murders of Admiral Coligny and the scholar Peter Ramus; the accession of Henri III (1584); the murder of the Duc de Guise (December 23, 1588); and the murder of Henri III (August 2, 1589).

For all these there are abundant sources in the semi-journalistic histories and news pamphlets of the time. There are particularly close resemblances between Marlowe's play and the tenth book of a volume called *Three Partes of Commentaries containing the whole and perfect discourse of the Ciuill Wares of France* (1574). The authorship is ascribed to Jean de Serres, author of numerous other works on the French wars of religion. Three Latin editions had preceded the English text. Two appeared in Geneva in 1570 and 1571 as *Commentariorum de Statu Religionis in regno Galliae Partes V*, though only the first three parts seem actually to have appeared at this time. The book appeared in London in 1573 as *De furoribus Gallicis*, and was in this edition attributed to one Ernestus Vagamundus, who has been identified both as François Hotman and as Jean de Serres. In the following year, the *Three Partes* appeared in English, and there seems to be very little doubt that Marlowe made some use of it.

The book presents a number of striking similarities to the play. Unlike other similar works, it reports the murder of Admiral Coligny almost exactly as it appears in *The Massacre*, and with one close resemblance in phraseology. After the Admiral has been killed in the play, the Duke of Guise commands:

> Then throw him down.

In the *Three Partes* this very phrase occurs:

Then said the Duke of *Guise*, our Cheuelier (meaning King *Henries* bastard abouesaide) vnlesse he see it with his eyes will not beleeue it: *throw him down* at the window.[23]

[23] *Massacre*, 310; *Three Partes*, bk. X, fol. 14v.

This is, of course, a natural expression for anyone to use in such a scene; but as a matter of fact the other contemporary authors do not use it at all. De Serres comes closest to it in his *Historical Collection*, the English version of which did not appear until after Marlowe's death.

A further borrowing from the *Three Partes* appears in Marlowe's lines:

> Cut of his [the Admiral's] head and handes,
> And send them for a present to the Pope.

In *Three Partes*, this appears as follows:

Then a certaine Italian of *Gonzagues* band, cut off the Admirals head, & sent it preserued with spices to *Rome* to the Pope and the Cardinall of *Loreine*. Other cut off his hands.[24]

The *Three Partes* reports the wounding of the Admiral as follows:

Beholde, a Harquebuzier out of a window of a house neere adioyning, shot ỹ Admiral with two bullets of leade *through both the armes*. When the Admirall felte himselfe wounded, nothing at all amazed, but with the same countenance that he was accustomed, he sayde, throughe yonder windowe it was done: goe see who are in the house: What manner of trecherie is this?

According to Marlowe, the Admiral is "shot through the arme"; and the exact nature of the wound is reiterated in the play when the Duke of Guise, observing the body after the assassination which follows the first, unsuccessful attempt on the Admiral's life, says:

> See where my Souldier shot him through the arm.[25]

In another book, de Serres says that one of the Admiral's fingers was also shot away, but of this Marlowe says nothing.[26]

None of these parallels are very close, however, and most of the facts could readily have been taken from other books. The story of the first attempt on the Admiral's life is told in a violently Protestant pamphlet, *Le Tocsain contre les Massacreurs* (1579), which is quite as close to Marlowe's version. It may

---

[24] Ll. 320–321; *Three Partes*, bk. X, fol. 14*v*.
[25] Ll. 201, 314; *Three Partes*, bk. X, fol. 10, *r* and *v*.
[26] *History of France*, p. 792.

have influenced Marlowe in this episode, as it certainly influenced him in the story of Peter Ramus. The passage runs:

Il luy tira subitement vn coup d'harquebouse chargee de basles de cuiure, qui luy perça le bras gauche, & luy couppa vn doigt de la main droicte. . . . Le Roy de Nauarre, le Prince de Condé, le Conte de la Roche-foucault vindrent visiter l'Admiral, en aiant fait penser ses plaies, en allerent faire plainte au Roy: . . . Sur cela il promit auec blasphemes d'en faire vne punition si exemplaire que tous auroient occasion de se contenter.[27]

The account of the Admiral's assassination diverges from Marlowe's:

. . . Le Duc de Guise fit entrer en sa chambre quelque nombre de soldats. . . . Estant donc ainsi tué par ceste bande de meurtriers, son corps fut ietté par Sarlaboux emmi la cour de son logis, par le commandement des Ducs de Guise, le voulant voir mort auant que departir de la place. . . . Ils resolurent de l'enuoier au gibet, où il fut pendu par les piedz.[28]

In one respect Marlowe also departs sharply from the *Three Partes*: The Huguenot preacher, Loreine, is killed in the play. In the *Three Partes*,[29] he is saved.

Marlowe's account of the slaughter of the scholar, Peter Ramus, is far closer to the *Tocsain* than to the *Three Partes* and probably comes from one or the other, since most accounts overlook it entirely. The *Three Partes* says merely that there was killed "among the rest *Petrus Ramus* that renoumed man throughout the worlde." [30] The *Tocsain* is more specific:

On n'espargna les hommes doctes non plus que le vulgaire, ains s'attacha on à eux à l'imitation des Turcs, & autres Barbares ennemis des lettres. Car Pierre de la Ramee Professeur du Roy en eloquence, homme docte, & renommé par toute l'Europe, aiant r'achepté sa vie de grande somme de deniers, fut tué en son College de Presle, son corps ietté au milieu des rues, & trainé par les fanges iusques en la riuiere.

The play mentions Ramus' efforts to buy his life:

Come *Ramus*, more golde, or thou shalt haue the stabbe,

a detail given by the *Tocsain* but not by the *Three Partes*.[31]

[27] *Tocsain*, pp. 113–115.   [28] *Tocsain*, pp. 122–123.   [29] Sig. Diij.
[30] *Three Partes*, bk. X, p. 19r. On p. 271v of bk. III, tribute is again paid to Ramus' eminence as a scholar and he is wrongly given as the author of the *Commentaries*.
[31] *Tocsain*, pp. 130–131; *Massacre*, 380.

The high value which the unknown author of the *Tocsain* sets on the personal safety of scholars is refreshing, and just the sort of thing to attract Marlowe, in whose works there are several references to the value of scholarship or the scholar's poverty.[32] But the correspondence with the play is by no means perfect.

The accurate rendering of Ramus' philosophical ideas, which Marlowe gives, nowhere appears in the newsbooks. It is presumably a recollection of the dramatist's days at Cambridge. After 1574 the *Dialectica* of Ramus began to replace the *Organon* of Aristotle in English universities, and an edition was published at Cambridge in 1584, while Marlowe was in residence.[33] The "Rethorica Rami" had already been entered in the *Stationers' Register* for November 11, 1577,[34] and Sir Nicholas Bacon had presented *Rami arithmetica* and *Ramus in artes liberales* to the Cambridge University Library in 1574.[35] The new ideas took an especial hold at Cambridge, which soon became the leading school of Ramist philosophy. Marlowe's eager mind had been strongly attracted by the novel doctrine; hence the quite unnecessary discussion of philosophy while the murder is in progress.

It is especially interesting to note that Sir Francis Walsingham was personally acquainted with Ramus. His diary contains the entry, "Monsr. Ramus came to viset me" on December 19 and 25, 1571.[36]

In the conclusion of his version of the massacre — which is, of course, not the conclusion of the play itself — Marlowe again follows the *Three Partes*. Guise orders:

> *Gonzago* poste you to Orleance, *Retes* to Deep,
> *Mountsorrell* vnto Roan, and spare not one
> That you suspect of heresy.

The source reads:

Messengers were sent in post into all the partes of the Realme, with oft

---

[32] Notably in *Hero and Leander*, I. 470–472; *Massacre*, 380–384; *Doctor Faustus*, 16.

[33] STC 15243. See also CHEL, IV. 317; J. B. Mullinger: *Hist. Univ. Cambridge*, II. 411–412.

[34] Arber's Reprint, II. 143a. See also Frank Pierrepont Graves: *Peter Ramus and the Educational Reformation of the Sixteenth Century*, pp. 212–213.

[35] *Catalogus Librorum* MS. (Donors' Book); Charles Sayle: *Annals of the Cambridge University Library*, p. 49.

[36] *Journal of Sir Francis Walsingham*, p. 13. Camden *Miscellany*, vol. 6; *Royal Hist. Soc. Publications*, vol. 104.

shifting their horsses for hast, to commaunde all other Cities in the Kings name to followe the example of *Paris*, and to cause to be killed as many as they had among them of the reformed Religion.[37]

The maltreatment of the Admiral's body also appears in the *Three Partes*:

The Admirals body being hanged vp by the heeles vpon the common gallowes of *Paris*, . . . the Parisians went thither by heapes to see it. And the Queene mother to feede hir eyes with that spectacle, had a mynde also to goe thither, and she caryed with hir the King and both hir other sonnes.[38]

Marlowe also brings Catherine de' Medici, the Queen Mother, and the King to see the Admiral's body, which in this scene is hanged in a street, but which in an earlier line has already been ordered taken to Montfaucon, the hill where the Parisian gallows stood.

The murder of the Old Queen of Navarre with the poisoned and perfumed gloves, which occurs early in the play and has no structural relation to it, is, of course, an old and familiar story. It made a great impression, is often mentioned in the histories of the day, and appears in English literature as late as Sir Richard Steele's *The Funeral*: "The *Italians*, they say, can readily remove the too much intrusted — Oh their pretty scented Gloves!" [39]

The *Three Partes* hints at the suspicions which were abroad:

Not long before this, *Ioane* Queene of *Nauarre* aboue mentioned, died in the Court at *Paris*, of a sodaine sicknesse, beeing about the age of fortie and three yeres, where as the suspition was great that she dyed of poyson, and hir body being for that cause opened by the Phisitions, there were no tokens of poyson espied. But shortely after, by the detection of one A. P. it hath ben founde that she was poysoned with a venomed smell of a payre of perfumed gloues, dressed by one *Renat* the Kings Apothicarie, an Italian, that hath a shop at *Paris* vpon S. Michaels bridge, neare vnto the Pallace: which could not be espied by the Phisitions whiche did not open the heade nor loked into the brayne.[40]

---

[37] Ll. 450–452; *Three Partes*, bk. X, fol. 16*v*.
[38] Ll. 487–504 and 323; *Three Partes*, bk. X, fol. 2*or*. Cf. II. 81 for the same material in the *Tocsain*.
[39] *The Funeral*, I. i; *Dramatick Works* (1723), p. 11.
[40] *Three Partes*, bk. X, fol. 9*r*.

Essentially the same story is repeated in the *Fourthe Parte of the Commentaries* (1576):

THE Queene of *Nauar* being poysoned to death with a payre of perfumed gloues (as is sayde in the tenth booke) the King, Queene, and the whole court seemed to take hir death very grieuously. . . . The phisitions taking a viewe of $\tilde{y}$ body, reported that she dyed of a pleurisie: the more secret cause, which was the poysoning of the brayne, being not found, for that they did not search the head.

In the play, Marlowe is very specific as to the effect of the poison on the brain. The dying queen exclaims:

> . . . the fatall poyson
> Workes within my head, my brain pan breakes.[41]

The same story is told in the *Discours merveilleux de la vie . . . de Catherine de Medicis*,[42] which mentions Master René, who prepared the poisoned gloves. Marlowe brings him in simply as "the Pothecarie," without naming him.

The refusal of Henry of Navarre, as bridegroom, to attend the nuptial mass, which Marlowe recounts in lines 17–25, is thus described:

The bryde was with great traine and pompe led into the Church to heare Masse, and in the meane time the brydegrome who mislyked these ceremonies, togither with *Henrie* Prince of *Conde*, sonne of *Lewes*, and the Admirall, and other noble me*n* of the same Religion, walked without the Churche dore.[43]

Whatever sources Marlowe may have used for the first part of his play, he must necessarily have depended on newsbooks and political pamphlets for the three scenes in which the Duc de Guise, the Cardinal of Lorraine, and Henri III are assassinated. All these episodes were voluminously reported in numerous partisan pamphlets, from which Marlowe seems to have chosen what he needed. It is again impossible to designate any single pamphlet as a source. Probably he used several, just as one would today read several newspapers. It is possible, however, to indicate numerous passages in contemporary newsbooks

---

[41] *Additions to the tenth Booke*, p. 17; *De Furoribus Gallicis*, pp. xxxiv–xxxv; *Massacre*, 187–188.

[42] Ed. of 1660, pp. 60, 90, 91.

[43] *Three Partes*, bk. X, p. 9; *De Furoribus Gallicis*, p. xxxvi.

which correspond exactly with the dramatic version and which were available to the dramatist.[44]

One unimportant passage shows this use of the newsbooks with especial clarity. Much has been made of the line,

> Yet *Cæsar* shall goe forth,[45]

uttered by Marlowe's Guise when warned that he may be assassinated if he leaves the room in which he stands. Immediately after the assassination, the line is repeated by the dying Guise:

> Thus *Cæsar* did goe foorth, and thus he dyed.

This almost exactly parallels the lines of Shakespeare's hero in *Julius Caesar*:

> Cæsar shall go forth

and

> Yet Cæsar shall go forth.[46]

Scholars have been divided as to whether Marlowe was borrowing from Shakespeare or vice versa. J. M. Robertson and William Wells [47] have even argued that Marlowe wrote a source play on Julius Caesar, which Shakespeare rewrote.

Examination of another possible source for *The Massacre at Paris* makes it clear that the line is original with Marlowe and that Shakespeare is the borrower. This possible source is the *Firste Booke*, which is bound up with J. de Serres's *Historical Collection* (1598).[48] This makes it entirely clear that "Caesar" was a nickname which the League conventionally applied to the Duc de Guise:

Such was the end of the Duke of *Guise*, a Prince (without all doubt) of valour and courage, the League called him her *Cæzar*, and made goodly comparisons betweene them.

---

[44] Studies by Dr. Paul H. Kocher, University of Washington, soon to be published, will provide additional detail. See also "Christopher Marlowe and the Newsbooks," by the present author, *Journalism Quarterly*, 14: 18–22 (1937).

[45] Line 1005.

[46] Line 1027; *Julius Caesar*, II. ii. 10, 28, and 48. See II. 257.

[47] *Shakespeare Canon*, pp. 106–113; preface to William Wells' *Authorship of Julius Caesar*.

[48] Page 203. The paging begins anew after the book reaches p. 310. This is the second p. 203.

Here follow four pages of detailed comparison, on two of which almost every paragraph begins with the italicized word, "Cæzar." As a fair sample, we may take the following comparison of the two men's deaths:

Cæzar was slaine with blowes of rapiers: the Duke of *Guise* with poinyards. *Cæzar* fell dead at the feete of the Image of *Pompey*, whom hee had so cruelly pursued. The Duke of *Guise* died at the kings chamber doore, where hee had made so many brauadoes, and so much despising of the kings authoritie. . . .
Cæzar was slaine in the Senat: the *Duke* of *Guise* at the Parliament, when hee came out of the Councell chamber.[49]

From this or some similar source, Marlowe picked up the comparison. Later Shakespeare, being thoroughly familiar with Marlowe's work, reproduced the line consciously or unconsciously when drafting a similar scene, as he does on other occasions.[50]

It is perhaps worth mentioning that the de Serres *Historical Collection* specifically mentions that the body of Admiral Coligny "was borne to the Gibbet of *Montfaucon*, and there hanged by thee feete." [51] Few contemporary accounts give the location of the gibbet, to which Marlowe refers specifically:

Vnto mount Faucon will we dragge his coarse.[52]

The *Three Partes* refers merely to the "gallowes of *Paris*." [53]

Two other pamphlets give accounts of the murder more or less resembling Marlowe's. The closest similarity exists between the dramatist's account and that in *Le Martire des deux Freres* (1589). In this pamphlet, the Duke receives a warning, just as in Marlowe, though it comes not from one of the assassins, as in Marlowe, but from a certain Monseigneur d'Albauf. The Duke brushes aside this warning and goes to his death, which is described as follows:

Ce Prince . . . apres s'estre long temps combatu à coup de poin, en fin est terrassé par ces bourreaux, & tõbant . . . cria, mon Dieu ayez

[49] *Firste Booke*, p. 207. This is the second page of that number. Bound with *Historical Collection* in NYPL.
[50] See II. 208–211.
[51] *Firste Booke*, p. 256. This is the first page of that number.
[52] Line 323.
[53] See II. 83.

pitié de moy, cela dit: ietta le pan de son manteau sur son visage pour mieux mediter au ciel.[54]

In describing the murder of the Cardinal of Lorraine, Marlowe emphasizes the fact that the assassins strangle him because their scruples over shedding a churchman's blood make it impossible to use the dagger.[55] In the pamphlet they also use the rope, though they have no hesitation over using weapons which shed blood at the same time:

Ce Prince agenouillé cōtre vne muraille auquel à grand peine permirent-il dire vne seule oraison, & icelle finie, se couure de ses mains recommandāt son âme à Dieu ces pendars, bourreaux a l'instant tirant le cordeau que ja ils luy auoient mis au col, luy lancent plusieurs coups de poignards, & d'allebardes au trauers de son sacré corps.

Other contemporary accounts miss the detail of the rope, and *Les cruavtes sanginaires* (1589) does not even mention the strangling but says that the Cardinal was simply stabbed.

Newsbooks dealing with the assassination of Henri III were as numerous, as violent, and as completely partisan as those dealing with the murders of the Duke and Cardinal. There is a long account in the *Veritable recit, ov vraye histoire, de la mort subite, de Henry de Valois, Roy de France* (1589). After describing the reception of the priest who killed the King, the pamphlet goes on:

Il le mena en son Cabinet, ou estant il leust plusieurs petites lettres & memoires que le Religieux lui presenta, & ne scait on d'où elles venoient: & comme le Roy eut acheué de lire le dernier memoire, il luy demanda s'il n'eu auoit plus: luy respondit le dit Iacobin, qu'il en auoit encores vn, Et faisant semblant de le tirer de sa manche, au lieu d'vne lettre il tira vn couteau assé petit, mais de la largeur de deux doigts ou enuiron, dont soudainement il donna vn coup au Roy au dessoubz du nombril, lequel coutteau il laissa dedans son ventre, dont le Roy le retirant eslargit la playe. Ce fait s'ingera de donner du mesme coutteau dans la gorge dudit Iacobin, sur le cry que feit le Roy se sentant blesçé, entrerent quelques gens dedans le Cabinet.[56]

In the play, the King kills the assassin himself. In the pamphlet, he merely attacks him with the knife, while one of the

---

[54] *Le Martire*, pp. 29–31.
[55] Ll. 1105–1116; p. 40 of the pamphlet.
[56] Sig. A2v. This and the *Cruavtes sanginaires* are bound up with the *Martire* and other pamphlets in NYPL.

attendants gives the death blow. In the pamphlet there is no mention of a poisoned blade. In the play, Marlowe says that the letters came from "the President of Paris." [57] In the pamphlet their origin is a mystery.

A Catholic version of the tragedy, *Admirable et prodigieuse mort de Henri de Valois* (1589?), says that they were "lettres de creance d'aucuns Politiques," [58] but being violently hostile in tone, this account gives the King no credit for his self-defense. It does refer to the monk's knife, "qu'il auoit souz son habit." It is interesting to find here an allusion to the King's "migmons heretiques." [59] No real source has ever been discovered for Marlowe's treatment of Mugeroun and Epernoun, the royal favorites. *Le Martire des deux Freres* makes similar scandalous allusions to "lasciuetez, meschancetez, ordures & sodomies," and specifically mentions the name of Iean d'Espernon.[60]

Otherwise the newsbooks are silent on this matter. Marlowe may, however, have read Jean Boucher's pamphlet on Gaveston, the favorite of Edward II, which was published in 1588 with satirical allusions to the Duc d'Espernon. He may also have read the Latin original, which was published even earlier. This work alludes to both the two favorites who figure in his two plays. The frequency with which Marlowe uses the word "minion" in *Edward the Second* suggests that the French court was more or less in his mind. As one commentator observes, "Gaveston, as he lived for Marlowe, is the pet and darling of another Henri Trois." [61]

It may, then, be definitely concluded that Marlowe was acquainted with the *Three Partes of the Commentaries*, attributed to Jean de Serres. This was probably the main source for the first part of the play. Marlowe supplemented it, however, with newsbooks and controversial pamphlets, with books of recent history, and with reminiscences of his study of philosophy at Cambridge. It is not quite certain that he used the *Three Partes*, however, since he could have found practically all of the details given there by piecing together the accounts given in several

---

[57] Ll. 1169, 1181.
[58] Sig. A[iv]*r*.
[59] Sig. Aij*v*.
[60] *Martire des deux Freres*, p. 7.
[61] J. A. Nicklin: "Marlowe's 'Gaveston.'" *Free Review*, 5: 324 D 1895 [LC].

other books. It is also highly probable that he derived his knowledge of the Massacre of St. Bartholomew's from Sir Francis Walsingham, from Sir Walter Raleigh, perhaps from the younger (fifth) Thomas Walsingham, son of his patron, or from his friend Thomas Watson, the poet.

Stage History

The first record of a stage performance of *The Massacre at Paris* is Henslowe's entry, recording his production of January 30, 1592/3.[62] The date is not very clearly indicated, but can be deduced from the position of the entry in a list of a series of productions by Lord Strange's men at the Rose in January and February of this year. Greg believes, however, that the correct date is really January 26.

Henslowe marks the play "ne," and the takings, being the highest of the season, confirm him. There are no further productions for some time, because the plague had forced the theatres to close. We next find *The Massacre* being performed by the Admiral's men, again at the Rose Theatre, on June 19, 1593. There are ten performances between that date and September 25. The whole series may be tabulated as follows:

Date	Henslowe's Title	Takings
January 30, 1593/4	gvyes	£3. 14s.
June 19, 1594	Gwies	54s.
June 25, 1594	masacer	36s.
July 3, 1594	masacer	31s.
July 8, 1594	masacer	27s.
July 16, 1594	masacare	31s.
July 27, 1594	masacar	22s.
August 8, 1594	masacare	23s. 6d.
August 17, 1594	masacar	20s.
Sept. 7 [6], 1594	mesacar	17s. 6d.
September 25, 1594	masacar	14s.

There are various entries in the *Diary* relating to costuming and properties for *The Massacre*. Four years later Henslowe enters: "Lent vnto w^m Bor[ne] the 19 of november 1598 vpon a longe taney [tawny] clocke of clothe the some of xij^s wch he sayd

---

[62] Greg's ed., I. 15 ff. Henslowe's original entry is 1592, but the "2" is struck out and "3" substituted. By modern reckoning, this is 1594. In the first September date, "6" has been struck out and "7" substituted. See Greg, p. xlviii.

yt was to Jmbrader his hatte for the gwisse . . . xij^s." [63] On November 27 the same actor gets twenty shillings "to bye his stockens fo^r the gwisse," and William Birde gets the same amount "to bye a payer of sylke stockens to playe the gwisse in." [64] Three years later there is a further expenditure of three pounds to "bye stamell cllath for a clocke for the gwisse," [65] and others of thirty shillings "Lent vnto the company to lend the littell tayller to bye fuschen [fustian] and lynynge for the clockes for the masaker of france"; twenty shillings "Lent vnto the companye the 8 of november 1601 to paye vnto the littell tayller vpon his bell for mackeynge of sewtes for the gwesse"; another twenty shillings "Lent vnto the companye the 13 of november 1601 to paye the littell tayllor Radford vpon his bill for the gwisse"; and, finally, 24s. 6d. "pd at the apoyntment of the company vnto the littell tayller in fulle payment of his Bille for the gwisse the 26 of november 1601." [66]

Henslowe's record of *The Massacre* ends January 18, 1602, when the Admiral's men buy the "massaker of france" from Edward Alleyn, paying six pounds for three plays, of which it is one.[67] The play, then, must have been Alleyn's personal property, and he had presumably brought it with him when he reorganized the Admiral's Company in the spring of 1594. It was probably part of his share in the stock of Lord Strange's Company, most of whose members at that time became the Lord Chamberlain's Company, while Alleyn resumed independent acting.[68]

There is some doubt whether all these entries really relate to Marlowe's play. Henslowe never actually uses the title *The Massacre at Paris*, and John Webster (1580–c. 1625) is known to have written a play, now lost, called *Guise*. Henslowe can hardly be referring to this play, however, for Webster was at this time a boy in his earliest teens. A forged reference to Webster, interpolated in the "stamell cllath" entry quoted above,

[63] Greg's ed., I. 78; MS. fol. 41v.

[64] *Ibid.*, I. 72; MS. fol. 38v.

[65] *Ibid.*, I. 149; MS. fol. 94r. The entry is regarded as genuine by Greg, but the interlineation of Webster's name is a forgery. See Greg, *op. cit.*, I. 231.

[66] *Ibid.*, I. 150–151; MS. fols. 94v and 95r.

[67] *Ibid.*, I. 153; MS. fol. 96r.

[68] Malone Society reprint (ed. W. W. Greg), p. vi.

is probably Collier's handiwork, since Collier attempts to use this forged entry to connect Webster with a late version of Marlowe's play.[69]

From Henslowe's day to this, *The Massacre* seems to have gone unproduced until the Yale Dramatic Association produced it October 21, 22, and 23, 1940, with a cast of freshmen under the direction of Burton G. Shevelove. Samuel Hemingway wrote a special prologue. The "jig" dubiously attributed [70] to Marlowe was performed, and a soloist sang "The Passionate Shepherd."

EDITIONS AND MANUSCRIPT

Although fairly successful on the stage, the published play seems to have been a failure. It has come down to us in a single edition, undated but probably issued some time between 1594 and 1600, or perhaps even later, following the stage revival of 1601. The book is typographically similar to the 1605–06 *Tamburlaine* and is issued by the same publisher, Edward White. It was not reprinted until 1818, when W. Oxberry brought it out separately, shortly before his collected edition of Marlowe's works. Thereafter it was usually reprinted in collected editions but never reprinted separately until W. W. Greg brought out his Malone Society Reprint in 1928. In nearly four centuries there have been only three separate editions, an eloquent commentary on posterity's literary evaluation of the play. Eleven copies are known, the abundance of the single early edition suggesting that the books were little read and so not worn out.

The Massacre at Paris is the only Marlowe play of which a leaf of manuscript has survived in a contemporary hand. (Mary Clarke's version of the supposed 1593 *Edward the Second* [71] is certainly not contemporary.) This is the so-called "Collier Leaf," now in the Folger Shakespeare Library. It contains the scene between the Soldier, the King's Minion (Mugeroun), and the Duke of Guise, corresponding to lines 812–827 of Brooke's (1910) edition. The manuscript adds several lines and various textual variants to the printed text.

[69] HEDP, III. 101. See also E. K. Chambers: *Eliz. Stage*, III. 511–512; F. L. Lucas: *Complete Works of John Webster*, II. 321.
[70] See II. 291–292.
[71] See II. 6–7.

The first allusion to this interesting manuscript appears in the introduction to Collier's edition of *The Jew of Malta*, printed in the 1825 Dodsley. According to this account:

A curious MS. fragment of one quarto leaf of this tragedy came into the hands of Mr. Rodd [the book-dealer] of Newport-street not long since, which, as it very materially differs from the printed edition, is here inserted *literatim*: it perhaps formed part of a copy belonging to the theatre at the time it was first acted, and it would be still more valuable should any accident hereafter shew that it is in the original hand-writing of Marlow.[72]

Collier later reprinted a different text, also purporting to reproduce the manuscript, in the first (1831) edition of his *History of English Dramatic Poetry*.[73] Since at that time the manuscript had not been seen by any other scholar, its authenticity and even its existence were doubted, especially as Collier's other frauds became known.

Collier at first stated that he had merely seen the manuscript in the hands of Rodd, the London dealer. In his *History* he says that it is in his own possession. At some time before 1879, it passed out of his collection, probably by direct sale to J. O. Halliwell-Phillips, for in the second edition of the history, published in that year, Collier implies that he is no longer the owner.[74] It appears in Halliwell-Phillips' *Calendar of Shakespearean Rarities*, where it is described as "the only vestige of the tragedy in the state in which it left the hands of the author." [75] Halliwell-Phillips seems to have retained it until his death in 1889.[76] With the rest of his collection it was bought in 1897 by Marsden J. Perry, of Providence, R. I., from whom it passed to H. C. Folger and thence to the Folger Shakespeare Library.[77]

The manuscript is now inlaid in a large sheet of heavy paper and bound with blank leaves, in full green levant morocco, the work of Francis Bedford. The binding was presumably made

[72] VIII. 244–245.

[73] III. 133–135.

[74] HEDP (1831), III. 133–134; (1879), II. 510–512.

[75] No. 287, p. 85 (1st ed., 1887), p. 91 (2nd ed., 1891).

[76] Dr. Samuel A. Tannenbaum is probably wrong in thinking (*Shaksperian Scraps*, p. 178) that the MS. passed from Halliwell-Phillips to the Warwick Castle Collection. Cf. De Ricci, *op. cit.*, pp. 145–146, and J. Q. Adams, *Library*, 14: 447–448 Mr 1934.

[77] De Ricci, *op. cit.*, p. 148.

for Halliwell-Phillips. The leaf itself measures $7\frac{1}{8}$ inches in height by $7\frac{7}{8}$ inches in width,[78] and is creased vertically along its whole length, as if from folding. The ink varies from a very dark to a very light brown, some letters having faded almost to invisibility (the last lines on the recto being pale throughout) and in some cases with a succession of four or five pale words. The hand is partly "secretary" and partly Roman. Collier regarded the manuscript as "an original contemporary MS. of this play, possibly as it came from the hands of Marlow." [79] Halliwell-Phillips thought it was "the unique fragment of a contemporary prompt-copy." [80]

Dr. Tannenbaum thinks the manuscript is neither a prompt-book nor the author's original. He believes it is not the kind of copy a theatrical prompter needed and points out that the right margin is narrow, whereas in his opinion a real prompt-book would have a wide right margin for the insertion of stage business. He doubts whether the manuscript can possibly be the author's original, because he thinks the blunders are not the sort a writer is likely to make in his own work and because there is no suggestion of revision. His final conclusion is that the leaf is merely another of Collier's mystifications.[81]

He bases his assertion that the leaf is a forgery on the arguments: (1) that he believes he detects two writing fluids, used alternately to suggest the contrast between dark and pale ink and thus indicate age; (2) that the handwriting seems slow and laborious, as in forgery; (3) that the writing seems to have been done after the paper had been creased, a proceeding likely enough in forgery because the forger has to use such old paper as he can get, but unlikely in a genuine document; (4) that one place looks as if the writing runs over on the modern paper in which the leaf is inlaid; (5) that the writing does not fill the page; (6) that the document has no history before Collier reported it; and (7) that Shakespearean echoes and certain obscenities characteristic of Collier's forgeries are present.

[78] Dr. J. Q. Adams' measurements (*Library*, 14: 447–448 Mr 1934). Dr. Tannenbaum gives $7\frac{1}{4}$ x $7\frac{15}{16}$ inches.

[79] J. P. Collier: HEDP (1831), III. 133–134.

[80] Halliwell-Phillips, *op. cit.* (1st ed., 1887), p. 14; (2nd ed., 1891), p. xvi. On pp. 85, 91 respectively it is called the "fragment of an original contemporary manuscript."

[81] Cf. *Shaksperian Scraps*, pp. 177–186.

The paper is generally admitted to be of genuine Elizabethan manufacture, with the pitcher watermark then used. Nothing, however, is more common than for a forger to strengthen his position by working on authentic paper of the correct period.

If all Dr. Tannenbaum's arguments could be sustained, they would certainly throw doubt on the genuineness of the document, though they would hardly prove it definitely to be a forgery. After all, Collier made many genuine discoveries; some people do write laboriously; it is not certain that two writing fluids were really used; people sometimes write on creased paper; and we do not know enough about Elizabethan prompt-books or authors' manuscripts to be sure exactly what all of them were like. As for the Shakespearean echoes, Marlowe's admittedly genuine work often sounds like Shakespeare because Shakespeare frequently borrowed from him. It would be more reasonable to say that the early Shakespeare frequently sounds like Marlowe; [82] but most people are naturally more familiar with the greater writer, borrower though he be. As for obscenity, the Elizabethan drama frequently *was* obscene, especially when it portrayed a private soldier endeavoring to be humorous about cuckoldry.

Dr. Tannenbaum's article, however, provoked a reply from Dr. J. Q. Adams, of the Folger Library staff. [83] This revealed the surprising fact that Dr. Tannenbaum had worked largely from photostats and had seen the original manuscript only cursorily "during the course of a few hours' visit." [84]

Dr. Adams' conclusions, after a study of the original, are very different from Dr. Tannenbaum's. He finds the handwriting "natural and fluent." [85] The ink is actually of normal uniformity, Dr. Tannenbaum having been deceived by shadows made in photographing. The leaf was not originally creased down the center, but was wrinkled after the writing had been done. The photographs made the wrinkle look like a crease. The apparent carrying over of the writing on to the modern paper in which it is inlaid is due to the binder, Bedford, who apparently

---

[82] See II. 208–211.
[83] "The *Massacre at Paris* Leaf," *Library*, 14: 447–469 Mr 1934.
[84] *Op. cit.*, p. 454.
[85] *Op. cit.*, p. 458.

frayed the edges of the original and the modern sheet and joined the fibres under pressure.

These conclusions by Dr. Adams were supported later in the same year by B. A. P. van Dam, writing at The Hague, who held that the manuscript's "authenticity is above suspicion." [86] In spite of Dr. Tannenbaum's view that this cannot be the author's holograph, Dr. Adams suggests that we have here one of the "foul sheets" on which the author drafted his play. In that case, the document is an example of Marlowe's handwriting; but since his signature on the Benchkyn will is the only authenticated specimen with which the Folger manuscript can be compared, proof is difficult. The signature certainly does not closely resemble the handwriting of the manuscript.

INFLUENCE

The Massacre at Paris is unique among Marlowe's plays in that it had political repercussions. In 1602 Sir Ralph Winwood, English ambassador at Paris, protested to the French government that "certaine *Italian Comedians* did set up upon the Corners of the Passages in this Towne [Paris], that that Afternoone they would plaie *l'Histoire Angloise contre la Roine d'Angleterre*." He reported this matter to Cecil on July 7, 1602.[87]

The French replied that an English play, which they did not name, but which was almost certainly *The Massacre*, was equally offensive to their government. As Sir Ralph described the incident in his report to Cecil:

It was objected to me before the [French] Counsaile by some Standers by, that the Death of the Duke of *Guise* hath ben plaied at *London*; which I answered was never done in the Life of the last King [of France]; and sence, by some others, that the *Massacre of St. Bartholomews* hath ben publickly acted, and this King represented upon the Stage.

Nothing further is known of the incident. Both the French and Spanish governments seem to have been sensitive on such points. The French ambassador protested George Chapman's *Tragedy of Charles, Duke of Biron*, and cited a prohibition

---

[86] "The Collier Leaf," *English Studies* (Amsterdam), 16: 172 O 1934.
[87] Edmund Sawyer: *Memorials of Affairs of State* (1725), I. 425.

against the representation on the stage of any living Christian king.[88] The Spanish government resented Middleton's *Game at Chesse*, and the Privy Council demanded that "passages in it reflecting in matter of scorne and ignominy vpon ye King of Spaine some of his Ministers and others of good note and quality" be omitted. The actors were placed under bond of three hundred pounds, and the play was eventually "antiquated and sylenced." The English government also insisted on revision of Philip Massinger's *Believe As You List*, to avoid giving offense to Spain.[89]

The Massacre's influence upon the course of the English drama has been very slight. The French protest seems to indicate that two plays on the subject were already in existence; and, in all, four other plays on much the same theme are now known. One of these is John Webster's lost *Guise*, to which he alludes in a list of "some of my other Works" in the dedication of *The Devil's Law Case* (1623).[90] *Guise* reappears in Archer's play list (1656) as a comedy, and in Kirkman's list (1661) as a tragedy. Since Webster shows Marlowe's influence clearly in *The Devil's Law Case*,[91] he presumably showed it also in the lost *Guise*. *Henslowe's Diary* alludes to a play by "mr dickers" which was "called the 3 parte of the syvell wares of france," [92] now lost, which may have some relation to Marlowe.

Still another lost play on the Duke of Guise was entered on the stationers' books in 1653 in the name of Henry Shirley. Two other plays on the same theme appeared after the Restoration. One was *The Duke of Guise* (1682), signed by John Dryden and Nathaniel Lee. This was mainly a revision of Lee's *Massacre of Paris*, which had been written some years previously but had not at that time been produced, the parallel with British political conditions under James II being too close for comfort. Lee's original play was eventually produced at the Drury Lane Theatre in November, 1689.[93] Neither of these two plays shows any

---

[88] Cazamian and Legouis: *Hist. Eng. Lit.*, I. 284.

[89] CHEL, VI. 166–167. See also Collier: HEDP, I. 431; C. M. Ingleby: *Shakespere Controversy*, p. 314. The British Museum MS. Eg. 2623, fol. 26, contains the Lord Chamberlain's letter (1624) relative to the *Game at Chesse*.

[90] F. L. Lucas' ed. (1928), II. 235.

[91] III. iii. 1 ff. See I. 374.

[92] Greg's ed., I. 99; MS. fol. 99*r*.

[93] CHEL, VIII. 211; Allardyce Nicoll: *Restoration Drama*, pp. 360, 367.

resemblances to Marlowe's beyond those to be expected from similarity of theme. Except perhaps for Webster, Marlowe's contemporaries and successors seem to have paid no attention to the play at all.

One can hardly blame them. There is little to be said for *The Massacre at Paris*, either as literature or as drama. It is a blood-sodden piece of hack work, relieved by occasional purple patches, to which the author himself appears to have been indifferent, and to which his editors have paid but perfunctory attention. In *The Jew of Malta* we have plain evidence of Marlowe at his best for the first part of the play, and then a sudden falling-off. *The Massacre at Paris*, on the other hand, seems to be Marlowe's unsuccessful handiwork all through, save for the occasional passages in which he rises for a moment into his greater manner.

In a sense, *The Massacre at Paris* is typically Elizabethan. It is crude, violent, gory, relieved by vivid and sometimes poetic interludes between assassinations. It has no unity except such as is given it by the theme of religious conflict and the characterization of the Duke of Guise — a typically Marlowe hero, a violently ambitious superman, reaching eagerly for unattainable heights and falling in the end as Faustus fell, and Barabas, and Tamburlaine.

Marlowe has missed many chances to get into his play materials that lay ready to his hand. As usual, his women characters are rather wooden, though he had a superb opportunity to equal Lady Macbeth in his picture of Catherine de' Medici, the sinister incarnation of mother love gone wrong. Instead, she is allowed to remain a mere puppet. The gallant old Queen Jeanne of Navarre, dignified, indomitable, and honest in a day when treachery was a commonplace of statesmanship, is brought on stage merely to be slain. The innumerable picturesque amours of her son Henri are — perhaps excusably — ignored. After all, we meet the king upon his wedding day. But we might at least expect more about his bride, the bad and brilliant mischief-maker, Margaret of Navarre, who is merely allowed to appear on her way to the nuptial mass and then fades from the picture forever.

Of authentic dramatic quality *The Massacre at Paris* has few traces. Such limited success as it enjoyed in its own day was due to its liberal use of a peculiarly Elizabethan variety of "hokum," and its appeal to national and religious prejudice. Its lack of genuine dramatic quality is best evidenced by the total neglect with which it has met since stage fashions changed. But, with all its faults, the old play is worth reading — though hardly worth producing — if only because it shows Marlowe's limitations so distinctly and at the same time, in the finer passages, without being great itself, shows the promise of his greatness elsewhere.

CHAPTER XIII

HERO AND LEANDER

. . . that partly excellent Poem of Maister Marloe's.
GEORGE CHAPMAN: Preface to Musaeus

ERO AND LEANDER is a fragment, left incomplete at Marlowe's death but in form finished and complete, so far as he had gone with it. The other poems, except for one exquisite lyric, are insignificant or doubtful. The plays, except for *Edward the Second*, are either early work in which Marlowe's tendency to rant overshadows the true, fine, and high poetic passion of which he was capable, at his best; or else they have been butchered in unknown hacks' ruthless adaptation to a commercial stage.

The first two sestiads of *Hero and Leander* are untouched and unspoiled — Marlowe at his best; and the poet has carried his work far enough to display the beauty of what he meant to do. The two poets who later undertook to complete Marlowe's poem fortunately do not mingle their own inferior work with the authentic lines of the original. One does not have to pause and wonder, ever and anon, how much is Marlowe's, how much adulterant inserted by some well-meaning fool. And with the intrinsic fascination of the verse itself goes the quite extrinsic but touching, wistful charm of the sadness of its incompletion and the cause.

Though there are none of the customary puzzles as to the authorship of this passage or that, some aspects of the poem's history are not without the shade of doubt usual in Elizabethan letters.

DATE

Hero and Leander has been variously dated; but all agree that it must come either at the beginning or at the close of Marlowe's career. For the earlier date, the arguments advanced are the classical subject matter and the presumably early dates

of Marlowe's translations of Ovid and Lucan and of his classical play on *Dido*.[1] It is sometimes, rather fallaciously, argued
further that Elizabethan poets — Shakespeare, Spenser, and
Drayton are examples — often began with short poems before
attempting plays or longer poems. But this view overlooks the
fact that *Hero and Leander* was, in intention at least, a long
poem; and that such a rule is based mainly on coincidence and
is certain to be broken. Two fairly early allusions to the story
of the lovers prove very little about the date of Marlowe's poem,
since they may easily be allusions to the original Greek of the
legendary Musaeus. One of these is in *The Pleasauntest Workes
of George Gascoigne Esquire*, which was published in 1587:

> Both deepe and dreadfull were the Seas
> Which held *Leander* from his loue.[2]

The other is in Greene's *Neuer Too Late* (1590):

Appoint what I shall doe to compasse a priuate conference. Thinke
I will account of the seas as *Leander*, of the wars as *Troylus*.[3]

Both sound very much like the ordinary classical allusion of
which most Elizabethan writers were extremely fond.

For the later date, the arguments are: the incomplete state
of the poem, which looks as if it might have been interrupted by
Marlowe's violent death, at a time when the theatres had been
closed and he was likely to be turning to narrative poetry; the
amazing maturity, beauty, and finish of the verse; and the
immense superiority to all Marlowe's other work on classical
themes. Chapman's statements, confused and halting though
they are, certainly seem to indicate that Marlowe asked him to
finish the poem.[4] This suggests a poet's concern for a work new
begun, and not a suddenly recollected anxiety for a poem about

---

[1] Cf. Ernest Faligan: *De Marlovianis Fabulis*, pp. 215–216; Léonce Chabalier: *Héro
et Léandre*, pp. 21–22.

[2] *Complete Poems*, edited by W. C. Hazlitt (Roxburghe Club, 1869), I. 493.

[3] Grosart's Greene, VIII. 41–42.

[4] The following views are typical:

> Malone (MS. note): "This was, I believe, Marlowe's *last* work." [Quoted by
> Tucker Brooke, PMLA, 37: 391 (1922)]

1887. Ernest Faligan: "Poema cui *Hero and Leander* titulus, compositum fuit, ut veri-
simile est, temporibus iisdem quibus scripta fuerunt, et poemata de quibus
modo agebatur et primae Marlovii fabulae, id est, sive quum Cantabrigiensium
Athenarum incola esset, sive quum Londinii recens, et memoria studiorum qui-

which Marlowe had not troubled himself since leaving the
university some years before.

The finished beauty of the first two sestiads in itself provides
a sufficient argument for the late date. Marlowe's capacity for
writing exquisite lines is apparent from the beginning — in
Tamburlaine, even in *Dido*. But in the beginning he is not capable of sustained beauty and the mighty lines are scattered here
and there among exceedingly weak ones; whereas in *Hero and
Leander* he rarely falters.

Quite probably the poem was begun during his enforced leisure at Scadbury in 1593, when the plague raged in London and,
the theatres being closed, playwrights had no employment.
Critics have been by no means unanimous, but the weight of
their opinion inclines to the later date.

SOURCE

There has never been any doubt about the source of *Hero and
Leander*, which is plainly indicated both by the title and the
content, as well as by contemporary references. Marlowe based
his poem on a Greek poem of Hero and Leander, attributed to
a certain Musaeus, probably an Alexandrian scholar of the
fourth or fifth century. Renaissance scholars, however, usually
attributed it to the Musaeus mentioned by Homer and by
Vergil, and assigned it an antiquity quite impossible in view of

---

bus deditus fuerat illectus, majorem quam posterius fervorem ad bonarum artium
disciplinas adhiberet, et laudum cupidissimus esset." [*De Marl. Fab.*, p. 215]

1904. Ingram: "That it was the product of his latest life all things seem to testify."
[*Christopher Marlowe and His Associates*, p. 214]

1910. Brooke: "Probably the latest of Marlowe's writings." [*Works*, p. 485]

1911. Léonce Chabalier: "M. Faligan émet l'opinion qu'*Héro et Léandre* ne doit pas
être attribué aux dernières années du poète, mais bien à la période universitaire. . . . Cette conjecture paraît assez plausible." [*Héro et Léandre*, pp. 21–22]

1922. Brooke: "It is reasonable to assume, as has commonly been done, that it is one
of Marlowe's latest works, left unfinished at his death." [PMLA, 37: 391]
(1922)

1927. Ellis-Fermor: "To the early months of 1593 (n.s.) is generally assigned his
poem, *Hero and Leander*, which bears internal evidence of being late (in fact, his
latest) work. . . . Marlowe's last poem." [*Christopher Marlowe*, pp. 6, 123]

1932. L. C. Martin: "It is commonly believed that *Hero and Leander* was Marlowe's
last work. . . . Yet something may be said for the view that it was written before Marlowe became a playwright, while he was still at Cambridge, and abandoned because he found dramatic activity more congenial." [Marlowe's *Poems*,
p. 3]

1932. Douglas Bush: "The notion of a date earlier than 1593 does not seem untenable." [*Mythology and the Renaissance Tradition*, p. 124]

the dialect in which it is written — good (if not especially inspired) literary Attic of the decadent Alexandrine period. It
has not the remotest resemblance to the Greek of Homer or of
Hesiod, and is held by classical scholars to show the influence of
Nonnus, a fifth-century epic poet.[5]

At the very least, Musaeus was, like Mrs. Malaprop's Cer-
berus, "three gentlemen at once." Greek literature and tradition include three — perhaps even four or five — poets of this
name, their identities being hard to establish and equally hard
to disentangle. Suidas, whose *Lexicon* was in the University
Library, Cambridge, when Marlowe was a student,[6] discusses
them all. One is the mythical pupil of Orpheus, to whom Aristophanes alludes in *The Frogs* and Vergil in the *Aeneid*, not to
mention passing references in other classical authors.[7]

A second Musaeus was an Ephesian courtier of the kings of
Pergamum, author of a *Perseis* and poems on Eumenes and
Attalus.[8] The third, an Alexandrian scholar of the fourth, fifth,
or sixth century, Musaeus Grammaticus, is now generally regarded as the author of the poem on which Marlowe based his
Hero and Leander. A love lyric on the story of Alpheus and
Arethusa [9] is ascribed to him. His poem on Hero and Leander
— if it is indeed his — is undoubtedly one of the most beautiful works of a rather decadent age; but it is difficult to compre-
hend the opinion of Julius Caesar Scaliger, who passed upon it
one of the queerest of all his queer literary judgments, averring
that "si Musaeus ea quae Homerus scripsit, scripsisset; longe
melius eum scripsisse judicemus." [10]

Suidas lists a fourth and even a fifth Musaeus. One of these
is described as a "philosopher among the Greeks," but, as his
name is linked with Hesiod, there is an obvious confusion with
the first legendary poet. The fifth is "Musaeus the Theban,"
but the reading is not above suspicion and the correct reading
may be "Athenian," in which case this individual is identical

[5] Wilmer Cave Wright: *Short History of Greek Literature*, p. 469; Gilbert Murray:
History of Greek Literature, p. 395.

[6] See the old *Catalogus Librorum MS.*, p. 49, and Charles Sayle: *Cambridge University
Library Annals*, under the year 1574.

[7] *Frogs*, 1033; *Aeneid*, VI. 665; Suidas: *Lexicon* (ed. Gaisford, rev. Bernhardy, 1853),
II. 890; Pausanias, I. 25. 8; Herodotus, VII. 6; VIII. 96; IX. 43.

[8] Suidas: *Lexicon*, *loc. cit.*

[9] *Anthol. Pal.*, IX. 362.   [10] J. B. Gail's ed. of Musaeus, p. vii.

with the first and legendary Musaeus. This is the more probable, since both are also connected with Eleusis.[11]

The name Musaeus is at best suspiciously eponymous, and the embarrassing multiplicity of poets who bear it may be due wholly to the fact that the Greek common noun μουσείον and the Greek proper name Μουσαῖος are nearly alike in most of the oblique cases. Confusion thus arose between companies of scholars — μουσεία — and the name of an individual. This was the easier because Suidas was writing in the late tenth century after Christ,[12] nearly two thousand years after any possible historical prototype of the first Musaeus to whom he refers.

Renaissance scholars, needless to say, were untroubled by doubts of this sort. At best highly uncritical, they were inclined to accept the authorship of the legendary Musaeus — now frequently known as the Pseudo-Musaeus — as genuine. The first English writer to express doubts was Sir Robert Stapylton, who published a *Musæus on the Love of Hero and Leander* in 1647.[13]

Marlowe had no particular difficulty in gaining access to his source. *The historie of Leander and Hero, written by Musæus, and Englished by me a dozen yeares ago, and in print* is mentioned by Abraham Fleming in his edition of Vergil's *Georgics* in 1589, though it has since disappeared.[14] There were, however, editions in Greek, Latin, French, and Italian in Marlowe's time, and earlier, beginning with Aldus' edition, which may have been published as early as 1484, though 1494 is a more probable date.[15] Henri Estienne, the younger, included Musaeus in his *Poetae Graeci Principes*, published in 1566. Bernardo Tasso's translation appeared in 1537, Juan Boscan Almogaver's in 1543, Clément Marot's in 1541, and Bernardino Baldi's in 1585. There is some ground for thinking Marlowe may have used the Latin version in F. Paulinus' *Centum Fabulae ex Antiquis*, which appeared in 1587, the year when he left Cambridge. Sir Sidney

[11] Suidas: *Lexicon* (ed. Gaisford, rev. Bernhardy, 1853), II. 890.
[12] 976 A.D., according to Leonard Whibley: *Companion to Greek Studies*, p. 748.
[13] Douglas Bush, in MLN, 43: 101 F 1928.
[14] H. R. Palmer: *List of English Editions and Translations . . . of the Classics*, p. 74. Cf. MLN, 43: 101 (1928).
[15] Chabalier, p. 5, followed by L. C. Martin in his introduction to the *Poems*, p. 5. The grounds for accepting 1494 as the date are given by T. F. Dibdin: *Bibliotheca Spenceriana*, II. 177, 181.

Lee, however, says that Marlowe's poem is part of Marot's "progeny," and that "Marlowe followed Marot," a view for which he gives no evidence.[16]

No matter which version Marlowe used, his main source was unquestionably Musaeus, though with the material thus provided he makes exceedingly free. *Hero and Leander* has often been described as a translation. It is, in fact, nothing of the sort. The English poet has used his Greek original as a storehouse of material with which he could take any liberty he wished — precisely as he had used his other sources in his playwriting. The clearest evidence of this is the comparative length of the two poems. Musaeus tells the whole story in 343 lines,[17] whereas Marlowe's share of the English poem, that is, the first two sestiads, leaves the story unfinished after 818 lines.

Marlowe expands and elaborates the older story at every opportunity. In Musaeus, Hero has a single slave, whom she mentions once; in Marlowe, the slave becomes an old nurse, who quite possibly gave Shakespeare a hint for *Romeo and Juliet* and who may also have some relation to the nurse of Ascanius, in the Marlowe-Nashe *Dido*. Musaeus' Hero is an ingenue; Marlowe's, a highly sophisticated lady of Elizabeth's court. Marlowe introduces a note of sensuality and a wealth of glittering imagery, absent in Musaeus' unpretentious idyll; invents Hero's flight from her lover; omits the story of the torch set up to guide him; introduces long personal descriptions of the lovers themselves, their first meeting, and the Temple of Venus; brings in the episode of Mercury, the country maid, and Cupid; and gives a detailed description of Leander's swim across the Hellespont, delaying the seduction scene to the second meeting of the lovers.

Chapman, perhaps carrying out a plan of Marlowe's, lets Leander perish while swimming to his third rendezvous; Musaeus permits his lovers to meet all summer, undisturbed, and only the storms of winter bring about Leander's death. Marlowe also supplies the interview of Leander and his father, while Chapman adds a sister, to whom Leander confides his love. Both are unknown to Musaeus.

[16] *French Renaissance in England*, pp. 112, 126.
[17] Ed. Ludwig Schaub, Tübingen, 1876.

Musaeus was not, however, the sole source of Marlowe's entire poem. The story of Hero and Leander is alluded to by Ovid and Lucan, classical writers with whom he was certainly familiar; and there is some reason for believing that Marlowe also borrowed from Caxton's *Recuyell of the Historyes of Troye*.

Of these, the most important is Ovid, a poet of whom Marlowe makes free use in almost all his works. The *Heroides* contain imaginary letters of the two lovers,[18] and there is further allusion to them in the *Amores*,[19] which Marlowe translated as *Ovid's Elegies*:

> Saepe petens Heron iuvenis transnaverat undas;
> Tum quoque transnasset, sed via caeca fuit.

> The youth oft swimming to his *Hero* kinde
> Had then swum ouer, but the way was blinde.[20]

Even if Marlowe's interest in Ovid were not so well-established, some acquaintance with the Roman poet might almost be taken for granted in a sixteenth-century university man of literary tastes. University training of the day included some of Ovid's poems, and Golding's translation of the *Metamorphoses* (1565–67) had increased Elizabethan interest. In *Scillaes Metamorphosis*, also called *Glaucus and Scilla*,[21] Thomas Lodge had by 1589 or earlier begun to draw on this great storehouse of material for original verse in English.

His poem may perhaps have made two small contributions to Marlowe. The robe of Venus in *Glaucus and Scilla* has embroidered on it "the yong Adonis wrack"; Hero's robe also has a picture of Adonis. There is one pair of parallel passages, but the parallel is at best a commonplace which might have occurred to each poet independently:

> But loue resisted once, growes passionate,
> And nothing more than counsaile louers hate.
> [H&L, II. 139–140]
> . . . nor words, nor weeping teares
> Can fasten counsaile in the louers eares.
> [G&S, Hunterian Club ed., p. 20]

[18] XVIII, XIX.
[19] II. xvi. 31–32.
[20] II. xvi. 31–32. Marlowe is here translating line for line.
[21] *Complete Works of Thomas Lodge* (Hunterian Club ed., 1883), vol. I.

Marlowe's episode of Mercury and the country maid [22] may have had its origin in Ovid's story of Mercury's love for Herse in the second book of the *Metamorphoses*. The allusion to Mercury's putting Argus to sleep, which comes from the first book of the *Metamorphoses*,[23] strengthens the view that Marlowe developed the rest of the story from the second book.

The language of many passages in *Hero and Leander* is plainly borrowed from Ovid's *Heroides* and from Marlowe's own translation of the *Amores*, which he called *Elegies*.[24] The following examples make this clear:

> . . . Treason was in her thought,
> And cunningly to yeeld her selfe she sought.
> [H&L, II. 293–294]
> And striuing thus as one that would be cast,
> Betray'd her selfe, and yelded at the last.
> [El. I. v. 15–16]

> My words shall be as spotlesse as my youth,
> Full of simplicitie and naked truth.
> [H&L, I. 207–208]
> My spotlesse life, which but to Gods giues place,
> Naked simplicitie, and modest grace.
> [El. I. iii. 13–14]

> Beautie alone is lost, too warily kept.
> [H&L, I. 328]
> Vnmeete is beauty without vse to wither.
> [El. II. iii. 14]

> . . . The rites
> In which Loues beauteous Empresse most delites,
> Are banquets, Dorick musicke, midnight-reuell,
> Plaies, maskes, and all that stern age counteth euill.
> [H&L, I. 299–302]
> Festiuall dayes aske *Venus*, songs, and wine,
> These gifts are meete to please the powers diuine.
> [El. III. ix. 47–48]

[22] H&L, I. 385–484.
[23] H&L, I. 386–388; *Metamorphoses*, I. 668–721.
[24] See Douglas Bush in PMLA, 44: 760–761 (1929); Gertrud Lazarus: *Technik und Stil von Hero and Leander*, pp. 77, 94, 101; and II. 124–125, 130 of the present work, for parallels similar to the first pair.

But as her naked feet were whipping out.
[H&L, II. 313]
In skipping out her naked feete much grac'd her.
[El. III. vi. 82]

Dang'd downe to hell her loathsome carriage.
[H&L, II. 334]
And early mountest thy hatefull carriage.
[El. I. xiii. 38]

She trembling stroue, this strife of hers (like that
Which made the world) another world begat
Of vnknowne ioy. Treason was in her thought,
And cunningly to yeeld her selfe she sought.
[H&L, II. 291–294]
And her all naked to his sight displayd,
Whence his admiring eyes more pleasure tooke
Than *Dis*, on heapes of gold fixing his looke.
[H&L, II. 324–326]
I snacht her gowne, being thin, the harme was small,
Yet striu'd she to be couered there withall.
And striuing thus as one that would be cast,
Betray'd her selfe, and yelded at the last.
Starke naked as she stood before mine eye,
Not one wen in her body could I spie.
[El. I. v. 13–18]

Vessels of Brasse oft handled, brightly shine.
[H&L, I. 231]
Brasse shines with vse.   [El. I. viii. 51]

For as a hote prowd horse highly disdaines
To haue his head control'd, but breakes the raines,
Spits foorth the ringled bit, and with his houes
Checkes the submissiue ground: so hee that loues,
The more he is restrain'd, the woorse he fares.
[H&L, II. 141–145]
I saw a horse against the bitte stiffe-neckt,
Like lightning go, his strugling mouth being checkt.
When he perceiud the reines let slacke, he stayde.
[El. III. iv. 13–15]

'Tis wisedome to giue much, a gift preuailes,
When deepe perswading Oratorie failes.
[H&L, II. 225–226]

Let *Homer* yeeld to such as presents bring
(Trust me) to giue, it is a witty thing.
                              [El. I. viii. 61–62] [25]

Rich robes themselues and others do adorne,
Neither themselues nor others, if not worne.
                              [H&L, I. 237–238]
. . . good garments would be worne.
                              [El. I. viii. 51]

Marlowe borrows also from the Latin text of the *Heroides.*
Thus

And pray'd the narrow toyling *Hellespont*
To part in twaine, that hee might come and go,
But still the rising billowes answered no.
                              [H&L, II. 150–152]
Vana peto; precibusque meis obmurmurat ipse
    quasque quatit, nulla parte coercet aquas.
                              [*Heroides*, XVIII. 47–48]

O that these tardie armes of mine were wings!
                              [H&L, II. 205]
Nunc daret audaces utinam mihi Daedalus alas.
                              [*Heroides*, XVIII. 49]

And as he spake, vpon the waues he springs.
                              [H&L, II. 206]
fortiter in summas erigor altus aquas.
                              [*Heroides*, XVIII. 84]

The allusion to the story of Hero and Leander in the ninth
book of Lucan's *Pharsalia* must have been familiar to Marlowe,
since he translated the first book. But it does not seem to have
had any particular influence upon his work. The passage runs:

Threiciasque legit fauces et amore notatum
Aequor et Heroas lacrimoso littore turris,
Qua pelago nomen Nephelias abstulit Helle. [26]

There is a curious parallel between a scene in *The Recuyell of
the Historyes of Troye* and the scene of Hero's final yielding in
Marlowe's poem. The passage describes the wooing of **Danäe**
as follows:

[25] See II. 126–127 for a similar parallel.
[26] *Pharsalia* (ed. C. M. Francken, 1896), IX. 954–956.

Danes was so sore abasshed whan she felt herself so kyste/ that she crept wyth in the bedde. Iupiter nyghed neer so fer that he descourid her face for to speke to her/ wherof she beyng a frayd opend her eyen and whan she wiste that hit was Iupiter/ and was allone by her bedde side/ she made a ryght grete shryche and crye/ whan Iupiter herd this crye he was not right well assured/ Neuertheles he poursued his aduenture tornyng her to hym ward and confortyng her by hys swete spekyng/ he declared to her in the ende that hit was force that she muste be his wyf promyttyng to come and to fecche her in short tyme/ and so longe he held her in suche deuyses/ that he vnclothed hym self/ and that in spekyng to here he sprange in to the bed and laye by her side. how well that she wythsayd and wythstode hit wyth alle her myght Thanne sayde the mayde that she was betrayed And wepynge tenderly she wende to haue fled and dide her beste to haue gon away But Iupiter toke good hede/ And at the lepe that she sup-posid to make caught and helde her by the Arme/ And made her to lye doun agayn And beclypt her and kyste her agayn/ And so ap-pesed her in suche facion that she lefte her wepynge.[27]

The scene hardly provides conclusive evidence that Marlowe used the *Recuyell* — such episodes are much alike in all ages — but the parallel is very close, and the coincidence is the more striking because it was perfectly possible for Marlowe to know all of Caxton's books at first hand.

Analogies with the Nausicaa episode in the *Odyssey* have also been suggested, but are not close enough to be convincing.[28]

THE TWO CONTINUATIONS

The poem left unfinished at Marlowe's death was completed in two independent versions, one by Henry Petowe and the other by George Chapman. Petowe's version, a wretched per-formance, has been almost completely forgotten, and Chap-man's is the only one that has ordinarily been reprinted in com-pany with Marlowe's. It is probable, however, that Petowe's was the first published, since an inferior and comparatively un-known writer would scarcely have ventured to compete with Chapman, an author of established position, to whom Meres re-fers in this very year as a renowned scholar, tragedian, and comedian. Petowe's first and only edition is dated 1598, whereas

[27] *Recuyell* (ed. Heinrich Oskar Sommer), I. 129. Cf. H&L, II. 244–334. The parallel was first noted by Douglas Bush, PMLA, 44: 764 (1929).
[28] M. H. Jellinek: *Die Sage von Hero und Leander in der Dichtung*, p. 22.

Chapman's continuation, appearing in the same year, was re-printed in nine editions, ending with the *Hero and Leander* of 1637, and has been continuously associated with Marlowe's poem ever since. It looks very much as if both writers had worked independently on the same theme, and then had suffered the not uncommon misfortune of simultaneous publication. Chapman's version was so obviously superior that nothing further was heard of Petowe's.

Henry Petowe was an obscure writer, of whom very little is known except that in 1612 and later he was Marshal of the Artillery Garden,[29] where the gunners from the Tower of London trained; and that he published various obscure works, only one of which, *Elizabeth Quasi-Viuens, Eliza's Funerall*, reached a second edition. This has no date but obviously preceded Petowe's celebration of James I's accession in *Englands Caesar. His Majesties Most Royall Coronation* (1603). Another work, *Philochasander and Elanira* (1599), seems to deal with Petowe's own courtship and may owe something to Marlowe's work. He also wrote a book called *The Country Ague* (1626).[30]

Original editions of Petowe's continuation of *Hero and Leander* are almost unknown, and his part of the poem has been only once completely reprinted — by Léonce Chabalier, who refuses even to mention him in the title of his *Héro et Léandre. Poème de Christopher Marlowe et George Chapman*. Dyce re-printed a few selections from Petowe with a view to demonstrating his exceeding badness.

Although professing reverence for "that admired Poet *Marloe*," Petowe disdains to follow his example in basing his work on the original Greek of Musaeus. In his "Epistle Dedicatorie," he claims to have been "inriched by a Gentleman a friend of mine, with the true Italian discourse, of those Lovers further Fortunes"; but there is room for suspicion that he invented the rest of his story himself, since no copy of the "true Italian discourse" has ever come to light. A writer of our day would be ashamed to admit the use of a source; Petowe, the

---

[29] In Teasel Close, now Artillery Lane, Bishopsgate Street Without. Cf. E. H. Sugden: *Topographical Dictionary of Shakespeare and His Fellow Dramatists*, pp. 31-32.
[30] Warton: *Hist. Eng. Poetry* (1781), III. 434n, and Ronald Bayne: article "Petowe," DNB, XV. 975-976; STC 19803-19808.

Elizabethan hack, feels that a source is necessary to literary respectability. It is a curious instance of a complete reversal of literary attitudes. Dyce agrees that the alleged source is merely "an ingenious fiction," and adds: "It is at least certain that the wretched style in which he relates the very foolish incidents is all his own." [31]

Dyce is, however, too severe. Petowe's poem is at least mercifully brief — it extends to but 628 lines — and has the merit of giving a tribute to Marlowe which has some interest:

> . . . this suppos'd *Apollo*,
> Conceit no other, but th'admired *Marlo*:
> *Marlo* admir'd, whose honney flowing vaine,
> No English writer can as yet attaine.
> Whose name in Fames immortall treasurie,
> Truth shall record to endles memorie,
> *Marlo* late mortall, now fram'd all divine.[32]

Petowe's version of the later history of Hero and Leander, told in extremely obscure verse that rarely rises to the level of respectable mediocrity, is painfully dull. Venus is indignant at her priestess. Juno joins in her plaints, while Jupiter defends Hero. Then follows the apostrophe to Marlowe, and then the resumption of the tale proper. Duke Archilaus courts Hero and banishes Leander. Archilaus dies and is succeeded by his brother, Euristippus, who accuses Hero of poisoning Archilaus. She submits her fate to ordeal by battle. Leander returns, champions Hero, slays Euristippus, and becomes "heire of Sestos right." The lovers live happily "full many yeares" and are at death transformed into two trees, like Baucis and Philemon.

Chapman's continuation of Marlowe's poem begins with what is now the third sestiad. Marlowe had written what is contained in Blount's 1598 edition. This was all one section of the poem, without division. Chapman cut it up into two sestiads — a word that he seems to have derived from the town of Sestos — and added an "argument" to each, corresponding to the "argument" preceding each of his own subsequent sestiads.

[31] Dyce's 1850 ed., xlix–l.
[32] Chabalier, *op. cit.*, pp. 184–185.

Certain early critics have held that somewhere in Chapman's continuation are imbedded a hundred lines of authentic Marlowe. This idea originated with Edmund Malone,[33] who based it on a misunderstanding of the 1600 edition of *England's Parnassus*. In his unpublished notes Malone asserted that Marlowe wrote the first two sestiads and about a hundred lines of the third, and supposed that the compiler of *England's Parnassus* had the complete, though unfinished, text of Marlowe before him. Malone repeated this idea in his notes, but later added other notes retracting it and accepting the view that Marlowe's work ends with the second sestiad. There is really nothing in *England's Parnassus* which can be interpreted as assigning anything more to Marlowe.

Malone's error did not die so easily, however. He had told Thomas Warton [34] of his opinion that Marlowe had written a hundred lines of the third sestiad, and Lieutenant-Colonel Francis Cunningham [35] took up the idea in his edition. Apparently Cunningham knew nothing of the Malone manuscripts; but he ventured the opinion that the extra hundred lines were "not to be looked for in the place assigned to them, where all is manifestly Chapman's, but in the episode of Teras,[36] and other portions of the fifth Sestiad, where the higher hand of Marlowe seems to me easily discernible." By "the place assigned to them" he apparently means the first hundred lines of the third sestiad.

With other critics, the idea that Marlowe's hand is to be felt somewhere in the sestiads usually assigned to Chapman and claimed for him in the early editions has never found very wide acceptance. Tucker Brooke admits [37] that the tale of Teras is one of the finest passages in the continuation, but scoffs [38] at the idea that it is Marlowe's. Though Chapman may have had a few manuscript notes of Marlowe's, and though it is possible

[33] The passage referred to corresponds with III. 109–144 in Brooke's edition. It appears on pp. 454–456 of the reprint of *England's Parnassus* included in Heliconia (vol. III, ed. T. Park, 1815) and on p. 379 of the 1600 ed. See Tucker Brooke, PMLA, 37: 391–393 (1922), and Malone's MS. notes in Bodleian 131, facing p. 345.

[34] *Hist. Eng. Poetry* (1875), p. 906n.

[35] Cunningham's ed., p. xvii.

[36] *Hero and Leander*, V. 90 ff.

[37] *Works*, p. 487.

[38] PMLA, 37: 393 (1922).

that a few authentic specimens of the mighty line may be imbedded here and there in the continuation, there is no good
reason for doubting that the last four sestiads are Chapman's
and his alone.

The exact conditions under which Chapman undertook the
task are by no means clear. It has ordinarily been assumed that
the dying Marlowe charged his friend Chapman to complete the
poem that he left unfinished. So long as the circumstances of
Marlowe's death remained a mystery, Chapman's obscure hints
could be thus interpreted; but, thanks to Dr. Hotson's discovery of the exact circumstances of the assassination, it is now
clear that this is impossible.

Marlowe died suddenly and violently, in an obscure and
squalid tavern brawl. There would have been no time for dying
injunctions, even had Chapman been present — as he certainly
was not. It remains possible that Marlowe, knowing the extreme personal danger in which he stood in the last few months
of his life,[39] may have suggested something of the sort to Chapman, with whom he was probably acquainted. The delay of
five years in completing the poem after Marlowe's violent
taking-off is not unnatural. Chapman had been working on his
translation of Homer and in fact published seven books of the
Iliad in the very year in which the first complete edition of
Hero and Leander appeared. Publication of Petowe's continuation in that same year is undeniably odd, but seems to be mere
coincidence.

The lines which seem to suggest that Marlowe urged Chapman to continue *Hero and Leander* appear in the third sestiad:

> Then thou most strangely-intellectuall fire,
> That proper to my soule hast power t'inspire
> Her burning faculties, and with the wings
> Of thy vnspheared flame visitst the springs
> Of spirits immortall; Now (as swift as Time
> Doth follow Motion) finde th'eternall Clime
> Of his free soule, whose liuing subiect stood
> Vp to the chin in the Pyerean flood,
> And drunke to me halfe this Musean storie,
> Inscribing it to deathles Memorie:
> Confer with it, and make my pledge as deepe,

[39] See I. 106 ff.

That neithers draught be consecrate to sleepe.
Tell it how much his late desires I tender,
(If yet it know not) and to light surrender
My soules darke ofspring, willing it should die
To loues, to passions, and societie.[40]

This is obscure with a more than Elizabethan obscurity; yet the allusion is plainly in some way to Marlowe; and "his late desires" are most reasonably interpreted as meaning the continuation of the poem. Precisely when or how or why those desires were expressed, we shall probably never know; but it is quite possible that Chapman was of Kentish birth and part of a literary group which included the Walsinghams, Oxindens, and Manwoods, and that Marlowe actually did ask him, as a friend, to finish the poem in the event of his own sudden death.[41]

Chapman's share of the poem is like Marlowe's in being a mere expansion of the Musaean story, the chief variations being the insertion of the tale of Teras and the speeding up of the catastrophe. Musaeus had allowed the lovers an entire summer of happiness, which Chapman denies them. The lovers are at length transformed by Neptune

Like two sweet birds surnam'd th' *Acanthides*,
Which we call Thistle-warps, that neere no Seas
Dare euer come, but still in couples flie,
And feede on Thistle tops, to testifie
The hardnes of their first life in their last.[42]

INFLUENCE

Hero and Leander was an extremely popular poem. It was published in ten extant editions, of which the two earliest appeared in 1598. It exercised a powerful influence over poets for the half century following its publication and was still being imitated during the nineteenth century. This success was probably largely responsible for the flood of amatory verse that followed, though Thomas Lodge's *Glaucus and Scilla*, which probably preceded Marlowe's poem, may have had some share

---

[40] *Hero and Leander*, III. 183–198.
[41] W. C. Hazlitt: *Shakespear: The Man and His Work*, p. 211.
[42] *Hero and Leander*, VI. 276–280.

in setting up this fashion. In many cases, however, borrowers or imitators openly acknowledge their debt, and in other cases direct quotations, parallel passages, or obvious imitation give plain evidence of Marlowe's literary influence.

One of the characteristics of *Hero and Leander* most frequently imitated is the "myth-making" which Marlowe introduces. The long, interpolated mythological episode, like the story of Mercury and the country maid, was already familiar, but Marlowe often introduces in a line or two a bit of mythology of his own devising, as when he explains night as Nature's mourning for Hero's misfortunes:

> . . . in signe her treasure suffred wracke,
> Since *Heroes* time, hath halfe the world beene blacke.
> [H&L, I. 49–50]

Certain other lines are quite as popular as his myth-making, and are quoted by so many poets that one cannot always be sure whether they are quoting their great original or merely each other.

So numerous are the imitations and quotations that a chronological table is necessary to avoid confusion. The one which follows includes the more important instances, excluding Shakespeare, who requires a separate chapter:

1589–1593. Walter Raleigh: *Ocean to Scinthia*
1592. Abraham Fraunce: *Countess of Pembroke's Ivychurch*
1593–1594. Michael Drayton: *Endimion and Phoebe*; *Peirs Gaveston*
1594. Richard Barnfield: *Affectionate Shepherd*
1596. Thomas Edwards: *Narcissus*; *Cephalus and Procris*
1596. Dunstan Gale: *Pyramus and Thisbe*
1597. Anonymous: *Pilgrimage to Parnassus*
1596. Bartholomew Griffin: *Fidessa*
1598? Ben Jonson: *Every Man in His Humour*, and later works
1598. John Marston: *Pygmalion*
1599. Henry Petowe: *Philocassander and Elanira*
1600. Anonymous: *England's Parnassus*
1600. John Bodenham: *Belvedere*
1602. Anonymous: *Salmacis and Hermaphroditus*
1603. Phineas Fletcher: *Venus and Anchises*

1607. William Barksted: *Mirrha; Hiren*

1607. Edward Sharpham: *The Fleire*

1609. Thomas Heywood: *Troia Britannica*

1610? Edmund Bolton: *Hypercritica*

1613. Samuel Page: *Loves of Amos and Laura*

1614. John Cooke: *Greene's Tu Quoque or the City Gallant*

1614. Ben Jonson: *Bartholomew Faire*

1615. Richard Braithwaite: *Strappado for the Diuell*

1621. Richard Braithwaite: *Natures Embassie*

1621. Robert Burton: *Anatomy of Melancholy*

1621. John Taylor: *Praise, Antiquity, and commodity of Beggery, Beggers, and Begging*

1622. Patrick Hannay: *Philomela*

1626? William Bosworth: *Arcadius and Sepha*

1630. John Taylor: "Motto" in the *Works*

1635. Thomas Heywood: *Hierarchie of the Blessed Angels*

Many of these poems date from a period earlier than 1598, when the two earliest editions of *Hero and Leander* now extant were published. The influence of Marlowe's poem may be ascribed either to the well-known Elizabethan practice of circulating verse in manuscript, or to the possible existence of a still earlier edition of 1593, all copies of which have since disappeared. The poem had been entered in the *Stationers' Register* on September 28, 1593, but no copies of an edition of that date are now known. This, however, is not remarkable, since many early editions are now represented by single copies only.

In Samuel Daniel's *Complaint of Rosamond*, sometimes dated 1592, the "seeming Matron yet sinfull Monster" lures the virtuous Rosamond to her destruction with arguments very like Leander's; but these ideas are at best commonplaces, and as the *Complaint* may antedate Marlowe's poem, the relationship between them is doubtful.

Marlowe's poem was much quoted, both seriously and satirically. Not only did *England's Parnassus* (1600) reprint something over a hundred lines, but John Bodenham's *Belvedere* (1600) quotes a great many more.[43] Ben Jonson's plagiarizing

---

[43] Tucker Brooke in *Trans. Conn. Acad.*, 25: 362 (1922); Charles Crawford in *Englische Studien*, 43: 206 (1910).

poetaster, Master Matthew, misquotes the first sestiad in the second, anglicized version of *Every Man in His Humour*.[44] The first, Italianate version had appeared in 1598, the year when *Hero and Leander* was first published, and the dramatist's certainty that his audience would recognize Marlowe's lines is evidence of their popularity. Jonson had reverence enough for Marlowe's memory to condemn Matthew's plagiarism:

A filching rogue, hang him! — and from the dead! it's worse than sacrilege.

The lawyer-dramatist, Edward Sharpham (fl. 1607), used parts of the same comic misquotations in his play *The Fleire*, which is supposed to have been acted in 1606.[45]

Edmund Bolton's *Hypercritica* (1610?), in its Rawlinson manuscript version, includes "Marlowe his excellent fragment of Hero and Leander" among works "out of which wee gather the most warrantable English," but the passage is omitted from the printed version of 1722.[46]

SIR WALTER RALEIGH: THE OCEAN TO SCINTHIA

Sir Walter Raleigh, in *The Ocean to Scinthia*, echoes *Hero and Leander* once:

> On Sestus shore Leanders late resorte
> Hero hath left no lampe to Guyde her love.[47]

Raleigh had begun this poem at least as early as 1589 and continued to work on it until about 1592 or 1593. This was the period when he and Marlowe — and probably Spenser — were in closest association.[48]

JOHN MARSTON: PYGMALION

John Marston's *Pygmalion* differs from other poems of the sort in its satiric or jocular tone, which anticipates seventeenth-

[44] H&L, I. 199–204, 221–222; *Every Man in His Humour*, IV. i, p. 600 of the Everyman ed.

[45] H&L, I. 199–204; *Fleire*, Act I. See Hunold Nibbe in *Materialien*, 1912, p. 10.

[46] Brooke, *op. cit.*, p. 363; J. Haslewood: *Ancient Critical Essays* (ed. 1815), II. 246; Rawlinson MSS. Misc. I, p. 13.

[47] Bk. XI, ll. 487–488. See Hatfield MSS. (Salisbury Papers), no. 144. Hist. MSS. Comm. Cf. Agnes M. Latham's ed. of Raleigh's *Poems*, p. 93.

[48] See I. 208–209; and Latham, *op. cit.*, pp. 173, 179.

century treatment of the same theme. It owes something to *Hero and Leander*, but the parallels are rarely close. Perhaps the clearest echo is in the lines: [49]

> But you are faire (aye me) so wondrous faire,
> So yoong, so gentle, and so debonaire.
> > [H&L, I. 287–288]
> . . . Call her wondrous fair,
> Virtuous, divine, most debonair.
> > [*Pygmalion*, 13–14]

In other poems [50] Marston ridicules lovers' sighs of "aye me," as does Drayton in his sonnet "To the Reader." [51] In the second satire of his *Scourge of Villaine*,[52] Marston obviously alludes to the episode of Mercury and the country maid in *Hero and Leander*:

> Here Jove's lust-pander, Maia's juggling son,
> In clown's disguise, doth after milkmaids run.

The following parallel passages have some relation to each other:

> The more a gentle pleasing heat reuiued.
> > [H&L, II. 67]
> Whose liuely heat like fire from heauen fet,
> Would animate grosse clay, and higher set
> The drooping thoughts of base declining soules.
> > [H&L, II. 255–257]
> Thy favours, like Promethean sacred fire,
> In dead and dull conceit can life inspire.
> > [*Pygmalion*, p. 250]
> . . . that warmth and wishèd heat
> Which might a saint and coldest spirit move.
> > [*Pygmalion*, 219–220]

> And her all naked to his sight displayd.
> > [H&L, II. 324]
> And naked as it stood before his eyes.
> > [*Pygmalion*, 19]

[49] The exact title is *The Metamorphosis of Pigmalion's Image*. References are to Bullen's Marston, vol. III. See II. 139 for possible relation to Milton.
[50] *Scourge of Villaine*, VI. 18; VIII. 33, 52; Bullen's ed., III. 340, 355, 356.
[51] Brett's ed., p. 28.
[52] *Scourge*, II. 27–28; Bullen's ed., III. 312.

Many would praise the sweet smell as she past.
                    [H&L, I. 21]
So sweet a breath, that doth perfume the air.
                    [*Pygmalion*, 39]

        . . . Hee thus replide: The rites
In which Loues beauteous Empresse most delites,
Are banquets, Dorick musicke, midnight-reuell,
Plaies, maskes, and all that stern age counteth euill.
                    [H&L, I. 299–302]
"Thou sacred queen of sportive dallying"
(Thus he begins), "Love's only emperess,
Whose kingdom rests in wanton revelling. . . ."
                    [*Pygmalion*, 133–135] [53]

With that hee stript him to the yu'rie skin.
                    [H&L, II. 153]
And therefore straight he strips him naked quite.
                    [*Pygmalion*, 149]

Me in thy bed and maiden bosome take.
                    [H&L, II. 248]
. . . deign for to take me in.
                    [*Pygmalion*, 155]

MICHAEL DRAYTON

Michael Drayton's *Endimion and Phoebe* is likewise in the mood of *Hero and Leander*, showing several parallels in phrasing, though no other marked similarities. Of these, the more important are: [54]

Some swore he was a maid in mans attire.
                    [H&L, I. 83]
Thinking some Nymph was cloth'd in boyes attire,
                    [E&P, p. 200]

an idea which reappears in Shakespeare's twentieth sonnet.

The lining purple silke . . .
        . . . her vaile reacht to the ground beneath.
                    [H&L, I. 10–18]
An Azur'd Mantle purfled with a vaile.
                    [E&P, p. 200]

[53] See II. 127 for a similar parallel.
[54] References are to the Roxburghe Club ed. of Drayton's *Poems* (1856), edited by J. P. Collier, vol. I. See II. 129, 132, 134, 263 for other similar parallels.

About her necke hung chaines of peble stone.

> [H&L, I. 25]

About her neck a chayne, twise twenty fold,
Of Rubyes set in lozenges of gold.

> [E&P, p. 200]

Buskins of shels all siluered vsed she,
And brancht with blushing corall to the knee.

> [H&L, I. 31–32]

Her dainty Buskins lac'd vnto the knee.

> [E&P, p. 201]

Drayton also alludes to "the sweet Museus of these times," [55] and plainly echoes the "Passionate Shepherd":

Thy Ewes (qd. she) with Milk shall daily spring,
And to thy profit yeerely Twins shall bring;
And thy fayre flock (a wonder to behold)
Shall haue their fleeces turn'd to burnisht gold; . . .
Thou in great Phoebes Iuory Coche shalt ride,
Which, drawne by Eagles, in the ayre shall glide.[56]

Drayton's *Peirs Gaveston* has at least one reminiscence of *Hero and Leander*:

Or as Muse-mervaile *Hero*, when she clips
Her deer *Leanders* byllow-beaten limms,
And with sweet kisses seazeth on his lips,
When for her sake deep Hellespont he swimms,
    Might by our tender-deer imbracings prove,
    Fayre *Heros* kindnes, and *Leanders* love.[57]

There is a faint echo of *Hero and Leander* in one line of *Idea's Mirror* (1594):

Vnfained loue in naked simple truth,[58]

which resembles

My words shall be as spotlesse as my youth,
Full of simplicitie and naked truth.

> [H&L, I. 207–208]

Naked simplicitie, and modest grace.

> [El. I. iii. 14]

---

[55] *Op. cit.*, p. 226.
[56] *Op. cit.*, pp. 204–205. For imitations of this poem by other writers, see II. 157–160.
[57] Cf. J. William Hebel, MLN, 41: 250 Ap 1926. The passage is in Hebel's ed. of Drayton (1932), I. 198, ll. 1417–1422. This poem should not be confused with Drayton's *Legend of Peirs Gaueston* or with Gaveston's letter in *England's Heroicall Epistles*.
[58] Amour 38, p. 168 Roxburghe Club ed. See also II. 106, 129.

This is also echoed in Beaumont and Fletcher's *Faithful Shepherdess*:

> My language shall be honest, full of truth,
> My flames as smooth and spotless as my youth.[59]

SALMACIS AND HERMAPHRODITUS

Salmacis and Hermaphroditus, published anonymously in 1602 [60] and republished in editions of 1640 and later with Francis Beaumont's name on the title page, probably owes a good deal to Ovid and to *Venus and Adonis*,[61] but its imitation of *Hero and Leander* is unmistakable. The poem imitates the personal descriptions of Hero [62] and of Leander [63] and the description of the temple.[64] It also reproduces the amorous arguments which Marlowe had made conventional and represents the meeting of Bacchus and Salmacis as resembling the meetings of Hero with Leander and of Mercury with the country maid.[65]

There are certain parallels in the phrasing:

> . . . Her on the ground hee layd,
> And tumbling in the grasse, he often strayd
> Beyond the bounds of shame.
> [H&L, I. 405–407]
> And kist the helplesse Nymph vpon the ground,
> And would haue stray'd beyond that lawful bound.
> [S&H, p. 114]

> . . . leapt liuely in.
> [H&L, II. 154]
> . . . leapt liuely from the land.
> [S&H, p. 125]

> . . . I could tell ye,
> How smooth his brest was, & how white his bellie.
> [H&L, I. 65–66]

[59] Dyce's (1843) ed., II. iv. 9–10.
[60] STC 1666 ff.
[61] Cf. Douglas Bush: *Mythology and the Renaissance Tradition*, pp. 180–183. The poem is reprinted in the *Shakespeare Society's Papers*, 3: 94–126 (1847), to which page references are given above. The only known copy of the 1602 ed. is in the Bodleian.
[62] H&L, I. 5–50; S&H, p. 104.
[63] H&L, I. 51–90; S&H, pp. 103–104.
[64] H&L, I. 135–157; S&H, p. 107.
[65] H&L, I. 160–484; S&H, pp. 112–114.

So soft a belly, such a lustie thigh.

[S&H, p. 104]

The wals were of discoloured *Iasper* stone.

[H&L, I. 136]

Which seat was builded all of iasper stone.

[S&H, p. 107]

Ioue slylie stealing from his sisters bed,
To dallie with *Idalian Ganimed.*

[H&L, I. 147–148]

The wanton vnseene stealths of amorous Ioue.

[S&H, p. 107]

Where *Venus* in her naked glory stroue.

[H&L, I. 12]

. . . the naked pride
Of louely Venus in the vale of Ide.

[S&H, p. 107]

THOMAS EDWARDS

The *Cephalus and Procris* and the *Narcissus* of the mysterious
Thomas Edwards [66] are certainly part of the general group of
amatory tales to which *Hero and Leander* belongs.

In many instances, there is room for reasonable doubt
whether we have a direct influence exerted by Marlowe's poem
or a mere casual similarity due to the Elizabethan fondness for
love stories in verse, which begins in the last decade of the sixteenth century. In Edwards' poems there is no possibility of
doubt.

In his versified *Narcissus* Edwards alludes directly to Marlowe, under a transparent pseudonym, and quotes him almost
verbatim. The envoy alludes to "Collyn," "Rosamond,"
"Amintas," and "Leander," in whom [67] are obviously recognizable Spenser, author of *Colin Clout*; Samuel Daniel, author
of *The Complaint of Rosamond*; Marlowe's friend, Thomas

[66] Cf. DNB and the Roxburghe Club ed., pp. xi–xv, for guesses at his identity. Also
C. C. Stopes, MLR, 16: 209 ff. (1921).

[67] Watson is twice referred to as "Amintas" in Richard Barnfield's *Affectionate
Shepherd*, pt. III, stanzas xix and xxxiii, pp. xxxvi and 4 of Grosart's ed. (Roxburghe
Club, 1876). Peele makes a similar reference in the prologue ("Ad Maecenatum Pro-
logus") to *The Honour of the Garter*, as does Spenser in *Colin Clout* (l. 434): "Amyntas
quite is gone."

Watson, author of *Amintae Gaudia*, for which Marlowe wrote a dedication; and Marlowe himself.[68]

Watson had died in 1592 and Marlowe in 1593. Hence Edwards' lines:

> *Amintas* and *Leander's* gone,
>   Oh deere sonnes of stately kings,
> Blessed be your nimble throats,
>   That so amorously could sing.[69]

Edwards was presumably writing in the very year of Marlowe's death, since his work is entered in the *Stationers' Register* October 22, 1593, though it was not published until 1595.[70]

Between Marlowe's poem and the two poems of Edwards there are many parallels, not of lines, but of mere phrases, which in isolation would be meaningless, but which become significant because they are so numerous and because there is other evidence for a relationship between the two writers. One of the most interesting of these is "*Ioues* high court," which appears in *Hero and Leander*, in *Narcissus*, and — doubtless by accident — as "Jove's court," in Milton's *Comus*.[71]

Ougly night.	[H&L, II. 332; C&P, p. 12] [72]
Tralucent.	[H&L, I. 296; C&P, p. 4]
Naked truth.	[H&L, I. 208; C&P, p. 12]
Dang'd downe.	[H&L, II. 334]
Downe dingeth.	[C&P, p. 7]
Yu'rie skin.	[H&L, II. 153]
Yuorie limbes.	[C&P, p. 11]
Slacke muse.	[H&L, I. 72]
Slow Muse.	[*Narcissus*, p. 61]
Shot a shaft.	[H&L, I. 72]
Shot a dart.	[C&P, p. 14]

[68] References are to the Roxburghe Club ed. (1882), edited by W. E. Buckley. See II. 208 for discussion of the Elizabethan practice of referring to writers by the titles of their works.

[69] See p. 62.

[70] Reg. B., fol. 302r; Arber's reprint, II. 639.

[71] H&L, I. 299; *Narcissus*, p. 59; *Comus*, 1.

[72] Also in *Troilus and Cressida*, V. viii. 6; I *Tamb.*, 1057; *Locrine*, I. i. 9; Drummond of Hawthornden: *Poems* (2nd ed., 1616), E-1v. See also II. 281.

Another *Phaeton*.   [H&L, I. 101; C&P, p. 7]

The golden tree.   [H&L, II. 299–300]
This same golden tree. [C&P, p. 10]

In *Narcissus* Edwards occasionally quotes Marlowe almost verbatim. Thus the lines:

> Welcome *Leander*, welcome, stand thou neere,
> Alacke poore youth, what hast thou for a pawne,
> What, not a rag, where's *Heroes* vale of lawne

are clearly reminiscent of Marlowe's line:

> The outside of her garments were of lawne,

which is followed a little later by allusions to Hero's "vaile." [73] Again, Edwards' line (immediately following an allusion to Leander and to Musaeus):

> For without men alacke they nothing are,

is obviously borrowed from Marlowe's

> . . . mayds are nothing then,
> Without the sweet societie of men.[74]

Among other parallels of the same sort, the following are worth noting:

> . . . Exceeding his
> That leapt into the water for a kis.
>   [H&L, I. 73–74]
> Amidst the spring I leapt.
>   [*Narcissus*, p. 60]

> As pittying these louers, downeward creepes.
>   [H&L, II. 100]
> And wrung her hands, & downwards would haue crept.
>   [*Narcissus*, p. 55]

> Treason was in her thought,
> And cunningly to yeeld her selfe she sought.
> Seeming not woon, yet woon she was at length.
>   [H&L, II. 293–295]

---

73 H&L, I. 9; *Narcissus*, p. 43.
74 H&L, I. 255–256; *Narcissus*, p. 44.

Women doo yeeld, yet shame to tell vs so.
                    [*Narcissus*, p. 57]
She (as some say, all woemen stricktly do,)
Faintly deni'd what she was willing too.
                    [C&P, p. 19] [75]

So ran the people foorth to gaze vpon her.
                    [H&L, I. 117]
So on report of any passing faire,
The greedie people in the streetes do runne.
                    [*Narcissus*, p. 40]

With that *Leander* stoopt, to haue imbrac'd her.
                    [H&L, I. 341]
For as I thought downe stouping to haue kist her.
                    [*Narcissus*, p. 53]

Hero, *Venus* Nun. . . . *Venus* Nun.
                    [H&L, I. 45, 319]
. . . the queene of dalliance and her Nuns.
                    [*Narcissus*, p. 56]

Cephalus and Procris opens with a passage described as "a
pariphrisis of the Night," [76] which seems curiously to echo the
marginal note in *Hero and Leander*, "A periphrasis of night." [77]
Edwards imitated Marlowe's luxuriant descriptions, his arguments against virginity, his myth-making, and many of his in-
cidental phrases. Buckley lists thirty borrowings,[78] and there
are probably others. Shakespeare and Spenser are also echoed,
and there is a single parallel (the first listed below) with Chapman's continuation of Marlowe's poem:

To beate back *Barbarisme*, and *Auarice*.
                    [H&L, III. 138]
To blind-fold Enuie, barbarisme scorning.
                    [C&P, p. 3]

His dangling tresses that were neuer shorne.
                    [H&L, I. 55]
His amber-couloured tresses, neuer yet cut.
                    [C&P, p. 12]

[75] See II. 106, 130 for other parallels.
[76] Page 6.
[77] H&L, I. 190.
[78] Roxburghe Club ed. (1882), *passim*.

Danaes statue in a brazen tower.
[H&L, I. 146]
Where *Ioue* in likenes of a golden shower,
Rauisht faire *Danae*.
[C&P, p. 9]
In brazen tower had not *Danae* dwelt,
A mothers ioy by *Ioue* she had not felt.
[*Elegies*, II. xix. 27–28]

His bodie was as straight as *Circes* wand.
[H&L, I. 61]
Rode he vpright as any heisell wan.
[C&P, p. 11] [79]

. . . Then treasure is abus'de,
When misers keepe it; being put to lone,
In time it will returne vs two for one.
[H&L, I. 234–236]
. . . Loue me againe.
Then I am thine, is it not heartie gaine,
Vpon aduantage to take double fee?
[C&P, p. 16] [80]

And to this day is euerie scholler poore.
[H&L, I. 471]
How schollers fauourites waxe ouer poore.
[C&P, p. 11]

All headlong throwes her selfe the clouds among.
[H&L, II. 90]
Therewith away she headlong postes along.
[C&P, p. 6]

. . . And with his houes
Checkes the submissiue ground.
[H&L, II. 143–144]
Whose ouer head-strong prauncing checkt the earth.
[C&P, p. 11]

'Tis wisedome to giue much, a gift preuailes,
When deepe perswading Oratorie failes.
[H&L, II. 225–226]

[79] See II. 132 for a similar parallel.
[80] See II. 264–265 for a similar passage in the *Sonnets*.

What there did want in wordes most subtilly,
By liberall giftes he did the same supply.
                    [C&P, p. 20] [81]

Loue is not ful of pittie (as men say)
But deaffe and cruell, where he meanes to pray.
                    [H&L, II. 287–288]
"For loue is pittilesse, rude, and impartiall,
    When he intendes to laugh at others fall.
                    [C&P, p. 14]

Leander now like Theban *Hercules*,
Entred the orchard of *Th'esperides*.
                    [H&L, II. 297–298]
Along'st she passed by *Hesperides*.
                    [C&P, p. 9]

And faine by stealth away she would haue crept,
. . . Leauing *Leander* in the bed alone.
                    [H&L, II. 310–312]
Whereat she starts, and in a desperate moode,
Skipt from the bed, all wrathfull where she stoode.
                    [C&P, p. 21]

                              . . . The rites
In which Loues beauteous Empresse most delites,
Are banquets, Dorick musicke, midnight-reuell,
Plaies, maskes. . . .
                    [H&L, I. 299–302]
As Reuels, Maskes, and all that *Cupids* mother
Could summon to the earth.   [C&P, p. 29] [82]

BARTHOLOMEW GRIFFIN: FIDESSA

Bartholomew Griffin's *Fidessa, more chaste than kind* (1596) [83]
probably alludes to Marlowe's poem in the lines:

Compare me to LEANDER struggling in the waves,
    Not able to attain his safety's shore,[84]

---

[81] See II. 107–108 for a similar parallel.
[82] See II. 119 for a similar parallel.
[83] Reprinted in Sidney Lee: *Elizabethan Sonnets*, III. 261–296 (*An English Garner*, vol. IX [Westminster: Constable, 1904]), and in Martha Foote Crowe: *Elizabethan Sonnet-Cycles* (London: Kegan Paul, Trench, Trübner & Co., 1892), pp. 73–138.
[84] Sonnet XIII.

though this might conceivably be borrowed directly from the Greek original. Marlowe emphasizes this part of the story rather more and at greater length than Musaeus does. A passage in Sonnet LIV, alluding to the episode of Mercury and the country maid, almost certainly comes from Marlowe:

> If Heaven's-winged herald HERMES had
> His heart enchanted with a country maid.

The fact that the two passages appear in the same work probably indicates that Griffin had been reading *Hero and Leander*.

HENRY PETOWE: PHILOCASSANDER AND ELANIRA

Since Henry Petowe published his continuation of *Hero and Leander* in 1598, it is not surprising that his *Philocassander and Elanira*, published in the following year, shows Marlowe's influence very strongly. Both of the lovers in the original poem are named,[85] and there are several obvious reminiscences. The following are the most important:

> ... the rising yu'rie mount he scal'd,
> Which is with azure circling lines empal'd,
> Much like a globe, (a globe may I tearme this,
> By which loue sailes to regions full of blis.
> [H&L, II. 273–276]
> The couering Canopie of pleasures globe.
> A globe wherein a man did neuer see,
> Such pleasant fertill countries as there be.
> [P&E, sig. B4r]

> ... liuely heat.   [H&L, II. 255; P&E, sig. Br]

> *Leander* stoopt, to haue imbrac'd her.
> [H&L, I. 341]
> ... had thought to kist her.
> [P&E, sig. D4v]

The poem contains a few reminiscences of *Tamburlaine* and uses Marlowe's characteristic word, unusual elsewhere, "ruinate." [86]

---

[85] Sigs. C1r, D2v, D3v. There is a copy of this book in the British Museum.
[86] Sig. A4r.

WILLIAM BARKSTED

The actor, William Barksted (fl. 1611), shows the influence of *Hero and Leander* in two poems — *Mirrha the Mother of Adonis* (1607) and *Hiren or the faire Greek* (1611).[87] In *Mirrha* the familiar arguments against virginity are rehearsed, especially the line

> To *Vesta* dedicate do not expire

with its following allusion to "cold fruitlesse Virginitie." There is a typical touch of Marlowe's myth-making in a passage about the sun:

> Then blusht he first, and backward would ha fled
> And euer since in rising hee's still red,

which is doubtless an imitation of Marlowe's

> And to this day is euerie scholler poore [88]

at the close of the episode of Mercury and the country maid. There are perhaps vague reminiscences of Marlowe in the lines:

> My heart is the true index of my tongue.
> And by my naked wordes you may discouer,
> I am not traded like a common Louer.[89]

Mirrha's costume is very like Hero's in the line:

> & vail'd her face with lawne, not halfe so white.

Marlowe dresses his Hero in garments of lawn and twice alludes to her veil. Hiren's costume is even closer to Hero's than Mirrha's:

> In a silke mantle, and a smocke of lawne . . .
> And siluer buskins on her feete she wore.[90]

---

[87] The poems are STC 1428 and 1429. There are copies in the Bodleian Library. Both were reprinted by Grosart in his *Occasional Issues of Very Rare Books* (1876), vol. III, but, as only fifty copies of the work were issued, even this is rather rare. There are copies in the Peabody Institute, Baltimore, and in the Columbia University Library. The Harvard College Library has a copy of *Hiren* in a dissertation by W. G. Rice: *Turk, Moor, and Persian in English Literature* (1926), pp. 543–548. Page references here are to Grosart's reprint. The first quotation is on p. 19.

[88] *Mirrha*, p. 41; H&L, I. 471.

[89] *Mirrha*, p. 14; H&L, I. 207–208; *Elegies*, I. iii. 14. Cf. II. 120 for a parallel in Drayton, and also II. 106.

[90] *Mirrha*, p. 15; *Hiren*, st. 33; H&L, I. 9, 18–19, 31. Cf. II. 119 for a similar parallel in Drayton, both the veil and buskins appearing in separate passages. Also II. 132, 134.

Marlowe's "buskins of shels all siluered" are plainly the source
of the second line.

The poem on Hiren not only echoes *Hero and Leander* in this
and other passages, but has two stanzas in imitation of "The
Passionate Shepherd," written in the characteristic "invitation
to love" vein which began with Marlowe's lyric.[91] It is here
forced to serve Mahomet's wooing of his fair captive, Hiren:

> Wilt thou be his, on thee shall waite and tend,
> A traine of Nymphs, and Pages by thy side,
> With faunes, horse, coach, & musicke which shall lend
> The spheares new notes in their harmonies pride,
> When thou wilt walke, and publikly be ey'd,
> To bring thee on, thy hie way cloath'd with flowers
> Shall sent like *Tempe* when the graces send,
> To meet each other in those fragrant bowers.
>
> At home shall comick Masques, & night-disports
> Conduct thee to thy pillow, and thy sheetes,
> And all those reuels which soft loue consorts,
> Shall entertaine thee with their sweetest sweets.

Some of the parallel passages that follow are commonplaces
of erotic verse, but the number of the correspondences makes it
certain — if more evidence were needed — that Barksted was
modeling his work on Marlowe's:

> Dang'd downe to hell her loathsome carriage.
> [H&L, II. 334]
> And darknesse from the aire to hell is hurld.
> [*Hiren*, st. 82]
>
> Some amorous rites or other were neglected.
> [H&L, II. 64]
> Making vs know when lips are sweetly linck't,
> That to those Kickshawes 'longs more dainty meate.
> [*Hiren*, st. 59] [92]
>
> Seeming not woon, yet woon she was at length,
> In such warres women vse but halfe their strength.
> [H&L, II. 295–296]
> Women were made to take what they reproue.
> [*Hiren*, st. 58] [93]

[91] See II. 158–160. The quotation is from st. 41 and 42 of *Hiren*.
[92] See II. 132, 133 for a similar parallel.   [93] See II. 106, 124–125 for similar parallels.

And now she wisht this night were neuer done,
And sigh'd to thinke vpon th'approching sunne.
                              [H&L, II. 301–302]
And wishes *Phœbus* blinde all night, no day.
                              [*Hiren*, st. 81]

PILGRIMAGE TO PARNASSUS AND AFFECTIONATE SHEPHERD

There are also traces of *Hero and Leander* in the anonymous *Pilgrimage to Parnassus* and in Richard Barnfield's *Affectionate Shepherd*, both of which draw on the same passage: [94]

And to this day is euerie scholler poore,
Grosse gold from them runs headlong to the boore.
                              [H&L, I. 471–472]
Though I foreknewe that gold runns to the boore
Ile be a scholler, though I live but poore.
                              [*Pilgrimage*, 63–64]
That he [Learning] and *Pouertie* should alwaies kis.
                              [H&L, I. 470]
Learninge and povertie will ever kiss.
                              [*Pilgrimage*, 76]
That gives rich Churles great store of golde and fee,
And lets poore Schollers live in miserie.
                              [*Affectionate Shepherd*,
                                pt. III, st. xvi, p. 41]

DUNSTAN GALE: PYRAMUS AND THISBE

Dunstan Gale's *Pyramus and Thisbe* frequently echoes and sometimes deliberately imitates *Hero and Leander*.[95] His Thisbe, for instance, excites admiration as she walks about, precisely as does Marlowe's Hero. There is not so much lush eroticism in Gale's poem as in Marlowe's and some of his other imitators' work; but the traces are clear in such passages as the following:

And as a brother with his sister toyed.
                              [H&L, II. 52]
For why, they lou'd like sister & like brother.
                              [P&T, st. 5]

[94] References are to W. D. Macray's ed. (Oxford, 1886), from which the date of the play is taken. J. W. Hales (*Folia Literaria*, p. 167) would date it 1598/9. References to *The Affectionate Shepherd* are to Grosart's Roxburghe Club ed. (1876).
[95] Douglas Bush, *Mythology and the Renaissance Tradition*, p. 311.

> . . . Yet he suspected
> Some amorous rites or other were neglected.
> [H&L, II. 63–64]
> And cast her done, but let her lye alone,
> For other pastimes *Pyramus* knew none.
> [P&T, st. 5]⁹⁶

> As he [Cupid] imagyn'd *Hero* was his mother.
> [H&L, I. 40]
> As purblind Cupid tooke her for his mother.
> [P&T, st. 13] ⁹⁷

> The outside of her garments were of lawne.
> [H&L, I. 9]
> Her upper garment was a robe of lawne.
> [P&T, st. 14] ⁹⁸

> Her wide sleeues greene, and bordered with a groue,
> Where *Venus* in her naked glory stroue.
> [H&L, I. 11–12]
> In which by cunning needle-worke she drew,
> Loue-wounded Venus in the bushie groue.
> [P&T, st. 14]

> His bodie was as straight as *Circes* wand.
> [H&L, I. 61]
> Her middle straight as any wand.
> [P&T, st. 5] ⁹⁹

> Guiltie of True-loues blood.   [H&L, I. 1]
> Stain'd with true loues bloud.   [P&T, st. 14]

PHINEAS FLETCHER: VENUS AND ANCHISES

Phineas Fletcher's *Venus and Anchises* shows general similarity of tone and numerous parallel passages. The poem was originally published in 1628 as *Brittain's Ida*, with Spenser's name on the title page. In 1926, however, Miss Ethel Seaton published a manuscript copy which she had discovered, and confirmed Grosart's suspicion, based on internal evidence, that

---

⁹⁶ See similar parallels on II. 130, 133.
⁹⁷ See II. 137 for a similar parallel.
⁹⁸ See II. 119, 129, 134 for similar parallels.
⁹⁹ See II. 126 for a similar parallel.

Fletcher was the real author. His authorship had been suspected in the eighteenth century by W. Thompson.[100]

The parallel passages are as follows:

Leander, thou art made for amorous play.

[H&L, I. 88]

His lovelie limbs . . . Were made for playe.

[V&A, st. 4]

Darke night is *Cupids* day.   [H&L, I. 191]

Night is Loues holyday.   [V&A, st. 12]

Lesse sinnes the poore rich man that starues himselfe,

In heaping vp a masse of drossie pelfe.

[H&L, I. 243–244]

Too foolish is the man that starves to feed his treasure.

[V&A, st. 16]

. . . . Yet he suspected

Some amorous rites or other were neglected.

[H&L, II. 63–64]

He thinks that somewhat wantes for his requiring.

[V&A, st. 56] [101]

Whose liuely heat like fire from heauen fet,

Would animate grosse clay.

[H&L, II. 255–256]

Kindlie heat enflaming his desiring.

[V&A, st. 56]

Which taught him all that elder louers know.

[H&L, II. 69]

That now he perfect knowes what ever blisse

Elder love taught and he before did misse.

[V&A, st. 59]

WILLIAM BOSWORTH: ARCADIUS AND SEPHA

William Bosworth, or Boxworth (1607–1650?), was a poet who never fulfilled his earlier promise. He finished, apparently in 1626, when he was nineteen, a poem called *Arcadius and*

[100] References are to Ethel Seaton: *Venus and Anchises* (Oxford University Press, 1926). See also F. S. Boas' ed. of the *Poetical Works* of Giles and Phineas Fletcher (Columbia University Press, 1909), II. xiii–xxi, and Alexander B. Grosart: *Who Wrote 'Brittain's Ida'?* (London: Blackburn, 1869).

[101] See II. 130, 131 for similar parallels.

Sepha, which was posthumously published in 1651. A certain "R. C.," who edited it, admits the author's indebtedness to Marlowe in so many words.

"The strength of his fancy," he observes, "and the shadowing of it in words, he taketh from Mr. Marlow in his *Hero and Leander*" — adding, with refreshing frankness: "You shall find our Author everywhere in this imitation." [102]

Not only is imitation of the general plan of Marlowe's poem quite as apparent throughout *Arcadius and Sepha* as one might expect from this, but there are three references to Leander, three to Hero, and various echoes, of which the following are the most important:[103]

> The outside of her garments were of lawne,
> The lining purple silke, with guilt starres drawne.
> > [H&L, I. 9–10]
> Her upper garments were of milky hue,
> And under them a coat of azure blue;
> Some stars of gold there were. . . .
> > [A&S, I. 636–638] [104]

> Chast *Hero* to her selfe thus softly said:
> Were I the saint hee worships, I would heare him.
> > [H&L, I. 178–179]
> While Sepha, overcome with passion, said,
> So loud that he might hear, 'Were I the saint
> To whom he prays, sure I would hear his plaint.'
> > [A&S, II. 135–137]

> Some say, for her the fairest *Cupid* pyn'd.
> > [H&L, I. 37]
> Some say the fairest Cupid being mov'd,
> Mourn'd as he went, and thinking on her pin'd.
> > [A&S, I. 911–912]

CRITICAL OPINION

Hero and Leander owes its existence to the vogue of graceful, highly ornamental, and highly erotic poetry which marked the

---

[102] George Saintsbury (ed.): *Minor Poets of the Caroline Period,* II. 527; Douglas Bush: *Mythology and the Renaissance Tradition,* pp. 193–195; Sidney Lee: article "Bosworth, William," DNB, II. 904.

[103] References are to Saintsbury's ed.

[104] See II. 119, 129, and 132 (especially the last) for similar parallels.

last two decades of Elizabethan literature. To this fashion we owe poems — on the higher level — like *Venus and Adonis*, *The Rape of Lucrece*, and *Hero and Leander* itself; while — on the lower level — we owe it also clumsier work like *Salmacis and Hermaphroditus* or such bits of unblushing bawdry as Nashe's *Choyse of Valentines*. The young man from Canterbury at least helped to set this fashion, while the young man from Stratford seems to have fallen under its influence almost immediately. This was natural enough, for beginning writers are usually under the influence of their immediate predecessors, while love and death are the traditional themes of youthful bards in all lands and in all times.

Both lifted mere eroticism high above its earthy origin (even if they left its roots there) into the realm of transcendent beauty. More exquisite English verse than some passages in these three poems was never to be written; yet no one of them can be reckoned among the supremely great poems of English literature. Whatever date we assign to *Hero and Leander*, all of them must have been written within a few years of each other. All were young men's work — work which the greater poet lived vastly to improve and which the lesser left tragically unfinished when he died.

The exceeding beauty of Marlowe's verse, which already, in the sixteenth century, had much of the almost cloying sweetness and perfection that were to reappear in Keats, did not escape his more discerning contemporaries. The poem was generally applauded and the allusions of other writers of the day are uniformly appreciative. Abraham Fraunce, who observed in 1592 that "Leander and Heroe's loue is in euery man's mouth," [105] may not be alluding to Marlowe at all, since he quotes from Boscan's translation of Musaeus, but Chapman is certainly attempting praise of Marlowe's poem when he pens his rather cryptic lines on the author, who

> . . . stood
> Vp to the chin in the Pyerean flood,
> And drunke to me halfe this Musean storie,
> Inscribing it to deathles Memorie.[106]

[105] *Third Part of the Countess of Pembroke's Ivychurch*, p. 46. [MLA Photostatic Facsimiles, no. 75.] NYPL.   [106] H&L, III. 189–192. See also I. 187.

Francis Meres in the second part of his *Palladis Tamia*, published in 1598, the year of the first two known editions of *Hero and Leander*, follows this almost immediately with further praise, observing that Musaeus has in England "two excellent poets, imitators of him in the same argument and subiect, Christopher Marlow and George Chapman." [107] Meres does not even mention Petowe.

Richard Carew (d. 1620) may have been even earlier with his praises in his *Excellencie of the English Tongue* (which Sir Sidney Lee dates about 1596)[108] though his printer makes an unfortunate error which obscures the allusion. Carew compares "Shakespeare and Barlowe's fragment" to Catullus. This can hardly mean anything but *Hero and Leander*.

Thomas Heywood observes in his rather wooden measures in *The Hierarchie of the Blessed Angels* (1635) [109] that

> . . . his *Hero and Leander* did
> Merit addition rather,

and follows Marlowe in his story of Jupiter and Callisto, in *Troia Britanica* (1609).[110]

John Taylor (1580–1654), the "water poet," a mere boy of thirteen when Marlowe was killed, had a special liking for the poem. In his *Praise, Antiquity, and commodity of Beggery, Beggers, and Begging* (1621), he quotes Marlowe's passage on the poverty of scholars, almost verbatim:

> For as a learned Poet* wrote before,
> Grosse Golde runnes headlong from them, to the Bore:
> For which this vnauoyded Vow Ile make,
> To loue a Begger for a Poets sake.[111]

The asterisk refers to the marginal note, "Chris. Marlo." Taylor seems to have known *Hero and Leander*, or portions of it, by heart. In his "Motto," he writes:

[107] Page 282. Cf. G. Gregory Smith: *Elizabethan Critical Essays*, II. 318.

[108] *Life of Shakespeare* (1916), p. 143n. The passage appears in Carew's ed. of 1713, p. 13. There is a copy of this ed. in NYPL. Cf. G. Gregory Smith, *op. cit.*, II. 293; Camden's *Remaines* (1614), p. 43.

[109] Page 206. Cf. Dyce (1850), I. xxxviii, and Halliwell-Phillips: *Life of Shakespeare*, p. 190. See also I. 188.

[110] Canto 2, st. 53–54. See also Douglas Bush in MLN, 42: 211–217 (1927). Copy in BM.

[111] Sig. B3*v*. Copy in HCL. First noted by Dr. Gertrude Noyes, Connecticut College, who has kindly placed the allusion at my disposal.

It chanc'd one evening, on a Reedy banke,
The Muses sate together in a ranke;
Whilst in my boat I did by water wander,
Repeating lines of *Hero* and *Leander*.[112]

Sidney Lee [113] takes this to mean that Marlowe's poem was so
familiar to the general Elizabethan public that the Thames
boatmen, plying across the river to the theatres on the Bank-
side, used to sing it — a view for which there is no real evidence.
Taylor was no ordinary waterman.

Leander's wooing is imitated by Samuel Page, Izaak Walton's
friend, in his *Love of Amos and Laura* (1613), and also by
Richard Braithwaite in his *Strappado for the Diuell* (1615). The
latter's book, *Natures Embassie* (1621), also shows traces of
Marlowe. The most striking parallels in Page's work are: [114]

So yoong, so gentle, and so debonaire.
[H&L, I. 288]
. . . for her the fairest *Cupid* pyn'd . . .
As he imagyn'd *Hero* was his mother.
[H&L, I. 37–40]
So sweete, so proper, and so debonaire,
The strangers tooke her for to be none other,
Than *Venus* selfe, the god of *Loues* owne Mother.
[*Amos and Laura*]

The wals were of discoloured *Iasper* stone, . . .
Ioue slylie stealing from his sisters bed,
To dallie with *Idalian Ganimed*.
[H&L, I. 136–148]
The pauement Marble was, the walls of Glasse:
Whereunder was so liuely caru'd the Story
Of *Ioues* loue, his wondrous works and glory.
[*Amos and Laura*]

Braithwaite imitates Marlowe's myth-making, his description of the pictures in the Temple of Venus, and his phrasing.
The closest parallels are: [115]

[112] *Works* (1630), p. 55. See p. 215 of the Spenser Society reprint (1869).
[113] Article "Marlowe," DNB, XII. 1071.
[114] There is a copy of Page's work in the British Museum. Quotations here are from
Douglas Bush, MLN, 42: 215 (1927). For similar parallels, see II. 118, 139.
[115] References are to the eds. by J. W. Ebsworth, 1877, 1878. See especially *Strappado*,
pp. 216, 253; *Embassie*, pp. 58–59. See also H&L, I. 143–156; *Strappado*, pp. 43–44.

... the rising yu'rie mount he scal'd,
Which is with azure circling lines empal'd,
Much like a globe, (a globe may I tearme this,
By which loue sailes to regions full of blis.)
[H&L, II. 273-276]
Her brests two iuory mounts, mounts may I cal them
for many vales of pleasant veines empall'd them.
[*Strappado*, p. 256]

And crying, Loue I come, leapt liuely in.
[H&L, II. 154]
For now he cries, *Hero* I come to thee.
[*Natures Embassie*, p. 59]

Patrick Hanney's *Philomela* (1622) imitates one passage: [116]

Loue deepely grounded, hardly is dissembled.
[H&L, I. 184]
Where love's deep grounded, theres no wit
Can his sure signs dissemble.
[*Philomela*, 361-362]

Robert Burton, in the *Anatomy of Melancholy* (1621), quotes repeatedly, [117] and a perplexed lover in John Cooke's comedy, *Greene's Tu Quoque; or, the City Gallant* (1614), exclaims:

There's no good to be done by praying for her,
I see that; I must plunge into a passion:
Now for a piece of Hero and Leander;
'Twere excellent, and (praise be to my memory),
It has reach'd half a dozen lines for the purpose:
Well, she shall have them —

after which he recites ten of Marlowe's lines.[118]
Critics of the day were not slow to see (what the cynical booksellers had doubtless seen long before) that the popularity of Marlowe's poem was not due wholly to its beauty but largely also to the highly sexed story that it told. This is the point of Thomas Middleton's allusion when he makes his character Hairbrain in *A Mad World My Masters* exclaim:

[116] Saintsbury: *Minor Poets of the Caroline Period*, I. 626. See also Douglas Bush, MLN, 42: 211-217 (1927).
[117] Eds. 1652, 1660, pp. 457, 458, 464, 468.
[118] Hazlitt's Dodsley, XI. 250-251; H&L, I. 255-264.

I have conveyed away all her wanton pamphlets; as *Hero and Leander*, *Venus and Adonis*; O, two luscious marrow-bone pies for a young married wife![119]

This was not long after 1600 — Middleton's play was published in 1608 and had certainly been acted before that — when Marlowe's poem was appearing in one after another of those editions which have come down to us in so few copies [120] that it is clear they must have been read, literally, to pieces. Middleton also alludes to it in his *Family of Love*.[121]

All these poems of the erotic school seem to have been regarded by contemporaries in much the same light. In Cranley's *Amanda, or the Reformed Whore* (1635), *Venus and Adonis* and *Salmacis and Hermaphroditus* are mentioned together as forming part of a courtesan's library.[122]

This fact makes it all the stranger that the poem should have influenced John Milton. Some of the apparent resemblances may be due solely to a common classical background; others must certainly be echoes of *Hero and Leander*.[123] Thus the naturalistic arguments of Comus against chastity are very like those in Marlowe's poem. *Il Penseroso* has lines closely resembling the last few lines of the Second Sestyad. *L'Allegro* seems oddly to combine Shakespeare and Marlowe:

> So yoong, so gentle, and so debonaire.
> [H&L, I. 288]
> So buxom, blithe, and debonair.
> [*L'Allegro*, 24]
> So buxom, blithe, and full of face.
> [*Pericles*, I. i. 23]

Even *Paradise Lost* shows at least one parallel:

> . . . of three that in Mount Ida naked strove.
> [PL, V. 382]

[119] Dyce's Middleton (1840), II. 340, Act I, sc. ii.
[120] See Bibliography.
[121] III. ii.
[122] Not *Hero and Leander*, as Bullen says. Cf. his *Works of John Marston* (1887), I. xviii; J. P. Collier: *Shakespeare* (1858), VI. 481. The passage quoted above appears in the ed. of *Amanda* by Frederic Ouvry, ll. 52–54, p. 46.
[123] See also David Masson (ed.): *Milton's Poems* (Globe Poets, 1909), p. 410; Douglas Bush: *Mythology and the Renaissance Tradition*, p. 267; E. M. W. Tillyard: *Milton* (London: Chatto & Windus, 1930), p. 19. L. C. Martin in his edition suggests various traces of Milton in his notes to the First Sestyad.

Where *Venus* in her naked glory stroue.

[H&L, I. 12]

The suggestion that "On the Death of a Fair Infant" owes something to *Hero and Leander* may be absurd, but it is not at all absurd to think that the versification is influenced by Marlowe's.

Hero and Leander also became a popular subject for the tapestries woven at Mortlake by weavers brought across from Flanders in 1620 and later, and the subject was reproduced over and over again. The set representing the history of the immortal lovers was designed by Francis Cleyn, or Clein, and occupied 284 Flemish ells. Sir Sackville Crow, who was in charge of the manufacture of the tapestries in 1670, wrote the Countess of Rutland that this was one of the six designs in England "worth the making." [124] Charles I purchased a set for £1,704, and another set was on the list of tapestries to be purchased for Cromwell, though there is some doubt whether the grim Lord Protector ever received this strange adornment for a Puritan palace. The only complete set of the Mortlake Hero and Leander tapestries now known is in the Royal Swedish Collection. We may thus credit Marlowe with a small influence on textile art in England, since without the inspiration of his poem the subject would hardly have been chosen.

As it passed from literature into art, the poem's popularity slowly waned, and there is no mistaking the significant fact that the edition of which most copies have survived is the last, that of 1637. After a publisher's "run" of at least forty years, *Hero and Leander* ceased to interest the reading public. People stopped reading — and buying — it. Publishers therefore stopped publishing it, and during the harsh years of Civil War, the old poem was nearly forgotten. Under the Puritan régime, *Hero and Leander* could not possibly find any but surreptitious readers, though William Bosworth's *Arcadius and Sepha* appeared as late as 1651.

Toward the end of the seventeenth century, readers began to remember *Hero and Leander*, of which copies still lingered in old libraries. But under the Merry Monarch, the passion and

[124] Cf. William George Thomson: *Tapestry Weaving in England*, pp. 82, 124, 148; George Leland Hunter: *Decorative Textiles*, II. 305.

sincerity and beauty of Marlowe's poem missed their mark. Wit and cynicism were the fashion, and the tale of the tragic lovers now became the basis of a long series of burlesques. This had begun in some slight degree under James I, with the puppet show in Ben Jonson's *Bartholomew Faire* (1614) and Thomas Nashe's *Lenten Stuffe* (1599). Jonson introduces *The ancient modern history of Hero and Leander, otherwise called the Touchstone of true Love* as part of a puppet show at the Fair; and his actors decline to "play it according to the printed book," explaining: "that is too learned and poetical for our audience: what do they know what *Hellespont* is, *guilty of true love's blood*? or what *Abydos* is? or *the other, Sestos hight*." [125] The puppet-master Littlewit has

only made it a little easy, and modern for the times, sir, that's all. As for the Hellespont, I imagine our Thames here; and then Leander I make a dyer's son about Puddle-wharf: and Hero a wench o' the Bank-side, who going over one morning to Old Fish-street, Leander spies her land at Trig-stairs, and falls in love with her.

In *Lenten Stuffe* Thomas Nashe devotes a section called "Prayse of the Red Herring" to "Leander and Hero, of whome diuine *Musæus* sung, and a diuiner Muse than him, *Kit Marlow*." This practically tells Marlowe's story over again, in prose parody, and at the end Hero springs after Leander into the sea, "and so resignd vp her Priesthood, and left worke for *Musæus* and *Kit Marlowe*." [126]

It is sometimes supposed that there is one faint echo of Marlowe in Milton's *Il Penseroso*:

> And with his flaring beames mockt ougly night.
> [H&L, II. 332]
> And, when the sun begins to fling
> His flaring beams.
> [*Il Penseroso*, 131–132] [127]

---

[125] *Bartholomew Faire*, V. iii. Cf. H&L, I. 4. Edward Copleston (1776–1849) used part of this scene as a horrible example of unfair distortion in his *Advice to a Young Reviewer* (Stratford: Shakespeare Head; Boston: Houghton Mifflin), p. 15. The italicized lines are from Marlowe.

[126] McKerrow's Nashe, III. 195, 198; Grosart's Nashe, V. 262, 267.

[127] See incomplete allusion in index to Columbia University Milton. Also Todd's Variorum Milton, V. 136.

As parodies and burlesques of the classics became fashionable in the seventeenth century, *Hero and Leander* did not escape. Nashe had, indeed, already made it one of the first victims, even before the century opened. The fashionable taste for burlesque in England was largely due to French influence, especially that of Paul Scarron (1610–1660), which became strongest under Charles II, but which had begun to make itself felt even before the Royal Charles brought home the exiled monarch.

As early as 1651 the poem was being very freely handled by an anonymous author, as *The Loves of Hero and Leander*. This was only three years after publication of the first book of Scarron's *Virgile Travesty*.[128] The burlesque of *Hero and Leander* was popular enough to require a new edition in 1653 and another in 1661, after which the burlesque of 1669, usually attributed to William Wycherley, replaced it in popular esteem. Both these parodies are in much the same vein. The story remains, but the idyllic grace of Musaeus and the exquisite beauty, mingled with a sensuality that is at least delicate in Marlowe's poem, become heavy-handed and smirking obscenity. To the seventeenth century this may have appeared humorous; to the twentieth it is merely dull.

Travesties of the classics now sprang up on every hand, both in France and England. In France, Furetier, Dufresny, and d'Assoucy followed Scarron's example, with Ovid, Lucan, and Juvenal as their victims. Boileau remarked that Parnassus now spoke the language of the market place and Apollo had become a Tabarin.

The 1651 burlesque of *Hero and Leander* appears to have been the earliest classical parody in England — a fact not hitherto recognized; but it had abundant successors.[129] In 1664 Charles Cotton (1630–1687) published his *Scarronides, or Virgil Travestie*, based on Scarron and the first book of the *Aeneid*. He followed this six years later with a parody of the fourth book, and later put Lucan into "English fustian" as a *Burlesque upon Burlesque, or the Scoffer Scoff'd*. Another *Scarronides*, by a certain Monsey, of Pembroke Hall, Cambridge,

128 CHEL, IX. 287.
129 Ben Jonson parodied *Hero and Leander* earlier, as did Nashe, but neither was very complete.

followed; and John Phillips in *Maronides* parodied the fifth and sixth books of the *Aeneid*. In 1664, almost simultaneously with Cotton's poem, James Scudamore published *Homer à la Mode. A Mock Poem upon the first and second Books of Homer's Iliads* [plural], which was followed fifty years later by "Sir Iliad Doggerell's" *Homerides: or Homer's First Book Modernized.* "Naso Scarronimus" published *Ovidius Exulans*, and Alexander Radcliffe wrote an *Ovid Travestie*.

Unimportant in themselves, these poems have a certain historical significance because they paved the way for *Hudibras*. It is odd to think that Marlowe, of all poets, by providing material for the earliest classical burlesque was, even though in a rather strained sense, a forerunner of Samuel Butler.

After the brutal parody of Wycherley [130] all interest in *Hero and Leander* seems to have ceased. The eighteenth century, regarding even Shakespeare as slightly barbarous, would none of Marlowe, nor were even his heroic couplets sufficient to mollify its judgments. In Germany, Schiller had told the story, and Goethe had meditated a poem on it,[131] but in England the poem did not come into its own again until the nineteenth century. Even as late as the end of the eighteenth century, it was being treated merely as a theme for a burletta, *Hero and Leander*, by Isaac Jackson (fl. 1795).[132] Byron, in "The Bride of Abydos," made use of the old tale, and his feat of swimming the Hellespont was probably inspired by emulation of Marlowe's Leander. Leigh Hunt, in his *Hero and Leander* (1819), retells the old story, but Hunt himself professed to believe that Marlowe's poem was "not comparable with his plays." [133]

Keats's references in the sonnet, "Come hither all," are probably due to his friend Hunt rather than to Marlowe. It is possible, however, that there is a single echo of Marlowe:

> His plump white arms, and shoulders, enough white
> For Venus' pearly bite.
> [*Endymion*, IV. 213-214]

[130] Reprinted by Chabalier.
[131] See I. 322.
[132] There were at least three editions of this, one by John Murray, 1787; one by C. Wiley, New York, 1824; and one in a collection entitled *The British Drama* (London, 1824), I. 213-218.
[133] See Douglas Bush: *Mythology and the Romantic Tradition*, p. 179.

Euen as delicious meat is to the tast,
So was his necke in touching, and surpast
The white of *Pelops* shoulder.

[H&L, I. 63–65]

Thomas Hood also wrote a *Hero and Leander* (1827), in which certain lines suggest a resemblance to Marlowe, but Hood avoided too close comparison by inventing a good deal of the story. There are, however, resemblances:

Far from the towne (where all is whist and still,
Saue that the sea playing on yellow sand,
Sends foorth a ratling murmure to the land.

[H&L, I. 346–348]

Now, lay thine ear against this golden sand,
And thou shalt hear the music of the sea,
Those hollow tunes it plays against the land.

[Hood: H&L, st. LXVIII]

And as she wept, her teares to pearle he turn'd,
And wound them on his arme, and for her mourn'd.

[H&L, I. 375–376]

Whence being shed, the liquid crystalline
Drops straightway down, refusing to partake
In gross admixture with the baser brine,
But shrinks and hardens into pearls opaque,
Hereafter to be worn on arms and ears;
So one maid's trophy is another's tears!

[Hood: H&L, st. LXXXIII]

There are other suggestions of Marlowe's influence in Hood's "Plea of the Midsummer Fairies" (1827). Tennyson's "Hero to Leander" (1830) may owe something to Hood but does not show resemblance to Marlowe. Oscar Wilde's "Charmides," [134] with its conventional mention of virginity, its lament over the drowned lover, and its general theme, may have a remote relation to Marlowe's poem. One passage may be a verbal resemblance:

And crying, Loue I come, leapt liuely in.

[H&L, II. 154]

[134] For a list of European works on the Hero and Leander theme, see M. H. Jellinek: *Die Sage von Hero und Leander* (Bonn Diss., 1915). On the Victorian poets and Marlowe, see Douglas Bush, *op. cit.*

Laughed loud for joy, and crying out "I come"
Leapt from the lofty poop into the chill and churning foam.

["Charmides," st. 46]

These poems reflect the enthusiasm for Elizabethan letters which had begun with the dawning of the nineteenth century and with the romantic movement. Swinburne, who always took fire easily from Elizabethan torches, had an especial enthusiasm for Marlowe, perhaps because the magnificent sound (with sometimes insignificant sense) of Marlowe's lines united Swinburne's own strength with his own weakness. Nowhere does Marlowe come closer to the Swinburnian mood than in *Hero and Leander*. Hence the famous passage in which this most un-Victorian of Victorian poets avers that

Marlowe's poem of *Hero and Leander*, closing with the sunrise which closes the night of the lovers' union, stands alone in its age, and far ahead of the work of any possible competitor between the death of Spenser and the dawn of Milton. In clear mastery of narrative and presentation, in melodious ease and simplicity of strength, it is not less pre-eminent than in the adorable beauty and impeccable perfection of separate lines or passages.[135]

It was a subject to which Swinburne liked to return. This poem, he wrote in his essay on George Chapman,

stands out alone amid all the wide and wild poetic wealth of its teeming and turbulent age, as might a small shrine of Parian sculpture amid the rank splendour of a tropic jungle. . . . Faultless indeed this lovely fragment is not; it also bears traces of Elizabethan barbarism, as though the great queen's ruff and farthingale had been clapped about the neck and waist of the Medicean Venus; but for all the strange costume we can see that the limbs are perfect still.[136]

This poem was, to Swinburne, "the only not faultless poem of Marlowe," [137] whereas Shakespeare's *Venus and Adonis*, "with all its overcrowding beauties of detail," seemed to him "on the whole a model of what a young man of genius should not write on such a subject."

W. J. Courthope, in his *History of English Poetry*, wrote, with rather more restraint: "Though his style is coloured with the

---

[135] "Christopher Marlowe," in *The Age of Shakespeare* (Works, Bonchurch ed., 1926), XI. 280. Originally written for the *Encyclopædia Britannica*.
[136] "Contemporaries of Shakespeare" (Works, Bonchurch ed., 1926), XII. 229.
[137] *Ibid.*, XII. 230.

conceits and mannerism of the period, yet, as compared with the diction of contemporary Euphuistic writers, it has a fiery strength and vigour not to be found in any other man." [138] But Courthope compares Marlowe unfavorably with other men who have dealt with the same theme: "Compared with *Troilus and Criseyde*, his *Hero and Leander* lacks dramatic interest, variety, and relief. It never reaches the depths of pathos which Virgil sounds in the fourth *Aeneid*, nor the heights of spiritual feeling of which Spenser has given us examples in the *Faerie Queene*. Fortune favored him in obliging him to leave his poem a splendid fragment."

A. H. Bullen, in his edition of Marlowe, praising the poem as an "exquisite fragment," also dwells upon "the music of Marlowe's rhymed heroics," concluding that "the clear, rich, fervent notes of *Hero and Leander* were heard but once." [139]

That is not quite true. They were heard again — after the lapse of something more than two hundred years — from the lips of John Keats, another young poet who was cut down upon the very threshold of his career. The strange similarity between the narrative verse of Keats and Marlowe — a similarity of sound rather than of sense, and of intonations rather than of mood — has scarcely been noted, save in one passage of Swinburne's. He alludes to *The Eve of Saint Agnes*, "in which the figure of Madeline brings back upon the mind's eye, if only as moonlight recalls a sense of sunshine, the nuptial picture of Marlowe's Hero and the sleeping presence of Shakespeare's Imogen." [140]

The similarity is difficult to explain and quite impossible to prove; but it is so easy to feel, that proof is perhaps unnecessary. There are many passages in the works of either poet which could be slipped almost indistinguishably into the works of the other, or could, at least, were not the poems of both so thoroughly familiar to all literate readers. A pair of parallel passages are perhaps sufficient to demonstrate the resemblance between

> And soon his eyes had drunk her beauty up,
> Leaving no drop in the bewildering cup,

[138] II. 326.
[139] I. xlix–lii.   [140] "Keats," in Works (Bonchurch ed., 1926), XIV. 298.

which is Keats, and

> These louers parled by the touch of hands,
> True loue is mute, and oft amazed stands,

which is Marlowe.[141]

Superficially, this resemblance is due to the fact that both were writing rhymed heroics. More truly, we may say that partly it is due to the strong influence upon both of the classics, which Marlowe, the university man, knew at first hand, and which Keats, through the doubtful medium of translations, absorbed so thoroughly that he seemed almost intuitively a Greek. Partly, too, no doubt, it is due to an emotional kinship — both reaching for an unattainable something which eluded both their grasps: Marlowe for knowledge infinite; Keats for love and for life itself. Prosaically, also, this kinship in mood may be due to the similarity of social position of two young Englishmen of lowly birth, whose genius, in lifting them to associations above their original status, had left room for many regrets.

We must leave it at that; for evidence of the sort beloved by the *Quellenstudent* there is none.[142] Shakespeare's influence on Keats, like Milton's influence on Keats, is clear enough; for the testimony of occasional parallelism in each case is supported by allusions in Keats's letters. Strange to say, he never alludes to Marlowe. Keats did, however, know some of the Elizabethans, and, as he lived in the period when Lamb and others were rediscovering Marlowe, it is reasonable to suppose that he had some acquaintance with his great predecessor. There is, moreover, the glorious testimony of a great sonnet that Keats was well acquainted with Chapman's Homer, so that he might easily have known also the poem which Chapman completed and which many passages of *Hyperion* resemble.

The rhymed heroics of *Hero and Leander* were a kind of prophecy of what was to come in English poetry. The poem is, as Mr. J. St. Loe Strachey puts it, "memorable for lighting a torch in men's hearts." [143] Its literary effect did not cease. Pre-eminently a romantic poem, it foreshadows not only Keats's, but also

[141] *Lamia*, I. 251–252; H&L, I. 185–186.
[142] But see Claude Lee Finney: *Evolution of Keats's Poetry*, I. 162, 192–193, 247, 285, 377, 555, 670.
[143] *Spectator*, 133: 471, 24 O 1924; *New York Times Book Review*, 12 O 1924, p. 2.

Wordsworth's love of nature, Coleridge's tendency to philosophize in verse rather fantastically, the rich sensuousness of Swinburne, and even the phrasing of so modern a person as James Elroy Flecker.

So much one might have expected; but there are traces of its influence elsewhere. Donne borrowed directly, Crabbe is occasionally indebted, and, strange to say, *Hero and Leander* also contains hints of Dryden and even examples of Pope's mannered, artificial couplet with its end-stopped lines, antitheses, and half-line caesura, all plain to see or hear:

> It lies not in our power to loue, or hate,
> For will in vs is ouer-rul'd by fate.

> Like *Æsops* cocke, this iewell he enioyed,
> And as a brother with his sister toyed.

> Loue is not ful of pittie (as men say)
> But deaffe and cruell, where he meanes to pray.

> Seeming not woon, yet woon she was at length,
> In such warres women vse but halfe their strength.[144]

Here are perfectly typical Elizabethan lines in the very tone and accent of the eighteenth century. A curious, unexpected illustration of the range of Marlowe's talent, one more tantalizing hint of what might have been expected of him, had life — and death — been a little kinder.

[144] *Hero and Leander*, I. 167–168; II. 51–52, 287–288, 295–296.

MINOR WORKS AND TRANSLATIONS

> *. . . Immortall flowers of Poesy,*
> *Wherein as in a myrrour we perceiue*
> *The highest reaches of a humaine wit.*
> I *Tamburlaine,* 1947–1949

THERE WAS NONE of the decorous and respectable competence of the minor poet in the work of Christopher Marlowe. He wrote either in letters of fire or in the dregs of the ink bottle, with no mediocre work between his extremes of good and bad. His best work is eternally a precious part of the imperishable heritage of the English-speaking peoples; his worst approaches insignificance.

Marlowe's translations and his shorter lyrics belong, with one, possibly two, exceptions, to the latter class. Most of them are so obscure that they are well-nigh unknown, even to professed students of English literature. "I Walked Along a Stream" might possibly be regarded, by a very charitable critic, as a lyric of some distinction; but only one of Marlowe's shorter poems is known and admired wherever English poetry is read.

That is the poem entitled "The Passionate Shepherd to His Love," but more commonly known by its first line, "Come live with me and be my love." One of the most beautiful lyrics in English literature, and one which has exercised a powerful influence upon three centuries of English verse, this has usually — in spite of occasional efforts to question the attribution — been regarded as Marlowe's.

It appears first in Shakespeare's *Passionate Pilgrim* (1599),[1] where only four stanzas are printed. These lines are unsigned, are grouped with doubtfully Shakespearean poems at the back of the book, and are separated from the undoubtedly Shakespearean work by a second title page, *Sonnets to Sundry*

[1] Sig. D4*v.*

Notes of Music, which does not carry Shakespeare's name as author. With Marlowe's poem is printed one stanza of the reply — usually called "The Nymph's Reply" — elsewhere attributed to Sir Walter Raleigh.

"The Passionate Shepherd" was reprinted the following year in *England's Helicon* (1600) [2] with the signature "Chr. Marlow," and with the reply in full, plus a second reply signed "Ignoto." Marlowe's lyric here appears with six stanzas.

Izaak Walton printed different versions both of Marlowe's poem and of Raleigh's reply, in the 1653 and 1655 editions of his *Compleat Angler*, describing the original poem as "that smooth Song which was made by *Kit Marlow*, now at least fifty years ago." [3] In the 1655 edition he adds a stanza to Marlowe's poem and another to Raleigh's. As a matter of fact, Marlowe had been dead exactly sixty years when the first edition of the *Compleat Angler* was printed; and since Raleigh was forty-one at the time of Marlowe's death, he can hardly be said to have written the reply "in his yonger dayes," as Walton says. Walton, however, had probably no idea that his dates would be taken literally.

The Roxburghe Ballads, in the British Museum,[4] include a broadsheet which has the two poems printed together; and there are also versions in Birch's edition of Sir Walter Raleigh's works [5] and in Percy's *Reliques*.[6]

Five manuscript copies exist: two at the Bodleian, two at the Folger Shakespeare Library, and one in the possession of Dr. A. S. W. Rosenbach. The two Bodleian manuscripts are Ashmolean MS. 1486, ii, fol. 6 verso, and Rawlinson Poet. MS. 148, fols. 96 verso and 97 recto.

The Ashmolean manuscript is probably the oldest. The volume in which it appears bears the inscriptions: "This is Robarte garlandes Booke, practizioner in the arte spagericke, año dõ. 1596," and "Whoso*ever* on me dothe looke, I am Robarte garlands booke." [7] It contains a mass of heterogeneous

[2] Sig. Aa2r.
[3] See the 1653 ed., pp. 63–64, 67, and pp. 105–106, 108–109 of the 1655 ed.
[4] I. 250.
[5] See the 1751 ed., II. 394.
[6] Ed. 1765, ser. I, bk. II.
[7] Ashmolean MS. 1486, fols. 1 and 27r.

notes, most of which relate to alchemy and which include an experiment for producing silver, attributed to "Sr W. Rawley."[8] Marlowe's poem and the reply do not seem to be in Garland's hand and may not be so old as the rest of the book. The date 1596 may carry the text back to within three years of Marlowe's death, though there is no exact way of ascertaining when it was written. No author is given for either poem, and part of the reply has been torn away. The Rawlinson manuscript is among the material gathered by Richard Rawlinson in the eighteenth century, but nothing further is known of its origin.

The history of the Folger manuscripts is obscure. The Thornborough Commonplace Book (Folger MS. 297.3, fol. 100) is said by a note at the end to have been kept by John Thornborough (1551–1641), who was successively chaplain to Henry Herbert, Earl of Pembroke, chaplain to the Queen, Dean of York, and Bishop of Worcester. His wife was a friend of Lady Audrey Walsingham.[9] The book consists of 232 pages, enclosed in a limp leather cover, stamped with curious devices, and believed to date from the sixteenth century. The contents are largely contemporary records and theological notes.

It was owned by Lieutenant-Colonel Carew, of Crowcombe Court, Somerset, whose library was sold at Sotheby's May 6, 1903. It may have come from the sale of the Duke of Chandos' books in 1746, at which Colonel Carew is known to have bought heavily.[10] It is supposed to have been bought by a certain Cotton at Colonel Carew's sale for £3 15s., but was sold at Sotheby's June 19, 1903, Lot 525, for £192, an astonishing mark-up. Pearson sold it to the late H. C. Folger, with whose books it passed to the Folger Library. Neither of the two commonplace books names the author or suggests the date. There is a good deal of doubt whether the Folger book was really kept by Bishop Thornborough.

Folger MS. 621.1, fol. 2, contains both lyrics with the titles "The Milke Maids Song" and "The Milke Maids Mothers answer." These suggest some relationship to Walton. The

---

[8] *Ibid.*, i, no. 6.

[9] See the section devoted to Lady Audrey in Chapter VI.

[10] *Hist. MSS. Commission, 4th Report*, 1873, p. 368, and Claire Grece in TLS, 33: 460, 28 Je 1934. Edward Irving Carlyle: article "Thornborough, John," DNB, XIX. 766–767, does not mention the Commonplace Book.

manuscript is a small volume of 76 leaves containing notes on English history, topography, and nobility, and poems by Jonson, Donne, and others. The earliest known owner appears to have been Edward Brookes, probably before 1700. On the flyleaf, in a hand that does not elsewhere appear, is the note: "Mr John Oldhams Booke." Presumably this is John Oldham, the poet.

Equally little is known of the history of the Rosenbach manuscript. The inside of the front cover contains the bookplate of William Horatio Crawford, Lakelands, Cork, and a number of poems have marginal annotations in what seems to be the hand of John Payne Collier. Collier certainly knew the manuscript, since as early as 1846 he published one of its poems and in 1865 published its version of "The Lie." Chappell refers to the book and to Collier's ownership.[11] It measures $5\frac{3}{4} \times 7\frac{1}{2}$ inches and is bound in vellum. There are no folio numbers, and the first few leaves have been stained by damp, the front leaf being defective at bottom. It is in Gothic or English secretary hand with many titles in Roman. Apparently there were three writers. Many poems are highly erotic. In spite of Collier's ownership, no suspicion of forgery has arisen.

External evidence for Marlowe's authorship thus rests on the 1600 edition of *England's Helicon* and the 1653 edition of the *Compleat Angler*. One might add to these the manuscript catalogue of the poems in *England's Helicon*, now preserved in the British Museum and supposed to be the work of Francis Davison (fl. 1600), which also names Marlowe.[12] Otherwise, the the early versions are silent as to authorship.

A far more powerful, indeed a conclusive, argument for Marlowe's authorship is the fact that the theme, the mood, and even the words of the lyric appear and reappear throughout Marlowe's work from first to last. Mr. R. S. Forsythe [13] has detected fourteen traces of the lyric in Marlowe's plays, beginning with *Dido* and ending with *Edward the Second*. Some of these are obvious echoes; a few, if they stood alone, might be doubt-

---

[11] See Samuel A. Tannenbaum in PMLA, 45: 809–821 (1930); Collier: *Biographical and Critical Account* (1865), p. 224; Chappell: *Popular Music*, II. 774.

[12] Harleian MS. 280, fol. 101r. See also Agnes M. C. Latham: *Poems of Sir Walter Raleigh*, p. 147.

[13] "Passionate Shepherd and English Poetry," PMLA, 40: 692–742 (1925).

ful; but taken together they offer a perfectly clear demonstra-
tion of what was happening in the poet's mind.

Marlowe had the theme of the lyric running in his head. He
wrote hastily, he habitually repeated favorite lines and phrases,
and the idea suggested itself to him again and again, now in one
form, now in another. Whenever it did suggest itself, he used
it, quite unaware that he was repeating. He never edited his
own works, and he therefore never detected the repetitions.
Everyone who writes has had similar experiences. Shakespeare
repeats again and again, notably in the famous comparison of
life and a stage.[14]

The clearest of Marlowe's repetitions is in *The Jew of Malta*,
where the blackguard Ithamore quotes a whole line of "The
Passionate Shepherd" to his mistress.[15] Tamburlaine woos the
Princess Zenocrate with the question: "Disdaines *Zenocrate* to
liue with me?" and promises:

> A hundreth Tartars shall attend on thee,
> Mounted on Steeds, swifter than *Pegasus*.
> Thy Garments shall be made of Medean silke,
> Enchast with precious iuelles of mine owne:
> More rich and valurous than *Zenocrates*.
> With milke-white Hartes vpon an Iuorie sled,
> Thou shalt be drawn amidst the frosen Pooles,
> And scale the ysie mountaines lofty tops:
> Which with thy beautie will be soone resolu'd.[16]

Marlowe's other characters frequently employ similar terms
when seeking to persuade. A few lines further on, Tamburlaine
uses much the same arguments in winning over the Persian
general Theridamas, including the line

> If thou wilt stay with me, renowmed man.[17]

In Part II, the captive Turkish prince, Callapine, bribing his
jailer, makes promises in the same vein:

> The Grecian virgins shall attend on thee,
> Skilful in musicke and in amorous laies:
> As faire as was *Pigmalions* Iuory gyrle,
> Or louely *Io* metamorphosed.
> With naked Negros shall thy coach be drawen.[18]

---

[14] *Macbeth*, V. v. 25; *Merchant of Venice*, I. i. 78; *As You Like It*, II, vii. 139; Sonnet
XXIII. [15] See I. 333. [16] I *Tamb*. 289-297.
[17] I *Tamb*. 383. [18] II *Tamb*. 2527-2531.

The whole passage, which is much longer, is distinctly in the mood of the lyric.

Dido also contains a number of similar lines, notably those at the opening, in which Jupiter promises various things to Ganymede "if thou wilt be my loue." [19] Venus bribes Ascanius to stay with her:

> Ile giue thee Sugar-almonds, sweete Conserues,
> A siluer girdle, and a golden purse. [20]

Later, the nurse's invitation to Cupid is couched in similar terms, [21] and Dido, begging Aeneas to remain, makes much the same promises. [22] The identity of mood and the frequency of the repetition, unusual even for Marlowe, suggest that the play and the lyric were written about the same time.

In *Edward the Second* three passages resemble "The Passionate Shepherd," notably the letter which opens the play:

> Then liue and be the fauorit of a king. [23]

There are clearer examples in Gaveston's plan for entrancing the weak King:

> And in the day when he shall walke abroad,
> Like *Syluan* Nimphes my pages shall be clad,
> My men like Satyres grazing on the lawnes,
> Shall with their Goate feete daunce an antick hay, [24]

and in the passage where the King proclaims that he will

> . . . eyther die, or liue with *Gaueston*. [25]

Mr. Forsythe, in his eagerness to prove his case, includes some less convincing passages, but inexplicably omits the grim wooing of Faustus' soul to its own destruction by Mephistophilis:

> Ile cull thee out the fairest curtezans,
> And bring them eu'ry morning to thy bed.
> She whome thine eie shall like, thy heart shal haue. [26]

One can thus approximately fix the date at which the lyric was composed. When *Dido* and *Tamburlaine* were being writ-

[19] *Dido,* 49.
[20] *Dido,* 600–601.
[21] *Dido,* 1374–1383.
[22] *Dido,* 747–767.

[23] *Edward the Second,* 5.
[24] *Edward the Second,* 57–60.
[25] *Edward the Second,* 138.
[26] *Doctor Faustus,* 585–587.

ten, the poem was merely running in Marlowe's mind. By the time Marlowe reached *The Jew of Malta*, he had apparently finished "The Passionate Shepherd," since he was able to quote a line of it word for word. This ingenious theorizing, however, neglects the possibility that in the Ithamore scene in *The Jew of Malta* Marlowe simply happened to strike out a lucky line entire, which he later worked up into a complete lyric. If that be true, the dating fails.

The argument occasionally set up for Shakespearean authorship of "The Passionate Shepherd" rests on two facts and one assumption. It is a fact that the poem first appears in a book attributed to Shakespeare. It is also a fact that Shakespeare quotes from it in *The Merry Wives of Windsor*,[27] where Sir Hugh Evans sings a few lines with variations of his own. It is assumed that Shakespeare would not have taken such liberties with any lyric but his own — not a very convincing argument, seeing that an Elizabethan dramatist habitually used anything he could lay his hands on.

Internal evidence gives no help either way. Each poet was quite capable of writing the lyric; but the Shakespearean arguments are on the whole rather weak. Given the methods of Elizabethan publishers, it is not remarkable to find a poem of Marlowe's in a book with the greater man's signature, especially in a part of the volume not specifically attributed to Shakespeare. There are undoubtedly other poems in this collection not from his pen either. Both poets quote lines from "The Passionate Shepherd," but we know that Shakespeare quotes, or half-quotes, from Marlowe rather frequently.[28] Nor would an Elizabethan dramatist necessarily hesitate to insert other men's work in a book of his own, least of all a lyric poem. Ben Jonson's translation of the fifteenth elegy of the first book of the *Amores* appears in Marlowe's Ovid. The lyric "What Bird So Sings Yet So Does Wayl?" appears both in Lyly's *Alexander and Campaspe* and in Ford and Dekker's *The Sun's Darling*; while another lyric, "O for a Bowl of Fat Canary," appears both in Lyly's play and in Middleton's *A Mad World My Masters*.

There is no real reason, then, for assigning the poem to

[27] III. i, 17–29.   [28] See II. 208–211.

Shakespeare, and there is every reason to assign it to Marlowe. The way in which it permeates his other work is in itself convincing. Charles Lamb wrote to Southey: "I need not tell *you* that Marlow was author of that pretty madrigal," and copied it with his own hand into the manuscript book of verses made for his adopted daughter.[29]

"The Nymph's Reply," usually printed as a companion piece, first appears in full in *England's Helicon*, together with "Another of the same nature." The latter has attracted little attention. One stanza of "The Nymph's Reply" had already appeared in *The Passionate Pilgrim*.

The usual attribution of this poem to Sir Walter Raleigh rests entirely on Izaak Walton's assertion that it is his, and on Marlowe's known association with Raleigh. Bullen's assertion that the original signature was "S.W.R.," and that this had been hidden by a cancel slip bearing the word "Ignoto," is apparently a mistake. At least the Folger, British Museum, Bodleian, and John Rylands copies have the signature "Ignoto" on the page itself with no sign of a cancel slip. The Rylands copy, however, bears the manuscript note, "alias Sr. Walt. Ralegh" in an early hand. Several signatures of other poems have been altered by cancel slips, and this seems to have confused Bullen.[30] Even if Bullen were correct, the initials "S.W.R." would hardly stand for "Sir Walter Raleigh," since it would be very odd for a knight to use his title in this way. Francis Davison's manuscript catalogue [31] of these poems gives no author. One of Oldys' annotated copies of Langbaine, now at the British Museum, attributes the poem to Raleigh solely on the basis of Walton's assertion.[32]

Sources

Several Greek and Latin poems may have served as models for "The Passionate Shepherd." Marlowe certainly knew the

---

[29] *Letters* (ed. W. C. Hazlitt, 1886), I. 197. Lamb's MS. copy is in the hands of Quaritch, London. See Hyder Edward Rollins' ed. of *England's Helicon*, II. 188.

[30] Bullen's reprint of *England's Helicon* (London: Lawrence & Bullen, 1899), p. xxix. See also Henrietta C. Bartlett in TLS, 24: 335, 14 My 1925, and pp. 257 and 352 of the same volume; Miss Bartlett's *Mr. William Shakespeare*, no. 304; Hugh Macdonald's ed. of *England's Helicon* (Haslewood Books), p. 245.

[31] British Museum, Harleian MS. 280, fol. 101r.

[32] See Dyce (1858), p. xlv n; Bullen's Marlowe, III. 258n.

passage in Ovid's *Metamorphoses* [33] which tells of the wooing of Galatea by Polyphemus, who offers his orchards, his flocks, to his prospective love, and concludes:

Jam, Galatea, veni; nec munera despice nostra.[34]

The same story is told in the eleventh Idyll of Theocritus, where the Cyclops lists his inducements to love, and in the twenty-seventh idyll, where the lover promises:

πᾶσαν τὰν ἀγέλαν, πάντ' ἄλσεα καὶ νομὸν ἕξεις.

Corydon makes similar promises to Alexis in Vergil's second Eclogue, and, if we may trust the Baines libel, Marlowe referred to this Eclogue in conversation.

INFLUENCE

"The Passionate Shepherd" seems to have been a general favorite from the beginning. N. Breton in his *Poste with a Packet of Mad Letters* (1603) refers to it:

You shall heare the old song that you were wont to think well of, sung by the blacke brows with the cherrie-cheeke, under the side of the pide cow, *Come Live with me and be my love.*[35]

In his *Choice, Chance, and Change, or Conceites in their Colours* (1606) Breton also refers to it: "Why, how now, do you take me for a woman, that you come upon me with a ballad of *Come live with me and be my love?*" [36] In the following year Thomas Deloney, the novelist and ballad-writer, sets a ballad "to the tune of *Come live with me and be my love.*" [37] Deloney seems to glance at it even earlier in his novel, *Jack of Newbury*, which was registered in March, 1596/7.[38]

The tune is given in Corkine's *Second Book of Ayres* (1612), and there is a variant in Steevens' edition of Shakespeare. It is also given, from a manuscript of Sir J. Hawkins in Malone's

[33] *Metamorphoses*, bk. XIII.

[34] *Op. cit.*, l. 839. Cf. R. S. Forsyth, *loc. cit.*, who lists similar classical passages that did *not* influence Marlowe.

[35] Ed. 1637, p. 59; Dyce, p. xlvi n. Copy in Huntington.

[36] Ed. 1606, p. 3. Cf. *Notes and Queries*, 2nd ser., 10: 206, 15 S 1860. There is a copy of *Choice, Chance, and Change* in the Bodleian. Grosart edited a reprint as no. 33 in his series of "Occasional Reprints of Very Rare Books" (Manchester: C. E. Simms, 1881), and the Library of Congress has a copy of this.

[37] *Strange Histories*, etc. (1607).

[38] *Works* (ed. Mann), p. 49, ll. 19–23.

Shakespeare, edited by the younger Boswell,[39] in Chappell's *Popular Music of the Olden Time*,[40] and in Chappell's *National English Airs*.[41]

Izaak Walton, then, was only repeating earlier opinion when he wrote of "The Passionate Shepherd," calling it "The Milkmaid's Song":

> Her voice was good, and the Ditty fitted it; for 'twas that smooth Song which was made by *Kit Marlow*, now at least fifty years ago; and the Milk maids mother sung an answer to it, which was made by Sir *Walter Raleigh* in his yonger dayes.
>
> They were old fashioned Poetry, but choicely good, I think much better then that now in fashion in this Critical age.[42]

Later editions read "much better than the strong lines that are now in fashion in this critical age." But, as a matter of fact, many of the "strong lines" then in fashion, and others in fashion for some three hundred and fifty years afterward, show clear evidence of the influence of Marlowe's lyric. "The Passionate Shepherd" set a fashion of its own, the "invitation to love" poem. Nothing like it had existed in English before, with the possible exception of "Quia Amore Langueo," once attributed to Lydgate; a casual passage in the January Eclogue of Spenser's *Shepherd's Calendar*, a work with which Marlowe was undoubtedly acquainted; [43] and Sidney's *May Lady*.

The first evidence of the lyric's influence is in Greene's *Menaphon* (1589), where Marlowe's traces are to be found twice. The name Menaphon is taken from *Tamburlaine*, and the resemblance to "The Passionate Shepherd" is too clear to be mistaken. The shepherd Menaphon displays to his love Samela his flocks and pastures, promising her garlands, milk from his ewes, wool for her weaving, walks in the mountains and valleys, ending: "As much as Menaphon owes [i.e., owns] shall be at *Samela's* command if she like to live with *Menaphon*." [44] Greene, not Marlowe, is clearly the borrower, since,

---

[39] VIII. 104.

[40] Pp. 213–215.

[41] II. 130–140.

[42] The quotation is from p. 67 of the 1653 ed. See pp. 108–109 of the 1655 ed., and II. 150 of the present work.

[43] For Marlowe's borrowings from Spenser, see I. 205–209.

[44] Grosart's Greene, VI. 59.

as we have seen, the theme had been running through Marlowe's work from the beginning.

Richard Barnfield, in "The Affectionate Shepherd" (1594), obviously is borrowing from the promises of "The Passionate Shepherd." This is especially clear in Stanza XX of the First Part:

> And when it pleaseth thee to walk abroad,
> (Abroad into the fields to take fresh ayre:)
> The Meades with *Floras* treasure should be strowde,
> (The mantled meaddowes, and the fields so fayre,)
>   And by a siluer Well (with golden sands)
>   Ile sit me downe, and wash thine yuory hands.[45]

There is another close echo of the poem in the pseudo-Shakespearean *Mucedorus*:

> If thou wilt loue me thou shalt be my queene:
> I will crowne thee with a chaplet made of Iuie,
> And make the rose and lilly wait on thee:
> Ile rend the burley braunches from the oke,
> To shadow thee from burning sunne.[46]
> The trees shall spred themselues where thou dost go.

After the original theme had been set by Marlowe, devoted lovers offer catalogues of delights to soften the hard hearts of obdurate ladies — not without some monotony — for three hundred years and more. Some of these were conscious imitators; others doubtless were merely following a literary convention, of whose origin in Marlowe's lyric they had no suspicion; but the almost complete absence of such poems before Marlowe and their abundance after Marlowe leave very little room for doubt.

Charles Cotton, who knew Marlowe's poem at first hand, since he had continued *The Compleat Angler*, writes an imitation in his "Invitation to Phyllis." Other imitations are Donne's "The Bait," Herrick's "To Phyllis to Love and Live with Him," and Sir Edward Sherburne's "A Shepherd Inviting a Nymph to his Cottage." Milton's *Allegro* and *Penseroso* give the invitation poem a new direction, but they contain elements

[45] Pt. I, st. XVII–XXXIII; pt. II, st. VII–XVIII. English Scholar's Library (ed. Arber), no. 14.

[46] The whole passage is much longer. See IV. iii. 24–55, C. F. Tucker Brooke: *Shakespeare Apocrypha*, pp. 119–120.

plainly Marlowe's in their use of the octosyllabic couplet, the invitation, the list of promised delights, and certain verbal echoes. Milton may also have taken hints from *Hero and Leander*.[47]

His lyric "On the Death of a Fair Infant" has also been supposed to be in the Marlowe tradition.[48] The "invitation to love" motif creeps into dramatic dialogue in *Iacke Drums Entertainment*,[49] which also copies *The Jew of Malta*.

VERSES IN ENGLAND'S PARNASSUS

A fragment without title is ascribed to Marlowe in *England's Parnassus* (1600) under the general heading, "Description of Seas, Waters, Riuers, &c." These lines have sometimes been regarded as part of a published poem of Marlowe's which has been lost; but this view is based on the belief, now questioned, that the anthology was originally chosen solely from works already in print and never from manuscript. There is no good reason for believing that the verses were ever previously in print. They may well represent the only surviving fragment of a poem circulated in manuscript among the poet's friends.

Charles Crawford, however, as late as 1906, still argued that Marlowe had at some time made a more elaborate version of "The Passionate Shepherd," and that the fragment was all that remained of this much longer lost poem.[50] He believed that from this work Richard Barnfield (1574–1627) had borrowed fragments for his "Affectionate Shepherd" (1594) and "Cynthia" (1595). The former, as we have seen, borrows from Marlowe's known work,[51] and both have a strong resemblance to it. There is, however, no real evidence for this view; and it was natural that Barnfield should be acquainted with Marlowe, since both he and Marlowe were intimate friends of Thomas Watson's.[52]

Whatever the story of their origin may be, the lines in *England's Parnassus* have the genuine Marlowe ring, and there is no reason for questioning their authenticity — especially as

[47] See II. 118, 123, 139–141.
[48] E. M. W. Tillyard: *Milton* (London: Chatto & Windus, 1930), p. 19.
[49] Cf. II. 491.
[50] *Collectanea*, 1st ser. (1906), pp. 8–9.   [51] See I. 269–270, II. 37, 131.
[52] Edmund Gosse: article "Barnfield, Richard," DNB, I. 1163.

five of the twenty-four lines are run on, much in Marlowe's manner, which was by no means common at this period.[53]

The verses appear to be an experiment in ottava rima. The editor of the anthology quotes only the end of one stanza, rhyming *abcc*, two whole stanzas rhyming *abababcc*, and the beginning of a fourth stanza rhyming *abab*.

The verses have especial significance as the only extant example of Marlowe's verse written in a complex stanza form. "They are," says Professor Brooke, "a valuable evidence of Marlowe's versatility, for they indicate the possession of an aptitude for graceful stanzaic verse after the Spenserian fashion which no other extant production of his attests." [54] He regards them, probably correctly, as "work of the poet's full maturity, parallel in date as in tone with *Hero and Leander*." Marlowe's mastery of this difficult stanza form suggests that other work of the same sort has probably been lost, since it is unlikely that such dexterity was attained at a single bound. This makes it the more probable that Marlowe's lost sonnets may have been genuine.[55]

THE MANWOOD EPITAPH

Two Latin compositions, long held doubtful, can now be shown to be Marlowe's work. One of these is the epitaph on Sir Roger Manwood, the other the dedication to Thomas Watson's *Amintae Gaudia*.

The Manwood epitaph was first printed among Marlowe's works by Dyce in his 1850 edition, and it was retained in later issues. Dyce based his text on that discovered on the flyleaf of the Prideaux copy of the 1629 *Hero and Leander*, by Collier. The authenticity of this inscription need not be questioned, since it was in the book before Collier saw it; [56] but the epitaph was not there specifically ascribed to Marlowe, and matters were not helped by the subsequent disappearance of the book itself in 1917. The epitaph was not used on Sir Roger's tomb, which still exists at St. Stephen's, near Canterbury.

Marlowe's editors have almost uniformly refused to accept this Latin poem as authentic. Cunningham and the anonymous

[53] See II. 184–185.
[54] PMLA, 37: 396 (1922).

[55] See II. 290.
[56] See I. 116–117.

editor of the 1905 Newnes edition, later reprinted by Simpkin Marshall, are the only ones who are willing to include it. Tucker Brooke excludes it from his (1910) edition of the *Works*, and it is not even mentioned among "poems attributed to Marlowe" by L. C. Martin in his 1931 edition of the poems.

Sir Roger Manwood was a Kentishman, whose home was at St. Stephen's, also called Hackington, near Canterbury. His family was related by marriage to the Walsinghams, and Sir Roger was on the bench when Marlowe and Thomas Watson, associates of Sir Roger's friend and neighbor, Sir Thomas Walsingham, were charged with the murder of William Bradley.[57] Either the lenient treatment of the two poets on that occasion or Sir Roger's acquaintance with the Walsinghams might have prompted Marlowe to write the flattering epitaph; and Marlowe might also have remembered that Sir Roger had been a friend of his own benefactor, Archbishop Parker.

The authorship is definitely ascribed to Marlowe in the Oxinden Commonplace Book, which contains two copies of the epitaph.[58] An ascription by a literary amateur, living at Barham, Kent, near Canterbury, and made within half a century of the poet's death cannot very well be questioned, especially as the owner of the Commonplace Book was undoubtedly acquainted with friends of Marlowe's, if not with Marlowe himself. The epitaph must henceforth be regarded as a genuine part of the poet's work, though it sheds little luster on his name.

The Latin dedication of Watson's *Amintae Gaudia*, signed "C. M.," must also be included among Marlowe's genuine writings, since Mr. Mark Eccles' discovery that Watson and Marlowe were friends.[59] It had previously been questioned because of doubts whether Marlowe ever had any relationship of any kind with the Pembroke circle. *Edward the Second* had, of course, been produced by Pembroke's men, but that fact was hardly sufficient evidence.

Most writers have simply neglected these two pages of Latin. The catalogue of the John Rylands Library, Man-

57 See I. 98–102.
58 See I. 119–123.   The idea that Sir Roger was the benefactor who sent Marlowe to Cambridge has, of course, long been abandoned, but see Cunningham, p. ix; and Keltie: *Works of the British Dramatists*, p. 97; Woodruff and Cape: *Schola Regia*.
59 See I. 98, 269, and Eccles: *Marlowe in London*, pp. 163–171.

chester, hazarded the guess that the initials might stand for
Christopher Marlowe, but both Mr. Tucker Brooke and Miss
U. M. Ellis-Fermor remained skeptical.[60]

Like the Manwood epitaph, these two pages of Latin prose
do not add to Marlowe's literary stature; but the fact that the
signature "C. M." in this case turns out to stand for Marlowe
makes one less certain that the Bodleian pamphlet on *The
Natvre of a Woman* may not have claims to be considered
authentic.[61]

THE TRANSLATION OF LUCAN

Marlowe's translation of the first book of Lucan's (39–65 A.D.)
Pharsalia, which recounts the wars of Caesar and Pompey, is
chiefly important because it is the only known example of
Marlowe's nondramatic blank verse and because it influences
Milton. It is one of the earliest English blank verse poems.
The translator reproduces the Latin practically line for line,
with perhaps as many, but not such grave, inaccuracies of rendering as in the Ovid, and with rather more maturity in phrasing and greater metrical skill.

Marlowe fails wretchedly with Lucan's most famous line:

> Victrix causa deis placuit sed victa Catoni,

which he renders:

> *Cæsars* cause
> The gods abetted; *Cato* likt the other.[62]

In another passage,

> Ingentesque animo motus bellumque futurum
> Ceperat,

he mistakes the noun *motus* for the participle, and translates:

> His mind was troubled, and he aim'd at war.[63]

Actually, *motus* is the fourth declension noun, and the meaning
of the line is: "He had grasped in his mind gigantic turmoils
and the war to come."

---

[60] PMLA, 37: 414 S 1922; *Christopher Marlowe*, p. 9.
[61] See II. 294–295.
[62] Ll. 128–129.   [63] Line 186.

Publication of the Lucan is in some obscure way connected with *Hero and Leander*. The two poems are entered together in the *Stationers' Register* on the same day, September 28, 1593, both in the name of John Wolf. The 1600 edition of *Hero and Leander* has on its title page the line: "Whereunto is added the first booke of Lucan *translated line for line by* the same Author." The publisher is now John Flasket.

The translation of Lucan does not appear in the book at all, in spite of the title page; but in the same year Thomas Thorpe brought out the only known edition, a quarto dedicated to Edward Blount with an allusion to Blount's "old right in it." Sir Sidney Lee asserts that "it was through Blount's good offices that Peter Short undertook to print Thorpe's manuscript of Marlowe's 'Lucan,' and Walter Burre agreed to sell it at his shop in St. Paul's Churchyard." [64] This is probable enough, but Sir Sidney gives no authority for his statement.

Apparently the Lucan manuscript had been in the hands of various publishers before it appeared. Wolf seems to have made over his right in it to Edward Blount, though the *Register* has no record of the transaction. On March 2, 1597/8, Blount assigned to still another publisher, Paul Linley, his rights in *Hero and Leander*; and Linley presumably secured the Lucan at the same time. When on June 26, 1600, Linley transferred twenty-four books to John Flasket, "Hero and Leander with the j. booke of *Lucan* by Marlowe" were among them.

Flasket actually did publish *Hero and Leander*. Apparently he intended to publish the Lucan with it and then changed his mind after the title page had been printed. How Thorpe secured his manuscript, and why he makes acknowledgments to Blount but none to Flasket, is not clear.

Though Marlowe's *Lucan* is generally regarded as a rather dull poem, it has a special interest because of its possible influence on John Milton's *Paradise Lost*. There is absolutely no definite evidence that Milton ever read Marlowe, much less imitated him, but the idea has a distinct plausibility. The most marked resemblance between the two is their characteristic use of colorful or resounding geographic names, a char-

[64] *Shakespeare* (1916), p. 672. On Thorpe and Blount, see Sir Sidney Lee: "An Elizabethan Bookseller," *Bibliographica*, 1: 474-498 (1895).

acteristic too well-known to require comment. There are certain parallels with Marlowe's other works, too close to be entirely accidental. And there are in the translation any number of passages which sound nearly as much like Milton as they sound like Marlowe. Thus, for example, the lines:

> As when against pine bearing *Ossa's* rocks
> Beates *Thracian Boreas*; or when trees bowde down,
> And rustling swing vp as the winds fets breath
> *[Lucan,* 390–392]

are very like Milton's

>   . . . as when the force
> Of subterranean wind transports a hill
> Torn from Pelorus, or the shattered side
> Of thundering Ætna, whose combustible
> And fuelled entrails, thence conceiving fire,
> Sublimed with mineral fury, aid the winds.
> *[Paradise Lost,* I. 230–235]

So, too, Marlowe's

> And others came from that vncertaine shore,
> Which is nor sea, nor land, but oft times both
> *[Lucan,* 410–411]

might easily have suggested Milton's

>   . . . till on dry land
> He lights — if it were land that ever burned
> With solid, as the lake with liquid fire.
> *[Paradise Lost,* I. 227–228]

Innumerable other passages in Marlowe's *Lucan* are so like Milton in mood and sound that they might almost be palmed off as his work.[65] More striking are occasional verbal parallels, such as Marlowe's "*Emathian* bandes" and Milton's "great *Emathian* Conqueror"; Marlowe's "new factions rise," which occurs a few lines further on, and Milton's "new foes arise"; or the preference both poets show for the forms "Nilus" and "Rhene" for "Nile" and "Rhine." [66] All this gives added

---

[65] Examples are ll. 15–20, 73–74, 100–106. I owe most of the parallels here cited to Charles Graves, Esq., of the *Scotsman*, Edinburgh.

[66] *Lucan,* 687, 691; Sonnets, VII. 10, "To the Lord General Cromwell." See also *Paradise Regained,* III. 290.

plausibility to the Marlowe-Milton parallels suspected in other poems.

Though the Lucan was published in 1600, eight years before Milton's birth, other works by Marlowe continued to be published until 1663, only eleven years before his death, so that the Puritan poet could hardly have escaped some knowledge of his predecessor — a knowledge which the parallels in other works almost compel us to believe he possessed. The "ciuil broiles" with which the *Pharsalia* dealt gave it a painfully immediate interest during the English Civil War, particularly to a literary man who, like Milton, was employed by the government.

THE TRANSLATION OF OVID

The translations of Ovid's *Amores*, which Marlowe called "Elegies" because of the Latin elegiac verse in which they were written, add nothing to his reputation. They are significant only as one more evidence of his devotion to the Roman poet, quotations from whom abound throughout his work.

The poems are rather free translations into English heroic couplets. In several glaring instances Marlowe plainly does not understand the Latin.

> Snakes leape by verse from caues of broken mountaines

is intended as a rendering of

> Carmine dissiliunt, abruptis faucibus, angues.

The correct translation is: "Through song, serpents burst asunder, their fangs drawn out." [67] Another striking mistranslation is Marlowe's rendering of *canebat frugibus* as "did sing with corne." The correct translation is: "were white with corn." Marlowe mistook *caneo* for *cano*. Equally clumsy is his rendering of

> ante eat effuso tristis captiva capillo
> si sinerent laesae, candida tota, genae,

which is Englished as

> Let the sad captiue formost with lockes spred
> On her white necke but for hurt cheekes be led.[68]

---

[67] "Song bursts the serpent's jaws apart and robs him of his fangs." — Grant Showerman's translation, Loeb Classical Library.

[68] *Elegies*, II. i. 25; III. ix. 39; I. vii. 39–40.

The correct version is: "Let the captive girl walk before, downcast, with her hair loose, all white, did her wounded cheeks allow."

All these errors suggest inadequate Latinity, but not every deviation from the Latin is of this kind. Some are free renderings to meet the exigencies of verse. Others are probably correct translations of faults in the sixteenth-century Latin texts from which Marlowe was working. The text of Ovid, which has since been much improved, was at that time particularly faulty.

Minor slips on Marlowe's part include the mistranslation of *gravis* in the line

> Thee pompous Birds, and him two Tygers drew.

Ovid had written,

> Tu gravis alitibus, tigribus ille fuit,[69]

which really means

> Thou wilt be dread with thy span of birds; with tigers dread was he.

Marlowe has mistaken the third declension singular nominative, *gravis*, for an ablative plural. Most of the blunders in Latin grammar are of this sort — often elementary but rarely distorting the meaning completely.

Where necessary, the poet makes deliberate changes for the sake of rhyme, rhythm, or English idiom. Thus in the couplet,

> When I (my light) do or say ought that please thee,
> Turne round thy gold-ring, *as it were to ease thee*,[70]

he has simply inserted the italicized words to make a none too brilliant rhyme. Again, in the couplet,

> Constrain'd against thy will giue it *the pezant*,
> Forbeare sweet wordes, and be your sport vnpleasant,[71]

Marlowe has supplied "the pezant" to find a rhyme. It is a fair translation of Ovid's mood but not of any particular word in the original Latin.

No one sixteenth-century edition of Ovid explains all Mar-

[69] I. ii. 48.
[70] I. iv. 25–26.   [71] I. iv. 65–66.

lowe's textual blunders, but two of them explain a good many. These are *P. Ovidii Nasonis Amatoria* (Basel, 1568) and *P. Ovidii Nasonis Heroidum Epistolae, Amorum libri III* (Antwerp, 1575). Presumably, Marlowe at one time or another used both.[72] Thus, in the second elegy of the first book, he translates *errorque* as "fear," obviously because he read *terrorque*.[73] In the sixth elegy he translates

> What ere thou art, farewell, be like me paind,

because early Latin texts of Ovid read

> . . . sentique abeuntis amorem

— "feel the love of one departing." [74] Even so, Marlowe's translation is very free, though well enough in view of the license required in verse translation. But modern texts of Ovid read *honorem* — "take the honor of my parting word," which has no possible relation to Marlowe's version.

Marlowe's nineteenth-century editors did not realize how many of these discrepancies in the Latin text existed, and therefore charged him with mistranslations for which he was not responsible.

Other errors seem to be due to ignorance of the customs of antiquity. Thus the line

> Tutaque deposito poscitur ense rudis [75]

is translated

> His sword layed by, safe, though rude places yeelds.

Marlowe simply did not know that a Roman gladiator, when discharged from his perilous profession, was presented with a wooden foil (*rudis*). Again, the allusion to the stingy lover who fails to make gifts loses its entire point through mistranslation.

> If he giues nothing, let him from thee wend.

[72] L. C. Martin's ed., p. 16; Boas: *Christopher Marlowe*, p. 35. There is a copy of the 1568 ed. in the University of Chicago library.

[73] I. ii. 35.

[74] I. vi. 71.

[75] II. ix. 20. There is an excellent discussion of these and other errors, with further examples, in Boas: *Christopher Marlowe*, pp. 29–42.

The Latin reads,

> Si dederit nemo, Sacra roganda Via est.[76]

That is, the Via Sacra, shopping center of ancient Rome, is the neglected lady's only hope. Marlowe here misses the point. When he comes to

> . . . quid nunc Aegyptia prosunt
> Sistra,

he gives up entirely and omits the line,[77] evidently because he did not know that the *sistrum* was a metallic rattle used by the Egyptians.

The translation of Ovid seems to have been seized upon after Marlowe's death and linked with the salacious epigrams of Sir John Davies, by some keen and not very scrupulous publisher, intent upon a *succès de scandale*. If this is the case, the translations might be regarded as early work of his university days which he had not himself thought worth publishing. It is, on the other hand, just possible that the translations were made on a publisher's order, after Marlowe had reached London. In this case, his errors might conceivably be attributed to a Latinity rusty with disuse. More probably, however, the translation is early work and Marlowe makes the blunders of a raw collegian for the very good reason that he was a raw collegian at the time.

All editions of the Marlowe Ovid purport to have been printed at Middleburg, in Holland. Two of the six extant editions, however, bear a peculiar form of signature marking used only by Robert Waldegrave, King's Printer in Edinburgh, who had been driven out of England because he had printed Puritan tracts! The Middleburg imprint was probably a joke, since that Dutch town was frequently the place of publication of English religious tracts written for the Brownist and other Puritan sects which would have been banned in England itself.[78]

The ecclesiastical authorities were not unnaturally perturbed by the elegies and epigrams; and in 1599 John Whitgift, Archbishop of Canterbury, and Richard Bancroft, Bishop of London, included the poems in a list of books to be burned.

---

[76] I. viii. 100.   [77] III. ix (viii). 33–34.
[78] William A. Jackson: *Catalogue of the Carl H. Pforzheimer Library*, no. 413.

The publisher had probably foreseen difficulties of this sort, for all clue to his identity is carefully concealed. The bishops list for the fire nine works, whose titles leave little doubt as to the motives of the episcopal condemnation. The books ordered burned were Joseph Hall's *Virgidemiarum*, John Marston's *Pigmalion* [79] and *Scourge of Villanye*; *The Shadowe of truthe in Epigrams and Satyres*; [80] *Snarling Satyres*; [81] Thomas Cutwode's *Caltha Poetarum*; "DAVYes *Epigrams*, with MARLOWes *Elegyes*"; "The booke againste woemen viz, *of marriage and wyvinge*"; and *The xv ioyes of marriage.*[82]

The bishops' order concludes with instructions: [83]

That noe *Satyres* or *Epigrams* be printed hereafter
That noe Englishe historyes be printed excepte they bee allowed by some of her maiesties privie Counsell/
That noe playes be printed excepte they bee allowed by suche as haue aucthorytie/
That all NASSHes bookes and Doctor HARVYes bookes be taken wheresoeuer they maye be found and that none of theire bookes bee euer printed hereafter/
That thoughe any booke of the nature of theise heretofore expressed shalbe broughte vnto yow vnder the hands of the Lord Archebisshop of CANTERBURYE or the Lord Bishop of LONDON yet the said booke shall not bee printed vntill the master or wardens haue acquainted the said Lord Archbishop, or the Lord Bishop with the same to knowe whether it be theire hand or no/

JO[HN WHITGIFT] CANTUAR
RIC[HARD BANCROFT] LONDON

Suche bookes as can be found or are allready taken of the Argumentes aforesaid or any of the bookes aboue expressed lett them bee presentlye [i.e., immediately] broughte to the Bishop of LONDON to be burnte/

JO CANTUAR
RIC LONDON

Sic examinatur/

[79] See II. 117-119 for relation of this poem to Marlowe.
[80] Better known as *Skialetheia*.
[81] *Microcynicon. Sixe Snarling Satyres*, by T. M. — perhaps Thomas Middleton.
[82] Most of these objectionable books have since been reprinted by industrious antiquaries without discoverable damage to public morals.
[83] *Stationers' Register*, C, f. 316 v. Arber's reprint, III. 316–317, 677, 678. Cf. N&Q, 3rd ser., 12: 436–437 30 N 1867. Cf. also pp. 374–375 and Warton: *Hist. Eng. Poetry* (1840), III. 394. Charles Edmonds' transcription in N&Q, cited above, does not always agree with Arber's, whose text is used here.

The banning of Harvey's and Nashe's books was probably due as much to their savage controversial tone as to such casual bits of bawdry as Nashe's "Choyse of Valentines." The bishops were plainly as much interested in censoring the bitter satires in which the Elizabethans indulged as they were in censoring licentiousness.

The orders were delivered June 1, 1599, to the wardens of the Stationers' Company, who signed two copies, one for each bishop. "The aforesaid Commaundements" were published to the Stationers' Company and to the fourteen unprivileged printers who might conceivably try to print the forbidden books. Seven of the nine works were burned on June 4. *Caltha Poetarum* and the *Satires* of Joseph Hall (who himself became a bishop in 1641) were "staid," and the further order was given: "WILLOBIES *Adviso* to bee Called in," but as this work appeared in new editions of 1605, 1609, and 1635, the censorship was presumably later lifted.

Most of the books ordered burned had been published in 1598 and 1599. The Davies epigrams had probably been going about from hand to hand, either in manuscript or in print, since 1596 or earlier. The date usually accepted is 1596. This is based on an allusion in Sir John Harington's *Metamorphosis of Ajax*, published in that year. "My good friend M. Davies," wrote Sir John, "said of his epigrams, that they were made like doublets in Birchin-lane, for everyone whom they will serve." [84] Such a work might easily circulate for several years without coming to the attention of the two reverend fathers in God who suppressed it.

Their wrath was probably directed mainly at the Davies epigrams, which could not be disguised as anything but simple pornography, whereas Marlowe's Ovid had the respectability of the classics. The epigrams are signed merely "J. D." in all editions, but are connected with Sir John Davies (1569–1626), sometime attorney-general for Ireland, through certain "Gullinge Sonnets," by "Mr. Dauyes," which A. H. Bullen declares "evidently from the same hand as the epigrams." [85] Thomas

[84] Page 133 of the Chiswick Press ed. (1814). There is another unmistakable allusion to one of the epigrams — that on the lady's glove (XIV) in the same book (p. 42).

[85] Farmer MS., Chetham Library; Spenser Society Reprint (1888); Harleian MS. 1836.

Bastard in *Chrestoleros, Seuen Bookes of Epigrams*, has two allusions to the Davies epigrams. One is indirect and deals with the boastful soldier Scilla [86] in a way that seems reminiscent of two epigrams by Davies. The other allusion is direct:

> *Heywood* goes downe saith *Dauie*, sikerley,
> And downe he goes, I can it not deny.
> But were I happy, did not fortune frowne.
> Were I in heart I would sing *Dauy* downe. [87]

This is an obvious reply to Epigram XXIX by Davies:

> *Haywood* that did in Epigrams excell,
> Is now put downe since my light Muse arose. [88]

In Book III of *Chrestoleros* the third epigram gives the full name of Iohannes Dauis, and contains the lines:

> *Heywood* sang others downe, but thy sweete note
> *Dauis*, hath sang him downe. [89]

It is diverting to find that Archbishop Whitgift, who had ordered the epigrams burned, is praised in this same volume. [90] Marlowe's translation of Ovid had also probably been known for some years. Nashe quotes two lines in *The Unfortunate Traveller*, [91] which is dated June 27, 1593, just after Marlowe's death, and which also alludes to Davies. Otherwise, there are only two known allusions to the work, or to be strictly accurate, quotations from it. Shakespeare quotes, or seems to quote, a line; [92] and Ben Jonson incorporates the fifteenth elegy of Book I in his *Poetaster*. [93] Many editions of the Ovid print this version together with Marlowe's. It is signed "B.I." Marlowe's contemporaries seem to have realized that the translations added little to his reputation, and the rest, so far as they are concerned, is silence.

[86] Bk. I, no. 22.
[87] Bk. II, no. 15.
[88] Cf. pp. 14 and 36, Publ. Spenser Society (Manchester, 1888), no. 47.
[89] *Chrestoleros*, pp. 54–55.
[90] *Chrestoleros*, IV, no. 8, p. 82.
[91] McKerrow's Nashe, II. 238; the lines are II. iii, 3–4.
[92] See II. 209.
[93] I. i.

CHAPTER XV

THE MIGHTY LINE

. . . how farre thou didst our Lily *out-shine,*
Or sporting Kid, *or* Marlowes *mighty line.*
BEN JONSON in the First Folio

ENGLISH POETRY provides an exception to the usual rule that a literature begins with blank verse. Greek and Latin poetry never attempted rhyme until their great periods were over. Rhyme does not develop in Latin until the Silver Age, and Greek poets never employed it to any great extent until relatively modern times. Early French poetry — the *Chanson de Roland* is a convenient example — had at best a rude kind of assonance. Chinese and Japanese poetry, because of the structure of their languages, could not employ rhyme.

English blank verse, on the other hand, begins only after ten centuries either of internal initial rhyme (alliteration) or end rhyme; and even then the early experiments are only rather crude imitations of Latin hexameters, introduced as a means of translation into an English measure which the early translators fondly believed to be more or less equivalent. Old English versification might conceivably — by a rather wild stretch of the term — be called blank. It certainly lacks end rhyme; but the alliteration which is its most characteristic feature is with equal certainty a kind of rhyme. When, under the French influence which began after the Conquest, English poets in courtly circles broke away from the ancient traditions, they took over, along with other aspects of French versification, the end rhyme for which French poetry had developed a passion.

It would be false to say that end rhyme would never have developed in English without French models; for one can see its first faint beginnings clearly enough — in odd combination with the old alliterative verse — in such rough, post-Conquest popular poetry as *King Horn* and other popular romances. In these, the rhyme seems more or less accidental. The poet stumbles into a couplet by accident and then, finding it agreeable to the ear, goes on adding rhyme to successive rhyme so long as his ingenuity holds out. In one passage of *Havelock the Dane* there are nineteen successive lines all ending in the same syllable.[1]

Entranced by the melody of "rhyme-words coming aptly in," English poets abandoned alliteration entirely; but in exchanging alliteration for end rhyme no one seems to have thought of abandoning both kinds of rhyme. Until a few years before Elizabeth ascended the throne, all English poetry and all English plays were written either in alliteration or end rhyme, the latter being employed for dramatic literature. As late as 1582 Stephen Gosson in his *Plays Confuted in Five Actions*[2] could declare that "Poets send theire verses to the Stage vpon such feete as continually are rowled vp in rime at the fingers endes" — without even mentioning blank verse as a possibility.

This slavery to rhyme was a sad handicap to the English drama. It seems rarely, if ever, to have occurred to the playwrights who wrote the mystery, miracle, and morality plays, or the earliest plays of the Elizabethan period, that it was possible to write prose dialogue. They were as blind as Monsieur Jourdain to the fact that prose might be literature and even drama. They insisted on writing verse; and verse to them meant rhyming verse. Hence their characters often talked in elaborate stanza forms — an affectation from which even Shakespeare, with his sonnet imbedded in the blank verse of *Love's Labour's Lost*, was not wholly free. This limitation lent an inevitable unreality and air of artifice to early English dramatic writing, against which the first dramatists struggled in vain.

The moment, however, that the blank verse which the Earl of Surrey had introduced[3] was tried on the stage, it swept everything before it. Rhyme, except as an ornament — which the young Shakespeare and a few others continued to use with

---

[1] Skeat's ed., revised by K. Sisam (Oxford, 1923), ll. 87-105.
[2] STC 12066. Cf. p. 201 of the reprint in W. C. Hazlitt: *English Drama and Stage* (Roxburghe Library, 1869).
[3] Cazamian and Legouis: *Hist. Eng. Lit.*, I. 144.

extreme freedom for some years — vanished from the stage, though it naturally remained in the lyrics which Elizabethan dramatists freely introduced into their plays. The speed with which this transformation took place is best illustrated by the two parts of a play attributed to Robert Wilson (d. 1600) just before and just after the innovation. *The Three Ladies of London*, printed in 1584, was written in rhyme. Its second part, *The Three Lords and Three Ladies of London*, which appeared in print in 1590, was entirely in blank verse.[4]

The reasons for the swiftness of this change are clear enough. Dramatic writing is necessarily emotionally toned — there would be no drama, otherwise; and, as every writer knows, every emotional passage tends to take on a degree of rhythm. The Elizabethans might well have written in rhythmic prose, but the English prose of Marlowe's day was hardly developed enough to serve as a dramatic vehicle. Rhythmic prose of a kind that the actors could make effective on the stage was therefore out of the question.

The Elizabethan drama had necessarily to be written in meter, and the meter ideally adapted to the drama was the unrhymed, ten-syllable line. This was near enough to the speech of everyday life, heightened and refined as literary dialogue must always be, to make stage illusion possible. Its beauty to some degree atoned for the scantiness of Elizabethan staging. It did not have the patent unreality and artificiality of rhyme. Neither did it hamper a swift interchange between characters of line for line, or even fractions of lines. This is so nearly impossible with rhymed verse that even Dryden complained that the couplet made one-line speeches difficult and reduced dramatic dialogue to a neat set of epigrams.

Playwrights, ever conservative folk, were slow to see this. They even ridiculed the first blank verse to appear upon the boards. Though he was, or at one time had been, Marlowe's collaborator, Thomas Nashe sneered at his friend's "bragging blanke verse" and "drumming decasillabon," in a famous passage already quoted.[5] Though Ben Jonson praised the "mighty line" in his verses prefixed to the First Folio, he is also credited

---

[4] STC 25783 and 25784. Cf. J. P. Collier, HEDP (1831), III. 124.
[5] "To the Gentlemen Students," prefixed to Greene's *Menaphon* (1587). See I. 195.

with the rather disparaging remark that Marlowe's mighty lines "were examples fitter for admiration than for parallel." [6]

It was not until other writers had for some thirty years indulged in rather desultory experiment with blank verse in nondramatic poems that Marlowe first used the blank decasyllable in a play.[7] *Tamburlaine* was quite probably the first blank verse play on the popular stage, although some critics believe that Kyd's *Spanish Tragedy*, also in decasyllables, preceded it. However that may be, it is quite certain that *Tamburlaine* was the first blank verse play of permanent literary value — a quality which no one is likely to attribute to the *Spanish Tragedy*, however important it may be to the historian of the stage.[8]

The earliest English blank verse, the Earl of Surrey's translation of the second and fourth books of the *Aeneid*, appears to have been an effort to reproduce in English the quantitative Latin verse with which their classical studies had made all Elizabethan writers familiar. It is difficult today to realize how long, how serious, and how stubborn was the English effort to force English verse into the quantitative mold, for which we now see the substance of the language to be wholly unfit. The effort was futile and doomed to inevitable failure; but it had the merit of contributing to the movement which eventually provided Marlowe, Shakespeare, and their fellows with an instrument essential to their work.

Surrey is supposed by W. J. Courthope to have been influenced by an Italian translation of the second book of the *Aeneid* attributed to Francesco-Maria Molza (1489–1544) but published under the name of Cardinal Ippolito de' Medici (d. 1535) in 1541 — an early example of the modern practice of "ghost-writing." This was in *versi sciolti* (*sc. della rima*), i.e., verses of eleven syllables without rhyme. Surrey may also, as Warton thinks,[9] have been influenced by Giovanni Giorgio Trissino

[6] Preceding William Bosworth's *Chast and Lost Lovers* [*Arcadius and Sepha*] (1651). See George Saintsbury: *Minor Poets of the Caroline Period*, II. 527.

[7] Critics as late as Coleridge fell into the error of attributing this innovation to Shakespeare. Dryden remarks in his preface to *The Rival Ladies* (1664) that Shakespeare "was the first who, to shun the pains of continual rhyming, inventing that kind of writing which we call blank verse." (*Dramatic Essays*, Everyman ed., pp. 185–186.) Coleridge says that "Shakespeare's blank verse is an absolutely new creation." (*Lectures and Notes on Shakespeare*, Bohn ed., 1834, p. 545.)   [8] See II. 207.

[9] Thomas Warton: *Hist. English Poetry* (Hazlitt's 1871 ed.), IV. 39.

(1478–1550), who is credited with having introduced *versi sciolti* into Italian poetry with his epic, *Italia liberata dai Goti* and his drama *Sofonisba*.[10] The influence of Luigi Alamanni (1495–1556) has also been suggested by Sir Sidney Lee;[11] and it is possible that the occasional decasyllables in Chaucer's two prose Canterbury Tales may have had influence.

On the title page to Book Four in the second edition of Surrey's work, the foreign character of the new versification is pointed out, and the blank verse is described as a "straunge meter." English poets continued for some years to employ it with a rather dubious air, as something rich, perhaps, but certainly strange and foreign.

Two narrative poems by Nicholas Grimald (1519–1562) in *Tottel's Miscellany* (1557) are the next experiments in the new meter.[12] They are both short, "The Death of Zoroas" containing but 115 lines and "Marcus Tullius Ciceroe's Death" but 88. From about this time also must date the translation of passages from the second act of Seneca's *Hercules Oetaeus*, attributed to Queen Elizabeth and preserved at the Bodleian in manuscript.[13]

The blank verse of both Grimald and Surrey is curiously stiff, awkward, and unmusical. The opening lines of Grimald's "Zoroas" are a fair example:

> Now clattering arms, now rayging broyles of warr
> Gan passe the noyes of tarantara clang:
> Shrowded with shafts, the heven: with clowd of darts,
> Covered, the ayre: against fulfatted bulls,
> As forceth kindled ire the Lions keene:
> Whose greedy gutts the gnawing hoonger pricks:
> So Macedoins against the Persians fare.

One gets an idea of the advance made by Marlowe when one contrasts a passage from Surrey's translation of the *Aeneid*

[10] J. Schipper: *Hist. English Versification*, p. 220.
[11] Article "Wyatt, Thomas," DNB, XXI. 1101.
[12] Hyder E. Rollins' ed. (1929), I. 115–120; II. 247–254; Arber's (1870) ed., pp. 120–125.
[13] Bodleian Library, MS. E. Mus. 55 [3499 in the Catalogue of 1697], fols. 48–49. The manuscript is headed "A Translation by Queen Elizabeth," but is not in the Queen's hand. It appears to have been written in the latter sixteenth or early seventeenth century, and was presented by Dr. Robert Clay about 1620. It is printed in Horace Walpole's *Catalogue of Noble and Royal Authors*, I. 102–109.

with a paraphrase of the same passage from Marlowe's *Dido*, even though the latter is early work and far from Marlowe's best. Surrey writes:

> Sinon, preserved by froward destiny,
> Let forth the Greeks enclosed in the womb:
> The closures eke of pine by stealth unpinn'd,
> Whereby the Greeks restored were to air.
> With joy down hasting from the hollow tree,
> With cords let down did slide unto the ground
> The great captains. . . .

Marlowe, who in this passage is practically giving a free translation of Vergil, renders it:

> Some surfetted, and others soundly slept.
> Which *Sinon* viewing, causde the Greekish spyes
> To hast to *Tenedos* and tell the Campe:
> Then he vnlockt the Horse, and suddenly
> From out his entrailes, *Neoptolemus*
> Setting his speare vpon the ground, leapt forth,
> And after him a thousand Grecians more,
> In whose sterne faces shin'd the quenchles fire,
> That after burnt the pride of *Asia*.
> By this the Campe was come vnto the walles,
> And through the breach did march into the streetes,
> Where meeting with the rest, kill, kill they cryed.[14]

Blank verse reached the stage slowly, and was used at first only in plays that seem to have been meant for the fastidious ears of private audiences. *Jocasta* (1566), from which Marlowe probably borrowed a scene in *Tamburlaine*,[15] is entirely in blank verse, but it is the wooden blankness of the early experimenters. George Peele, in his *Arraignment of Paris*, which was published in 1584 and probably produced some years earlier,[16] ventures a few scenes of blank verse which show advancing skill, but he hesitates to use the new medium freely and falls back upon couplet, quatrain, and a variety of meters. Both these plays preceded any of Marlowe's known work and probably influenced him, since he takes various hints in stagecraft from

---

[14] *Aeneid*, II. 326–339; *Dido*, 474–485.

[15] See I. 239.

[16] Fleay's statement (*Chron. Hist. . . . London Stage*, II. 152) that the play dates from 1581 assumes that the Children of the Chapel stopped playing in 1582. They continued until 1584. Cf. Chambers: *Eliz. Stage*, III. 459.

Jocasta and was probably personally acquainted with Peele.

Marlowe did not invent English blank verse, which had been in use for more than a decade before his birth. He did not invent the decasyllabic line, which (with rhyme) had been used by Chaucer. He was not the first to employ the ten-syllable unrhymed line on the stage, for at least two plays besides the *Spanish Tragedy* had been written in it before his dramatic career began. *Gorboduc* had appeared in 1561, three years before his birth, and *Jocasta* when he was two years old; and there were probably others, now lost.

Neither was Marlowe the inventor of the various devices whose skilful use gave his verse much of its melody. Enjambement, the substitution of trochees, epic and lyric caesuras, pyrrhic endings, the occasional mingling of alexandrines with the decasyllables, and rhyming tags at the ends of scenes (which Marlowe occasionally used, while Shakespeare used them very frequently) all appear in English blank verse from the very beginning.

It is not even certain — as some scholars so positively state — that Marlowe was the first to employ blank verse on the popular stage, since the laurels of priority remain in dispute between the *Spanish Tragedy* and *Tamburlaine*. Thomas Hughes's *Misfortunes of Arthur* can be definitely dated no later than 1588, for it was performed before the Queen in that year; but, as it never reached the public stage, it does not enter the problem. Marlowe's partisans insist that *Tamburlaine* came first and that the resounding but hopelessly bombastic verse of *The Spanish Tragedy* is merely the effort of a popular poetaster to reach the stage quickly with his imitation of a dramatic form whose future popularity was instantly evident on its first appearance. Mr. T. W. Baldwin, on the other hand, argues that "Kyd had ceased writing for the stage when Marlowe, Greene, and Shakespeare began." [17]

The controversy has no great significance, for it is not actually important who first used the decasyllable on the English popular stage. Marlowe is the first writer of really great blank verse in English, the first that can possibly be called the "mighty line" — and of that no one has any doubts at all.

[17] "Chronology of Thomas Kyd's Plays," MLN, 40: 349 (1925).

Both *The Spanish Tragedy* and *Tamburlaine* created an immense impression, which is attested by innumerable references in the literature of the time, references which extend over a long period of years. That impression was partly due to the verse, but partly also to the constant and lively action of both plays and above all to their immense violence, which, however crude to modern taste, precisely suited the Elizabethan palate. The difference between them lay in their poetic quality and especially in the quality of the versification. Kyd's verse was decasyllabic and even rose at times to a certain music, but it was not the mighty line. Neither, at all times, was Marlowe's; but throughout *Tamburlaine*, in spite of its perpetual rant and its occasional bathos, there runs a strain of varied music which had not been heard before on the English stage. Sometimes it has a barbaric violence, like the beginning of Tamburlaine's lament over Zenocrate:

> Blacke is the beauty of the brightest day.[18]

But even here it rises to lyric quality in the latter part of this very passage, with its refrain,

> To entertaine diuine *Zenocrate*.

In this measure Marlowe wrote, from the very opening of his career, some of the supremely beautiful things in English letters, now with a majesty strongly suggestive of the Milton that was to come, in passages like

> Nay could their numbers counteruail the stars
> Or euer drisling drops of Aprill showers,
> Or withered leaues that Autume shaketh downe:
> Yet would the Souldane by his conquering power,
> So scatter and consume them in his rage,
> That not a man should liue to rue their fall,

now with all the piercing melody of Keats in passages like

> If all the pens that euer poets held,
> Had fed the feeling of their maisters thoughts,
> And euery sweetnes that inspir'd their harts,
> Their minds, and muses on admyred theames:
> If all the heauenly Quintessence they still
> From their immortall flowers of Poesy,

[18] II *Tamb.* 2969.

Wherein as in a myrrour we perceiue
The highest reaches of a humaine wit.
If these had made one Poems period
And all combin'd in Beauties worthinesse,
Yet should ther houer in their restlesse heads,
One thought, one grace, one woonder at the least,
Which into words no vertue can digest.[19]

This begins with *Tamburlaine*, and, though it is refined and developed as Marlowe grows older, it never loses a certain characteristic quality that is Marlowe's own — never ceases, in other words, to be the mighty line.

Marlowe's verse, through the various plays and poems, shows a curious mixture of sameness and development. He begins his earliest work with the same intensity of feeling, vehemence of expression, melody, and lyric grace with which he ends; but with each successive play he learns better and better how to adapt his line to the mood which it expresses. The monotony of *Tamburlaine* has already become in *Doctor Faustus* a skilful adaptation of sound to sense, and this process goes further in the genuine half of *The Jew of Malta*, reaching its climax in *Edward the Second* and *Hero and Leander*.

One gets a very clear idea of this growth by comparing the death scenes which conclude the Second Part of *Tamburlaine*, *Doctor Faustus*, and *Edward the Second*. The catastrophe of *The Jew of Malta* can hardly be included, since it is obviously a grotesque horror botched up by a stage manager to send the groundlings shuddering home.

The verse of Tamburlaine's dying speech is the same robustious, bragging measure of his triumphal speeches. Marlowe has not yet been able to suit his verses to express the weak and halting speech of a dying man. Compare the

> I am dying, Egypt, dying

of Shakespeare's Antony with Tamburlaine's last lines:

> Farewel my boies, my dearest friends, farewel,
> My body feeles, my soule dooth weepe to see
> Your sweet desires depriu'd my company,
> For *Tamburlaine*, the Scourge of God must die.[20]

---

[19] I *Tamb.* 1402–1407, 1942–1954.
[20] *Antony and Cleopatra*, IV. xv. 41; II *Tamb.* 4638–4641.

The whole of Tamburlaine's dying speech occupies thirteen
lines. Shakespeare's single line is the gasp of a man barely able
to talk. Marlowe's elaborate speech for his dying hero is an
exercise in rhetoric which demands the sturdy lungs of an
Edward Alleyn who is very much alive. Even Shakespeare
relapses into purely Elizabethan rhetoric in the dying Antony's
final speech.

In the magnificent last speech of *Doctor Faustus*, in which
Marlowe reaches very nearly the top of his performance, the
dramatist has learned a little more about reality. In the
broken verse, interrupted with caesuras, we have the gasping
utterance of a man in the last paroxysms of utter terror:

> My God, my God, looke not so fierce on me:
> Adders, and Serpents, let me breathe a while:
> Vgly hell gape not, come not *Lucifer*,
> Ile burne my bookes, ah *Mephastophilis*.[21]

In these four lines there are seven sharp pauses, in which one
can almost hear the terrified gasps of the damned magician,
damned by his own consent and all too well aware of the horrors
that await him.

Edward the Second dies in a mood of resignation, mingled with
grief, both emotions being clearly mirrored in the verse. Thus
his perturbation is well expressed in

> Know that I am a king, oh at that name,
> I feele a hell of greefe: where is my crowne?
> Gone, gone, and doe I remaine aliue?

and his resignation is equally clear in

> I am too weake and feeble to resist,
> Assist me sweete God, and receiue my soule. . . .
> O spare me, or dispatche me in a trice.[22]

These contrasting passages show clearly enough which way
Marlowe was advancing — toward calmness, skill, knowledge
of humanity, and the restraint which he so badly needed yet
never quite achieved.

It is frequently asserted that the magic of great verse defies

[21] *Doctor Faustus*, 1474–1477.
[22] *Edward the Second*, 2537–2539, 2556–2559.

analysis or explanation. This is true, in part. In all genuine art there is an indefinable personal quality that is the mark of the individual who created it, a statement that holds true of painting, sculpture, music, and poetry alike. But the painter, the sculptor, the musician, and the poet all use machinery — a technique which *can* be analyzed and which to a very large extent helps to explain the abiding and mysterious and partly inexplicable thing which is sheer genius.

It is, no doubt, like laying some gorgeously plumaged tropical bird on the dissecting table to attempt to analyze the mighty line. Yet much of its magic and its beauty are due to certain definite technical devices, which Marlowe did not, indeed, originate; but which he used more freely and more skilfully than any writer before him. English blank verse before Marlowe had been dull and monotonous, a procession of wooden soldiers, marching in columns of five. Marlowe made it the proud march of Tamburlaine and his hosts from the stately tent of war, and used it later to bring Helen back from the realm of shades, to project the mind of Faustus, still climbing after knowledge infinite, the lust of wealth, the soul of a miser, "the reluctant pangs of abdicating royalty." [23]

He did this mainly by the use of a variety of devices to alter his meter or his music and fit it to the changing mood that he had to express. Doubtless the use of this machinery was not always conscious, but the machinery was there, nevertheless. These devices include:

1. Enjambement of the normally end-stopped line.
2. The introduction of occasional alexandrines.
3. The use of "tumbling" endings, which have much the effect of alexandrines, and may have been meant as such.
4. Feminine endings.
5. A more artful use of both epic and lyric caesura.
6. A freer substitution of other feet for the basic iambus, including trochees, dactyls, anapaests, spondees, and a characteristic use of pyrrhics.
7. The nine-syllable line.
8. Interpolated and extra-metrical syllables.

[23] Charles Lamb's description of Edward II's abdication. ("Characters of Dramatic Writers," *Works*, ed. Percy Fitzgerald, 1876, IV. 215.)

9. Tetrameters and even shorter lines.
10. Breaking of lines between characters to give a livelier, more conversational pitch to certain passages.
11. Occasional alliteration.
12. A very sparing use of rhyme, so sparing indeed that one almost feels that Marlowe, pre-eminently a blank verse poet, distrusted rhyme and used it, even as ornament, as little as he could.
13. A careful choice of vowel sounds.
14. The development of the "verse paragraph."

Special caution is required in any generalization with regard to Marlowe's scansion until we are quite sure what Marlowe really wrote. Until Tucker Brooke's edition of the *Works* appeared in 1910, it was not possible to be sure of a given passage without consulting the sixteenth- and seventeenth-century editions; for the editors of the two following centuries were obsessed with the idea of a completely regular decasyllabic line. They did not hesitate to cut down alexandrines (which they regarded as mere oversights on the poet's part or accidents of printing), to pad out tetrameters, and to indulge their favorite fancies in some rather wild emendations. Furthermore, they seem to have had no idea how frequently Marlowe employed the light, pyrrhic foot.

All illustrative passages in the present chapter, therefore, are taken from Brooke's edition, with due consideration to the variant quarto readings if they affect the scansion.

1. The run-on line (enjambement) had already appeared in Surrey's *Aeneid*, rather rarely in his translation of the second book and more frequently as he progressed in the fourth book. Schipper [24] counts 35 examples in the first 250 lines, and Emerson [25] 198 in the first 500 lines. Enjambement also appears occasionally in *Gorboduc* (1561) in such passages as

> And with his owne most bloudy hand he hath
> His brother slaine, and doth possesse his realme

and

> And hearing him oft call the wretched name
> Of mother, and to crye to her for aide.[26]

[24] J. Schipper: *Hist. Eng. Versification*, p. 221.
[25] Oliver Farrar Emerson: "Development of Blank Verse," MLN, 4: 466–472 (1889).
[26] *Gorboduc*, III. i. 161–162; IV. ii. 211–212. References are to J. M. Manly: *Specimens of Pre-Shakespearean Drama* (Athenaeum Press Series, Ginn & Co., 1897).

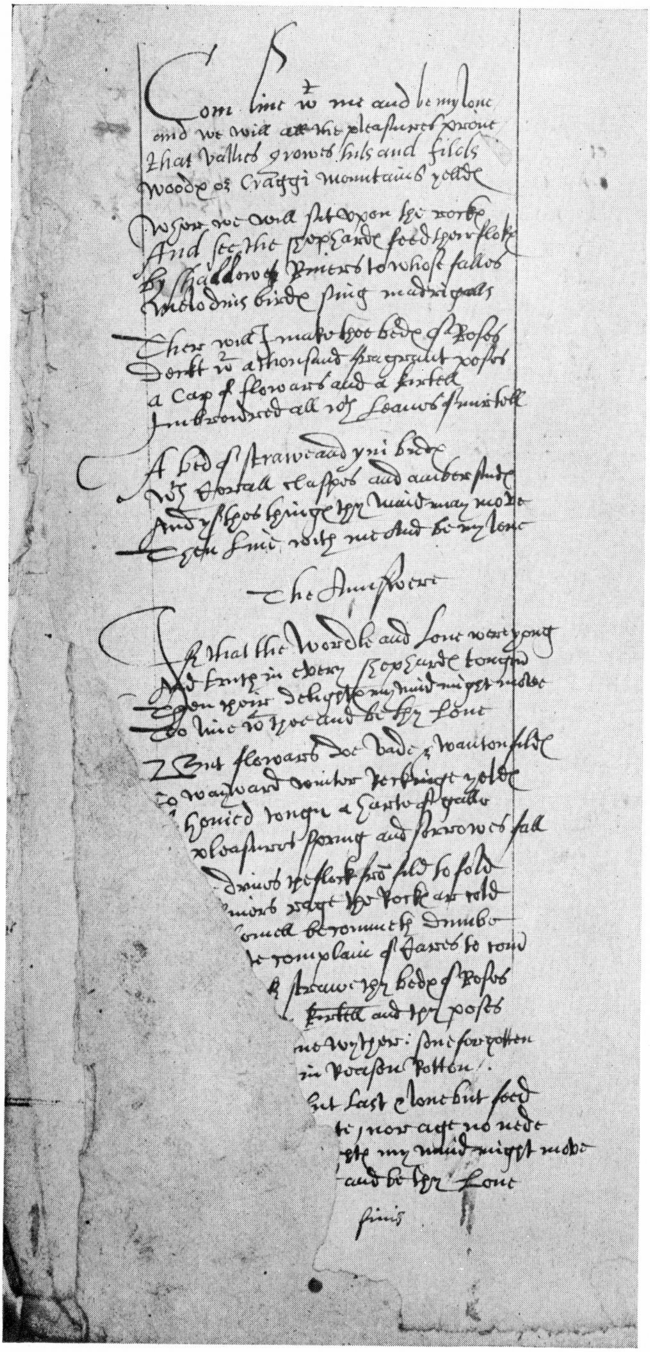
Com live with me and be my love
and we will all the pleasures prove
that valleis groves hils and fields
woods or craggi mountains yelde

Where we will sit upon the rocke
And see the shepardes feed ther flockes
by shallow rivers to whose falls
melodius birde sing madrigalls

Ther will I make the beds of roses
Deckt with a thousand fragrant poses
a cap of flowers and a kirtell
Imbrodered all with leaves of mirtell

A bed of strawe and yvi buds
with corall clasps and amber studs
And if these thinges thy maid may move
Then live with me and be my love

The Answere

If that the World and love were yong
And truth in every shepardes tonge
Then those delightes my maid might move
To live with thee and be thy love

But flowers doe fade & wanton fildes
to wayward winter reckning yeldes
honied tonge a hart of galle
pleasures spring and sorrowes fall

...

fin[is]

MS. COPY OF "THE PASSIONATE SHEPHERD," *c.* 1596

But it is here used very sparingly, and the end-stopped line
predominates. In general, all writers of blank verse between
Surrey and Marlowe make a very cautious use of enjambement,
which often appears to be accidental rather than deliberate.
Even Marlowe uses it very cautiously in his earlier plays. In
Tamburlaine the proportion of run-on lines is small, rising with
each successive play until it reaches its climax in *Edward the
Second*.

As he became freer and freer in the use of enjambement,
Marlowe produced a verse that linked line to line in a free
flowing-forward of both sense and rhythm, and thus gradually
came to write that type of verse paragraph which is one of the
marked beauties of his work. Take, for example, these lines
from *Edward the Second*:

> . . . A heauie case,
> When force to force is knit and sword and gleaue
> In ciuill broiles makes kin and country men
> Slaughter themselues in others and their sides
> With their owne weapons gorde, but whats the helpe? [27]

Here line flows smoothly into line as the thought moves forward, and the verse pauses only when the thought, completed,
pauses too.

Even so, Marlowe's use of this device is cautious compared
to that made of it by a poet like Keats.[28] One must read *Hero
and Leander* and *Endymion* together to appreciate how great the
development was in the intervening two centuries.

2–3. The introduction of alexandrines into pentameter verse
is characteristic of Marlowe, though one or two predecessors
had used it and the device became fairly frequent among later
dramatists. Marlowe was, however, probably the first dramatic
poet to employ it. In certain cases, even in Marlowe's works,
it may be accidental; and in certain other cases it is hard to tell
whether the poet intends to write a so-called "tumbling ending" — that is, a feminine ending with two extra weak syllables
at the end instead of one — or whether he expects the line to
scan as an alexandrine with one of his characteristic weak
pyrrhic feet at the end. Examples of these doubtful cases are

[27] *Edward the Second*, 1751–1755.
[28] For similarities between Marlowe and Keats, see II. 135, 143–147, 192, 202–204.

Yet wíl/ I cáll/ on hím:// oh spáre/ me *Lúc*/ *ifer*   [DF, 1435]
But fór/ we knów/ thou árt/ a nób/ le gént/ leman [E II, 1239]

On the other hand, there are some cases where one is inclined to feel sure that the line scans with five feet and an indubitable "tumbling ending," notably in lines like

Yet nót/ your wórds/ ónely,// but míne/ owne fán/ tasie
[DF, 131]

Whát, is/ great *Méph*/ *astóph*/ *ilís*/ so páss/ ionate
[DF, 319]

Why mán,/ they sáy/ there ís/ great éx/ ecú/ tion
[E II, 1700]

Sometimes this may be due merely to haste and bad workmanship, the poet relying on the actor's voice to read the line with sufficient skill to prevent its redundance from becoming apparent, or else failing to realize that he had added extra syllables.

Something of the sort must have happened in one odd line of Tamburlaine's address to Zenocrate:

A faíre/ *Zenóc*/ *raté*,// diuíne/ *Zenóc*/ *raté*
[I *Tamb.* 1916]

where there is no real accent in the third and sixth feet. The line can be scanned as an alexandrine by making a secondary accent into a primary accent (as good poets often do); but Marlowe quite possibly thought of this line as one of his occasional tetrameters, treating the name of Tamburlaine's love as a single foot with a single real stress.

There are, at any rate, plenty of unquestionable alexandrines, often with masculine endings, in which the last syllable is so emphatic that no one will doubt Marlowe meant us to feel the rhythm of a full six-beat pulse. The most famous example of this is in the almond-tree simile in the Second Part of *Tamburlaine*, already mentioned.[29] This has usually been treated as a mere piece of inadvertence on Marlowe's part. Borrowing, consciously or unconsciously, from Spenser, whose work he

[29] See I. 205, 209. Mr. T. S. Eliot, in his essay, "The Blank Verse of Marlowe," in *The Sacred Wood* (p. 88), seems to think that this was first noticed by Mr. J. M. Robertson. Actually, however, it is noted by J. P. Collier, HEDP (1831), III. 118, and by practically all succeeding editors. Cf. Bullen, II. 201; Dyce (1850), I. 200 (1858), p. 66; Mermaid, p. 149.

knew well,[30] he is supposed to have failed to note the extra syllables. But as it was Marlowe's practice to include alexandrines
in passages undoubtedly his own, he may well have let this one
stand with full deliberation. *Tamburlaine* alone contains some
thirty clear specimens of the alexandrine line, and they are frequent elsewhere.[31] The following examples illustrate Marlowe's
practice in all his plays:

They wíll/ talk stíll/ my Lórd,// if you dóe/ not bríd/ le thém.
[II *Tamb.* 4258]

To máke/ me mís/ eráb/ le:// héere/ recéiue/ my crówne.
[E II, 2083]

O léu/ ell áll/ your lóokes/ vpón/ these dár/ ing mén.
[E II, 2304]

Awáy.// Poore *Gáu/ estón*,// that hást/ no fríend/ but mé.
[E II, 1021]

Yóu that/ were né're/ possést/ of wéalth,/ are pleás'd/ with wánt.
[JofM, 434]

Me thínkes/ that tówne/ there shóuld/ be *Tróy*, yon Í/ *das* híll.
[*Dido*, 302]

Surrey had used a few alexandrines, and Bishop Joseph Hall,
who ridiculed Marlowe fiercely, interspersed them among the
pentameters of his satires, as did John Marston. Shakespeare,
probably in imitation of Marlowe, uses an occasional alexandrine, but it is an exaggeration to say that "there is not a
play of Shakespeares in which alexandrines do not frequently
occur." [32] Unlike Marlowe, Shakespeare seems to have come to
dislike alexandrines and to have cut them out of his own work
when revising. The 1597 quarto of *Romeo and Juliet* contains
ninety-two such lines, but in the 1599 quarto there are only six.
In *Richard III* the alexandrine

And húgd/ me ín/ his árms,// and kínd/ ly kíst/ my chéeke

is later revised and reappears as

And pít/ tied mé,// and kínd/ ly kíst/ my chéeke.[33]

[30] See II. 205–209 and Georg Schoeneich: *Litterarische Einfluss Spensers auf Marlowe*; Charles Crawford: *Collectanea*, I. 47–100.
[31] Tucker Brooke: "Marlowe's Versification and Style," SP, 18: 191 Ap 1922; J. P.
Collier: HEDP (1831), III. 119.
[32] Boswell's Malone (1821), I. 537; *Troilus and Cressida*, IV. v. 243; V. ii. 178.
[33] Furness Variorum *Richard III*, p. 163; James Spedding in Shakspere Society
Transactions, ser. 1, no. 2, 1875–76, pp. 41–48.

Bartholomew Griffin, known to have been under Marlowe's influence,[34] also mingles alexandrines with pentameter lines, as do Massinger, Jonson, and Marlowe's friend Thomas Watson. John Fletcher has fifty-two in his play, *The Loyal Subject*. As other examples, we have:

When once he smiles, to laugh: and when he sighs, to grieve.
[Hall's *Satires*, I. vii]
In mightiest Inkhornismes he can thither wrest.
[*Ibid.* I. viii]
And be not outward sober, inlye impudent.
[Marston: *Satire* IV]
Compare me to Leander struggling in the waves.
[Griffin: *Fidessa*]
Compare me to Pygmalion with his image sotted.
[*Ibid.*]
With that away she went, and I did wake withall.
[*Ibid.*]
Melissa mother is and fautrix to the bee.
[Watson: *Hecatompathia*, 92]

In *Tamburlaine* Marlowe usually employs alexandrines to open or close speeches.[35] Sometimes they are used to give emphasis to a special appeal or entreaty, as when Tamburlaine begins:

Ortigius and Menaphon, my trustie friendes,[36]

and the fact that such appeals are likely to come at the beginning of speeches accounts in part for the large number of alexandrines in this position. In the great soliloquy of Barabas, with which *The Jew of Malta* opens, there is the odd but effective line,

Bágs (x)/ of fiér/ y óp/ als,// sáp/ phires ám/ ethýsts,

which is mathematically an alexandrine, but in which Alleyn's voice and gesture probably gave the single word, "bags," the effect of a whole line.[37]

---

[34] See II. 127-128.

[35] Ll. 309, 1318, 1569, 1916 begin speeches; ll. 404, 1986, 2277, 4195, 4329 close speeches. Line 454 closes an act. Cf. Brooke, *op. cit.*, p. 191.

[36] I *Tamb.* 734.

[37] *Jew of Malta*, 60. See Chris. Brennan in *Beiblatt zur Anglia*, 16: 208 (1905).

It is not always possible, as we have seen, to distinguish between genuine alexandrines and lines with two redundant
syllables at the end, instead of the usual feminine ending with
one redundant syllable. Marlowe himself may not always have
been clear which he was writing, for he probably knew less about
his own theory of prosody than the modern students who
analyze him. Technique was, as always in the arts, at least
partly an unconscious process. If the result pleased the poet's
ear and the actor's and the audience's, that was quite enough.

4. Marlowe makes relatively slight use of the feminine ending, but he represents an advance on Kyd and Greene, who
make practically no use of it at all. In *Tamburlaine* feminine
endings appear in only 2 per cent of the lines. As early as
Love's Labour's Lost, Shakespeare is using feminine endings in
7.7 per cent of his blank verse lines, and this percentage rises
steadily, reaching its height in *All's Well That Ends Well*,
where 29.4 per cent of the lines have feminine endings. The
later Elizabethan drama carried this to still further extremes,
mainly under the influence of John Fletcher.[38] Marlowe, on the
other hand, whose work falls wholly in the very early period,
increases his use of feminine endings very little, so that even in
Edward the Second, a late play, the proportion has risen only to
3.8 per cent.

5. Marlowe's verse also shows an increased subtlety in variation through the use of the caesura. Here, again, he uses no devices which are unknown to his predecessors — Schipper even
asserts that in this respect "he differs little from his predecessors." [39] But, in fact, Marlowe uses the caesura with a more
skilful and conscious artistry; or, if the process is not wholly
deliberate, with a far surer taste. This is partly because Marlowe — short though his literary life was — wrote more blank
verse than any English poet before him, and wrote very little
else.[40] He had, therefore, more opportunity for developing his
blank verse technique, which shows the improvement one might
expect in the later plays as contrasted with the earlier.

[38] Tucker Brooke in SP, 19: 189 (1922), and Neilson and Thorndike: *Facts about
Shakespeare*, pp. 71–72.
[39] J. Schipper: *Hist. Eng. Versification*, p. 223.
[40] For Marlowe's lost and doubtfully attributed work, see Chapter XVII.

Surrey had employed the epic caesura occasionally, after the second foot — as, for example, in the line:

Líke to/ th'ádder// with vén/ emous hér/ bes féd.[41]

Marlowe usually places his caesura after the second or third foot, but occasionally, especially for emphasis, places it after the first. Thus we have it after the second foot (fourth syllable) in such lines as

Thóusands/ of mén// drówn'd in/ *Asphál/ tis* Láke.
[II *Tamb.* 4315]

In *Gér/ manỳ,*// withín/ a tówne/ calld *Rhódes.*
[DF, 12]

Now *Má/ homét,*// if thóu/ haue án/ y pówer.
[II *Tamb.* 4298]

Sweete fáth/ er héere,// vntó/ thy múr/ dered ghóst.
[E II. 2667]

Farewéll/ faire Quéene,// wéepe not/ for *Mór/ timér.*
[E II, 2632]

We have it after the third foot (sixth syllable) in such lines as

And bríng/ my fún/ erall róbes:// accúr/ sed héad.
[E II, 2663]

Forbíd/ not mé/ to wéepe,// hé was/ my fáther.
[E II, 2602]

Distrést/ *Olým/ piá,*// whose wéep/ ing éies.
[II *Tamb.* 3882]

Wrétched/ *Zenóc/ raté,*// that líu/ est to sée.
[I *Tamb.* 2101]

Ah faíre/ *Zenóc/ raté,*// diuíne/ *Zenóc/ raté.*
[I *Tamb.* 1916]

Wél sáid/ *Theríd/ amas,*// spéake in/ that móod.
[I *Tamb.* 1138]

These ár/ guménts/ he v́s'de,// and mán/ y móre.
[H&L, I. 329]

Stríu'd with/ redóub/ led stréngth:// the móre/ she stríued.
[H&L, II. 67]

We also have the caesura after the first foot (second syllable) in lines like

Táke it:// whát are/ you moóude,// pítie/ you mé?
[E II, 2088]

---

41 Page 131 of the Aldine ed. (London: Bell & Daldy, 1886).

My lórd,// I féare/ me ít/ will próoue/ too trúe.
[E II, 2645]
Confésse;// what méane/ you, Lórds,/ whó should/ confésse?
[JofM, 2028]
Whose thís?// Fáire *Ab*/ igáll/ the rích/ Iewes dáughter.
[JofM, 608]
Amásde,// swim v́p/ and dówne/ vpón/ the wáues.
[II *Tamb.* 4318]

Sometimes Marlowe places a caesura after the third syllable, squarely in the middle of the second foot. Thus the lines:

Techél/ *les*,// drówne/ them áll,// mán, woman/ and child.
[II *Tamb.* 4281]
Thérefore/ cóme,// dál/ liance dán/ geréth/ our líues.
[E II, 2268]
Art thóu/ kíng,// must/ I díe/ at thý/ commáund?
[E II, 2435]
Faire créat/ ure,// lét/ me spéake/ withóut/ offénce.
[H&L, I. 199]

Marlowe sometimes omits the caesura altogether, or — since it is probably impossible to write a decasyllabic verse with no pause whatever — makes it so slight as to be almost imperceptible. Mayor asserts that "most lines have only the final pause," [42] but this is exaggeration. The caesura has certainly, however, very nearly disappeared in such lines as

Why should I dye then, or basely dispaire?
[DF, 642]
Carolus the fift, at whose pallace now
[DF, 918]

but even in these lines one feels faint, slight pauses after "then" and "fift." On the other hand, while it is possible to force caesuras into these lines, the natural impulse of the voice runs smoothly and evenly from end to end, as in most of the lines below.

One gets the full effect of Marlowe's alternation of these rhythmic variations in scanning this passage from *Edward the Second*:

The greefes of priuate men are soone allayde,
But not of kings,// the forrest Deare being strucke,
Runnes to an herbe that closeth vp the wounds,

[42] Joseph B. Mayor: *Chapters on English Metre* (1886), p. 144.

But when the imperiall *Li*ons flesh is gorde,
He rends and teares it with his wrathfull pawe,
[And] highly scorning, that the lowly earth
Should drinke his bloud,// mounts vp into the ayre: [43]

This is, on the whole, extremely regular verse. Yet it is saved
from monotony by the two caesuras and by the substitution of
a trochee for an iambus in the third and seventh lines and a
single anapaest at the end of the second.

6. Though he is the most resourceful in variation of this
kind among the early writers of blank verse, Marlowe's reper-
toire of metrical substitutions is by no means large. Compared
with the verse of a Keats, his is singularly unvaried; for, though
Marlowe does vary more than other Elizabethans of his decade,
he still adheres closely to the strictly iambic line with five regular stresses — what Tucker Brooke has called "the heady music
of the five marching iambs." The least appreciated wonder of
Marlowe's poetry is the wide range of effect he produced with
means so limited.

His most frequent device is the introduction of a trochee for
an iambus. He uses spondees and his characteristic pyrrhic
feet occasionally, but the latter are such as can, by a little forc-
ing, be scanned as iambic, and as such the poet may have regarded them. He employs anapaests freely, but makes very
little use of the dactyl. In spite of these substitutions, his verse
is far more conservatively regular than Shakespeare's, especially in Shakespeare's final period; and it seems positively
ironclad when compared with the extreme freedom in substitution of Fletcher and other dramatists in the later years of the
drama, just before the outbreak of the Civil War.

Marlowe substituted both trochee and anapaest at any point
in his line. His use of the trochee is illustrated in two lines of
Tamburlaine:

Áh sac/ red *Máh*/ omét,// thóu that/ hast séene
Míllions/ of Túrkes// pérish/ by *Tám*/ burláine.[44]

This is much like the use of a trochee for emphasis at the beginning of a line, which we find in Surrey's *Aeneid*:

Trápt by/ decéit;// some, fór/ ced bý/ his téars.

[43] Ll. 1994–2000.   [44] Ll. 4357–4358.

Examples of the same device used for emphasis in mid-verse are:

> But stíl/ the pórts/ were shút://villaine/ I sáy.
> [II *Tamb.* 4207]
> And hágs/ hówle for/ my deáth/ at *Chár*/ ons shóre.
> [E II, 1957]

As illustrations of Marlowe's use of anapaests, often in pairs, we may take the following lines:

> Áre but/ obéyd/ in their séu/ erall próu/ incés.
> [DF, 86]
> Alréad/ y Faús/ tus hath ház/ arded thát/ for thée.
> [DF, 465]
> Spéake *Faus*/ *tus*,// dó/ you delíu/ er thís/ as your déede?
> [DF, 543]
> Sweete *Hél*/ *en*,// máke/ me immór/ tall wíth/ a kísse.
> [DF, 1330]
> And wíth/ the rést/ accóm/ panie hím/ to his gráue.
> [E II, 2656]

The fourth foot of the last example — "panie him" — is read by Mayor [45] as an anapaest; but these are syllables over which an actor would pass lightly and swiftly, the aspirate barely sounding. It is probably a pyrrhic rather than an anapaest. The very last foot of the line, on the other hand — "to his graue" — is an unquestionable anapaest.

Dactyls, though rare, are used with exquisite skill when they are used at all, as in the lines:

> Shádowing/ more béau/ tie ín/ their áy/ rie brówes
> [DF, 157]
> Shalbé/ at mý/ commaúnd,// Émperours/ and Kíngs
> [DF, 85]
> Hé being/ a nóu/ ice, knéw/ not whát/ she méant.
> [H&L, II. 13]

The prolonged foot in each case gives emphasis as well as musical variety, the dactyl falling, according to Marlowe's usual method, either in the first or the fourth foot.

Use of the amphibrach is very rare. Few of the prosodists who have analyzed Marlowe's verse admit that he used it at all.

---

[45] *Op. cit.*, p. 143.

It is usually the result of an extra light syllable in the last foot, as in the following examples:

> And whát/ he díd/ she wíl/ linglý/ requíted.
> [H&L, II. 28]
> And túrn'd/ asíde,/ and tó/ her sélfe/ laménted.
> [H&L, II. 34]
> Loue ál/ waies mákes/ those él/ oquént/ that háue it.
> [H&L, II. 72]

Spondees, always difficult to identify in accentual verse, though clear enough in Greek or Latin quantitative verse, rarely appear in Marlowe. He seems to use this foot most frequently in half-completed lines where the scansion is doubtful, and where he may have been relying on the actor's voice or the actor's gesture to help him out. As examples we find:

> Me thínkes/ thát tówne/ thére shóuld/ be *Tŕoy*.
> [*Dido*, 302]
> Wéll dóone,/ *Néd*.
> [E II, 98]
> My Lórd/ Cárdin/ all óf/ Loráine,/ téll mé.
> [MP, 636]
> Héare, héare,/ O héare/ *Iár*/ *bus* pláin/ ing práyers.
> [*Dido*, 1102]

The last example could, of course, be scanned as an alexandrine with pauses in the first two feet.

Use of the light, practically unstressed pyrrhic foot is a marked characteristic of Marlowe's early verse, particularly at the end of the line, where it becomes the so-called "pyrrhic ending." In Marlowe's later plays it gradually becomes less frequent, though it never entirely disappears. This is part of the general tendency which the plays show toward increasing simplicity and verisimilitude in style and vocabulary, as well as in meter. In the beginning Marlowe had a habit of sounding *-ion*, which we should ordinarily make into one syllable today, as two syllables. This accounts for a great many, though not by any means all, of his pyrrhic feet.

Much has been made of this characteristic of his pronunciation; but, as a matter of fact, the university-bred poet was merely following rather more carefully than other dramatists

the accepted pronunciation of his day. The modern pronunciation with *sh* or *zh* of such words as *nation* or *vision* had not yet
developed. Careful speech made *-ion* into two syllables, though
for metrical purposes it might be sounded either as one or two,
a liberty of which most poets took full advantage.[46] The authors of *Gorboduc*, for some reason, habitually sounded *-ion* as one
syllable.

Marlowe also makes pyrrhic feet with many other syllables,
in words such as "follower," "senator," "warrior," "barbarous," and "idolaters." He also frequently used the letters *r*, *l*,
m, *n* as syllables, so that pronunciations like "Eng(e)land,"
"Eu(o)rope" are necessary to make his verses scan.

All this gave a lightness and grace — what Tucker Brooke
calls "a tripping flow" — to his verse; and its gradual abandon-
ment in later plays by no means contributes to the improvement of Marlowe's verse. His verse did improve, but this
change was hardly one of the improvements. Examples are
abundant:

And séeke/ not tó/ inrích/ thy fól/lowérs.
[I Tamb. 205]

Nóbly/ resólu'd,/ sweet fríends/ and fól/lowérs.
[I Tamb. 256]

And míght/ ie kíngs/ shall bé/ our Sén/ atórs.
[I Tamb. 393]

But gíue/ him wár/ ning ánd/ more wár/ rióurs.
[I Tamb. 808]

Let nót/ a mán/ so víle/ and bár/ baróus.
[I Tamb. 1011]

But ére/ I díe/ those fóule/ Idól/ atérs.
[I Tamb. 1337]

But íf/ these thréats/ mooue nót/ submís/ sión,
Bláck are/ his cóll/ ours, blácke/ Pauíl/ ión.
[I Tamb. 1430–1431]

Befóre/ we párt/ with óur/ possés/ sión.
[I Tamb. 340]

I, wéal/ thier fárre/ then án/ y Chrís/ tián.
[JofM, 166]

I, pól/ icíe?/ that's théir/ profés/ sión.
[JofM, 393]

[46] Henry Bradley: "Shakespeare's English." In *Shakespeare's England* (ed. Sidney
Lee, 1916), II. 542.

To énd/ thy life/ with rés/ olú/ tión.
                                    [JofM, 2364]
That íf/ withóut/ effús/ ión/ of blóud.
                                    [E II, 1468]
To máke/ my prép/ ará/ tión/ for Fráunce.
                                    [E II, 1396]

7. Marlowe's verse is marked by a number of "irregulari-ties." He employs various devices which break the perfect correctness of the verse — omitted syllables, single vowels sounded twice, and interpolated, extra-metrical words — which justify themselves either by the variety they give to the line or by their dramatic appropriateness.

An omitted syllable, resulting in a nine-syllable line, is some-times used to give the effect of a sob of horror or anger, or merely to provide emphasis, as in the following examples:

O Góds,/ is thís// (x) *Tám*/ *burláine*/ the thíefe?
                                    [I *Tamb.* 704]
Iniúr/ ious víl/ laines,// thiéues,// (x) rún/ nagátes.
                                    [I *Tamb.* 1323]
How prét/ ilié/ he laúghs,// (x) góe/ ye wágge.
                                    [*Dido*, 1390]
Héere, (x)/ héere: (x)/ (x) nów/ sweete Gód/ of heáuen.
                                    [E II, 2093]
And nóne/ but wé/ shall knów/ (x) whére/ he lieth.
                                    [E II, 2184]

In these cases Marlowe has contented himself with omitting the unaccented syllables. Occasionally he went even further in his irregularity and dropped a beat, allowing a full foot to be represented only by its light syllables, as in

Yóu are/ *Achát*/ *es*, (x)// or Í/ decíu'd,
                                    [*Dido*, 344]

where the actor's method of delivery is all that can make the difference between verse and prose.

Marlowe must also have relied on the actor's voice to roll out a vowel or deliberately make a liquid or nasal consonant into a full syllable and save the meter. His habit of vocalizing *r*, *l*, *m*, *n*, which has already been alluded to, was not peculiar to himself, but was common Elizabethan practice, or became so not long after his day. It is a natural device for a poet in difficulties with hasty work for the stage. Examples are:

> Creáte/ him Pró/ (o)réx/ of *Áf/ fricá.*
> [I *Tamb.* 97]
> As món/ st(e)róus/ as *Gór/ gon,* prínce/ of Héll.
> [I *Tamb.* 1389]
> How fár/ hence líes/ the Gál/ ley, sáy/ (y) yóu?
> [II *Tamb.* 2545]
> And máde/ a vóy/age ín/ to *Eú/ (o)rópe.*
> [II *Tamb.* 2777]

8. Another general Elizabethan practice was the free introduction of an entirely extra-metrical word, usually an emphatic negative, a vocative, or a complete phrase of direct address, even if it contained two beats and today seems to add two full feet to the decasyllabic line. This practice seems to have originated with Marlowe and to have been retained throughout the Elizabethan and Jacobean periods. It would doubtless have persisted even after the Restoration had it not been for the rigid refining process which verse underwent at the hands of John Dryden. In some of Marlowe's passages, freedom in adding or omitting syllables reaches very nearly the utmost possible license, and suggests how easy and natural was the gradual transition to the extraordinary freedom which developed a few decades after him, when Fletcher and his fellows ended by reducing blank verse very nearly to the level of highly rhythmic prose.

In the following examples, Marlowe's hypermetrical syllables are italicized:

> *Tám/ burláine?*// A Scýth/ ian Shép/ heard, só/ imbél/ lishéd?
> [I *Tamb.* 350]
> *No, nó.*/ Then wíl/ I héad/ long rúnne/ intó/ the eárth.
> [DF, 1440, 1441]
> *No,*/ for thís/ exám/ ple Í'le/ remáine/ a Iéw.
> [JofM, 1705]
> *No,*/ but wásh/ your fáce/, and sháue/ awáy/ your béard.
> [E II, 2296]
> *No,*/ vnlésse/ thou bríng/ me néwes/ of *Éd/wards* déath.
> [E II, 2377]

Irregularities of this sort greatly scandalized the editors of the nineteenth century, who resorted to various devices to patch up the poet's work on behalf of his reputation. They would have done better to let the passages stand, for they are clearly what Marlowe intended, and his example was followed by Shakespeare himself:

I tell thee,/ He dúrst/ as wéll/ have mét/ the dévil/ alóne.
[I *Henry IV*, I. iii. 115]

O, sir,/ your prés/ ence ís/ too bóld/ and pér/ emptóry.
[*Ibid.* I. iii. 17]

'Sblood!/ When yóu/ and hé/ came báck/ from Ráv/ enspúrgh.
[*Ibid.* I. iii. 248]

Certain of these lines, both Marlowe's and Shakespeare's, could be scanned as alexandrines. Many, however, add two beats instead of one, and, as the extra words are always of about the same sort, they are probably best treated as mere interpolations. This view is the more persuasive because Shakespeare, though he did use an occasional alexandrine, certainly did not share Marlowe's fondness for the six-stress line.

9. Not only did Marlowe add or drop syllables — he also wrote occasional lines of four beats, three beats, two beats, or even one beat, where dramatic exigency required a short, sharp interchange. Many of the hypermetrical lines may be ascribed to the one-beat line which has been printed as part of the decasyllable.

These abbreviated lines are not due to a breaking up of the regular decasyllabic line between two or more characters. Instead, for short periods the playwright simply drops out of the decasyllabic scansion entirely and returns only when the mood of the dialogue changes. The brutal scenes in which the captives are ill-treated in *Tamburlaine* contain many abrupt verses of this sort, as do other passages intended to suggest the bluntness of the soldier:

Bring óut/ my fóot-stoole.
[I *Tamb.* 1445]

Chíde her/ *Aníppe.*
[*Ibid.* 1515]

Put him ín/ agáine.
[*Ibid.* 1526]

Cóme (x)/ bring ín/ the Túrke.
[*Ibid.* 1570]
Wél sir,// (x) whát/ of thís?
[II *Tamb.* 2509]
What nów?/ In lóue?
[I *Tamb.* 302]
Néwes (x)/ néwes (x).
[*Ibid.* 305]
How nów,/ whát's the/ mátter?
[*Ibid.* 306]
Cóme (x)// let vs mártch.
[*Ibid.* 332]

Sometimes the poet seems merely to have counted wrong, left out a foot, and produced a tetrameter by inadvertence. Lines like the following give no effect that could not have been secured with the conventional decasyllable:

Where ís/ this Scýth/ ian *Tám*/ *burláine*?
[I *Tamb.* 348]
My Lórd,/ how cán/ you súf/ fer thése?
[I *Tamb.* 1664]
Tis bráue/ indéed/ my bóy,// wél dóne.
[II *Tamb.* 4261]
Then sháll/ the Cáth/ olick fáith/ of Róme.
[MP, 644]
Cárthage,/ my fríend/ ly hóst,/ adúe.
[*Dido,* 1151]

Where there is swift interchange in a dialogue, Marlowe is very likely to write a series of these short lines which cannot possibly be combined to fit into the decasyllabic mold. There is a plain example of this in the dialogue between the Persian king, Mycetes, and Tamburlaine; and another in the dialogue between Faustus and Mephistophilis after signing their compact.[47]

10. Marlowe has already learned the trick of dividing an orthodox decasyllable between two characters. This device appears even in so irregular a scene as that between Faustus and Mephistophilis. Thus:

Fau. . . . Tel me, where is the place that men call hell?
Me. Vnder the heauens.
Fau. I, but where about? [48]

[47] I *Tamb.* 679–705; *Doctor Faustus*, 548–611.   [48] *Doctor Faustus*, 548–550.

This is a commonplace of later dramatic prosody, but Marlowe makes surprisingly little use of it, especially in the earlier plays, preferring his own abrupt, irregular lines — perhaps because he worked in haste, perhaps because he did not care.

11. Spenser's strong influence on Marlowe inclined him to alliteration, especially at the beginning of his career. *Dido* in particular has many alliterative passages, such as

> The surges, his fierce souldiers, to the spoyle.
> [69]
> Ay me! the Starres supprisde like *Rhesus* Steedes.
> [72]
> The rest we feare are foulded in the flouds.
> [279]

This kind of thing tends to disappear in later plays, like most of Marlowe's overelaboration, but alliterative passages are plentiful in *Tamburlaine*, where rich ornateness is deliberately sought. Thus we have lines like:

> . . . the man of fame,
> The man that in the forhead of his fortune,
> Beares figures of renowne and myracle.
> [I *Tamb.* 456–458]
> To see his choller shut in secrete thoughtes,
> And wrapt in silence of his angry soule.
> [I *Tamb.* 1055–1056]
> Blacke is the beauty of the brightest day.
> [II *Tamb.* 2969]

Marlowe also alliterates on two sounds at once, as in the lines:

> And from their shieldes strike flames of lightening)
> All fearefull foldes his sailes, and sounds the maine.
> [I *Tamb.* 1066–1067]

12. Though he could use rhyme to exquisite effect, as his poems show, Marlowe was not a rhymer. On the stage, he seems to have deliberately avoided rhyme — no one can miss the note of contempt in the opening lines of *Tamburlaine* for

> . . . iygging vaines of riming mother wits,
> And such conceits as clownage keepes in pay.

Unlike Shakespeare, he rarely uses a rhyming tag to round off a scene. Only one such couplet appears in *Tamburlaine* [809–

810], and even there the final line is broken. On the other hand, Marlowe frequently does use blank verse distichs to round off scenes, and he may thus have unconsciously led the way to the later use of rhymed couplets for this purpose by Shakespeare and other writers of a younger day.

The first part of *Tamburlaine* has only 67 rhymed lines out of a total of 2316; and *Doctor Faustus* has but eight.[49] Yet so easily did music come to the point of Marlowe's pen that one can see him again and again barely avoiding rhyme by slipping into assonance in lines which end: ". . . witnesses . . . for this [30–31]; . . . home . . . Dame [73–74]; . . . followers . . . Emperours [262–263]; . . . one . . . possession [339–340]." If he had followed Marlowe more closely, the young Shakespeare would have avoided the excesses of *Love's Labour's Lost*, where almost two-thirds of the play is in rhyme.

13. Marlowe's finest lyrics are really passages imbedded in his dramatic dialogue. Faustus' address to Helen, the apostrophe to poetry and beauty in *Tamburlaine*, and the lament over Zenocrate [50] are as truly lyrical as "The Passionate Shepherd." They cry aloud for music. It is true that they do not rhyme and they are not in stanzaic form, but there is such music in the blank verse that it could easily be sung. A modern stage manager (if he could get anything like them) would probably let his players speak them over music.

All this because Marlowe is the first of the Elizabethan dramatists to see that, in addition to rhyme and rhythm, poetry has yet another resource — the music of speech itself. This is the most vexed of all questions in the technique of verse. The textbooks of metrics are usually either silent or absurd; but no one who can hear verse at all can fail to distinguish between a definitely harsh line like Matthew Arnold's

> Who prop, thou askst, in these bad days my mind,

and the melody of

> Charm'd magic casements, opening on the foam
> Of perilous seas, in faery lands forlorn.[51]

[49] Ruth Janet Barber: *Certain Elements of the Structure of Pre-Shakespearean Dramatic Blank Verse* (Stanford Master's Thesis, 1923, MS.), p. 10.

[50] *Doctor Faustus*, 1328–1347; I *Tamb.* 1942–1954; II *Tamb.* 2969–3005.

[51] Arnold: "To a Friend" (Oxford ed., 1913), p. 40. Keats: "Ode to a Nightingale," st. 7.

Keats himself makes the distinction:

> Forlorn! the very word is like a bell.

As a matter of coldly scientific fact, it *is* like a bell, and it is the boom of the *o* vowels and the liquid and nasal consonants that produce the effect, an effect which poets have employed since Homer's

Δεῦρ' ἄγε νῦν, πολύαιν' 'Οδυσεῦ, μέγα κῦδος 'Αχαιῶν [52]

but which the English poetry of Marlowe's day had yet to rediscover.

Such effects were rare before Marlowe and were usually confined to lyric poetry. One finds passages like that in Chaucer. One finds them in Sidney. One does not find them, nor does one find anything like them, in *Gorboduc* or *The Spanish Tragedy* or *The Misfortunes of Arthur*. One does find them in Marlowe's verse, find them everywhere, and find them ever after on the Elizabethan stage. From them — probably, but also, alas! unprovably — Milton and Keats learned some valued and valuable lessons.

Lines like these do not ordinarily occur in the strictly dramatic portions of Marlowe's verse. The rush and bustle of the stage would have obscured his music. But in moments of spiritual high tension, in lyric moments and apostrophes, Marlowe falls into melodious, almost Keatsian music, using the sounds of *o* and *l* and *m* and *w* as carefully as Keats himself in lines like

> And all combin'd in Beauties worthinesse.
> [I *Tamb.* 1951]
> When wandring *Phoebes* Iuory cheeks were scortcht.
> [II *Tamb.* 4625]
> This is the ware wherein consists my wealth.
> [JofM, 68]
> Are smoothly gliding downe by *Candie* shoare.
> [JofM, 81]
> As faire as was *Pigmalions* Iuory gyrle,
> Or louely *Io* metamorphosed.
> [II *Tamb.* 2529–2530]

[52] *Odyssey*, XII. 185. Some texts give the opening words as Δεῦρ' ἄγ' ἰών.

Marlowe saves lines like these for moments when the bustle of his mimic world is stilled for an instant and pure beauty may come uppermost — on Aristotle's principle that ornamented language is appropriate only to the quiet moments of the plot.[53]

14. Marlowe was the first Elizabethan dramatist to develop the "verse paragraph," in which the thought flows on freely from line to line, often without pause, or with end-stopped lines distributed irregularly, so as not to break the thought or the mood. He clung, it is true, to the end-stopped line more meticulously than his successors, and so never fully developed this device, but one finds it frequently in all the plays, most notably in the famous passage beginning

> If all the pens that euer poets held . . .

in *Tamburlaine*.[54]

The first experimenters with blank verse in England seem to have felt that the blank verse pentameter line was simply the heroic couplet with the rhyme left off. Blank verse before Marlowe was usually a succession of blank verse distichs, in which pairs of unrhymed lines were held together by the pauses, by the meter, or by the thought. The pairs formed units that often were complete sentences with a slight pause at the end of the first line and a marked pause at the end of the second.

Marlowe, in his emotional passages, broke wholly free from this and let his thought and the white heat of his feeling pour on from line to line until they reached an end, logical at once in thought, in emotion, and in metre.

Such were the implements with which the mighty line was produced; but it is well to remember that they were not new implements. Practically all of them had been used before. A few had been used by Spenser quite as skilfully as by Marlowe. And yet nothing like the mighty line had ever sounded on an English stage, and rarely in a page of English verse, before. Out of old materials, subtly fused in the fiery emotions of that passionate, agonized soul, out of Marlowe's perpetual reach for

[53] *Poetics*, XXIV. xxiii.
[54] I *Tamb*. 1942. See II. 184–185.

everything that always eluded his grasp, the mighty line was made, a line that Milton [55] and Keats were sometimes to alter, sometimes technically to improve, but never, at its best, to surpass in beauty, melody, or the heights of intense feeling and lyric or dramatic emotion.

[55] Swinburne remarks (*North American Review*, 203: 746 My 1916): "Milton long afterwards prolonged and intensified by reverberations 'Marlowe's "mighty line." '" John Forster also refers to Marlowe, "to the modulation and music of whose verse Milton had large obligations" (*Catalogue of the Printed Books and Manuscripts Bequeathed by the Reverend Alexander Dyce*, p. xix). See also the introduction to the edition of *Doctor Faustus* by S. C. Sarcar, p. xxii.

CHAPTER XVI

MARLOWE AND SHAKESPEARE

Was it the proud full sail of his great verse,
. . . That did my ripe thoughts in my brain inhearse?

Sonnet LXXXVI

THE EXACT RELATIONSHIP between the work of
Marlowe and the work of Shakespeare will remain in
doubt forever. It is perfectly clear — and is, indeed,
universally admitted — that such a relationship did
exist; and that Marlowe, as Swinburne says, "guided Shakespeare into the right way of work." [1] But speculation as to
the precise nature of this relationship between the two poets
ranges from one extreme, which would assign the shoemaker's
son of Canterbury a fair share of all the plays ordinarily regarded as the work of the tanner's son of Stratford, to another
extreme, which admits at most some slight borrowing and early
imitation on Shakespeare's part.

Where so much uncertainty reigns, it is well to make sure
first of the undisputed facts, before attempting either to survey
the opposing views of warring schools of Elizabethan critics or
to set up new views in their stead.

We may begin, then, with the undoubted fact — or rather,
since there is no absolute evidence, with the generally admitted
opinion — that Christopher Marlowe wrote more plays than
have come down to us. For a modern playwright, seven plays
in approximately five years would be a rich harvest; and a
series of resounding successes like the two parts of *Tamburlaine*,
Doctor Faustus, and *The Jew of Malta* would provide an income
more than adequate for the brief period of Marlowe's active
literary life. But even when Elizabethan theatrical conditions
had become more regularized and somewhat more favorable to
the dramatist, in the decades after Marlowe's death, the ut-

[1] *Encyclopædia Britannica*, article "Marlowe." See his article on "King Lear,"
Harper's, 106: 3 D 1902, and *Age of Shakespeare*, p. 14. See also Ward, HEDL, I. 361.

most profit that a play could possibly yield the author was from four to ten pounds.

Even assuming that Marlowe added secret service work to playwriting, or that he was for a time an actor, he could hardly have made a living answering at all to his apparently luxurious tastes from these notoriously ill-paid professions. Nor, from what we know of Elizabethan patrons, is it likely that Sir Thomas Walsingham's bounty made up the necessary difference.

Presumably, therefore, Marlowe wrote plays that have not come down to us. At least the name of one survives — that *Maiden's Holiday* the manuscript of which Warburton's cook destroyed to make coverings for her pies;[2] and there are vague rumors of a play on Helen of Troy, which may be due to the famous "thousand ships" passage in *Doctor Faustus*, to the translation of Coluthus,[3] or to confusion with *Dido*.[4] The attribution of *Lust's Dominion* to Marlowe on the title page of the 1657 edition is no doubt false, but it suggests that the publisher at least had reason to expect his public to believe that Marlowe had written plays other than those now known for his; and it may even mask the rewriting of a genuine earlier Marlowe play, now lost.[5]

There is nothing unusual in the total disappearance of Elizabethan plays, even by famous pens. The dramatic companies — usually eager to keep their manuscripts out of publishers' hands so long as there was a chance of stage profit from them — sometimes forgot to squeeze out the last drop of profit by selling the manuscript for publication after the play's welcome had been worn out on the boards. In many cases, the public may have been so tired of certain plays that there was no chance of interesting a bookseller any longer. Hence the total disappearance of plays like Kyd's *Ur-Hamlet*; Ben Jonson's *Richard Crookback*, which seems to have vanished even in his own lifetime; and three plays which Jonson wrote in collaboration — *Hot Anger Soon Cold*, with Porter and Chettle; *Page of*

[2] See II. 277.
[3] See II. 293–294.
[4] James T. Foard: "Joint authorship of Christopher Marlowe and William Shakespeare," *Gentleman's Magazine*, (OS) 288, (NS) 64: 140 F 1900.
[5] See II. 269–276.

Plymouth, a domestic tragedy, with Dekker; and *Robert II, King of Scots,* with Dekker and Chettle.

The lack of contemporary allusions to plays of Marlowe's other than those of the accepted canon is not especially surprising. Silence enshrouds the work of Shakespeare at this same period, and there is no really clear contemporary allusion to Marlowe as the author of *Tamburlaine,* nor any indication of his authorship on any of the early title pages,[6] though no one for a moment doubts his authorship. Many of the earlier Shakespearean quartos lack the author's name and, were it not for rare later quartos or the folios, would have to be assigned on internal evidence alone.

Marlowe is in this respect in no worse a plight than some of his lesser fellows. The attribution to Robert Greene of *George à Greene, the Pinner of Wakefield,* rests on the very slender evidence of manuscript notations in a copy of the 1590 edition, formerly in the Duke of Devonshire's library and now in the Folger Shakespeare Library.[7] That Elizabethan landmark, *The Spanish Tragedy,* is assigned to Kyd on the basis of a casual allusion in Thomas Heywood's *Apologie for Actors* (1612). Here even internal evidence fails, for there is not enough dramatic work definitely known to be Kyd's to make possible any reliable analysis of style, phrasing, or meter.[8]

Presumably, then, some of Marlowe's plays have been lost, especially if we accept Fleay's assertion that "Marlowe probably wrote two plays a year from 1587–1593," though we now have but seven "acknowledged as his." [9] Some of his lost work was probably written in collaboration and may have been signed by other writers. There is, it is true, no clear evidence that Marlowe ever collaborated with any author except Thomas Nashe, with whom he wrote *Dido*; but, given his undoubted financial need, the opportunities that the eager stage afforded him, and the well-known Elizabethan practice of frequent collaboration, it is not unreasonable to suppose that he may have

---

[6] See I. 190–191.

[7] The authenticity of this inscription has been questioned. See Samuel A. Tannenbaum: *Shaksperian Scraps,* pp. 42–50.

[8] CHEL, V. 151–152, 178; Ward, HEDL, II. 211; Chambers, *Eliz. Stage,* III. 395–397.

[9] *Chron. Hist. . . . Shakespeare,* p. 281.

done so. Since *Doctor Faustus* and *The Jew of Malta* were certainly revised by other pens, some of Marlowe's work, now unknown, may have been similarly revised, but so thoroughly that it is now unrecognizable.

Though Marlowe may have collaborated with, or been revised by, others, it is to his relations with his great successor that most interest attaches; and fortunately his relationship to Shakespeare is clearer than any other. That Shakespeare knew Marlowe's work is plain enough. Several of their characters can be paired off, one against the other, Shakespeare having obviously borrowed from Marlowe, since he had barely begun to write for the stage at the time of Marlowe's murder. Thus Barabas and Shylock; Abigail and Jessica; Edward II and Richard II; Kent in *Edward the Second* and Kent in *King Lear*; Young Mortimer and Hotspur; the Duke of Guise and Aaron; the murderers of the two little princes and the murderers of Edward II show many points of close resemblance. If Marlowe had never conceived these characters as he did, Shakespeare's characters would have been quite other than they are.

Shakespeare quotes Marlowe or alludes to his plays repeatedly. He lays *Tamburlaine*, *Doctor Faustus*, *Edward the Second*, *The Jew of Malta*, *The Massacre at Paris*,[10] *Dido*, *Hero and Leander*, the translation of Ovid, and "The Passionate Shepherd" under contribution — practically the whole of Marlowe's work as it is now known. The most famous of these borrowed passages is

> Dead shepherd, now I find thy saw of might,
> "Who ever loved that loved not at first sight?"

in *As You Like It*.[11] This is a double allusion. "Shepherd" refers to Marlowe's famous lyric, in the usual Elizabethan way of naming a poet indirectly by one of his works.[12] The second line is verbatim from *Hero and Leander*. Shakespeare again alludes to "How young Leander cross'd the Hellespont," in *Two*

[10] See II. 85–86.
[11] *As You Like it*, III. v. 81–82; *Hero and Leander*, I. 176. Also quoted by Thomas Heywood in *The Captives* (II. ii. 139–141), and by George Chapman, with slight changes, in *The Blinde Beggar of Alexandria* [*Comedies and Tragedies* (1873 ed.), I. 47]: "None euer loud but at first sight they loud." It was, of course, natural for Chapman to quote from a poem to which he had written the conclusion.
[12] See II. 122–123.

Gentlemen of Verona.[13] He quotes from Marlowe's translation of Ovid in *The Merchant of Venice*:

> Peace, ho! the moon sleeps with Endymion.

Marlowe had written:

> The Moone sleepes with *Endymion* euery day,[14]

a translation of Ovid's original Latin:

> Adspice, quot somnos iuueni donarit amato Luna,

so free that Shakespeare cannot possibly be quoting directly and translating for himself. In *Henry IV* mine Ancient Pistol parodies the "pamper'd jades" speech.[15] In *The Merry Wives of Windsor* Shakespeare allows Sir Hugh Evans to garble "The Passionate Shepherd," and also permits him an allusion to "three German devils, three Doctor Faustuses."[16] In *Hamlet* he at least seems to draw upon *Dido* for the Player King's speeches,[17] and he draws twice on *Edward the Second*. The lines of Young Mortimer, as he faces death:

> . . . Weepe not for *Mortimer*,
> That scornes the world, and as a traueller,
> Goes to discouer countries yet vnknowne

irresistibly recall a famous passage in Hamlet's soliloquy.[18] The method by which King Claudius causes Hamlet's father to be murdered is very like the villainy of Marlowe's Lightborne:

> . . . To take a quill
> And blowe a little powder in his eares,[19]

and there is an obvious echo in the lines:

> Before the Moone renew her borrowed light.
>   [I *Tamb.* 77]
> Thirty dozen moons with borrowed sheen.
>   [*Hamlet*, III. ii. 167]

[13] I. i. 22–27.
[14] *Merchant of Venice*, V. i. 109; *Elegies*, I. xiii. 43.
[15] 2 *Henry IV*, II. iv. 176–180. Cf. I. 238–240.
[16] *Merry Wives of Windsor*, III. i. 15–27; IV. v. 70–71.
[17] *Hamlet*, II. ii. Cf. II. 67–68.
[18] *Hamlet*, III. i. 79–80; *Edward the Second*, 2632–2634.
[19] *Hamlet*, I. v. 63; *Edward the Second*, 2366–2367.

There is a plain allusion to the "thousand ships" passage in *Troilus and Cressida*:

> . . . Why, she is a pearl,
> Whose price hath launch'd above a thousand ships,[20]

while Marlowe's "Is this the face" reappears in *Richard II*.[21]

Much Ado About Nothing contains a character named Hero and an allusion to "Leander the good swimmer." [22] The fifth act of *Midsummer-Night's Dream* probably makes two allusions to Marlowe and his work. One is an allusion by the play-acting clowns to "Limander" as the lover of "Helen," [23] which may be a malapropism for Hero and Leander. The other is the well-known passage beginning:

> The lunatic, the lover, and the poet,[24]

one of whom "sees more devils than vast hell can hold," while another "sees Helen's beauty," and the last possesses "the poet's eye, in a fine frenzy rolling." There is some Marlowe here, if only for Faustus' sake, and Helen's.

Other supposed echoes of Marlowe by Shakespeare are more doubtful, though close enough to be worth considering. Marlowe translated Ovid's "longas hiemes" as "winters lasting rage." This reappears in *Edward the Second* as "biting winters rage," and in *Cymbeline* as "winter's rages." [25] Again, Marlowe translated Ovid's

> Quem metuit quisque, perisse cupit

as "whom we feare, we wish to perish." This is very like Shylock's question,

> Hates any man the thing he would not kill? [26]

The Latin line in *Doctor Faustus*,

> Solamen miseris socios habuisse doloris,[27]

---

[20] *Troilus and Cressida*, II. ii. 81–82; *Doctor Faustus*, 1328. Cf. McKerrow's Nashe, III. 185.

[21] *Richard II*, IV. i. 281–286; *Doctor Faustus*, 1328. See II. 243.

[22] *Much Ado About Nothing*, V. ii. 30–31.

[23] *Midsummer-Night's Dream*, V. i. 199–200.

[24] *Midsummer-Night's Dream*, V. i. 7 ff.

[25] *Amores*, I. viii; *Elegies*, I. viii. 114; *Edward the Second*, 863; *Cymbeline*, IV. ii. 259.

[26] *Amores*, II. ii. 10; *Elegies*, II. ii. 10; *Merchant of Venice*, IV. i. 67.

[27] *Doctor Faustus*, 474.

seems to be translated in *The Rape of Lucrece*:

> It easeth some, though none it ever cured,
> To think their dolour others have endured,[28]

but the idea is an Elizabethan commonplace.

Mr. Oliver W. F. Lodge believes that Touchstone's allusion to Ovid and the Goths [29] is really an allusion to the burning of Marlowe's Ovid in 1599,[30] which some regard as the date of Shakespeare's *As You Like It*. This play certainly does refer to Marlowe elsewhere,[31] and if Mr. Lodge is correct, the reference to "great reckoning in a little room," [32] which follows the passage on Ovid, is all the more significant.

Shakespeare makes three further adaptations of *The Jew of Malta*, which, though not very significant in themselves, become so in the light of all his other borrowings. Barabas uses "Poppy and cold mandrake juyce" as an opiate. Can it be accident that Shakespeare writes in *Othello*:

> Not poppy, nor mandragora,
> Nor all the drowsy syrups of the world? [33]

Again, Barabas asks, "Let me haue law," and is ironically told, "You shall haue law." Shylock also says, "I crave the law," and is twice told, "The law allows it" and "The law doth give it." [34]

A further parallel may be due to Marlowe's suspected share in *Henry VI*:

> These armes of mine shall be thy Sepulchre.
> [JofM, 1192]
> These arms of mine shall be thy winding-sheet;
> My heart, sweet boy, shall be thy sepulchre.
> [3 *Henry VI*, II. v. 114–115]

---

[28] *Rape of Lucrece*, 1581–1582. The line reappears in Peele's *Honour of the Garter* (1593), Dekker's *Seven Deadly Sinnes* (1606), and Robert Chester's *Love's Martyr* (1600), but the two latter poems may be quoting from *Lucrece*. The idea enters English literature in Chaucer's *Troilus and Criseyde* [I. 708–709], and is probably even older. Its source in classical literature is obscure. Cf. B. Buchman: *Geflügelte Worte*, p. 333 (1912 ed.); *Baconiana*, 6: 154 Jy 1908; Boas' ed. of *Doctor Faustus*, p. 82n; R. M. Theobald: *Shakespeare Studies*, chap. V.

[29] *As You Like It*, III. iii. 9–10.

[30] See II. 169–171.   [31] See II. 208.   [32] See I. 373–374.

[33] *Jew of Malta*, 2083; *Othello*, III. iii. 330.

[34] *Jew of Malta*, 2040, 2042; *Merchant of Venice*, IV. i. 206, 303, 300.

Argument of this sort, from parallel passages, must always be used with the utmost caution. Often, what appear to be parallels are only pairs of commonplaces. The following passages, for example, are almost exactly alike, and yet their likeness proves nothing whatever:

> I arrest you of high treason.
> [*Edward II*, 1924]
> I arrest thee of high treason.
> [*Henry V*, II. ii. 145]
> I do arrest thee, traitor, of high treason.
> [2 *Henry IV*, IV. ii. 107]
> I arrest thee of high treason.
> [*Henry VIII*, I. i. 200]

Sometimes parallels represent merely common allusion to a common practice, or familiar proverb, as in these examples:

> And with my hand turne Fortunes wheel about.
> [I *Tamb.* 370]
> Giddy Fortune's furious fickle wheel.
> [*Henry V*, III. vi. 29]

> Into what corner peeres my *Halcions* bill?
> [JofM, 74]
> ... turn their halcyon beaks
> With every gale and vary of their masters.
> [*Lear*, II. ii. 85]

Other parallels are merely typical Elizabethan attitudes in similar situations. Hamlet's mad grief at Ophelia's grave is very like Tamburlaine's rant after the death of Zenocrate. Shakespeare may possibly have been thinking of Marlowe, but it would be injudicious to be positive about it. On the other hand, where the influence of one writer on another is known to exist, parallels so slight as to be otherwise negligible may have significance.

In the relationship of Marlowe to Shakespeare one further question — which is borrower and which lender — rarely arises, since Marlowe had been slain before Shakespeare began to write his most important plays. Where resemblance can be shown, the presumption therefore is that Shakespeare borrowed; and that such resemblances are fairly abundant, the passages already quoted suffice to prove.]

The abundance of Shakespeare's quotations, echoes, and allusions is especially important because he lets his other literary contemporaries severely alone.[35] At the very least, this shows a relationship of some kind between the two dramatists, even if Marlowe is not the rival poet of the Sonnets, against the "proud full sail" of whose "great verse" Shakespeare complains.[36] The description fits Marlowe's mighty line so perfectly that one is inclined to accept the passage as an allusion to him, though both Chapman and Peele have also been suggested by certain scholars of repute.[37] The traces of Machiavelli in Shakespeare may also be due to Marlowe; and, finally, there is a kind of rumor, not very well founded but persistent, that Marlowe and Shakespeare were friends.[38]

[It is not strange that the work of the young Shakespeare shows many evidences of Marlowe's influence; it would be strange if it did not, for that influence was all-pervasive in the English drama when Shakespeare was beginning to write.] In so small a world as theatrical London, it would have been almost equally strange for the promising young beginner from Stratford not to have some kind of acquaintance with the most brilliantly successful playwright of the day. They had tastes

[35] J. Q., Adams: *Life of Shakespeare*, pp. 132, 291.

[36] Sonnet LXXXVI.

[37] Cf. Arthur Acheson: *Shakespeare and the Rival Poet* (London and New York: John Lane, 1903), and Charles Crawford in *Jahrb*. 36: 117 (1900). Crawford tentatively suggests Peele because, though he had dedicated his *Honour of the Garter* to the Earl of Northumberland, he had also dedicated other work to the Earl of Southampton, Shakespeare's patron. See, however, N&Q, 11th ser., 5: 190 (1912), and R. M. Alden's ed. of the *Sonnets*.

[38] Tycho Mommsen, however, advances the theory that Marlowe and Shakespeare were unfriendly rivals. He thinks that Marlowe must have resented Shakespeare's adaptation of the mighty line and finds most of Shakespeare's quotations from Marlowe slightly derisive. (*Marlowe und Shakespeare*, pp. 2–6.) He regards Marlowe's lines in *Hero and Leander* (I. 471–472):

> And to this day is euerie scholler poore,
> Grosse gold from them runs headlong to the boore,

as a fling at Shakespeare's early success. This view overlooks the fact that Marlowe saw practically none of Shakespeare's work; that many other writers took up the mighty line; that the financial plight of scholars is a commonplace; and that these very lines are used by several other writers. (See II. 131.) E. Hermann in his *Shakespeare der Kämpfer* (Abt. II, pp. 623 ff.) believes that Shakespeare satirizes Marlowe in an unfriendly way, but his argument is based on doubtful allusions.

in common; they were about of an age; and they probably lived near each other, Marlowe in Norton Folgate and Shakespeare in Shoreditch.[39] More positive evidence of their acquaintance, indeed adequate evidence of any kind, is lacking; but their acquaintance, though hard to prove, is even harder to doubt.

In view of the common Elizabethan practice of collaboration between playwrights, it would have been natural, as soon as young William Shakespeare showed an interest in dramatic writing and some talent for it, to tell him off to work with Marlowe, an established figure, who would thus be able to take full advantage of his initial success, rushing play after play on the boards. The close similarity of *The Contention* and *The True Tragedie* both to Marlowe's and to Shakespeare's work would thus be explained, likewise the coupling of the two men in Greene's malicious *Groats-worth of Witte*.

But there are difficulties to be urged against this tempting opinion. There is no real external evidence that either Shakespeare or Marlowe ordinarily worked in collaboration with anyone, whatever other Elizabethan dramatists may have done. It is the less likely that Marlowe and Shakespeare worked together because they seem to have written for rival companies.

It was, however, easy for the manuscripts of one company to fall into the hands of another by legitimate purchase, especially at the dissolution of a group of players. The old manuscripts thus acquired, and also old manuscripts which had long been in the possession of a single company, usually required furbishing up to fit them for the stage anew. The mixture of recognizable bits of Marlowe and equally recognizable bits of Shakespeare may, therefore, be due to Shakespeare's revision of Marlowe's work, after Marlowe himself was dead. On the whole, this is in most cases a plausible conjecture; while in other cases Shakespeare is a conscious or unconscious imitator.

After years of speculation on this subject, three facts are demonstrable: (1) Certain plays ordinarily included in the Shakespearean canon reveal definite traces of Marlowe which can hardly be due to mere imitation. Notable among these are the first two parts of *Henry VI*, *Richard II*, *Richard III*, *Titus Andronicus*, and *Julius Caesar*. (2) To these may be added a

---

[39] See I. 103–104.

few plays of doubtful authorship which have a definite relation to Shakespearean plays. Notable among these are *The Contention*, *The True Tragedie*, and *The Taming of a Shrew*. (3) The traces of Marlowe consist first of whole lines or short passages from plays known to be Marlowe's; second, of words typical of Marlowe's vocabulary, not typical of Shakespeare's, and not known to be typical of any other playwright; and third, of obvious examples of Marlowe's structure, mood, and style.

Taken together, all this affords good reason for believing in a direct relationship of some kind between Marlowe and Shakespeare. The question remains, however, exactly what that relation was.

Wild as the theorizing on this tantalizing subject has been, few have pretended that Marlowe imitated Shakespeare.[40] There are four other possible ways of accounting for the admitted facts; and it is at least conceivable that in each of the four there lurks at least a germ of truth.

The first and obvious suggestion is that Shakespeare wrote, as most young writers do, under the powerful influence of the foremost author of the moment.

The second is that the two writers collaborated, Marlowe perhaps aiding in the construction — which in most of these plays is usually typical of his workmanship — and the less experienced dramatist doing most of the actual writing, except for very important scenes. Over the whole result Marlowe may have cast a critical eye, and into it, in rewriting, he may have worked the typical and unmistakable mighty lines which stud these plays.

The third is that Marlowe actually wrote the plays in question and that their attribution to Shakespeare is entirely erroneous.

Still a fourth view, one which also accords well with Elizabethan stage practice, is that Shakespeare used as sources early Marlowe plays, which were already forgotten and have now

---

[40] Except a certain Robert Cartwright, M.D., who wrote: "Let any person read 'Tamburlaine' and 'Faustus,' then let him read the 'Jew of Malta,' and he will readily perceive how diligently and earnestly the author must have studied the Shaksperian plays." See his *Papers on Shakspere*, p. 13, and his *Footsteps of Shakspere*, p. 139. Richard Simpson in his *Shakspere Allusion-Books* (pt. I, p. xlvii, 1874) wrote: "The very structure of *Edward II.* seems to bear witness to the counsel and aid of Shakspere."

been lost completely; and that in reworking them he had intelligence and literary feeling sufficient to let the more magnificently sonorous passages stand unchanged.

The most fantastic claim made for Marlowe — one that must at least be mentioned, though there is neither evidence to prove it nor even ground for taking it seriously — is that of Mr. Archie Webster, who in 1923 asserted that Marlowe wrote all of Shakespeare's plays, the sonnets, and the other poems, and survived to 1623 to revise the First Folio![41] Ironically enough, this preposterous idea was set forth only a little while before Dr. Hotson's discovery established once for all the full facts of Marlowe's death, the date of which had, in any case, never been in doubt for the last century.

More rational than this, but still sufficiently extreme, are the theories of the Rt. Hon. J. M. Robertson. He believes that Marlowe's contributions to the text are important in the *Henry VI* plays, *Henry V*, *Richard II*, *Richard III*, *Julius Caesar*, and *The Comedy of Errors*, a list which is certainly alarmingly inclusive. His theories are based on criteria of three sorts. In the first place, on purely literary grounds, he receives from these plays a disquieting impression that they are non-Shakespearean in style. In the second place, he believes that he is able to detect "clues" to the presence in these plays of the work of other dramatists. Finally, he applies the metrical tests originally introduced by Fleay,[42] which he describes as "inexorable," and treats as infallible.

The most cogent criticism of these methods was made by Sir Edmund K. Chambers in his lecture on *The Disintegration of Shakespeare*, before the British Academy in 1924. Sir Edmund pointed out that Mr. Robertson's theory amounts to treating Shakespeare as an infallible personage, and not as a very human though extraordinary writer, subject to the influence of other writers, doing better work at some times than at others, frequently forced to bow to the exigencies of a commercial theatre, and by no means always employing the same style.

He pointed out also that the supposedly inexorable metrical tests were very considerably modified by Fleay himself in his

---

[41] "Was Marlowe the Man?" *National Review*, 82: 81–86 S 1923.
[42] *Shakespeare Manual* (1876); *Life and Work of Shakespeare* (1886); "On the Metrical Tests as Applied to Dramatic Poetry," *New Shakspere Society Trans.*, 1874, pt. I.

later writings; and that even when thus modified they were far from infallible. As for the frequent resemblances in Shakespeare's work to the work of other men — which admittedly occur — he suggested that, after all, the Elizabethan dramatists all wrote "a common poetic diction, much of it ultimately traceable to Spenser and to Sidney." Resemblances were, therefore, to be expected and prove very little.[43]

At the other extreme from Mr. Robertson's are the views of critics like the late Professor John Semple Smart, Mr. Alfred W. Pollard, and Mr. Peter Alexander, who deny Marlowe any particular share in the plays accepted as Shakespeare's, and dismiss the numerous parallel passages as mere interpolations due to actors' faulty memories.[44]

Speculation has been particularly wild on this aspect of the matter. Not only the plays of the Shakespeare Canon, but also several apocryphal plays, have been assigned to Marlowe — so many, indeed, that, were all the attributions to be accepted as authentic, Marlowe would have had to live to a ripe old age, working with more than conceivable industry, to write them all.

Discarding the extremes of speculation, we may make the following list of Shakespearean plays and three of Shakespeare's source plays in which the influence of Marlowe appears to be important:

Merchant of Venice	*Richard III*
Henry VI	*Taming of a Shrew*
Contention and *True Tragedie*	*Titus Andronicus*
Richard II	*Julius Caesar*

There are faint traces of Marlowe in

Romeo and Juliet	*King Lear*
Antony and Cleopatra	*Hamlet*
Henry IV	*Much Ado About Nothing*
As You Like It	*King John*
Merry Wives of Windsor	*Sonnets*
Midsummer-Night's Dream	*Lucrece*
Troilus and Cressida	*Venus and Adonis*

[43] Annual Shakespeare Lecture, British Academy, 1924, pp. 10 ff.

[44] See Peter Alexander: *Shakespeare's Henry VI and Richard III*, with an introduction by Alfred W. Pollard (Cambridge: University Press, 1929); John Semple Smart: *Shakespeare: Truth and Tradition* (London and New York: Longmans, 1928).

Shakespeare borrows ideas wholesale from *The Jew of Malta* and from *Edward the Second*. Otherwise his debt is a general one to the tradition, the verse, and the manner which Marlowe established. He also owes something to *Hero and Leander*, the translation of Ovid, *Doctor Faustus*, and *Tamburlaine*. He has, therefore, laid all of Marlowe's best work under contribution for more than half of his own plays. It is striking to note that, while other Elizabethan dramatists admiringly plundered the rant of *Tamburlaine* wholesale, Shakespeare alludes to it only in ridicule.

THE MERCHANT OF VENICE

In *The Merchant of Venice*, as in *Richard II*, Shakespeare borrows certain characters, and with them certain elements of his plot, from Marlowe. The *Merchant* is in no sense a mere revision of Marlowe's *Jew of Malta*, nor is there the faintest reason to suspect collaboration.[45] Traces of Marlowe's manner are unusually few, as if Shakespeare had very nearly attained independence of his predecessor's style even when drawing on him for material.

Shakespeare simply found a Jew in *Il Pecorone*, one of his sources, and in developing the character drew on another Jewish character, whom Marlowe had already made famous. Jessica was presumably invented to correspond to Abigail, since the Jew in Shakespeare's source has no daughter. The other elements in the story of *The Merchant of Venice* — the caskets, the pound of flesh, and Portia's legal masquerade — owe nothing whatever to Marlowe.

Shakespeare makes no effort to disguise his borrowing. In each play we have a rich Jew, portrayed as a usurer and as, in general, an unsympathetic character. Barabas, at his first appearance (I: i) enumerates his argosies and his wealth; Shylock at his first appearance (I: iii) enumerates the argosies of Antonio.[46] Each Jew has a daughter whom he loves, but who falls in love with a Christian. Each Jew is more or less devout in his own faith, but each hates Christians. Each daughter

---

[45] See also I. 367–369.
[46] Cf. Ward, HEDL, I. 346; F. C. Waldron's (unsigned) ed. of Jonson's *Sad Shepherd* (London: C. Dilly, 1783), pp. 208–212.

deserts her father and steals his money. Each Jew, as might be expected, rages. Each, in the end, succumbs to the Christians, his stratagems having failed. Each is stripped of his wealth and pressed to turn Christian.

The numerous variations between the two characters may be partly due to a deliberate effort on Shakespeare's part to differentiate his own character, but are far more largely due to his superior skill in characterization. Barabas is an incredible monster of iniquity; Shylock is human and believable, even when he drives his bargain for the pound of flesh. Barabas is an avowed criminal; Shylock is always within the letter of the law — a merchant whom "the Venetian law cannot impugn." [47] Both are avaricious, but with Barabas avarice is an overmastering passion and religion nothing; Shylock never subordinates religion. In the end Barabas is defiant, Shylock almost tragic. Barabas is always a little bit vulgar; Shylock never loses dignity. Barabas is a highly educated man, a merchant prince, a musician, a physician, an engineer — in other words, a typical Marlowe hero, whose reach exceeds any normal human grasp; Shylock is simply a Jewish merchant. Barabas obviously loves his daughter Abigail less than Shylock loves his daughter Jessica. Marlowe, the Cambridge scholar, betrays himself when he allows Barabas a wealth of classical allusions but only a few scriptural allusions from the Book of Job, whereas Shylock always makes strictly Jewish allusions to the Old Testament.[48]

Shakespeare's treatment of his character is on the whole vastly more tolerant and free from prejudice. Both characters were no doubt played as semicomic parts for the groundlings; [49] but, over and above and around the comedy, Shakespeare wrote in something which gives his Shylock, at the end, a strange pathos that is wholly lacking in Marlowe's Barabas.

The verbal parallels are numerous and striking. In the first set quoted below, both Shakespeare and Ben Jonson seem to have borrowed from the same passage of Marlowe:

[47] *Merchant of Venice*, IV. i. 178–179.
[48] See I. 354–356. Cf. Otto Jespersen: *Growth and Structure of the English Language* (4th ed., 1923), p. 215.
[49] See I. 367–369.

Oh my girle,
My gold, my fortune, my felicity;
. . . Oh girle, oh gold, oh beauty, oh my blisse!
    [JofM, 688–695]

My daughter! O my ducats! O my daughter!
Fled with a Christian! O my Christian ducats!
Justice! the law! my ducats, and my daughter!
    [MofV, II. viii. 15–17]

Gold, gold, man-making gold; another star!
Drop they from heaven? no, no, my house I hope,
Is haunted with a fairy. My dear Lar,
My household god, my fairy, on my knees —
. . . O sweet voice,
Musical as the spheres! see, see, more gold.
    [Jonson: *Case is Altered*, V. ii]

These are the Blessings promis'd to the Iewes,
And herein was old *Abrams* happinesse.
    [JofM, 143–144]
[Reference to Jacob and Abraham]
This was a way to thrive, and he [Jacob] was blest;
And thrift is blessing, if men steal it not.
    [MofV, I. iii. 90–91]

What? bring you Scripture to confirm your wrongs?
    [JofM, 343]
The devil can cite Scripture for his purpose.
    [MofV, I. iii. 99]

You haue my goods, my mony, and my wealth,
My ships, my store, and all that I enioy'd;
And hauing all, you can request no more;
Vnlesse your vnrelenting flinty hearts
Suppresse all pitty in your stony breasts,
And now shall move you to bereave my life.
    [JofM, 371–376]
Nay, take my life and all; pardon not that.
You take my house when you do take the prop
That doth sustain my house; you take my life
When you do take the means whereby I live.
    [MofV, IV. i. 374–377]

I learn'd in *Florence* how to kisse my hand,
Heave vp my shoulders when they call me dogge,
And ducke as low as any bare-foot Fryar.
    [JofM, 784–786]

Still have I borne it with a patient shrug,
For sufferance is the badge of all our tribe.
You call me misbeliever, cut-throat dog. . . .
[MofV, I. iii. 110–113]

Hee that denies to pay, shal straight become a Christian.
[JofM, 306]
. . . that, for this favour,
He presently become a Christian.
[MofV, IV. i. 386–387]

I must haue one that's sickly, and be but for sparing
vittles: 'tis not a stone of beef a day will maintaine
you in these chops; let me see one that's somewhat
leaner.
[JofM, 886–890]
. . . Thou shalt not gormandise,
As thou hast done with me, . . . a huge feeder.
[MofV, II. v. 2–3; 46]

Shylock's angry exclamation:
. . . I have a daughter;
Would any of the stock of Barrabas
Had been her husband rather than a Christian! [50]

is probably an allusion to the New Testament rather than to
Marlowe's play, but the choice of this particular name may
indicate that Marlowe's Barabas was in Shakespeare's mind.

Henry VI

The authorship of the plays collectively known as the "King
Henry VI plays" has long been disputed. The group includes
five plays in all — that is, the two source plays, *The First part
of the Contention betwixt the two famous Houses of Yorke and
Lancaster* and *The true Tragedie of Richard Duke of Yorke*; and
the three plays usually admitted to the Shakespeare canon as
the First, Second, and Third Parts of *King Henry VI*.

It is universally admitted that *The Contention* was the source
for the Second Part of *Henry VI*, and *The True Tragedie* for
the Third Part. It is somewhat less generally admitted that
Marlowe (and perhaps others) pretty certainly had something

[50] *Merchant of Venice*, IV. i. 295–297.

to do with both *The Contention* and *The True Tragedie*. It is usually agreed that the admission of the three *Henry VI* plays to the Shakespeare canon has at least something to justify it, if nothing more than a final revision by Shakespeare's pen.

Beyond this point there is no agreement. Peele, Greene, Lodge, and Kyd are put forward as authors or co-authors (with or without Marlowe) of the two source plays; and Shakespeare's share in *Henry VI*, even as a reviser, has been called in question.

Where so much uncertainty reigns, it is well to be sure from the start of such facts as are definitely ascertainable. These are lamentably sparse and relate mainly to the circumstances of publication. Both *The Contention* and *The True Tragedie* were printed for the bookseller, Thomas Millington. *The Contention* was entered in the *Stationers' Register*, March 12, 1593/4, and appeared the same year. There is no entry for *The True Tragedie*, which was published by Millington in 1595. Millington reprinted both plays in 1600; and in 1602 Thomas Pavier entered in the *Register*, by assignment from Millington, *The First and Second Parts of Henry VI*.

Pavier did not publish any book under the title of *Henry VI*; but in 1619 he did publish *The Whole Contention betweene the two Famous Houses, Lancaster and Yorke*, which unites in a single volume revised versions of the two source plays. The title page declares that they are "Written by *William Shakespeare*, Gent." This is the first mention of Shakespeare's name in relation to these plays, since Francis Meres's list in *Palladis Tamia* (1598) does not even include the canonical *Henry VI*.

In 1623 — obviously in preparation for publishing the First Folio — Blount and Jaggard entered in the *Register*, *The Thirde Parte of Henry the Sixt*, which is usually assumed to be identical with the play now known as the First Part. To Blount and Jaggard it was the third part in order of composition, not in order of historical chronology.

Both *The True Tragedie* and the Third Part of *Henry VI* seem to be connected with Shakespeare in the famous passage in Greene's *Groats-worth of Witte*, in which Greene refers to "an vpstart Crow, beautified with our feathers, that with his *Tygers heart wrapt in a Players hide*, supposes he is as well able to bumbast out a blanke verse as the best of you: and being an

absolute *Iohannes fac totum*, is in his owne conceit the onely
Shake-scene in a countrie." [51]   The line,

> O tiger's heart wrapt in a woman's hide!

appears both in *The True Tragedie* and in the Third Part of
Henry VI.[52]

Greene's malice is the only clear thing in this troublesome
passage. Apparently, Shakespeare is described as an upstart
actor (crow) beautified in the feathers (that is, deriving his success from the writings) of the established dramatists. He has
the impudence to believe that he can write blank verse as well
as recite it. He is, therefore, a mere Jack-of-all-trades (Johannes
fac totum), proverbially master of none. The allusion to the
"Tygers heart" and the pun on his name — Shake-scene —
are thrown in to make identification easy.

Greene uses similar language a few lines earlier, assailing
actors as "those Puppits . . . that speake from our mouths,
those Anticks garnisht in our colours." In his *Neuer Too Late*
(1590) he compares an actor to "*Esops* Crow, being pranct
with the glorie of others feathers." [53]   There is, therefore, little
justification for the view sometimes urged, that by the phrase
"beautified with our feathers" Greene implies literary plagiarism by Shakespeare. Some weight is lent to it, however, by
a poem called "Greene's Funeralles," signed "R. B.," in which
appear the lines:

> Nay more the men, that so eclipst his fame:
> Purloynde his Plumes, can they deny the same? [54]

Where external evidence as to the authorship of the source
plays and their relationship to *Henry VI* is so slight, Elizabethan scholarship has necessarily had recourse to internal
evidence, some of which is fairly convincing, while some is
highly dubious and based mainly on the individual critic's
confidence in his own ability to detect authorship by his feeling
for style. The literature is voluminous and the opinions fre-

[51] First pointed out by Thomas Tyrwhitt. See Boswell's Malone, XVIII. 551.
The text here is from Grosart's Greene.
[52] *True Tragedie*, I. iv, Praetorius Facsimile, p. 20, l. 137; 3 *Henry VI*, I. iv. 137.
[53] Grosart's Greene, VIII. 132.
[54] Page 81 of the reprint by R. B. McKerrow (Stratford: Shakespeare Head, 1922).

quently contradictory. Among the more important are the following:

1797 (or earlier). Dr. Richard Farmer (d. 1797) suggests Marlowe's authorship of *The Contention* and of *Henry VI*. [Boswell's Malone (1821), II. 313, XXI. 260]

1798. First known copy of *The True Tragedie* appears in sale of Dr. Samuel Pegge's library (April 2). [George Chalmers: *Supplemental Apology*, p. 293n]

1799. George Chalmers: "Henry VI. *The Third Part* . . . being copied from a previous play of Marlow, entitled *The true Tragedy*." [*Supplemental Apology*, p. 292]

1812 (or earlier). Malone (d. 1812): Inclined to believe "that Marlowe was the author of one, if not both [*Contention* plays]." [Boswell's Malone (1821), II. 313]

1831. Collier: "There is nothing to fix any of these [*Contention* plays and *Henry VI*] as the property of Marlow." [HEDP, III. 145] Collier: "By whom it [2 *Henry VI*] was written we have no information." [*Shakespeare*, V. 107] "There is no ground for giving it [*The True Tragedie*] to Marlowe." [*Shakespeare*, I. xlix]

1839. Charles Knight: "Marlowe could not have been the author of these two dramas." [*Pictorial Shakespeare*, II. 464]

1843. J. O. Halliwell-Phillips: "Many passages [in the *Contention* plays] . . . seem almost beyond the power of any of Shakespeare's predecessors or contemporaries, perhaps even not excepting Marlowe." [*Supplement to Dodsley*, Shakespeare Society Reprints, p. xix]

1843. Hallam: "It seems probable that the old plays . . . were in great part by Marlowe." [*Introd. Lit. Europe* (1843), II. 171]

1850. Dyce: "We have full warrant for supposing that Marlowe was largely concerned in the composition of *The First Part of the Contention* and of *The True Tragedie*." [*Works*, I. lx–lxi]

1857. Dyce: "*The Contention* and *The True Tragedie* were most probably by Marlowe." [*Shakespeare*, I. clxxv]

1859. Richard Grant White: "*The First Part of the Contention, The True Tragedy* and, probably, an early form of The First Part of *King Henry the Sixth* unknown to us, were written by Marlowe, Greene and Shakespeare (and perhaps Peele) together." [*Pictorial Shakespeare*, II. 485; *Works* (ed. 1865), p. 407]

1864. W. C. Clark and W. A. Wright: Shakespeare "had a considerable share in their [*Contention* plays'] composition." [Cambridge *Shakespeare*, V. xii]

1865. H. Ulrici: Certain scenes "unmöglich von Marlowe herrühren
können." [*Jahrb.*, 1 : 72]

1874. George Lockhart Rives: "A part, and a part only, of the two
old plays is the work of Shakespeare. . . . During the year
1591, Greene, Marlowe, and Shakespeare, — then a mere actor
in the Blackfriars [*sic*] company, — produced the two parts of
the Whole Contention." [*Essay on the Authorship of Henry
the Sixth*, pp. 29, 45]

1875–76. Jane Lee: "Marlowe and Greene, and possibly Peele, were
the writers." Marlowe may have collaborated with Shakespeare in 2 and 3 *Henry VI*. [*Transactions*, New Shakspere
Society, p. 275]

1875. Fleay: Marlowe plotted 1 *Henry VI* and with Kyd (or Greene),
Peele, and Lodge wrote it and 2 *Henry VI*. Marlowe alone
wrote 3 *Henry VI*. *The Contention* and *True Tragedie* are
abridged acting versions for provincial tours. [*Chron. Hist. . . .
Shakespeare* (1886), pp. 273–274]

1876. Swinburne: "Marlowe was more or less concerned in the production, and Shakespeare in the revision, of these plays."
[*Fortnightly Review*, 109: 26 Ja 1876]

1886. A. W. Verity: "He [Shakespeare] became associated with
Marlowe in the revision of the earlier sketches of *Henry VI*,
Parts II. and III." [*Influence of Christopher Marlowe*, p. 93]

1902. Schelling: "Shakespeare, whether in revision or in independent
authorship, was working either with Marlowe or directly under
his influence." [*English Chronicle Play*, p. 75]

1903. W. J. Courthope: "There are no sufficient internal reasons to
warrant us in resisting the testimony of the folio of 1623 that
Titus Andronicus and *King Henry VI* are the work of Shake-
speare. . . . If *King Henry VI* is the work of Shakespeare, *The
Contention* and *The True Tragedy* are also his." [*Hist. Eng.
Poet.*, IV. 470]

1905. Stopford Brooke: "These plays were originally written by
other men than Shakespeare and were, as some conjecture,
revised by Shakespeare and Marlowe in partnership. If so,
Shakespeare worked afterwards upon them alone, after Marlowe's death." [*On Ten Plays*, p. 71]

1910. A. H. Thorndike: "[In *Henry VI*,] Marlowe's influence, if not
his hand, is dominant." [*Minor Elizabethan Drama* (Everyman
Series), I. xiii]

1913. Tucker Brooke: "Marlowe, the only Elizabethan writer who,
in my opinion, has any demonstrable interest in these [*Contention*] plays." [*Trans. Conn. Acad.*, 17: 148 (1913)]

1916. Sir Sidney Lee: "The theory that Robert Greene, with George Peele's co-operation, produced the original draft of the three parts of 'Henry VI,' which Shakespeare twice helped to recast, can alone account for Greene's indignant denunciation of Shakespeare. . . . Signs are not wanting that it was Marlowe . . . whom Shakespeare joined in the first revision." [*Life of William Shakespeare*, 3rd ed., p. 122]

1919. H. Dugdale Sykes: "Internal evidence of Peel's hand in the three parts of *King Henry VI.*, and the two earlier historical dramas." [*Sidelights on Shakespeare*, p. 102]

1923. J. Q. Adams: "For the Pembroke's Men Marlowe wrote *Edward II*, *The True Tragedy*, *The Contention*, and possibly other plays." [*Life of William Shakespeare*, p. 132]

1923. E. K. Chambers: "The various claims of Marlowe, Kyd, Greene, Peele, Lodge, and Shakespeare himself to the *Contention* can only be discussed in relation to Shakespeare's revision." [*Elizabethan Stage*, IV. 8]

1929. Alfred W. Pollard: "As to Marlowe I fall back on an old formula of my own by which, until my class at King's College, London, dragged me into it, I kept out of this controversy: (i) if Shakespeare ever set himself to imitate Marlowe what he wrote would be indistinguishable from Marlowe at his best; (ii) there is no room for both Shakespeare and Marlowe in any one of the four plays. . . . I cannot deny that the bright gallantry [of Richard Crookback] may be a sketch by Shakespeare in rivalry with Marlowe. . . . Is it justifiable to call in Marlowe when it is possible to do without him, and if we refrain from calling in Greene, Nashe or Marlowe is it reasonable to call in Peele . . . ?" [Introd. to Peter Alexander: *Shakespeare's Henry VI and Richard III*, p. 24]

1929. Peter Alexander: "Marlowe is either the author of the whole of 2 and 3 *Henry VI* or there is no room for him here at all. . . . Marlowe must be excluded, for there are two other reasonable explanations of the parallel passages: Marlowe may have known 2 and 3 *Henry VI* and reproduced lines or phrases consciously or unconsciously when writing *Edward II*, or Shakespeare may be the imitator." [*Op. cit.*, p. 146]

These opinions reduce themselves to three main views:

First, that both *Henry VI* and the two source plays are Shakespeare's authentic work;

Second, that *The Contention* and *True Tragedie* are the work of a group of collaborating playwrights, probably including Peele, Greene, Marlowe, Lodge, and perhaps the youthful

Shakespeare himself, which were later revised by someone, perhaps Shakespeare, and then found their way into the First Folio;

Third, that *The Contention* and *True Tragedie* are, at least in very large part, authentic Marlowe which Shakespeare revised, and to which he added the First Part of *Henry VI*.

This third view is probably correct. It is based on six main considerations:

First, the general characteristics of *The Contention* and *The True Tragedie*, including style, structure, the frequent parallels with canonical Marlowe plays, and the appearance of Marlowe's typical vocabulary;

Second, the versification;

Third, the curious way in which historical facts, correctly stated in *The Contention* and *The True Tragedie*, turn up as slightly warped allusions in Marlowe's admitted work, as if an unconscious memory of what he had previously written lingered in the poet's restless brain;

Fourth, the appearance of Marlowe's habitual self-repetition;

Fifth, the dramatic companies known to have produced the plays; and

Sixth, general probability arising from the dates at which *The Contention*, *The True Tragedie*, and *Henry VI* seem to have been written.

Many of the facts involved were unknown or imperfectly known to the earlier scholars dealing with the problem. The eminence of those who have in the past opposed these views need not, therefore, necessarily disturb us. Most of the later critics, with the full array of facts before them, have been willing to admit that Marlowe had at least some share in the *Contention* plays.

I. Dramatic Structure

Taking these six considerations in the order given, we find in the first place that the general style of *The Contention* and *The True Tragedie* is Marlowe's. There is the same loose dramatic structure — episodic and relatively plotless. There is the absence of "such conceits as clownage keepes in pay" — an absence typical of Marlowe's work, but very unusual in Elizabethan chronicle histories, where comic relief was valued. There is Marlowe's usual emphasis on ruthless ambition. The characters who obviously most interest the dramatist are typical of Marlowe's heroes — savagely but splendidly egoistic villains; while the virtuous characters are weak and bloodless, made of milk and water, like Edward of York, or the good King Henry VI, himself. They are exactly like Edmund in *Edward the Second* or Henry of Navarre in *The Massacre at Paris*. Indeed, the most striking change made by the reviser who reworked the source plays into *Henry VI* was the transformation of King Henry himself into a sympathetic and credible figure.

II. Versification

The verse of *The True Tragedie* and of *The Contention* is woefully beneath that of Marlowe at his best; but one catches fairly frequent echoes of the mighty line, and the general average is no worse than in *The Massacre at Paris*. It presents the main characteristics of Marlowe's prosody: the predominately end-stopped line with enough enjambement to relieve monotony; the poet's obvious fondness for the pyrrhic ending; and his equally obvious dislike of the eleven-syllable line — the last two characteristics reversing Shakespeare's practice in the unquestioned plays. Mr. Tucker Brooke [55] has summed all this up statistically:

Plays	Per cent Pyrrhic Feet	Per cent 11-Syllable Lines	Per cent Run-On Lines	Total Metrical Lines
Contention	7−	4−	4+	1254
2 *Henry VI* (Additions)	11−	14−	10	2148
The True Tragedie	10	7	5	1865
3 *Henry VI* (Additions)	8−	14−	7.5	1550
Edward II	13.5	4.33	6.66	2519
Massacre	14	2	7.25	1039
Jew of Malta	18−	3	10.5	1811
Richard III	9	19+	13+	3412

There are two apparent discrepancies in this table. The first is the relatively small number of run-on lines in the Third

[55] *Trans. Connecticut Acad.*, 17: 181 (1912).

Part of *Henry VI* — only 7.5 per cent as against 10 per cent in the additions to the Second Part. It will be observed, however, that these additions are 600 lines shorter than the others. The adapter (presumably Shakespeare) had very little opportunity to add run-on lines, as he was usually writing very short bits of verse, here and there throughout the play. The second and more surprising fact is that the proportion of pyrrhic endings is actually smaller in *The Contention* than in the Second Part of *Henry VI*. This is probably to be explained by Professor Brooke's suggestion that the Second Part of *Henry VI* preserves additional pyrrhic feet, which were cut out of the later *Contention* manuscript but were preserved in the earlier manuscript from which Shakespeare worked.[56]

Otherwise the figures support the theory of Marlowe's authorship. The eleven-syllable lines have a consistently low percentage — 4 — to 7 — in *The Contention* and *True Tragedie*. They have nearly the same percentage — 2 to 4.33 — in the canonical Marlowe plays. On the other hand, the percentage is consistently high — 14 — to 19+ — in the additions and in *Richard III*, which are presumably Shakespeare's work.

Similarly, run-on lines are relatively infrequent in *The Contention* and *True Tragedie*. They are also infrequent in the canonical Marlowe plays, while they increase sharply in the additions to *Henry VI* and in *Richard III*. It is also striking that whereas *The Contention* and *The True Tragedie* abound in pyrrhic endings, typical of Marlowe, the reviser seizes every opportunity to make them over into eleven-syllable lines, typical of Shakespeare. This strongly suggests Shakespeare revising Marlowe.[57] As examples:

Before/ his legs/ can beare/ his bod/ ie vp
[*Contention*, p. 32, l. 100]

---

[56] Mr. Brooke's views are adversely criticized by Dr. Madeleine Doran in *Henry VI, Parts II and III. Their Relation to the Contention and True Tragedy* (University of Iowa Humanistic Studies, vol. IV, no. 4), pp. 69–70. Her chief objection is that we have no adequate basis for figures such as these. The source plays, she argues, have probably not come down to us in the state in which Marlowe left them — if he was indeed the author. Furthermore, some of Marlowe's lines may actually be imbedded in *Henry VI* and yet have dropped out of the source plays.

[57] All references are to the Praetorius Facsimiles of the *Contention* plays. See Brooke, *op. cit.*, pp. 179–180, for further examples. For Shakespeare's similar treatment of alexandrines, see II. 187.

Before/ his legs/ be firm/ to bear/ his body
[2 *Henry VI*, III. i. 190]
Of ash/ ie sem/ blance, pale/ and blood/ (e)lesse
[*Contention*, p. 37, l. 59]
Of ash/ y sem/ blance, meag/ re, pale,/ and bloodless
[2 *Henry VI*, III. ii. 162]

III. HISTORICAL FACTS

Much of this might, of course, be ascribed to the imitation of Marlowe which began with *Tamburlaine*. More striking, and exceedingly difficult to explain on any ground other than Marlowe's authorship or part authorship of the *Contention* plays, is an argument first advanced by Mr. Tucker Brooke[58] in 1913: Where *The Contention* alludes to historical facts, they are usually correct. When, however, *Edward the Second*, which is unquestionably Marlowe's, alludes to these same facts, the allusion is either incorrect or inappropriate to the dramatic situation in which it is made. A similar but reversed relationship exists between *The True Tragedie* and *The Massacre at Paris*. Where *The Massacre*, known to be Marlowe's work, alludes to historical events, the allusions are usually correct. Where the two *Contention* plays allude to the same events, the allusion is incorrect or inappropriate.

This situation is perfectly comprehensible if we assume *The Contention* and *The True Tragedie* to be Marlowe's work; it is quite incomprehensible on any other grounds. According to this theory, Marlowe, who notoriously repeats himself, wrote *The Contention* before *Edward the Second* and *The Massacre at Paris* before *The True Tragedie*. Since the sources for *The Contention* and *The Massacre* were clearly in Marlowe's mind, his historical allusions are correct. Later, when he wrote *Edward the Second*, his sources were less clear in his mind; but, as usual, what he had previously written was still running in his head. Hence he repeated bits of what he had already written, but either dragged in allusions inappropriately or positively incorrectly. The same thing happened when he wrote *The True Tragedie*.

[58] *Trans. Connecticut Acad.*, 17: 172–177 (1913). George B. Churchill, in his *Richard III Up to Shakespeare*, pp. 482–483, had just missed the same discovery in 1900.

It is impossible to believe that some unknown dramatist first wrote his historical allusions in *The Contention* correctly and that Marlowe later dragged them into *Edward the Second* incorrectly. It is equally hard to suppose that the hypothetical unknown dramatist wrote incorrect historical references in *The True Tragedie* and that these by some miracle fitted correctly into *The Massacre at Paris*. Assume, however, that the same dramatist wrote all four, that he had the allusions — sometimes clearly and sometimes rather vaguely — in his head, and the whole situation is accounted for.

Specific examples will make this rather clearer. In *The Contention* Queen Margaret says to Suffolk:

> I tell thee *Poull,* when thou didst runne at Tilt,
> And stolst away our Laidaies hearts in *France,*
> I thought King *Henry* had bene like to thee,
> Or else thou hadst not brought me out of *France.*[59]

This fits Margaret's character and accords with the facts of history. During Henry's courtship of Margaret there *were* magnificent jousts in France, in which Suffolk was a leading figure.

An obvious echo appears in *Edward the Second*:

> Tell *Isabell* the Queene, I lookt not thus,
> When for her sake I ran at tilt in Fraunce,
> And there vnhorste the duke of *Cleremont.*[60]

These lines are intensely pathetic when spoken by the imprisoned and abused king; but, in spite of their dramatic effect, they have no relation to history. The historical Edward was not a hero of the tiltyard; instead, his obvious effeminacy was only too apparent at the wedding.

References to the Irish family of O'Neill are likewise accurate in *The Contention* and inaccurate, though dramatic, in *Edward the Second*. The lines in *The Contention*:

> The wild Onele my Lords, is vp in Armes,
> With troupes of Irish Kernes that vncontrold,
> Doth plant themselues within the English pale,[61]

---

[59] *Contention,* p. 13, ll. 59–61. Repeated in 2 *Henry VI,* I. iii. 53–56.
[60] *Edward the Second,* 2516–2518.
[61] *Contention,* p. 33, ll. 134–136.

correctly describe the exploits of Henry O'Neill, then conspicuous in Irish revolts against the English. But when in *Edward the Second* we find the lines:

> The wilde *Oneyle*, with swarmes of Irish Kernes,
> Liues vncontroulde within the English pale,[62]

this self-evident echo of *The Contention* has no relation to history at all. There was no Irish rebellion while the Gaveston of history was governor of Ireland. No O'Neill of the period was sufficiently important to be listed in the *Dictionary of National Biography*.[63] Again, *The True Tragedie* has the lines

> . . . Sterne *Fawconbridge*
> Commands the narrow seas,[64]

a perfectly accurate statement of history. But in *Edward the Second*, Young Mortimer's reproach to Edward for his incompetent rule:

> The hautie *Dane* commands the narrow seas,
> While in the harbor ride thy ships vnrigd,[65]

has nothing to do with history. No Danish vessels kept English ships in port while Edward was on the throne, though during Marlowe's lifetime Frederick II, King of Denmark (1571–1588), forced foreign ships to strike their sails to Danish men-o'-war.[66]

In *The Massacre at Paris* the Duke of Guise employs an appropriate simile when he says:

> As ancient Romanes ouer their Captiue Lords,
> So will I triumph ouer this wanton King,
> And he shall follow my proud Chariots wheeles.[67]

But Duke Humphrey, lamenting his wife's punishment, is vastly less appropriate in *The Contention* when he uses the same language:

[62] *Edward the Second*, 966–967.
[63] W. D. Briggs attempts to make this an allusion to Turlough O'Neill, who died in 1595, a contemporary of Marlowe, not of Edward II. Cf. his ed. of the play, pp. 141–142.
[64] *True Tragedie*, I. i. 210–211, p. 11.
[65] *Edward the Second*, 970–971.
[66] Briggs, *op. cit.*, p. 143.
[67] *Massacre*, 989–991.

Sweete Nell, ill can thy noble minde abrooke,
The abiect people gazing on thy face, . . .
That earst did follow thy proud Chariot wheeles,
When thou didst ride in tryumph through the streetes.[68]

The echo from the famous line in *Tamburlaine*:

And ride in triumph through *Persepolis*,[69]

is also less fitting here than in its original place.

Again, in *The Massacre*, Dumayn, expecting death himself and aware that the Guise faction is crushed by the death of their leader, says appropriately enough:

Sweet Duke of *Guise* our prop to leane vpon,
Now thou art dead, heere is no stay for vs.[70]

But Edward, in *The True Tragedie*, expresses merely personal sorrow in the words:

Sweet Duke of *Yorke* our prop to leane vpon.
Now thou art gone there is no hope for vs.[71]

Indeed, in the lines immediately following he expresses hope for the fortunes of his party!

IV. REPETITION

Marlowe's habitual repetition of his own lines appears very frequently in both *The Contention* and *The True Tragedie*. Both plays borrow numerous lines from the accepted Marlowe canon. While it is true that most of the Elizabethan dramatists borrowed occasional lines from each other and that many of them borrowed heavily from Marlowe, these repetitions are too close and too frequent to be of the same nature. It is especially significant that the author of the source plays practically ignores other Elizabethan authors. Moreover, both *The Contention* and *The True Tragedie* borrow from each other with the utmost freedom, as if Marlowe were running true to form even in his unsigned work and repeating himself as usual.

The evidence for all this is almost embarrassing in its

[68] *Contention*, p. 27, ll. 6–10.
[69] I *Tamb.* 755.
[70] *Massacre*, 1122–1123.
[71] *True Tragedie*, p. 23, ll. 45–46.

abundance. The following examples, collected by Mr. Tucker Brooke,[72] illustrate the parallelism between the two source plays and Marlowe's canonical work:

> *Aeneas* no, although his eyes doe pearce.
>> [*Dido*, 1007]
> Her lookes did wound, but now her speech doth pierce.
>> [*Contention*, p. 4, l. 30]

> Oh fatall was this mariage to vs all.
>> [*Massacre*, 206]
> Ah Lords, fatall is this marriage . . .
>> [*Contention*, p. 5, l. 79]

> For this, I wake, when others think I sleepe
>> [*Massacre*, 105]
> Watch thou, and wake when others be asleepe.
>> [*Contention*, p. 8, l. 156]

> As though your highnes were a schoole boy still,
> And must be awde and gouernd like a child.
>> [*Edward II*, 1336–1337]
> But still must be protected like a childe,
> And gouerned by that ambitious Duke.
>> [*Contention*, p. 12, ll. 49–50]

> Furies from the blacke *Cocitus* lake.
>> [I *Tamb.* 1999]
> Wherein the Furies maske in hellish troupes,
> Send vp I charge you from Sosetus lake.
>> [*Contention*, p. 17, ll. 15–16]

> Nay, to my death, for too long haue I liued.
>> [*Edward II*, 2651]
> Euen to my death, for I haue liued too long.
>> [*Contention*, p. 25, l. 10]

> A griping paine hath ceasde vpon my heart:
> A sodaine pang, the messenger of death.
>> [*Massacre*, 542]
> For sorrowes teares hath gripte my aged heart.
>> [*Contention*, p. 25, l. 17]
> See how the panges of death doth gripe his heart.
>> [*Ibid.*, p. 42, l. 12]

[72] *Trans. Connecticut Acad.*, 17: 164–171 (1913).

How inlie anger gripes his hart.
[*True Tragedie*, p. 21, l. 156]

Or looke you, I should play the Orator?
[I *Tamb.* 325]
Our swordes shall play the Orators for vs.
[I *Tamb.* 328]
Doubt not, my lord, I'll play the orator.
[*Richard III*, III. v. 94]
To trie how quaint an Orator you were.
[*Contention*, p. 39, l. 127]
Nay, I can better plaie the Orator.
[*True Tragedie*, p. 12, l. 2]
Full wel hath *Clifford* plaid the Orator.
[*Ibid.*, p. 29, l. 42]

For he hath solemnely sworne thy death.
Muge. I may be stabd, and liue till he be dead.
[*Massacre*, 783–784]
Lord Say, Iacke Cade hath solemnely vowde to haue thy head.
Say. I, but I hope your highnesse shall haue his.
[*Contention*, p. 49, ll. 6–7]

The sworde shall plane the furrowes of thy browes.
[*Edward II*, 94]
Giue me a look, that when I bend the browes,
Pale death may walke in furrowes of my face.
[*Massacre*, 158]
Deepe trenched furrowes in his frowning brow.
[*Contention*, p. 57, l. 53]
The wrinkles in my browes now fild with bloud
Were likened oft to kinglie sepulchers.
[*True Tragedie*, p. 68, ll. 10–11]

Weaponles must I fall and die in bands
[*Edward II*, 1289]
And die in bands for this vnkingly deed.
[*True Tragedie*, p. 10. l. 177]

Here, take my crowne, the life of *Edward* too.
[*Edward II*, 2043]
Off with the crowne, and with the crowne his head.
[*True Tragedie*, p. 19, l. 92]

Inhumaine creatures, nurst with Tigers milke.
[*Edward II*, 2057]
But thou art sprung from *Scythian Caucasus*,
And Tygers of *Hircania* gaue thee sucke.
[*Dido*, 1566–1567]
But you are more inhumaine, more inexorable,
O ten times more then Tygers of *Arcadia*. 73
[*True Tragedie*, p. 21, ll. 139–140]

For which thy head shall ouer looke the rest
As much as thou in rage out wentst the rest.
[*Edward II*, 1547–1548]
Off with his head and set it on *Yorke* Gates,
So Yorke maie ouerlooke the towne of *Yorke*.
[*True Tragedie*, p. 21, ll. 164–165]

And we are grac'd with wreathes of victory.
[*Massacre*, 794]
Thus farre our fortunes keepes an vpward Course,
and we are grast with wreathes of victorie.
[*True Tragedie*, p. 39, ll. 30–31]

Your Lordship shall doe well to let them haue it.
[JofM, 274]
Your highnesse shall doe well to grant it then.
[*True Tragedie*, p. 43, l. 9]

The royall vine, whose golden leaues
Empale your princelie head, your diadem.
[*Edward II*, 1472–1473]
Did I impale him with the regall Crowne.
[*True Tragedie*, p. 52, l. 118]

Since thou hast all the Cardes within thy hands
To shuffle or cut, take this as surest thing:
That right or wrong, thou deale thy selfe a King.
[*Massacre*, 146–148]
But whilst he sought to steale the single ten,
The king was finelie fingerd from the decke.
[*True Tragedie*, p. 66, ll. 32–33]

A loftie Cedar tree faire flourishing,
On whose top-branches Kinglie Eagles pearch.
[*Edward II*, 818–819]

---

73 "Hircania," in 1623 ed. The allusion here and in Shakespeare (*Macbeth*, III. iv.
101) is to *Aeneid*, IV. 367, "Hyrcanaeque admorunt ubera tigres."

Thus yeelds the Cedar to the axes edge,
Whose armes gaue shelter to the princelie Eagle.
[True Tragedie, p. 68, ll. 6–7]

. . . I stand as Ioues huge tree,

And others are but shrubs compard to me.
[Edward II, 2579–2580]

Whose top branch ouerpeerd Ioues spreading tree.
[True Tragedie, p. 68, l. 9]

Shaking their swords, their speares and yron bils,
Enuironing their Standard round, that stood
As bristle-pointed as a thorny wood.
[I Tamb. 1397–1399]

See brothers, yonder stands the thornie wood,
Which by Gods assistance and your prowesse,
Shall with our swords yer night be cleane cut downe.
[True Tragedie, p. 71, ll. 35–37]

Frownst thou thereat, aspiring Lancaster?
[Edward II, 93]

Highly scorning, that the lowly earth
Should drinke his bloud, mounts vp into the ayre.
[Edward II, 2000–2001]

What? will the aspiring bloud of Lancaster
Sinke into the ground, I had thought it would haue mounted.
[True Tragedie, p. 76, ll. 50–51]

As might be expected, Marlowe's habitual repetition is equally evident within each of the two source plays and also from play to play. As examples:

Till terme of eighteene months be full expirde.
[Contention, p. 4, l. 39]

Till terme of 18. months be full expirde.
[Ibid., p. 5, l. 60]

The common people swarme about him straight,
Crying Iesus blesse your royall exellence,
With God preserue the good Duke Humphrey,
And many things besides that are not knowne.
[Contention, p. 6, ll. 98–101]

See you not how the Commons follow him
In troupes, crying, God saue the good Duke Humphrey,

And with long life, Iesus preserue his grace,
Honoring him as if he were their King.
                    [*Ibid.*, p. 30, ll. 9–12]

Ile laie a plot to heaue him from his seate.
                    [*Contention*, p. 6, l. 104]
Weele quickly heaue Duke *Humphrey* from his seate.
                    [*Contention*, p. 6, l. 111]

And put them from the marke they faine would hit.
                    [*Contention*, p. 6, l. 108]
For thats the golden marke I seeke to hit.[74]
                    [*Ibid.*, p. 7, l. 150]

Cold newes for me, for I had hope of *France*,
Euen as I haue of fertill England.
                    [*Contention*, p. 7, ll. 144–145]
Cold newes for me, for I had hope of France,
Euen as I haue of fertill England.
                    [*Ibid.*, p. 31, ll. 34–35]

My mind doth tell me thou art innocent.
                    [*Contention*, p. 23, l. 171]
My conscience tels me thou art innocent.
                    [*Ibid.*, p. 32, l. 70]

If our King Henry had shooke hands with death,
Duke Humphrey then would looke to be our King.
                    [*Contention*, p. 33, ll. 118–119]
As I bethinke me you should not be king,
Till our *Henry* had shooke hands with death.
                    [*True Tragedie*, p. 19, ll. 86–87]

You bad me ban, and will you bid me sease?
                    [*Contention*, p. 40, l. 165]
Bids thou me rage? why now thou hast thy will.
                    [*True Tragedie*, p. 20, l. 128]

Make hast, for vengeance comes along with them.
                    [*Contention*, p. 62, l. 63]
Awaie my Lord for vengance comes along with him.
                    [*True Tragedie*, p. 38, l. 61]

[74] Cf. *Contention*, pp. 35, 60.

For strokes receiude, and manie blowes repaide,
Hath robd my strong knit sinnews of their strength,
And force perforce needes must *I* rest my selfe.

[*True Tragedie*, pp. 33–34]

For manie wounds receiu'd, and manie moe repaid,
Hath robd my strong knit sinews of their strength,
And spite of spites needes must I yeeld to death.

[*Ibid.*, p. 68, ll. 25–27]

Her lookes are all repleat with maiestie.

[*True Tragedie*, p. 45, l. 64]

Thy lookes are all repleat with Maiestie.

[*Ibid.*, p. 63, l. 19]

Lent me a heart repleat with thankfulnesse.

[*Contention*, p. 4, l. 21]

For I am not yet lookt on in the world.

[*True Tragedie*, p. 47, l. 107]

For yet I am not lookt on in the world.

[*Ibid.*, p. 78, l. 22]

And free King *Henry* from imprisonment,
And see him seated in his regall throne.

[*True Tragedie*, p. 59, ll. 52–53]

And pull false *Henry* from the Regall throne.

[*Ibid.*, p. 63, l. 58]

Awaie with him, I will not heare him speake.

[*True Tragedie*, p. 65, l. 3]

Awaie I will not heare them speake.

[*Ibid.*, p. 72, l. 50]

My Lord, this harmefull pittie makes your followers faint.

[*True Tragedie*, p. 29, l. 55]

My gratious Lord, this too much lenitie,
And harmefull pittie must be laid aside.

[*True Tragedie*, p. 28, ll. 8–9]

. . . tell false *Edward* thy supposed king,
That *Lewis* of France is sending ouer Maskers
To reuell it with him and his new bride.
Bona. Tell him in hope heele be a widower shortlie,
Ile weare the willow garland for his sake.
Queen. Tell him my mourning weedes be laide aside,
And I am readie to put armour on.

War. Tell him from me, that he hath done me wrong,
And therefore Ile vncrowne him er't be long.

[*True Tragedie,* p. 52, ll. 135–143]

. . . tell false *Edward* thy supposed king,
That *Lewis* of France is sending ouer Maskers,
To reuill it with him and his new bride. . . .
Tel him quoth she, in hope heele proue a widdower shortly,
Ile weare the willow garland for his sake. . . .
Tell him quoth shee my mourning weeds be
Doone, and I am ready to put armour on. . . .
Tell him quoth he, that he hath done me wrong,
And therefore Ile vncrowne him er't be long.

[*Ibid.,* p. 56, ll. 64–66, 69–70, 74–75, 79 ff.]

The last parallel is, of course, accounted for by the fact that an ambassador is repeating at the English court the message given him at the French court. But only a dramatist with a strong tendency to repeat would give the report in words so closely resembling the original.

V. DRAMATIC COMPANIES

Further strength is lent to Marlowe's claim to authorship of the two source plays by the fact that both were produced by Pembroke's Company. We know from the title page of *The True Tragedie* that it was "sundrie times acted by the Right Honourable the Earle of Pembrooke his seruantes." Since each play is meaningless without the other, it is obvious that *The Contention* was also a Pembroke play.

Now, Pembroke's Company produced Marlowe's *Edward the Second,* though most of his other plays seem to have been written for the Admiral's men. Dr. Eleanor Grace Clark [75] argues that only six men could have written the two source plays — Robert Wilson, Kyd, Peele, Greene, Shakespeare, and Marlowe. Of these, only Kyd, Shakespeare, and Marlowe wrote for Pembroke's men. Of these three, only Marlowe had any connection with Lord Strange's men or any of the other companies financed by Henslowe. The two source plays eventually turn up in *Henslowe's Diary,* and "the only author who could have taken Pembroke's plays to the Rose [Henslowe's theatre] was Marlowe."

[75] *The Pembroke Plays* (Bryn Mawr Diss., 1928), p. 21.

Pembroke's men never produced any of Shakespeare's undisputed works, and their performance of the highly dubious *Titus Andronicus* may be regarded as evidence of Marlowe's authorship,[76] or part authorship. Shakespeare seems to have written only for his own dramatic company, whose patrons were successively Lord Strange, Lord Derby, Lord Hunsdon, the Lord Chamberlain, and the King.[77] It would be strange indeed for Shakespeare to lend his aid against his own financial interest to collaborate with the chief dramatist of a rival organization. It would be even stranger for that rival organization to ask the still relatively unimportant young man from Stratford to aid the sensationally successful Marlowe.

VI. Date

Finally, force is added to the argument for Marlowe's authorship of *The Contention* and *The True Tragedie* by the probable dates of production — roughly 1590–92 — which fall within the period of his greatest dramatic activity, and a period when Shakespeare was at best but a beginner.

It is reasonable to conclude that the greater part of *The Contention* and *The True Tragedie* is Marlowe's handiwork; and that the large portions of both plays taken over in *Henry VI* represent wholesale borrowing on Shakespeare's part.

Richard II

Richard II at first glance shows less obvious traces of Marlowe's influence than a play like *Richard III*, with the single dominating figure of Richard Crookback and his cynical self-revelation of his own villainy, in the manner of Marlowe's Guise or Barabas. When one analyzes the structure of both plays, however, one finds that *Richard II* shows Marlowe's influence less obviously, simply because Shakespeare is here imitating *Edward the Second*. Since this is the least typical of Marlowe's plays, especially in its lack of the usual dominant

[76] See II. 258–263.

[77] It has been asserted on doubtful grounds that Shakespeare *did* write for the Pembroke Company; but the arguments are questionable and it has even been questioned whether a Pembroke Company existed at the time. Cf. A. W. Pollard's Introduction to Peter Alexander's *Shakespeare's Henry VI and Richard III*, and J. Q. Adams: *Life of Shakespeare*, p. 131.

Marlowe hero, the extent of Shakespeare's borrowing is not at once apparent. Actually, his imitation of *Edward the Second* in *Richard II* is almost as close as Robert Greene's imitation of *Tamburlaine* in *Alphonsus, King of Aragon*.[78]

Shakespeare's play, like Marlowe's, has a fiery dispute near the beginning. In *Richard II* this is between Bolingbroke and Mowbray; in *Edward the Second*, between the king and his nobles. In each play the quarrel serves to bring the opposing factions into line against each other and reveal the general nature of the plot at once. In each play there are three king's favorites: Gaveston and the two Spensers in *Edward the Second*; Busby, Green, and Bagot in *Richard II*. Each dramatist brings in a fourth timeserver who is less important: Baldock in *Edward the Second*; the Earl of Wiltshire, who is repeatedly mentioned but who does not come on the stage, in *Richard II*. Each king makes a levy upon his subjects' property, and each dramatist uses this fact to help on the catastrophe. Each king is caught unprepared by the return of an absent enemy. Each is forced, after a hesitation of which each author makes full dramatic use, to abdicate. Each, in his anger, destroys a physical object: Edward a letter, Richard a mirror. Each is eventually murdered, and the coffin of each is brought on the stage in the final scene.

Granting that most of this is history, that each play contains other elements not used in its companion-piece, and that the emphasis — especially on the exact roles of the two sets of favorites — is different, it is nevertheless hard to believe that Shakespeare's choice and his structural combination of historical incidents were uninfluenced by Marlowe's.

The favorites are put to death on much the same grounds in each play. In *Edward the Second* Mortimer says,

> The proud corrupters of the light-brainde king
> Haue done their homage to the loftie gallowes.

In *Richard II* Busby and Green are executed after Bolingbroke's accusation,

> You have misled a prince, a royal king.[79]

[78] See I. 248–252.
[79] *Edward the Second*, 2144–2145; *Richard II*, III. i. 8.

This is especially striking because Shakespeare's version does not accord with history. The Busby, Bagot, and Green of actual fact were not responsible for the real king's misdeeds. Gaveston and the Spensers were. Shakespeare found the accusation dramatically effective and took it over from Marlowe in blithe indifference to fact.

Again, in *Richard II*, Bolingbroke condemns Busby and Green because

> You have in manner with your sinful hours
> Made a divorce betwixt his queen and him,
> Broke the possession of a royal bed,[80]

which is true enough of Edward's favorites but not of Richard's. Shakespeare's king and queen were actually in entire harmony. In both these cases Shakespeare kept Marlowe's play a little too closely in mind.

Beyond this, the relationship between the two plays is slight. The style and structure are more typically Shakespearean than in *Richard III*, with less of Marlowe. The verse is typically Shakespearean, with abundant rhyme, which Marlowe practically never used in dramatic writing.[81] Rhyme in *Richard II* is in a proportion of 1 : 4, while in *Edward the Second* it is in a proportion of 1 : 23.[82]

Shakespeare's play does contain a few lines that remind one of Marlowe, but they are very few. The clearest borrowing is in the abdication scene, especially the episode with the mirror, at the end of Act IV.[83] Richard's hesitancy and reluctance are plainly modeled on those of Edward in the same situation. The mirror scene is certainly an imitation — conscious, unconscious, or derisive — of the most famous passage in *Doctor Faustus*:

> . . . Was this face the face
> That every day under his household roof
> Did keep ten thousand men? Was this the face
> That, like the sun, did make beholders wink?
> Is this the face which fac'd so many follies,
> That was at last outfac'd by Bolingbroke?

---

[80] *Richard II*, III. i. 11–13.   [81] See II. 202–203.

[82] Paul Kühl: *Verhältnis von Shakesperes Richard II zu Marlowes Edward II* (Greifswald Diss., 1923, MS.), p. 100.

[83] The abdication scene is in *Richard II*, IV. i. 162–320. The mirror episode is IV. i. 281–286. Edward II abdicates in ll. 1987–2114 of Marlowe's play. Cf. *Doctor Faustus*, 1328–1347.

A passage in the third act seems to have been drawn from the scene in which Tamburlaine condemns to death the virgins of Damascus. Shakespeare wrote:

> . . . Within the hollow crown
> That rounds the mortal temples of a king
> Keeps Death his court, and there the antic sits,
> Scoffing his state and grinning at his pomp.

Marlowe's Tamburlaine says of his sword's point:

> For there sits Death, there sits imperious Death,
> Keeping his circuit by the slicing edge.[84]

In *Henry VI* the phrase "antic Death" recurs.[85]

German scholars have endeavored to trace more detailed parallels.[86] Few others, however, have been inclined to lay much stress on Shakespeare's further borrowings. Stopford Brooke says simply that, while *Edward the Second* possibly suggested *Richard II*, "it may be so, I do not know." [87] A. W. Verity thought that Shakespeare's play was "written on a model furnished by Marlowe." [88] Felix Schelling says that "in Richard II. Shakespeare passes beyond the period of interpolation, revision and imitation, but he still has his great rival in view." [89] Mr. William Allan Neilson thinks that "the subject may have been suggested by Marlowe's *Edward II*; but the style shows a marked departure from the Marlowesque rhetoric of *Richard III*, and takes it out of the period when Shakespeare was most under the influence of his great predecessor." [90] Sidney Lee thought that in both the Richard plays and in *The Merchant of Venice* "Shakespeare plainly disclosed a conscious and a prudent resolve to follow in the dead Marlowe's footsteps," and that in *Richard II* "again there is a clear echo of Marlowe's 'mighty line.' " [91] Miss Priscilla Fletcher says that it is "mod-

---

[84] *Richard II*, III. ii. 160–163; I *Tamb.* 1892–1893.
[85] I *Henry VI*, IV. vii. 18.
[86] Paul Kühl: *op. cit.*; M. Dametz: *Marlowes Edward II und Shakespeares Richard II, Ein literar-historischer Vergleich. 53ter Jahresbericht* (K. K. Staats-Realschule, Vienna, 1903–04).
[87] *Ten Plays*, p. 71.
[88] *Influence of Christopher Marlowe*, p. 94.
[89] *English Chronicle Play*, p. 96.
[90] *Shakespeare* (Cambridge ed., 1906), p. 506.
[91] *Life of William Shakespeare* (1916), pp. 123–126.

elled certainly upon Marlowe," [92] and Alfred Stern says: "Marlowes 'Edward II.' hat auch mit Shakespeares 'Richard III.' einige Züge gemein, die dieser jenem entlehnte." [93]

RICHARD III

Richard III is, next to *The Merchant of Venice* and *Henry VI*, the clearest example of Marlowe's powerful and direct influence upon Shakespeare's earlier work. Elsewhere we are usually confronted with a tedious array of doubtful and frequently contradictory possibilities. In these three plays we have clear ones. *Richard III* is obviously in Marlowe's vein — a one-character play, centering around a single unscrupulous, ambitious Machiavellian superman. The course of action is outlined at the very start in an introductory soliloquy typical of Marlowe and found in *The Jew of Malta*, *Doctor Faustus*, and *The Massacre at Paris*.[94] There is an absence of comic relief, also typical of Marlowe but very uncharacteristic of Shakespeare, and the inadequate characterization of women equally typical of Marlowe and unusual in Shakespeare.

Marlowe's Machiavellianism and thirst for power are quite as recognizable in Richard as in Tamburlaine, Faustus, Barabas, or Guise. Richard further resembles Marlowe's rather than Shakespeare's handiwork in that his character is complete and unchanging, the same throughout the play, showing no development. It is, moreover, brutally driven home to the audience by its sheer blazing force and audacity, not dextrously insinuated by the numberless touches, strokes, and hints of character-painting typical of Shakespeare's method.

That Marlowe's influence is dominant in all this, no one will for a moment deny, though critics have not been wanting to affirm more extreme theories. It has been asserted that Marlowe himself wrote *Richard III*; that he collaborated with Shakespeare; that Shakespeare revised his work; and that the play, though more than a mere revision, is at least based upon an earlier play, now lost, which was entirely Marlowe's. So

---

[92] *Study of English Blank Verse* (1907), p. 49.
[93] *Archiv*, 156: 197 (1929).
[94] *Richard III*, I. i. 1–40; *Jew of Malta*, 1–35; *Doctor Faustus*, 29–91; *Massacre*, 91–166.

clear is the Marlowe influence, indeed, that the usual claims for Peele, Greene, or Lodge have rarely been made. Fleay is alone in regarding *Richard III* as based by Shakespeare on an unfinished original by Peele.[95]

The Marlowe characteristics in the play have been summed up as follows by Sir Israel Gollancz:

(*a*) Richard, like Tamberlaine [*sic*] or Faustus, or Barabas, monopolises the whole action of the Drama; (*b*) the characters of this play of passion seem intended, for the most part, merely to set off the hero's "ideal villainy"; (*c*) the absence of evolution of character in the hero; (*d*) the hero's consciousness and avowal of his villainy; (*e*) the tone of the play is often lyrical or epical rather than dramatic (*e.g.*, the lamentation of the women, II, ii; IV, i.); (*f*) blank verse is used throughout, while prose and the lyrical forms found in the earlier plays are conspicuously absent.[96]

In contrast with this, however, it is well to note Judge Samuel S. Ashbaugh's list of the Shakespearean characteristics obviously lacking in *Richard III*. These include:

(a) An ever-present sweetness of spirit and a benignant worldly wisdom readily quoted; (b) a kindly and spontaneous humor, which in his tragedies lies close to an immeasurable pathos; (c) a dramatic development of plot which aids in the evolution of the leading characters; (d) an unclouded insight into the moral law as worked out in human affairs; (e) a richness of language and a variety of measure which breaks the monotony and increases the music of the blank verse; (f) the inclusion of one or more female characters in each play bearing his own stamp and impress.[97]

None of these qualities, according to this critic, appear in *Richard III*, "except in the 'purple patches' of revision."

From this Judge Ashbaugh drew the conclusion that *Richard III* is Marlowe's work, perhaps revised by Shakespeare — a view shared by a surprising number of critics, as the following table will show:

1799. George Chalmers: "Shakespeare had received so many hints from the perusal of Marlow's *True Tragedie* . . . that he was induced, immediately, to continue the *Historie* of Richard the third. [*Supplemental Apology* (1799), p. 303]

[95] F. C. Fleay: "Who Wrote Henry VI?" *Macmillan's Magazine*, 33: 60 N 1875.
[96] Introduction to the Temple ed., p. x.
[97] Samuel S. Ashbaugh: *On the parts of Marlowe and Shakespeare in Richard III*, p. 10.

1875. Jane Lee: "*Richard III*, no less than 2 and 3 *Henry* [*VI*,] is full of the influence of Marlowe's soul and spirit; and, though I think it more than improbable that Marlowe actually wrote any part of this play, yet in many passages we seem to catch echoes of his voice." [*Trans. New Shakspere Society*, ser. 1, p. 310 (1875)]

1875. Edward Dowden. "A certain resemblance, not elsewhere to be found in Shakspere's writings, to the ideal manner of Marlowe." [*Mind and Art*, p. 180]

1883. James Russell Lowell: "It seems to me that an examination of *Richard III* plainly indicates that it is a play which Shakespeare adapted to the stage, making additions, sometimes longer and sometimes shorter; and that, towards the end, either growing weary of his work or pressed for time, he left the older author, whoever he was, pretty much to himself. [Address to the Edinburgh Philosophical Institution, quoted by Ashbaugh, *op. cit.*, p. 2]

1885. P. A. Daniel: "Not of Shakespeare's original composition, but the work of the author or authors of the *Henry VI.* series of plays; his part in this as in those, being merely that of reviser or re-writer." [Introd. to Facsimile Quarto 1597, p. iv]

1885. A. W. Verity: "Shakspere was writing altogether on the lines of Marlowe." [*Influence of Christopher Marlowe*, p. 90]

1886. F. G. Fleay: "Bears strong internal evidence of Marlowe's craftsmanship, but was no doubt completed and partly rewritten by Shakespeare." [*Chron. Hist. . . . Shakespeare*, p. 23]

1902. F. E. Schelling: "The essential difference between Shakespeare's *Richard III.* and his other historical plays has long been recognized. . . . All this has been . . . variously explained: some assigning to Marlowe a hand in *Richard III.* and regarding it as a joint production of Shakespeare and Marlowe; others denying Marlowe's hand, but confessing his influence. The latter is assuredly the wiser view." [*English Chronicle Play*, pp. 92–94]

1908. F. E. Schelling: "*Richard III* shows the influence of Marlowe to a greater degree than any play of Shakespeare's shows any single influence." [*Eliz. Drama*, I. 275]

1921. Samuel S. Ashbaugh: "Shakespeare . . . must have taken a *Richard III*, written by Marlowe but now lost, and revised it into the *Richard III* subsequently ascribed to him by the pirate publishers. . . . There is far more of Marlowe than of Shakespeare in *Richard III*." [*Op. cit.*, pp. 5, 31]

1929. Alfred W. Pollard: "There is no room for both Shakespeare and Marlowe." [Introd. to Peter Alexander: *op. cit.*, p. 24]

If no critic has attempted to question the strong influence which Marlowe obviously exerts over *Richard III*, neither has any critic of importance attempted to deny that in its present form it is more or less (and more rather than less) Shakespearean. It is definitely attributed to Shakespeare in Meres' list, published in 1598, early in Shakespeare's career. It is metrically in accord with Shakespeare's work at this time and just as definitely out of accord with Marlowe's, except for the lack of rhyme.[98] The percentage of pyrrhic feet — a typical quality of Marlowe's verse — is far lower than in Marlowe's canonical plays. On the other hand, the percentage of eleven-syllable feet and of run-on lines — Shakespearean qualities both — is far higher. Furthermore, though the verse is often powerful, it is hardly the mighty line, and Marlowe's usual self-repetition is lacking.

The evidence for Marlowe's influence is clear and cogent. Evidence for any other relationship is doubtful. It is best to be content with the assertion of a marked influence by Marlowe and leave other views to the limbo of hypothesis.

THE TAMING OF A SHREW

The problem presented by *The Taming of a Shrew*, the play which Shakespeare recast to make *The Taming of the Shrew*, is simpler than that presented by other Shakespearean or pseudo-Shakespearean plays in which Marlowe's influence is felt. It is quite impossible to suppose that either Marlowe or Shakespeare wrote the earlier play. Indeed, it is not quite accurate to speak of Marlowe's "influence" at all. *A Shrew* shows no trace of his thought, his dramatic structure, his characterization, nor — except in purple patches very clumsily sewn in from Marlowe's known plays — of his mighty line. The humor of the play is wholly out of Marlowe's vein.

There are only two reasons for discussing it here at all. One is the ruthless rifling to which *Tamburlaine* and *Doctor Faustus* were subjected whenever the unknown author felt that his play needed poetical ornamentation which he himself was unable to supply. The other is the fact that it did serve as a source for Shakespeare.

[98] See II. 202–203, 228–230.

In all, some sixteen quotations from both parts of *Tambur-laine* and from *Doctor Faustus* have been detected. The author lets Marlowe's other plays alone, perhaps because they had not yet been written. These cannot be examples of Marlowe's self-repetition. They are too long — running up to six lines at a time; and they are too accurate to be anything but deliberate copying, probably with the original open before the author as he wrote. They often fit so badly into the text of the play that one can hardly imagine Marlowe misplacing his own lines so grotesquely; and the style of the play as a whole is far below the level of the stolen passages.

One may see an example of the unknown author's abrupt tumble into bathos the moment he ceases to quote, in the open-ing of the Induction. This introduces the frolicsome nobleman and the tale of Christopher Sly's dream in the source play at rather more length than Shakespeare gave it. The nobleman opens with a word-for-word quotation from *Doctor Faustus* for five lines and then stumbles suddenly in the next two:

> Now that the gloomy shadow of the night,
> Longing to view Orion's drizzling looks,
> Leaps from th' Antarctic world unto the sky,
> And dims the welkin with her pitchy breath,
> And darksome night o'ershades the crystal heavens,
> Here break we off our hunting for to-night:
> Couple up the hounds and let us hie us home.[99]

A more dismal example of that inappropriate stitching of purple patches on a commonplace garment against which Horace warns it would be hard to find.

The play has a good many passages that one simply cannot imagine Marlowe's writing — as this:

> A large dowry he shall be sure to have,
> For her father is a man of mighty wealth,
> And an ancient citizen of the town,
> And that was he that went along with them.[100]

Since the text is not notably corrupt, this is an integral part of

---

[99] *A Shrew*, Induction, 9–15; *Doctor Faustus*, 235–239.
[100] *A Shrew*, I. i. 56–59. References are to the ed. by F. S. Boas (Shakespeare Clas-sics), New York: Duffield; London: Chatto and Windus, 1908.

it. Hence this is what the author wrote, and hence that author is emphatically not Christopher Marlowe.

A further reason for doubting Marlowe's authorship is found in the quite ridiculous errors that are occasionally made. Marlowe's scholarship was by no means impeccable, but these errors would have been impossible for a Cambridge Master of Arts. No Cambridge scholar would have made Pegasus the horse "that ran so swiftly o'er the Persian plains," [101] a blunder plainly based on a passage in *Tamburlaine* [102] which refers first to Pegasus and then in the next line to "Medean silke." Neither would a Cambridge scholar have supplied the Egyptian deity Ibis with a golden beak, though Marlowe does introduce this deity in an oath appropriate to the Soldan of Egypt who utters it.[103]

The play is, to adapt a famous remark, a very pretty play, but you mustn't call it Marlowe.

We have here, quite plainly, an unknown playwright — who has been identified, on no adequate ground, with both Greene and Kyd. He is not without comic gifts, a talent for construction, and an ardor for magnificent language without any great gift that way. He is evidently writing at some time in 1593, when Marlowe is at the height of his reputation. The Marlowe trick of using resounding geographic names is plainly borrowed, and two characters, Sander and the Boy, are adapted from Wagner and Robin in *Doctor Faustus*. Occasional lines have a ring like Marlowe's, but it is a hollow ring; and it is noticeable that Shakespeare, in *The Shrew*, gets rid of both the authentic and the imitation Marlowe, neither being of great value in farcical comedy.

The older play has, however, an unexpected value in that two of its quotations [104] are from the so-called 1616 text of *Doctor Faustus* — that is, they correspond to the quarto first published in that year, which differs widely from the earlier editions.[105] Now, *The Taming of a Shrew* is certainly an early play.

---

[101] *A Shrew*, Induction, ii. 20–21.
[102] I *Tamb.* 290–291.
[103] *A Shrew*, II. i. 151; I *Tamb.* 1607.
[104] See II. 249. *Doctor Faustus*, 235, has "earth" for "night" until 1616. Lines 351–353 differ even more widely.
[105] See I. 293–297.

It is entered in the *Stationers' Register* May 2, 1594; the first edition appears in that year; and a passage in Greene's *Menaphon* [106] suggests that it was on the stage as early as 1589. The quotations therefore indicate that the 1616 text of *Faustus* is really very early; and since it is being quoted the year after Marlowe's death at latest, it is probably his authentic work. Since the early nineteenth century, however, no one has pretended that *The Taming of a Shrew* is genuine work of Marlowe's. [107]

Four of the borrowings from Marlowe are so nearly verbatim that they need not be repeated. These are: I *Tamburlaine*, 1003–1005 (*A Shrew*, II. i. 67–69); I *Tamburlaine*, 1856–1860 (*A Shrew*, I. i. 61–64); *Doctor Faustus*, 235–236 (*A Shrew*, Induction, i. 9–12); *Doctor Faustus*, 640 (*A Shrew*, III. vi. 32). The other borrowings, which have undergone a little adaptation, are as follows:

> *Zenocrate*, the loueliest Maide aliue,
> Fairer than rockes of pearle and pretious stone,
> The onely Paragon of *Tamburlaine*,
> Whose eies are brighter than the Lamps of heauen.
> [I *Tamb.* 1215–1218]

> But stay; what dames are these so bright of hue,
> Whose eyes are brighter than the lamps of heaven,
> Fairer than rocks of pearl and precious stone.
> [*A Shrew*, I. i. 22–24]

> . . . pale and ghastly death:
> Whose darts do pierce the Center of my soule.
> Her sacred beauty hath enchaunted heauen,
> And had she liu'd before the siege of *Troy*,
> *Hellen*, whose beauty sommond Greece to armes,
> And drew a thousand ships to *Tenedos*,
> Had not bene nam'd in *Homers* Iliads.
> [II *Tamb.* 3051–3057]

> Oh, might I see the centre of my soul,
> Whose sacred beauty hath enchanted me,
> More fair than was the Grecian Helena

[106] Cf. Albert H. Tolman: *Shakespeare's Part in The Taming of the Shrew*, p. 15; Grosart's Greene, VI. 119.

[107] Cf. N&Q, 1st ser., 1: 347, 30 Mr 1859; Richard Simpson: *op. cit.*, pt. I, p. xlvii; Ingram: *op. cit.*, p. 211; Boas' ed., p. xxxiii; Alexander, *op. cit.*, pp. 68–70.

For whose sweet sake so many princes died,
That came with thousand ships to Tenedos!
[*A Shrew*, I. i. 81–85]

Now, bright *Zenocrate*, the worlds faire eie,
Whose beames illuminate the lamps of heauen,
Whose chearful looks do cleare the clowdy aire
And cloath it in a christall liuerie.
[II *Tamb.* 2570–2573]

Come, fair Emelia, my lovely love,
Brighter than the burnished palace of the sun,
The eyesight of the glorious firmament,
In whose bright looks sparkles the radiant fire.
[*A Shrew*, II. i. 56–59]

And show your pleasure to the Persean,
As fits the Legate of the stately Turk.
[I *Tamb.* 961–962]

And I sat downe, cloth'd with the massie robe,
That late adorn'd the Affrike Potentate.
[II *Tamb.* 3313–3314]

As was the massy robe that late adorned
The stately legate of the Persian King.
[*A Shrew*, II. i. 131–132]

Zenocrate, louelier than the Loue of *Ioue*,
Brighter than is the siluer Rhodope,
Fairer than whitest snow on Scythian hils.
[I *Tamb.* 283–285]

Sweet Kate, lovelier than Diana's purple robe,
Whiter than are the snowy Apennines.
[*A Shrew*, II. i. 148–149]

That restes vpon the snowy Appenines.
[II *Tamb.* 2436]

Thy Garments shall be made of Medean silke,
Enchast with precious iuelles of mine owne.
[I *Tamb.* 291–292]

And Christian Merchants that with Russian stems
Plow vp huge furrowes in the Caspian sea.
[I *Tamb.* 389–390]

The Terrene main wherein *Danubius* fals.
[II *Tamb.* 2362]

Thou shalt have garments wrought of Median silk,
Enchased with precious jewels fetched from far,

By Italian merchants that with Russian stems
Ploughs up huge furrows in the Terrene Maine.
[*A Shrew*, II. i. 156–159]

The headstrong Iades of *Thrace*, *Alcides* tam'd,
That King *Egeus* fed with humaine flesh,
And made so wanton that they knew their strengths.
[II *Tamb.* 3991–3993]

Were she as stubborn or as full of strength
As were the Thracian horse Alcides tamed,
That King Egeus fed with flesh of men.
[*A Shrew*, III. i. 49–51]

Ransacke the Ocean for orient pearle,
And search all corners of the new found world.
[DF, 111–112]

To seek for strange and new-found precious stones,
And dive into the sea to gather pearl.
[*A Shrew*, II. i. 79–80]

Wag. Sirra boy, come hither.
Clo. How, boy? swowns boy, I hope you haue seene
many boyes with such pickadevaunts as I haue.
Boy, quotha?   [DF (1604), 351–354]
Wag. Come hither sirra boy.
Clo. Boy? O disgrace to my person: Zounds boy in
your face, you haue seene many boyes with
beards, I am sure.   [DF (1616), 351–353]
Boy. Come hither, sirrah boy.
San. Boy, oh, disgrace to my person! Souns! boy, of
your face! You have many boys with such pick-
adevants, I am sure!   [*A Shrew*, II. ii. 1–4]

And had you cut my body with your swords,
Or hew'd this flesh and bones as small as sand.
[DF (1616), 1252–1253]

This angry sword should rip thy hateful chest,
And hewed thee smaller than the Lybian sands.
[*A Shrew*, IV. ii. 60–61]

JULIUS CAESAR

When we enter upon the question of Marlowe's influence on
Shakespeare's *Julius Caesar*, we enter a morass of controversy,
conjecture, and doubtful evidence, remarkable even in the study
of Elizabethan drama. To most readers, the play has always

appeared to be entirely Shakespeare's, even though it may owe a good deal to one or more earlier plays and a little to the influence — perhaps even to the pens — of fellow-dramatists. If the play shows any traces of other writers, Marlowe is certainly one; and various turns of phrase and echoes of lines suggest that Francis Beaumont may be another. Yet on the whole it appears to be right Shakespeare, characteristic and unmistakable. This view can be based on internal grounds, which there is no good external evidence to confute.

There is, however, a more extreme view, represented chiefly by Mr. J. M. Robertson (who is never willing to allow anything to Shakespeare that can possibly be assigned elsewhere); by a one-book enthusiast, Mr. William Wells; and by the far more conservative and scholarly Dr. E. H. C. Oliphant. These writers would very largely parcel out the play between Marlowe and Beaumont, allowing Shakespeare relatively little. Mr. Wells doubts whether Shakespeare contributed more than the first fifty-seven lines. Mr. Robertson is sure that whatever else is Shakespeare's in the play, these lines are not. Both profess a high regard for each other's views; but such a discrepancy is likely to give the judicious pause.

Their views, set forth in full, with an elaborate list of parallel passages, require several hundred pages; but their conclusions, differing only in detail, may be summarized as follows:

J. M. Robertson
Shakespeare   Drayton?
Marlowe   Chapman?
Beaumont?

William Wells
Shakespeare: I. i, 1–57
Beaumont: V. ii; V. iii. 1–22; II. iii (?) and iv (?)
Marlowe; the rest of the play, Shakespeare in collaboration with
    Beaumont

E. H. C. Oliphant
Shakespeare: I. ii a (to Caesar's first exit) and three speeches preceding Caesar's first re-entry; iii (containing perhaps a little Marlowe); II. i a (to "stands as the Capitol, directly here"); also from "*Cas.* Nay we will all of us," to Calpurnia's entry; iii a (the prose); iv; all of Act III; IV. i; V. i b (last twelve speeches); iv; v (probably based on Marlowe)

Marlowe: II. iii b (the verse); V. i a; ii; iii
Beaumont: IV. ii
Marlowe and Shakespeare (jointly): I. i; ii; II. i b; ii b
Beaumont and Shakespeare: I. ii b; IV. ii (both outside and inside
  the tent)

It is evident that there is very little agreement here, except that all find traces of three writers in the play; and that both Wells and Robertson agree in denying to Shakespeare Antony's oration over the body of Caesar. These widely disparate results of three critics working by essentially the same methods — intuitive recognition of style and parallel passages — suggest that their conclusions cannot be accepted save in the most general way. They may, perhaps, show that there are non-Shakespearean traces in *Julius Caesar*, some of which are quite probably due to Marlowe, and a few others which may conceivably be due to Francis Beaumont. The average, unprejudiced reader will be likely to feel, however, that it is high time to get back to the *terra firma* of external evidence. Of that, happily, there is a good deal, and it all points strongly to Shakespeare.

In the first place, it is pretty clear that there were two or three plays on Julius Caesar before the present Shakespeare play came into being, perhaps by recension, about 1599 or 1600. At most, then, Shakespeare was simply working from a source, as usual. In view of the classical taste of the Elizabethan age, Caesar was too good a subject to be missed. An extant play called *Caesar and Pompey* [108] either is itself one of these earlier plays or bears traces of them. We have also numerous allusions to Caesar and his deeds scattered through other Elizabethan plays. These may be mere allusions to Roman history, but they sound very much more like allusions to contemporary stage successes. For example, Peele's *Edward I*, Marlowe's *Edward the Second*, Greene's *Alphonsus of Aragon*, and Shakespeare's *Henry V* [109] all allude in this way to Caesar's triumphal entry into Rome. No such scene appears in any extant play, but the passages resemble similar references to Tamburlaine's famous

---

[108] Usually regarded as Chapman's.
[109] *Edward I*, Dodsley (1825), XI. 12; *Edward the Second*, 173–174; *Alphonsus*, I. i. (p. 12, Mermaid ed.); *Henry V*, Prologue, 28.

entry with the captive kings.[110] Other allusions to Caesar in Greene's *Orlando* and his *Friar Bacon and Friar Bungay* and in Peele's *Alphonsus, Emperor of Germany*, may also refer to stage productions. The last play even has the lines:

> Methinks I now present Mark Antony,
> Folding dead Julius Caesar in mine arms.[111]

As a second bit of evidence for the existence of earlier plays, we may note that Shakespeare's play, as it stands in the Folio text, pretty clearly points to a predecessor. It is named for Caesar, a character who disappears in the beginning of the third act. This may be the result of compressing at least two and perhaps three earlier plays, one on the triumph of Caesar, another on the death of Caesar, and still another on the avenging of Caesar's death. A further bit of evidence for this view is the odd way in which Portia's death is twice reported in the same scene. Brutus has scarcely confided his sorrow to Cassius,[112] when a messenger enters with the same news, which Brutus receives as if it really were still news. This looks as if a reviser had failed to notice the overlapping of two old plays. The Elizabethan actors doubtless corrected the blunder for stage purposes, but being in manuscript it slipped into print.

There is further Ben Jonson's famous gibe in *Discoveries*,[113] in which he ridicules Shakespeare for his line

> Cæsar did never wrong, but with just cause.

Now, this line does not appear in the text as we have it today. Instead, this passage reads:

> Know, Caesar doth not wrong, nor without cause
> Will he be satisfied.[114]

This is plain evidence that someone has been revising, perhaps Jonson himself, as final editor of a much revised play. Strength is lent to the idea that Jonson was the reviser by the curious

[110] See I. 239–240.

[111] *Alphonsus, Emperor of Germany*, p. 124 of Karl Elze's (Leipzig, 1867) ed., which has two other references. Elze attributes the play to Chapman.

[112] IV. iii. 147–162.

[113] Page 29 of G. B. Harrison's ed. (Bodley Head Quartos. London: John Lane; New York: Dutton, n.d.).

[114] III. i. 47–48.

fact that the First Folio uses the spelling "Antony" only in *Julius Caesar*, and elsewhere employs the anglicized "Anthony" — a useful bit of evidence which is obscured by the uniformity of modern editions. "Antony" was the spelling always used by Jonson in his Roman plays.

Undue stress has hitherto been laid on two bits of evidence that seem to link Marlowe with *Julius Caesar*. These lose their value when placed in proper perspective. One of these is a passage in Robert Greene's *Neuer Too Late* (1590), containing the words: "The Cobler hath taught thee to say *Aue Caesar*." [115] Given the undoubted facts that Greene hated Marlowe and that Marlowe's father was a shoemaker, this has been taken as an allusion to a play by Marlowe on Julius Caesar. It need not, however, be an allusion to Marlowe at all; and if the passage alludes to any Elizabethan play, it is to the anonymous *Edward III*, in which this very line occurs. [116]

Equal stress has been laid on the exact parallel of the line "Caesar shall go forth," which occurs repeatedly in *Julius Caesar* and *The Massacre at Paris*. [117] If this is a borrowing at all, it is a borrowing from Marlowe, as has already been shown; but the phrase is natural in the context and the similarity may go back to a common origin in the newsbooks. [118]

With these two arguments destroyed, it is still possible to believe that there was a pre-Shakespearean play, or several of them, on which Shakespeare based his tragedy. It is no longer possible, however, to father the earlier plays on Marlowe. *Julius Caesar* is, at best, not much like Marlowe's known work. The theme is not ambition but the danger of ambition, which must be thwarted. We lack the usual Machiavellian hero with his cynical avowal of his purposes. We have in Portia a woman character never fashioned by Christopher Marlowe. We may have occasional verbal parallels, but we lack anything like the constant thunder of the mighty line. We need at most write down *Julius Caesar* as perhaps influenced by Marlowe, but (in its present form) very remotely.

[115] Grosart's Greene, VIII. 132.
[116] See II. 282 and *Edward III*, I. i.
[117] See II. 85–86.
[118] See William Wells: *Authorship of Julius Caesar*; E. H. C. Oliphant: *Plays of Beaumont and Fletcher*, pp. 320–321.

One clear parallel should, however, be noted:

The glorie of this happy day is yours.
[II *Tamb.* 3664]
To part the glories of this happy day.
[JC, V. v. 81]

TITUS ANDRONICUS

Extremists who would claim the most improbable plays for
Marlowe are happily silenced in the case of *Titus Andronicus*
by the date of composition, which can be pretty accurately
fixed about the middle of the year 1593/4, after Marlowe had
been slain at Deptford.[119] This does not rule out Marlowe's
influence nor the possibility that Shakespeare was reworking
an old play of his; but it does make tolerably certain that
Marlowe had no hand in the play as it now stands.

Shakespeare's own claim to the complete authorship of this
bloody production is not very strong. His name does not appear on the title pages of the quartos, though the play is included among his in Meres' list. Attribution to him rests on
this fact, on its inclusion in the folios, and on the Shakespearean
ring of certain passages. As usual, critics, though quite certain
that they can detect the genuine vein of Shakespearean gold,
usually pick different passages as containing it. Coleridge
selects V. ii. 20–60; Swinburne, IV. iii; while Arthur Symons
believes that he detects brief lyrical passages by Shakespeare
scattered throughout the play.[120]

---

[119] Evidence for the date is abundant and fairly conclusive. Much has been made of
Ben Jonson's statement in the introduction to *Bartholomew Fair*, first produced in
1614, "He that will swear, *Jeronimo* or *Andronicus*, are the best plays yet, shall pass
unexcepted at here, as a man whose judgment shews it is constant, and hath stood
still these five and twenty or thirty years." This would, if strictly interpreted, give
1589 or 1584 as the date of composition; but Jonson is obviously not trying to be precise. There is better reason for thinking 1593/4 the more probable date. Henslowe
notes "Titus and Ondronicus" as "ne" on January 23, 1593/4. On February 6,
1593/4, John Danter enters "A Noble Roman Historye of Tytus Andronicus," and the
first quarto — as played by Derby's, Pembroke's, and Sussex's men — appears in the
same year.

Charles Crawford even believes ("Date and author of Titus Andronicus," *Jahrb.*,
36: 109–121 [1900]) that he can date the play definitely in July of the year 1593,
basing this view on the abundant phrasal echoes from George Peele's *Honour of the
Garter*, which commemorated the installation of new knights on June 26, 1593, just
after Marlowe's death.

[120] Introduction to the Facsimile Quarto (1600).

The evidence against Shakespearean authorship is both external and internal. The chief bit of external evidence is a statement by Edward Ravenscroft, who adapted *Titus Andronicus* for the stage in 1678 and published it in 1687: "I have been told by some anciently conversant with the Stage that it was not Originally his [Shakespeare's], but brought by a private Author to be Acted, and he only gave some Master-touches to one or two of the Principal Parts or Characters." [121] If this is true, it does not greatly help the critics who uphold the claims of Marlowe, Lodge, Peele, Greene, or Kyd to the authorship or partial authorship, since they were all well-known playwrights, who can hardly be regarded as "private authors." [122] Thus if we bow Shakespeare politely out of the door on Ravenscroft's testimony, we bow the chief candidates for his place out with him.

There is, however, grave doubt of Ravenscroft's veracity. He is called a liar to his face by Langbaine, who in his edition of 1691 charges that Ravenscroft's chief aim in minimizing Shakespeare's share in the play is to magnify his own. Color is lent to this suspicion by the odd fact that when he came to publish his adaptation Ravenscroft pretended to have lost the prologue. Langbaine, however, was able to quote some half dozen lines from it, which showed clearly that at the time of the stage presentation Ravenscroft had declared the play to be Shakespearean:

> To-day the poet does not fear your rage,
> Shakespeare, by him revived now treads the stage;
> Under his sacred laurels he sits down,
> Safe from the blast of any critic's frown.
> Like other poets, he'll not proudly scorn
> To own that he but winnowed Shakespeare's corn.[123]

As for internal evidence, idolaters of Shakespeare usually have qualms about admitting that Shakespeare could possibly have written this gory drama, with its rape, its three amputated hands, and its fourteen killings. Indeed, Fleay asserted

---

[121] Preface to his version, 1687.

[122] But see Alexander B. Grosart: "Was Robert Greene Substantially the Author of Titus Andronicus?" *Englische Studien*, 22: 390 Ag 1896.

[123] Gerard Langbaine: *Account of the English Dramatic Poets* (1691), pp. 464–465; (1698), p. 117. Cf. H. Bellyse Baildon: Introduction to *Titus Andronicus* (Arden ed., 1904), p. xxiii.

that the introduction of rape as a subject for the stage would be "sufficient to disprove" Shakespeare's authorship.[124] It is an odd argument when one remembers the general theme of *Lucrece*.

On the whole, it is probably better to admit that this is Shakespeare's work, or at least his adaptation, remembering that Shakespeare was an extremely practical man of the theatre and that *Titus Andronicus* seems to have been a huge commercial success. That it is mainly Shakespeare's work does not, however, remove the possibility that it may display the influence or actual handiwork of other playwrights, notably Marlowe, Greene, Kyd, Lodge, and Peele, all of whose styles various critics think they detect.

Evidence of Marlowe's influence is abundant, though actual examples of the mighty line are absent. Aaron is a typical, self-revealed Marlowe villain, a kind of link between Barabas and the later and subtler Shakespearean scoundrels, like Iago. Titus is in several respects much like Tamburlaine. He appears in the first scene, bringing the coffin of his son, much as Tamburlaine carries about the coffin of Zenocrate. Like Tamburlaine, he is a conqueror not to be resisted; like Tamburlaine, he is ready to sacrifice his sons to his ideal of military honor and discipline; like Tamburlaine, he is tender toward one woman.[125] Marlowe's influence is apparent in theme, structure, and to some degree in the versification; in the rant which recalls his less happy moments; and in the general Machiavellian atmosphere.

There are a few parallels, none of very great importance and most of them rather remote:

> Ah Shepheard, pity my distressed plight.
> > [I *Tamb.* 203]
> Comfort his distressed plight.
> > (*Titus Andronicus*, IV. iv. 32]

> Threatning the world.
> > [I *Tamb.* 5]
> Threat'ning the welkin.
> > [*Titus Andronicus*, III. i. 224]

---

[124] *Chron. Hist. . . . William Shakespeare*, p. 280.
[125] Alois Brandl carries the comparison even further in *Göttingische gelehrte Anzeigen*, 153: 711 (1891).

And Angels diue into the pooles of hell.
[II *Tamb.* 4425]
I'll dive into the burning lake below.
[*Titus Andronicus*, IV. iii. 43]

Some critics have not hesitated to ascribe the entire play to Marlowe, but opinion is much divided, as the following table shows:

1780. Edmund Malone: "Written by Marlowe." [Supplement, I. 163]

1797 or earlier. Richard Farmer: Kyd was "probably original author of Andronicus." [Quoted by Steevens "from a loose scrap of paper, in the handwriting of Dr. Farmer." Boswell's Malone (1821), XXI. 260]

1818. S. T. Coleridge: "Shakspere wrote some passages." [*Lectures and Notes on Shakespere* (Bohn ed.), p. 304]

1821. James Boswell, Jr.: "Much more in the style of Marlowe." [Boswell's Malone (1821), XXI. 261]

1821. William Hazlitt: "Marlowe has a much fairer claim to be the author of 'Titus Andronicus' than Shakespeare, at least from internal evidence." [*Lectures on the Dramatic Literature of the Age of Elizabeth* (3rd ed. 1840), p. 61]

1846. Hermann Ulrici: "Even more than 'Henry the Sixth,' exhibits a certain resemblance to the style of Marlowe." [*Shakspeare's Dramatic Art*, p. 411]

1853. J. P. Collier: "We feel no hesitation in assigning 'Titus Andronicus' to Shakespeare. . . . The lines . . . are scarcely inferior to the later and better productions of Marlowe." [*Shakespeare*, VI. 271–272]

1866. Gerald Massey: "Mapped out and partly written by Marlowe." [*Shakspeare's Sonnets*, p. 584]

1885. A. W. Verity: "It is, I suppose, fairly safe to assume that *Titus Andronicus* is in great part the work of Marlowe. . . . It is practically certain that Marlowe was a part author." [*Influence*, pp. 97n, 104]

1891. M. M. Arnold Schröer: "Ich habe in der ganzen mir zugänglichen zeitgenössischen Litteratur Englands nichts gefunden, das sich wie Marlowe's *Tamburlaine* und *Jew of Malta* als Vorlage für *Titus* und *Aaron* wahrscheinlich machen liesse. Und diese beiden Dramen, bez. die Gestalten *Tamburlaine*, *Bajazeth*, *Barabas*, *Ithimore* genügten auch vollständig, die des *Titus* und *Aaron* zu veranlassen." [*Über Titus Andronicus*, p. 121]

1896. Alexander B. Grosart: "Robert Greene was substantially the author of *Titus Andronicus*." [*Englische Studien*, 22: 400]

1897. Gregor Sarrazin: "Auf Grund der Stilähnlichkeit könnte man den Tit. Andr. mit viel grösserem Recht Thomas Kyd, als Greene oder Marlowe zuschreiben." [*William Shakespeares Lehrjahre*, p. 41]

1899. A. W. Ward: "I should not care to decide whether large parts of this play were written by Marlowe, or by so great a *virtuoso* in imitation as Greene; but the evidence of vocabulary favours the latter hypothesis." [HEDL, II. 56]

1900. Charles Crawford: "The idea that Shakespeare did not write the whole of *Titus Andronicus* is based upon a fiction." [*Jahrb.*, 36: 110 (1900)]

1901. H. de W. Fuller: "I believe Shakspere to be the author of practically every line." [PMLA, 16: 65 (1901)]

1904. H. Bellyse Baildon: "A strong case can be made out in favour of Shakespeare's authorship. . . . I do not maintain that every line and passage is Shakespeare's *own original* writing." [Introduction to *Titus Andronicus*, Arden Shakespeare, pp. lxx, lxxxiv]

1904. John Churton Collins: "He [Shakespeare] had probably never written blank verse before [*Titus Andronicus*], so he took that of Marlowe, Greene and Peele as his models. . . . The blank verse bears a closer resemblance to that of Greene and Peele than to that of Marlowe." [*Studies in Shakespeare*, p. 121]

1905. J. M. Robertson: "It is when we apply the final tests of plot and structure that Marlowe is most clearly acquitted of any serious share in *Titus*, while Peele, Kyd, and Greene are more or less certainly implicated." [*Did Shakespeare Write 'Titus Andronicus'?* p. 217]

1905. Georg Brandes: "The evidence for the Shakespearean authorship of this drama of horrors, though mainly external, is weighty and, it would seem, decisive." [*Introduction to Titus Andronicus*, Brandes ed., p. v]

1908. F. E. Schelling: "Unmistakable traces of the master's regulating hand." [*Elizabethan Drama*, I. 221]

1909. Wilhelm Creizenach: ". . . tritt der Einfluss Marlowes im Titus Andronicus gänzlich zurück." [*Ges. d. neur. Dramas*, IV. 643]

1916. H. D. Gray: "My conclusion so far is that only Shakespeare could have written the main portion of this play, and that the subject and treatment were entirely possible for him at the very beginning of his dramatic career." [He regards Greene and Peele as revisers.] [*Flügel Memorial Volume*, p. 121]

1916. Sidney Lee: "The play was in all probability written originally in 1591 by Thomas Kyd, with some aid, it may be, from Greene or Peele, and it was on its revival in 1594 that Shakespeare improved it here and there." [*Life of William Shakespeare* (1916 ed.), p. 131]

1919. H. Dugdale Sykes: ". . . good reasons to suspect that Peele was in some way concerned." [*Sidelights on Shakespeare*, p. 108]

1919. T. M. Parrott: "*Titus Andronicus* was originally an old, pre-Shakespearean play, dating apparently between 1584 and 1589. . . . the reviser was none other than Shakespeare and . . . this revision gave us the play to all intents as we have it to-day. . . . Shakespeare's revision was superficial. . . . I am inclined, however, to agree with Robertson that Kyd had a hand, perhaps the main hand, in shaping the original plot, and that the present text shows conclusively the hand of Peele." [MLR, 14: 17 and note on p. 36, Ja 1919]

1923. J. Q. Adams: "Mainly, if not entirely, by George Peele . . . revised by Shakespeare." [*Life of William Shakespeare*, pp. 134–135]

THE POEMS

Hero and Leander influenced Shakespeare directly and powerfully when he was writing *Venus and Adonis*, and to a somewhat less degree in the *Sonnets* and *Lucrece*. The influence of Marlowe's poem is not so obvious as the influence of his plays; but there is no doubt whatever that it does exist. Shakespeare had read *Hero and Leander*, since he quotes from it, since his scheme and treatment are essentially similar in *Venus and Adonis*, and since this poem and *Lucrece* are both part of the tradition to which Marlowe gave the main impetus.

The best known of the verbal parallels is the phrase "rose-cheek'd Adonis," which occurs in both *Venus and Adonis* and in *Hero and Leander*,[126] but there is a similarity quite as close in Shakespeare's adaptation of a line of Marlowe's:

> Stain to all nymphs, more lovely than a man.

This obviously parallels Marlowe's

> Some swore he was a maid in mans attire.[127]

---

[126] *Venus and Adonis*, l. 9; H&L, I. 83. Sir Israel Gollancz, in his ed. of the poem (1896, p. viii), insisted that Marlowe was the borrower. But see also Malone's ed. (1790), pp. 14, 73; Lee's ed. (1905), pp. 29–34; Pooler's ed. (1911), p. xxii; and Chambers: *William Shakespeare*, I. 245.   [127] See II. 119.

The following additional parallels have been noted:

> . . . leapt into the water for a kis
> Of his owne shadow.
> > [H&L, I. 74–75]
>
> Died to kiss his shadow in the brook.
> > [V&A, 162] [128]

> *Hero* . . . fell downe and fainted.
> He kist her, and breath'd life into her lips.
> > [H&L, II. 1–3]
>
> . . . she lies as she were slain,
> Till his breath breatheth life in her again.
> > [V&A, 473–474]

> . . . Then treasure is abus'de,
> When misers keepe it; being put to lone,
> In time it will returne vs two for one.
> > [H&L, I. 234–236]
>
> But gold that's put to use more gold begets.
> > [V&A, 768]

> Thence flew Loues arrow with the golden head.
> > [H&L, I. 161]
>
> Love's golden arrow at him should have fled.
> > [V&A, 947]

> Loue is too full of faith, too credulous,
> With follie and false hope deluding vs.
> > [H&L, II. 221–222]
>
> O hard-believing love, how strange it seems
> Not to believe, and yet too credulous!
> > [V&A, 985–986]

Shakespeare at least seems to draw on *Edward the Second* in one instance:

> Wet with my teares, and dried againe with sighes.
> > [*Edward II*, 2105]
>
> . . . she with her tears
> Doth quench the maiden burning of his cheeks;
> Then with her windy sighs and golden hairs
> To fan and blow them dry again she seeks.
> > [V&A, 49–52]

---

[128] See Douglas Bush in PQ, 6: 297 (1927). Other doubtful parallels may exist between H&L, I. 27, V&A, 1082; H&L, I. 441 ff., V&A, 733 f.; H&L, I. 191, V&A, 443–444; H&L, II. 141–145, V&A, 720; H&L, I. 469 ff., V&A, 1135–1136. See also Hyder E. Rollins' Variorum ed. of Shakespeare's *Poems, passim.*

Lucrece presents similarities to *Hero and Leander*, but they are both few and faint. "Quenchless fire" [129] is almost certainly an echo of Marlowe, who uses it three times, whereas it does not occur elsewhere in Shakespeare. "Quenchless fury" in *Henry VI* is presumably another Marlowe echo. One other pair of parallels may possibly be more than coincidence or common use of a special poetic diction:

> . . . with azure circling lines empal'd,
> Much like a globe.
> [H&L, II. 274–275]
> Her breasts, like ivory globes circled with blue.
> [*Lucrece*, 407]

Several verbal similarities in the *Sonnets* are close enough to *Hero and Leander* to be regarded as echoes:

> The richest corne dies, if it be not reapt,
> Beautie alone is lost, too warily kept.
> [H&L, I. 327–328]
> Thy unused beauty must be tomb'd with thee.
> [Sonnet IV. 13]

> Then treasure is abus'de,
> When misers keepe it; being put to lone,
> In time it will returne vs two for one.
> [H&L, I. 234–236]
> Profitless usurer, why dost thou use
> So great a sum of sums.
> [Sonnet IV. 7–8] [130]

> One is no number, mayds are nothing then,
> Without the sweet societie of men.
> [H&L, I. 255–256]
> Thou single wilt prove none.
> [Sonnet VIII. 14]

OTHER WORKS

There are faint traces of Marlowe in other Shakespearean works which at first sight seem to be wholly free from his influ-

[129] II *Tamb.* 3529; *Edward II*, 2030; *Dido*, 481. Cf. *3 Henry VI*, I. iv. 28; II *Tamb.* 2945; *True Tragedie*, 351; *Lucrece*, 1554.

Other doubtful parallels have been suggested between H&L, II. 327–334, *Lucrece*, 1079–1084; H&L, I. 143, *Lucrece*, 1380.

[130] See II. 126, 264.

ence. The rough, blunt, faithful Kent of *Edward the Second* foreshadows the faithful Kent of *King Lear*, and there is a faint suggestion of parallels in a few lines of *King John*:

> Nature doth striue with Fortune and his stars
> To make him famous.
> > [I *Tamb.* 487–488]
>
> Nature and Fortune join'd to make thee great.
> > [*King John*, III. i. 52]

> These lookes of thine can harbor naught but death.
> I see my tragedie written in thy browes.
> > [*Edward II*, 2521–2522]
>
> For I do see the cruel pangs of death
> Right in thine eye.
> > [*King John*, V. iv. 59–60]

Romeo, Juliet, and the Nurse perhaps owe something to Aeneas, Dido, and the nurse of Ascanius, or to the similar trio in *Hero and Leander*, though all these groups of characters certainly have a debt to the tradition established by Seneca.

Presumably Marlowe's lines:

> But stay, what starre shines yonder in the *East*?
> The Loadstarre of my life,

suggested Romeo's similar and more famous lines.[131] There is strong similarity between other passages:

> Gallop a pace bright *Phœbus* through the skie,
> And duskie night, in rustie iron carre,
> Betweene you both, shorten the time I pray.
> > [*Edward II*, 1738–1740]
>
> Gallop apace, you fiery-footed steeds,
> Towards Phœbus' lodging; such a waggoner
> As Phaethon would whip you to the west,
> And bring in cloudy night immediately.
> > [R&J, III. ii. 1–4]

Mercutio's casual allusion to Hero is probably due to Marlowe, and his mock conjuring of Romeo is a patent parody of *Doctor Faustus*, a play which was then fresh in the mind of every

---

[131] *Jew of Malta*, 680–681; *Romeo and Juliet*, II. ii. 2–3; II. iv. 44; II. i. 6–29.

theatregoer and of every reader. The line in *Troilus and Cressida*:

I'll learn to conjure and raise devils,[132]

is probably another allusion to Faustus.

Shakespeare's Cleopatra perishes with a last assumption of royal state:

Give me my robe, put on my crown,

like Marlowe's Zabina, wife of Bajazeth, who also dies in defeat and despair:

Make ready my Coch, my chaire, my iewels, I come, I come, I come.[133]

Faint echoes, indeed, but echoes none the less. Shakespeare, who had learned so much from Marlowe, never quite forgot the touch of the vanished hand that had guided him as a raw and youthful beginner in the theatre.

[132] *Troilus and Cressida*, II. iii. 6.
[133] I *Tamb.* 2100; *Antony and Cleopatra*, V. ii. 282.

CHAPTER XVII

THE MARLOWE APOCRYPHA

... alms for oblivion.
Troilus and Cressida, III. iii. 146

GIVEN THE LARGE NUMBER of Elizabethan
plays and poems for which no definite authorship can
be established and the practical certainty that not
all of Marlowe's work has come down to us,[1] it was
natural that as soon as interest in Elizabethan literature began
to develop in the latter eighteenth century, scholars should attempt to assign to Christopher Marlowe a few of the better
plays and some poems which still lacked authors. They were
encouraged to do so because several important Elizabethan
plays, the ascription of which is no longer questioned, had
originally appeared without their authors' names on the title
pages, and had been authoritatively assigned by an adroit
combination of internal and external evidence.

It was equally natural that the earlier, uncritical Elizabethan
scholars should have little hesitation in assigning to Marlowe
a wild congeries of unrelated plays which had little in common
save their unknown authorship. Some of these could not possibly be the work of the same author; and most of them, on
internal evidence alone, must be removed from any possible
Marlowe canon. Marlowe's style, dramatic method, and attitude toward life are very marked; and although there is a clear
development and improvement in his work, he never abandons
the general literary method and the intellectual and emotional
attitude with which he set out. Few of the doubtful plays show
enough of these qualities to be regarded as even partially his.

Resemblances to Marlowe's writing, even though numerous,
do not prove a play his, for Marlowe exercised a powerful influence on his contemporaries and immediate successors and was
widely imitated; but the absence of characteristics which ap-

[1] See II. 205–206.

pear in all his known work is plain evidence that a play is not his. Several of the doubtful plays assigned him are excellent work of their kind; but it is such a kind that it cannot possibly be Marlowe's. The older critics seem frequently to have assigned them to him mainly because they could think of no one else.

The absurdity of some of these attributions is apparent the moment one sets down the list:

Play	Attributed by
Lust's Dominion	Title pages, 1657, 1658, 1661. Langbaine and critics prior to Collier.
Maiden's Holiday . . . . (In collaboration with Day)	Warburton, Stationers' Register
Selimus	Malone, Crawford
Locrine	Malone, Hickson, Foard
Edward III (in part) . . .	Fleay, Lee, Greg, Foard
Troublesome Raigne of King John	Malone, Fleay (plot only)
True History of George Scanderbage	Gabriel Harvey (?), Fleay
Alarum for London . . .	Collier, Bullen, Robertson
Arden of Feversham . . .	Oliphant (part only)

The opening lines of Doctor Faustus,

> Not marching now in fields of Thracimene,
> Where Mars did mate the Carthaginians,

have been taken to allude to a lost play on Hannibal, but this is pure speculation, wholly unsupported by evidence. There are some strange parallels with Leir, the source of Shakespeare's play, but no one has as yet suggested Marlowe's collaboration or authorship.[2]

LUST'S DOMINION

Of all the doubtful plays, Lust's Dominion is attributed to Marlowe with the best show of reason. His name appears on the title page of the first edition in 1657, and on the title pages,

[2] See II. 288–289.

which alone survive, of the new editions or re-issues of the old one, in 1658 and 1661.[3] The play is attributed to him by William Winstanley's *Lives of the English Poets* (1687), by Langbaine's *Momus Triumphans* (1688) and his *Lives and Characters* (1698), and by Anthony à Wood's *Athenae Oxonienses*,[4] but is not mentioned at all in many early catalogues of plays.

If we regard the prologue to *Doctor Faustus* as referring to Marlowe's other plays, the lines,

> . . . Sporting in the dalliance of loue
> In courts of Kings where state is ouerturnd,

may be taken as describing *Lust's Dominion* with perfect accuracy. But this may well be regarded as pure coincidence.

In addition to this external evidence, there is some fairly cogent internal evidence. The villainous Moor, Eleazar, is a typical Marlowe villain-as-hero and practices the self-revelation typical of Marlowe's villains. He is, in short, a not very adroit combination of the villainy of Barabas in *The Jew of Malta* and that of Aaron in *Titus Andronicus*. The verse and phrasing of certain passages sound very much like authentic Marlowe, and one or two echo lines from *Doctor Faustus* and *Edward the Second*. Certain passages which ring most clearly like Marlowe may well preserve lines taken over from an early and authentic Marlowe play, now lost.

One could hardly ask for a more typical example of the villain's self-revelation, such as Marlowe uses in *The Jew of Malta* and *The Massacre at Paris*, than this passage spoken by Eleazar:

> Ha, ha, I thank thee provident creation,
> That seeing in moulding me thou did'st intend,
> I should prove villain, thanks to thee and nature
> That skilful workman; thanks for my face,
> Thanks that I have not wit to blush.[5]

While this tangled verse is anything but Marlowe's, there are other passages in the play where one seems for an instant to

---

[3] William Rufus Chetwood, or Chetwode: *British Theatre* (1752), p. 8, mentions a 1604 ed. of which no trace survives.
[4] See table on II. 274–275.
[5] *Lust's Dominion*, 925–931.

hear his very voice. "We have heard much of 'Marlowe's mighty line,'" wrote William Hazlitt, "and this play furnishes frequent instances of it. There are a number of single lines that seem struck out in the heat of a glowing fancy, and leave a track of golden fire behind them." [6] Hazlitt had no doubt of Marlowe's authorship and in his lectures discussed *Lust's Dominion* to the neglect of *Tamburlaine*. Among the lines [7] that he selected as typical of Marlowe were:

> I know he is not dead, I know proud Death
> Durst not behold such sacred majesty.
>
> [434-435]
>
> ... From discontent grows treason,
> And on the stalk of treason death.
>
> [912-913]
>
> Hang both your greedy ears upon my lips,
> Let them devour my speech, suck in my breath.
>
> [936-937]

These passages are really far less like Marlowe than such lines as:

> Why stares this Divell thus, as if pale death
> Had made his eyes the dreadfull messengers
> To carry black destruction to the world.
>
> [663-665]

The phrase "pale death" appears and reappears in plays known to be Marlowe's and others suspected of being his. [8] There are also some striking verbal parallels:

> Had I as many soules as there be starres.
> [DF, 338]
> Had I as many soules as I have sins.
> [LD, 485]

> Sometime a louelie boye ...
> Crownets of pearle about his naked armes ...
> Shall bathe him in a spring.
> [*Edward II*, 61-66]

---

[6] *Lectures on the Dramatic Literature of the Age of Elizabeth*, chap. II.

[7] References are to J. LeGay Brereton's ed. (Louvain, 1931).

[8] II *Tamb.* 3051; *Dido*, 410; II *Tamb.* 3051 ("pale and ghastly death"); *Selimus*, 665, 1311; *Locrine*, 30; I *Henry VI*, IV. ii. 27, 38 ("pale destruction," "pale, and dead") See also II. 66, 281.

. . . These two wanton boies, . . .
. . . with coronets of pearle,
And bells of gold, circling their pretty arms
In a round Ivorie fount these two shal swim,
And dive to make thee sport.
[LD, 73–81]

. . . a naked Lady in a net of golde.
[II *Tamb.* 3742]
And in a net of twisted silk and gold
In my all-naked arms, thy self shalt lie.
[LD, 84–85]

There is no other reason for regarding *Lust's Dominion* as
Marlowe's work, nor is the evidence just stated by any means
conclusive. Ascriptions on early title pages are notoriously
open to question. Frequently they were inserted by the publisher for sales purposes, as was the case with several doubtful
Shakespearean plays. It is true, however, that Marlowe's name
may have been placed on the title page in good faith, on the
basis of some now-forgotten theatrical tradition that he had had
something to do with its plot or with the earlier play that may
have preceded it. This is especially probable, since Marlowe
was so nearly forgotten by the middle of the seventeenth century that his name would have had no very great sales value.[9]

The early writers on the theatre do not always deserve much
greater credence than the title pages, from which they seem to
have taken much of their evidence. The prologue to *Doctor
Faustus* is at best obscure — we do not even know whether it
refers to plays written by one author or to plays produced by
one company. Traces of the mighty line may be survivals of
Marlowe's genuine work in a lost source play.

The workmanship, general tone, and versification suggest a
date around 1600, a view confirmed by the central importance
to the plot of King Philip's death, which occurred in 1598,
when Marlowe had been dead five years. This episode is too
closely wrought into the general structure to be set down as
another example of the common Elizabethan practice of writing
in allusions to contemporary events.[10] The date makes it im-

9 See I. 243–244.
10 This opinion is vigorously controverted in N&Q, 1st ser., 7: 253–254 Mr 1853.

possible to regard Marlowe as the author, but it also confirms the idea that *Lust's Dominion* was written at a time when Marlowe was still much imitated — a period, also, when doubtless his unpublished manuscripts still lay about the playhouses, inviting the attention of the revising hacks.

Even the source pamphlet was not published until 1589, and it is so close to the text of the play that there can be no question of their relationship. This *True and brief declaration of the sickness and last words of Philip the Second, king of Spain*, shows the following passages resembling the text of *Lust's Dominion*:[11]

> . . . when I am embalm'd,
> Apparel me in a rich Roial Robe,
> According to the custome of the Land;
> Then place my bones within that brazen shrine.
> [LD, 358–361]
> Commanding that this my body so soon as ever
> my soul shall be separated from the same be embalmed; then apparelled with a royal robe and so
> placed in this brazen shrine.
> [Harl. Misc. II. 378]

> . . . Have care to *Isabel*,
> Her virtue was King *Philips* looking-glasse.
> [LD, 379–380]
> I pray you haue a great Care and regard to your
> Sister, because shee was my Looking-glasse.
> [Harl. Misc. II. 379]

> Dry your wet eies, for sorrow wanteth force
> T'inspire a breathing soul in a dead coarse.
> [LD, 323–324]
> My Friends and Subiects, your Sorrowes are of
> no Force to recouer my Health, for no humane
> Remedie can profit me.
> [Harl. Misc. II. 378]

> Heavens hands I see are beckning for my soul.
> [LD, 402]

[11] First pointed out by J. P. Collier in his *Select Collection of Old Plays* (3rd ed. of Dodsley), II. 311, 313. Cf. Robinson (Pickering ed., 1826), I. xii, and Brereton's ed., pp. xv and 251. The pamphlet is reprinted in Lord Somers' Collection, IX. 113 ff., and is in the British Museum's Harleian Misc. II.

We, *Philip*, . . . commend my Soule into his blessed
Hands.

[Harl. Misc. II. 378]

I do commend him to thee for a man
Both wise and warlike.

[LD, 390–391]

Remember, I commend vnto you Don *Christofer* for
the most faithfull Seruant which I euer had.

[Harl. Misc. II. 379]

In spite of all this, the play was pretty generally accepted
as Marlowe's work for many years. Charles Lamb and Charles
Wentworth Dilke, as well as Hazlitt, held this view. But other
early nineteenth-century critics began to be skeptical. E. G.
Robinson, the only editor who has admitted *Lust's Dominion*
to a collected edition, did so with misgivings.[12]

Speculation as to the real author's identity has been fruitless.
Brereton [13] suggests Dekker, with possible aid from Haughton
and Day. Fleay, Greg, and E. H. C. Oliphant take much the
same view, except that Oliphant also suspects "a writer not
found elsewhere." [14] There is a possible clue in Collier's tentative identification — later supported by Swinburne, Fleay, and
Greg — of *Lust's Dominion* with *The Spanish Moor's Tragedy*,
which Dekker, Day, and Haughton were writing for the Admiral's men in 1600.[15] These are independently suggested as
authors of *Lust's Dominion* by A. W. Ward and A. H. Bullen.

One can see the gradual shift of critical opinion away from
the idea of Marlowe's authorship in the following table:

1674. Edward Phillips: Not listed. [*Theatrum Poetarum*, p. 25]

1687. William Winstanley: Listed as Marlowe's. [*Lives of the English
Poets*, p. 134]

1688–1698. Gerard Langbaine: Listed as Marlowe's.

1691. Anthony à Wood: Listed as Marlowe's. [*Ath. Oxon.* (ed. 1691),
I. 288]

1723. Giles Jacobs: Listed as Marlowe's. [*Poetical Register*, II. 171]

---

[12] Pickering ed. (1826), I. xii.

[13] *Op. cit.*, pp. xviii–xxv.

[14] See comparative table in Brereton, p. xxx.

[15] Cf. Fleay: *Chron. Hist. Eng. Drama*, I. 272; Greg's ed. of *Henslowe's Diary*, II. 211;
Collier, HEDP, III. 97; Chambers: *Elizabethan Stage*, III. 427, II. 173n; Mary L.
Hunt: *Thomas Dekker*, p. 63; Sykes: *Sidelights on Elizabethan Drama*, p. 107; N&Q,
12th ser., 1: 84.

1764. David Erskine Baker: Listed as Marlowe's. [*Companion to Playhouse* (ed. 1764), II. sig. X2v; (ed. 1782), I. 301]

1807, 1814. William Beloe: Listed as Marlowe's. [*Anecdotes of Literature and Rare Books*, I. 313–314]

1808. Charles Lamb: Listed as Marlowe's. [*Specimens*, Percy Fitzgerald's ed. (1876), IV. 214–215]

1814. Anon. The production "of Marlowe." [*Monthly Review*, 75: 226 N 1814]

1814, 1815, 1816. Charles Wentworth Dilke: Listed as Marlowe's. [OEP, I. 7]

1818. W. Oxberry: Included as Marlowe's. [*Works*, no. 4]

1819. Thomas Campbell: "Marlowe's tragedy." [*Specimens*, II. 160; ed. 1841, p. 42]

1821. Anon. Listed as Marlowe's. [Preface to Singer reprint of *Hero and Leander*]

1821. William Hazlitt: Discussed as Marlowe's. [*Lectures on the Dramatic Literature of the Age of Elizabeth*, p. 65.]

1822. Anon. Listed as Marlowe's. [*Retrospective Review*, 4: 173–181 (1822)]

1823. Anon. Listed as Marlowe's. [*Edinburgh Review*, 38: 188 F 1823]

1825. Collier: "Unquestionably not his." [3rd ed. of Dodsley, OEP, II. 311]

1826. E. G. Robinson: "Pretty clear that it is the composition of a later writer." [*Works*, I. xii]

1830. James Broughton: Authorship questioned, following Collier. [*Gentleman's Magazine*, 100: 594 (Supplement) 1830]

1831. Collier: "Marlow had nothing to do with the authorship." [HEDP (1831), III. 73n, 140]

1845. Collier: "Absurdly included in . . . the works of Marlowe." [*Henslowe's Diary*, p. 165]

1850. Dyce: "Could not have been the work of Marlowe." [*Works*, I. lviii]

1853. "B.R.I.": "Many passages which at least *might* have been written by Marlowe." [N&Q, 1st ser., 7: 254, 12 Mr 1853]

1860. Halliwell-Phillips: "This play has been often wrongly ascribed to Marlowe, but it was certainly not written until after the death of that writer." [*Dict. of Old English Plays*, p. 158]

1862. Karl Moritz Rapp: "Nicht von Marlowe." [*Stud. über d. engl. Theater*, p. 136]

1875. William Carew Hazlitt: "This play was printed . . . with the name of Christopher Marlowe on the title as the author, than which few things are more improbable." [*Hazlitt's Dodsley*, XIV. 95]

1884. John Addington Symonds: "Direct imitation of Marlowe is obvious." [*Shakespeare's Predecessors* (ed. 1900), p. 392]

1885. Arthur Symons: "Assigned by Mr. Collier, with great probability, to Dekker, Haughton, and Day." [*Stud. Eliz. Drama*, p. 70]

1887. Algernon Charles Swinburne: "Attributed — of all poets in the world — to Christopher Marlowe, by a knavish and ignorant bookseller of the period." [*19th Century*, 21: 92 Ja 1887]

1893. Sidney Lee: "Unjustifiably ascribed to Marlowe." [DNB, XII. 1071]

1897. Edward Meyer: "A palpable imitation of Marlowe and Shakspere." [*Machiavelli and the Elizabethan Drama*, p. 92]

1908. W. W. Greg: "A good deal that is Marlowan." [*Henslowe's Diary*, II. 211]

1908. F. E. Schelling: "Certainly not Marlowe's." [*Eliz. Drama*, I. 223; *English Literature in the Lifetime of Shakespeare* (1910), p. 100]

1911. Tucker Brooke: "Ascription to Marlowe seems to be unsupported by any evidence." [*Tudor Drama*, p. 219]

1922. Tucker Brooke: "Impossible to take very seriously the claim of the title-page. . . . The tragedy may have had its inception in 1591, when Marlowe and Kyd were by the latter's testimony 'wrytinge in one chamber.'" [PMLA, 37: 406–412 (1922)]

1928. S. R. Golding: "Originally written by an imitator of Marlowe." [N&Q, 155: 402, 8 D 1928]

1929. Eduard Eckhardt: "Marlowe im Titel als Verfasser angegeben, ein . . . Irrtum." [*Eng. Drama d. Spätrenaissance*, pp. 46–47]

1931. J. LeGay Brereton: "Compiled by a lively imitator." [Brereton's ed., p. xiii][16]

THE MAIDEN'S HOLIDAY

Speculation as to the lost *Maiden's Holiday*, which apparently was never either published or produced, is impossible for lack of evidence. The play undoubtedly existed, and there is no reason to doubt that Marlowe had a hand in it, for it is ascribed to him and to John Day (c. 1574–c. 1619) in the *Stationers' Register*, April 8, 1654.[17] The publisher was Moseley.

---

[16] In a letter to C. F. Tucker Brooke in 1909, Brereton wrote that there was "not a trace of Marlowe's hand in it." Cf. PMLA, 37: 411n (1922).

[17] Transcript 1640–1708. I. 145.

The entry is interesting for two reasons. It provides the only suggestion that Marlowe ever wrote comedy, and it records the only play in which there is external evidence of collaboration, except *Dido*.[18] Since, however, Day is not known as a dramatist prior to 1599, six years after Marlowe's death, he may have completed an unfinished script or brought an old play of Marlowe's up to date.

The only known manuscript of *The Maiden's Holiday* survived in the collection of John Warburton (1682–1759) until it was "unluckily burnd or put under pye bottoms"[19] by his too-famous cook. The entry in Warburton's own list reads, "The Mayden Holaday by Chris. Marlowe,"[20] making no mention of Day. Apparently, Marlowe's name stood alone on the manuscript. Warburton seems never to have read it, and there is no record whatever of its contents. In spite of the entry in the *Stationers' Register*, there is nothing to indicate that it was ever published except mention by David Erskine Baker in his *Companion to the Playhouse* (1764) of the fact that Marlowe "also joined with Day in the Maiden's Holyday. 1654."[21] This suggests that Baker had seen the play in print, but it may have simply been taken from the *Register*. If there ever was an edition, all copies have disappeared. This is improbable, since the later editions of Marlowe's works usually survive in several copies. The 1633 *Jew of Malta*, the 1637 *Hero and Leander*, and the 1657 *Lust's Dominion*, for example, are fairly plentiful.

Dyce hazarded the opinion[22] that the *Dialogue in Verse* which Collier claimed to have found among the Alleyn Papers at Dulwich College was a remnant of the lost play; but these verses are almost certainly not Marlowe's and were probably never part of an ordinary play for the professional stage.[23]

---

[18] See II. 41–46.
[19] Steevens and Reed: *Shakespeare* (1803), II. 371–372; Frederick Thornhill: "Old Dramas in Mr. Warburton's Collection," *Gentleman's Magazine*, (OS) 118 (NS) 85: 217–222 S 1815; William Prideaux Courtney: article "Warburton, John," DNB, XX. 755; W. W. Greg: "Bakings of Betsy," *Library*, 3rd ser., 2: 225–259 Jy 1911; Egerton Bridges: *Censura Literaria* (1807), V. 273.
[20] British Museum, Lansdowne MS. 807.
[21] Cf. *Biographica Dramatica* (1812), pt. II, p. 493.
[22] Dyce's ed. (1850), I. lviii; III. 303n.
[23] See II. 291–292.

SELIMUS

The anonymous plays of *Selimus* and *Locrine* are clearly related to each other. Both have been assigned to Marlowe by
some critics, to Shakespeare by others, and to Robert Greene
by still others. Only one critic, however, has definitely assigned
all of *Selimus* to Marlowe. This is Charles Crawford, who calls
it "a tragedy from the pen of Christopher Marlowe" and suggests that it was "Marlowe's first play and was immediately
followed by *The First Part of Tamburlaine*," at the same time
denying Marlowe's authorship of *Locrine*.[24] He argues that
Selimus airs Marlowe's characteristic anti-religious views; that
it has an obvious relation to *Tamburlaine* and *Doctor Faustus*;
and that it borrows from Spenser passages that Marlowe also
borrows. There are several direct allusions to Marlowe's play
— one to "Tamburlaine the scourge of nations" and to Bajazeth's fate; one to "mighty Tamburlaine"; and another, in
Marlowe's very words, to the "Scythian thiefe." [25]

The whole problem is confused by attribution of the play in
its second edition (1638) to a mysterious "T. G.," who has been
identified with Thomas Goffe, author of various plays on Turkish history. Unfortunately for this theory, Goffe was born in
1591, and the first edition of *Selimus* was published in 1594. A
more probable author is Robert Greene, to whom six passages
from *Selimus* are attributed in *England's Parnassus* (1600).
"R.A.," the editor of this book, is identified with Robert
Allott, whose reputation for accuracy is not all that it might be.
Nevertheless, the play is given to Greene by Grosart, while
Fleay would treat it as collaboration between Greene and
Lodge.[26] Charles Mills Gayley denies Greene's authorship and
tentatively suggests Lodge alone.

Churton Collins, who denied Greene's authorship, thought it
"perfectly clear that the play was originally one of the old-
fashioned rhymed plays, and that it had been re-cast and interpolated with blank verse in consequence of the popularity of

---

[24] *Collectanea*, I. 47, 59, 66, 79, 99. Cf. his article in N&Q, 9th ser., 7: 61, 26 Ja 1901.
[25] I *Tamb.* 44; Huth Library, XIV, ll. 1588, 2290, 2389.
[26] Grosart's Greene, I. lxxi–lxxvii; Temple ed., pp. ix–xiii; Tucker Brooke: *Shakespeare Apocrypha*, p. xix; Fleay, *Chron. Hist. Eng. Drama*, II. 315; Gayley: *Rep. Eng.
Comedies*, I. 420.

Marlowe's innovations." [27] The abundant classical allusions suggest one of the University Wits as author but afford no clue to his individuality. Of the forty-five such allusions, nineteen are used elsewhere by Greene, eighteen by Peele, and seventeen by Marlowe.[28]

Selimus is not really in the Marlowe formula. It has multiple heroes, whereas Marlowe habitually builds his plays around a single central figure. The plot is disjointed, whereas Marlowe's plots, though simple, move directly forward. Rhyme is abundant, whereas Marlowe rarely uses rhyme. There is little sheer poetry, which is always abundant in Marlowe. The situations lack the striking originality which he shows even when at his crudest. On the whole, Mr. C. F. Tucker Brooke is justified in consigning the theory of Marlowe's authorship to "the limbo of rash and unbalanced criticism." [29]

Like Marlowe, however, the author borrows heavily from Spenser,[30] and there are various parallels with Marlowe's known plays. The most interesting of these appears in both *Selimus* and *Locrine*:

> What means this diuelish shepheard to aspire
> With such a Giantly presumption,
> To cast vp hils against the face of heauen.
> > [I *Tamb.* 812–814]
>
> That darted mountaines at her brother *Ioue*:
> > [I *Tamb.* 2293]
>
> Than he that darted mountaines at thy head.
> > [II *Tamb.* 3802]
>
> Flung forth a hundreth mountains at great Jove.
> > [*Selimus*, 2435]
>
> Flung forth a hundred mountains at great Jove.
> > [*Locrine*, II. v.]

> Behold my sword, what see you at the point?
> . . . There sits imperious Death.
> > [I *Tamb.* 1889–1892]
>
> Upon my sword's sharp point standeth pale Death.[31]
> > [*Selimus*, 665]

[27] *Life and Works of Robert Greene*, I. 63.
[28] A. F. Hopkinson's ed., pp. vi, xix.
[29] *Shakespeare Apocrypha*, p. xix.
[30] *Collectanea*, I. 47–100.   [31] See II. 271n.

I know sir, what it is to kil a man,
It works remorse of conscience in me.
[II Tamb. 3700–3701]

. . . For I am none of those
That make a conscience for to kill a man.
[Selimus, 1729–1730]

I hold the Fates bound fast in yron chaines,
And with my hand turne Fortunes wheel about.
[I Tamb. 369–370] [32]
Thou hast not Fortune tièd in a chain.
[Selimus, 2420]

The chiefest Captaine of Mycetes hoste.
[I Tamb. 66 (1605 4to)]
Chief captain of the Tartar's mighty host.
[Selimus, 712]

When she that rules in Rhamnis golden gates.
[I Tamb. 635]
Chief patroness of Ramus' golden gates.
[Selimus, 682]

Tamburlaine's irreligious rant is echoed when Selimus declares that God, religion, heaven, and hell are but "bugbears to keep the world in feare." [33] This is strangely like the opinion, attributed to Marlowe in the Baines libel,[34] that "the firste beginnynge of Religion was only to keep men in awe."

LOCRINE

Malone was the only one of the early critics who attributed *Locrine* to Marlowe; but he has been followed in more recent years by Samuel Hickson and by James T. Foard.[35] Malone's argument for Marlowe's authorship is based mainly on verse technique and general style. Marlowe's pyrrhic endings are abundant — there are four examples in the first half page.[36]

---

[32] See I. 251, 264, 265. See *Collectanea*, I. 94–99, for other passages which may be parallels.   [33] Line 333.

[34] On the Baines libel, see I. 110–113. Cf. British Museum, Harl. MS. 6853, fol. 307 (previously numbered 320); Harl. MS. 6848, fol. 185; Mermaid ed., p. 428; Brooke: *Life*, p. 98.

[35] Malone's *Supplement to Shakespeare* (1780), II. 187–264, *passim*; N&Q, 1st ser., 1: 194, 26 Ja 1850; *Gentleman's Magazine*, 288: 147 F 1900. There is a copy of the Malone *Supplement* in the Folger Shakespeare Library.

[36] Cf. Tucker Brooke: *Shakespeare Apocrypha*, p. 39 — Prologue, l. 2; I. i. 1, 3, 4. *Locrine*, I. i. 9–24.

The dying speech of Brutus is very like the dying speech of Tamburlaine:

> Blacke vgly death, with visage pale and wanne,
> Presents himselfe before my dazeles eies,
> And with his dart prepared is to strike.
> These armes my Lords, these neuer daunted armes,
> That oft have queld the courage of my foes,
> Now yeeld to death. . . .
> This heart, my Lords, the neare appalled heart,
> That was a terror to the bordring lands,
> A doleful scourge vnto my neighbor Kings,
> Is clove asunder.

Allusions to death as "pale" and "ugly," [37] though natural enough, occur with suspicious frequency both in plays and poems known to be Marlowe's and in those suspected of being his.

There is patent imitation of Tamburlaine's lament over Zenocrate in the lines:

> Behold the heauens do waile for *Guendoline.*
> The shining sunne doth blush for *Guendoline.*
> The liquid aire doth weep for *Guendoline.*
> The verie ground doth grone for *Guendoline.*[38]

This is Marlowe's trick of repeating a name. The phrase "high resounding noyse" is strangely like Tamburlaine's "high astounding tearms." Locrine falls in love with his fair captive Estrild, as Tamburlaine with Zenocrate. Geographical names are used for sonority, as in Marlowe, and there is much repetition.[39]

But none of this proves Marlowe's authorship, however clearly it proves his influence. Hickson adduced no further evidence, simply asserting that Marlowe was the author, a view "in favour of which I conceive there to be either internal or external evidence." Foard, in some obscure way, persuades himself that the prologue to *Doctor Faustus* contains an allusion to *Locrine,* which is patent nonsense; he gives no real evidence for

---

[37] See II. 271n. and II. 279 for "pale"; II. 123 and n. for "ugly."

[38] II *Tamb.* 2969–3005; *Locrine,* V. ii. 19–22.

[39] I *Tamb.* 5; *Locrine,* I. i. 77. For repetitions, cf. *Locrine,* II. ii. 64; II. ii. 67; II. ii. 103–105; III. i. 68, 70; IV. i. 56–57; IV. i. 107–108; V. iii. 12 and V. iv. 102. For use of geographic names, see V. iv. 9–20.

his assertion that Marlowe's "footprints are clearly traceable in every line of 'Locrine'." [40]

All this represents little real advance on Malone, who in 1780 had written: "my creed, therefore, relative to this piece is, that it was written by Christopher Marlowe, whose style it appears to me to resemble more than that of any other known dramatick author of that age." [41] Malone assumes that there was a revision after Marlowe's death, which makes his views a little more plausible, and quotes Dr. Farmer, who believes that *Locrine, Titus Andronicus*, and the player's speech in *Hamlet* were all by the same hand. Apparently Farmer made this remark in conversation, as it does not appear in print.

EDWARD III

There is no valid reason for assigning *Edward III* to Marlowe. Only Halliwell-Phillips and Fleay have attempted to do so, the latter qualifying his attribution by adding, "with alterations by Shakespeare." [42] Their view is based mainly on a passage in Greene's *Neuer Too Late* (1590), addressed by the poet Archias to Roscius, "the prowd Comedian":

Why *Roscius*, art thou proud with *Esops* Crow, being pranct with the glorie of others feathers? of thy selfe thou canst say nothing, and if the Cobler hath taught thee to say *Aue Cæsar*, disdain not thy tutor. [43]

The passage has all Greene's usual obscurity, but it is true that the words "Ave Caesar" occur in *Edward III* [44] and in no other Elizabethan play now extant. The allusion to the cobbler may be a taunt against Marlowe's parentage, but it may merely allude to a fable. [45]

A better reason for attributing the play to Marlowe is the development of the character of Edward III at the end of Marlowe's *Edward the Second*. A. W. Ward [46] comments on this and suggests that Marlowe may perhaps have written an early play later revised — perhaps by Shakespeare. This is not very satis-

---

[40] *Gentleman's Magazine*, 288: 146 F 1900.
[41] *Supplement*, II. 190. Cf. I. 371.
[42] *Outlines* (1883), p. 109; *Chron. Hist. Shakespeare*, pp. 23, 118–119.
[43] Grosart's ed., VIII. 132.
[44] See II. 257.
[45] Cf. Fleay, *op. cit.*, pp. 23, 282; *Biog. Chron. Eng. Drama*, II. 62.
[46] Ward: HEDL (1899), I. 352, 359–360; II. 223.

factory, nor do the few passages suggesting Marlowe's style strengthen the argument. Any of them can be accounted for on Swinburne's theory that "the author of 'King Edward III.' was a devout student and humble follower of Christopher Marlowe." Mr. A. F. Hopkinson [47] denies any relationship between this play and Marlowe's work, on the ground that it is singularly free from rant and bombast and that the characterization, treatment, style, and versification are all unlike Marlowe's. The abundance of rhyme strengthens this opinion.

Most critics who have attempted to identify the author at all have preferred Shakespeare. It is worth noting that the line,

> Lilies that fester smell far worse than weeds,

appears both in the *Sonnets* and in this play.[48] The odd phrase, "scarlet ornaments," appears in both works, and "laurel victory" appears in *Antony and Cleopatra* as well as in *Edward III*.[49] There are other less striking parallels. None of the evidence is sufficiently conclusive to justify identification of the author.

TROUBLESOME RAIGNE OF KING JOHN

Malone attempted, without notable enthusiasm, to prove that *The Troublesome Raigne of King John*, the source of Shakespeare's play, was Marlowe's handiwork. Fleay regarded it as the work of Greene, Peele, and Lodge, working on a plot by Marlowe; or else as the work of Peele, Marlowe, and Lodge working jointly.[50] It is far more probable that the play is by some imitator of Shakespeare during the period when he was still strongly under Marlowe's influence.

The chief arguments for the views of Fleay and Malone are an allusion to Tamburlaine in the opening lines, a few parallel passages, and a rather dubious interpretation of the prologue to *Doctor Faustus*. The opening lines of the *Troublesome Raigne*:

> You that with friendly grace of smoothed brow
> Haue entertaind the Scythian Tamburlaine,

[47] *Shakespeare's Doubtful Plays*, pp. 14–15.
[48] Sonnet XCIV, *Edward III*, II. i. 451; Sonnet CXLII, *Edward III*, II. i. 10.
[49] *Antony and Cleopatra*, I. iii. 100; *Edward III*, III. iii. 190.
[50] *Chron. Hist. . . . Shakespeare*, p. 27; *Chron. Hist. . . . Eng. Drama*, II. 53; see also his ed. of *King John*, p. 34.

> And giuen applause vnto an Infidel:
> Vouchsafe to welcome (with like curtesie)
> A warlike Christian and your Countreyman,

certainly do not prove that their author is likewise the author of *Tamburlaine*. In the prologue to *Doctor Faustus* Marlowe seems to give a list of his previous plays; and this passage has been regarded as a similar attempt. Carefully read, however, it seems rather to invite the audience to disregard *Tamburlaine* — a singular plea for the author to make.

Rogers' and Ley's play lists of 1656 attributed the play to Shakespeare. This attribution is somewhat weakened by their equally confident assertion that *Edward the Second* is also Shakespeare's. There is no real reason for making any definite assertion as to authorship.

TRUE HISTORY OF GEORGE SCANDERBAGE

The true historye of George Scanderbage was entered in the *Stationers' Register*, July 3, 1601; but no copies have survived, and internal evidence is therefore lacking. Fleay attempted to assign it to Marlowe on the basis of some sneering lines in the Foure Sonets, which form part of his *New Letter of Notable Contents* (1593):

> . . . Is that Gargantua minde
> Conquerd, and left no Scanderbeg behinde? [51]

These are coupled with sneering allusions to *Tamburlaine* and seemed to Fleay to indicate Harvey's affected surprise that Marlowe had not published a play on Scanderbeg as well as his play on Tamburlaine. This passage, he thought, "surely attributes its authorship to Marlow." [52] He misses, however, the further allusion, evidently to Marlowe:

> Have you forgot the Scanderbegging wight?

and fails to note that the historical Tamburlaine is discussed together with the historical Scanderbeg in *Two very notable Commentaries* (1562), which Marlowe may have used in writing *Tamburlaine*. [53]

[51] See I. 143.
[52] *Biog. Chron. Eng. Drama*, II. 65.
[53] See I. 198–199.

While, therefore, Sir Edmund K. Chambers may be right in thinking that "there seems no adequate reason for ascribing this to Marlowe," it is by no means impossible that Marlowe did write a play on this subject and that in some forgotten library a copy will one day be unearthed.[54]

ALARUM FOR LONDON

An Alarum for London, also called *A 'Larum for London*, is assigned to Marlowe by Collier, and his view is supported by the usual suspicious document. Among moderns, only Mr. J. M. Robertson agrees with the attribution, on internal evidence. Marlowe must have had a hand in the play, he thinks, so often does it suggest his rhythm and style. He suggests Greene, Lodge, and Marston as possible co-authors.[55]

Collier had in his possession a copy of the play with "doggeral rimes written by some early possessor on its title page":

> Our famous Marloe had in thys a hand
> As from his fellowes I do understand
> The printed copie doth his muse much wrong
> But natheless manie lines ar good *and* strong
> Of paris massaker such was his fate
> A perfitt coppie came to hand to late.

Bullen regarded this as "a very ridiculous piece of forgery," [56] and modern rediscovery of the manuscript note fully confirms him. Collier had written his own name on the title page, "J. Payne Collier," and then inked his signature over to read "S. Leighe Collier." The note itself is so obviously forged that an indignant later owner has noted "no pretext for assigning a single line to Marlow." Even if authentic, the inscription would prove only Marlowe's assistance or revision, not his authorship.

ARDEN OF FEVERSHAM

Mr. E. H. C. Oliphant has argued vigorously for Marlowe's part authorship of *Arden of Feversham*. He thinks that "Marlowe's hand is to be seen in *Arden*," but that "another writer,

---

[54] Chambers: *Eliz. Stage*, IV. 400.
[55] *Marlowe*, pp. 115, 126 ff.; *Did Shakespeare Write Titus Andronicus?*, p. 179.
[56] *Works*, I. lxxiv. The book itself is now in HCL.

probably Kyd, was concerned." [57] As we have Kyd's own testimony that he was sharing a room with Marlowe about 1591,[58] this is probable enough, especially as other scholars — notably Crawford and Sykes [59] — think that Kyd wrote the play. Crawford is at pains to deny Marlowe any share in the authorship at all.

There are several reasons for Mr. Oliphant's view. The verse is often much like Marlowe's and much better than Kyd could write. The wording, especially of ejaculations and epithets, suggests Marlowe. The play shows an intimate knowledge of Kent, and Marlowe was (except for Lyly, who is out of the question here) the only Kentishman among the early dramatists. Mr. Oliphant notes the quarrel scene especially [60] as one of the passages which he thinks beyond "the reach of every dramatist of the time" save Marlowe and Shakespeare. Francis Thynne, whose cousin, Sir John Thynne, seems to have been part of the Raleigh-Marlowe circle,[61] helped edit the 1586/7 Holinshed, which discusses the murder,[62] and might have called the material to Marlowe's attention.

The argument from the wording is rather striking. Marlowe's favorite exclamation, "tush," appears ten times. "Seeing" is used for "since" seventeen times in *Arden* and nine times in *Edward the Second*. "Peasant," "slave," "groom," and "ungentle" are more frequent than in the dialogue of other dramatists. The word "tush" appears in only two lines in all Shakespeare's plays; and the other words are frequent only in those Shakespearean plays in which Marlowe's hand has been suspected — as may be seen in any concordance.

These views are supported by an imposing array of parallels, some of which are merely the usual echoes of the mighty line, while others are of a more peculiar and personal sort. Crawford

[57] *Criterion*, 4: 89 Ja 1926. Cf. *Modern Philology*, 8: 420 (1911); PMLA, 37: 401 S 1922.

[58] Letter to Sir John Puckering, Harl. MS. 6849, fol. 218; Tucker Brooke, *Life*, p. 104.

[59] *Collectanea*, I. 101 ff.; *Sidelights on Shakespeare*, p. 48.

[60] III. v. 80–134. Cf. *Criterion*, 4: 86 Ja 1926. George Chapman, whose early life is obscure, may have been a Kentishman. Cf. W. C. Hazlitt: *Shakespear: The Man and His Work*, p. 211.

[61] See I. 131.

[62] Lionel Cust, *Archæologia Cantiana*, 34: 112 (1920).

asserted that at least thirty passages in *Arden* were inspired by *Edward the Second*, but he listed only four and continued to deny Marlowe's authorship.[63]

Among the echoes of a more familiar sort are such lines as

> The rancorous venome of thy mis-swolne hart

in *Arden of Feversham*, which might well be an imitation of

> Swolne with the venome of ambitious pride

from *Edward the Second*;[64] while the line

> With mightye furrowes in his stormye browes

resembles passages in *Tamburlaine* like "the folded furrowes of his browes" or "the furrowes of his frowning browes";[65] in *Edward the Second*, like "the furrowes of thy browes";[66] in *The Contention*, like "deep-trenched furrowes in his frowning browes" or in *Soliman and Perseda*, like "furrowes of her clowding brow."[67]

The words of the Queen in *Edward the Second*:

> Nay, to my death, for too long haue I liued,

find an echo in Mistress Alice Arden's repentant:

> But beare me hence, for I haue liued too long.

The lines are uttered in similar situations — in each case by an adulteress who has connived at murder and is being led to punishment. Almost the same line appears in *The Contention*:

> Even to my death, for I have lived too long.[68]

As another set of parallels, we have

> He weares a lords reuenewe on his back.
> [*Edward II*, 704]
> She beares a duke's whole revenues on her back.
> [*Contention* (3rd 4to), I. iii]

[63] *Jahrb.*, 39: 80 (1903); *Collectanea*, I. 114–115.
[64] *Edward the Second*, 238; *Arden*, I. i. 327.
[65] I *Tamb.* 1838; II *Tamb.* 2646; *Arden*, II. i. 53.
[66] *Edward the Second*, 94.
[67] *Contention*, 1728; sig. Cv. See Crawford: *Collectanea*, I, 127–129, for parallels between this play and *Arden*.
[68] *Edward the Second*, 2651; *Arden*, V. v. 36; *Contention*, sc. VII. 10.

She bears a duke's revenues on her back.
                    [2 *Henry VI*, I. iii. 83]
She'll lay her husband's benefice on her back.
                    [*Leir*, sc. 6]

I haue my wish, in that I ioy thy sight.
                    [*Edward II*, 151]
I haue my wish in that I joy thy sight.
                    [*Arden*, V. i. 349]

Is this the loue you beare your soueraigne?
Is this the fruite your reconcilement beares?
                    [*Edward II*, 832–833]
Is this the end of all thy solemne oathes?
Is this the frute thy reconcilement buds?
                    [*Arden*, I. i. 186–187]

Looke vp my lord. *Baldock*, this drowsines
Betides no good, here euen we are betraied.
                    [*Edward II*, 1911–1912]
This drowsiness in me bodes little good.
                    [*Arden*, III. ii. 17]

Or like the snakie wreathe of *Tisiphon*,
Engirt the temples of his hatefull head.
                    [*Edward II*, 2031–2032]
That lyke the snakes of blacke Tisiphone
Sting me with their embraceings.
                    [*Arden*, V. i. 156–157]

. . . a shaggy totter'd staring slaue,
That when he speakes, drawes out his grisly beard,
And winds it twice or thrice about his eare.
                    [JofM, 1858–1860]
A lean faced writhen knaue,
Hawk-nosed and very hollow-eyed. . . .
A mustachio, which he wound about his ear.
                    [*Arden*, II. i. 51–56] [69]

And witnesse heauen how deere thou art to me.
                    [*Edward II*, 463]
Heauens can witnesse, I loue none but you.
                    [*Edward II*, 1112]
The heauens can witnes. [*Arden*, I. i. 195; IV. iv. 116]

[69] This comes from the same passage in *Arden* as the "furrowed brows" line quoted
on II. 287.

... the lowlie ground. [*Edward II*, 397]
... the lowly earth. [*Edward II*, 1999]
... the lowly earth. [*Arden*, I. i. 255]

There is another group of parallels, simple little phrases, some of them Elizabethan commonplaces, such as a man once in the habit of using them employs unconsciously. No one would imitate these deliberately, and it is unlikely that the two dramatists would have identical habits of this sort. These appear in *Arden*. They also appear in two known Marlowe plays — *The Massacre at Paris* and *Edward the Second* — as well as in four plays — *The Contention*, *The True Tragedie*, *Leir*, *Soliman and Perseda* — in which other traces of Marlowe have been discovered. Thus we have:

Hell of greefe. [*Edward II*, 2538]
Hell of griefe. [*Arden*, V. v. 12]

The raylingest knaue in christendome.
                [*Arden*, IV. iv. 54]
The lyingest knave in Christendom.
                [*Contention*, II. i]
The bragging'st knave in Christendom. [S&P, I. i]

... hauing bought so deare a friend.
                [*Edward II*, 607]
And purchase friends. . . .
                [II *Henry VI*, I. i. 223]
His company hath purchest me ill frends.
                [*Arden*, V. i. 194]
Your company hath purchased me ill freends.
                [*Arden*, V. i. 221]

There are similar parallels between *Arden*, *Leir*, and *Soliman and Perseda* [70] which have no relation to Marlowe's canonical plays.

None of these facts can be taken as proving Marlowe's authorship, though there is something of him in the play, whether it is stray samples of his handiwork, deliberate thefts, or unconscious echoes. On the other hand, style and theme are entirely different from his. Marlowe was too much in love with "high

[70] Many examples are given by Crawford: *Collectanea*, I. 100–130.

astounding terms" to take any very great interest in domestic tragedy and its necessarily homely dialogue.

Lost Poems

Sundry odds and ends of nondramatic verse have at various times been ascribed to Marlowe. A group of manuscript poems, bearing the signature "Infortunatus Ch.M.," turned up in 1850. They formed part of a copy of Henry Howard's translation of the last instructions given by the Emperor Charles V to his son Philip, and are supposed to have been transcribed by one Paul Thompson about the end of the sixteenth century. The poems were in a hand different from that of the rest of the manuscript. An account of them was sent to *Notes and Queries* [71] by an anonymous correspondent, who unfortunately failed to make a transcript. No trace of the manuscript has since been discovered.

The poems included sixteen sonnets, each signed "Ch.M." There was also an eclogue of some length, the first line of which ran:

> For shame, man, wilt thou never leave this sorrowe?

This had the title, "Amor Constans," and the same signature as the sonnets. Four lines of one sonnet were also given:

> Whilest thou in breathinge cullers, crimson white,
>   Drewst these bright eyes, whose language sayth to me,
>   Loe! the right waye to heaven; Love stoode by the[e],
> *Seager!* fayne to be drawne in cullers brighte.

This appears to be an allusion to an Elizabethan painter named Seager, of whom nothing else is known. If genuine, the lost poems are remarkable as including Marlowe's only known experiment in sonnet form.

Ignoto

More doubt attaches to the verses entitled "Ignoto," beginning:

> I love thee not for sacred chastity.

These are unsigned and have been excluded from all editions

---

[71] N&Q, 1st ser., 1: 469–470, 18 My 1850.

except Cunningham's. The only ground for ascribing them to Marlowe is their appearance in the duodecimo edition of the *Epigrammes and Elegies.* The verses are unsigned and appear immediately after Davies' epigrams. Then follows a second title page with Marlowe's name, and then his translation of Ovid. As the verses are in the part of the book attributed to Davies under the initials "J.D.," they are probably his work, which they closely resemble.

DIALOGUE IN VERSE

Still less importance is to be attached to the *Dialogue in Verse* found by Collier among the papers at Dulwich College.[72] Someone has written "Kitt Marlowe" on the back of the sheet, and on that very slight ground this typical Elizabethan "jig" is sometimes included in Marlowe's works. Discovery of a genuine Marlowe signature shows that the alleged autograph cannot possibly be his. Not even the spelling of the name corresponds, and the handwriting is entirely unlike Marlowe's.

The verse limps sadly and has absolutely none of Marlowe's style. Dyce, Cunningham, and Bullen are the only editors who have included it. George F. Warner prints a partial transcript in his catalogue of the Dulwich College manuscripts.

The manuscript itself consists of a single page. Until the scribe reaches the last eight lines, everything is run together, as if written in prose. It is, however, in verse form, or, rather, it can be reduced to verse form by some rather heroic carpentry on the part of modern editors, who have had to cut and trim and even supply some words and several lines. The version printed by Collier and followed by later editors omits several lines which cannot be forced into stanzaic mold.

Genuine or not, the dialogue is a good example of the English "jig," specimens of which are rather scarce. It was given a stage production at the University of Chicago in 1916, as part of a series illustrating the development of the English drama, and was produced at Yale in 1940. Professor C. R. Baskervill, who produced the *Dialogue* at Chicago, says: "Though I did not take the fact into account in producing the verses, they

[72] Henslowe Papers, fol. 272. Now in the library at Dulwich College. See also Warner's Catalogue (1881) and *Alleyn Papers* (Shakespeare Society, 1843), pp. 8-11.

may have come from the body of a play as Dyce suggests, for the last lines are couplets. But the context shows that the verses must have been accompanied with dance, and there is little doubt that they were written to be sung, so that the piece seems to be a dramatic jig, whether performed at the end of a play or not. It seems to belong to a type of jig that developed out of folklore." [73]

UNIDENTIFIED POEM

Marlowe is listed as one of the "Modern and extant Poets" from whose work John Bodenham (fl. 1600) says he made selections for his *Bel-vedére or the Garden of the Muses* (1600). None of the verses in this book are signed, but Charles Crawford [74] has identified forty-three brief excerpts from *Hero and Leander* and seven from *Edward the Second*. It is possible that the book contains other examples of Marlowe's work and even, perhaps, verse not included in his acknowledged works; but if so the loss to his reputation is probably not very great. It is odd to find him named in 1600 among the living poets instead of among the dead, who are in a separate list.

THE LYE

A poem called "The Lye" appears in a miscellany entitled *Davison's Poems, or a Poetical Rhapsody.*[75] This was once supposed to have been written by Raleigh on the night before his execution, October 29, 1618. It is an obvious imitation of the Emperor Hadrian's address to his soul,[76] especially the line, "hospes comesque corporis":

> Goe, soule, the bodies guest,
> Upon a thankelesse arrant;

[73] From a letter quoted by Tucker Brooke, PMLA, 37: 413 (1922). Cf. C. R. Baskervill: *English Jig and Related Song Drama* (University of Chicago Press, 1929), pp. 252–254.

[74] *Englische Studien*, 43: 198–228. See especially pp. 206, 216, 217. Reprinted in Publications of the Spenser Society, no. 17 (1875). See also Jesse Franklin Bradley and Joseph Quincy Adams: *Jonson Allusion Book*, pp. 7–8.

[75] Eds. in 1602, 1608, 1611, 1621. Modern eds. by the Lee Priory Press (1814), Pickering (1826), and A. H. Bullen (1890). Sir Egerton Brydges brought out a privately printed ed. of one hundred copies. "The Lye" also appears in Harl. MS. 6910, fol. 141, believed to date from 1596, in Harl. MS. 2296, fol. 135, and in a commonplace book in the possession of Dr. A. S. W. Rosenbach.

[76] *Oxford Book of Latin Verse*, no. 287, p. 349.

Feare not to touche the best,
The truth shall be thy warrant:
Goe, since I needs must die,
And give the world the lye. . . .

So, when thou hast, as I
Commaunded thee, done blabbing,
Although to give the lye
Deserves no less than stabbing,
Yet stab at thee who will,
No stab the soule can kill. ·

The allusion to stabbing suggests the circumstances of Marlowe's rather than Raleigh's death; and the anonymous writer of "Marlowe and His Works" [77] claimed it as Marlowe's. Since it appears in the 1608 and 1611 editions of Davison's collection, it was certainly not written just before Raleigh's execution in 1618. The anonymous critic held that "the poem was written by some one before his death" — and who so likely as Marlowe? Since 1887, however, we have learned more about the manner of Marlowe's violent taking-off and know that the dying poet had no time for versifying.[78]

COLUTHUS: RAPTUS HELENAE

No trace remains of a rhymed translation of the *Raptus Helenae* by Coluthus, an obscure Greek poet of the late fifth and early sixth centuries, A.D., which Marlowe is supposed to have written in 1587. Thomas Warton, the younger, refers to the translation in his *History of English Poetry*, admitting that he has never seen the book and giving "the manuscript papers of a diligent collector of these fugacious anecdotes," namely Coxeter, as his authority.[79] Malone, in his annotated Langbaine,[80] says: "Coluthus's *Rape of Helen* was translated into English rhime [*sic*] by Marlowe and published in 1587 — in 1595 was entered on the Stationers' Books by R. Jones [who published Marlowe] 'a booke entituled *Raptus Helenae*, Helens Rape by the Athenian Duke Theseus.' M." [81]   In his collection of Marlowe's

---

[77] *Book Lore* (London), 5: 99–100 My 1887.
[78] Cf. *Poems of Raleigh and Wotton* (ed. Hannah, 1845, 1875).
[79] Ed. 1781, III. 433; reprint, 1875, p. 906.
[80] Bodleian Library, Malone 131.
[81] *Stationers' Register* B, fol. 131*v*, April 3, 1595; Arber's reprint, II. 296. See W. C.

works now at the Bodleian (Arch. G.d.48), Malone remarks: "Mr Coxeter says in his Ms notes that Marlow translated Coluthus's *Rape of Helen* into English rime in 1587. . . . The same has been paraphrased in Latin Verse by T. Watson in 1586 — in wch year it was printed in Lo."

Warton suggested that this subject was probably suggested to Marlowe by Watson's paraphrase. Warton's guess is probably correct, especially since Mr. Mark Eccles' discovery that Marlowe and Watson were friends.[82]

Nature of a Woman

Perhaps the most impudent effort to palm off the work of some hack of the 1590's as Marlowe's posthumous writing is a queer little black-letter pamphlet of twenty-two pages, the unique copy of which is now in the Bodleian.[83] The title page reads:

THE/ SECOND PART OF/ THE HISTORIE, CALLED/ THE NATVRE OF A WOMAN:/ Contayning the end of the ftrife betwixt/ *Perfeus* and *Thefeus*./ Compiled by *C. M.*/ [Ornament]/ AT LONDON,/ Printed by the Widow *Orwin* for *Clement*/ *Knight*, and are to be fold at his fhop at the little/ North-doore of S. Paules Church./ 1596.

A first part is frequently alluded to in the text; but all traces of it have disappeared. It is, however, entered in the *Stationers' Register* December 30, 1595.[84] There is no entry for the second part.

The book recounts the struggles between Perseus and Theseus, which are finally solved by making the son of Perseus, who is named Adrianus, king. The story of Adrianus is the familiar legend of the child reared by wild beasts. Not enough of Marlowe's prose is now extant to make possible a critical opinion, but it is hard to believe that this undistinguished tale is really his. The occasional snatches of verse show no similarity to the mighty line.

Marlowe was much discussed and very popular at this time.

Hazlitt: *Handbook of Early-English Literature*, p. 373, which gives Coxeter as authority.

[82] See I. 98–100. Arch. G.d.48 was formerly Mal. 133.

[83] STC 17127. The Bodleian number is Malone 630.

[84] Arber's reprint, III. 6.

The famous initials would therefore have only one meaning to the reading public of the day. Malone, who once owned the pamphlet, wrote on the flyleaf, "probably C.M. means Christopher Marlowe," but his successors have disagreed with him so completely that the pamphlet has never been included in Marlowe's *Works* nor even mentioned by any editor. J. P. Collier disposes of the whole matter by saying: "We are quite sure, after a patient perusal, that Marlowe had nothing to do with the authorship of it." [85]

THE FRAUDULENT PEELE LETTER

The forged letter supposed to have been written to Marlowe by George Peele may be included here, though it of course purports to be Peele's writing and not Marlowe's. As originally printed by George Steevens in the *Theatrical Review*,[86] it runs as follows:

Friende Marle,

I must desyre that my syster hyr watche, and the cookerie booke you promysed, may be sente by the man. — I never longed for thy companie more than last night; we were all verie merrie at the globe, when Ned Alleyn did not scruple to affyrme pleasauntely to thy friende Will, that he had stolen hys speeche about the excellencie of acting, in Hamlet hys Tragedie, from conversaytions manyfold whych had passed betweene them, and opiniones gyven by Alleyn touchyng that subjecte. Shakespear did not take thys talke in good sorte, but Jonson put an ende to the stryfe wyth wittielie sayinge, thys affaire needeth no contentione, you stole it from Ned no doubte; do not marvel; have you not seene hym acte tymes out of number? — believe me most syncerelie

Harrie
Thyne
G. PEEL.

This astonishing production abounds in internal evidence of fraud, but John Berkenhout, quoting it in his *Biographia Literaria* (1777), naïvely remarks: "Whence I copied this letter, I do not recollect; but I remember that at the time of transcribing it, I had no doubt of its authenticity." [87] No one else

---

[85] *Biographical and Critical Account of the Rarest Books in the English Language* (ed. 1866), II. 315.

[86] *Theatrical Review*, 1:64, 1 F 1763. File in HCL.

[87] Berkenhout, *op. cit.*, p. 399, n. g.

is likely to share this simple faith. As originally published by Steevens, it is addressed to "Henrie Marle" — a fact which is ignored in subsequent quotation. Even if this were regarded as an error in transcription — a large assumption — internal evidence would still suffice to proclaim the fraud. The Globe Theatre, to which the forger alludes, was not built until after Marlowe's death. At the time of the Deptford tragedy, Jonson was a boy of twenty, Shakespeare was barely beginning to be known as a poet and was scarcely known as a dramatist. Whatever may be said of the *Ur-Hamlet*, Shakespeare's *Hamlet* had certainly not been written. That distinguished theatrical figures like Marlowe, Peele, and Alleyn were on terms of extreme intimacy with such neophytes is hard to believe. Worse still, Steevens gives the letter the date 1600 — two or three years after Peele's death, the date of which was not known until some time later, and seven years after Marlowe's death, the date of which was not known until the early nineteenth century.

Steevens probably supplied the letter — perhaps after forging it himself — to Berkenhout, but silently omitted the date and intimated that the original could no longer be found.

The document is, as Mr. Tucker Brooke says, "a very obvious forgery," [88] though it is by no means certain that Berkenhout shared Steevens' guilt. Its chief importance is as an illustration of the perils that beset the literary historian, and proof that there were forgers before Collier.[89] It is remotely possible that some of the crimes imputed to that otherwise eminent scholar may have been due to a predecessor.

[88] *Trans. Connecticut Acad.*, 25: 391 (1922).
[89] For a more detailed history of this sorry fraud, see Sidney Lee: *Life of William Shakespeare* (ed. 1916), p. 646; J. M. Farrer: *Literary Forgeries*, pp. 246–247; H. M. Paull: *Literary Ethics*, p. 33; Chester L. Riess: *Christopher Marlowe and Atheism*, p. 38 (New York M.A. Thesis, 1932); and John H. Ingram: *Christopher Marlowe and His Associates*, p. 259. The two latter suggest that the original is in the Lansdowne MSS., but the catalogue shows nothing of the sort and the British Museum authorities know nothing of it.

BIBLIOGRAPHY

BIBLIOGRAPHY

BIOGRAPHIES

1830. James Broughton. "Of the dramatic writers who preceded Shake-speare, and especially of Christopher Marlowe." *Gentleman's Magazine*, (OS) 100 (NS) 23: 3–6, 121–126, 222–224, 313–315, 593–597, Ja–Ap and supplement, 1830.

1870. Rudolf Gabel. *Über Marlowes leben und dramatische werke.* Rostock Diss. 1870. Göttingen: E. A. Huth, 1870. [HCL]

1890. J. G. Lewis. *Christopher Marlowe: his life and works. A lecture written by J. G. Lewis of the Inland Revenue and delivered at Canterbury on the 8th May 1890, in aid of the Marlowe Memorial Fund by Ralph Stewart, Elocutionist.* Canterbury: W. E. Goulden; London: Hamilton Adams, n.d. [Royal Museum and Public Library, Canterbury, JB]

1891. J. G. Lewis. *Christopher Marlowe: outlines of his life and works.* Canterbury: W. W. Gibbings. [The two Lewis pamphlets are almost identical.] [HCL, CUL, NYPL, JB]

1904. John H. Ingram. *Christopher Marlowe and his associates.* London: Grant Richards. [Attacked by R. M. Theobald, *Baconiana*, 3rd ser. 3: 5–19 Ja 1905; reviewed by J. G. Brereton, *Hermes* (Sydney, Australia), 18 O 1904, reprinted in his *Elizabethan drama: notes and studies.* Sydney: William Brooks & Co., 1909, pp. 7–10.]

1914. John H. Ingram. *Marlowe and his poetry.* London: Harrap. [Poetry and Life Series.]

1922. Wladyslaw Tarnawski. *Krzysztof Marlowe: jego zycie, dziela i znaczenie w literaturze angielskiej.* Warsaw: Bibljoteka Polska. [Bibljoteka historyczno-literacka.] [This work has an English summary.] [HCL, NYPL]

1927. U[na] M[ary] Ellis-Fermor. [See General Section.]

1930. C[harles] F[rederick] Tucker Brooke. *Life and Dido.* London: Methuen; New York: Dial.

1931. J[ohn] M[ackinnon] Robertson. *Marlowe: a conspectus.* London: Routledge. [Reviewed, RES, 8: 329–330 (1932).]

1935. Aurelio Zanco. "La biografia di Christopher Marlowe alla luce degli studi moderni." *Annali della Facultà di Filosofia e Lettere della R. Università di Cagliari,* 5: 155–182 (1933–1935). [HCL]

1936. John Bakeless. *Christopher Marlowe: a biographical and critical study.* Harvard Diss. 1936 [MS.] *Harvard . . . Summaries of Theses,* 1936, pp. 302–307.

1937. John Bakeless. *Christopher Marlowe: the man in his time.* New York: William Morrow & Co.

1937. Philip Henderson. *And morning in his eyes.* London: Boriswood.

1937. Benvenuto Cellini. *La vita e il carattere di Christopher Marlowe.* Rome: Angelo Signorelli. [SAT, JB]

1938. John Bakeless. *Christopher Marlowe*. London: Jonathan Cape. [Abbreviation of the American edition of 1937.]

1940. Frederick S[amuel] Boas. *Christopher Marlowe*. Oxford University Press.

Charles Crawford. *Marlowe Concordance*. Louvain: A. Uystpruyst; Leipzig: O. Harrassowitz; London: David Nutt, 1911 and later. [See *Jahrb.* 48: 345–346 (1912).]

Canterbury

Will of Richard Marley, 1521. Consistory Registry, Canterbury, vol. XIII, fol. 61. PRO, Cant., 32/13. [Transcribed by Brooke.]

Will of Christopher Marley, 1539/40. Archdeaconry Register, Canterbury, vol. XXI, fols. 258 ff. PRO, Cant., 17/21. [Transcribed by Brooke.]

Will of John Hobbes, father-in-law of Christopher Marley, 1545/6. Archdeaconry Register, Canterbury, vol. XXIV, fol. 62. PRO, Cant., 17/24. [Transcribed by Brooke.]

Will of Dorothy Arthur, 1597. Archdeaconry Register, vol. L, fol. 361. PRO, Cant., 17/50. [Transcribed by Brooke.]

Will of John Marlowe, father of the dramatist, 1604/5. Archdeaconry Register, vol. LII, fol. 373. PRO, Cant., 17/52. [Transcribed by Brooke.]

Will of Katherine Marlowe, mother of the dramatist, 1605/6. Archdeaconry Register, vol. LIV, fol. 267. PRO, Cant., 17/54. [Transcribed by Brooke.]

Treasurer's Accounts, King's School, Canterbury. [In the Cathedral Library.]

Register Book of St. George the Martyr, Canterbury. [In custody of the rector.]

Register of St. Andrew's, Canterbury. [Now in care of the rector of St. Margaret's, Canterbury.]

Register of St. Mary Bredman, Canterbury. [Now in care of the rector of St. Margaret's, Canterbury.]

Chamberlain's Accounts, Royal Museum and Public Library, Canterbury. [This includes material printed by J. M. Cowper in his *Roll of the Freemen* and *Intrantes of Canterbury*.]

Bunce MSS., Royal Museum and Public Library, Canterbury. [These are MS. extracts from the Canterbury records, made by Alderman Cyprian Rondeau Bunce. They ran serially in the *Kentish Gazette*, 1800–1801. A few galley proofs were bound up without title. There seems to have been no regular book publication. The MSS. were received by the library in 1899. It also has a set of the proofs and a file of the *Kentish Gazette*.]

Transcripts of Parish Records. [These are duplicate copies of the parish registers, made for the archbishop and archdeacon. They do not always agree either with each other or with the registers. They are now preserved in Christ Church Gate, Canterbury Cathedral.]

Entries of marriage licenses. [The original licenses have disappeared, but the remaining entries provide information on John Marlowe's business as a bondsman. Christ Church Gate.]

Will of Katherine Benchkyn, 1585. PRO, Cant., 16/86. [Discovered by Frank W. Tyler, Esq., former sub-librarian of the Cathedral Library, 1939. Contains the only known signature of Christopher Marlowe (Marley).]

Deposition of John Marlowe (Marley) with regard to the Benchkyn Will, October 5, 1586. PRO, Cant., 39/11, fol. 237. [Discovered by Mr. Tyler, 1939.]

A second deposition of John Marlowe (Marley) in an action of distraint. *Depositions of Witnesses, 1591–94*, X, ii, 6, fol. 147b. [Discovered by Mr. Tyler, 1939.]

A third deposition of John Marlowe (Marley) in Hunte vs. Aplegate, February 19, 1565. PRO, Cant., 39/5. [Discovered by Mr. Tyler, 1940.]

A fourth deposition of John Marlowe (Marley) in Byssell vs. Johnson, October 2, 1602. PRO, Cant., 39/26. [Discovered by Mr. Tyler, 1940.]

Signature of John Marlowe (Marley). Records of St. Mary Bredman, Christ Church Gate, Canterbury. [Discovered by author, 1936. This was the first signature discovered and settled the question of John Marlowe's literacy. All signatures now known agree perfectly.]

Cambridge

"C.C.C.C. Chapter Book. 1569–1626." [This contains, after fol. 292, the Registrum Parvum, which has two entries relating to Marlowe's admission — both transcribed by G. C. Moore Smith and John H. Ingram. The Chapter Book itself contains much valuable information as to the life of the college. It is preserved in the strong room of the Estates Bursary.]

Buttery Books. CCC. [Discovered by the college authorities and placed in the strong room of the Estates Bursary, 1935. Marlowe entries discovered by the writer, 1936. The records give a week-by-week account of the poet's purchases and thus a clue to his comings and goings from 1580 to 1586. It thus covers the year 1585–86 missing from the Audits.]

Statuta, & c. & c. [The book of MSS. thus labeled and now in the Spencer Room, CCC, contains many of the indentures relating to the Norwich and Canterbury scholars.]

Audit Books. Estates Bursary, CCC. [Transcribed by Smith, Ingram, and Brooke.]

Cambridge University Grace Book Delta, 1542–1589. University Registry, Cambridge. [See also Venn, John, Chap. III.]

Matriculation Book. University Registry, Cambridge.

Supplicats for B.A. and M.A. degrees. University Registry, Cambridge. [Transcribed by Smith and Ingram.]

Lansdowne MS. 33, fols. 84–85. "The names of all the Readers and Auditors of eueri of the Lectures in cambrige año dõi 1581. the nũber of them is. 1862." [British Museum.]

T. R. B. Sanders: Bursary Books & Documents, 1935. [MS.] [Estates Bursary, CCC.]

London

Acts of the Privy Council, June 29, 1587, May 18, 20, 1593. MS. Vols. VI and XI. Dasent's reprint, XV. 141, XXIV. 244. PRO. [First reference to Marlowe discovered by Sidney Lee and printed in DNB. See *Athenaeum*, no. 3486: 235–236, 18 Ag 1894. Second reference discovered by John Leslie Hotson, *q.v.*]

Petition of William Bradley, Queen's Bench Controlment Roll, K. B. 29/226. membrane 119 verso. PRO. [Transcribed by Eccles, the discoverer.]

Coroner's inquest on William Bradley. Chancery Miscellanea, Bundle 68, File 12, no. 362. PRO. [Transcribed by Eccles, the discoverer.]

Marlowe and Thomas Watson at Newgate Prison. Middlesex Sessions Roll, 284, no. 12. Middlesex Guildhall, London. [Transcribed by Eccles, the discoverer.]

Marlowe's Recognizance. Middlesex Sessions Roll, 284, no. 1. Middlesex Guildhall, London. [Discovered by Sidney Lee. See *Athenaeum*, no. 3486: 235–236, 18 Ag 1894.]

Gaol Delivery Roll, October 3, 31st Elizabeth, nos. 1 and 2. Middlesex Guildhall, London. [Transcribed by Eccles, the discoverer.]

Constables' appeal for court protection against Marlowe. Middlesex Sessions Roll, 309, no. 13. Middlesex Guildhall, London. [Transcribed by Eccles, the discoverer.]

Baines Libel. Harleian MS. 6848, fols. 185–186, and Harleian MS. 6853, fols. 307–308 (formerly numbered 170–171 and 320–321 respectively). British Museum.

Another spy's report. Harleian MS. 6848, fol. 191. British Museum.

Thomas Kyd's two letters to Sir John Puckering. Harleian MS. 6848, fol. 154, and Harleian MS. 6849, fol. 218. [BM.] [There is reference to at least one of these in William Oldys' annotated Langbaines at the British Museum.]

Heretical papers found among the effects of Thomas Kyd. Harleian MS. 6848, fols. 187–189 (formerly numbered 172–174). British Museum. [Printed by F. S. Boas: *Works of Kyd*, pp. cx–cxiii; Samuel A. Tannenbaum: *Book of Sir Thomas More*, pp. 103–104; W. D. Briggs, SP, 20: 153–159 (1923); F.-C. Danchin, *Revue germanique*, 9: 567–570, N–D 1913.]

Notations in the 1629 *Hero and Leander*, Prideaux copy. Present location unknown. [A photograph, said to have been made for the late A. H. Bullen, has also disappeared.]

Commonplace Book of Henry Oxinden. Folger Shakespeare Library.

Another Commonplace Book of Henry Oxinden. British Museum Addit. MS. 28012, fols. 514–515. See also fols. 492, 495, 496.

Oxinden Amici. Folger Shakespeare Library. [Contains a poem identifying the individual stated in the Commonplace Books to have been under Marlowe's influence.]

"Remembraunces of wordes and matters against Ric[hard] Cholmeley." Harleian MS. 6848, fol. 190 (formerly numbered 175). British Museum.

Investigation of Raleigh's religious beliefs. Harleian MS. 7042, fol. 401. British Museum. [Printed by G. B. Harrison in his edition of *Willobie's Avisa* and by F.-C. Danchin in *Revue germanique*, 10: 578–581 (1914).]

[Forged] Atheist's Tragedie. British Museum Addit. MS. 32380, fols. 16–12. [Folios in reverse because the forger, presumably J. P. Collier, worked on the verso of a genuine MS. of the *Eikon Basilike*. Collier printed part of the Marlowe forgery in *New Particulars* (1836), p. 47n. The museum bought the MS. at Collier's Sale, August 11, 1884, Lot 214. See *Catalogue of Additions to the Manuscripts of the British Museum* (1889), p. 110.]

Philip Henslowe's Diary. [MS.] Dulwich College. [Reprinted by Collier and Greg, the latter indicating Collier's forgeries clearly.]

Henslowe Papers. Dulwich College.

Original MS. Calendar of Patent Rolls for 35 Elizabeth. PRO.

Coroner's Inquest on Marlowe. Chancery Miscellanea, Bundle 64, File 8, no. 241b. PRO.

Writ of Certiorari. Chancery Miscellanea, Bundle 64, File 8, no. 241a. PRO.

Pardon of Ingram Friser. Patent Rolls of Chancery, 1401, 35 Elizabeth (June 28, 1593). PRO.

Burial Register. Church of St. Nicholas, Deptford. [Discovered by James Broughton, *q.v.* See *Athenaeum*, no. 3486: 235, 18 Ag 1894.]

"Newe metamorphosis." British Museum Addit. MSS. 14824–14826. [Signed "J. M." and attributed to Jervis, or Gervase, Markham, also to John Marston. Often dated about 1600 but probably not finished until ca. 1615. See John Henry Hobart Lyon: *Study of the Newe metamorphosis*. Columbia Diss. 1918. New York: Columbia University Press, 1919.]

Woodleff vs. Friser. Chancery Proceedings, Elizabeth, Bundle W. 25, no. 43. PRO.

"Collier Leaf." A scene from *The Massacre at Paris* roughly corresponding to Brooke's edition, lines 812–823. Folger Shakespeare Library.

Aubrey MS. 6, fol. 108, recording an erroneous account of Marlowe's death at the hands of Ben Jonson. Bodleian Library.

Ashmolean MS. 1486, ii (Ash), fol. 6, verso, containing a version of "The Passionate Shepherd." Bodleian Library.

Thornborough Commonplace Book, containing another version of "The Passionate Shepherd." Folger Shakespeare Library.

Commonplace Book of unknown origin, containing a third version of "The Passionate Shepherd." In the possession of Dr. A. S. W. Rosenbach. [Reprinted by Dr. Samuel A. Tannenbaum in PMLA, 45: 809–821 (1930).]

Manuscript notes by Edmund Malone, especially in his copy of Langbaine and in Arch. G.d. 48. Bodleian Library. [See also under Langbaine.]

Hunter's *Chorus Vatum*, Addit. MS. 24488, fols. 372–380. British Museum. [Photostats, JB, New York Public Library, Newberry Library.]

Three letters by Algernon Charles Swinburne to Sidney Lee on the Marlowe Memorial (1888). MS. eng. misc. d. 180 f. 417. In correspondence of Sir Sidney Lee. Bodleian Library. [See also fol. 185.]

Charles Lamb's holograph MS. of "The Passionate Shepherd." Quaritch.

Check List of Extant Early Editions

Tamburlaine

1590. Black letter octavo. Parts I. and II. [STC 17425]. — 2 copies known: Bodleian; Huntington, the latter also possessing two leaves of a third copy.

1592. Black letter octavo. Parts I. and II. [STC 17426]. — Unique copy at the British Museum. Sometimes erroneously described as a 1593 copy. No such edition exists.

1597. Black letter octavo. Parts I. and II. [STC 17427]. — Unique copy in Huntington.

1605. Black letter quarto. Part I. only. [STC 17428]. — 11 copies known: British Museum, 2 copies; Bodleian; Dyce; Huntington, 2 copies; Boston Public Library; Rosenbach (White copy), New York; Magdalene College, Cambridge; Parke-Bernet, New York; Folger.

1606. Black letter quarto. Part II. only. [STC 17428a]. — 9 copies known: British Museum, 2 copies; Bodleian; Dyce; Huntington; Rosenbach (2 copies, White and Clawson); Worcester College, Oxford; Folger.

Doctor Faustus

1604. Black letter quarto. [STC 17429]. — Unique copy at Bodleian.

1609. Black letter quarto. [STC 17430]. — 2 copies: Hamburg; Huntington.

1611. Black letter quarto. [STC 17431]. — Unique copy at Huntington.

1616. Black letter quarto. [STC 17432]. — Unique copy at British Museum.

1619. Black letter quarto. [STC 17433]. — Unique copy: Robert Garrett, Baltimore.

1620. Black letter quarto. [STC 17434]. — 3 copies: British Museum; Worcester College, Oxford; Carroll Wilson, New York.

1624. Black letter quarto. [STC 17435]. — Unique copy: British Museum.

1628. Black letter quarto. [Unknown to STC]. — 2 copies: Lincoln College, Oxford; Kungliga Biblioteket, Stockholm.

1631. Black letter quarto. [STC 17436]. — 8 copies: British Museum, Bodleian, 2 copies; National Library of Scotland; Huntington; Harvard; Yale; Barnet J. Beyer, New York (Clawson copy).

1663. Quarto. [Not listed in STC, being later than 1640]. — 8 copies: British Museum, 2 copies; Dyce; Huntington; Harvard; Yale; Carl H. Pforzheimer, New York; Worcester College, Oxford.

Jew of Malta

1633. Quarto. [STC 17412]. — 42 copies known.

Edward the Second

1594. Quarto. [STC 17437]. — 2 copies: Landesbibliothek, Kassel; Zentralbibliothek, Zurich.

1598. Quarto. [STC 17438]. — 7 copies: British Museum, 2 copies; Bodleian; National Library of Scotland; Huntington, 2 copies; Folger.

1612. Quarto. [STC 17439]. — 6 copies: British Museum; Dyce; Huntington, 2 copies; Harvard; John E. Hannigan, Boston.

1622. Quarto. [STC 17440 and 17440a]. — 13 copies: British Museum, 2 copies; Bodleian; Dyce; Yale; Harvard; Boston; New York Public Library; Rosenbach; Nationalbibliothek, Vienna; Huntington; Worcester College, Oxford; Folger.

Dido

1594. Quarto. [STC 17441]. — 3 copies: Bodleian; Huntington; Folger.

Massacre at Paris

(No date). Octavo. [STC 17423]. — 11 copies: British Museum; Bodleian; Dyce; Magdalene College, Cambridge; Huntington; Williams College; Folger; Charles W. Clark, New York; Rosenbach; Library of Congress; John Bakeless, New York.

Hero and Leander

1598A. Quarto. [STC 17413]. — Unique copy at Folger.

1598B. Quarto. [STC 17414]. — 2 copies: British Museum; Huntington (Lamport copies).

1600. Quarto. [STC 17415]. — 3 copies: British Museum; Huntington; Rosenbach.

1606. Quarto [STC 17416]. — 4 copies: British Museum; Bodleian; Morgan; Wellesley (Rowfant copy).

1609. Quarto. [STC 17417]. — 3 copies: Dyce; Folger; Rosenbach (W. A. White copy).

1613. Quarto. [STC 17418]. — 2 copies: British Museum; Huntington.

1616. Ghost Edition. No copies known. It probably never existed, though many books refer to it.

1617. Quarto. [STC 17419]. — 4 copies: Huntington, 2 copies; Rylands Library, Manchester; Worcester College, Oxford.

1622. Quarto. [STC 17420]. — 3 copies: Huntington; Yale; Estate of F. B. Bemis, Boston.

1629. Quarto. [STC 17421]. — 10 copies: British Museum; Dyce; Bodleian; Trinity College, Cambridge; Library of Congress; Huntington; Folger; Williams College; John E. Hannigan, Boston; Prideaux copy (in hands of unknown owner since 1917).

1637. Quarto. [STC 17422]. — 14 copies: British Museum, 2 copies; Dyce; National Library of Scotland; Trinity College, Cambridge, 2 copies; Rylands Library, Manchester; Huntington; Folger; Harvard; Morgan; University of Texas; Williams College; Carl H. Pforzheimer, New York.

Lucan

1600. Octavo. [STC 17415]. — 5 copies: British Museum; Bodleian; Huntington; Folger; Rosenbach.

Ovid

The translations of Ovid exist in six separate editions. Having been surreptitiously printed without printer's name or date, the editions can be distinguished only by choosing a check-copy of each edition and naming the whole edition for it. The ornaments on the title pages are different on each edition and these are given in parenthesis in the list below:

1. Check-copy: Mason AA 207 (Bodleian). 6 asterisks in two rows of 3 each, the whole in brackets. Octavo. — 3 copies: Bodleian; Dyce; Huntington.

2. Check-copy: Douce o 31 (Bodleian). Ornamental band at top of page; lower on page a long band made up of 2 dolphins, 2 birds, and a head. Octavo. Unique copy at Bodleian.

3. Check-copy: Isham copy found at Lamport Hall. Quarto. 2 lace designs. Unique copy at Huntington.

4. Check-copy: Bindley copy (C 34.a.28) British Museum. Quarto. One lace ornament. — 2 copies: British Museum; Carl H. Pforzheimer, New York.

5. Check-copy: Malone 368 (Bodleian). 3 leaves above 2 hands. Octavo. — 16 copies: Bodleian; British Museum; Dyce; Huntington; Morgan; Wellesley; Yale; Carl H. Pforzheimer, New York; John Bakeless, New York; Quaritch; Myers, London; Corpus Christi, Cambridge; Worcester College, Oxford; Folger (2 copies); Dr. James Hubert Norman, London.

6. Check-copy: Malone 133 (Bodleian). Square formed of four smaller squares, that in the upper left corner being turned the wrong way. Octavo. — 8 copies: British Museum, 2 copies; Bodleian; Huntington; Folger; Harvard; Emmanuel College, Cambridge; George Arents, Jr., New York.

COLLECTED EDITIONS

[This portion of the Bibliography lists complete or nearly complete editions of Marlowe's works in all languages. Separate editions and extracts are listed under individual plays and poems.]

UNDATED. Edmund Malone made a collected edition of Marlowe for his own private use by binding together early editions and manuscript copies. This book (Malone 133 = Arch. G. d. 48) is now in the Bodleian. A note by Malone says: "Of the various pieces in this volume, together with the paper into which they are let in, the expence [*sic*] of the inlaying, and the binding, cost five guineas. The two manuscript plays are not included in this estimate. They are two of the rarest plays extant. Mr Capel sought for the tragedy of *Dido* for 30 years in vain. This is, I believe, the only complete collection of Marlowe's works, now extant."

The collection now includes no manuscript plays but only manuscript poems. The *Dido*, now bound in, cost Malone £17 17s.[1] The collection must therefore have been modified after the note was written.

---

[1] *European Magazine*, 2: 457 (1787).

The British Museum has a similar collection from the library of George III.

King Charles II possessed still a third (entirely distinct from that of his successor), which passed into the hands of the Earl of Charlemont, then into the Huth Library, and then disappears — probably broken up by a dealer. It contained only three plays.[2]

1818-20. *Dramatic works of Christopher Marlowe, with prefatory remarks, notes, critical and explanatory.* By W. Oxberry, comedian. London: W. Simpkin and R. Marshall. [No date on title but the individual plays, which were also issued separately, bear dates from 1818 to 1820.]

1826. *Works of Christopher Marlowe.* 3 vols. London: William Pickering. [Often called "Pickering's Edition," also the "Wreath Edition," from ornament on title page. No editor's name appears, but the editor is identified as E. G. Robinson, or George Robinson, in N&Q, 4th ser. 11: 295, 5 Ap 1873, and by John H. Ingram: *Christopher Marlowe and his associates*, p. 280. BM copy has MS. notes, probably by J. Broughton. Reviewed in *Gentleman's Magazine*, (OS) 169 (NS) 15: 45-48 Ja 1841.]

1850. *Works of Christopher Marlowe with notes and some account of his life and writings.* By the Rev. Alexander Dyce, 3 vols. London: William Pickering. [Reprinted 1858. Revised edition in one volume, 1861, 1865, 1870, and ca. 1885. Reviewed in *Fraser's Magazine*, 47: 221-234 F 1853. A BM copy has MS. notes, probably by J. P. Collier.]

1856. *Poems of Greene and Marlowe.* [Edited by Robert Bell.] London: J. W. Parker & Sons, 1856; London: C. Griffin and Co. 186?; London: G. Bell & Sons, 1889; New York: Hurst, n.d. [Bell's Annotated Edition of the English Poets.] [Contains a memoir of Marlowe, and the second edition contains the portrait of Lord Herbert of Cherbury that reappears in Cunningham's edition as a portrait (false) of Marlowe. Later editions change the title and include Jonson.] [NYPL, BM, JB]

1870. *Works of Christopher Marlowe.* Edited with notes and introduction. London: Crocker Brothers. [Later editions, 1871, 1872, 1897, and 1902.]

1870. *Works of Marlowe including his translations.* Edited with introduction and notes by Lieut.-Col. Francis Cunningham. London: John Camden Hotten, n.d. [Reprinted with minor alterations from same plates at intervals until 1912, when Chatto & Windus brought out a reprint. Reviewed by J. A. Symonds in *Academy*, 12: 308-310, 10 S 1870, reprinted *Living Age*, 107: 177-178, 15 O 1870.]

1885. *Works of Christopher Marlowe.* Edited by A. H. Bullen, B.A., in three volumes. London: Nimmo; Boston: Houghton Mifflin, 1885. [British edition limited to 400 copies, American to 350. Reviewed in *Academy*, 26: 315-316, 15 N 1884; *Athenaeum*, no. 2977: 634-635, 15 N 1884; *Literary World*, 15: 325, 4 O 1884; (New York) *Nation*, 40: 423-424, 444-446, 21, 28 My 1885; *Spectator*, 58: 713-714, 30 My 1885; *Bookmart*, 5: 175-177, 217-218, O, N 1887.]

---

[2] Huth Cat., IX. Addenda, p. 2275, No. 8258.

1885. *[Selected] Dramatic works of Christopher Marlowe*. Edited by Percy E. Pinkerton. With a prefatory notice, biographical and critical. London: W. Scott; New York: J. Pott & Co. [Canterbury Poets.] [Also an 1889 edition.] [NYPL, LC]

1885–89. *Marlowes werke historisch-kritische ausgabe*. Von Hermann Breymann . . . und Albrecht Wagner. Heilbronn: Gebr. Henninger. [Englische Sprach- und Literatur-Denkmale.] [This edition was never completed. Reviewed in ES, 14: 137–142 (1890); *Zeitschrift für vergleichende litteraturgeschichte und Renaissance-Litteratur*, 4: 263–265 (1891); *Jahrb*. 7: 359–360 (1872); 21: 282 (1886).]

1887. *Best plays of the old dramatists. Christopher Marlowe*. Edited by Havelock Ellis. With an introduction by J. A. Symonds. London: Vizetelly & Co., 1887. [Mermaid Edition.] [First edition unexpurgated. Slight changes in editions of 1903, 1905, and later. There was also a 1930 edition, Boston: Cornhill; London: Benn. The original Vizetelly edition was taken over by Unwin in England and Scribner's in America and is kept constantly in print. The circumstances of its expurgation are given in Houston Peterson: *Havelock Ellis* [London: Allen & Unwin, n.d.], p. 177; and in Havelock Ellis: *My Life* [Boston: Houghton Mifflin, 1939], pp. 208–210. The edition is reviewed in *Dial*, 8: 97–100 S 1887; *Spectator*, 60: 802–803, 11 Je 1897. Symonds' introduction is also in *Shakespeare's Predecessors*, *q.v.*]

1889. *Théâtre. Traduction de Félix Rabbe avec une préface par J. Richepine*. 2 tom. Paris: A. Savine. [BN, BM]

1902? *Passages from the works of Marlowe*. Selected and edited for young students by J. Le Gay Brereton, B.A. Sydney [Australia]: Kealy & Philips, n.d. [Australian Tutorial Series.] [Now very rare. There are copies in author's collection and in Mitchell Library, Sydney, the principal Australian depository, though the University of Sydney, where Brereton was librarian, has none. The author's copy was originally given to A. Wagner by Brereton himself and has many proposed changes in his handwriting.]

1905. *Plays & poems of Christopher Marlowe*. London: George Newnes; New York: Scribner's. [From same plates as 1930 edition by Simpkin Marshall, Hamilton Kent & Co., *q.v.*]

1906. *Dramatic works of Christopher Marlowe*. London: Routledge; New York: Dutton. [Muses Library.] [JB, BM]

1909. *Plays of Christopher Marlowe*. Introduction by Edward Thomas. London: Dent; New York: Dutton. [Everyman Library.] [Constantly reprinted.]

1910. *Works of Christopher Marlowe*. Edited by C[harles] F[rederick] Tucker Brooke. Oxford: Clarendon Press. [Standard text on which all subsequent study has been based. Constantly reprinted. See *Jahrb*. 46: 331–332 (1910).]

1912. *Christopher Marlowe*. With an introduction by William Lyon Phelps. New York: American Book Company. [Masterpieces of the English Drama.] [Introduction reprinted in *Essays on books*, *q.v.*]

1917. *Doctor Faustus Edward the Second The Jew of Malta.* Leipzig: Tauchnitz; Paris: Librairie Henri Gaulon. [Collection of British and American Authors.] [Text based on Dyce.]

1930. *Plays and poems of Christopher Marlowe.* London: Simpkin Marshall, Hamilton Kent & Co., Ltd.; New York: Scribner's. [From same plates as Newnes edition of 1905, *q.v.*]

1930–33. *Works and life of Christopher Marlowe.* General Editor: R. H. Case. London: Methuen; New York: Dial Press. *Life of Marlowe and the tragedy of Dido*, by C[harles] F[rancis] Tucker Brooke (1930); *Tamburlaine the great*, by U[na] M[ary] Ellis-Fermor (1930); *Jew of Malta and the Massacre at Paris*, by H. S. Bennett (1931); *Poems*, by L. C. Martin (1931); *Tragical history of Doctor Faustus*, by Frederick S[amuel] Boas (1932); *Edward II*, by Charlton and Waller (1933).

1932–. De luxe edition of the *Works*. London: Golden Hours Press. Incomplete. Three works only: *Doctor Faustus*, *Jew of Malta*, and *Hero and Leander*.

1939. *Plays of Christopher Marlowe.* Oxford University Press. [World's Classics.]

Marlowe as a Literary Subject

1828. Johann Ludwig Tieck. *Das fest zu Kenelworth.* Reprinted as *Dichterleben* in Tieck's *Gesammelte werke*. Berlin: Reimer, 1852–54. Translated as *The Life of poets.* Leipzic: Fischer, 1830. Review with extracts in *Blackwood's*, 42: 394–404 S 1837. Various modern editions. [Introduces Peele, Greene, Marlowe, and Shakespeare as characters. Marlowe is slain by the footman "Ingeram."] See also Allen W. Porterfield: "Poets as heroes in German literature." MP, 12: 70–72 (1914).

1837. R[ichard] H[enry, later changed to Hengist] Horne. *Death of Marlowe.* London: Thomas Hales Tracy, 1870, 5th ed. [Lacy's acting edition of plays . . ., vol. 89. Reprinted by Bullen, III. 315–353.] [This piece was attacked by Swinburne but praised by Bullen as a "noble and pathetic tragedy." It was also praised by Leigh Hunt, to whom it was dedicated, and by Elizabeth Barrett Browning, an old friend of the author's. It is accompanied by a poem on Marlowe by J. W. Dalby.]

1844. Elizabeth Barrett Browning. "Vision of poets." In *Poems.* London: Chapman & Hall, II. 3–62.

1865. Karl Kösting. *Shakespeare, ein winternachtstraum. Dramatische gedichte.* Wiesbaden: Niedner, 1865.

1878, and later. Algernon Charles Swinburne. *Poems and ballads*, 2nd series. Stanzas 8–40 of "In the Bay" are supposed to refer to Marlowe.

Channel passage and other poems
  "Prologue to Doctor Faustus"
  "Afterglow of Shakespeare"
  "Prologue to Arden of Feversham"
  "Prologue to The Broken Heart"

Sonnets on the Elizabethan dramatists
        "Christopher Marlowe"
Astrophel
        "Inscriptions for the four sides of a pedestal"
        [Also in *Bibelot*, 1: 141 (1895).]

1884. Ernst von Wildenbruch. "Christoph Marlow. Trauerspiel in vier akten." In *Gesammelte Werke*. Berlin: Grote, 1911–24, VIII. 361–375. [More influenced by the Tieck story than by fact. See TLS, 23: 477, 31 Jy 1924; Allen W. Porterfield: "Poets as heroes in German literature." MP, 12: 76–78 (1914).]

1884. William Watson. [No title.] In *Epigrams of art, life, and nature*. Liverpool: Gilbert G. Walmsley, no. VII. Reprinted in *Collected poems*. New York and London: John Lane, p. 86.

1890. W. L. Courtney. "Kit Marlowe's death." *Universal Review*, 6: 356–371, 15 Mr. Reprinted in *Studies at Leisure*. London: Chapman and Hall, 1892, pp. 1–24. [Produced by Arthur Bourchier, with Cyril Maud in the cast, at the Shaftesbury Theatre, London, 4 Jy 1890; revived at the St. James Theatre, 1892. See also *Quarterly Review*, 262: 249 Ap 1934.]

1894. Ernest Rhys. "Marlowe." [Poem.] In *London Rose*. London: Elkin Matthews and John Lane; New York: Dodd Mead, p. 91.

1896. J[ohn] Le Gay Brereton. "Kit Marlowe." [Poem.] In *Song of brotherhood*. London: George Allen, pp. 57–58. [NYPL]

1896. James Dryden Hosken. *Christopher Marlowe, a tragedy*. London: Henry and Company. [BM]

1897. Arthur A[lbert] D[awson] Bayldon. "Marlowe." In *Poems*. Brisbane, Queensland: W. H. Wendt & Co., pp. 139–140. Also in *Western track*. Sydney: H. T. Dunn, 1905, p. 85, and in *Eagles: the collected poems*. Sydney: H. Wise & Co., p. 21. [NYPL]

1899. "To Christopher Marlowe." [Poem.] *Critic*, 35: 888–889 O.

1900. Wilhelm Schäfer. *Wilhelm Shakespeare. Schauspiel aus der Renaissancezeit Englands*. Zürich: Selbstverlag.

1901. Josephine Preston Peabody. *Marlowe, a drama in five acts*. Boston: Houghton Mifflin. [First produced at Radcliffe College, Cambridge, Mass., 19, 20 Je 1905.]

1905. Sarah Hawks Sterling. *Shakespeare's sweetheart*. Philadelphia: G. W. Jacobs & Co. [Based on the story of Anne Hathaway and introducing Marlowe as an actor playing Tybalt in *Romeo and Juliet*.]

1913. Alfred Noyes. *Tales of the Mermaid Tavern*. New York: Stokes.
        "A coiner of angels," pp. 17–41
        "Sign of the Golden Shoe," pp. 71–96
    Also in *Blackwood's*, 193: 216–225, 342–346 F, Mr 1913, and in *Collected poems*. Edinburgh: Blackwood; New York: Stokes, 1913, 1920, 1927, pp. 274–433.

1913. Horace Van Offel. *Une nuit de Shakespeare, conte en trois actes*. Préface de Grégoire Le Roy. Brussels: Librairie Moderne. [Collection "Junior."]

1919. L. A. G. Strong. "C. Marlye." [Poem.] *Coterie*, no. 3: 37 D. [HCL]

1919. James Branch Cabell. "The episode called porcelain cups." *Century*, 99: 20–29 N 1919. Reprinted in *Line of love: Dizain des mariages*. New York: McBride, 1921; London: John Lane, 1929. The story does not appear in the 1905 edition. Reprinted in *Bedside book of famous American stories*. Edited by Angus Burrell and Bennett A. Cerf. New York: Random House, 1936. [Anticipates in fiction Dr. Hotson's discovery that Marlowe was killed in a brawl over a tavern reckoning.]

1921. Harold F[rederick] Rubinstein and Clifford Bax. *Shakespeare: a play in five episodes*. Boston: Houghton Mifflin.

1922. Clemence Dane [pseudonym of Winifred Ashton]. *Will Shakespeare. An invention in four acts*. London: Heinemann. [Shakespeare accidentally kills Marlowe.]

1923. J. Lindsay. "Death of Marlowe." [One-act play.] *Vision*, 1: 23–26 Ag. [NYPL]

1924. Ernest Milton. *Christopher Marlowe*. Prologue by Walter de la Mare. London: Constable. 2nd ed., 1929. [Reviewed in TLS, 23: 460, 24 Jy 1924.]

1925. Douglas Ainslie. "Christopher Marlowe." [Poem.] *English Review*, 41: 578 O. [Written for recitation at William Poel's production of selections from Marlowe, Haymarket Theatre, London, 24 Jy 1925.]

1925. J[ohn] Le Gay Brereton. "For Marlowe." [Sonnet.] In *Marlowe's dramatic art*. [See Chap. VII.] [HCL, JB]

1928. J[ohn] Le Gay Brereton. "Marlowe." [Poem.] In *Swags up!* London: Dent, p. 40. [NYPL]

1928. H[enry] H[amby] Hay. *Great Elizabeth*. Boston: R. G. Badger. [NYPL]

1928. Charles Williams. *Myth of Shakespeare*. Oxford University Press. [Excerpts in *Periodical*, 14: 80–81 Je 1929.]

1928?–1932? n.d. Philip Owens. *Marlowe*. [Play.] New York: McKee.

1929. Arista Edward Fisher. *To the Sun*. New York: Cosmopolitan; London: John Murray.

1929. Charles Norman. "Exequy on the death of Marlowe." In *Poems*. New York: Knopf, pp. 59–67.

1930. Charles Edward Lawrence. "The Reckoning. Telling possibly the truth of the death of Marlowe." [Play in one act.] *Cornhill*, 69: 10–28 Jy.

1930. William Robinson Leigh. *Clipt wings: a drama in 5 acts*. New York: Thornton W. Allen Co.

1930. Austin Melford. *Kit Marlowe*; *a play in one act*. London: S. French. [French's Acting Editions, no. 762.]

1930. Clinton Scollard. "Of Kit Marlowe." [Poem.] *Sewanee Review*, 38: 132 Ap.

1931. Lionel R[oy] McColvin. "*To kill the queen;*" (*a pageant play in 3 acts*). London: N. Douglas. [NYPL]

1932. Philip Lindsay. *One dagger for two*. London: Cassell.

1934. H[enry] H[amby] Hay. *As Shakespeare was*. London: E. Matthews Marot, Ltd. [SAT gives publication date as 1931 and publisher as Douglas.]

1935. T. Jennings. *This side idolatry*. [Unpublished play in seven scenes.] [MS.] [SAT]

1936. Maria M. Coxe. *Kit Marlowe*. Produced by Hedgerow Players, Moylan-Rose Valley, Pa. [MS.]

1936. Elizabeth Jenkins. *Phoenix nest*. London: Gollancz; Toronto: Ryerson.

1937. George Cronyn. *Mermaid Tavern. Kit Marlowe's story*. New York: Knight Publications.

1938. Rupert Sargent Holland. *Boy who lived on London Bridge*. Philadelphia: Macrae Smith. [Marlowe is a character.]

1938. Cryn Jones. *Garland of bays*. New York: Macmillan.

1940. John Brophy. *Gentleman of Stratford*. New York: Harper. [Chap. VIII deals with Marlowe's death.]

UNDATED. T. R. S. Temple. *Shakespeare: a romantic drama in 3 acts*. [MS.] [SAT]

UNDATED. L. Cowen and H. Gingold. *Shakespeare: a play in 4 acts and an epilogue*. [M. H. Spielmann Collection, Upland, Folkestone, Kent.]

EARLY PRINTED BOOKS

1588. Robert Greene. *Perimedes the blacke-smith*. London: J. Wolfe f. E. White.

1589. Thomas Nashe. "To the gentlemen students of both universities." Preface to Robert Greene's *Menaphon*. London: T. O[rwin] f. S. Clarke.

1591. Robert Greene. *Greene's farewell to folly*. London: T. Scarlet f. T. Gubbin a. T. Newman.

1592. Robert Greene. *Groats-worth of witte*. London: W. Wright.

1592-93? Henry Chettle. *Kind harts dreame*. London: W. Wright.

1593? Thomas Nashe. *Strange Newes, of the intercepting certaine letters*. London: [J. Danter]. [Doubtful allusion.]

1593. Thomas Nashe. *Christs teares ouer Jerusalem*. London: J. Roberts, solde by A. Wise.

1593. Gabriel Harvey. *New letter of notable contents*. London: J. Wolfe.

1593. Gabriel Harvey. *Pierces supererogation*. London: J. Wolfe.

1593? George Peele. Prologue to *The honour of the Garter*. London: Widdowe Charlewood f. J. Busbie.

1595. Thomas Edwardes. "L'Envoy" to *Narcissus*. London: John Wolfe. [Unique copy at Peterborough Cathedral.]

1595-96? R[ichard] C[arew]. "Excellencie of the English tongue." In William Camden: *Remaines of a greate worke concerning Britaine*. London: J. Legatt f. S. Waterson.

1596. Thomas Nash. *Haue with you to Saffron-Walden.* London: J. Danter.

1597. Thomas Beard. *Theatre of Gods judgments.* London: A. Islip.

1598. Francis Meres. *Palladis Tamia; Wit's treasury.* London: P. Short f. C. Burbie. [See Don Cameron Allen. "Francis Meres's treatise . . . a critical edition." Illinois Diss. 1931. *Ill. Studies in Language and Literature*, 16: 343–500 (1933).]

1598. Edward Blunt's dedication of *Hero and Leander.* London: A. Islip f. E. Blount.

1598. George Chapman's continuation of *Hero and Leander.* London: F. Kingston f. P. Linley.

1598. Henry Petowe. *The second part of Hero and Leander.* London: T. Purfoot.

1599. Thomas Nash. *Nashes Lenten stuffe.* [T. Judson a. V. Sims] f. N. L[ing] a. C. B[urbie.]

1600. John Bodenham. *Bel-vedére, or the garden of the muses.* F. K[ingston] f. H. Astley.

1600. William Vaughan. *Golden grove.* London: S. Stafford.

1600. John Lane. *Tom Tel-Troth's message.* London: f. R. Howell.

1605–06? Anon. *Returne from Pernassus.* London: G. Eld f. J. Wright.

1607. Thomas Dekker. *Knights conjuring.* T. C[reed] f. W. Barley.

1610? Edmund Bolton. "Choise of English." Bodleian Library, Rawlinson MS., D 1 [formerly Misc. 1], p. 13. Reprinted by Anthony Hall in *Nicolai Triverti annalium continuatio* (1722); Joseph Haslewood: *Ancient critical essays.* London: Robert Triphook, 1815, II. 247.

1615. Edmond Howes. *Annales, or Generall Chronicle of England, begun first by maister Iohn Stow.* London: Thomas Adams, 1615, p. 811. [NYPL]

1618. Edmund Rudierd. *Thunderbolt of Gods wrath.* London: W. I[ones?] f. T. Pavier.

1623. Ben Jonson: "To the memory of . . . Mr. William Shakespeare." First Folio.

1627. Michael Drayton. "To my most dearely-loved friend Henery Reynolds, Esquire, of Poets and Poesie." In "Elegies" at end of *Battaile of Agincourt.* London: [A. Mathewes] f. W. Lee. [Not in 1620 and 1619 editions.]

1628. John Earle. *Micro-cosmographie.* London: W. S[tansby] f. E. Blount.

1635. Thomas Heywood. *Hierarchie of the blessed angells.* London: A. Islip.

1646. Sa[muel] Clarke. *Mirrour or looking-glasse for both saints and sinners.* London: Ric. Cotes f. John Bellamy. [BM]

1653. Izaak Walton. *Compleat Angler.* London: T. Maxey f. R. Marriot.

1675. Edward Phillips. *Theatrum poetarum.* London: Smith. [See Walter Albrecht. *Über das theatrum poetarum von Milton's neffen Edward Phillips.* Berlin Diss. 1928. Weimar: Uschmann; Leipzig: Mayer & Muller, 1928.]

1687. William Winstanley. *Lives of the most famous English poets.* London: H. Clark f. Samuel Manship.

1687. Gerard Langbaine. *Momus triumphans; or the plagiaries of the English stage exposed in a catalogue.* Oxford: Nicholas Cox; London: Sam Holford. [See DNB, XI. 534–535.]

1688. Gerard Langbaine. *New catalogue of English plays.* London: N. Cox [First authorized edition. Actually appeared in December, 1687.]

1691. Gerard Langbaine. *Account of the English dramatick poets.* Oxford: G. West and H. Clements. [Bodleian has Malone's copy with notes. British Museum has copies with notes by William Oldys, J. Haslewood, Richard Wright, and others. See DNB, XI. 534–535, and Alun Watkin-Jones. "English dramatick poets," *Essays and Studies,* 21: 75–85 (1936).]

1691–92. Anthony à Wood. *Athenae Oxonienses.* London: Tho. Bennett.

1698–99? Gerard Langbaine. *Lives and characters of the English dramatic poets.* London: Tho. Leigh and William Turner. [Revised by Charles Gildon.]

GENERAL

Agate, James (ed.). *English dramatic critics.* London: Arthur Barker Limited, n.d. [ca. 1932]. Articles by Joseph Knight and St. John Ervine.

Åkerlund, Alfred. *On the history of the definite tenses in English.* Cambridge: Heffer, 1911, pp. 61 ff. [Casual allusions only.] [NYPL]

Aksenov, I. A. Гамлет и другие опыты. [*Hamlet and other essays.*] Moscow: Federatsiya, 1930, pp. 27–31. [HCL]

Alden, Raymond Macdonald. *Rise of formal satire in England under classical influence.* Philadelphia: Ginn & Co. for the University of Pennsylvania, 1899, pp. 124–125, 201. [Publications of the University of Pennsylvania, vol. VII, no. 2.]

Anon. *Playhouse pocket-companion, or theatrical vade-mecum.* London: Richardson and Urquhart, 1779. [Passing references to Marlowe on pp. 21, 91.]

Anon. "Ancient drama." *Monthly Review,* 75: 225–239 N 1814.

Anon. "English tragedy." *Edinburgh Review,* 38: 177–208 F 1823, especially pp. 187–190.

Anon. "Christopher Marlowe." *Fraser's Magazine,* 47: 221–234 F 1853. [Review of Dyce.]

Anon. "Dr. Bliss's selections from the old poets." N&Q, 2nd ser. 10: 204–205, 15 S 1860.

Anon. *Footsteps of Shakspere.* London: John Russell, 1862, pp. 138–159. [BM]

Anon. "Marlowe." *Every Saturday,* 1: 670, 15 O 1870.

Anon. "Marlowe." *Eclectic Magazine,* 76: 241–243 F 1871. [Review of Cunningham from *Academy.*]

Anon. "Shakespeare's Fellows." *Atlantic Monthly,* 56: 851–854 D 1885.

Anon. "Marlowe and his works." *Book Lore,* 5: 98–102 Mr 1887.

Anon. Various news stories on the Marlowe Memorial at Canterbury: London *Times,* 16 N 1888, p. 3b; 15 D 1888, p. 14b; 17 Ja 1889, p. 5f; 19 Ag

1890, p. 14d; 24 Jy 1889, p. 13a; 2 Ja 1889, p. 6e; 5 Ja 1889, p. 10b; 20 Jy 1891, p. 6b; 17 S 1891, p. 6d.

Anon. "Marlowe Memorial." *Shakespeariana*, 5: 530 (1888).

Anon. News stories on the Marlowe Memorial in the *Kentish Gazette and Canterbury Press*: "Unveiling of the Marlowe Memorial by Sir Henry Irving [on Sept. 16, 1891]," 211: 8, 19 S 1891; "The Marlowe memorial at Canterbury," 253: 2, 27 O 1928; same title [three statuettes added; unveiling by Sir Hugh Walpole], 253: 7, 3 N 1928.

Anon. "Unveiling of Marlowe's Memorial." *Saturday Review*. [London], 72: 318, 19 S 1891.

Anon. "Marlowe." *Spectator*, 67: 381, 19 S 1891.

Anon. "Christopher Marlowe." *Lyceum*, 5: 40–42 O 1891. [Chicago Public Library.]

Anon. Article "Christopher Marlowe" in *New International Encyclopaedia*. New York: Dodd Mead, 1916, XV. 110.

Anon. *History and description of the Marlowe monument. Canterbury, 1890–1928*. Marlowe Memorial Committee, 1929.

Anon. *Columbia University Course in Literature*. New York: Columbia University Press, 1928, XI. 214–228.

Anon. "Canterbury to honor Marlowe." *New York Times*, 22 O 1933.

Anon. Bibliography. Pratt Institute. School of Library Service. *Lectures*, II. 428–429. [NYPL]

Anon. "Marlowe (Cristobal)." In *Enciclopedia universal ilustrado*. Barcelona: Hijos de J. Espasa, XXXIII. 248–249.

Adams, William Davenport. *Dictionary of drama*. London: Chatto and Windus; Philadelphia: Lippincott, 1904. [Earliest edition apparently 1878. No article on Marlowe, but short articles on individual plays.]

Arber, Edward. *Transcript of the register of the Company of Stationers of London, 1554–1640, A.D.* London: privately printed, 1875–77; Birmingham, 1894.

Archer, William. *Old drama and the new*. Boston: Small Maynard, 1923; New York: Dodd Mead, 1926.

Armas y Cardenas, José de. *Ensayos criticos de literatura inglesa y española*. Madrid: V. Suarez, 1910, pp. 13–106.

Aronstein, Philipp. "Das nationale erlebnis im englischen Renaissancedrama." *Jahrb.* 55: 87–128 (1919). [Especially pp. 97–99.]

Aronstein, Philipp. *Das englische renaissancedrama*. Leipzig and Berlin: Teubner, 1929, pp. 42–47.

Baker, David Erskine. "Marloe, Mr. Christopher," in *Companion to the playhouse*. London: 1764, vol. III, sig. X2. Later editions, 1782, 1812.

Baker, George Pierce. "Dramatic technique in Marlowe." *Essays and studies*, 4: 172–182 (1913).

Baker, George Pierce. *Development of Shakespeare as a dramatist*. New York: Macmillan, 1920.

Baker, H[enry] Barton. *History of the London stage and its famous players (1596–1903)*. London: Routledge; New York: Dutton, 1904.

Baker, James Ernest. "Marlowe memorial." *Academy*, 37: 206, 22 Mr 1890.

Barth, Hermann. *Das epitheton in den dramen des jungen Shakespeare und seiner vorgänger*. Göttingen Diss., 1913. Göttingen: no publisher named, 1913. [HCL]

Bartlett, Henrietta C. *Mr. William Shakespeare*. New Haven: Yale University Press, 1922.

Baskervill, Charles Read; Heltzel, Virgil B.; and Nethered, Arthur N. *Elizabethan and Stuart plays*. New York: Holt, 1934. Biographical notes, pp. 307–308.

Bayley, Harold. *Shakespeare symphony*. London: Chapman & Hall, 1906. Discussion of Collier's forged ballad, pp. 10–13.

Beljame, A. "Premières œuvres dramatiques de Shakespeare." *Revue des cours et conférences*, 6: 402–409; 496–504; 585–593; 743–752; 788–796 (1898). Other lectures of this series deal with other Elizabethans.

Beloe, William. *Anecdotes of literature and science*. London: Rivington, 1907, II. 311–315.

Biesterfeld, Peter Wilhelm. "Die oberbühne bei Marlowe." [Herrig's] *Archiv f. d. Studium d. neueren Sprachen u. Litteraturen*, 160: 51–60 (1931).

Blair, Nancy Brown. *Women in the dramas of Lyly, Peele, Marlowe, Kyd, and Greene*. Colorado M. A. Thesis, 1905. [MS.]

Blessing, Carmen Urcell. *Study in the creation of atmosphere on the Elizabethan stage by means of poetic description, figurative language, and hints of speech, as determined from the plays of Marlowe, Dekker, Chapman, and Webster*. Colorado M. A. Thesis, 1928. [MS.]

Boas, F[rederick] S[amuel]. *Works of Thomas Kyd*. Oxford University Press, 1901.

Boas, F[rederick] S[amuel]. *University drama in the Tudor age*. Oxford University Press, 1914.

Boas, F[rederick] S[amuel]. *Shakespeare and his predecessors*. New York: Scribner's, 1896, 1904.

Boas, F[rederick] S[amuel]. *Shakespeare and the universities*. Oxford: Blackwell, 1923.

Boas, Frederick S[amuel]. *Marlowe and his circle*. Oxford University Press, 1929; revised ed. 1931. Reviewed in *Quarterly Review*, 255: 231–246 O 1930; TLS, 28: 919, 14 N 1929; RES, 7: 86–89 Ja 1931; *Queen's Quarterly*, 38: 214–219; *Manchester Guardian*, 16 O 1929; MLR, 25: 201–203 (1930); MLN, 45: 329–331 (1930); *Criterion*, 9: 555–557 Ap 1930.

Boas, F[rederick] S[amuel]. *Introduction to Tudor drama*. Oxford University Press, 1933.

Boas, F[rederick] S[amuel]. "Elizabethan Literary Society, 1884–1934." *Quarterly Review*, 262: 242–257 Ap 1934. Reprinted by John Murray, London. Contains data on the Marlowe Memorial.

Bodenstedt, Friedrich Martin. *Shakespeares zeitgenossen und ihre werke*. Berlin: Decker, 1860, III. 155–172.

Boecker, Alexander. *Christopher Marlowe as a transformer of the English drama*. New York University M.A. Thesis, 1906. [MS.]

Bormann, Edwin. *300 Geistesblitze und anderes von Bacon-Shakespeare-Marlowe.* Leipzig: E. Bormann, 1902.

Bormann, Hermann. *Der jurist in der drama der Elisabethanischen zeit.* Halle Diss. n.d. Halle: Heinrich John, 1906. [Marlowe has no legal characters.]

Bouterwek, Friedrich. *Geschichte der poesie und beredsamkeit.* Göttingen: Rower, 1809, VII. 206–209. [Also called *Geschichte der kunste und wissenschaften.*]

Bradbrook, M[uriel] C[lara]. *Themes and conventions of Elizabethan tragedy.* Cambridge University Press, 1935.

Bradley, A[ndrew] C[ecil]. [Ward's] *English Poets.* New York: Macmillan, 1912, I. 411–423.

Bradley, Jesse Franklin, and Adams, Josiah Quincy. *Jonson allusion-book.* New Haven: Yale University Press, 1922. [Cornell Studies in English, VI.]

Brennan, Chris. "Marlowe." *Beiblatt zur Anglia,* 16: 207–209 (1905).

Brereton, J[ohn] LeGay. "Notes on the text of Marlowe." *Beiblatt zur Anglia,* 16: 203–207 (1905). Also in his *Elizabethan drama: Notes and studies.* Sydney, Australia: William Brooks & Co., 1909, pp. 1–6.

Brereton, J[ohn] LeGay. "Marlowe, some textual notes." MLR, 6: 94–96 Ja 1911. [On five plays.]

Brink, Eveadell. *Elizabethan dramatists' treatment of morality before and after 1603.* Iowa M. A. Thesis, 1933. [MS.]

Brooke, C[harles] F[rederick] Tucker. "Marlowe canon." PMLA, 37: 367–417 (1922).

Brooke, C[harles] F[rederick] Tucker. "Reputation of Christopher Marlowe." *Transactions of the Connecticut Academy of Sciences,* 25: 347–408 (1922).

Brooke, C[harles] F[rederick] Tucker. *Life of Marlowe.* London: Methuen; New York: Dial Press, 1930. Bound with Brooke's edition of *Dido* in vol. I of the complete Marlowe edited by R. H. Case.

Broun, Heywood. "It seems to me." *New York World-Telegram,* 8 D 1938.

Brown, John Mason. *Letters to greenroom ghosts.* New York: Viking, 1934. "Christopher Marlowe to Eugene O'Neill," pp. 71–118.

Büchner, Alexander. *Geschichte der englischen poesie.* Darmstadt: Diehl, 1855, I. 226–236. [Now hopelessly out of date.]

Burchardt, Carl. "Christopher Marlowe." *Edda* [Christiania, Norway]. 18: 120–133 (1922).

Buland, Mable. *Presentation of time in the Elizabethan drama.* Yale Diss. n.d. New York: Holt, 1912. [Yale Studies in English, no. 44.]

Butler, James Madison. *Christopher Marlowe: his personality in his plays.* Virginia M.A. Thesis, 1924. [MS.]

Cabell, James Branch. *Beyond life.* New York: R. M. McBride, 1919. Modern Library ed. (1923), p. 86.

Campbell, Lucien Quitman. *Characterization in the dramatic works of Marlowe.* Texas M.A. Thesis, 1924. [MS.]

Chalmers, Alexander. *General biographical dictionary*. London, 1815 (new ed.), XXI. 329–332.

Chambers, Edmund K[erchever]. *Elizabethan stage*. Oxford University Press, 1923, III. 418–427.

Chambers, Edmund K[erchever]. *William Shakespeare*. Oxford University Press, 1930.

Chambers, Edmund K[erchever]. *Shakspere allusion book*. Oxford University Press, 1932.

Chandler, Josephine. *Lyricism in Marlowe's death scenes*. Columbia M.A. Thesis, 1925. [MS.]

Cheney, Sheldon. *The Theatre*. London: Longmans, 1929, pp. 266–269.

Chetwode, or Chetwood, William Rufus. *British Theatre*. London, 1752.

Chreitzberg, Margaret. *Prevailing types of women in English drama from its beginning to 1640*. North Carolina M.A. Thesis, 1928. [MS.] [Abstracted in University of North Carolina *Record*, Graduate School Series, 19: 49–50 (1928).]

Cibber, Colley. *Lives of the poets*. London, 1753, I. 85–87. [Said to have been written by Robert Shiels. Cf. Boswell's Johnson.]

Clark, Eleanor Grace. *Elizabethan fustian: a study in the social and political backgrounds of the drama, with particular reference to Christopher Marlowe*. New York: Oxford Press, 1937.

Clark, Eleanor Grace. *Ralegh and Marlowe. A study in Elizabethan fustian*. New York: Fordham University Press, 1941.

Clark, John Scott and Odell, John Price. *Study of English and American writers*. Chicago: Row Peterson and Company, 1916, pp. 31–40.

Clayton, F. T., *Marlowe's plays; charts*. [MS.] [HCL]

Collier, John Payne. "On the English dramatic writers who preceded Shakespeare." *Edinburgh Magazine*, 3: 525–531; 4: 127–131; 409–414; 5: 104–110; 522–527; 7: 517–522; 8: 149–154 D 1818; F, Ap, My, Ag, D 1819; Je 1820; F 1821. [This appears to be Collier's first draft for his *History*. It is signed variously, "I.P.C.," "J.P.C.," and "C.P.J." There is a file in NYPL. The Folger Shakespeare Library has Collier's own clippings with a few MS. alterations in vol. II of *MS. Bibliog. Coll.* (J. P. Collier).]

Collier, John Payne. MS. emendations and notes in old printed plays. In possession of Dr. A. S. W. Rosenbach.

Collier, John Payne. *Poetical Decameron*. Edinburgh: Constable, 1820.

Collier, John Payne. *History of English dramatic poetry*. London: John Murray, 1831; 2nd ed., London: George Bell & Sons, 1879. [The second edition is rather rare. There is a copy in the Washington Square College Library, New York University.]

Collier, John Payne. *Memoirs of Edward Alleyn*. London: Shakespeare Society, 1841. [Publications, vol. 1.]

Collier, John Payne. "History of English drama and stage in the time of Shakespeare." In *Works of Shakespeare*, I. ii–xlvi. New York: Redfield, 1853.

Collier, John Payne. *Bibliographical and critical account of the rarest books in the English language*. London: 1865.

Collins, John Churton. "Predecessors of Shakespeare." In *Essays and Studies*. London: Macmillan, 1895, pp. 91–192, especially pp. 152–160.

Compton-Rickett, Arthur. "Kit Marlowe, pioneer." *Poetry Review*, 6: 107–116 Mr 1915; *Living Age*, 2: 348–352, 8 My 1915.

Conrad, Hermann. "Christopher Marlowe." *Preussische jahrbuecher*, 134: 115–147 (1908). [See *Jahrb.* 45: 284 (1909).]

Courtney, W. L. "Christopher Marlowe." *Fortnightly Review*, 78: 467–484; 678–691, S, O 1905. [See *Jahrb.* 43: 294–295 (1907).]

Cowling, G. H. *Music on the Shakespearian stage*. Cambridge University Press, 1913. [Specific reference to Marlowe as well as Shakespeare.]

Cox, J. Charles. *Canterbury: A historical and topographical record of the city*. London: Methuen, 1905.

Creizenach, Wilhelm. *English drama in the age of Shakespeare*. London: Sidgwick and Jackson, 1916.

Crofts, Ellen. *Chapters in the history of English literature*. London: Rivington, 1884, pp. 171–194.

Cunliffe, John W[illiam]. *Influence of Seneca on Elizabethan tragedy*. London: Macmillan, 1893; New York: Stechert, 1925, pp. 58–62.

Cunningham, George Godfrey. *Lives of eminent and illustrious Englishmen*. Glasgow: A. Fullarton & Co., 1837, II. 267–269. [NYPL, LC]

Cunningham, George Godfrey. *English nation; or a history of England in the lives of Englishmen*. Edinburgh and London: A. Fullarton & Co.; New York: Fullarton, McNab & Co. [ca. 1863], I. 755–757. [CUL]

Danchin, F.-C. "Trois corrections au texte de Marlowe." *Revue anglo-américaine*, 10: 330 Ap 1933.

Deighton, K. *The old dramatists*. Westminster: Constable, 1896.

Dezsö, Rózsa. "Shakespeare elözöi. I. Marlowe." *Magyar Shakespeare-Tár*, 5: 19–65 (1912). [HCL]

Dimock, Elizabeth Ricker. "Marlowe's works as an exponent of the Renaissance." *Vassar Miscellany*, 31: 353–358 My 1902.

Doi, S. *On the earlier plays of Christopher Marlowe*. Tokyo University, Graduation Thesis, 1935. [MS.]

Dowden, Edward. "Christopher Marlowe." In *Transcripts and Studies*. London: Paul, Trench, Trübner, 1892, 2nd ed. Cf. *Fortnightly Review*, 13: 69–81, 1 Ja 1870.

Drake, Nathan. *Shakespeare and his times*. London: Cadell and Davies, 1817; Paris: Baudry's European Library, 1838. Reviewed in *New Monthly Review*, 89: 361 Ag 1819.

Duboc, Julius. *Tragik vom standpunkt des optimismus*. Hamburg: Grüning, 1886, pp. 116–117. [CUL]

Eagle, R. "Marlowe problems." *Baconiana*, 3rd ser. 13: 219–227 O 1915.

Eckhardt, Eduard. *Englische drama im zeitalter der Reformation und der Hochrenaissance*. Berlin and Leipzig: de Gruyter, 1928, pp. 86–95.

Eekhoud, Georges. "La Pléiade Shakespearienne." *Société nouvelle*, 21 (Année 11): 188–202; 641–656 (1895).

Eliot, T. S. "Four Elizabethan dramatists." *Criterion*, 2: 115–123 F 1924.

[Henslowe, Philip.] *Henslowe's diary*. Edited by W[alter] W[ilson] Greg. London: A. H. Bullen, 1904–1908.

Hertel, Wilhelm. *Rollenhäufung bei der aufführung der dramen Christopher Marlowes*. (*Ein beitrag z. Gesch. d. Admiralstruppe*.) Leipzig Diss. 1926. [MS.]

Herz, E[mil]. *Englische schauspieler und englisches schauspiel zur zeit Shakespeares in Deutschland*. Hamburg and Leipzig: Voss, 1903, pp. 74–75, 84–85. [Theatre Geschichtliche Forschungen, no. 18.]

Hirtel, Helmuth. *Entwicklung des prologs und epilogs im früh-neuenglischen drama*. Giessen Diss. 1915. Giessen: Justus Christ, 1928, pp. 18–19.

Hohn, M. T. *Recent investigations concerning Christopher Marlowe*. Colorado M.A. Thesis, 1927. [MS.]

Hood, Arthur. "Vindication of the character and work of Marlowe: Shakespeare's great contemporary." *Poetry Review*, 25: 17–33 (1934).

Hüdepohl, Adolf. *Tragische ironie in der Englischen tragödie und historie vor Shakespeare*. Halle Diss. 1914. Halle: Ehrhardt Karras, 1915, pp. 76–93.

Ingleby, C. M. *See* Munro, John.

Ingram, John H. "Shakespeare's Associates." *The Key*, pt. XVI, pp. 264–265, May 1864. [BM.] [Ingram in his own bibliography erroneously gives the date as April 23, 1864.]

Ingram, John H. "New View of Marlowe." *Universal Review*, 4: 380–399 (1889).

Ingram, John H. "Christopher Marlowe Bibliography." *Athenaeum*, no. 4080: 18, 6 Ja 1906.

[Jacob, Giles]. *Poetical Register*. London, 1719, 1723, I. 171–172.

J. M. H. "Christopher Marlowe." *Eagle* (St. John's Coll., Camb.), 17: 632–646 Je 1893. [CUL]

Jones, Iva Marie. *Two centuries of Marlowe allusion*. Stanford M.A. Thesis, 1934. [MS.]

Jusserand, Jules. *Le Théâtre en Angleterre depuis la conquête jusqu'aux prédécesseurs immediats de Shakespeare*. Paris: E. Leroux, 1881. (1st ed. 1878.)

Jusserand, Jules. *Histoire littéraire du peuple anglais*. Paris: Firmin-Didot et Cie., 1894. Translated as *Literary history of the English people*. New York: Putnam, 1926 (3rd ed.), III. 133–148.

Kashiwagura, S. *Some considerations on the art of Marlowe*. Tokyo University Graduation Thesis, 1927. [MS.]

Keltie, John S. *Works of the British dramatists*. London: Nimmo, 1870. Biographical notes, pp. 97–98.

King, William Henry. *Bookland*. London: G. Philip & Son, 1921 [New Era Library], pp. 51–62.

Kingsley, Henry. "Father of irregular drama." In *Fireside studies*. London: Chatto and Windus, 1876, II. 1–90.

Klein, J[ulius] L[udwig]. *Geschichte des dramas*. Leipzig: Weigel, 1865–76, XIII. 607–807.

Kocher, Paul Harold. *Ethics of the early Elizabethan drama as exemplified in the plays of the university wits.* Stanford Diss. 1935. [MS.] [Marlowe is discussed on pp. 134–320.] See also *Abstracts of Diss.,* 11: 51–52 (1935–36).

Kocher, Paul H[arold]. "Development of Marlowe's character." PQ, 17: 331–350 (1938).

Koeppel, E. *Ben Jonson's wirkung auf zeitgenossische dramatiker.* Heidelberg: Carl Winter, 1906, pp. 6–19, 80–82.

Koldewey, Eva. *See* Chap. XVI.

Lamb, Charles. "Characters of dramatic writers contemporary with Shakespeare." *Works* (ed. Percy Fitzgerald). London: Moxon, 1876, IV. 213–226, especially pp. 214–221. [Reviewed in *Monthly Review,* 58: 349–356 Ap 1806.]

Landau, M. "Zum dreihundertsten todestage der dichters der ersten Fausttragödie." *Ueber Land und Meer,* 70: 819 O 1893. [NYPL]

Lanier, Sidney. *Shakespeare and his forerunners.* New York: Doubleday, 1902.

Lansberry, Julius Robert. *Bulk character emphasis in Marlowe's chief plays.* Idaho M.A. Thesis, 1931. [MS.]

Lardner, Dionysius (ed.). *Cabinet cyclopædia . . . eminent literary and scientific men.* London: Longmans, 1837.

Larkins, Dorothy. *Christopher Marlowe, his life and works.* Columbia M.A. Thesis, 1920. [MS.]

Lawrence, C. E. "Christopher Marlowe, the man." *Quarterly Review,* 255: 231–246 (1930). [Review of Brooke and Boas.]

Lawrence, W[illiam] J[ohn]. *Elizabethan playhouse and other studies.* Stratford: Shakespeare Head, 1912–13.

Lawrence, W[illiam] J[ohn]. *Pre-Restoration stage studies.* Cambridge: Harvard University Press, 1927.

Lederer, Franz. *Die ironie in den tragödien Shaksperes.* Berlin: Mayer & Müller, 1907.

Liening, Martin. *Personification unpersönlichen hauptwörter bei den vorläufern Shakespeares.* Münster Diss. 1904. Borna-Leipzig: R. Noske, 1904.

Lindabury, Richard Vliet. *Study of patriotism in the Elizabethan drama.* Princeton Diss. 1930. Princeton University Press, 1931.

Lindley, Mabel Clare. *Nature and classical elements in the plays of Green [sic], Peele and Marlowe.* Indiana M.A. Thesis, 1902. [MS.]

L. J[oubert?]. "Marlowe ou Marloe, Christopher." In *Nouvelle Biographie générale.* Paris: Didot, 1860, XXXIII, 860–863.

Löhrer, Alfred. *Swinburne als kritiker der literatur.* Zürich Diss. 1926. Weida i. Thür.: Thomas & Hubert, 1925.

Lott, Bernhard. *Der monolog im englischen drama vor Shakespeare.* Greifswald Diss. n.d. Greifswald: Julius Abel, 1909. [See *Jahrb.* 46: 191 (1910).]

Lounsbury, Thomas R. *Text of Shakespeare.* New York: Scribners, 1906, pp. 15, 27, 503, 506. [Reputation.]

Lowe, Robert W. *Bibliographical account of English theatrical literature.* New York: J. W. Bouton; London: Nimmo, 1888.

Lowell, James Russell. "Marlowe." In *Old English dramatists. Works*, XI. 212–238. Boston: Houghton Mifflin, n.d. Also in *Harper's*, 85: 194–203 Jy 1892. See *Shakespeariana*, 4: 243–244 (1887).

Lowry, Mildred Ellen. *Christopher Marlowe, his work, influence, and reputation.* Colorado College Honors Diss. 1926. [MS.]

Lucas, Hippolyte. *Curiosités dramatiques et littéraires.* Paris: Garnier frères, 1855, pp. 123–126. [BN]

Luick, Karl. "Zur geschichte des englischen dramas in XVI jahrhundert." In *Forschungen z. neueren literaturgeschichte Festgabe f. Richard Heinzel.* Weimar: E. Felber, 1898, pp. 131–187. [Reviewed in *Jahrb.* 35: 298–299 (1890).]

Madden, D[odgson] H[amilton]. *Shakespeare and his fellows.* London: Smith, Elder & Co., 1916, pp. 137–169.

Magnus, Laurie. *General Sketch of the history of literature in the centuries of romance.* London: Kegan Paul, 1918, pp. 307–309, 332–337.

Magnus, Laurie. *Dictionary of European literature.* London: Routledge; New York: Dutton, 1926, pp. 324–325.

Magnus, Laurie. *History of European literature.* London: Ivor Nicholson and Watson, Ltd., 1934.

Mantzius, Karl. *History of theatrical art.* Translated by Louise von Cassel. London: Duckworth, 1903–21, vol. III.

Marshall, Geoffrey. *Theory of the Elizabethan drama, with special reference to Marlowe as one of the earliest Elizabethans.* Louisiana State University M.A. Thesis, 1911. [MS.]

Mathew, Frank. *Image of Shakespeare.* London: Cape, 1922, pp. 151–163.

McBreen, Thomas J., and others. "Christopher Marlowe: a symposium." *Manhattan Quarterly*, 11: 264–273 Ja 1915. [By undergraduates of Manhattan College.] [NYPL]

Mennechet, Edouard. *Matinées littéraires. Cours complet de littérature moderne.* Paris: Langlois et Leclercq, 1857, II. 83–124. [BN]

Meyn, Heinrich. *Beteuerung und verwunschungen bei Marlowe, Kyd, Lyly, Greene und Peele.* Kiel Diss. 1914. Kiel: Schmid & Klaunig, 1914.

Mézières, A[lfred Jean François]. *Contemporains et successeurs de Shakespeare.* Paris: Charpentier, 1864. See also *Magasin de librairie*, 2: 406–421 (1859).

Miller, Vida. *Terminology of supernatural beings in Chapman, Daniel, Drayton, Marlowe, and Spenser.* North Carolina M.A. Thesis, 1934. Abstracted in *University of North Carolina Record, Graduate School Series*, 28: 45 (1934).

Mills, Abraham. *Literature and the literary men of Great Britain.* New York: Harper, 1851, pp. 283–288. [NYPL]

Mincoff, Marco K. "Christopher Marlowe: a study of his development." *Studia Historico-Philologica Serdicensia*, 1: 1–112 (1937). [In English in a learned journal of Sofia, Bulgaria. Ulpia Serdica was the name given to Sofia by the Emperor Trajan.] [JB]

Minto, William. *Characteristics of English poets from Chaucer to Shirley.* Edinburgh: Blackwood; Boston: Ginn, 1891, 1897, pp. 230–240. [NYPL]

Mitchell, Donald G[rant]. *English lands letters and kings.* New York: Scribner's, 1889, I. 269–273.

M[itford], J[ohn]. "Retrospective Review" [of Pickering's edition]. *Gentleman's Magazine,* 15 (NS): 45–48 Ja 1841.

Mitford, John. "Additional Notes." In *Cursory notes on various passages.* London: John Russell Smith, 1856, pp. 54–55.

Mizuta, I. *Plays of Christopher Marlowe.* Tokyo University Graduation Thesis, 1934. [MS.]

Montgomery, Robert M. *Study of setting in Christopher Marlowe's plays.* Pittsburgh M.A. Thesis, 1931 [MS.]. Summarized in *University of Pittsburgh Bulletin,* 28: 339–340 (1931).

Moosmann, Eberhard. *Englische literaturstunde auf der oberstufe.* Marburg: N. G. Elwert, G. Braun, 1927–28. [Die neueren Sprachen . . . Beiheft Nr. 12 a–b.]

Morley, Henry. *Journal of a London play-goer from 1851 to 1866.* London: G. Routledge & Sons, 1866.

Morley, Henry. *English writers.* London: Chapman and Hall, 1864–67; Cassell, 1887–95. [Especially vols. VIII–X.]

Morley, Henry. *English plays.* London: Cassell, 1880, pp. 113–128. [Cassell's Library of English Literature.]

Morris, Hortense. *Marlowe's villains.* West Virginia Bachelor's Thesis, 1902. [MS.]

Mortland, Maizie. *Morality elements in Christopher Marlowe's plays.* Iowa M.A. Thesis, 1925. [MS.]

Moulton, Clark Wells. *Library of literary criticism.* Buffalo: Moulton, 1901, I. 346–358.

Munn, James B. *Development of plot and characterization in early Greek and early Elizabethan tragedy.* Harvard Diss. 1917. [MS.]

Munro, John (ed.). *Shakspere allusion book: a collection of allusions to Shakspere from 1591 to 1700.* London: Chatto & Windus; New York: Duffield, 1909. Based on C[lement] M[ansfield] Ingleby. *Shakspere's century of prayse.* London: Trübner, 1874, 2nd ed. revised by Lucy Toulmin Smith, 1879; and Fred[eric]k J. Furnivall. *Some 300 fresh allusions to Shakspere from 1594 to 1694.* London: Trübner, 1886. [New Shakspere Society publications, ser. IV.]

Murray, John Tucker. *English dramatic companies, 1558–1642.* London: Constable, 1910.

Naujocks, E. *Gestaltung und auffassung des todes bei Shakespeare.* Berlin Diss. 1916. Berlin: Mayer and Müller, n.d.

Neele, Henry. *Lectures on English poetry.* London: Joseph Thomas, 1839 (3rd ed.), pp. 85–86. [NYPL]

Nelle, Paul. *Das wortspiel im englischen drama des 16. jahrhunderts vor Shakspere.* Halle Diss. 1900. Halle: Heinrich John, 1900.

Newbern, Jefferson Lamar. *Marlowe's audience (in the light of contemporary chronicles and references).* Georgia M.A. Thesis, ca. 1920. [MS. not dated.]

Nicoll, Allardyce. *Introduction to dramatic theory*. London: Harrap, 1923, pp. 122–126.

Nicoll, Allardyce. *Theory of drama*. London: Harrap, 1931, pp. 166–171.

Nicoll, Allardyce. *British drama*. London: Harrap, 1932, pp. 78–86, 90–94.

Norman, Charles. "Marlowe, the muses' darling." *Bookman*, 75: 135–143 My 1932.

Norman, Charles. *Marlowe & Co.: Elizabethans*. [In preparation.]

Norton, C[harles] E[liot]. "Marlowe and his times." *Harvard Monthly*, 1: 50–57 N 1885.

Noyes, Alfred. "Christopher Marlowe." In *Great Tudors* [edited by Katharine Garvin]. London: Ivor Nicholson & Watson, 1935, pp. 449–460.

Noyes, Alfred. "Marlowe." In *Pageant of Letters*. New York: Sheed & Ward, 1940, pp. 14–29.

"Old Fag" [G. H. Vallins]. "Letters to John Doe." *John O'London's Weekly*, 35: 874, 19 S 1936.

Ordish, T. Fairman. *Early London theatres*. London: Eliot Stock, 1894 [Camden Library], pp. 160–163.

Owlett, F. C. "Eulogy of Marlowe." *Poetry Review*, 26: 5–18 F, Mr 1935; Reprint, London: privately printed, 1935; also in *Spacious days*, London: Herbert Joseph, Ltd., 1937, pp. 47–90.

Paletta, Gerhard. *Fürstengeschick und inner-staatlicher machtkampf im Englischen Renaissance-drama*. Breslau: Priebatsch, 1934 [Sprache und Kultur der Germanischen und Romanischen Völker, no. 16], pp. 48–57.

Patrick, Ada Belle. *Tragedies of Christopher Marlowe*. Vanderbilt M.A. Thesis, 1928. [MS.]

Patterson, Richard Ferrar. *Six centuries of English literature*. London: Blackie, 1933, II. 34–36.

Pearce, T[homas] M[atthews]. "Christopher Marlowe — figure of the Renaissance." *University of New Mexico Bulletin*, 1: 5–43 (1934).

Phelps, William Lyon. "Marlowe." In *Essays on books*. New York: Macmillan, 1922, pp. 233–254. Also as preface to 1912 edition of the plays.

Philippi, Adolf. *Christoph Marlowe: eine literar-historische abhandlung*. Düsseldorf: Hermann Voss, 1851. [Programm der Realschule zu Düsseldorf.] [CUL]

Piccoli, Raffaello. *Drammi elisabettiani*. Paris: Gino Laterza & Figli, 1914, II. 271–276.

Powys, Llewellyn. "Christopher Marlowe." In *Thirteen worthies*. New York: American Library Service, 1923; London: Richards, 1924. Also in *Freeman*, 6: 584–585 F 1923.

Praz, Mario. "Christopher Marlowe." *English Studies* [Amsterdam], 13: 209–223 D 1931.

Proelss, Robert. *Geschichte des neueren dramas*. Leipzig: B. Schlicke, 1882.

Ransom, Harry. "Some legal elements in Elizabethan plays." *Studies in English, No. 16. University of Texas Bulletin*, no. 3626: 53–76, 8 Jy 1936.

R.B.H.T. "Aeschylus and Marlowe." *Eagle* [St. John's College, Cambridge], 37: 236–239 Mr 1916. [CUL]

Rébora, Piero. *L'Italia nella dramma inglese (1558–1642)*. Milano: Modernissima, 1925. [NYPL]

Rébora, Piero. Article, "Marlowe, Christopher." In *Enciclopedia italiana*. Rome: Instituto della . . . 1934, XXII, 363–364.

Reed, Isaac. In *Select Collection of Old Plays*. London: H. Hughs for J. Dodsley.

Reynolds, L. J. *Study of the patterns of bombast*. Oregon M.A. Thesis, 1929. [MS.]

Richardson, Abby Sage. "Christopher Marlowe." *Appleton's Journal*, 6: 347, 23 S 1871.

Robertson, J[ohn] M[ackinnon]. *Marlowe: a conspectus*. London: Routledge, 1931. [Reviewed in RES, 8: 329–330 (1932).]

Rowse, A[lfred] L[eslie], and Harrison, G[eorge] B[agshaw]. *Queen Elizabeth and her subjects*. London: G. Allen; Toronto: Nelson, 1935, pp. 68–78.

Russell, Edward R. "Estimate of Marlowe." *Proceedings of the Literary and Philosophical Society of Liverpool*, 46: 81–106 (1892). [LC]

Sander, G. H. *Das moment der letzten spannung in der englischen tragödie bis zu Shakespeare*. Berlin: Mayer & Müller, 1902, pp. 29–39.

Sawyer, Charles J., and Darton, F. J. *English books, 1475–1900*. Westminster: Chas. J. Sawyer, Ltd.; New York: Dutton, n.d. [1927], I. 134–136.

Schau, Kurt Ehrhard. *Sprach und grammatik der dramen Marlowes*. Leipzig Diss. 1901. Halle: H. John, 1901.

Schelling, Felix E[manuel]. *English chronicle play*. New York: Macmillan, 1902.

Schelling, Felix E[manuel]. *Elizabethan drama*. Boston: Houghton Mifflin, 1908.

Schelling, Felix E[manuel]. *English literature during the lifetime of Shakespeare*. New York: Holt, 1910.

Schelling, Felix E[manuel]. *English drama*. London: Dent; New York: Dutton, 1914, pp. 66–75, 81–83.

Schelling, Felix E[manuel]. *Foreign influences in Elizabethan plays*. New York: Harper, 1923.

Schelling, Felix E[manuel]. *Elizabethan playwrights*. New York: Harper, 1925.

Schlegel, W. *Zur szenenführung bei Christopher Marlowe*. Leipzig Diss. 1926. [MS.]

Schick, J. "Christopher Marlowe: seine personlichkeit und sein schaffen." *Jahrb.* 64: 159–179 (1922). [Lecture preceding the Weimar production of *Doctor Faustus*, April 23, 1928.]

Schneider, Reinhold. "Idyll und tragödie (Die dichter)." *Deutsche rundschau*, 47: 582–588.

Schneider, Reinhold. "Christopher Marlowe, der dichter der macht." *Literatur*, 38: 215–218 F 1936. [Popular summary.]

Schröder, Otto. *Marlowe und Webster*. Halle Diss. n.d. Halle: Heinrich John, 1907.

Seccombe, Thomas. *See also* Swinburne, Algernon Charles, in General Section.

Seccombe, Thomas, and Allen, J. W. *Age of Shakespeare.* London: Bell, 1925.

Seccombe, Thomas, and Nicoll, W. Robertson. *Bookman history of English literature.* London: Hodder & Stoughton, 1905–1907, I. 71–75.

Sharpe, Robert Boies. *Real war of the theatres.* Boston: Heath; London: Oxford University Press, 1935. [M.L.A. Monograph Series.]

Shurter, E[lijah] T[oles]. "Christopher Marlowe." *Williams Literary Monthly,* 2: 95–103 Jy 1886.

Sibley, Gertrude Marian. *Lost plays and masques.* Ithaca: Cornell University Press, 1933.

[Slater, J. H.?] "Marlowe and his works." *Book Lore,* 5: 98–102 Mr 1887.

Slater, J. H. "Some Marlowe riddles." *Athenaeum,* no. 4065: 411–412, 23 S 1905. *See also* pp. 552, 868.

S[mith], G. B. "Christopher Marlowe." *Cornhill,* 30: 329–348 S 1874. [Author identified by John H. Ingram.]

Smith, G. C. Moore. "Marlowe and Kyd." *Cambridge history of English literature.* Cambridge University Press, 1910, V. 142–164.

Smith, Lucy Toulmin. *See* Munro, John.

Smith, Marian Love. *Christopher Marlowe, Shakespeare's greatest predecessor.* Thiel College [Greenville, Pa.] B.A. Thesis, 1929. [MS.]

Snider, Denton Jaques. "History of the Faust legend." In *Goethe's Faust.* St. Louis: Sigma Publishing Co., 1886, I. vii–lvi.

[Steevens, George.] "Life of Mr. Edward Alleyn, comedian." *Theatrical Review* [London], 1: 61–66; 134–137 F, Ap 1763. [Signed "Critique." For the attribution to Steevens, see Sidney Lee: *Life of Shakespeare,* p. 646. Contains the forged letter to "Marle," though the context does not directly allude to Christopher Marlowe.]

Storer, Agnes C. "Two Elizabethan dramatists: a contrast." *Catholic World,* 75: 609–618 Ag 1902.

Storozhenko, Nikolai Il'ich. Англійская драма до смерти Шекспира. ["English drama to the death of Shakespeare."] In Всеобщая исторія литературы. [*General history of literature.*] Edited by V. Th. Korsh and A. Kirpichnikov. St. Petersburg: Karl Rikker, 1888, III. 522–537.

Storozhenko, Nikolai Il'ich. Оцеркъ исторіи западно-европейской литературый. [*Outline of the history of western European literature.*] Moscow: Lisener and Sobko, 1900 (2nd ed.), pp. 169–172; G. Lissner, 1910; A. I. Mamontov, 1916.

Straforello, Gustavo. "I poeti drammatici inglesi contemporanei di Shakspeare." *Rivista contemporanea,* 19: 123–140 (1859).

Strohm, Inez Honadel. *Three centuries of Marlowe as a playwright.* Columbia M.A. Thesis, 1925. [MS.]

Stuart, Donald Clive. *Development of dramatic art.* New York: Appleton, 1928, pp. 187–240.

Swinburne, Algernon Charles. "Early English dramatists. No. 1. Christopher Marlowe and John Webster." *Undergraduate Papers* [Oxford], 1:

7–15, 1 D 1857. [BM, Bodleian, JB.] Written while Swinburne was still a student and interesting both for its content and for its anticipation of his later enthusiasm. See Sir Edmund Gosse's *Life* (4th ed.) included in the Bonchurch edition of Swinburne's *Works* (1926), XIX. 42–43; *Literary anecdotes of the nineteenth century*, edited by W. R. Nicoll and T. J. Wise, II. 291.

Swinburne, Algernon Charles. *Study of Shakespeare.* New York: R. Worthington, 1880.

Swinburne, Algernon Charles. *Contemporaries of Shakespeare.* Edited by Edmund Gosse and Thomas James Wise. London: Heinemann, 1919, pp. 1–12.

Swinburne, Algernon Charles. Article, "Marlowe, Christopher," in *Encyclopaedia Britannica.* [This appears in the 9th (1883), 11th (1911), and 14th (1929) editions. It is not brought up to date until 1932, but a bibliography by Thomas Seccombe is added to the 11th and later editions. There are short, unsigned articles on Marlowe in the 3rd (1797) and 8th (1857) editions.]

Swinburne, Algernon Charles. *Age of Shakespeare.* New York and London: Harper, 1908.

Swinburne, Algernon Charles. "Christopher Marlowe in relation to Greene, Peele, and Lodge." *Fortnightly Review*, (OS) 105 (NS) 99: 764–769 My 1916. A note by Sir Edmund Gosse on p. 769 says: "From the original manuscript, purchased from Watts-Dunton in 1910, by Mr. Thos. J. Wise." The same article appears under the title, "Christopher Marlowe and some minor contemporaries," in the *North American Review*, 203: 742–748 My 1916, and also in *Contemporaries of Shakespeare* (see above). An edition of twenty copies was printed by T. J. Wise in 1914. There is a copy in the University Library, Cambridge. See also *Current Literature*, 45: 661–663 D 1908.

Symonds, John Addington. *Shakespeare's predecessors.* London: Smith Elder; New York: Scribner's, 1900. Chap. XV is on "Marlowe." [Edition of 1884 reviewed in *Quarterly Review*, 161: 330–331 O 1885. See also under Ellis' edition. Partial reprint in *Shakespeariana*, 2: 553–576 (1885).]

Symons, Arthur. "Note on the genius of Marlowe." *English Review*, 36: 306–316 Ap 1923.

Taine, H. A. *History of English literature.* Translated by H. van Laun. Edinburgh: Edmonston and Douglas, 1872, I. 237–244.

Talbot, Ethel. "Aspects of tragedy." *Academy*, 80: 334–335, 400–401, 18 Mr, 4 Ap 1911.

Tannenbaum, Samuel A. *Christopher Marlowe: a concise bibliography.* New York: Scholars' Facsimile Reprints, 1937.

Tannenbaum, Samuel A[aron]. *Christopher Marlowe (a concise bibliography).* New York: Scholars' Facsimile Reprints, 1937. Supplement, 1937.

Tannenbaum, Samuel A. "Additions to *Christopher Marlowe: a concise bibliography.*" *Shakespeare Association Bulletin*, 12: 252–255 (1937).

Tanner, Thomas. *Bibliotheca Britannico-Hibernica.* Edited by David Wilkins. London: G. Bowyer, 1748. [See p. 512 for notes on Marlowe, mainly bibliographical.]

Taylor, Rupert. "Tentative chronology of Marlowe's and some other Elizabethan plays." PMLA, 51: 643–688 S 1936.

Texte, Joseph. "Christophe Marlowe." *Revue des deux mondes*, 309: 892–915 F 1890.

Theobald, Bertram G. "Bacon-Marlowe problems." *Baconiana*, 23: 58–65 O 1935.

T. H. K. "Christopher Marlowe, M.A." *Dramatic Magazine*, 2: 236–244 S 1830. [HCL]

Thorndike, Ashley H. *Tragedy*. Boston: Houghton Mifflin, 1908, pp. 88–99, 113–126.

Thorp, Willard. *Triumph of realism in Elizabethan drama*. Princeton Diss. 1926. Princeton University Press, 1928. (Princeton Studies in English, no. 3), pp. 39–50. [The Princeton university library also has a MS. copy.]

Tilley, M. P., and Ray, James K. "Proverbs and proverbial allusions in Marlowe." MLN, 50: 347–355 Je 1935.

Tomlinson, Warren E. *Herodes-charakter im englischen drama*. Leipzig: Mayer & Müller, 1934 (*Palaestra*, 195). [Discussion of Marlowe on pp. 60–67.]

Turner, Charles Edward. *Our great writers*. St. Petersburg, Russia: A. Münx, 1864. Eighth Lecture, pp. 117–136.

Uvarov, S. «Марло, одинъ изъ предшественніковъ Шекспира.» ["Marlowe, one of Shakespeare's predecessors."] *Русское Слово* [Russkoe Slovo], 1: 5–53, 221–284 F, Mr 1859.

Vallins, G. F. *See* "Old Fag."

Van der Spek, Cornelis. *Church and the churchman in English dramatic literature before 1642*. Amsterdam Diss. 1930. Amsterdam: H. J. Paris, 1930.

Vehse, Eduard. *Shakespeare als protestant, politiker, psycholog und dichter*. Hamburg: Hoffman und Campe, 1851, I. 218–221.

Villemain, [A. F.]. [No title.] *Journal des savants*. [No vol. number]: 5–23, 129–142, 257–275 (1856).

Vogt, Richard. *Das adjektiv bei Christopher Marlowe*. Berlin Diss. 1906. [n.p., n.d.] [See *Jahrb*. 45: 271 (1909).]

Wagner, Wilhelm. "Emendationen und bemerkungen zu Marlowe." *Jahrb*. 11: 70–77, 363 (1876).

Wallis, N. Hardy. "Christopher Marlowe as a poet." In *Ethics of criticism*. London: Chapman and Hall, 1924, pp. 81–102.

Ward, A[dolphus] W[illiam]. *History of English dramatic literature*. London and New York: Macmillan, 1875, 1899.

Ward, Thomas Humphrey. *English poets. Selections with critical introductions*. London: Macmillan, 1880.

Warner, Charles Dudley (ed.). *Warner's library of the world's best literature*. New York: International Society, 1897, XXIV. 9719. [Earlier edition copyright 1896.]

Warton, Thomas. *History of English poetry*. London, 1774–78–81; new ed., 1824–40–71.

Watt, Robert. *Bibliotheca Britannica*. Edinburgh: Constable, Longmans, Hurts, 1824.

Watt, Lauchlan Maclean. *Attic and Elizabethan tragedy*. London: Dent; New York: Dutton, 1908.

Wegener, Richard. *Bühneneinrichtung des Shakespeareschen theaters*. Halle: Max Niemeyer, 1907. [Passing references only.]

Weidensall, Clara Jean. "Christopher Marlowe." *Vassar Miscellany*. 32: 319–324 Ap 1903.

Wells, Henry W. *Poetic imagery illustrated from Elizabethan literature*. New York: Columbia University Press, 1924.

Wells, Henry W. *Elizabethan and Jacobean playwrights*. New York: Columbia University Press, 1939.

Welsh, Alfred H. *Development of English literature and language*. Chicago: S. C. Griggs & Co.; London: Trübner, 1882, I. 313–321.

Wendell, Barrett. *William Shakespeare*. New York: Scribner, 1899, pp. 56, 62, 98–100.

Wendell, Barrett. *Temper of the seventeenth century in English literature*. New York: Scribner's, 1904, pp. 33–37.

Westmore, B. F. *Development of the plays of Marlowe*. Colorado M.A. Thesis, 1906. [MS.]

Whipple, Edwin P[ercy]. *Essays and reviews*. Boston: Ticknor and Fields, 1856, II. 7–24.

Whipple, E. P. *Literature of the age of Elizabeth*. Boston: Houghton Mifflin, 1876, 1883, 1886, 1893, 1897. [Lowell Lectures, 1859, which ran serially in the *Atlantic Monthly*, 1867–68.]

White, Margaret Martha. *Influence of Seneca on the University Wits with special reference to Marlowe*. Marquette M.A. Thesis, 1926. [MS.]

Williams, W[illiam] H[enry]. "Marlowe." *A. H. R.* [under which appears, on title page, *Australian Home Reader*], 2: 111–115 Ag 1893. [Paper read at first meeting of the Hobart Group, Australian Home Reading Union. Copy in Fisher Library, University of Sydney.]

Wills, Mary Matheson. *Christopher Marlowe and the classics*. Southern California Diss. 1936. [MS.]

Wills, Mary Matheson. "Marlowe's role in borrowed lines." PMLA, 52: 902–905 S 1937.

Withington, Robert. *Excursions in English drama*. New York: Appleton-Century, 1937.

Wood, Louise Meyer. *Materials for a Marlowe glossary*. Indiana M.A. Thesis, 1903. [MS.] [All copies lost.]

Woodberry, George Edward. "Marlowe." In *Inspiration of poetry*. New York: Macmillan, 1911 [Lowell Lectures, 1906], pp. 29–57.

Woodward, Parker. "Kit Marlowe." In *Euphues, the peripatician*. London: Gay & Bird, 1907, Chap. IV, pp. 71–81.

Woodward, Parker. "Bacon as playwright." *Baconiana*, 3rd ser. 9: 102–109 Ap 1911.

Wynne, Arnold. *Growth of English drama.* Oxford: Clarendon Press, 1914, pp. 193–269.

Wynne, D. A. *Swinburne as a critic of the drama of Marlowe and Jonson.* New York M.A. Thesis, 1916. [MS.]

Yearsley, [Percival] Macleod. *Doctors in Elizabethan drama.* London: John Bale, 1933, pp. 24, 43–45, 108.

Young, William Lesquereux. *Possession of power as a motive for tragedy: a study of Aeschylus Marlowe and Echegaray.* Ohio State M.A. Thesis, 1916. [MS.]

Zanco, Aurelio. *Christopher Marlowe, saggio critico.* Firenze: La Nuova Italia, 1937.

CHAPTER I: MARLOWE AND HIS FAMILY

Anon. *Pilgrim's guide to the royal and ancient city of Canterbury.* Canterbury: Gibbs and Sons, 1936.

Anon. *Index of wills proved in the Prerogative Court of Canterbury . . . and now preserved in the Principal Probate Registry, Somerset House,* London. London: British Record Society, 1893–1922.

Armytage, Geo. J. (ed.), and Chester, Col. Joseph Lemuel (ed.). *Allegations for marriage licenses issued from the Faculty Office of the Archbishop of Canterbury at London, 1543 to 1869.* London: Harleian Society, 1886.

Bakeless, John. "Marlowe and his father." TLS, 36: 12, 2 Ja 1937. [See Seaton, below.]

Bennett-Goldney, Francis. *Story of the Westgate.* Canterbury: J. A. Jennings, 1933.

Brent, John. *Canterbury in the olden time.* London: Simpkin Marshall & Co., 1879 [2nd ed.].

Cowper, Joseph Meadows. *The booke of regester of the Parish of St. Peter in Canterbury for christninges, weddings and buryalls, 1560–1800.* Canterbury: Cross & Jackman, 1888.

Cowper, Joseph Meadows. *Canterbury marriage licenses, first series.* Canterbury: Cross & Jackman, 1892. [102 copies privately printed.]

Cowper, Joseph Meadows. *Intrantes: a list of persons admitted to live and trade within the City of Canterbury, on payment of an annual fine, from 1392 to 1592.* Canterbury: Cross & Jackman, 1904. [56 copies privately printed.]

Cowper, Joseph Meadows. *Memorial inscriptions in the church and churchyard of Holy Cross, Westgate, Canterbury.* Canterbury: Cross & Jackman, 1888.

Cowper, Joseph Meadows. *The names of them that were crystened marryed and buryed in the paryshe of Saynt Mary Magdalene.* Canterbury: Cross & Jackman, 1890.

Cowper, Joseph Meadows. *The register booke of christeninges, marriages and burialls in Saint Dunstan's Canterbury, 1559–1800.* Canterbury: Cross & Jackman, 1887.

Cowper, Joseph Meadows. *The register booke of the Parish of St. George the*

Martyr, within the citie of Canterburie, of christenings, mariages and burials. 1538–1800. Canterbury: Cross & Jackman, 1891.

Ingram, John H. "Literary gossip." *Athenaeum*, no. 4114: 244, 1 S 1906. [See Symons, below, and *Jahrb*. 43: 295 (1907).]

Nichols, John. *Progresses and public processions of Queen Elizabeth*. London: Nichols, 1823.

Page, John T. "Marlowe: date of his birth." N&Q, 10th ser. 1: 491–492, 18 Je 1904.

Platt, Isaac Hull. "Marlowe: date of his birth." N&Q, 10th ser. 1: 408, 21 My 1904. Cf. pp. 491–492, 18 Je.

Seaton, Ethel. "Marlowe and his father." TLS, 36: 428, 5 Je 1937. [See Bakeless, above.]

Symons, Arthur. "Gleanings from parish registers." *Athenaeum*, no. 4112: 187, 18 Ag 1906. [See Ingram, above, and *Jahrb*. 43: 295 (1907).]

Tonks, C. F. *Parish church of S. George the Martyr, Canterbury*. Canterbury: Gibbs and Sons, n.d.

Woodruff, C. Eveleigh. *Sede vacante wills: a calendar of wills proved before the Commissary of the Prior and Chapter of Christ Church, Canterbury*. Canterbury: Cross and Jackman, 1914. [Kent Records, vol. III.]

CHAPTER II: EDUCATION: THE KING'S SCHOOL

Benndorf, Cornelie. *Die englische pädagogik in 16. jahrhundert*. Wiener Beiträge. XXII (1905).

Brown, J. H. *Elizabethan schooldays*. Oxford: Blackwell, 1933.

G[alpin], A. J. "Schoolroom windows." *Cantuarian* [no volume number], N 1898 and My 1899. Reprinted separately by the King's School, Canterbury, n.d. [The *Cantuarian* is the magazine of the King's School.]

Gardiner, Dorothy. *Literary tradition of Canterbury*. Cambridge University Press, 1930.

Stowe, A. R. Monroe. *English grammar schools in the reign of Queen Elizabeth*. New York: Teachers' College, Columbia, 1908.

Watson, Foster. *English grammar schools to 1660*. Cambridge University Press, 1908.

Watson, Foster (ed.). *Tudor school-boy life. Dialogues of Juan Luis Vives*. London: Dent, 1908.

Woodruff, C[harles] E[veleigh], and Cape, H[arry] J[ames]. *Schola regia cantuarensis*. London: Mitchell, Hughes, & Clarke, 1908.

CHAPTER III: EDUCATION: CAMBRIDGE

Almond, A. G. *Gowns and gossip*. Cambridge: Bowes and Bowes, 1925. [NYPL]

Almond, A. G. *Cambridge robes for doctors and graduates*. Cambridge: Almond, 1909; revised edition, 1934. [LC has the first, CUL the second edition.]

Anon. "Education at the universities." *Baconiana*, 3rd ser. 3: 19–27 Ja 1905.

Anon. "The other Marlowe." London *Times*, 23, 24, 27 Je 1925.

Anon. *Documents relating to the university and colleges of Cambridge.* London: H. M. Stationery Office. Published by Longmans, 1852.

Atkinson, Thomas Dinham. *Cambridge described and illustrated.* London: Macmillan and Bowes; Cambridge: Bowes and Bowes, 1897.

Bradshaw, Henry. *Collected papers.* (Edited by F. J[enkinson].) Cambridge: University Press, 1889.

Braun [or Bruin], Georg. *Beschreibung und contrafactur der vornembsten statt der welt.* Cölnn, 1574. [Including a map of Cambridge. French and Latin editions also exist.]

Brooke, Iris. *English costume in the age of Elizabeth.* London: A. & C. Black, 1933.

Caius, John. *Historia Cantabrigiensis Academiae ab vrbe condita.* London, 1574. [ULC]

Clark, J[ohn] W[illis]. *Endowments of the University of Cambridge.* Cambridge University Press, 1904. [ULC]

Clark, J[ohn] Willis, and Gray, Arthur. *Old plans of Cambridge.* Cambridge: Bowes and Bowes, 1921. [ULC, NYPL]

Cooper, C[harles] H[enry]. *Annals of Cambridge.* Cambridge: Warnock, 1842–52. [Vol. IV has the imprint of Metcalfe.] [NYPL, ULC, CUL]

Cooper, C[harles] H[enry], and Cooper, Thompson. *Athenae Cantabrigienses.* Cambridge: Deighton & Bell & Macmillan Co.; London: Bell & Doldy, 1861. [Especially II. 158–160 and bibliography.]

Dorrinck, [Karl] Alfred [Friedo]. *Die lateinischen zitate in den dramen der wichtigsten vorgänger Shakespeares.* Strassburg Diss. 1907. Strassburg: Schauberg, 1907, pp. 18–23. [See *Jahrb.* 43: 270–271 (1909).]

Fuller, Thomas. *History of the university of Cambridge.* Cambridge: J. & J. Deighton; London: T. Tegg, 1840.

Gollancz, Sir Israel. "The other Marlowe." London *Times*, 23 Je, 27 Jy, pp. 17e, 8e. [See also "Anon." above.]

Gray, A. K. "Some observations on Christopher Marlowe, government agent." PMLA, 43: 682–700 S 1928. [See *Jahrb.* (OS) 65 (NS) 6: 218 (1929).]

Harraden, Richard. *Cantabrigia depicta.* Cambridge: Harraden and Son; London: R. Cribb & Son, 1809. [CUL]

Henson, Canon Edwin. *Register of the English college at Valladolid, 1589–1862.* London: Catholic Record Society, 1930. [Publications of the Catholic Record Society, vol. XXX.] [Original archives still preserved in the College at Valladolid.]

Josseline, J. *Historiola Collegii Corporis Christi.* (Edited by John Willis Clark.) Cambridge: Antiquarian Society, 1880. [Josseline, Josselin, or Joscelyn, was Latin Secretary to Archbishop Parker, at whose request this work was written. There are four MSS., two at Corpus Christi, one at the University Registry, and one at the University Library.]

Lamb, John. *Collection of letters, statutes, and other documents from the MS. library of Corp. Christ. Coll., illustrative of the history of the University of*

Cambridge, during the period of the Reformation. London: John W. Parker, 1838. [ULC]

Lash, Joseph. *Marlowe — a youthful scholastic.* Columbia M.A. Thesis, 1932. [MS.]

Marquardsen, A. "Christopher Marlowe's kosmologie." *Jahrb.* 41: 54–80 (1905).

Masters, Robert. *History of Corpus Christi, Cambridge.* Cambridge: J. Bentham, 1753. [HCL]

Mullinger, James Bass. *History of Cambridge.* Cambridge University Press, 1884, II. 432.

Mullinger, James Bass. *History of the University of Cambridge.* London: Longmans Green & Co., 1888.

Petsch, Robert. "Naogeorgus und Marlowe." ES, 39: 153–157 (1908).

Sayle, Charles [Edward]. *Annals of the Cambridge University Library,* 1278–1900. Cambridge: University Library, 1916. Reprinted from *Library,* 3rd ser. 6: 38–76, 145–182, 197–227, 308–345 (1915).

Smith, G. C. Moore. "Marlowe at Cambridge." MLR, 4: 167–177 Ja 1909. [See *Jahrb.* 46: 200–201 (1910).]

Smith, G. C. Moore. *College plays performed in the University of Cambridge.* Cambridge University Press, 1923.

Smith, J. J. *Cambridge portfolio.* Cambridge: J. and J. J. Deighton; London: John W. Parker, 1890.

Stokes, H[enry] P[aine]. *Corpus Christi.* London: F. E. Robinson, 1898. [College Historical Series.]

Stokes, H[enry] P[aine]. *Cambridge scene.* Cambridge: Bowes and Bowes, 1921.

Stokes, H[enry] P[aine]. *Ceremonies of the University of Cambridge.* Cambridge University Press, 1927.

Tanner, J. R. *Historical registry of the University of Cambridge.* Cambridge University Press, 1917.

Venn, John. *Grace book Delta, containing the records of the University of Cambridge for the years 1542–1589.* Cambridge University Press, 1911.

Venn, John. *Book of matriculations and degrees . . . 1544–1659.* Cambridge University Press, 1913.

Venn, John. *Alumni Cantabrigienses.* Cambridge University Press, 1922–29.

Ward, B. M. "Alphonso Ferrabosco." RES, 8: 201–202 (1932). [On espionage.]

Westlake, H. F. "The other Marlowe." London *Times,* 24 Je 1925, p. 17d.

Whitmore, J. B. "The other Marlowe." London *Times,* 24 Jy 1933.

Willis, Robert, and Clark, John Willis. *Architectural history of the University of Cambridge.* Cambridge University Press, 1886.

CHAPTER IV: LONDON: THE LIFE OF LETTERS

Acheson, Arthur. *Shakespeare's lost years in London.* London: Quaritch, 1920.

Anderton, H. Ince. "Marlowe in Newgate." TLS, 33: 620, 13 S 1934.

Berkenhout, John. *Biographia litteraria.* London: J. Dodsley, 1777, I. 357–359, 399, note "e."

Baldwin, T[homas] W[hitfield]. "Thomas Kyd's early company connections." PQ, 6: 311–313 (1927). [*Jahrb.* (OS) 64 (NS) 5: 206 (1928).]

Beckwith, J. *See* Webb, E. A.

Boas, F[rederick] S[amuel]. *Works of Thomas Kyd.* Oxford University Press, 1901, pp. cviii–cxvi.

Boas, F[rederick] S[amuel]. "Marlowe in 1589–92." TLS, 36: 171, 6 Mr 1937. [*See* Brooks, E. St. John.]

Bray, William. *See* Manning, Owen.

Brooks, E. St. John. "Marlowe in 1589–92?" TLS, 36: 151, 27 F 1937. [*See* Boas, F. S.]

Collier, John Payne. *New particulars regarding the works of Shakespeare.* London: Thomas Rodd, 1836, pp. 47–48. [Includes the fraudulent ballad.]

Eccles, Mark. *Marlowe and Watson.* Harvard Diss. 1932 [MS.]. See also *Harvard . . . Summaries of Theses,* 1932, pp. 246–248.

Eccles, Mark. *Marlowe in London.* Cambridge: Harvard University Press, 1934. [Harvard Studies in English, no. 10.] [Development of the dissertation listed above. Reviewed TLS, 33: 389, 31 My 1934; MLR, 31: 565–567 (1936); RES, 12: 209–212 (1936); *Beiblatt zur Anglia,* 47: 116–118 (1936).]

Eccles, Mark. "Marlowe in Newgate." TLS, 33: 604, 6 S 1934. [See also Anderton, H. Ince.]

Fitzhopkins [No first name given]. "Dramatic." N&Q, 4th ser. 3: 134, 6 F 1869. [Contains an anecdote of Marlowe and King James II! This apparently comes from *The Theatre,* p. 91. The author was perhaps originally Th. Kenrick. The same story is said to have appeared in the *Penny Satirist,* 26 Ap 1834. I have been unable to follow these references further. The story itself is a chronological impossibility.]

Harrison, G[eorge] B[agshaw]. *Elizabethan journal.* New York: Richard R. Smith, Inc., 1931.

Harrison, G[eorge] B[agshaw]. *Shakespeare's fellows.* London: John Lane, 1923. [See also General Section.]

Hutton, Laurence. *Literary landmarks of London.* London: Unwin, 1885–88.

Ingleby, C[lement] M[ansfield]. "Spurious ballads, &c., affecting Shakspere and Marlowe." *Academy,* 9: 313, 1 Ap 1876.

Lee, Sidney. "Another new fact about Marlowe." *Athenaeum,* no. 3486: 235–236, 18 Ag 1894. Also H. P. Stokes, no. 3488: 299, 1 S 1894.

Manning, Owen, and Bray, William. *History and antiquities . . . of Surrey.* London: John White, 1809.

McKerrow, Ronald B. *Works of Thomas Nashe.* London: A. H. Bullen, 1914. [750 copies printed.]

Morley, Henry. "Spenser's 'Hobbinol.'" *Fortnightly Review,* 5: 264–283 My 1869. [On Gabriel Harvey, with special reference to Marlowe.]

Norman, Charles. "Marlowe's London." *Theatre Arts Monthly,* 23: 291–298 Ap 1939.

Read, Conyers. *Sir Francis Walsingham*. Cambridge: Harvard University Press, 1925, 3 vols.

Simpson, Richard. *See* Chap. XVI.

Stählin, Karl. *Sir Francis Walsingham und seine zeit*. Heidelberg: Carl Winter, 1908.

Watson, Thomas. (Edited by Edward Arber.) *Hekatompathia, Meliboeus, Teares of Fancie*. London: Constable, 1910.

Webb, E. A., Miller, G. W., and Beckwith, J. *History of Chislehurst*. London: George Allen, 1899. [Miss Eugénie de Kalb (TLS, 24: 351, 21 My 1925) calls this book "excellent and comparatively accurate" and asserts that it supersedes Hasted, *q.v.* under General Section.]

Woodward, Parker. "Sporting Kydd." *Baconiana*, 3rd ser. 5: 102–111 Ap 1907.

Woodward, Parker. "Elizabethan maze." *Baconiana*, 3rd ser. 7: 5–20 Ja 1909. [Deals especially with Thomas Watson.]

Woodward, Parker. "Masks or faces?" *Baconiana*, 3rd ser. 7: 86–93 Ap 1909. [Marlowe and Watson — a surprisingly early linking of their names.]

CHAPTER V: MARLOWE'S RELIGION

Anon. "Was Shakespeare a Roman Catholic?" *Quarterly Review*, 123: 146–185 Ja 1866.

Anon. "Religion in literature." *Edinburgh Review*, 207: 178–202 Ja 1908. [See pp. 192–194.] Reprinted in *Living Age*, 257: 67–84, 11 Ap 1908. [See pp. 77–78.]

Anon. "Poetry of atheism." *National Quarterly Review*, 38: 275–294 Ap 1879. [Deals mostly with Shelley. Attributed to G. W. Gunsaulus.]

Beau, J. "La religion de Sir Walter Raleigh." *Revue anglo-américaine*, 11: 410–422 Je 1934.

"Bibliothecary." "Marlowe and Mr. —— of Dover." N&Q, 5th ser. 12: 88, 2 Ag 1879.

Boas, F[rederick] S[amuel], and Hall, E. V[ine]. "Richard Baines, informer." *Nineteenth Century*, 112: 742–751 D 1932.

Boas, F[rederick] S[amuel]. "New light on Sir Walter Raleigh." *Literature*, 7: 96–98, 113–114, 11 and 18 Ag 1900.

Bradbrook, M[uriel] C[lara]. *School of night*. Cambridge University Press, 1936.

Brie, Friedrich. "Deismus und atheismus in der englischen Renaissance." *Anglia*, 48: 54–98, 105–156 (1924). [See especially pp. 119–144 and *Jahrb.* (OS) 63 (NS) 4: 220–221 (1927).]

Briggs, William Dinsmore. "On a document concerning Christopher Marlowe." SP, 20: 153–159 (1923). [See also *Beiblatt zur Anglia*, 34: 363 D 1923.]

Britton, S. "Marlowe the atheist." *Progress* [London], 6: 412–418, 443–449, 471–478 O, N, D 1886; 7: 11–17, 49–54 Ja, F 1887. [*Progress* was a small free-thought monthly, edited by G. W. Foote. File at Princeton.]

Buckley, George T. *Atheism in the English Renaissance.* University of Chicago Press, 1932, Chaps. I and II.

Buckley, George T. *Rationalism in sixteenth century English literature.* University of Chicago Press, 1933.

Buckley, George T. "Who was the late Arrian?" MLN, 49: 500–503 N 1934.

Camden, Carroll. "Marlowe and Elizabethan psychology." PQ, 8: 69–78 Ja 1929.

Colby, Elbridge. *English Catholic poets.* Milwaukee: Bruce Publishing Company, 1935, pp. 61–69. [Science and Culture Series.]

Cole, Grenville A. J. "Impiety of Marlowe." TLS, 20: 452, 14 Jy 1921.

Cummings, Charlotte Mary. *Evidence of religious skepticism in Christopher Marlowe and his dramas.* Iowa M.A. Thesis, 1929. [MS.]

Danchin, F.-C. "Études sur Christophe Marlowe." *Revue germanique,* 8: 22–33 Ja–F 1912; 9: 566–567 N–D 1913. [See *Jahrb.* 50: 144 (1914).]

Danchin, F.-C. "Authenticité des documents." *Revue germanique,* 10: 51–68 Ja–F 1914. [See *Jahrb.* 51: 221 (1915).]

de Kalb, Eugénie Walker. *Elucidation of the death of Christopher Marlowe through an examination of the lives and interests of certain of his associates.* Cambridge Diss. 1929. [MS.] [See also *Abstracts of Dissertations*, 1928– 29, pp. 59–61.] [JB]

Eccles, Mark. "Marlowe in Kentish tradition." N&Q, 169: 21–22, 39–41, 58–61, 134–135, 13, 20, 27 Jy, 24 Ag 1935.

Einstein, Lewis. *Italian Renaissance in England.* New York: Columbia University Press, 1927. [Studies in Comparative Literature.]

Einstein, Lewis. *Tudor ideals.* New York: Harcourt Brace & Co., 1921, pp. 225–229.

Ferrando, Guido. *See* Chap. VI.

Gardiner, Dorothy. *Oxinden letters.* London: Constable, 1933.

Grosart, Alexander B. (ed.). *Complete works in prose and verse of Edmund Spenser.* Manchester: Spenser Society, 1882–84.

Harvey, Gabriel. *Letter-book of Gabriel Harvey, A.D. 1573–1580.* (Edited by Edward John Long Scott.) London: Camden Society, 1884.

Herrington, Huntley Whatley. "Christopher Marlowe — rationalist." In *Essays in memory of Barrett Wendell.* Cambridge: Harvard University Press, 1926.

Horn, Francis Henry. *Plays of Peele, Greene, and Marlowe as an expression of the English Renaissance.* Virginia M.A. Thesis, 1934. [MS.]

Huberman, Edward. *Some aspects of atheism in Elizabethan literature.* Rutgers M.A. Thesis, 1930. [MS.]

Kempner, Nadja. *Raleghs staatstheoretische schriften: die einführung des Machiavellismus in England.* Leipzig: Tauchnitz, 1928. [Beiträge z. engl. Philol. Heft 7.]

Kocher, Paul H[arold]. "Marlowe's atheist lecture." JEGP, 39: 98–106 Ja 1940. [See also General Section.]

Lee, Sidney, and Laughton, John Knox. Article "Ralegh." DNB, XVI. 629–649.

Looten, Camille. *Shakespeare et la religion*. Paris: Perrin et Cie., 1929.

Marquardsen, H. "Christopher Marlowes kosmologie." *Jahrb*. 41: 54–80 (1905).

McCabe, Joseph. *Biographical dictionary of modern rationalists*. London: Watt, 1920.

Moore, [Frank] Hale. "Gabriel Harvey's references to Marlowe." SP, 23: 337–357 (1926). [See also *Jahrb*. (OS) 65 (NS) 6: 218 (1929).]

Morley, F. V. "Thomas Hariot, 1560–1621." *Scientific Monthly*, 14: 60–66 Ja 1921.

Mortland, Maizie. *Morality elements in Christopher Marlowe and his dramas*. Iowa M.A. Thesis, 1925. [MS.]

[Parsons, Robert.] *Elizabethae reginae Angliae edictum promulgatum Londini 29 Nouemb. Anni M.D.XCI. Andrae Philopatri ad idem edictum responsio*. [Device.] *Excusum M. D. XCIII*. . . . [There is also a German edition. Both German and Latin texts are in the Pierpont Morgan Library.]

Paul, F. "Marlowe and the heavy wrath of God." *American Catholic Quarterly Review*, 42: 584–588 O 1917.

Praz, Mario. "Un Machiavellico inglese: Sir Walter Raleigh." *La Cultura*, 8: 16–27 Ja 1929.

Riess, Chester L. *Christopher Marlowe and atheism*. New York M.A. Thesis, 1932. [MS.]

Ritson, Joseph. *Observations on the three first volumes of the history of English poetry, by Thomas Warton*. London: Stockdale and Faulder, 1782. [First appearance in print of the Baines libel.]

Sarrazin, Gregor. *Thomas Kyd und sein kreis*. Berlin: Emil Felber, 1892.

Sisson, Charles A. "Christopher Marlowe: atheist and Machiavellian." [Essay in preparation. Coker College.]

Sisson, Charles J. *Le goût public et le théâtre élisabéthain*. Dijon Thèse, 1921. Dijon: Darantière, n.d.

Smith, Winifred. *See* Chap. VIII.

Stevens, Henry Norton (ed.). *Thomas Hariot, the mathematician, the philosopher, and the scholar . . . with notices of his associates*. London: privately printed, 1900. [NYPL]

Stokes, H[enry] P[aine]. "Another new fact about Marlowe." *Athenaeum*, no. 3488: 299, 1 S 1894.

Stone, J. M. "Atheism under Elizabeth and James I." *Month*, 81: 174–187 Ja 1894.

Storer, Agnes C. "Two Elizabethan dramatists." *Catholic World*, 75: 609–618 Ag 1902. [Marlowe and Heywood.]

Warshaw, Jacob. *See* Chap. IX.

Williams, Arnold L. *Christopher Marlowe and the Raleigh circle*. North Carolina M.A. Thesis, 1930. [MS.] Abstracted in *University of North Carolina Record*, Graduate School Series, 22: 41 (1930).

Yates, Francis A. "Harriot and the 'School of Night.'" TLS, 35: 908, 7 N 1936.

Yearsley, [Percival] Macleod. "Rationalism of Kit Marlowe." *Rationalist Annual*, 1930, pp. 71-75. [NYPL]

CHAPTER VI: MARLOWE'S DEATH

Allen, Don Cameron. "Meres and the death of Marlowe." TLS, 31: 76, 4 F 1932.

Anderton, H. Ince. "More about Poole." TLS, 33: 620, 13 S 1934.

Anon. "Dismal Deptford." [London] *Daily Chronicle*, 10 D 1894, p. 5e. [A reference, partly erroneous, to Marlowe's burial. See also N&Q, 8th ser. 7: 229, 23 Mr 1895.]

Anon. "Memorial in Deptford Parish Church." [London] *Times*, 17 My 1919, p. 15d; 5 Je 1919, p. 6f.

Anon. "Kit Marlowe's murder out." Literary Digest, 85: 27-28, 13 Je 1925.

"Ayeahr." "Christopher Marlowe." N&Q, 8th ser. 7: 229, 23 Mr 1895. [Further comment on pp. 275, 353, and 499.]

Baldwin, T[homas] W[hitfield]. *See* Chap. XV.

Barker, James Ernest. "Christopher Marlowe's grave." [London] *Standard*, 25 Jy 1888, p. 2h. [Reply appears 28 Jy 1888, p. 3e. See under Warry, George.]

Beard, Thomas. *See* Early Printed Books.

Boas, F[rederick] S[amuel]. "New light on Marlowe and Kyd." *Fortnightly Review*, 71: 212-225 Fe 1899. [See *Jahrb.* 36: 329 (1900).]

Boas, F[rederick] S[amuel]. *Works of Thomas Kyd*. Oxford: Clarendon Press, 1901. [Documents on pp. cviii-cxvi.]

Boas, F[rederick] S[amuel]. "Robert Poley, an associate of Marlowe." *Nineteenth Century*, 104: 543-552 O 1928. [See letter of Eugénie de Kalb, 104: 715-71 N 1928, and reply by Boas, 104: 850 D 1928. Also *Jahrb.* (OS) 66 (NS) 7: 230 (1930).]

Boas, F[rederick] S[amuel], and Hall, E. Vine. "Richard Baines, informer." *Nineteenth Century*, 112: 742-751 D 1932.

Brandl, A[lois]. "Kyd an der Privy Council über Marlowe." *Archiv*, 142: 257 (1921).

Brereton, J[ohn] Le Gay. "Case of Francis Ingram." *Hermes*, 12: 57-60, 26 S 1906. Reprinted as no. 5 in the series on "Elizabethan dramatists" in *Sydney* [Australia] *University Library. Publications.* 1906. Also in Brereton's *Elizabethan drama: notes & studies*, pp. 11-15. [*Hermes* is a journal published by Sydney University, not to be confused with the archeological journal with the same name. The signature "XXX" there used was a common device of Brereton's.]

Brown, Ford K. "Marlowe and Kyd." TLS, 20: 355, 2 Je 1921.

Chambers, E[dmund] K[erchever]. "Death of Marlowe." TLS, 24: 352, 21 My 1925.

Chapman, William Hall. *Shakespeare the personal phase*. N.p. Privately printed, 1920, pp. 359-363.

Clarke, Samuel. *See* Early Printed Books.

Danchin, F.-C. "La mort de Marlowe." *Revue anglo-américaine*, 3: 48–53 O 1925.

de Kalb, Eugénie. "Death of Marlowe." TLS, 24: 351, 21 My 1925.

de Kalb, Eugénie. "Robert Poley — an associate of Marlowe." *Nineteenth Century*, 104: 715–716 N 1928. [Reply to F. S. Boas, *q.v.*]

de Kalb, Eugénie. "Robert Poley's movements as a messenger of the Court." RES, 9: 13–18 Ja 1933.

Dews, Nathan. *History of Deptford in the counties of Kent and Surrey, compiled from authentic records.* London: J. B. Smith, 1893, pp. 122–125. [BPL]

Donnelly, Ignatius. "Cecil tells the story of Marlowe." Chap. V in *The great cryptogram.* Chicago, New York, London: R. S. Peal & Company, 1888.

Earle, John. *See* Early Printed Books.

Eccles, Mark. "Jonson and the spies." RES, 13: 385–397 (1937).

Ferrando, Guido. "Com è morto Marlowe." *Il Marzocco*, 37: 2–3, 28 F 1932. [HCL, Cornell]

F[urnivall], F. J. "Marlowe's death: the Globe Theatre." N&Q, 5th ser. 3: 224, 20 Mr 1875.

Gallup, Elizabeth Wells. *Bi-lateral cypher of Sir Francis Bacon.* Detroit: Howard Publishing Company; London: Gay and Bird, 1899.

Gogarty, Oliver St. John. *I follow St. Patrick.* New York: Reynal & Hitchcock, 1938, pp. 31–32. [Badly misinformed.]

Gordon-Smith, Alan. *Babington plot.* London: Macmillan, 1936. [Poley.]

Gray, Arthur. "The Marlowe fiction." In *Chapter in the early life of Shakespeare.* Cambridge University Press, 1926, pp. 3–7.

Greenwood, George. "Death of Marlowe." TLS, 24: 384, 4 Je 1925.

Grinstead, T. P. *Last homes of departed genius.* London: Routledge, 1867, pp. 215–216. [NYPL]

Grubb, Marion. "Kyd's 'Libel' of 1593." *Saturday Review of Literature*, 9: 135, 24 S 1932.

Hall, E. Vine. "Christopher Marlowe's death at Deptford Strand, 1593. Wills of jurors at the inquest and some other wills." In *Testamentary papers*, III. London: Mitchell Hughes and Clarke, 1937.

Harman, Edward George. *Gabriel Harvey and Thomas Nashe.* London: Ouseley, 1923. [NYPL]

Harrison, G[eorge] B[agshaw]. "Death of Marlowe." In *Elizabethan plays and players.* London: Routledge, 1940, pp. 117–129.

Hotson, John Leslie. "Tracking down a murderer." *Atlantic Monthly*, 135: 733–741 Je 1925.

Hotson, John Leslie. "Marlowe among the churchwardens." *Atlantic Monthly*, 138: 37–44 Jy 1926.

Hotson, J[ohn] Leslie. *Death of Christopher Marlowe.* London: Nonesuch Press; Cambridge: Harvard University Press, 1925. [Reviewed in TLS, 24: 329, 14 My 1925; *Nation and Athenaeum*, 37: 238, 23 My 1925; *Saturday Review of Literature*, 1: 852, 27 Je 1925; *Spectator*, no. 5057: 892–893, 30 My 1925; *New Statesman*, 25: 256, 13 Je 1925; *Archiv*, 150: 256–

258 (1926); *Nation*, 121: 193–194, 12 Ag 1926; *English Studies*, 8: 188–189 (1926); JEGP, 26: 132–135 (1927); (London) *Poetry*, 8: 145–153 Je 1925.]

Ireland, Gordon. "Ingram Frizer laid more low than Marlowe." *Shakespeare Association Bulletin* [New York], 5: 192–194 (1930).

Kirby, J. W. "Slayer of Christopher Marlowe." TLS, 29: 592, 17 Jy 1930.

Lambin, Georges. "Destin de Christopher Marlowe." In *Théâtre elizabéthain. Cahiers du Sud*, 10: 166–169, 1er semestre, 1933. [NYPL]

Lodge, Oliver W. F. "Shakespeare and the death of Marlowe." TLS, 24: 335, 14 My 1925. [See also Chap. XVI, and TLS, 24: 384, 4 Je 1925, and 26: 12, 6 Ja 1927.]

Logeman, H[enri]. "Name of Christopher Marlowe's murderer." *Anglia*, (OS) 38 (NS) 26: 374–376 (1914). [Frezer or Frazer?]

Macaulay, Thurston. "Marlowe's burial register." TLS, 29: 514, 19 Je 1930. [Corrected on p. 554, 3 Jy.]

Moore, [Frank] Hale. *See* Chap. V.

Norman, Charles. "Marlowe, the muses' darling." *Bookman*, 75: 135–143 My 1932.

Poel, William. "Death of Marlowe." TLS, 24: 351, 21 My 1925.

[Ritson, Joseph.] *Bibliographia poetica*. London: Nicol, 1802, pp. 275–276.

"Sceptic." "Slaying of Christopher Marlowe." *Baconiana*, 3rd ser. 20: 61–62 F 1929.

Seaton, Ethel. "Marlowe, Robert Poley, and the Tippings." RES, 5: 273–287 Jy 1929.

Seaton, Ethel. "Robert Poley's ciphers." RES, 7: 137–150 (1931).

Slater, Gilbert. "Marlowe mystery." In *Seven Shakespeares*. London: Cecil Palmer, 1931. [Marlowe as Shakespeare.]

Tannenbaum, Samuel A. *Booke of Sir Thomas Moore*. New York: Tenny Press, privately printed, 1927. See also *Corrections and additions*. New York: privately printed, pp. 6–8. [Contains the signed Kyd letter, an eight-page supplement devoted to errata, and the Baines libel. Facsimiles. Reviewed in *Shakespeare Review*, 1: 198–200 (1928); [New York] *Nation*, 127: 132 O 1928; *Archiv*, 155: 143–144.]

Tannenbaum, Samuel A. *Assassination of Christopher Marlowe*. New York: privately printed, 1928. [100 copies only. Reviewed in MLN, 44: 487–488 (1929); *English Studies* (Amsterdam), 11: 152–153 (1929).]

Thom, W. W. ["N"]. "Death of Marlowe." *University of Virginia Magazine*, 12: 171–183 D 1873.

Warry, George. "Christopher Marlowe's grave." [London] *Standard*, 28 Jy 1888, p. 3e. [Letter from the senior churchwarden of St. Nicholas, Deptford, replying to James Ernest Baker, *q.v.*]

Williams, F. B., Jr. "Ingram Frizer." TLS, 34: 513, 15 Ag 1935.

CHAPTER VII: TAMBURLAINE

Translations

1854. Tycho Mommsen. "Proben aus Marlowe," nos. I–IX. In his *Marlowe und Shakespeare*. Programm, Eisenach Realgymnasium. [CUL has this as undated pamphlet bound with other Marlowe material as 823M34/09.]

1893. Adolf Friedrich, Graf von Schack. Scene. In *Die englischen dramatiker vor, neben und nach Shakespeare*. Stuttgart: Cotta, p. 89. [NYPL]

1893. Margarete Vöhl. *Der erste teil des Tamerlan des Grossen*. Helmsted: J. C. Schmidt. [CUL has this, bound with other Marlowe material as 823M34/09.]

Separate Editions

1738. Thomas Hayward. Extracts. In *British muse*. London: F. Cogan and J. Nourse, I. 27–28, 53–55, 72, 116–117, 181.

1740. [Thomas Hayward.] Extracts. In *Quintessence of English poetry*. London: O. Payne. [Page-for-page reprint.]

1845. Leigh Hunt. Extracts. In *Imagination and fancy*. New York: Wiley and Patterson, p. 103.

1894. Edward T. McLaughlin. Selections, with *Edward the Second* and the poems. New York: Holt. [English Readings.] [LC]

1896. Charles Dudley Warner. Extracts. In *Warner's Library*, XXIV. 9718–9722. [See General Section.]

1905. W[illiam] H[enry] Williams. *Specimens of the Elizabethan drama from Lyly to Shirley, A.D. 1580–A.D. 1642*. Oxford University Press, pp. 27–32. [Quarto text compared with Dyce and Cunningham.]

1907. G[race] E[leanor] and W[illiam] H[enry] Hadow. *Oxford treasury of English literature*. Oxford: Clarendon Press, II. 61–85. [Part II condensed.]

1911. William Allan Neilson. *Chief Elizabethan dramatists*. Boston: Houghton Mifflin; London: Harrap, pp. 57–79. [Part I only.]

1919. Edgar Montillion Woolley and Stephen Vincent Benét. New Haven: Yale University Press. [Yale, NYPL]

1923. William Allan Neilson. With *Doctor Faustus*. Boston: Houghton Mifflin. [Riverside Literature Series.]

1927. Albert A. Cock. Scenes. Together with *Doctor Faustus*. London: A. & C. Black. [Socrates Booklets, no. 14.]

1928. H[arry] C[hristian] Schweikert. *Early English plays*. New York: Harcourt, pp. 525–646.

1928. Anon. Extracts. *Columbia University course in literature*. New York: Columbia University Press, XI, 217–222.

1930. Reprint of the 1590 edition with five full page illustrations by R. S. Sherriff. London: Hesperides Press. [400 copies only.] [JB, BM]

1931. Felix E[manuel] Schelling and Matthew W[ilson] Black. *Typical Elizabethan plays*. New York: Harper, pp. 1–33. [Part I only.]

1931. Edwin Johnston Howard. *Ten Elizabethan plays*. New York: Nelson, pp. 57–94.

1933. C[harles] F[rederick] Tucker Brooke and N. Burton Paradise. *English drama, 1580–1642*. Boston: D. C. Heath, pp. 137–166. [Part I only.]

1933. Hazelton Spencer. *Elizabethan plays*. Boston: Little Brown, pp. 37–63.

1933. Richard Ferrar Patterson. Extract. In *Six centuries of English literature*. London: Blackie, II. 37–38.

1933. George Rylands. *Elizabethan tragedy*. London: G. Bell & Sons, pp. 1–90. [Part I only, with introduction and brief life.]

1934. Charles Reed Baskervill, Virgil B. Heltzel, and Arthur N. Nethered. *Elizabethan and Stuart plays*. New York: Holt, pp. 307–348.

Books and Articles

Allen, Don Cameron. "Tamburlaine." TLS, 30: 730, 24 S 1931.

Anon. " 'Tamburlaine the great.' Open air performance at Oxford." [London] *Times*, 13 Je 1933, p. 12d. See also 14 Je, first and second editions only.

Bagley, Walter. "Early contemporary evidence relating to the authorship of the Elizabethan drama." *Baconiana*, 3rd ser. 4: 216–233 O 1906.

Bakeless, John. *Marlowe's Tamburlaine: a new view of its source material*. Harvard University. Bowdoin Prize Essay, 1922. [MS.] [HCL, JB]

Baldwin, T. W. "On the chronology of Thomas Kyd's plays." MLN, 40: 343–349 Je 1925.

Baldwin, T. W. "Thomas Kyd's early company connections." PQ, 6: 311–313 Jy 1927.

Begley, Walter. "Authorship of *Tamburlaine* and the other Marlowe plays." *Baconiana*, 3rd ser. 5: 247–263 O 1907.

Booth, William Stone. *Some acrostic signatures of Francis Bacon*. Boston: Houghton Mifflin, 1909, pp. 200–222.

Brereton, John Le Gay. "Marlowe's dramatic art studied in his Tamburlaine." Australian English Association Leaflet, no. 5, N 1925; also Sydney: H. T. Dunn & Co. (reprint), 1925. [BM, HCL, JB]

Brereton, J[ohn] Le Gay. "Marlowe some textual notes." MLR, 6: 94–96 (1911). [See *Jahrb.* 48: 216 (1912).]

Brooke, C[harles] F[rederick] Tucker. "Marlowe's 'Tamburlaine.' " MLN, 25: 93–94 Mr 1910. [See *Jahrb.* 47: 258 (1911) and Bruce, below.]

Broughton, J. MS. notes on Tamburlaine in a copy of Pickering's 1826 edition. [BM, 11771.d.4]

Bruce, J. Douglas. "Three days tournament motif in Marlowe's *Tamburlaine*." MLN, 24: 257–258 D 1909. [See *Jahrb.* 46: 201 (1910) and Brooke, above.]

Bush, [John Nash] Douglas. "Marlowe and Spenser." TLS 12, 1 Ja 1938.

Butler, Pierce. "Stage mad-folk in Shakespeare's day." *American Journal of Insanity*, 73: 19–42 (1916). [Especially p. 27.]

Camden, Carroll, Jr. "Marlowe and Elizabethan psychology." PQ, 8: 69–78 Ja 1929.

Camden, Carroll, Jr. "Tamburlaine the choleric man." MLN, 44: 430–435 N 1929. [See also *Jahrb.* (OS) 66 (NS) 7: 231 (1930).]

Cawley, Robert Ralston. *Voyagers and Elizabethan drama.* Boston: Heath; London: Oxford University Press, 1938. [M.L.A. Monograph Series.]

Cellini, Benvenuto. *See* Biographies.

Chambers, E[dmund] K[erchever]. Review of Greg's edition of *Henslowe's Diary.* MLR, 4: 407–413 Ap 1909.

Chambers, E[dmund] K[erchever]. "Date of Marlowe's *Tamburlaine.*" TLS, 29: 684, 28 Ag 1930.

Chew, Samuel C[laggett]. *Crescent and the rose.* Oxford University Press, 1937.

Coghill, Nevill K. "Tamburlaine, the great." TLS, 32: 364, 25 My 1933.

Collier, John Payne. *Old man's diary.* London: Thomas Richards, 1872, pt. III, pp. 44–45, 92.

Cook, Albert S. "Notes on Marlowe's Tamburlaine." MLN, 21: 112–113 Ap 1906. [See *Jahrb.* 43: 296 (1907).]

Daffner, Hugo. "Selbstmord bei Shakespeare." *Jahrb.* 64: 90–131 (1928). [Especially pp. 94–95.]

Danchin, F.-C. "Études critiques sur Christophe Marlowe — en marge de la second partie de Tamburlaine." *Revue germanique,* 8: 22–33 (1912).

Deetjen, Werner. *See* Chap. VIII.

Degenhart, M. "Tamerlan in den literaturen des westlichen Europas." *Archiv,* (OS) 123 (NS) 23: 253–278 (1909) [See *Jahrb.* 47: 258 (1911).]

Delius, Nicolaus. "Klassische reminiscenzen in Shakespeare's dramen." *Jahrb.* 18: 81–103 (1883).

Dodsley, Robert, *et al. Select collection of old plays.* London: Septimus Prout, 1827, XII. 387–388.

Eisinger, Fritz. *See* Chap. XI.

Ellis-Fermor, Una M. "The '1592' 8vo of Tamburlaine." TLS, 28: 362, 2 My 1929.

Ellis-Fermor, Una Mary. "Tamburlaine the great." TLS, 32: 396, 8 Je 1933.

Flynn, J. G. "'Senseless lure' problem." TLS, 34: 464, 18 Jy 1935.

Fraenkel, Ludwig. "Zum stoffe von Marlowe's 'Tamburlaine.'" ES, 16: 459–462 F 1892.

Gayton, Edmund. *Pleasant notes on Don Quixote.* London: W. Hunt, 1654. [Also called *Festivous notes,* etc.] [See p. 271 for notes on provincial productions of *Tamburlaine* and *The Jew of Malta.*] Later edition, London: F. Newbery, 1768. [CUL]

Hart, H. C. "Robert Greene's prose works." N&Q, 10th ser. 5: 484–487, 504–506, 23, 30 Je 1906. [See *Jahrb.* 43: 295 (1907). (Primaudaye).]

Herford, C. H., and Wagner, A. "Sources of Marlowe's Tamburlaine." *Academy,* 24: 265–266, 20 O 1883.

Hubbard, F. G. "Possible evidence for the date of Tamburlaine." PMLA, 33: 436–438 S 1918.

Intze, Ottokar. *Tamerlan und Bajazet in den literaturen des Abendlandes.* Erlangen Diss. 1911. Erlangen: E. Th. Jacob, 1912. [HCL, NYPL]

Kellner, Leon. Review of Breymann and Wagner's edition. ES, 9: 297–301 Ja 1886. [Important for its original conjectures as to sources.]

King, Philip S. "Tradition about Tamburlaine." N&Q, 3rd ser. 12: 88–89 Ag 1867.

Kittredge, George Lyman. "On Marlowe's Tamburlaine." MLN, 5: 272–273 My 1890.

Köppel, Emil. "Beiträge zur geschichte des Elisabethanischen dramas." ES, 16: 357–374 (1892). [Includes a discussion of *Tamburlaine* and of *Titus Andronicus.*]

Lawrence, W[illiam] J[ohn]. *See* Chap. XII.

Lucas, F[rank] L[aurence]. *Seneca and Elizabethan tragedy.* Cambridge University Press, 1922, pp. 20–21, 103, 115, 129.

Lucius, Eberhard. *Gerichtsszenen im älteren englischen drama.* Giessen Diss. 1922. Giessen: Justus Christ, 1928, p. 41.

McDavid, Raven Ioor. *Military science as an Elizabethan literary motif.* Duke M.A. Thesis, 1933. [MS.]

Mills, L. J. "A note on I. *Tamburlaine,* I. ii. 242–243." MLN, 52: 101-103 (1937).

Mulholland, Vester Moye. *Power of fortune in Elizabethan tragedy.* Duke M.A. Thesis, 1927. [MS.]

Munn, James B. *See* General Section.

Nowak, Lothar. *Die alchemie und die alchemisten in der englischen literatur.* Breslau Diss. 1934. Breslau: Neumann, 1934. [Reference on p. 48 to the Theridamas-Olympia episode.]

Parks, George Bruner. *Richard Hakluyt and the English voyages.* New York: American Geographical Society, 1928, pp. 1–25. [General background in exploration.]

Rhoads, Francis Dale. *Oriental backgrounds of Marlowe's Tamburlaine.* Washington M.A. Thesis, 1932. [MS.]

Rogers, Frederick. "Tamburlaine the Great." *Academy,* 34: 244, 13 O 1888.

Rogers, Frederick. "Marlowe's Tamburlaine the Great." Paper before the Elizabethan Society, London, 1888–89. [Probably lost except for summary above.]

Schoembs, Jakob. *Ariosts Orlando Furioso in der englischen litteratur des zeitalters der Elisabeth.* Strassburg Diss. n.d. Soden: P. J. Pusch, 1898.

Schoeneich, Georg. *Litterarische einfluss Spensers auf Marlowe.* Halle Diss. n.d. Halle: Hohmann, 1907.

Scudder, Harold H. "An allusion in Tamburlaine." TLS, 32: 147, 2 Mr 1933.

Seaton, Ethel. "Marlowe and his authorities." TLS, 20: 388, 16 Je 1921.

Seaton, Ethel. "Marlowe's Map." *Essays and Studies,* 10: 13–35 (1924).

Seaton, Ethel. "Fresh sources for Marlowe." RES, 5: 385–401 O 1929. [See *Jahrb.* (OS) 66 (NS) 7: 231 (1930).]

Sencourt, Robert [pseudonym of R. E. G. George]. *India in English literature.* London: Simpkin Marshall, n.d. [ca. 1923], pp. 61–69.

Sheppard, J[ohn] T[hesidder]. *Aeschylus and Sophocles, their work and influence.* London and New York: Longmans, 1927, pp. 130–137 [Our Debt to Greece and Rome Series.]

Spence, Leslie. "Influence of Marlowe's sources on Tamburlaine." MP, 24: 181–199 (1928). [See also *Jahrb.* (OS) 63 (NS) 4: 221 (1927); (OS) 64 (NS) 5: 206 (1928).]

Spence, Leslie. "Tamburlaine and Marlowe." PMLA, 42: 604–622 (1927).

Spence, Leslie. *Tamburlaine in the light of its sources.* Wisconsin Diss. 1934. [MS.]

Spencer, Theodore. *Treatment of death in Elizabethan tragedy.* Harvard Diss. 1928. [MS.] See also *Harvard . . . Summaries of Theses,* 1928, pp. 145–148.

Spencer, Theodore. *Death and Elizabethan tragedy.* Cambridge: Harvard University Press, 1936.

Spens, Janet. *Essay on Shakespeare and tradition.* Oxford: Blackwell, 1916, pp. 68–70. [Greek tragedy.]

Spens, Janet. *Spenser's Faerie Queene.* London: Edward Arnold, 1934, pp. 63–65.

Symmes, Harold S. *Les débuts de la critique dramatique en Angleterre.* Paris: Leroux, 1903, pp. 150–151.

Thorp, Willard. "Ethical problems in Marlowe's Tamburlaine." JEGP, 29: 385–389 (1930).

Underhill, John Garrett. *Spanish literature in the England of the Tudors.* New York: Macmillan, 1899, pp. 258–259. [Columbia University Studies in Literature.]

Van Dam, B. A. P. "Marlowe's Tamburlaine." *English Studies* [Amsterdam], 16: 1–17; 49–58 F, Ap 1934.

Wann, Louis. "Oriental in Elizabethan drama." MP, 12: 423–447 (1915).

Warner, George F[rederick]. *Catalogue of the manuscripts and muniments of Alleyn's College of God's Gift at Dulwich.* London: Longmans Green & Co., 1881. [CUL]

Woodbridge, Benjamin M. "Marlowe and Jean de Meung." MLR, 14: 217 Ap 1919.

W. T. S. "Euripides and Marlowe." *Academy,* 67: 390–391, 29 O 1904.

Influence of "Tamburlaine"

Ayres, Harry Morgan. *See* Chap. XVI.

Behrend, Alfred. *Nicholas Rowe als dramatiker.* Königsberg Diss. 1907. Leipzig: A. Hoffman, 1907.

Boyd, Evelyn Mae. *Study of the characterization of Tamburlaine and evidence of its influence on drama from 1587–1605.* Chicago M.A. Thesis, 1920. [MS.]

Brown, J. M. "An early rival of Shakespeare." *New Zealand Magazine* [Dunedin, N. Z.], 2: 95–133 Ap 1877. [NYPL]

Cheffaud, P. N. *George Peele.* Paris: F. Alcan, 1913.

Collins, [John] Churton. *Plays & poems of Robert Greene.* Oxford: Clarendon Press, 1905. [Introduction discusses relation to Marlowe.]

Curtis, Verne Elizabeth. *Influence of Tamburlaine on Elizabethan drama to the year 1600.* Washington M.A. Thesis, 1930. [MS.]

Ehrke, Karl. *Robert Greene's dramen.* Greifswald Diss. 1904. Greifswald: Julius Abel, 1904. [Some reference to the influence of *Tamburlaine* and *Doctor Faustus.*]

Fane, Sir Francis. *The Sacrifice.* London: J. R. for John Weld, 1686. [CUL]

Geissler, Adolf. *Einfluss der Tamburlaine-rolle bis zum untergang des Elisabeth-Theaters.* Berlin Diss. 1925. [Printed but apparently never issued.] [Berlin, JB]

Grosart, Alexander B. *Life and complete works of Robert Greene.* London: privately printed, 1881–86. [Fifty copies only. Contains translations of Storojenko (also transliterated Storozhenko), excerpts from J. M. Brown (*q.v.*), and comments by Grosart.]

Hopkinson, A. F. *Tragical reign of Selimus.* London: M. E. Sims & Co., privately printed, 1916. [Valuable introduction.]

Hübener, E[mil]. *Einfluss von Marlowe's Tamburlaine auf die zeitgenossischen und folgenden dramatiker.* Halle Diss. 1901. Halle: no publisher named. [Reviewed by R. Fischer in *Jahrb.* 40: 256–257 (1904).]

Hunt, Mary. *Thomas Dekker.* New York: Columbia University Press, 1911. [Columbia University Studies in English.]

Jordan, John Clark. *Robert Greene.* New York: Columbia University Press, 1915, pp. 189–197. [Studies in English and Comparative Literature.]

Intze, O. *Nicholas Rowe.* Heidelberg: K. Groos Nachf., 1910.

Jung, Fritz. *Greene, Nash und die schauspieler.* Freiburg Diss. 1911. Freiburg: U. Hochreuther, 1911, pp. 12–46. [NYPL]

Keller, Wolfgang. "Wars of Cyrus." *Jahrb.* 37: 1–58 (1901).

Kroneberg, Erich. *George Peele's 'Edward the First.' Eine litterarhistorische untersuchung.* Jena Diss. 1903. Jena: A. Kämpfe, 1903.

Landsberg, Gertrud. *Der stil in Georg Peeles sicheren und zweifelhaften werke.* Breslau Diss. Breslau: H. Fleischmann, 1910.

Landsberg, Gertrud. *Ophelia.* Cöthen: Otto Schulze, 1918, pp. 21–25. [Neue Anglistische Arbeiten.]

Lawrence, W. J. "The earliest private-theatre play." TLS, 20: 514, 11 Ag 1921. [Discusses Marlowe's relation to *The Wars of Cyrus.*]

Lee, Sidney. *See* Chap. XII.

Lemmi, Charles W. "Tamburlaine and Greene's Orlando Furioso." MLN, 32: 434–435 N 1917.

Mühlfeld, Wilhelm. *Tragedie of Caesar and Pompey.* Münster Diss. n.d. Weimar: R. Wagner Sohn, 1912, pp. lviii–lix.

Schulze, Karl. *Die satiren Halls.* Berlin: Mayer & Muller, 1910. [Palaestra CVI.]

Sisson, Charles J. *Lost plays of Shakespeare's age.* Cambridge University Press, 1936, p. 175.

Storozhenko, Nikolai Il'ich. *See* General Section. [His *Life of Green* contains some material on the influence of *Tamburlaine*.]

Thaler, Alwin. *Shakspere's silences.* Cambridge: Harvard University Press, 1929, pp. 111–112. [Sir Thomas Browne.]

Van Dam, B. A. P. "R. Greene's Alphonsus." *English Studies* [Amsterdam], 13: 129–142 (1931).

White, Edith A. *Two hands in The Battle of Alcazar.* Hunter College M.A. Thesis, 1932. [MS.]

Wills, Mary Matheson. *See* General Section.

Wright, Ernest Hunter. *Influence of Christopher Marlowe on his immediate contemporaries.* Columbia M.A. Thesis, 1907. [MS.]

Thieme, Heinz. *Zur verfasserfrage des Dekkerschen stückes "The pleasant comedy of Old Fortunatus."* Leipzig Diss. 1934. Borna-Leipzig: Robert Noske, 1934. [NYPL]

Chapter VIII: Doctor Faustus

Translations

1818. Wilhelm Müller. *Doktor Faustus, tragödie von Marlowe . . . mit einer vorrede von L. A. von Arnim.* Berlin: Die Faustdichtung. [Reprinted in *Das Kloster*, 5: 922–1020 (1847); Reclams Universal-Bibliothek, no. 1128 (1879); *Pandora*, vol. II (1911); Rudolf Frank's *Wie der Faust entstand.* Berlin: Verlag Neues Leben, n.d. (ca. 1932); H[orst] W[olfram] Geisser's *Gestaltungen des Faust.* Munich: Parcus & Co., 1927, I. 135–210. Reviewed in *Euphorion*, 13: 94–104 (1906); *Jahrb.* 48: 344–345 (1912). Most of this material is in NYPL. *Pandora* is at the University of Chicago.]

1833. Amédée Pichot. Extracts. *Revue de Paris*, 48: 242–244 Mr.

1839. C. J. Linstrom, A. F. Wimmercranz, *et al. Doctor Faustus. Tragisk dikt., af Chr. Marlowe. Ofersattning med inledning.* Upsala: privately printed. [BM]

1850. Jean-Pierre-Antoine Bazy. *Histoire allégorique de la vie et de la mort du Docteur Jean Faust, drame de Christophe Marlowe.* Paris: Garnier Frères, 1850. [See his *Études historiques* in "Books and Articles" section.]

1855. Alexander Büchner. Extracts. In *Geschichte der englischen poesie.* Darmstadt: Diehl, I. 229–233.

1857. Adolf Böttger. *Christoph Marlowes Doctor Faust. (Gedichtet um das Jahr 1588). Und die alte englische ballade von D. Faustus.* Leipzig: Hartung. [Introduction on Marlowe and the Faustsage.] [BM]

1858. François Victor Hugo. *Le Faust de Christopher Marlowe.* Paris: Michel Lévy frères. [Collection Michel-Lévy.] [BM, BN, HCL]

1859. S. Uvarov. Angel scene. Русское Слово [*Russkoe Slovo*], 1: 27–29 F.

1859. Gustavo Strafforello. Scholar scene and final scene. *Rivista contemporaneo*, 19: 135–138.

1860. Mikh[ail] Mikhailov. Final scene. Русское Слово [*Russkoe Slovo*], 2: 416–418 F.

1860. Friedrich Martin Bodenstedt. *See* Collected Editions.

1870. Theophilo Braga. *Estudos da edade media. Philosophia da litteratura.* Porto. [Contains an article on "Leudo do Doutor Fausto," pp. 89–114, and translations, pp. 102–104, of the final scene, from the French of François Victor Hugo, *q.v.*]

1870. Alfred van der Velde. *Marlowe's Faust, die älteste dramatische bearbeitung der Faustsage. Ueberzetzt und mit einleitung und bemerkungen besehen.* Breslau? Diss. 1868. Breslau: A. Gosohorsky (L. F. Maske). [See *Jahrb.* 6: 361–362 (1871).] [BM, NYPL, HCL]

1871. Dmitri Minaev. Фаустъ [*Faust.*] Дѣло [*Dielo*], 5: 1–106 My 1871.

1875. Dmitri Minaev and Mikhail Mikhailov. Scenes. In Англійскіе поэты въ біографіяхъ и образцахъ [*Angliskie poeti v biografiyach i obraztsach. English poets in biographies and specimens.*] St. Petersburg: A. M. Kotomin, pp. 24–33.

1880. W. Hertzberg. "Shakespeare und seine vorläufer." *Jahrb.* 15: 360–409 (1880). [Contains some original translation.]

1882. Erich Schmidt. "Faust und das sechszehnten jahrhundert." *Goethe Jahrb.* 77: 131.

1887. Albert Verwey. "De tragische historie van Dr. Faustus." *De Nieuwe Gids* [Amsterdam], 3: 12–64. [NYPL, Yale]

1887. R. S. Tjaden Modderman. *Het oudste Faust-drama. Marlowe's tragische historie van Dr. Faustus. Vertaald en toegelicht door.* Groningen. [BM]

1889. Final scene. *Rassegna italiana*, 48: 667, 16 Ag.

1893. Adolf Friedrich, Graf von Schack. Scenes. In *Die Englischen dramatiker vor, neben und nach Shakespeare.* Stuttgart: Cotta, pp. 72–82. [NYPL]

1894. *La tragique histoire du docteur Faust. Notice par Alfred Ernst.* Paris: H. Gautier. [Nouvelle Bibliothèque Populaire.]

1898. A. Halling. *Doktor Faustus oversat af A. Halling.* Copenhagen: Philologisk Historisk Samfund. [Studien fra Sprog- og Oldtids forskning, no. 35.] [BM]

1898. Eugenio Turiello. *La tragica storia del dottor Fausto . . . primo traduzione italiana.* Naples: Guiseppe Golia. [With a "breve notizia."] [BM]

1899. K. D. Balmont (?). Трагическая исторія Доктора Фауста. [*Tragical history of Doctor Faustus.*] In Жизнь (*Zhizn*), 7: 178–216; 11–42 Jy, Ag. [Pagination of this volume is eccentric.] [NYPL]

1911. Don José Alcalá-Galiano. *La trágica historia del Doctor Fausto . . . traducción en verso al castellano . . . con un prólogo de D. José de Armas.* Madrid: Victoriano Suarez. [Based on the 1604 text.] [BM]

1912. J. Kasprowicz. *Tragiczne dzeije doktora Fausta.* [Arcydziela europejskiej poezyi dramatycznej. Vol. I.] Lwow: Nakladem Tow. Wydawniczego; Warsaw: I. Wende i Spólka. [NYPL, BM] [Based on Mermaid edition.]

1916. Rózsa Dezsö. "*Doktor Faustus tragikus története.* Fordította Rózsa Dezsö." *Magyar Shakespeare-Tár*, 9: 131–193 (1916). [HCL]

1920. Constantin Castera. *La tragique histoire du docteur Faust*. Paris: Jouve. [BN]

1926. J[erome] Decroos. *Rondom Shakespeare . . . III. Doctor Faustus, treurspel van Christopher Marlowe*. Antwerp: De Sikkel; Santport: C. A. Mees. [See *Jahrb*. (OS) 63 (NS) 4: 217 (1927); *English Studies* (Amsterdam), 17: 25–31; 91–95 (1935).]

1927. Mario Giobbe. *Mefistofele; tragedie in cinque atti, dal primo Faust di W. Goethe e della tragica storia del Dottor Faust di Cristoforo Marlowe, con prefazione di Benedetto Croce*. Milan: Bietti. [Adaptation.] [NYPL]

1928. A. Morsbach and A. Rapp. MS. translation for German Shakespeare Society's Weimar production. [See *Jahrb*. (OS) 64 (NS) 5: 240–242 (1928).] [1604 text with some additions from 1616.]

1935. F.-C. Danchin. *La tragique histoire du Docteur Faust*. Paris: Les Belles Lettres. [Translation of the shorter text.]

Separate Editions

1697. William Mountfort (adapter). *Life and death of Doctor Faustus*. London: E. Whitlock. [BM] [There is also an 1863 reprint in Englische Sprach- und Literaturdenkmale.]

1720. William Mountfort (adapter). In *Six plays*. London: Tonson, II. 373–409. [BM, NYPL] [The various editions of *The Necromancer, or Harlequin Doctor Faustus* are not here included. There is a copy of the 1723 edition in HCL.]

1724. William Mountfort (adapter). *Life and death of Doctor Faustus*. London: W. Mears.

1814. C[harles] W[entworth] Dilke. *Old English plays*. London: Whittingham and Rowland, I. 1–88. [With short introductory notes.]

1816. C[harles] W[entworth] Dilke. *Old plays: being a continuation of Dodsley's collection*. London: Rodwell and Martin, I. 1–88. [Same as preceding with new title page.]

1818. [S. Penley (ed.)?] Reprint of the 1624 edition, with collation of 1616–1624 editions. London: J. Chappell, Jr.

1830. *Old English drama*. London: Thomas White, vol. IV, no. 2. [NYPL]

1839. *The famous tragedy of Doctor John Faustus, by Christopher Marlow [sic]. With an introduction, containing a memoir of Marlow, with a criticism on his Dr. Faustus, and an account of that illustrious magician*. Aberdeen: James Strachan. [National Library of Scotland]

1845. Leigh Hunt. Extract. In *Imagination and fancy*. New York: Wiley and Paterson, p. 102.

1870. John S. Keltie. *Works of the British dramatists*. Edinburgh: Nimmo, pp. 127–139. Reprint of the 1604 edition. Apparently reprinted 1872.

1874. Aug. Riedl. Based on Dyce's text. Berlin: Edwin Staude; Dresden: G. A. Kaufman. Also published at Salzwedel. [Sammlung Englischer Schriftsteller.]

1877. William Wagner. Reprint of 1609 text. New York: Longmans. [London Series of English Classics.] [Review in *Anglia*, 2: 518–526 (1879). *Jahrb.* 13: 306–307 (1878).]

1878. Reprint of 1604 edition, omitting some scenes. London: Cassell. [Cassell's Library of English Literature, III. 116–128.]

1878. A[dolphus] W[illiam] Ward. With *Friar Bacon and Friar Bungay* and elaborate apparatus. Oxford: Clarendon Press. Reissued 1887, 1892, 1901, with changes. [Review of second edition in *Shakespeariana*, 4: 378–379 (1887).]

1880. Henry Morley. *English plays.* London: Cassell, pp. 116–128. [Cassell's Library of English Literature. See 1878 edition.]

1881. English Library, no. 4. Zürich: Rudolphi and Klemm. [English Library, no. 4.] [Contains the ballad of Faustus. Heinemann in his bibliography calls it a "dirty little reprint."]

1883. Henry Morley. *Marlowe's Faustus — Goethe's Faust.* The latter translated from the German by John Anster. [Morley's Universal Library, no. 3.] [1604 text. Same in Excelsior Series, London: Routledge, 1887; World's Classics, Oxford University Press, 1901 and later.]

1886. [William] Mountfort. *Life and death of Dr. Faustus made into a farce.* Introduction by Otto Francke. Heilbronn: Henninger. [Englische Sprach- und Literaturdenkmale.]

1889. Hermann Breymann. 1604 and 1616 texts on opposite pages. Heilbronn: Gebr. Henninger. With apparatus. [Englische Sprach- und Literaturdenkmale.] Listed under "Complete Editions."

1896. Charles Dudley Warner. *Warner's Library.* XXIV. 9722–9724. [See General Section.]

1897. Israel Gollancz. London: Dent; New York: Dutton. [Temple Dramatists.] Later edition 1912.

1903. George Ansel Watrous. *Elizabethan dramatists.* New York: Crowell, pp. 1–64. [Handy Volume Classics.]

1903. John Masefield. Decorations by Charles Ricketts. Edinburgh: Ballantyne Press; London: Hacon & Ricketts; New York: John Lane. [Supplementary to the Vale Shakespeare, edited by T. Sturge Moore, and uniform with it. Printed for the benefit of the Romantic Stage Players, later the Literary Theatre Society. Text apparently from Bullen. Mr. Masefield says: "My own share in the book was mainly proof-correcting."]

1904. As revised by the Elizabethan Stage Society, under the direction of William Poel. London: A. H. Bullen. [NYPL]

1906. Mrs. J. S. Turner [Agnes Ward]. From the quarto of 1616. London: Horace Marshall. [Carmelite Classics.]

1907. F. J. Cox. Westminster: F. Griffiths. [Old English Plays.] [LC, BM]

1907. A[dolphus] W[illiam] Ward. [Introduction by.] *Marlowe's tragical history of Doctor Faustus and Goethe's Faust, Part I.* Translated by John Anster. Oxford University Press, 1907. [World's Classics Series.] [Later editions 1916, 1919, 1923, 1925. Not to be confused with Ward's edition of 1878 and later, *q.v.* See also school edition with notes by C. B. Wheeler, 1915.]

1909. Swan Dramatists. New York: Sturgis & Walton.

1909. Charles William Eliot (ed.). *Harvard Classics.* New York: Collier, XIX. 197–243.

1911. William Allan Neilson. *Chief Elizabethan dramatists.* Boston: Houghton Mifflin; London: Harrap, pp. 80–95.

1912. William Modlen. With introduction and notes. 1604 text. London: Macmillan. Reissued 1932.

1914. J. S. Farmer. Students Facsimile Texts. Amersham, England.

1915. Introduction by Adolphus William Ward and notes by C. B. Wheeler. Oxford University Press.

1916. S. C. Sarcar. Edited with introduction and notes. Calcutta: N. C. Sarcar; Dacca: Sarcar Bros. & Co. [BM]

1918. Little Theatre Classics. Adapted by Samuel A[tkins] Eliot, Jr. Boston: Little Brown, I. 105–176. Text used in production by Sam Hume at the Arts and Crafts Theatre, Detroit, 1918. [NYPL]

1923. William Allan Neilson. With *Tamburlaine.* Boston: Houghton Mifflin. [Riverside Literature Series.]

1924. R. S. Knox. London: Methuen. [Methuen's English Classics.]

1925. Robert Shafer. *From Beowulf to Thomas Hardy.* New York: Doubleday, I. 166–188.

1925. Kôchi Doi. *Marlowe's TRAGICAL HISTORY OF DOCTOR FAUSTUS and GOETHE'S FAUST, Part I.* Translated by Bayard Taylor. Tokyo: Kenkyusha, 1925. [Kenkyusha English Classics, no. 44.] [English text for Japanese students of English, with Japanese introduction and notes by Mr. Doi.]

1926. Felix E. Schelling and Matthew W. Black. *Typical Elizabethan plays.* New York and London: Harper, pp. 117–144.

1927. Albert A. Cock. *Scenes from Tamburlaine . . . together with Doctor Faustus.* London: A. & C. Black. [Socrates Booklets, no. 14.] [BM]

1927. J. B. Hubbell and J. O. Beaty. *Introduction to drama.* New York: Macmillan, pp. 137–162.

1928. Anon. *Columbia University course in literature.* New York: Columbia University Press, XI. 222–224.

1928. H[arry] C[hristian] Schweikert. *Early English plays.* New York: Harcourt Brace, pp. 647–690. [1604 text.]

1928. Robert Metcalf Smith. *Types of philosophic drama.* New York: Prentice-Hall, pp. 169–225. [World Drama Series.]

1928. A. H. Sleight. Cambridge University Press; New York: Macmillan. [English Literature for Schools.]

1928. J. K. Peel. New York: Knopf. [Borzoi Acting Versions of English Dramatists, no. 1.]

1928. H[arold] F[rederick] Rubinstein. *Great English plays.* New York: Harper, pp. 141–170.

1929. John Hampden. London and Edinburgh: T. Nelson & Sons. [Nelson Playbooks, 114.]

1929. E. H. C. Oliphant. *Shakespeare and his fellow dramatists*. New York: Prentice-Hall, pp. 151–182.

1929. P. R. Lieder, R. M. Lovett, R. K. Root. *British Drama*. Boston: Houghton Mifflin, pp. 43–70.

1929. John Robert Moore. *Representative English dramas*. New York: Ginn, pp. 37–91. [JB]

1930. George Raleigh Coffman. *Five significant English plays*. New York: Nelson, pp. 13–63.

1931. Edwin Johnston Howard. *Ten Elizabethan plays*. New York: Nelson, pp. 97–121. [Nelson's English Series.]

1931. Felix E[manuel] Schelling and Matthew W[ilson] Black. *Typical Elizabethan plays*. New York: Harper, pp. 117–143.

1931. Robert Shafer. *From Beowulf to Thomas Hardy*. New York: Doubleday, pp. 150–170.

1932. With engravings by Blair Hughes-Stanton. London: Golden Hours Press.

1932. *Eight famous Elizabethan plays*. New York: Modern Library, pp. 1–50.

1932. Harold Osborne. London: University Tutorial Press. [University Tutorial Series.] [BM]

1933. C[harles] F[rederick] Tucker Brooke and N. Burton Paradise. *English drama, 1580–1642*. Boston: D. C. Heath, pp. 167–192.

1933. B. H. Clark. *World drama*. New York: Appleton, pp. 375–398.

1933. Richard Ferrar Patterson. Extracts. In *Six centuries of English literature*. London: Blackie, II. 38–40.

1933. Hazelton Spencer. *Elizabethan plays*. Boston: Little Brown, pp. 37–63.

1933. Esther Cloudman Dunn. *Eight famous Elizabethan plays*. New York: Modern Library, pp. 2–50.

1934. Charles Reed Baskervill, Virgil B. Heltzel, and Arthur N. Nethered. *Elizabethan and Stuart plays*. New York: Holt, pp. 349–374.

1935. Rosalind Vallance. *Little plays from English drama*. London: Nelson, pp. 185–215. [Abridged and arranged for acting.]

1935. Edd Winfield Parks and R. C. Beatty. *English drama*. New York: Norton; Toronto: McLeod, pp. 378–419.

1936. George Benjamin Woods, Homer A. Watt, and George Kumber Anderson. *Literature of England*. Chicago: Scott, I. 446–471.

1940. Helen Louise Cohen [Stockwell]. *Milestones of the drama*. New York: Harcourt Brace, pp. 109–170.

Books and Articles

Anon. "Madame de Staël Holstein's L'Allemagne." *Quarterly Review*, 10: 355–409 Ja 1814. [Some mention of Marlowe and Goethe on p. 390.]

Anon. "Shelley's posthumous poems." *Edinburgh Review*, 40: 494–514 Jy 1824. [Casual reference only.]

Anon. "Ueber den Faust von Marlowe." *Jahrbuecher f. Drama, Dramaturgie, und Theatre*. [Leipzig], 1: 145–152 (1837).

Anon. "The two Fausts." *United States and Democratic Review*, 13: 315–323 S 1843.

Anon. "Zur litteratur der Faustsage." *Allgemeine Zeitung* [Augsburg], no. 224, *Beilage*, pp. 1786–1788; no. 225, *Beilage*, pp. 1795–1796 (1847). [CUL]

Anon. "Dutch version of Dr. Faustus." N&Q, 1st ser. 1: 169, 190, 12, 19 Ja 1850.

Anon. "German popular legend of Doctor Faustus." *Atlantic Monthly*, 2: 551–566 O 1859.

Anon. "Faustus, Bishop of Riez." N&Q, 3rd ser. 2: 169, 239, 30 Ag 20 S 1862.

Anon. "Faust on the stage." *All the Year Round*, (OS) 43 (NS) 23: 30–33, 28 Je 1879. [Comparison of Marlowe and Goethe.]

Anon. "Shakespeare societies." *Shakespeariana*, 3: 575 (1886).

Anon. "Clifton Shakespeare-Society." *See* Chap. X. [Trivial.]

Anon. "Marlowe's Faustus." *Temple Bar* [London], 98: 515–522 Ap 1893.

Anon. "Thurmond's Dr. Faustus." *Theater*, 25: 28–34, 1 Ja 1895.

Anon. "Doctor Faustus." *Saturday Review* [London], 82: 36–37, 11 Jy 1896.

Anon. "Marlowe on the stage." *Boston Evening Transcript*, 19 Mr 1910.

Anon. Notice of the Cambridge [England] production of *Doctor Faustus*. [London] *Observer*, 13 My 1923.

Anon. "Tragical history of Doctor Faustus." *London Mercury*, 13: 201–202 D 1925.

Anon. "Tavistock Little Theatre 'Dr. Faustus.'" [London] *Times*, 13 N 1937, p. 10c. [Also 15 N, p. 12d, first and second editions only.]

"Aeron." "The devil and the interlude of Dr. Faustus." N&Q, 2nd ser. 5: 295, 10 Ap 1858.

Agard, Arthur E. "Poetic personification of evil." *Poet Lore*, (OS) 9 (NS) 1: 206–216 Ap 1897.

Albers, J. H. "On Marlowe's 'Tragical history of Doctor Faustus.'" *Jahrb. f. romanische und englische Sprache und Literatur*, 15: 369–393 (1876). [Cf. Breymann, Hermann.]

Ashton, John. *Chap-books of the eighteenth century*. London: Chatto and Windus, 1882, pp. 38–52. [Reprint of the English Faust Book.]

Axon, William E. "Marlowe and Feuillet." N&Q, 7th ser. 11: 286, 11 Ap 1891.

Baer, Joseph & Co. *Faust-Bibliothek*. Frankfurt a. M.: Joseph Baer & Co., 1904, pp. 13–14. [HCL]

Baker, H. T. "On a passage in Marlowe's 'Faustus.'" MLN, 21: 86–87 Mr 1906. [See *Jahrb.* 43: 296 (1907).]

Balmont, K. D. «Нѣсколко словъ о типѣ Фауста.» ["A few words on the Faust type."] Русское Слово [*Russkoe Slovo*], 7: 171–177 Jy 1899. [NYPL]

Bang, W. "Bemerkungen zu *Faustus*." *Jahrb.* 39: 212–221 (1903).

Bang, W. "Zur bühne Shakespeares." *Jahrb.* 40: 223–225, 374 (1904). [See Keller, Wolfgang.]

Barbé, L. "Marlowe's 'Faustus.'" N&Q, 5th ser. 7: 388, 19 My 1877. Replies, pp. 493–494, and 8: 54–55, 21 Jy 1877.

Bazy, Jean-Pierre-Antoine. *Études histoiriques, littéraires et philosophiques sur C. Marlowe et Goethe.* Paris: Garnier Frères, 1850. [BN]

Beatty, Mary Annette (Powell). *Marlowe's and Goethe's Faust: a comparison.* Ohio B.S. Thesis, 1912. [MS.]

Begley, Walter. "Dr. Faustus." *Baconiana*, 3rd ser. 6: 145–155 Jy 1908.

Benezé [No first name given]. "Marlowes Faust also bühnenproblem." *Hamburger Nachrichten*, no. 484, 14 O 1911. [Reference to production by Lessing-Gesellschaft, 23 O 1911.]

Bianquis, Geneviève. *Faust à travers quatre siècles.* Paris: F. Droz, 1935, pp. 53–66. [Originally *leçons publiques* at the University of Dijon, 1932–1933.] [NYPL]

Bittner, Konrad. *Beiträge zur geschichte des volksschauspieles vom Doctor Faust.* Reichenberg: F. Kraus, 1922. [Prager Deutsche Studien, 27 Heft.] [NYU]

Bleibtreu, K. "Marlowe, Crabbe und Lenz." Wiener Rundschau, 4: 429–432, 15 D 1900. [Princeton]

Bøgholm, N. "Marlowe og Dr. Faustus." *Tilskueren*, 53: 427–434 Je 1936. [NYPL]

Borgmann, Albert Stephens. *Life and death of William Mountfort.* Cambridge: Harvard University Press, 1935, pp. 183–190. [Harvard Studies in English, XV.]

Boyd, James. *Goethe's knowledge of English literature.* Oxford University Press, 1933. [Oxford Studies in Modern Languages and Literature.]

Boyer, Charles Valentine. *Villain as hero in Elizabethan tragedy.* London: Routledge; New York: Dutton, 1914, pp. 40–59. [Originally a Princeton dissertation.]

Braga, Theophilo. "Leuda do Doutor Fausto." In *Estudos da Edade Media.* Porto: Ernesto Chardron, 1870, pp. 89–114. [Livraria Internacional.]

Breymann, Hermann. "Marlowe's Dr. Faustus und Herr J. H. Albers." ES, 5: 56–66 (1881). [Reply to Albers, *q.v.*]

Breymann, Hermann. "Zu L. Proescholdt's collation von Marlowe's Doctor Faustus." *Anglia*, 4: 288–291 (1881). [Discussion of Proescholdt's article, *q.v.*]

Breymann, Hermann. Review of Ward's edition [*q.v.*], ES, 12: 443–450 Ja 1889.

Brie, Friedrich. "Dissertations- und programmschau. I. Vorläufer und zeitgenossen." *Jahrb.* 46: 184–190 (1910). [On De Vries, Schröder, and Venzlaff, *qq.v.*]

Brie, Friedrich. "Roman und drama in zeitalter Shakespeares." *Jahrb.* 48: 125–151 (1912). [Especially pp. 142, 146–147.]

Briggs, W[illiam] D[insmore]. "Marlowe's Faustus." PQ, 12: 17–23 Ja 1933.

Brinton, G. E. *Tragedy in the time of Shakespeare, or Marlowe and his Faustus.* Franklin and Marshall Ph.B. Thesis, 1913. [MS.]

Brooke, C[harles] F[rederick] Tucker. "Notes on Marlowe's Doctor Faustus." PQ, 12: 17–23 Ja 1933.

Brooks, Edward. Report of a Browning Society paper on "Relation of music and science in Marlowe's 'Faustus,' Goethe's 'Faust,' and Browning's 'Fust and his friends.'" *Poet Lore*, 4: 109–111 (1892).

Brown, Beatrice Daw (Mrs. Carleton Brown). "Marlowe, Faustus, and Simon Magus," PMLA, 54: 82–121 (1939).

Brown, Esther. *Comparison of Marlowe's tragical history of Doctor Faustus and Byron's Manfred.* Washington M.A. Thesis, 1932. [MS.]

Brown, I. "Tragical history of Doctor Faustus." *Saturday Review* [London], 140: 501–502, 31 O 1925.

Bruinier, J. W. "Das volksschauspiel von Faust." *Zeitschrift f. deutsche Philologie*, 29: 180–195, 345–372 (1897); 30: 325–359 (1898); 31: 60–69, 194–231 (1899).

Budik, P. A. "Zur sage vom Dr. Faust." *Serapeum*, 8: 175 (1847).

Buehner, Valentin. *Marlowe's Doctor Faustus: sein verhältnis zum volksbuch von 1587 und zu Goethe's Faust.* Southern California M.A. Thesis, 1911. [MS.]

Bullen, A. H. "Miscellanea." *Athenaeum*, no. 2946: 484, 12 Ap 1884.

Cain, H. E. "Marlowe's French crowns." MP, 32: 11–31 Ag 1934. [See *Jahrb.* (OS) 71 (NS) 12: 141 (1935).]

Cardell, Richard Albert. *Henry Arthur Jones and the modern drama.* New York: Long and Smith, 1932. [Late traces of Marlowe's influence.]

Careil, Foucher de. "Les trois Faust." *Revue politique et parlementaire*, 2nd ser. 6: 1207–1211, 16 Je 1877.

Carner, Robert J[ordan]. *Comparative study of Marlowe's "Doctor Faustus" and Calderón's "El mágico prodigioso."* Virginia M.A. Thesis, 1924. [MS.]

Carpenter, W. Boyd. *Religious spirit in the poets.* New York: Crowell, 1901, pp. 81–102. Reprinted from "Religious element in the poets." [London] *Sunday Magazine*, (NS) 29: 442–447 (1900).

Casartelli, L. C. "Three Fausts." *Dublin Review*, 1st ser. 93: 2nd ser. 41: 3rd ser. 10: 245–259 O 1883.

Castle, Eduard. "Das erste zeugnis f. d. bekanntschaft mit Marlowes 'Dr. Faustus' in Deutschland." *Anzeiger* of *Zeitschrift f. deutsches Altertum u. deutsche Litteratur*, 35: 300–302, 4 D 1911. [See *Jahrb.* 49: 199 (1913).]

Castle, Eduard. "Das angeblich älteste Lateinische Faust-drama — eine mystification." *Theater der Welt*, 1: 51–56 Ja 1937. [NYPL]

"Chapin." "Tragical history of Doctor Faustus." *Stanford Daily* [Calif.], 7 My 1934. [Criticism of local production.]

Chew, Samuel C., Jr. *Dramas of Lord Byron.* Göttingen: Vandenhoef & Ruprecht; Baltimore: Johns Hopkins Press, 1915. [Hesperia. Ergänzungsreihe 3. Heft.] [*Manfred* shows Goethe's but not Marlowe's influence.]

Chudoba, F[rantisek?]. "Goethe a Christopher Marlowe." *Goethuv Sbornik*, 1932, pp. 364–370.

Clement I [Pope]. *Clementine homilies.* Edinburgh: T. & T. Clark, 1870. [Ante-Nicene Christian Library, XVII, pt. I.]

Cohen, Helen Louise. *See* Stockwell, Helen Louise Cohen.

Cohn, Albert. *See* Chap. XI.

Cook, Albert S. "Marlowe, *Doctor Faustus* 13. 106–9." MLN, 21: 145–147 (1906); 24: 166–167 (1909). [See *Jahrb.* 43: 296–297 (1907); 46: 201 (1910).]

Cook, Albert S. "Marlowe, *Faustus* 13. 91–92." MLN, 22: 35–37 (1907).

Courtney, W. L. "Faustus." *Fortnightly Review*, 84: 678–691 O 1905.

Cunningham, R[ichard] H[enry]. *Amusing prose chap-books.* London: Hamilton Adams & Co., 1889, pp. 286–289.

Cushman, Lysander William. *Die figuren des Teufels und des Vice in dem ersten englischen drama bis auf Shakespeare.* Göttingen Diss. 1900. Göttingen: Dieterich, 1900.

Cushman, Lysander William. *The Devil and the Vice in the English dramatic literature before Shakespeare.* Halle: Niemeyer, 1900. [*Studien z. englischen Philologie*, Heft VI.]

Danchin, F.-C. "Du nouveau sur Shakespeare." *Revue anglo-américaine*, 9: 224–232 F 1932.

Danchin, F.-C. "La date du *Doctor Faustus*." *Revue anglo-américaine*, 10: 515–516 Ag 1933.

Daniel, P. A. "Restoration of Marlowe's text." *Athenaeum*, no. 2555: 496, 14 O 1876.

Dawson, George. *Shakespeare and other lectures.* London: Kegan Paul, 1888, pp. 342–392. [HCL]

Dean, Ardys Thelo. *Magic in Elizabethan drama.* Stanford M.A. Thesis, 1928. [MS.]

Deetjen, Werner. "Goethe und Tiecks elisabethanische studien." *Jahrb.* (OSO) 65 (NS) 6: 175–183 (1929). [How Goethe may have become acquainted with Marlowe's work.]

Delius, Theodor. *Marlowe's Faustus und seine quellen.* Göttingen Diss. 1881. Bielefeld: Velhagen und Klasing, 1881.

De Vries, Harm R[everts] O[tten]. *Die überlieferung von Marlowe's Doctor Faustus.* Göttingen Diss. 1909. Halle: Ehrhardt Karras, 1909. [Expanded version in *Studien z. englischen Philologie*, Band 35. Halle: Max Niemeyer, 1909.]

Dibelius, Wilhelm. Reviews of Venzlaff, Schröder, and De Vries [*qq.v.*], *Archiv*, 126: 284–285 (1911).

Diebler, Arthur. "Faust- und Wagnerpantomimen in England." *Anglia*, 7: 341–354 (1884).

DuBois, Hamilton Graham. *Influence of the moralities and mysteries on Marlowe's Doctor Faustus.* Columbia M.A. Thesis, 1924. [MS.]

Düntzer, H. "Die sage von Doctor Johannes Faust." *Schatzgraber in d. literarischen u. bildlichen selteheiten d. mittelalters*, 1: 229–239 (1846). Reprinted in *Das Kloster*, 17: 229–238 (1847).

Düntzer, H. "Zu Marlowe's Faust." *Anglia*, 1: 44–54 (1877).

Edmonds, H[enry] M. "Marlowe's Doctor Faustus." *Tennessee University Magazine*, 12: 182–185 Mr 1899. [JB]

Edwards, Henry Sutherland. *The Faust legend: its origin and development.* London: Remington & Co., 1886. Also in *Macmillan's Magazine,* 34: 268–275 Jy 1876; *Eclectic Magazine,* 87: 351–358 S 1876.

Edwards, Henry Sutherland. *Lyrical drama.* London: W. H. Allen and Co., 1881.

Ellinger, Geax. "Zu den quellen des Faustbuches von 1557." *Zeitschrift f. vergleichende Litteraturgeschichte,* 2nd ser. 1: 156–181 (1887).

Eliot, T[homas] S[tearns]. *Shakespeare and the stoicism of Seneca.* Oxford University Press for the Shakespeare Association, 1927, pp. 10–11.

Elliott, Alvin Clarence. *Comparison of poems of temptation limited to Job, Doctor Faustus, Faust, Paradise Lost, and the Golden Legend.* Chicago M.A. Thesis, 1915. [MS.]

Engel, Carl. *Volksschauspiel Doctor Johann Faust.* Oldenburg: Schulzeschen Buchhandlung, 1874. [NYPL]

Engel, Karl. *Die zusammenstellung der Faust-schriften vom 16. jahrhundert bis mitte 1884.* Oldenburg: A. Schwarz, 1885. [Bibliotheca Faustiana.]

Errante, Vincenzo. *Il mito di Faust.* Bologna: N. Zanchelli, 1924, pp. 99–154. [NYPL]

"E. Tr." "Christopher Marlowe's: 'Doctor Faustus.'" *Frankfurter Zeitung,* no. 350: 1–2, 18 D 1903. [LC, JB]

Evans, M. B. "Notes on Faust and Faustus." JEGP, 31: 258–278 Ap 1932.

Faligan, Ernest. *Histoire de le légende de Faust.* Paris: Hachette, 1888. [See also General Section.]

Filmore, Lewis. *Faust. A tragedy.* London: W. Smith, 1846. [Smith's Standard Library.] [Translation of Goethe's play with an account of Marlowe's and excerpts from it, together with an account of Lessing's proposed play on the same theme.]

Fischer, Kuno. *Goethes 'Faust' nach seiner entstehung, idee, und composition.* Stuttgart: Cotta, 1887.

Fischer, Kuno. *Goethe's Faust.* Translated by Harry Riggs Wolcott. Manchester, Iowa: H. R. Wolcott, 1895, pp. 160–176. [HCL]

Flanagan, Hallie. "Hell hath no limits: Doctor Faustus at Malvern." *Theatre Arts Monthly,* 18: 871–873 N 1934.

Flasdieck, Hermann M. "Zur datierung von Marlowes Faust." ES, 64: 320–351 D 1929; 65: 1–25 F 1930. [See *Jahrb.* (OS) 66 (NS) 7: 231 (1930).]

Fleay, F[rederick] G[ard]. *Shakespeare Manual.* London: Macmillan, 1876, pp. 175–186.

Fluegel, E. "The irreverent Dr. Faustus." *Anglia,* 18: 332–334 [1896].

Förster, M. "Marlowe's 'Faustus' and its influence in Germany." *Jahrb.* 48: 344–345 (1912).

Francke, Kuno. *Lectures on the Harvard classics.* New York: Collier, 1914, pp. 398–401.

Francke, Otto. "Weimar: . . . Marlowes 'Faust.'" *Jahrb.* (OS) 64 (NS) 5: 240–242 (1928).

Fränkel, Ludwig. "Zu Doktor Fausts fortleben in England." *Goethe Jahrb.* 12: 256–258 (1891).

Fränkel, Ludwig. "Zu 'Dr. Faust in England.'" *Goethe Jahrb.* 14: 294–295 (1893).

Friswell, J. Hain. *Varia: readings from rare books.* London: S. Lowe, Son, and Marston, 1866, pp. 79–104.

Frohberg, George. "Fortleben des elisabethanischen dramas im zeitalter der Restauration." *Jahrb.* (OS) 69 (NS) 10: 72 (1933).

Gabriel, Gilbert W. "Legend of Dr. Faust." *Mentor,* 17: 1–13 F 1929.

Genevieve, Sister Mary, O.S.U. "Tragical history of Doctor Faustus." *Catholic Educational Review,* 32: 34–36 Ja 1934.

Graf, Arturo. "Il *Fausto* di Cristoforo Marlowe." In *Studii drammatici.* Torino: Ermanno Loescher, 1878, pp. 205–248. [CUL]

Grant, Charles. "The two Fausts." *Contemporary Review,* 40: 1–24 Jy 1881.

Greg, W[alter] W[ilson]. "Some notes on the Stationers' Registers." *Library,* 7: 376–386 (1927). [See especially p. 386.]

Greg, W[alter] W[ilson]. *Records of the court of the Stationers' Company.* London: Bibliographical Society, 1930, pp. lxx, lxxvii, 44. [Circumstances of publication.]

Grimm, Herman. "Die entstehung des volksbuches vom Dr. Faust." *Preussische Jahrbuecher,* 47: 445–465 My 1881.

Hart, H. C. "Robert Greene's prose works." N&Q, 10th ser. 5: 484–487, 23 Je 1906; 504–506, 30 Je 1906.

Hau, G. B. L. Article "Simon Magus" in *Encyclopedia of Religion and Ethics,* vol. XI.

Hauffen, Adolf. "Zur Faustsage." *Euphorion,* 5: 468–469 (1898).

Hayward, Abraham. *Faust: a dramatic poem by Goethe.* London: Hutchinson and others, 1833. Other editions, 1834, 1838, 1845, 1851, 1866, 1892, 1908. [References to Marlowe.]

Heinemann, William. *Essay toward a bibliography of Marlowe's "Tragical history of Dr. Faustus."* London: Elliot Stock; New York: Scribner and Welford, 1884. Also in *Bibliographer,* 6: 14–16 Je 1884; 40–46 Jy 1884. [Earlier instalment deals with Goethe also. Additions and corrections in (New York) *Nation,* 39: 312, 9 O 1884.]

Heller, Otto. *Faust and Faustus, a study of Goethe's relation to Marlowe.* Washington University Studies [NS]. Language and Literature, no. 2 (1931). [Reviewed by Mario Praz, *English Studies* (Amsterdam), 14: 83–88 Ap 1934; note by M. B. Evans in JEGP, 32: 81–82 Ja 1933. See also Walz, J. A., below. Heller's is the standard study of the subject.]

Herford, C[harles] H[arold]. *Studies in the literary relations of England and Germany in the sixteenth century.* Cambridge University Press, 1886.

Herrington, H[untly] W[hately]. "Witchcraft and magic in the Elizabethan drama." *Journal of American Folk Lore,* 32: 447–485 O-D 1919.

Herzfeld, Georg. "Zu Marlowe's 'Doctor Faustus.'" *Jahrb.* 41: 206–207 (1905). [Real devil on stage.]

H. E. W. Report on the production by Lessing-Gesellschaft, 23 O 1911.

Hamburger Nachrichten, no. 500, 24 O 1911. [Bibliothek der Hansestadt Hamburg.]

Holloway, Elma. *Satan in English literature.* Southern California M.A. Thesis, 1917. [MS.]

Holthausen, F. "Zur textkritik Marlowe's." *Beiblatt zur Anglia*, 21: 82–83 (1910).

Hooft, B. H. van't. *Das Holländische volksbuch vom Doktor Faust.* Haag: Martinus Nijhoff, 1926, pp. 1–19. [NYPL]

Horne, R. H. "Selling the soul." *Contemporary Review*, 33: 310–321 S 1878. [Special reference to Calderón.]

Housel, Alta Mae. *Marlowe's Doctor Faustus and its German sources.* Columbia M.A. Thesis, 1904. [MS.]

Housse, Ludwig. *Die Faustsage und der historische Faust. Eine untersuchung und beleuchtung nach positiv-Christlichen principien.* Luxemburg: Brück, 1862. [BPL, HCL, Michigan, Cleveland Public Library]

Hughes, Walter. "Early development of the Faust legend." *Papers of the Manchester Literary Club (Manchester Quarterly)*, 1: 101–124 (1882).

Hume, Sam. Setting for *Faustus. Theatre Arts Magazine*, 3: 109 Ap 1919.

Hurley, Jesse Raymond. *Textual difficulties in the 1604 quarto of Marlowe's Doctor Faustus.* Illinois B.A. Thesis, 1929. [MS.]

Ingram, John H. "Marlowe and his Doctor Faustus." *Rose, Shamrock and Thistle Magazine*, 1865.

Isaacs, Edith J. R. "Young race in its morning." *Theatre Arts Monthly*, 21: 184–185 My 1937.

J. G. R. In "Minor correspondence." *Gentleman's Magazine*, (OS) 188 (NS) 34: 234 S 1850.

Jones, Charles P. "Ordinary devils, special sun in Faustus." New Orleans *Times-Picayune*, 9 Je 1937, p. 4.

Jones, Florence. *Three representatives of evil as seen in Paradise Lost, Cain and Dr. Faustus.* Oregon M.A. Thesis, 1931. [MS.]

Jones, H[enry] A[rthur]. "Religion and the stage." *Nineteenth Century*, 17: 154–167 Ja 1885. [Especially pp. 162–163. Partial reprint in *Shakespeariana*, 2: 76–83 (1885).] [NYPL]

Keller, Wolfgang. "Nochmale zur bühne Shakespeares." *Jahrb.* 40: 225–227 (1904).

Kelman, John. "Two Fausts." In *Among famous books.* London: Hodder and Stoughton, 1912, pp. 63–88.

Kiesewetter, Karl. *Faust in der geschichte und tradition.* Leipzig: A. Spohr, 1893; Berlin: H. Barsdorf, 1921.

Kluge, Friedrich. "Ein zeugnis des 16. jahrhunderts über Dr. Faustus." *Zeitschrift f. vergleichende Litteraturgeschichte*, 6: 479–480 (1893).

Knortz, Karl. "Christopher Marlowe und seine Faustdichtung." In *Hamlet und Faust.* Zürich: Verlags-Magazin, 1888, pp. 30–55.

Koch, Max. "Zerstreute bemerkungen zu Marlowe's Faust." *Jahrb.* 21: 211–226 (1886).

Kocher, Paul H[arold]. "English *Faust Book* and the date of Marlowe's *Faustus.*" MLN, 55: 95–101 F 1940.

Koeppel, E. *See* General Section.

Kühne, August (ed.). *Historia von D. Johann Fausten dem weitbeschreiten zauberer und schwarzkunstler.* Frankfurt a.M. 1587. Reprinted with title: *Das alteste Faustbuch,* Zerbet: E. Lucce, 1868. [Original MS. in National Library, Vienna, closely related to this work.]

Kutcher, Joseph. *Character of Faust and Mephistopheles in the literature before Goethe.* New York M.A. Thesis, 1932. [MS.]

Law, Robert Adger. "Two parallels to Greene and Lodge's *Looking-Glass.*" MLN, 26: 146–148 (1911). See also *Jahrb.* 48: 216 (1912). [Influence of *Tamburlaine* and *Doctor Faustus.*]

Law, Robert Adger. "*A Looking glasse* and the Scriptures." *Studies in English* [University of Texas], 1939, pp. 31–47. [Influence of *Doctor Faustus,* pp. 43–47.]

Leutbecher, J. *Ueber den Faust von Goethe.* Nürnberg: Renner, 1838, pp. 135–140.

Leutbecher, J. "Die älteste dramatische bearbeitung der Faust-sage, oder der Marionetten-Faust." *Das Kloster,* 5: 718–728 (1847).

Leitner, Ph. von. "Mitteilungen über den Faust. 2) Marlowe's Faust." *Jahrbücher für Drama, Dramaturgie, und Theater,* 1: 145–152 (1837).

Leitner, Ph. von. "Ueber den Faust von Marlowe; Faust als puppenspiel und verwandtes." *Das Kloster,* 5: 698–717 (1847).

Lewes, George Henry. *Life and works of Goethe.* Boston: Ticknor and Fields, 1856; London: Dent, 1916.

Lewes, Louis. *Shakespeares frauengestalten.* Stuttgart: Krabbe, 1893. Translated as *Women of Shakespeare.* London: Hodder, 1894, pp. 44–50.

Logemann, Henri. *Faustus notes. A supplement to the commentaries on Marlowe's "Tragicall history of D. Faustus."* Ghent: H. Engelcke, 1898. [See also ES, 28: 435–437 (1900); *Jahrb.* 35: 342–343 (1899).]

Logemann, Henri. *English Faust-book of 1592.* Ghent: H. Engelcke; Amsterdam: Gebr. Schröder, 1900. [See *Jahrb.* 38: 285 (1902).]

MacCarthy, D. "Tragical history of Doctor Faustus." *New Statesman,* 26: 78–79, 31 O 1925.

MacDowall, H. C. "Faust of the marionettes." *Macmillan's Magazine,* 83: 198–203 Ja 1901.

Machule, P. "Bemerkungen zu Marlowes Faustus." *Archiv,* 86: 227–258 (1886).

MacKay, Charles. *New light on some obscure words and phrases in the works of Shakspeare and his contemporaries.* London: Reeves and Turner, 1884. [Comment on the name of Mephistopheles.]

M[aitland], H[enry]. "Marlowe's tragical history of the life and death of Doctor Faustus." *Blackwood's,* 1: 388–394 Jy 1817.

Malcolm, E. Hiscock. "Dr. Faustus: musical, dramatic, literary." *Sharpe's London Magazine,* (OS) 45 (NS) 30: 155–157 (1867).

Marmier, X[avier]. "Chronique de Faust." *Revue de Paris,* 5: 34–38 (1834).

Marmier, X[avier]. *Études sur Goethe*. Paris and Strasbourg: Levrault, 1935, pp. 76n, 105, 134–141. [University of Cincinnati.]

Marquardsen, A[nna]. *See* Chap. V.

Mary Genevieve, Sister. "Tragical history of Doctor Faustus." *Catholic Educational Review*, 32: 34–36 (1934). [NYPL]

Meek, H. C. *Johann Faust, the man and the myth*. Oxford University Press, 1930. [Reviewed in RES, 7: 227 (1931); TLS, 29: 331, 17 Ap 1930.]

Meissner, Johannes. *Die englischen commoedianten zur zeit Shakespeares in Oesterreich*. Vienna: Karl Konegan, 1884. [Beiträge z. Geschichte d. deutschen Lit. u. d. geistigen Lebens in Oesterreich. IV.]

Mengel, Arthur Robert. *Magic in Elizabethan drama to 1600*. Columbia M.A. Thesis, 1919. [MS.]

Merk, Charles. "Faust legend." *Academy*, 46: 12–13, 7 Jy 1894.

Mertching, R. A. G. *Some points of similarity and difference between Marlowe's Doctor Faustus and the Geiselbrecht, Ulm, Weimar, Simrock, and Engel German puppet-plays*. New York M.A. Thesis, 1918. [MS.]

Meyerstein, E. W. H. "Was this the face?" TLS, 27: 221, 22 Mr 1928.

Micou, R. D. "Faust dramas of Christopher Marlowe and Goethe." *University of Virginia Magazine*, 64: 393–402 Mr 1904.

Milchsack, Gustav (ed.). *Historia D. Johannis Fausti des zauberers nach der Wolfenbüttler handschrift nebst dem nachweis eines teils ihrer quellen*. Wolfenbüttel: Julius Zwissler, 1892. [University of Michigan.]

Modlen, W[illiam]. *Notes for the use of schools on Marlowe's Faustus*. Aberystwyth: Galloway, 1910.

More, Robert P. *See* Palmer, Philip M.

Morimoto, C. *On Marlowe and his Dr. Faustus in comparison with Goethe's Faust*. Tokyo Graduation Thesis, 1927. [MS.]

Morris, Max. *Goethe-studien*. Berlin: C. Skopnik, 1902, pp. 97–113.

Moulton, Richard G[reen]. *World literature and its place in general culture*. New York: Macmillan, 1911, pp. 220–294.

Münch, W. "Die innere stellung Marlowes zum volksbuch von Faust." No. 7, pp. 108–138 in *Festschrift zur begrüssung der XXXIV versammlung deutscher philologen und schulmänner zu Trier*. Trier: Lintz, 1879. [BM]

Neubert, Franz. *Vom Doctor Faustus zu Goethes Faust*. Leipzig: J. J. Weber, 1932. [NYPL]

Nevinson, H[enry] W. "Legend of Faust." In *Essays in freedom*. London: Duckworth, 1911, pp. 260–265.

Nichols, Dorothy. *"Production of Doctor Faustus."* Palo Alto [Calif.] *Times*, 7 My 1934. [JB]

Norman, Charles. "Faustus." *Theatre Arts Magazine*, 14: 309–312 Ap 1930.

Notter, Friedrich. "Zur Faustsage und der Faustliteratur." *Monatsblätter zur Ergänzung der Allgemeine Zeitung* [Augsburg], no volume number, pp. 133–145, 177–188, 589–610 (1847). [Partial file in CUL, including last instalment which deals with Marlowe.]

Ogborn, Jane. *Elizabethan production of Marlowe's* Doctor Faustus. Yale M.F.A. Thesis, 1932. [MS.]

Pagel, L. [of Liverpool]. *Doctor Faustus of the popular legend, Marlowe, the puppet-play, Goethe, and Lenau, treated historically and critically.* Two parts. Liverpool? Privately printed? 1883. [BM]

Palmer, Philip Mason, and More, Robert Pattison. *Sources of the Faust tradition from Simon Magus to Lessing.* Oxford University Press, 1936.

Pantin, W. E. P. "Sources of Marlowe's 'Dr. Faustus.'" *Academy,* 31: 449, 25 Je 1887. [See *Shakespeariana,* 4: 434 (1887).]

Paradise, N. Burton. *Thomas Lodge and his friends.* New Haven: Yale University Press, 1931. [Influence of *Faustus.*]

Perkinson, Richard H. "A restoration 'improvement' of Doctor Faustus." *Journal of English Literary History,* 1: 305–324 D 1934.

Peter, Franz. *Literatur der Faustsage bis ende des jahres 1850.* Leipzig: Voigt, 1851, nos. 135–136; *Zusätze,* 1857.

Peters, Sylvester G. *Faust story in Marlowe's Dr. Faustus and Byron's Manfred: a comparison of two plays.* Marquette M.A. Thesis, 1932. [MS.]

Petersen, Ottomar. "Beiträge zu Marlowes Doctor Faustus." *Zeitschrift für französischen und englischen Unterricht,* 13: 443–451 (1914).

Petsch, Robert. "Naogeorgus und Marlowe." ES, 39: 153–157 (1908). [See *Jahrb.* 45: 285 (1909).]

Petsch, Robert. "Der historische Doctor Faust." *Germanisch-romanische Monatsschrift,* 2: 99–115 (1910).

Petsch, Robert. "Die entstehung des volksbuches vom Doktor Faust." *Germanisch-romanische Monatsschrift,* 3: 207–224 (1911).

P. H. "Marlowe dramatic society" [production of *Doctor Faustus.*] *English Review,* 35: 342–344 O 1922.

Phillips, Stephen. "Diabolic in poetry." *Poetry Review,* 5: 143–147 O 1914. [Milton and Lucifer.]

Pichot, Amédée. "Trois Faust." *Revue de Paris,* 48: 237–253 Mr 1833.

Potter, Robert Russell. *Some aspects of the supernatural in English comedy from the origins to 1642.* North Carolina Diss. 1926. [MS.] Abstracted in *University of North Carolina Record,* Graduate School Series, 14: 42–45 (1926).

Price, Lawrence Marsden. *English⟩ German literary influences: bibliography and survey.* Berkeley: University of California, 1919–1920. [Publications in Modern Philology, no. 9.]

Proescholdt, Ludwig. "Eine collation der ältesten quarto von Marlowes Dr. Faustus." *Anglia,* 3: 88–96 (1880). [Criticism listed under Breymann, Hermann, *q.v.*]

Quekett, Arthur E. "Doubtful line of Marlowe's." N&Q, 6th ser. 1: 191, 6 Mr 1880. [Discussion by O. W. Tancock, p. 306 of this volume. See below under Tancock, O. W.]

Raleigh, Sir Walter. *Historie of the world.* London, 1614. [See Bk. I, Chap. XI: "Of the divers kinds of unlawful magic."]

Rascoe, Burton. *Titans of literature.* London and New York: Putnam, 1932. [Reviewed in *New York Times,* 27 N 1932, p. 2.]

Rascoe, Burton. *Bookman's day book.* New York: Liveright, 1929.

Reichlin-Meldegg, Karl Alex. von. "Die deutschen volksbücher von Johann Faust . . . und Christoph Wagner." *Schatzgräber in d. Lit. u. Bildl. Seltenheiten*, 6–8 (1848), I. 229–260. [NYPL]

Rhodes, R. C. "Tragical history of Doctor Faustus." [London] *Spectator*, 152: 270, 23 F 1934.

Richards, Alfred E. "Marlowe, *Faustus*, scene 14." MLN, 22: 126–127 (1907).

Richards, Alfred E. "Some *Faustus* notes." MLN, 22: 39–41 (1907). [See *Jahrb*. 43: 296 (1907); 44: 281–282 (1908). Faust known in England in 1572.]

Richards, Alfred E. *Studies in English Faust literature. I. The English Wagner book.* Berlin: Emil Felber, 1907. [Literarhistorische Forschungen, 35.]

Richards, Alfred E. "The English Wagner book of 1594." PMLA, 24: 32–39 (1909). [See *Jahrb*. 46: 201–202 (1910).]

Richardson, Ernest Cushing. "Faust and the Clementine Recognitions." *Papers of the American Society of Church History*, 6: 133–145 (1894). [NYPL]

Ristelhuber, P. *Faust dans l'histoire et dans la légende.* Paris: Didier et Cie., 1863, pp. 184–194.

Rodd, F. S. *Comparison between Dr. Faustus of Marlowe and Faust of Goethe.* Tulane M.A. Thesis, 1901. [MS.]

Roethe, Gustav. "Die Entstehung des 'Urfaust.'" *Sitzungsberichte d. preussischen Akademie d. Wissenschaften.* Jahrg. 1920. 32: 742–778 (1920).

Rohde, Richard. *Das englische Faustbuch und Marlowes tragödie.* Halle a.S.: Niemeyer, 1910. [*Studien zur englischen Philologie*, hrsg. L. Morsbach, no. 43.] [See *Jahrb*. 47: 360–362 (1911).]

Rohde, Richard. "Zu Marlowes Doctor Faustus." *Studien zur englischen Philologie*, 50: 223–232 (1913). [Festschrift f. Lorenz Morsbach.]

Root, Robert K. "Two notes on Marlowe's *Doctor Faustus*." ES, 43: 144–149 D 1910.

Root, Robert K. Review of De Vries, Schroeder, and Venzlaff [*qq.v.*], ES, 43: 117–134 (1910). [See *Jahrb*. 47: 258 (1911).]

Roscoe, Thomas. *German novelists.* London: H. Colburn, 1826, I. 256–413.

Rucker, Annabel. *Folklore and its influence upon "the University Wits." Greene, Marlowe, and Peele.* Columbia M.A. Thesis, 1926. [MS.]

Ryan, Elsa [assembler of MS.]. Complete working script. Federal Theatre production. Typewritten MS., blueprints, and plates of the production of Orson Welles at the Maxine Elliott Theatre, New York, beginning January 8, 1937. [NYPL]

Rudolf, Adalbert. "Eutychianos-Faustus senior und junior." *Archiv*, 68: 255–262 (1882).

Schade, Oskar. "Das puppenspiel Doctor Faust." *Weimarisches Jahrbuch*, 5: 241–328 (1856). [Puppenspiel text; unimportant discussion of Marlowe, pp. 245–248.]

Schade, Oskar. *Faust vom ursprung bis zur verklärung durch Goethe.* Berlin: Karl Curtius, 1912, pp. 138–167.

Scheible, J[ohan]. "Die sage vom Faust." *Das Kloster,* 5: entire (1847). [See also vols. 2, 3, and 11.]

Schelling, Felix E[manuel]. "Doctor Faustus and Friar Bacon: Examples of the superman then and now." [New York] *Nation,* 101: 12–13, 1 Jy 1915.

Schelling, Felix E[manuel]. *Foreign influences in Elizabethan plays.* New York: Harper, 1923.

Schelling, Felix E[manuel]. "Walls of brass: a fancy and a parallel." In *Shakespeare biography.* Philadelphia: University of Pennsylvania, 1937, pp. 133–143.

Schmid, E. "Marlowe's Faust und sein verhältnis zu den deutschen und englischen Faustbüchern." *Jahrb. f. romanische u. englische Sprache und Lit.,* 14: 42–62 (1875).

Schmidt, Erich. "Zur vorgeschichte des Goetheschen Faust." *Goethe Jahrb.* 4: 127–140 (1883). [CUL, NYPL]

Schmidt, Erich. *Charakteristiken.* Berlin: Weidmann, 1886, pp. 1–37.

Schneider, Rudolf. *See* Chap. IX. [Monks in drama.]

Scholderer, Victor. "Shakespeare's fools." *Library,* 2nd ser. 10: 201–207 (1909). [See *Jahrb.* 46: 225 (1910).]

Schröder, Kurt Rudolf. *Textverhältnisse und entstehungsgeschichte von Marlowe's 'Faust.'* Berlin Diss. 1909. Berlin: E. Elberling, 1909.

Schroer, K. J. "Zu Marlowe's Faust." *Anglia,* 5: 134–136 (1882).

Schwengberg, Maximilian. *Das Spies'sche Faustbuch und seine quelle.* Berlin and Leipzig: Oscar Parrisius, 1885.

Searle, John. "Marlowe and Chrysostom." TLS, 35: 139, 15 F 1936.

Sencourt, Robert. *See* Chap. VII.

Shaw, G[eorge] Bernard. "The spacious times." In *Dramatic opinions and essays.* New York: Brentano, 1906, II. 36–43.

Sheppard, J[ohn] T[hresidder]. *See* Chap. VII.

Simpson, Percy. "The 1604 text of Marlowe's 'Doctor Faustus.'" *Essays and Studies,* 7: 143–155 (1921).

Simpson, Percy. "Marlowe's tragical history of Doctor Faustus." *Ibid.* 14: 20–34 (1929). See also TLS 28: 231, 21 Mr 1929.

Simpson, Percy. [Review of Boas with original material.] MLR, 28: 379–384 (1933).

Smith, G. C. Moore. "Marlowe's 'Dr. Faustus.'" N&Q, 10th ser. 9: 65, 25 Ja 1908. [See *Jahrb.* 45: 285 (1909).]

Smith, James. "Marlowe's 'Dr. Faustus.'" *Scrutiny,* 8: 36–55 (1939).

Smith, Winifred. "Anti-Catholic propaganda in Elizabethan London." MP, 28: 208–212 N 1930.

Soanes, Wood. "Dr. Faustus is presented at Palo Alto." *Oakland [Calif.] Tribune,* 5 My 1934.

Spence, Lewis. "Ceremonial Magic," "Faust," and "Magic." In *Encyclopedia of occultism.* New York: Dodd Mead, 1920, pp. 98, 158, 258–261.

Spencer, Theodore. *See* Chap. VII.

Spivey, Gaynell Callaway. *Elizabethans in Victorian poetic drama.* North Carolina Diss. 1928. [MS.] Abstracted in University of North Carolina Record, Graduate School Series, 19: 46–47 (1928).

Stahl, Ernst Leopold. "Eine neue Shakespeare-bühne." *Jahrb.* 44: 229–239 (1908). [Especially the note on p. 238.]

Stahl, Ernst Leopold. *Der Hebbelverein in Heidelberg.* Heidelberg: Winter, 1911. [See *Jahrb.* 49: 160 (1913). Discussion of modern German productions.]

Stansell, James Julius. *Critical comparison of Christopher Marlowe's The tragical history of Doctor Faustus with two modern adaptations of the same play.* Oklahoma M.A. Thesis, 1938. [MS.]

"Staunch Baconian, A." "Faust puppet play." *Baconiana,* 3rd ser. 8: 79–88 Ap 1910.

Stieglitz, Christian Ludwig. "Die sage vom Doctor Faust." *Historisches Taschenbuch* [Brockhaus], 5: 125–210 (1834). [CUL]

Stockwell, Helen Louise Cohen. *Milestones of the drama.* New York: Harcourt Brace, 1940. [New York production.]

Summers, Montague. *History of witchcraft and demonology.* New York: Knopf, 1926. [History of Civilization Series.]

Sykes, H. Dugdale. *Authorship of . . . the additions to Marlowe's 'Faustus.'* London: Shakespeare Association, 1920. [Read, 28 February 1919.]

Sykes, H. Dugdale. *Sidelights on Elizabethan drama.* Oxford University Press, 1924, Chap. II, pp. 49–78.

Szamatólski, Siegfried. "Der historische Faust." *Vierteljahrsheft f. Litteraturgeschichte,* 2: 158–159 (1889).

Szamatólski, Siegfried. *Das Faustbuch des christlich meynenden nach dem druck von 1725.* Stuttgart: Goschen, 1891. [Deutsche Litteraturdenkmale des 18 u. 19 Jahrhunderts, no. 39.] [Contains three Faust portraits by Rembrandt.]

Tancock, O. W. "Marlowe's 'Faustus.'" N&Q, 5th ser. 11: 324, 26 Ap 1879.

Tapper, Bonno. "Aristotle's 'sweete analutikes' in Marlowe's *Doctor Faustus.*" SP, 27: 215–219 (1930). [See also *Jahrb.* (OS) 67 (NS) 8: 102 (1931).]

Taylor, A. E. "Marlowe's 'Dr. Faustus.'" TLS, 16: 597, 639, 6 D, 20 D 1917. [See *Jahrb.* 55: 192 (1919).]

Taylor, Bayard (tr.). *Faust, a tragedy.* Boston: Field, Osgood & Co., 1871. 2 vols. [Appendix III, vol. I, deals with Marlowe.]

Tegg, William. *Shakespeare and his contemporaries.* London: W. Tegg & Co., 1879.

Thaler, Alwin. "Churchyard and Marlowe." MLN, 38: 89–92 F 1923.

Thieme, Heinz. *See* Chap. VII.

Thoms, W. J. (ed.). *Early English prose romances.* London: Pickering, 1828; London: Nattali & Bond, 1858; revised and enlarged edition, London: Routledge; New York: Dutton, n.d. [1907?]

Tille, Alexander. "Neue Faustsplitter aus dem XVI., XVII. und XVIII.

Jahrhundert." *Zeitschrift f. vergleichende Litteraturgeschichte*, 9: 61–72 (1896).

Tille, Alexander. *Faustsplitter in der literatur des sechzehnten bis achtzehnten jahrhundert.* Berlin: E. Felber, 1900. [NYPL]

Tiller, Alexander. "Artistic treatment of the Faust legend." *Publications of the English Goethe Society*, no. VII. *Transactions, 1891–92*, pp. 151–224. [CUL]

Tilley, M. P. "Two notes on Dr. Faustus." MLN, 53: 494–498 (1935).

Traumann, Ernst. *Goethe's Faust.* Munich: Beck, 1914.

Tupper, Frederick. "Legacies of Lucian." MLN, 21: 76–77 (1906). [See also Cook, Albert S.]

"Urban." "Marlowe's 'Tragical history of Dr. Faustus.' " N&Q, 7th ser. 3: 285, 9 Ap 1887. [Comment by P. A. Daniel on p. 332.]

Van der Graaf, W. "Devil and his dam." ES, 32: 320 (1903).

Van der Velde, Alfred. *Ueber die Faustsage und ihre älteste dramatische bearbeitung. Breslau Phil. Diss.*, vol. 28, May 1868. [See *Verzeichnis der Breslauer Universitatsschriften 1811–1885*. Later republished with a translation. See under Translations.] [BM]

Venzlaff, Günther. *Textüberlieferung und entstehungsgeschichte von Marlowes "Doctor Faustus."* Greifswald Diss. 1909. Berlin: Egering, 1909. [Reviewed in ES, 43: 117–134 (1909).]

Wagner, W. "Zu Marlowe's Faustus." *Anglia*, 2: 309–313 (1879).

Walkley, A. B. "Renaissance play." In *Frames of mind*. London: Grant Richards, 1899, pp. 19–24. [Thomas Hardy reference.]

Walz, John A. "Notes on the puppet play of Doctor Faust." PQ, 7: 224–230 (1928).

Walz, John A. "Faust and Faustus; a study of Goethe's relation to Marlowe." JEGP, 31: 258–278 (1932). [Review of Heller, *q.v.*]

Warkentin, Roderick. *Nachklänge der sturm- und drangsperiode in Faust dichtungen.* Munich: Haushalter, 1896. [Forschungen zur Neueren Litteraturgeschichte.]

Wedmore, Frederick. "Performance of 'Doctor Faustus.' " *Academy*, 50: 39, 11 Jy 1896.

Werner, R. M. "Fauststudien. I. Die urgestalt von Marlowe's Faust. II. Marlowe und die deutsche drama." *Zeitschrift für die oesterreichischen Gymnasien*, 44: 193–205 (1893). [NYPL]

Wesser, Pauline. *Survey of Faust articles from 1926 to 1930.* New York M.A. Thesis, 1932. [MS.]

Williams, W. H. "Marlowe and Lucian." MLR, 10: 222 (1915). [See *Jahrb.* 55: 192 (1919).]

Witkowski, Georg. "Der historische Faust." *Deutsche Zeitschrift für Geschichtswissenschaft*, (OS) 13 (NS) 1: 298–350 (1896–97). [CUL]

Young, Stark. "Noctis equi." *New Republic*, 90: 46–47, 17 F 1937.

Zahn, T. *Cyprian von Antioch und die deutsche Faustsage.* Erlangen: A. Diechert, 1882, pp. 110–116.

Zarncke, Fr. "Das englische volksbuch vom Doctor Faust." *Anglia*, 9: 610–612 (1886).

Zender, Rudolf. *Die magie im englischen drama des Elisabethanischen zeitalters*. Halle Diss. 1907. Halle: Hohmann, 1907.

Z. Z. "Dr. Faustus." N&Q, 5th ser. 7: 67, 27 Ja 1877.

CHAPTER IX: THE JEW OF MALTA

Translations

1645. Gysbert de Sille. *Ioodt van Malta, ofte wraeck door moordt, treur-spel. Gerijmt door Gysbert de Sille.* Leyden: Iacob Roels, Boeckverkooper, Ende de Erfgenaemen van wijlen Ian Claesz. van Dorp. [Exact relation to Marlowe is not wholly clear. J. A. Worp: *Geschiedenis van het drama en van het tooneel in Nederland*, I. 326–327, believes it represents a re-working of the same material that Marlowe used. De Sille himself is obscure. The copy of his play in the University Library, Amsterdam, has an early manuscript note on the title page: "doenmaels student in de Regten, tot Leiden." The *Album studiosorum Academiae Lugduno Batavae 1575–1875*, col. 331, gives the "diem quo in membrum Academiae admitteretur" as 16 Maii 1642. He was then twenty years old and came from The Hague.] [BM, Amsterdam]

1831. [Karl] Eduard von Bülow. "Der Jude von Malta." In *Alt-englische schaubühne*. Berlin: G. Reimer. Part I, pp. 283–426. [CUL, BM]

1854. Tycho Mommsen. Extract. In *Marlowe und Shakespeare*, no. 11. [See Chap. XVI for bibliographical details.]

1860. Friedrich Martin Bodenstedt. *See* Collected Editions.

1882. M. Shelgunov. St. Petersburg. [No further details available.]

1889. "G." Scene in *Rassegna italiana*, 48: 664–666, 16 Ag.

1893. Friedrich Adolf, Graf von Schack. Extract. In *Die englischen dramatiker vor, neben und nach Shakespeare*. Stuttgart: Cotta, pp. 84–87. [NYPL]

1895. Israel Davidson. היהודי בספרות האנגלית. ["Ha-Yehudi be-sifrut haanglit, Jew in English literature."] *Ner Hamaaravi*, 1 (no. 6): 38–40; (no. 7): 7–15. [NYPL] [Essay illustrated with translations into Hebrew. Based on his *Sewanee Review* article. See Chap. XVI.]

1914. Rózsa Dezsö. "A máltai zsido. Fordította Rózsa Dezsö." *Magyar Shakespeare-Tár*, 7: 101–169. [HCL]

1920. Georges Duval. In *Les contemporains de Shakespeare*. Paris: Flammarion. [Meilleurs Auteurs Classiques Français et Étrangers.] [BN]

1925. Piero Rébora. Prologue. In *L'Italia nel dramma inglese (1558–1642)*. Milano: Modernissima, p. 176. [NYPL]

Separate Editions

No date. Pamphlet edition in NYPL. No editor or publisher given. [Call number NCO p. v. 552, no. 1.]

1780. Robert Dodsley. *Select collection of old plays*. London: H. Hughs for J. Dodsley, VIII. 299–395.

1810. Walter Scott. *Select collection of old plays*. London: W. Miller, I. 250–279.

1810. [W. Shone?] London: Reprinted by Reynell & Son and sold by Richardson. [Spelling "Marlo" still used and play said to be "imitated from the works of Machiavelli."] [BM]

1813. S. Penley. With alterations and additions. London: [Presumably the text of Kean's Drury Lane production, April 24, 1818.]

1825. Robert Dodsley. *Select collection of old plays*. London: Septimus Prowett, VIII. 241–327.

1845. Leigh Hunt. Extract. In *Imagination and fancy*. New York: Wiley and Putnam, pp. 100–101.

1890. W. R. Thayer. *Best Elizabethan plays*. Boston: Ginn and Co., pp. 23–112; 2nd ed. 1895.

1892. J. Scott Clark. Condensed. With introduction and explanatory notes. New York: Maynard & Co. [English Classics Series.] [NYPL, LC]

1894. Edward T. McLaughlin. With selections from *Tamburlaine* and the poems. New York: Holt.

1896. Charles Dudley Warner. *Library of the world's best literature*. Copr. by Peale and Hill, XXIV. 9727–9728.

1905. W[illiam] H[enry] Williams. *Specimens of the Elizabethan drama from Lyly to Shirley, A.D. 1580–A.D. 1642*. Oxford University Press, pp. 32–34. [Quarto text compared with Dyce and Cunningham.] [Princeton]

1909. Adapted acting version of the Williams College English Department. With a preface by Solomon Bulkley Griffin and an introduction by Lewis Perry. Williamstown, Mass. [LC, HCL, JB]

1911. William Allan Neilson. *Chief Elizabethan dramatists*. Boston: Houghton Mifflin; London: Harrap, pp. 96–121.

1928. Anon. Extracts. *Columbia University course in literature*. New York: Columbia University Press, XI. 227–228.

1933. Hazelton Spencer. *Elizabethan plays*. Boston: Little Brown; London: Macmillan, 1933, 1934, pp. 65–100.

1933. C[harles] F[rederick] Tucker Brooke and N. Burton Paradise. *English drama, 1580–1642*. Boston: D. C. Heath, pp. 193–224.

1933. Richard Ferrar Patterson. Extract. In *Six centuries of English literature*. London: Blackie, II. 41–42.

1933. With engravings by Eric Ravilious. London: Golden Hours Press.

1935. Edd Winfield Parks and R. C. Beatty. *English drama*. New York: Norton, pp. 480–547.

Books and Articles

Akers, Dorothy Dyer. *Scenic and costume design project for the Jew of Malta*. Iowa M.A. Thesis, 1935. [MS.]

Anon. Article 15 [no title]. *Monthly Review*, (NS) 67: 434–437 Ap 1812. [Review of the 1810 edition.]

Anon. Review of Kean's revival. *New Monthly Magazine*, 9: 444–445, 1 Je 1818.

Anon. "Jew of Malta." *Blackwood's*, 2: 260–266 D 1818.

Anon. "Clifton Shakespeare-Society. *See* Chap. X. [Trivial.]

Anon. "Jews in English fiction." *London Quarterly Review*, 88: 35–55 Ap 1897.

Anon. Reviews of Phoenix Society revival. [London] *Morning Post*, 7 N 1922; *Manchester Guardian Weekly*, 10 N 1922; *Blackwood's*, 212: 833–834 D 1922.

Bayne, Ronald. Article, "Patrick, Simon," DNB, XV. 490.

Begley, Walter. "Jew of Malta." *Baconiana*, 3rd ser. 6: 63–75 Ap 1908. [With note by R. M. Theobald at end.]

Birrell, Francis. "The Jews, or genius at play." *New Statesman*, 20: 175, 11 N 1922. [Another review of Phoenix Society revival.]

Booth, William Stone. *See* Chap. VII.

Bourchier, Arthur. "Jew in drama." *Contemporary Review*, 107: 376–384 Mr 1915.

Brennan, Chris. "Marlowe." *Beiblatt z. Anglia*, 16: 207–209 (1905).

Brereton, J[ohn] Le Gay. "Notes on the text of Marlowe." *Ibid.* 16: 203–207 (1905). [See also Chap. VII.]

Brie, Friedrich. "Romane und drama im zeitalter Shakespeares." *Jahrb.* 48: 15–151 (1912). [See especially pp. 141–142. See also Chap. XVI.]

Brooke, C[harles] F[rederick] Tucker. "Prototype of Marlowe's Jew of Malta." TLS, 21: 380, 8 Je 1922.

Browne, C. Elliot. "Marlowe and Machiavelli." N&Q, 5th ser. 4: 141–142, 21 Ag 1875. [Also discusses Gabriel Harvey.]

Calisch, Rabbi Edward W. *Jew in English literature*. Richmond, Va.: Bell Book and Stationery Co., 1909. [HCL]

Cardozo, Jacob Lopes. *Contemporary Jew in Elizabethan drama*. Amsterdam: H. J. Paris, 1925.

Carmoly, E. *Don Joseph Nassi Duc de Naxos*. Frankfort-sur-le-Main: C. Hess, 1868.

Cerewsak, E. M. *Machiavellianism in the Elizabethan drama, 1586–1620*. New York M.A. Thesis, 1926. [MS.]

Chang, Y. Z. *Jew in the drama of the English Renaissance*. Johns Hopkins M.S. Thesis, 1930. [MS.]

Chiarini, Guisseppe. *Studi Shakespeariani*. Livorno: R. Giusti, 1897.

Clark, Arthur Melville. *Thomas Heywood, playwright and miscellanist*. Oxford: Blackwell, 1931. [Appendix III. "Jew of Malta."]

Clouston, W. A. *See* Chap. XVI.

Cohn, Albert. *Shakespeare in Germany*. London: Asher & Co., 1895, pp. cxv–cxvii.

Coleman, Edward D. "Jew in English drama." New York Public Library *Bulletin*, 42: 827–850; 919–932 N, D 1938. [Reviewed in *New York Times Book Review*, 29 Ja 1939, p. 23.]

Collier, John Payne. "'To turn Turk.' — Jews in our early plays." *Athenaeum*, no. 1175: 475–476, 4 My 1850.

Cromwell, Otelia. *Thomas Heywood: a study in the Elizabethan drama of everyday life*. Yale University Press, 1926.

Danchin, F.-C. "Trois corrections au texte de Marlowe." *Revue anglo-Américaine*, 10: 330 Ap 1933.

Davidson, Israel. *See* Chap. XVI.

Deichert, Hans. *Der lehrer und der geistliche im Elisabethanischen drama*. Halle: Heinrich John, 1906, pp. 9–10.

Eckhardt, Eduard. *Die dialekte und ausländstypen des älteren englischen dramas*. Louvain: A. Uystpruyst, 1910, 1911. [Materialien zur Kunde des Älteren Englischen Dramas, nos. 27, 32.]

Gallup, E. Wells. *Bi-lateral cipher of Sir Francis Bacon*. Detroit: Howard Publishing Co.; London: Gay and Bird, 1900.

Graetz, Heinrich. *History of the Jews*. Philadelphia: Jewish Publication Society of America, 1894; New York: Dobsevage, 1927, vol. IV.

Greenlaw, Edwin A. "Influence of Machiavelli on Spenser." MP, 7: 187–202 (1909).

Holthausen, Ferdinand. "Zur textkritik von Marlowes Jew of Malta." ES, 40: 395–401 (1909).

Holthausen, F[erdinand]. "Zum vergleichende märchen- und sagenkunde. 5. Die geschichte vom buckligen." *Beiblatt zur Anglia*, 34: 192 (1923). [See also 21: 82–83 (1910).]

Hood, Arthur. "Vindication of the character and work of Marlowe: Shakespeare's great contemporary." *Poetry Review*, 25: 11–33 (1934).

Hume, Martin. "Spanish influences in Elizabethan literature." *Transactions of the Royal Society of Literature*, 2nd ser. 39: 1–34 (1909). [Read February 24, 1909. See also *Jahrb*. 46: 197–199 (1910).]

Hyamson, Albert M[ontefiore]. *History of the Jews in England*. London: Chatto & Windus, 1908; 2nd ed., 1928, pp. 132–134.

Judson, A. C. (ed.). *The Captives* [by Thomas Heywood]. New Haven: Yale University Press, 1921.

Kellner, Leon. "Die quelle von Marlowe's 'Jew of Malta.'" ES, 10: 80–111 (1886). [See also his *Shakespeare*. Leipzig: E. A. Seemann, 1900, and *Jahrb*. 37: 243–246 (1901).]

Kellner, Leon. Review of Breymann and Wagner's edition. ES, 14: 137–142 (1890).

Kittredge, G[eorge] L[yman]. "Notes on Elizabethan plays." JGP, 2: 13 (1898).

Knight, Joseph. *Theatrical notes*. London: Laurence and Britten, 1893, p. 277. Reprinted in James Agate: *English dramatic critics*. London: Arthur Barker, 1932, p. 186.

Koeppel, Emil. "Quellen von Thomas Heywoods 'The Captives.'" *Archiv*, 97: 323–329 (1896).

Kohler, Max J. "Jew in pre-Shakespearean literature." *Jewish Exponent*, 35: 1–2, 11 Jy 1902. [NYPL]

Lawrence, W[illiam] J[ohn]. *See* Chap. XII.

Landa, M[yer] J[ack]. "Marlowe's Jew of Malta." Chap. V in *Jew in drama*. London: King, 1926.

Landsberg, Gertrud. *See* Chap. VII.

Lee, S[idney] L. "Original of Shylock." *Gentleman's Magazine*, (OS) 246 (NS) 24: 185–200 F 1880.

Lee, Sidney L. "Elizabethan England and the Jews." *Trans. New Shakspere Society, 1887–1892*, pp. 143–166.

Levi, Harry. *Jewish characters in fiction*. Philadelphia: Jewish Chautauqua Society, 1903, pp. 13–20.

Levy, Moritz. *Don Joseph Nassi, Herzog von Naxos, seine familie und zwei judische diplomaten seiner zeit*. Breslau: Schaltter'sche Buchhandlung, 1859.

Mabon, Charles B. "Jew in English drama and poetry." *Jewish Quarterly Review*, 11: 411–430 Ap 1899.

Magnus, Laurie. *English literature in its foreign relations*. London: Kegan Paul; New York: Dutton, 1927, pp. 57–60. [Machiavelli's influence.]

M[aitland], H[enry]. "Analytical essays on the early English dramatists. No. III. *Jew of Malta*. — Marlow." *Blackwood's*, 2: 260–266 D 1817.

McEwan, Richard J., O.M.C. *Influence of Machiavelli on Marlowe through Raleigh*. Catholic University of America M.A. Thesis, 1934. [MS.]

McIntyre, Clara F. "Late career of the Elizabethan villain-hero." PMLA, 40: 874–880 (1925).

Meyer, Edward [Stockton]. *Machiavelli and the Elizabethan drama*. Weimar: E. Felber, 1897. [Litterarhistorische Forschungen, I.] [Also published in part as the author's Heidelberg dissertation. See *Jahrb*. 35: 274–276 (1899); ES, 24: 108–109 (1898).]

Meyer, Wilhelm. *Der wandel des jüdischen typus in der englischen literatur*. Marburg Diss. 1912. Borna-Leipzig: Noske, 1912.

Michelson, Hijman. *Jew in early English literature*. Amsterdam: H. J. Paris, 1926.

O'Brien, John F., O.S.A. *Character study of Barabas, "The Jew of Malta."* Catholic University of America M.A. Thesis, 1923. [MS.]

Passmann, Hanns. *Der typus der kurtisane im elisabethanischen drama*. Münster Diss. 1924. Borna-Leipzig: Noske, 1926.

Philipson, David. *Jew in English fiction*. Cincinnati: Robert Clarke Co., 1911. [Various other editions.]

Pichot, Amédée. "Le Juif de Malte." *Revue de Paris*, 47: 243–259 F 1833.

Pietzker, Annemarie. *Der kaufmann in der elisabethanischen literatur*. Freiburg Diss. 1930. Quakenbrück: C. Trute, 1931.

Poel, William. *See* Chap. XVI.

Porter, Whitworth. *History of the Knights of Malta*. London: Longmans Green & Co., 1893. [2nd ed.]

Praz, Mario. *Machiavelli and the Elizabethans*. British Academy Annual Italian Lecture, 1928. *Proceedings*, vol. 28.

Praz, Mario. *Machiavelli e gl'inglesi dell' epoca elisabettiana*. Firenze:

Vallecchi, 1930. [Quaderna di Civiltà Moderna.] [Revision of British Academy Lecture.]

Rébora, Piero. *L'Italia nel dramma inglese (1558–1642)*. Milano: Modernissima, 1925, pp. 65–67, 175–194. [NYPL]

Reinecke, Walter. *Der wucherer im älteren englischen drama*. Halle Diss. 1907. Halle: C. A. Kaemmerer & Co., 1907.

Rochlitz, A. R. *Machiavellian villain in Elizabethan drama*. New York M.A. Thesis, 1928. [MS.]

Sabatzky, Kurt. *Der jude in der dramatischen gestaltung*. Königsberg: Hartungsche Zeitung, 1930, pp. 13–14.

Schoeneich, Georg. *See* Chap. VII.

Schneider, Rudolf. *Der monch in der englischen dichtung bis auf Lewis's 'Monk' 1795*. Berlin: Mayer & Müller, 1928, pp. 88–89.

Seaton, Ethel. "Fresh sources for Marlowe." RES, 5: 385–401 (1929).

Spenser, Hazelton. "Marlowe's rice 'with a powder.'" MLN, 47: 35 (1932).

Stoll, Elmer Edgar. *John Webster*. Cambridge: Harvard Co-operative Society, 1905, Chap. IV, section IV.

Stoll, Elmer Edgar. "Shylock." JEGP, 10: 236–279 (1911).

Stonex, Arthur Bivins. "Usurer in Elizabethan drama." PMLA, 31: 190–210 (1916).

Swan, A. "Jew that Marlowe drew." *Sewanee Review*, 19: 483–497 O 1911.

Symons, Arthur. *Studies in two literatures*. London: Leonard Smithers, 1897, pp. 55–60. [Kyd.]

Taylor, Archer. "Dane Hew, Munk of Leicestre." MP, 15: 29–54 (1917).

Taylor, Rachel A. "Machiavelli and the Elizabethans." [London] *Bookman*, 71: 329–330 (1927).

Thimme, Margaret. *Marlowe's "Jew of Malta." Stil- und echtheitsfragen*. Halle a. S.: Max Niemeyer, 1921. [Studien z. Engl. Philologie, hrsg. v. L. Morsbach.] [Reviewed in *Jahrb*. 57: 108–109 (1921); *Zeitschrift f. franz. u. engl. Unterricht*, 21: 226–227 (1922); *Louvensche Bijdragen*, 14, Bijblad, 7–8 (1922).]

Turner, W. J. Review of the Phoenix Society revival. *London Mercury*, 7: 199–201 D 1922.

Turner, W. J. Another review of same. [London] *Spectator*, 129: 695–696, 11 N 1922.

Wahl, M. C. *See* Chap. X [page 83 only.]

Wann, Louis. *See* Chap. VII.

Warshaw, J. "Machiavelli in Marlowe." *Sewanee Review*, 24: 425–439 O 1916.

Wolf, Lucien. "Jews in Elizabethan England." *Trans. Jewish Historical Society of England*, 11: 1–91 (1924–27).

Wagner, Wilhelm. "Emendationen und bemerkungen zu Marlowe." *Jahrb*. 11: 70–77 (1875).

Wenger, Berta Viktoria. *Shylocks pfund fleisch. Eine stoffgeschichtliche untersuchung*. Munich Diss. 1928. Leipzig: Tauchnitz, 1929. Also in *Jahrb*. (OS) 65 (NS) 6: 92–174 (1929). [See especially pp. 147–152.]

CHAPTER X: EDWARD THE SECOND

Translations

1831. [Karl] Eduard von Bülow. "Eduard II." In *Alt-englische schaubühne.* Berlin: G. Reimer, Part I, pp. 125–282. [BM, CUL]

1859. S. Uvarov. Extracts. Русское Слово [*Russkoe Slovo*], 1: 232–258. [NYPL]

1860. N[ikolai Vas.] Gerbel. Scene with Lightborne. Русское Слово [*Russkoe Slovo*], 2: 413–416 F. [NYPL]

1864. N[ikolai Vas.] Gerbel. Three scenes. Современникъ [*Sovremennik*], 102: 201–214 Ag. [NYPL]

1870–90 (? n.d.). Robert Prölss. *Altenglische theatre.* Leipzig: Bibliographisches Institut, I. 137–282. [With long critical introduction.]

1875. N[ikolai Vas.] Gerbel. Excerpts in a free Russian translation. In Англійскіе поэты въ біографіяхъ и образцахъ [*Angliskie poeti v biographiyach i obraztsach, English poets in biographies and specimens.*] St. Petersburg: A. M. Kotomin, pp. 33–38. [NYPL]

1890. F. A. Gelbcke. In *Die englische bühne zu Shakespeare's zeit.* Leipzig: Brockhaus, 1890, I. 111–203. [With an introductory essay on Marlowe.] [CUL]

1893. Adolf Freidrich, Graf von Schack. Scenes. In *Die Englischen dramatiker vor, neben und nach Shakespeare.* Stuttgart: Cotta, pp. 63–72. [NYPL]

1895. J. B. Bury. Greek version of a part of the first scene. *Kottabos* [Dublin], 2: 296.

1896–97. G. Eeekhoud. *Société nouvelle,* 24: 619–640, 786–813; 25: 49–70 N, D, Ja.

1898. J. A. Webster. Greek version of *Edward the Second,* Act V, Scene I, 5. [Brooke's edition, lines 1991–2114.] Gaisford Prize, Oxford University. Oxford: Blackwell. [BM, JB]

1912. Alfred Walter Heymel. *Eduard II., tragödie von Christopher Marlowe.* Leipzig: Insel-Verlag, 1912, 1914. [Reviewed in *Jahrb.* 49: 182 (1913); 50: 162 (1914); 52: 262 (1916).]

1913. Rózsa Dezsö. "Másodic Edwárd. Fordította Rózsa Dezsö." *Magyar Shakespeare-Tár,* 6: 87–167. [HCL]

1914. Raffaello Piccoli. "Il regno travagliatto e la lamentabile morte di Eduardo Secondo." In *Drammi elisabettiani.* Bari: Laterza, I. 269–378. [Scrittori Stranieri, no. 9.] [BM]

1922. Ottokar Fischer. *Edvard Druhý. Tragedie o pěti dějstvích.* Kladno [Czechoslovakia]: J. Snajdr. [TLS, 21: 429, 29 Je 1922.]

1924. J[erome] Decroos. *Rondom Shakespeare . . . I.* [See Chap. VIII.]

1924. Bertholt Brecht and Lion Feuchtwanger. *Leben Eduards des Zweiten von England* [*nach Marlowe*]. Potsdam: Kiepenheuer, 1924. [JB] [See *Jahrb.* (OS) 61 (NS) 2: 154 (1925).]

Separate Editions

1738. Thomas Hayward. Extract. In *British muse*. London: F. Cogan and J. Nourse, III. 151.

1740. [Thomas Hayward.] Extract. In *Quintessence of English poetry*. London: O. Payne, 151. [Reprint of above.]

1744. Robert Dodsley. *Select collection of old plays*. London: Dodsley, II. 115–193.

1780. Robert Dodsley. *Select collection of old plays*. London: J. Nichols for J. Dodsley, II. 305–415.

1810. Walter Scott. *Ancient British drama*. London: I. 157–192.

1825. Robert Dodsley. *Select collection of old plays*. London: Septimus Prowett, II. 305–405; XII. 387–388.

1845. Leigh Hunt. Extract. In *Imagination and fancy*. New York: Wiley and Patterson, p. 103.

1870. J. S. Keltie. *Works of the British dramatists*. Edinburgh: Nimmo, pp. 100–127.

1871. Wilhelm Wagner. With introduction and notes. Hamburg: Boyes & Giesler. [BM]

1873. F. G. Fleay. [Collins School and College Classics.] London: Collins. [Also an 1877 edition.] [BM]

1879. O. W. Tancock. [Clarendon Press Series.] There are also editions of 1887 and 1899.

1894. Edward T. McLaughlin. With selections from *Tamburlaine* and the poems. New York: Holt. [English Readings.] [LC]

1896. Thomas Donovan. *English historical plays*. London: Macmillan, I. 97–170.

1896. Charles Dudley Warner. *Library of the world's best literature*, XXIV. 9725–9727. [See General Section.]

1905. W[illiam] H[enry] Williams. *Specimens of the Elizabethan drama from Lyly to Shirley A.D. 1580–A.D. 1642*. Oxford University Press, pp. 34–37. [Extracts from quarto text compared with Dyce and Cunningham.] [Princeton]

1911. William Allan Neilson. *Chief Elizabethan dramatists*. Boston: Houghton Mifflin; London: Harrap, pp. 122–152.

1913. A[rthur] W[ilson] Verity. Temple Dramatists. London: Dent; New York: Dutton.

1913. J. W. Holmes and T. S. Sterling. Edited with introduction and notes. London: Blackie. [BM]

1914. William Dinsmore Briggs. *Marlowe's Edward II*. London: David Nutt. [Reviewed in *Athenaeum*, no. 4506: 350–351, 7 Mr 1914; *Beiblatt z. Anglia*, 25: 312–314 (1914).]

1916. J[ohn] S. P. Tatlock and R. G. Martin. *Representative English plays*. New York: Century, pp. 74–118.

1923. R. S. Knox. [Methuen's English Classics.] London: Methuen.

1924. Brander Matthews and Paul Robert Lieder. *Chief British dramatists.* Boston: Houghton Mifflin, pp. 119–165.

1925. [Actually 1926.] W. W. Greg. Malone Society reprint. Oxford University Press. [Dated 1925 but contents show it was not finished until 1926.]

1926. Felix E[manuel] Schelling and Matthew W[ilson] Black. *Typical Elizabethan plays.* London and New York: Harper, pp. 195–242. [Also a 1931 edition.]

1927. Albert A. Cock. [Socrates Booklets.] London: A. & C. Black.

1928. H[arold] F[rederick] Rubinstein. *Great English plays.* New York: Harper, pp. 171–227.

1928. Anon. Extracts. *Columbia University course in literature.* New York: Columbia University Press, XI. 224–228.

1929. E[rnest] H[enry] C[lark] Oliphant. *Shakespeare and his fellow dramatist.* New York: Prentice-Hall, pp. 329–382.

1929. Anon. London: Aquila Press. [Illustrated with arms of all the characters. Fifty copies were printed on handmade paper with blazonings.]

1930. E. E. Reynolds. [English Literature for Schools Series.] Cambridge University Press. [Also a 1933 edition.] [NYPL]

1931. Felix E[manuel] Schelling and Matthew W[ilson] Black. *Typical Elizabethan plays.* New York: Harper, pp. 195–241.

1933. Hazelton Spencer. *Elizabethan plays.* Boston: Little Brown; London: Macmillan, 1933, 1934, pp. 101–142.

1933. C[harles] F[rederick] Tucker Brooke and N. Burton Paradise. *English drama, 1580–1642.* Boston: D. C. Heath, pp. 225–261.

1935. Edd Winfield Parks and R. C. Beatty. *English drama.* New York: Norton, pp. 225–262.

Books and Articles

A. G. C. "Edward II." N&Q, 8th ser. 11: 65, 23 Ja 1897.

Allen, Virginia Princehouse. *See* Chap. XVI.

Anon. "Edward II — Marlowe." *Blackwood's,* 2: 21–30 O 1817.

Anon. "Beaumont and Fletcher and their contemporaries." *Edinburgh Review,* 73: 209–224 Ap 1841.

Anon. "Shakespeare societies." *Shakespeariana,* 3: 575 (1886). [NYPL]

Anon. "Clifton Shakespeare-Society." *Jahrb.* 22: 273–276 (1886).

Anon. "Edward II at Oxford." [London] *Times,* 11 Ag 1903, p. 8.

Anon. "Phoenix Society at Daly's theatre." [London] *Times,* 7 N 1922, p. 10.

Anon. "Edward the Second." [London] *Sunday Times,* 25 N 1923.

Baldwin, Charles Sears. "Note on the history play." In *Shaksperian studies* (ed. Brander Matthews and Ashley Horace Thorndike). New York: Columbia University Press, 1916, pp. 303–310.

Bang, W. *See* Chap. VIII.

Baxter, James Phinney. *Greatest of literary problems.* Boston and New York: Houghton Mifflin, 1917, pp. 196–208, 480–484.

Bense, J. F. "Had I wist." N&Q, 11th ser. 4: 475, 9 D 1911.

Bent, J. Theodore. "Where did Edward the Second die?" *Macmillan's Magazine*, 41: 393–394 Mr 1880.

Bent, J. Theodore. "Where did Edward the Second die?" N&Q, 6th ser. 2: 381–383, 401–403, 13, 20 N 1880.

Berdan, John M. "Marlowe's 'Edward II.' " PQ, 3: 197–204 (1924).

Brereton, J[ohn] Le Gay. *See* Chap. VII.

Brie, Friedrich. "Shakespeare und die impresa-kunst seiner zeit." *Jahrb.* 50: 9–30 (1914). [See especially p. 27, and also *Jahrb.* 62: 178 (1926).]

Briggs, W[illiam] D[insmore]. "Meaning of the word 'lake' in Marlowe's 'Edward II.' " MLN, 39: 437–438 (1924).

Broadnax, Mrs. Robert. "Early dramas. I. Christopher Marlowe's 'Edward II.' " *American Shakespeare Magazine*, 3: 301–305 O 1897. [BPL]

Brooke, C[harles] F[rederick] Tucker. "On the date of the first edition of Marlowe's *Edward II.*" MLN, 24: 71–73 (1909). [See *Jahrb.* 46: 201 (1910).]

Carroll, Howard Brennan. *Christopher Marlowe's "Edward II" according to the standards of Aristotle's "Poetics."* Boston College Diss. 1937. [MS.]

Cholevius, E. *Marlowe's Edward the Second. Eine literar-historische studie.* Königsberg: G. Kemsies, 1900.

Conrad, Hermann. "Marlowe's Edward II in der ausgabe von Briggs mit einem seitenblick auf Fleays Shakspere. Forschung und englische text-kritik." *Zeitschrift f. französischen und englischen Unterricht*, 14: 298–315, 448–461 (1915).

Dametz, M. *See* Chap. XVI.

Davis, Blevins. "Edward II." In *Great Plays.* New York: Columbia University Press for National Broadcasting Co., 1939, pp. 20–22, 127–128.

Diestel, Heinrich. *Die schuldlos verdächtigte frau in elisabethanischen drama.* Rostock Diss. n.d. Rostock: Carl Hinstorff, 1909. [Discussion of Queen Isabell, pp. 3–5.]

Donovan, Thomas. *True text of Shakespeare.* London: Macmillan, 1923, p. 9.

Dühren, Eugen [pseudonym of Iwan Bloch]. *Englische sittengeschichte.* Berlin: Louis Marcus, 1912, II. 7–10.

Elze, Karl. "Noten und conjecturen zu Neu-Englischen dichtern. *Anglia*, 1: 348 (1878).

Genée, Rudolph. "Collation of the 1st edition of Marlowe's *Edward II*, (1594) . . . with Dyce's text of 1850, Marlowe's *Works*, Vol. ii." *New Shakspere Society Transactions*, Part II, 1875–76, pp. 445–451.

Genée, Rudolph. "Marlowe's tragödie 'Edward der Zweite.' Ein schatz der Kasseler Landes-Bibliothek." *Magazin f. d. Literatur des Auslandes*, no. 50: 722–725, 9 D 1876.

Getten, Helen. "Edward II and Richard II." *Silver Falcon* [Hunter College], pp. 31–38 (1935).

Grinden, Lee H. "Figurative language of Marlowe's 'Edward II.' " Paper of the Clifton Shakspere Society [Clifton, England]. Apparently never published, but summarized in *Academy*, 44: 592, 30 D 1893.

I. B. "Marlowe's 'Edward II.' " *Manchester Guardian Weekly*, 23 N 1923. [Review of Phoenix Society revival.]

K[eller?], W[olfgang?] "Wiederbelebung eines Marlowe'schen dramas." *Jahrb.* 40: 374 (1904). [Elizabethan Stage Society production.]

Klose, R. "Unterschied zwischen dem Casseler texte von Marlowe's Edward II und dem von 1598 edirt von Wilhelm Wagner." ES, 5: 242–245 (1881–1882).

Lewis, Wyndham. *Lion and the fox.* New York and London: Harper, n.d. [ca. 1928], pp. 156–158.

M[aitland], H[enry]. "Analytical essays on the early English dramatists. No. II. Edward II — Marlow." *Blackwood's*, 2: 21–30 O 1817.

Mills, Laurens J. "Meaning of Edward II." MP, 32: 11–31 (1934). [See *Jahrb.* (OS) 71 (NS) 12: 141–142 (1935).]

Mills, Laurens J. *One soul in bodies twain.* Bloomington, Ill.: Principia Press, 1937, pp. 245–250, 436–438.

Muir, Kenneth, and O'Loughlin, Sean. *Voyage to Illyria.* London: Methuen, 1937, pp. 94–96.

Nicklin, J. A. "Marlowe's historical play, Edward II, and his Gaveston." *Free Review*, 5: 323–327 D 1895.

Probst, Albert. *Samuel Daniels 'Civil Wars.'* Strassburg Diss. 1901. Strassburg: M. Du Mont-Schauberg, 1902, pp. 84–91.

Prölss, Robert. *Von den ältesten drucken der dramen Shakespeares.* Leipzig: F. A. Berger, 1905, pp. 110–111.

R. J. "Youth on the stage." *Spectator*, 136: 482, 13 Mr 1926.

Robinson, Chalfant. "Was King Edward the Second a degenerate?" *American Journal of Insanity*, 66: 445–464 (1910).

Sampley, Arthur M. "Peele's *Descensus Astraeae* and Marlowe's Edward II." MLN, 50: 506 (1935). [See *Jahrb.* (OS) 72 (NS) 13: 184 (1936).]

Schneider, Rudolf. *See* Chap. IX. [Monks in drama.]

Schoeneich, Georg. *See* Chap. VII.

Scholz, Wilhelm von. "Ein drama Marlowes." In *Gedanken zum drama.* Berlin and Munich: Georg Müller, 1915, pp. 254–267. [Also in *Der Tag*, no. 73, Mr 1912. See *Jahrb.* 49: 182 (1913).]

Shanks, Edward. "Edward II." [London] *Outlook*, 52: 394, 23 N 1923. [Review of Phoenix Society revival.]

Smith, G. C. Moore. "Edwardum occidere nolite timere. . . ." TLS, 27: 581, 9 Ag 1928. See also 16 Ag, p. 593.

Smith, Gertrude A. Young. *Marlowe's use of Holinshed in Edward the Second.* Texas M.A. Thesis, 1931. [MS.]

Smith, Robert Metcalf. *Froissart and the English chronicle play.* New York: Columbia University Press, 1915. [Studies in English and Comparative Philology, no. 14.]

Sprenger, R. "Zu Marlowe's Edward the Second." ES, 16: 156–157 (1891–92).

Summers, Montague. *Poems of Richard Barnfield.* London: Fortune Press, 1936, pp. xxi–xxii.

"Tarn." "Two Elizabethan plays." *Spectator*, 131: 792, 24 N 1923. [Review of Phoenix Society production.]

Thaler, Alwin. "Churchyard and Marlowe." MLN, 38: 89–92 F 1923.

Theobald, R. M. *Shakespeare studies in Baconian light.*

Tzschaschel, Curt. *"Marlowe's Edward II. und seine quellen.* Halle Diss. 1902. Halle: Heinrich John, 1902.

Wahl, M. C. "Das parömiologische sprachgut bei Shakespeare." *Jahrb.* 22: 45–130 (1887). [See p. 66.]

Walsingham, Thomas. *Ypodigma Neustriae vel Normanniae ab irruptione Normannorum usq; ad annum 6 regni Henrici Quinti.* Londini, in aedibus J. Daij, 1574. [See Lowndes, no. 2826. Author seems to have had no relation to the Walsingham family who were Marlowe's patrons.]

Walsingham, Thomas. *Historia anglicana.* (Ed. Henry Thomas Riley.) London: Longmans, 1863–64.

Wright, Ralph. "Marlowe and the Phoenix Society." *New Statesman*, 22: 210–211, 24 N 1923.

Young, Gertrude [A.]. *Marlowe's use of Holinshed in Edward the second.* Texas M.A. Thesis, 1931. [MS.]

Chapter XI: Dido, Queen of Carthage

Separate Editions

1825. *Old English drama.* London: Hurst, Robinson & Co.; Edinburgh; Constable, vol. II, separately paged. [NYPL]

1883–1885. A. B. Grosart (ed.). *Complete works of Thomas Nash.* London and Aylesbury: privately printed, VI. 1–79. [Huth Library.]

1904–1910. Ronald B. McKerrow. *Works of Thomas Nashe.* London: A. H. Bullen, II. 329–397; IV. 294–301. [See *Jahrb.* 46: 299 (1910).]

1914. John S. Farmer (ed.). Tudor Facsimile Texts. Amersham, England. [From Bodleian copy.]

1929. W[alter] W[ilson] Greg. Malone Society Reprint. Oxford University Press.

Books and Articles

Allen, Louise Virginia. *Dido Queene of Carthage and the Aeneid: a study in the use of source material.* Texas M.A. Thesis, 1924. [MS.]

Anon. "Notes on Sales." TLS, 22: 128, 22 F 1923. [Folger copy; Shakespeare.]

Blake, Harriet Manning. *Classic myth in the poetic drama of the age of Elizabeth.* Lancaster, Pa.: Steinman & Foltz, n.d. [1912?].

Brereton, J[ohn] LeGay. *See* Chap. VII.

Bruner, J. D. "Subsequent union of dying dramatic lovers." MLN, 22: 11–12 (1907). [See *Jahrb.* 44: 282 (1908).]

Crawford, Charles. *See* Chap. XVI.

Eisinger, Fritz. *Problem des selbstmordes in der literatur der englischen renaissance.* Freiburg Diss. 1925. Überlingen: Seebote, 1926, pp. 86–87.

Elze, K[arl], and "A. H." "Dido, Queen of Carthage, V. ii. 15." *Athenaeum*, no. 2950: 609–610, 644, 10 My, 17 My 1884.

Frey, Karl. *Die klassische götter- und heldensage in den dramen von Marlowe, Lyly, Kyd, Greene und Peele.* Strassburg Diss. 1909. Karlsruhe: Braun, 1909.

Friedrich, Jakob. *Die Didodramen des Dolce, Jodelle und Marlowe in ihrem verhältnis zu einander und zu Vergil's Aeneis.* Kempton: Kösel, 1888.

Fripp, Edgar I. "Shakespeare problem." TLS, 27: 593, 16 Ag 1928.

Gray, H. D. "Did Shakespeare write a tragedy of Dido?" MLR, 15: 217–222 (1920).

Herpich, Chas. A. "Green-Marlowe parallel." N&Q, 10th ser. 6: 185, 8 S 1906.

Höhna, Heinrich. *Physiologus in der elisabethanischen literatur.* Erlangen Diss. 1919. Erlangen: Höfer & Limmert, 1930, pp. 20–21.

Holthausen, F. *See* Chap. VIII.

Knutowski, Boleslaus. *Das Dido-drama von Marlowe und Nash; eine literarhistorische untersuchung.* Breslau Diss. 1905. Breslau: Grosser & Co., 1905.

Lawrence, W[illiam] J[ohn]. *Pre-Restoration stage studies.* Cambridge: Harvard University Press, 1927, pp. 264–265, 346–348.

Lee, Sidney. *See* Chap. XII.

Lodge, Oliver W. F. "Dido, Queen of Carthage." TLS, 29: 700, 4 S 1930.

Malone, Edmund. *Supplement to the edition of Shakspeare's plays published in 1778.* London: [various booksellers], 1780, I. 370–371. [Folger.]

Nicholson, BR. [*sic*]. "Marlowe's Dido." N&Q, 6th ser. 9: 508 28 Je 1884.

Nitchie, Elizabeth. *Vergil and the English poets.* New York: Columbia University Press, 1919, pp. 117–118.

Oliphant, E[rnest] H[unter] C[lark]. "Collaboration in Elizabethan drama: Mr. W. J. Lawrence's theory." PQ, 8: 1–10 (1929).

Pearce, Thomas Matthews. *Marlowe's "Tragedie of Dido" in relation to its Latin sources.* Pittsburgh Diss. 1930. [MS.] Summarized in University of Pittsburgh *Bulletin,* 27 [no. 3]: 141–149 (1930).

Prölss, Robert. *See* Chap. X.

Schaubert, E. Von. *See* Chap. XVI.

Sills, Kenneth C. M. "Virgil in the age of Elizabeth." *Classical Journal,* 6: 123–131 (1910–11).

Smith, G. C. Moore. *See* Chap. XVI.

Swain, Barbara. *Dido plays of Marlowe and Jodelle.* Columbia M.A. Thesis, 1924. [MS.]

Ulrici, Hermann. *Shakespeares dramatische kunst.* Halle: E. Anton, 1839; Leipzig: T. O. Weigel, 1874. [Translated as *Shakespeare's dramatic art.* London: Chapman Brothers, 1846; G. Bell, 1876.]

Wagner, Wilhelm. *See* Chap. IX.

CHAPTER XII: THE MASSACRE AT PARIS

Translation

1903. R. Faust. Scenes. *Neuphilologisches Centralblatt*, 17: 204–208.

Separate Edition

1928. W[alter] W. Greg. Malone Society reprint. Oxford University Press.

Books and Articles

Adams, Joseph Quincy. "Massacre at Paris Leaf." *Library*, 14: 447–469 (1934).

Bakeless, John. "Christopher Marlowe and the newsbooks." *Journalism Quarterly*, 14: 18–22 (1937).

Blass, Jakob. *See* Chap. X.

Crawford, Charles. "'England's Parnassus' 1600." N&Q, 10th ser. 11: 4–5, 502–503, 2 Ja, 26 Je 1909. [See also *Jahrb.* 46: 230 (1910). Discussion of quotation.]

Danchin, F.-C. *See* Chap. IX.

Deetjen, Werner. *See* Chap. VIII.

Guion, Ridie J. *Christopher Marlowe's 'Massacre at Paris.'* Columbia M.A. Thesis, 1917. [MS.]

Holthausen, F. *See* Chap. VIII.

Kirschbaum, Leo. "Census of bad quartos." RES, 14: 1–24 (1938), section XII.

Lawrence, W[illiam] J[ohn]. *Nut-cracking Elizabethans*. London: Argonaut Press, 1935, pp. 38, 84–85, 89.

Lawrence, W[illiam] J[ohn]. *Speeding up Shakespeare*. London: Argonaut Press, 1937, pp. 31–32, 129–130.

Lee, Sidney, *French Renaissance in England*. New York: Scribner's, 1910, pp. 430–435.

Press, Morris. *Preliminaries to the St. Bartholomew Massacre*. New York M.A. Thesis, 1923. [MS.]

Schneider, Rudolf. *See* Chap. IX. [Monks in drama.]

Smith, Arthur Harold. *Événements politiques de Frances dans le théâtre anglais du siècle d'Élisabeth*. Paris Thèse, 1906. Paris: Larose, 1906, pp. 11–27.

Tannenbaum, Samuel A. "Study of the Collier leaf." In *Shakesperian scraps and other Elizabethan fragments*. New York: Columbia University Press, 1933, pp. 177–186 [See *Jahrb.* (OS) 70 (NS) 11: 137 (1934).]

Thomann, Willy. *Die eifersüchtige ehemann im drama der Elisabethanischen zeit*. Halle Diss. 1908. Halle: Heinrich John, 1908, pp. 6–7.

Van Dam, B. A. P. "The Collier leaf. A text-critical detective story." *English Studies* [Amsterdam], 16: 166–173 (1934).

Wolcken, F. *See* Chap. XVI. [Caesar.]

CHAPTER XIII: HERO AND LEANDER

Translation

1925. Émile Legouis. *Dans les sentiers de la Renaissance anglaise*. Paris: Les Belles Lettres, p. 39. [Translation of I. 167–176 only.] [NYPL]

Separate Editions

1814–16. Egerton Brydges, or Bridges. In *Restituta*. London: Longmans et al., II. 112–129.

1820. Old English Poets, no. 5. London: C. Chapple. [NYPL]

1821. S. W. Singer. Select Early English Poets, no. 8. Chiswick: C. Wittingham.

1856. Robert Bell. *See* Collected Editions.

1874–75. Richard Herne Shepherd, with notes by A[lgernon] C[harles] Swinburne. *Works of George Chapman*. London: Chatto and Windus, II. 57–101.

1884. *Poems of Christopher Marlowe with memoir*. New York: Hurst & Co. [Hurst's Universal Library.] [University of Chicago.]

1894. With woodcuts by Charles Ricketts and Charles Shannon. London: Elkin Matthews and John Lane. [Printed by the Ballantyne Press in the style of the Kelmscott Press.] [NYPL]

1909. With preface by Joseph Hulton. London and Edinburgh: Joseph M. Dent. [500 copies only.] [LC, Newberry]

1924. Haslewood reprint, no. 2. London: F. Etchells and H. Macdonald. [Reviewed in TLS 23: 703, 6 N 1924.]

1927. Garrett Mattingly. With a signed note by the editor. New York: Maddox & Gray; San Francisco: Printed by the Brothers Johnson at the Windsor Press. [Morgan]

1933. With engravings by Lettice Sandford. London: Golden Hours Press.

1933. Richard Ferrar Patterson. Extract. In *Six centuries of English literature*. London: Blackie, II. 42–47.

1934. With one hundred black and white illustrations by Richard Jones. New York: Covici Friede. [LC]

1934. Reprint of the first 1898 edition (Islip for Blount). Handmade paper, initials and side notes in red and green. London: Stourton Press. [200 copies only.]

1936. J. William Hebel. First and second sestiads. In *Poetry of the English Renaissance*. New York: F. S. Crofts, pp. 168–187.

Books and Articles

Anders, Heinrich. "Randglossen zu 'Shakespeare's belesenheit.'" *Jahrb*. (OS) 62 (NS) 3: 158–162 (1926). [Anacreon and Marlowe, p. 161.]

Anon. [*Pseudo-*] *Musaeus*. Venice: Aldus, [1494?]. [*Editio princeps*. See Thomas Dibdin: *Bibliotheca Spenceriana*, II. 177, 181.]

Anon. *Ovid de arte amandi and the remedy of love, Englished with the loves of Hero and Leander, a mock poem*. London, 1672, 1677, 1682.

Arnold, Edwin. *Poems*. Boston: Roberts Brothers, 1892. [Translation of Musaeus.]

Begley, Walter. "Hero and Leander." *Baconiana*, 3rd ser. 8: 57–64 Ap 1910.

Biehringer, F. "Die sage von Hero und Leander." *Globus*, 89: 94–97, 8 F 1906.

Bradbrook, M. C. "Hero and Leander." *Scrutiny*, 2: 59–64 Je 1933. [NYPL]

Brunner, Karl. "Hero und Leander und die altenglischen elegien." *Archiv*, 142: 258–259 (1921).

Bush, [John Nash] Douglas. "Influence of Marlowe's *Hero and Leander* on early mythological poems." MLN, 42: 211–217 (1927). [See *Jahrb.* (OS) 64 (NS) 5: 206 (1928).]

Bush, [John Nash] Douglas. "Musaeus in English verse." MLN, 43: 101–104 (1928).

Bush, [John Nash] Douglas. "Notes on Marlowe's *Hero and Leander*." PMLA, 44: 760–764 (1929).

Bush, [John Nash] Douglas. *Mythology and the Renaissance tradition in English poetry*. Minneapolis: University of Minnesota Press, 1932. [Especially Chap. VI, though there are important allusions throughout the book.]

Bush, [John Nash] Douglas. *Mythology and the romantic tradition in English poetry*. Cambridge: Harvard University Press, 1937.

Bush, [John Nash] Douglas. *See also* Chap. VI.

Carew, Richard. *Epistle concerning the excellencies of the English tongue*. London, 1769. [With *Survey of Cornwall*.]

Chabalier, Léonce. *Héro et Léandre. Poème de Christopher Marlowe et George Chapman et sa fortune en Angleterre*. Paris Thèse, 1911. Paris: Hugonis, 1911.

Child, Harold H. "Michael Drayton." *Cambridge history of English literature*. Cambridge University Press, 1910, IV, 193–224.

Conley, Carey H. *First English translators of the classics*. New Haven: Yale University Press, 1927.

Courthope, W. J. *History of English poetry*. London: Macmillan, 1895–1910, II. 326–330.

Crathern, Alice T. "Romanticized version of *Hero and Leander*." MLN, 46: 382–385 (1931).

Ewig, Wilhelm. "Shakesperes Lucrece." *Anglia*, 22: 1–32, 343–363; 393–455; 449–453 (1899). [See especially the last section.]

Fawkes, F. "Loves of Hero and Leander." In *Anacreon*. London, 1760, pp. 293 ff.

Forsythe, R. S. "Note on Chapman." MLN, 26: 95 (1911). [See *Jahrb.* 48: 240 (1912).]

Foster, Finley M. K. *English translations from the Greek*. New York: Columbia University Press, 1918.

Gwynn, S. E. Paper on Hero and Leander read before the Clifton Literary Society. Apparently never published but reported in Academy, 44: 592, D 1893.

Hales, John Wesley. *Folia literaria*. New York: Macmillan, 1893. [Discussion of probable date, p. 167.]

Hebel, J. William. "Drayton and Shakespeare." MLN, 41: 248–250 (1926).

Hebel, J. William (ed.). *Endimion & Phoebe by Michael Drayton*. Oxford: Blackwell, 1925, pp. vii–xviii. [NYPL]

Herpich, Charles A. *See* Chap. XVI.

Höhna, H. *See* Chap. XI.

Holmes, Elizabeth. *Aspects of Elizabethan imagery*. Oxford: Blackwell, 1929.

Isaac, Hermann. "Die sonett-period in Shaksperes leben." *Jahrb.* 19: 176–264 (1884). [Especially pp. 248–251.]

Jellinek, M. H. *Die sage von Hero und Leander in der dichtung*. Berlin Diss. 1890. Berlin: Speyer und Peter, 1890.

Klemm, Johannes. *De fabula quae est de Herus et Leandri amoribus fonte et auctore*. Leipzig Diss. 1889. Leipzig: Max Hoffman, 1889.

Lathrop, H. B. *Translations from the classics into English from Caxton to Chapman (1477–1620)*. [University of Wisconsin Studies, no. 35.] Madison, 1933.

Lazarus, Gertrud. *Technik und stil von Hero and Leander*. Bonn Diss. 1919. Bonn: Rhenaniaverlag, 1915.

Lee, Sidney. *Shakespeare's Venus and Adonis* [Facsimile]. Oxford: Clarendon Press, 1905, pp. 29–38. [NYPL]

Morton, Robinson. *See* Chap. XIV.

Palmer, Henriette R. *List of English editions and translations of Greek and Latin classics before 1641*. London: Bibliographical Society, 1911.

Prideaux, W. F. "Marlowe's 'Hero and Leander.'" N&Q, 6th ser. 11: 305, 18 Ap 1865. Comment by C. M. Ingleby, *ibid.* 12: 15, 4 Jy 1885; 11th ser. 2: 24, 9 Jy 1910.

Quiller-Couch, Arthur. *See* Chap. XVI.

Shannon, G. P. "Petowe's continuation of *Hero and Leander*." MLN, 44: 383 (1929).

Strachey, J. St. Loe. "Hero and Leander." [London] *Spectator*, 133: 471–472, 4 O 1924; *New York Times Book Review*, 12 O 1924, p. 2. [Review of Haslewood reprint.]

Wills, Mary M. "Marlowe's rôle in borrowed lines." PMLA, 52: 902–905 (1927). [See also her MS. dissertation in General Section.]

CHAPTER XIV: MINOR POEMS AND TRANSLATIONS

Separate Editions

Ovid's Elegies

1830? Anonymous edition, tentatively so dated, in the British Museum. Thomas Grenville's copy, there preserved, has the note: "Only 50 printed & only 25 of them for Sale."

1902. *Antique Gems from the Greek and Latin. Ovid. The Amours*. Philadelphia: George Barrie & Son. Translations by Marlowe, Jonson, and others.

1925. With decorations engraved on wood by John Nash. London: Frederick Etchells and Hugh Macdonald. [625 copies, plus 35 additional signed by artist. Based on the Mason edition.]

1930. Illustrated by Alex Key. New York: Art Studies Books.

1931. Black and Gold Library. New York: Liveright.

Lucan's Pharsalia

1814–16. [Samuel] Egerton Brydges. In *Restituta*. London: Longmans *et al.*, III. 495–497.

Passionate Shepherd *

Translations

1855. Alexander Büchner. *Geschichte der englischen poesie*. Darmstadt: Diehl, I. 235.

1899. Leo Iosia Richardson. *Carmina Anglica Latine reddidit.* . . . Sancti Francisci: Apud Carolum A. Murdock, no. V. [CUL]. [Reprinted in *Classical Weekly*, 2: 174–175, 3 Ap 1909.]

1925. Émile Legouis. *Dans les sentiers de la Renaissance anglaise*. Paris: Les Belles Lettres, pp. 40–43. [NYPL]

Books and Articles

Passionate Shepherd

[See also List of Manuscripts.]

Anon. Casual notice, untitled, reprinted from *Chambers' cyclopedia*. *Living Age*, 1: 246, 8 Je 1844.

Anon. *Songs of England and Scotland*. London: James Cochrane & Co., 1835, I. xxix, 5–9, 287–290.

Bontoux, Germaine. *La chanson en Angleterre au temps d'Elizabeth*. Oxford University Press, 1936. [Edition limited to 500 copies.]

Bradley, A. C. *See* General Section.

Breslar, M. L. R. "Come, live with me." N&Q, 10th ser. 2: 89, 30 Jy 1904. Comment on pp. 153, 434, 20 Ag and 26 N.

"Ceylonensis." "Fair-lined slippers." N&Q, 2nd ser. 8: 285, 8 O 1859. Cf. 10: 206, 15 S 1860.

Chappell, William. *Popular music of the olden times*. London: Cramer Beake & Chappell, 1855–59. Republished as *Old English popular music*, London: Chappell; New York: Novello, Ewer & Co., 1893.

Crawford, Charles. *See* Chap. XVI, XVII.

Edwards, Edward. *Life of Sir Walter Raleigh*. London: Macmillan, 1868.

Elson, Louis C. *Shakespeare in music*. Boston: L. C. Page & Co., 1901, pp. 304–309.

Erskine, John. *Elizabethan lyric*. New York: Columbia University Press, 1905, p. 199. [Columbia University Series in English, II.]

Forsythe, R. S. "Passionate shepherd and English poetry." PMLA, 40: 692–742 (1925).

* Musical settings and reprintings, the latter mainly in anthologies, not listed.

Gosset, Adelaide L. J. *Shepherd songs of Elizabethan England.* London: Constable, 1912. [*Jahrb.* 49: 261 (1913).]

Hamilton, Walter (ed.). *Parodies of the works of English writers.* London: Reeves & Turner, 1884–89, IV. 36–38. [HCL has the MS. notebook used in preparation of this work.]

Hunt, Leigh. *Imagination and fancy.* London: Wiley and Patterson, 1845, pp. 104–105.

Lamson, Roy, Jr. "Musical settings. . . ." In *Variorum Shakespeare: The Poems* (ed. H. E. Rollins). Philadelphia: Lippincott, 1938, pp. 617–620.

Oldys, William. "Life of Ralegh." In *Ralegh's works.* Oxford University Press, 1829.

Roffe, A. *Handbook of Shakespeare music.* London: Chatto, 1878, pp. 50–52. [BM]

Rollins, H[yder] E[dward]. *Englands Helicon.* Cambridge: Harvard University Press, 1935, II. 186–189.

Tannenbaum, Samuel. "Unfamiliar verses of some Elizabethan poems." PMLA, 45: 809–821 (1930).

Watkins, W. B. C. *Johnson and English poetry before 1660.* Princeton University Press, 1936. [Princeton Studies in English, 13.] pp. 61–62, 71–72, 104–106.

Other Lyrics and Translations

Anon. Casual notice, untitled, reprinted from *Chambers' cyclopedia. Living Age,* 1: 246, 8 Je 1844.

Anon. *Songs of England and Scotland.* London: James Cochrane & Co., 1835, I. xxix, 5–9.

Bagley, Walter. "Ovid's elegies: translated by C. M." *Baconiana,* 3rd ser. 5: 24–28 Ja 1907.

Bond, R[ichard] Warwick. *Studia otiosa.* London: Constable, 1938, pp. 106–107. [Lucan.]

Bouchor, Maurice. "C'est au bord des limpides eaux." In *Chansons de Shakespeare.* Paris: L. Chailley, 1896, pp. 11, 86. [BN]

Brydges, [Samuel] Egerton. *Censura literaria.* London: Longmans, 1805–1809; 2nd ed., 1815, II. 137–145.

"Ceylonensis." *See above.*

Collier, J[ohn] P[ayne]. *Poetical decameron.* Edinburgh: Constable, 1820.

Cooper, Clyde Barnes. *Some Elizabethan opinions of the poetry and character of Ovid.* Chicago Diss. 1914. Menasha, Wis.: Banta, 1914.

Chattock, C. "The 'Soul's errand.'" N&Q, 5th ser. 3: 21–22, 9 Ja 1875.

Edmonds, Charles. "Destruction of books at Stationers' Hall in the year 1590." N&Q, 3rd ser. 12: 436–437, 30 N 1867. See also query by "Cuber," pp. 374–375.

Gillett, Charles Ripley. *Burned books.* New York: Columbia University Press, 1932, I. 90–91.

Mallory, Herbert S. (ed.). *Poetaster.* New York: Holt, 1905. [Yale Studies in English, no. 27], pp. xcvi–ci.

Morton, Robinson. *Marlowe's translations from the classics.* Columbia M.A. Thesis, 1924. [MS.]

Pound, Ezra. "Notes on Elizabethan classicists." In *Make it new.* New Haven: Yale University Press, 1935. Reprinted from *Egoist*, 4: 120–122; 135–136, S, O, 1917.

Rick, Leo. *Ovids metamorphosen in der englischen Renaissance.* Münster Diss. 1915. Münster: Westfalischen Vereinsdrückerei, 1915. [Part I only published as a dissertation; complete work in *Münsterschen Beiträge zur englischen Literaturgeschichte.*]

Robertson, J[ohn] M[acKinnon]. "Marlowe mystification." TLS, 23: 850, 11 D 1924.

Theobald, R. M. "Ovid *cum* Shakespeare *cum* Marlowe *cum* Ben Jonson." *Baconiana*, 3rd ser. 5: 20–24 Ja 1907.

Warton, Thomas. *History of English poetry.* London: 1774–78–81; 2nd ed., by W. C. Hazlitt, 1824–40–71, III. 394.

Whipple, T. K. *Martial and the English epigram.* Berkeley: University of California Press, 1935, pp. 337–344 and *passim.*

CHAPTER XV: THE MIGHTY LINE

Alden, Richard M. *English verse.* New York: Holt, 1903.

Anon. "Marlowe's mighty line." *Word Study* [G. and C. Merriam Co., Springfield, Mass.], 7: 1–2 Ap 1932. [HCL]

Anderson, J. J. *Classical metres in English from Ascham to Daniel.* New York M.A. Thesis, 1934. [MS.]

Baker, Howard. "Some blank verse written by Thomas Norton before 'Gorboduc.'" MLN, 48: 529–530 (1933). [See *Jahrb.* (OS) 70 (NS) 11: 162 (1934).]

Baldwin, T[homas] W[hitfield]. "Chronology of Thomas Kyd's plays." MLN, 40: 343–349 (1925). [See *Jahrb.* (OS) 64 (NS) 5: 206 (1928).]

Barber, Ruth Janet [Mrs. José Bornn]. *Certain elements of the structure of pre-Shakespearean dramatic blank verse.* Stanford M.A. Thesis, 1923. [MS.] [Author's name erroneously spelled "Barker" on library file copy.]

Barker, Granville. *See* Granville-Barker, Harley.

[Bathurst, C.] *Remarks on the differences in Shakespeare's versification.* London: Parker, 1857, pp. 7–11, 160–163.

Birnkraut, Maxim. *Devolopment of English blank verse considered as an index to the literary movements from the sixteenth to the nineteenth century.* New York M.A. Thesis, 1911. [MS.]

Bond, R[ichard] Warwick. *Complete works of John Lyly.* Oxford: Clarendon Press, 1902.

Brooke, [Charles Frederick] Tucker. "Marlowe's versification and style." SP, 19: 186–205, 2 Ap 1932.

Carpenter, Frederic Ives. *Metaphor and simile in the minor Elizabethan drama.* University of Chicago Press, 1895, pp. 33–48.

Collier, J[ohn] Payne. *History of English dramatic poetry.* London: John Murray, 1831, III. 107–146. [See also General Section.]

Compton-Rickett, Arthur. *See* General Section.

Courthope, W. J. *History of English poetry.* London: Macmillan, 1895–1910, II. 326–330, 403–422; IV. 9–11, 54–69.

Craik, George L[illie]. *Compendious history of English literature.* New York: Scribner, Armstrong & Co., 1875, I. 477–481, 490–491, 501–505. See also edition by Knight, London, 1845, III. 30–35, 47–49, 64–70.

Dukes, Ashley. "Forms of dramatic verse." *Theatre Arts Magazine,* 11: 521–529 Jy 1927.

Edmunds, Abe Craddock. *Christopher Marlowe's influence on blank verse and on William Shakespeare and John Milton.* Virginia M.A. Thesis, 1926. [MS.]

Eliot, T[homas] S[tearns]. "Notes on the blank verse of Christopher Marlowe." In *Sacred wood.* London: Methuen, 1920, pp. 86–94; 2nd ed., 1928. Reprinted with minor changes as "Marlowe" in *Selected essays, 1917–1932,* New York: Harcourt, 1932, pp. 100–105; again reprinted as "Christopher Marlowe" in *Elizabethan essays.* London: Faber, 1934, pp. 21–31.

Elton, Oliver. *English muse.* London: G. Bell & Sons, 1933, pp. 145–151.

Emerson, Oliver Farrar. "Development of blank verse. A study of Surrey." MLN, 41: 466–472 (1889).

Fest, Otto. *Ueber Surreys Virgilübersetzung.* Berlin: Mayer & Müller, 1903.

Fletcher, Priscilla. "*Study of English blank verse.* 1588–1632." *Colorado College Publications,* 2: 41–65 (1907). [M.A. Thesis.]

Gascoigne, George. *Certayne notes of instruction concerning the making of verse or rime in England.* (1575.) In Arber's Reprints.

Gerrard, E. A. *Elizabethan drama and dramatists, 1583–1603.* Oxford: J. Johnson, 1928, pp. 149–166.

Gilder, Rosamond. "Marlowe's mighty line." *New York Times,* 20 D 1936, section XI.

Granville-Barker, Harley. *On dramatic method.* London: Sidgwick & Jackson, 1931, pp. 43–62.

Grebanier, H. D. N. *Elizabethan discussion of prosody.* New York M.A. Thesis, 1930. [MS.]

Hadow, G[race] E[leanor], and W[illiam] H[enry]. "Development of blank verse." In *Oxford treasury of English literature,* Oxford: Clarendon Press, 1907, II. 55–60.

Hamer, Enid. *Metres of English poetry.* London: Methuen, 1930, pp. 45, 64–67.

Hasenfus, Nathaniel John. *Rise and fall of blank verse as a vehicle for the drama in the Elizabethan period, with particular attention to the progression and retrogression of truncated lines as seen in the plays of Christopher Marlowe, . . . William Shakespeare, . . . and James Shirley.* Boston College Diss. 1931. [MS.]

Heuser, Julius. "Der coupletreim in Shakespeare's dramen." *Jahrb.* 28: 177–272 (1893). [See especially pp. 181, 210, 225.]

Hubbard, Frank G. "Type of blank verse line found in the earlier Elizabethan drama." PMLA, 32: 68–80 (1917).

Hunter, Joseph. *Chorus Vatum.* British Museum, Addit. MSS. 2488, ff. 372–380. [Complete photostats at Newberry Library, Chicago, and NYPL. Marlowe sections only, JB.]

Imelmann, Rudolf. "Zu den anfängen des blankverses: Surreys Aeneis IV. in ursprunglichen gestalte." *Jahrb.* 41: 81–123 (1905).

Kellner, Leon. *Zur sprache Christopher Marlowes.* Vienna: Verlag der K. K. Staats-oberrealschule, 1887. [HCL, JB]

Klein, David. *Literary criticism from the Elizabethan dramatists.* New York: Sturgis and Walton, 1910.

König, Goswin. *Der vers in Shaksperes dramen.* Strassburg: Karl J. Trübner, 1888. [Quellen u. Forschungen, no. 61.]

Krumm, H. *Ueber die verwendung des reims im blankvers des englischen dramas vor Shakespeare.* Leipzig: Fock, 1889. [Jahresbericht der Oberrealschule zu Kiel, 1888–89.]

Littschwanger, Felix. *Alexandriner in den dramen Shakespeares.* Königsberg Diss. 1912. Berlin: E. Felber, 1912. [Also published as *Normannia*, no. 11.]

Lüders, Ferdinand. "Prolog und Epilog bei Shakespeare." *Jahrb.* 5: 274–291 (1870). [p. 278.]

Malone, Edmund. *Plays and poems of William Shakespeare.* London: Rivington, 1821. [See I. 507–585, "Essay on the phraseology and metre of Shakespeare and his contemporaries," especially pp. 579–581. The younger Boswell, who edited this edition, seems to have meant this to be ascribed to Malone himself. It is, however, attributed to Boswell on the title page of Malone's *Life of Shakespeare* (1821).]

Martin, Richard Hays. *Marlowe's poetic imagery and its implications.* Hamilton College M.A. Thesis, 1935. [MS.]

Matthews, Brander. *Study of versification.* Boston: Houghton Mifflin, 1911, pp. 209–212, 229–233.

Mayor, Joseph B[ickersteth]. *Handbook of modern English metre.* Cambridge University Press, 1912, pp. 133–145. [Originally published as *Chapters on English metre.* London: Clay, 1886; 2nd ed., 1901.]

Mommsen, Tycho. *Shakespeare's Romeo und Julia* [sic]. Oldenburg: G. Stalling, 1859, pp. 109–156.

Morton, Edward Payson. *Technique of English non-dramatic blank verse.* Chicago Diss. 1910. Chicago: R. R. Donnelly & Sons Co., 1910.

Padelford, Frederick Morgan. "Surrey's contribution to English verse." In *Poems of Henry Howard, Earl of Surrey.* Seattle: University of Washington Press, 1928, pp. 44–55.

Ramsay, Robert L. "Changes in verse-technic in the sixteenth century English drama." *Am. Journ. Philol.* 31: 175–202 (1910).

Robertson, John MacKinnon. "Evolution of English blank verse." *Criterion*, 2: 171–187 F 1924.

Saintsbury, George. *Historical manual of English prosody.* London: Macmillan, 1910.

Saintsbury, George. *History of English prosody.* London: Macmillan, 1906–10. 3 vols.

Schau, Kurt. *Sprache und grammatik der dramen Marlowes.* Leipzig Diss. 1901. Halle a. S.: Heinrich John, 1901.

Schelling, Felix E[manuel]. *Poetic and verse criticism of the reign of Queen Elizabeth.* Philadelphia: University of Pennsylvania Press, 1891. [Publications of the University of Pennsylvania. Series in Philology, Literature, and Archaeology, vol. I, no. 1.]

Schipper, Iacobus. *De versu Marlovii.* Bonn Diss. 1867. Bonnae: Typis Caroli Georgi, n.d.

Schipper, Jakob. *Englische metrik in historischer und systematischer entwicklung dargestellt.* Bonn: Emil Strauss, 1881–88, II. 275–284.

Schipper, Jakob. *Grundriss der englischen metrik.* Vienna: W. Braumüller, 1895. [Wiener Beiträge zur Englischen Philologie, Band II.]

Schipper, Jakob. *History of English versification.* Oxford: Clarendon Press, 1910.

Schröer, A. "Ueber die anfänge des blankverses in England." *Anglia,* 4: 1–72 (1881).

Shannon, George Pope. *Heroic couplet in the sixteenth and early seventeenth century.* Stanford M.A. Thesis, 1926. [MS.]

Smart, George K. "English non-dramatic blank verse in the sixteenth century." *Anglia,* 61: 370–397 (1937). [See *Jahrb.* (OS) 74 (NS) 15: 211–212 (1938).]

Smith, Egerton. *Principles of English metre.* Oxford: Milford, 1923, pp. 217–221.

Strachey, J. St. Loe. "Vicissitudes of blank verse." *London Mercury,* 6: 45–60 My 1922.

Stroheker, Friedrich. *Doppelformen und rhythmus bei Marlowe und Kyd.* Heidelberg Diss. 1913. Tübingen: H. Laup, Jr.; Heidelberg: Winter, 1913.

Symonds, John Addington. *Sketches and studies in Italy.* London: Smith Elder, 1879. [See especially Appendix, reprinting essay on blank verse from *Cornhill Magazine,* 1st ser. 15: 620–640 My 1867.]

Symonds, John Addington. "Lyrism of the English romantic drama." In *In the key of blue.* London: Elkin Matthews & John Lane; New York: Macmillan, 1893, pp. 241–264.

Symonds, John Addington. *Blank verse.* London: Nimmo, 1895. [Chap. II reprinted.]

Timberlake, Philip Wolcott. *Feminine ending in English blank verse; a study of its use by early writers.* Princeton Diss. 1926. Menasha, Wis.: Banta, 1931, pp. 36–45. [Also in MS. in Princeton Library.]

Todhunter, John. "Blank verse on the stage." *Fortnightly Review,* 77: 346–360 F 1902.

Van Dam, B. A. P., and Stoffel, C. *William Shakespeare's prosody and text.* Leyden: E. J. Brill, 1900. [Especially Chaps. X–XII.]

Van Dam, B. A. P., and Stoffel, C. *Chapters on English poetry, prosody, and pronunciation (1550–1700).* Heidelberg: Carl Winter, 1902. [Anglistische Forschungen, Heft 9.]

Vöhl, Margarete. *Der erste teil des Tamerlan des Grossen.* Helmstedt: J. C. Schmidt, 1893, pp. 135–139. [CUL]

Wagner, Max. *English blank verse before Marlowe.* [Programmabhandlung der städtischen höheren burgerschule zu Osterode in Ostpreussen.] Osterode, 1881–82. [Reviewed in ES, 5: 457–458 (1881–82); 8: 393 F 1885.]

Warton, Thomas. *See* Chap. XV.

Young, George. *English prosody on inductive lines.* Cambridge University Press, 1928, pp. 149–152.

CHAPTER XVI: MARLOWE AND SHAKESPEARE

Acheson, Arthur. *See also* Chap. IV.

Acheson, Arthur. *Shakespeare, Chapman and Sir Thomas More.* London: Quaritch, 1931, pp. 59–62.

Acheson, Arthur. *Shakespeare's sonnet story.* London: Quaritch, 1933.

Alexander, Bernard. "Shylock und Nathan." *Pester Lloyd* [Budapest], 71 Jahrgang, no. 51, 1 Mr 1924.

Alexander, Peter. *Shakespeare's Henry VI and Richard III.* Cambridge University Press, 1929. [Shakespeare Problems, no. 3.]

Alden, Raymond Macdonald. *Shakespeare.* New York: Duffield, 1922, pp. 66–68, 148–150, 160–161, 167–168, 239–241. [Master Spirits of Literature.]

Allen, Virginia Princehouse. *Comparison of Marlowe's treatment of history in "Edward II" with Shakespeare's treatment of history in "Richard II."* Claremont Colleges M.A. Thesis, 1930. [MS.]

Anders, H. R. D. *Shakespeare's books.* Berlin: George Reimer, 1904, pp. 90–101, 120–127.

Anon. *See* Chap. XI.

Anon. "Clifton Shakespeare-Society." *Jahrb.* 22: 273–276 (1886).

Anon. "Art. V. Shakspeare and his times." *Monthly Review,* 89: 357–372 Ag 1819. [See especially pp. 361–362 for an early Marlowe-Shakespeare suggestion.]

Anon. "Familiar parallism [*sic*] between Marlowe and Shakespeare." *New Shakespeareana,* 6: 73–76 (1907).

Archer, William. "Redistributing Shakespeare." *Contemporary Review,* 121: 746–753 Je 1922.

Arnold, Morris LeRoy. *Soliloquies of Shakespeare.* New York: Columbia University Press, 1911, pp. 12–14. [Columbia Studies in English, no. 30.]

Ashbaugh, Samuel S. *On the parts of Marlowe and Shakespeare in Richard III.* Washington: Service Press, 1921. [Address before the Shakespeare Society of Washington, January 14, 1921.]

Ayres, Harry Morgan. "Shakespeare's *Julius Cæsar* in the light of some other versions." PMLA, 25: 183–227 (1910). [See also *Jahrb.* 47: 267 (1911).]

Baxter, James Phinney. *See* Chap. X.

Benson, Nelson P. "Study in character delineation. Shylock in The Merchant of Venice and Barabas in The Jew of Malta." *Normal Bulletin* [Pennsylvania Central State Normal School, Lock Haven, Pa.], 13: 22–25

N 1912. Also in Arthur Huntington Nason: *Talks on theme writing*. New York: privately printed, 1909, pp. 117–119, 165–173. [NYPL, CUL]

Bermann, Edwin. *See* General Section.

Bidgood, Lee. "Marlowe's Edward II and Shakespeare's Richard II." *University of Virginia Magazine*, (OS) 66 (NS) 49: 375–383 Mr 1906.

Biesecker, Catherine Emma. *Comparison of the "Jew of Malta" and the "Merchant of Venice."* Ohio State M.A. Thesis, 1927. [MS.]

Boas, F[rederick] S[amuel] (ed.). *Taming of a Shrew*. London: Chatto & Windus; New York: Duffield and Company, 1908, pp. 91–98. [Shakespeare Library.]

Bodenstedt, Friedrich [Martin von]. "Marlowe und Greene als vorläufer Shakespeare's." In *Wissenschaftliche vorträge gehalten zu München im Winter 1858*. Braunschweig: Vieweg, 1858, pp. 221–259.

Borchers, Arthur. *Der characterkontrast in den dramen Shakespeares bis "Henry IV," 1 Teil*. Halle Diss. 1912. Halle a.S.: Kaemmerer, 1912. [*Jahrb.* 49: 174 (1913).]

Brandes, George. Introduction to *First part of King Henry VI*. New York: Dutton, 1905, pp. v–xii.

Bradford, Gamaliel. *Elizabethan women*. Boston: Houghton Mifflin, 1936, pp. 18–20.

Brandl, Alois. Review of Schröer [*q.v.*]. *Göttingen gelehrten Anzeiger*, 153: 708–728 (1891).

Brandl, Alois. *Shakespeare*. Berlin: E. Hofmann & Co., 1894; 2nd ed. 1923. [Geisteshelden, 8.]

Brandl, Alois. "Shakespeares vorgänger." *Jahrb*. 35: ix–xxiv (1899).

Brie, Friedrich. "Zur entstehung des 'Kaufmann von Venedig.'" *Jahrb*. 49: 97–108 (1913). [See especially pp. 98–99.]

Brooke, C[harles] F[rederick] Tucker. "Authorship of 'King Henry VI.'" *Trans. Connecticut Acad. Arts and Sciences*, 17: 141–211 Jy 1912.

Brooke, C[harles] F[rederick] Tucker. "*Titus Andronicus* and Shakespeare." MLN, 34: 32–36 Ja 1919.

Brooke, C[harles] F[rederick] Tucker (ed.). *King Henry the Sixth*. New Haven: Yale University Press, 1918, 1924, Pt. I, pp. 138–154, Appendix C; Pt. II, pp. 152–156, Appendix C; Pt. III, pp. 139–140, Appendix C. [Yale Shakespeare.]

Brown, J. M. "An early rival of Shakespeare." *New Zealand Magazine* [Dunedin, N. Z.], 2: 97–133 (1877). [Deals mainly with Greene.] [NYPL]

Bruner, James B. *See* Chap. XI.

Buland, Mabel. *Presentation of time in Elizabethan drama*. New York: Holt, 1912. [Yale Studies in English, no. 44.] [*Jahrb*. 49: 236 (1913).]

Bush, [John Nash] Douglas. "*Hero and Leander* and *Romeo and Juliet*." PQ, 9: 369–399 (1930).

Cartier, Général. "Le mystère Bacon-Shakespeare. Un document nouveau." *Mercure de France*, 158: 527–528, 1 S 1926. [Assigns both Marlowe's and Shakespeare's works to Francis Bacon.]

Cartwright, Robert. *Footsteps of Shakspere.* London: J. R. Smith, 1862, pp. 138–154.

Cartwright, Robert. "Shakspere and Marlowe." In *Papers on Shakspere.* London: J. R. Smith, 1877, pp. 13–17. [NYPL]

C. C. B. "Shakespeare's Sonnets: the rival poet." N&Q, 11th ser. 5: 190, 9 Mr 1912. See also *Jahrb.* 49: 182 (1913).

Chaffin, Pauline. *Evidence of Marlowe's and Lyly's influence upon Shakespeare.* Guilford [N.C.] College B.A. Thesis, 1928. [MS.]

Chalmers, George. *Supplementary apology for the believers in the Shakespeare-Papers* [Ireland forgeries]. London: Egerton, 1799.

Chambers, E[dmund] K[erchever]. *Disintegration of Shakespeare.* British Academy. Annual Shakespeare Lecture. Oxford University Press, 1924. [Read May 12, 1924.]

Clark, Arthur Melville. "Marlowe mystification." TLS, 24: 480, 16 Jy 1925.

Clouston, W. A. "Shylock and his predecessors." *Academy,* no. 789: 434, 18 Je 1887; no. 796: 89–91, 6 Ag 1887.

Collins, John Churton. *Studies in Shakespeare.* Westminster: Constable, 1904, pp. 96–126.

Conrad, H. "Christopher Marlowe." *Preussische Jahrbuecher,* 134: 115–147 O 1908.

Cowl, R. P. *Sources of the text of Henry the Fourth.* London: Elkin Mathews and Marrot Ltd.; Bruges: St. Catherine Press, 1928. [HCL]

Craig, Hardin. *Shakespeare; a historical and critical study.* Chicago: Scott, Foresman & Co., 1934, pp. 29–32, 42–44, 83–87, 104–107, 110–112.

Crawford, Charles. "Date and authenticity of Titus Andronicus." *Jahrb.* 36: 109–121 (1900). [Especially p. 116.]

Crawford, Charles. "Authorship of Arden of Feversham." *Jahrb.* 39: 74–86 (1903). [Especially pp. 80–81.]

Crawford, Charles. "Barnfield, Marlowe, and Shakespeare." N&Q, 9th ser. 8: 217–219, 277–279, 14 S, 5 O 1901. [See *Jahrb.* 38: 298–299 (1902).]

C.W.T. "Three parts of 'Henry the Sixth.'" *Shakespeariana,* 9: 99–113 (1892). [See p. 106.]

Dametz, Maximilian. *Marlowes Edward II. und Shakespeares Richard II. Ein literar-historischer vergleich.* [*Dreiundfünfzigster jahresbericht über die k. k. Staats-Realschule ... 1903/1904.*] Wien: Selbstverlag der k.k. Staats-Realschule, 1904.

Dannenberg, Friedrich. "Shakespeares Sonnette: herkunft, wesen, deutung." *Jahrb.* (OS) 70 (NS) 11: 36–64 (1934). [Especially pp. 45–62.]

Davidson, Israel. "Shylock and Barabas." *Sewanee Review,* 9: 337–348 Jy 1901.

Dean, Marguerite. *Comparison of Christopher Marlowe's Edward II and William Shakespeare's Richard II.* Colorado M.A. Thesis, 1914.

Dobrée, Bonamy. "Shakespeare and the drama of his time." In *Companion to Shakespeare studies* [Harley Granville-Barker and G. B. Harrison, ed.]. Cambridge University Press; New York: Macmillan, 1934, pp. 243–261.

Doran, Madeleine [Kathryn]. "*Henry VI, Parts II* and *III*: their relation to the *Contention* and the *True Tragedy*." University of Iowa *Humanistic Studies*, vol. IV, no. 4.

Dyde, S. W. "One point of contact between Marlowe and Shakespeare." *Queen's Quarterly*, 34: 320–325 Ja–Mr 1927. [HCL]

Eckhardt, Eduard. *Die dialekte und ausländertypen des älteren englischen dramas*. Louvain: A. Uystpruyst; Leipzig: Harrassowitz, 1911. [Materialien zur Kunde des Älteren Englischen Dramas, Bd. XXXII.] [See *Jahrb.* 48: 316 (1912).]

Edmunds, Abe Craddock. *See* Chap. XV.

Elze, Karl. "Zum Kaufmann von Venedig." *Jahrb.* 6: 129–168 (1871).

Ervine, St. John. *See* Agate, James, in General Section.

Farnham, Willard. "Lost innocence of poetry." In *Essays in Criticism* [edited by members of the Department of English, University of California]. Berkeley: University of California Press, 1929.

Farnham, Willard. *Medieval heritage of Elizabethan tragedy*. Berkeley: University of California Press, 1936, pp. 401–415.

Figgis, Darrell. *Shakespeare*. London: J. M. Dent, 1911. [See *Jahrb.* 48: 275–276 (1912).]

Fine, Nathaniel M. *Shylock and the Jew of the sixteenth century*. Columbia M.A. Thesis, 1918. [MS.]

Fischer, Rudolf. *Zur kunstentwicklung der englischen tragödie von ihren ersten anfangen bis zu Shakespeare*. Strassburg: K. J. Trübner, 1893, pp. 113–186. [See especially pp. 167, 172, 175, 179, 184.]

Fitzgerald, John T. *Shakespeare's indebtedness to Marlowe*. Boston College M.A. Thesis, 1931. [MS.]

Fitzhugh, Alexander. "Jew of Malta and the Jew of Venice." *University of Virginia Magazine*, (OS) 55 (NS) 38: 288–293 Ap 1895.

Fleay, Frederick Gard. "Who wrote Henry VI?" *Macmillan's Magazine*, 33: 50–62 N 1875.

Fripp, Edgar I. "Shakespeare's tribute to Marlowe." In *Shakespeare, man and artist*. Oxford University Press, 1938, II. 538–539. *See also* Chap. XI.

Furness, Horace Howard. *Merchant of Venice*. Philadelphia: J. B. Lippincott, 1888; 2nd ed., 1916 [New Variorum], pp. 322–324.

Furnivall, Frederick J[ames]. "Foreword" to *First part of the Contention* [Facsimile]. London: Charles Praetorius, 1889, pp. 3–xxii. [Shakspere Quarto Facsimiles, no. 37.] [Embodying the views of Grant White, *q.v.*] [CUL]

Furnivall, Frederick James. *Succession of Shakspere's work and the use of metrical tests in settling it*. London: Smith Elder & Co., 1874.

Gaw, Allison. *Origin and development of Henry VI in relation to Shakespeare, Marlowe, Peele, and Greene*. Los Angeles: University of Southern California, 1926. [Studies, 1st ser.]

Genée, Rudolph. *William Shakespeare in seinem werden und wesen*. Berlin: Reimer, 1905. [See *Jahrb.* 42: 241–244 (1906).]

Genée, Rudolph. *Shakespeare's leben und werke*. Leipzig: Bibliographisches Institut, 1872? pp. 21–25.

Godwin, Parke. *New study of the sonnets of Shakespeare*. New York: Putnam, 1900, pp. 199–200. [Marlowe as the rival poet.]

Gollancz, Israel. Preface to Temple edition of *Richard III*. London: Dent; New York: Dutton, n.d.

Gosse, Edmund W. "Marlowe and Shakespeare." *Academy*, 6: 612, 5 D 1874.

Gothein, Marie. "Die frau im englischen drama vor Shakespeare." *Jahrb.* 40: 1–50 (1904).

Grabau, Carl. "Zeitschriftenschau 1912." *Jahrb.* 49: 182, 188 (1913).

Graetz, Heinrich. *Shylock in der saga, im drama, und in der geschichte*. Krotoschin: Monasch & Co., 1899.

Granville-Barker, Harley and Harrison, G[eorge] B[agshaw]. *Companion to Shakespeare studies*. Cambridge University Press, 1934.

Gray, A. K. "Shakespeare and *Titus Andronicus*." SP, 25: 295–311 Jy 1928.

Gray, H. D. "Authorship of 'Titus Andronicus.'" In *Flügel memorial volume*. Stanford University, 1916, pp. 114–126. Criticized by C. F. Tucker Brooke: "*Titus Andronicus* and Shakespeare." MLN, 34: 32–36 (1919), with reply by author, "*Titus Andronicus* once more." MLN, 34: 214–220 Ap 1919.

Grosart, Alexander B. "Was Robert Greene substantially the author of Titus Andronicus." ES, 22: 389–436 (1896).

Halliwell-Phillips, James Orchard. "Remarks on the similarity of a passage in Marlowe's Edward II. and one in the first part of the Contention." *Shakspere Society Papers*, 1: 5–7 (1844).

Hamilton, Clayton. *Seen on the stage*. New York: Holt, 1920, pp. 41–44.

Harrison, G[eorge] B[agshaw]. *Shakespeare at work*. London: Routledge; New York: Holt, 1933, pp. 35–40. [American title: *Shakespeare under Elizabeth*.]

Hart, Alfred. *Shakespeare and the homilies*. Melbourne University Press in association with Oxford University Press, 1934.

Hastings, Emily Evelyn. *Comparative study of the Jew of Malta and the Merchant of Venice*. Ohio B.A. Thesis, 1913. [MS.]

Hawkins, F. "Shylock and other stage Jews." *Theatre*, 2: 191–198, 1 N 1879. [HCL]

Hermann, E. *Shakespeare der kämpfer*. Erlangen: Diechert, 1879, pp. 615–688. [Abteilung III of *Drei Shakespeare-studien*.]

Herpich, Charles A. "Marlowe and Shakespeare." N&Q, 10th ser. 1: 1–2, 2 Ja 1904. [Comment by E. F. Bates on p. 75.]

Hertzling, W. "Shakespeare und seine vorläufer." *Jahrb.* 15: 360–409 (1880).

Hickson, Samuel. "Marlowe and the old 'Taming of a shrew.'" N&Q, 1st ser. 1: 194, 226–227, 345–347, 26 Ja, 9 F, 30 Mr 1850.

Hickson, Samuel. "Shakspeare and Marlowe." N&Q, 1st ser. 2: 369–370, 2 N 1850.

Honigmann, D. "Ueber den charakter des Shylock." *Jahrb.* 17: 201–229 (1882).

Theobald, Robert M[asters]. *Shakespeare studies in Baconian light.* London: S. Low Marston and Co., 1901, pp. 415–488. [LC]

Theobald, William. *On the authorship of the plays attributed to Shakespere.* Budleigh Salterton [England]: T. Andrews, Printer, 1894. [LC]

Tiegs, A. *Zusammenarbeit englischer berufsdramatiker unmittelbar vor, neben, und nach Shakespeare.* Breslau Diss. 1933. Breslau: Eschenhagen, 1933.

Timon, Dr. [Pseudonym? No Christian name given.] *Shakespeare's drama in seiner natürlichen entwicklung dargestellt.* Leyden: E. J. Brill, 1889.

Turnbull, William Robertson. *Othello: a critical study.* Edinburgh: Blackwood, 1892, pp. 125–128.

Ulrici, H. "Christopher Marlowe und Shakespeare's verhältniss zu ihm." *Jahrb.* 1: 57–85 (1865).

Vatke, Theodor. "Shakespeare und Euripides. Eine parallele." *Jahrb.* 4: 62–93 (1869). [Especially pp. 75–76.]

Verity, Arthur Wilson. *Influence of Christopher Marlowe on Shakspere's earlier style.* Cambridge: Macmillan and Bowes, 1886.

Waldron, F. G. (ed.). *Jonson's Sad shepherd.* London: C. Dilly, 1783. [Cf. pp. 208–211. Waldron continued Whalley's edition.]

Weber, Alfred. *Der wahre Shakespeare.* Leipzig and Vienna: Anzengruber-Verlag, 1919, pp. 62–63. [Baconian.] [NYPL]

Webster, Archie. "Was Marlowe the man?" *National Review,* 82: 81–86 S 1923.

Weiner, Karl. *Die verwendung des parallelismus als kunstmittel im englischen drama vor Shakespeare.* Giessen Diss. 1915. Hamburger: Beingruber und Henning, 1916, pp. 54–60.

Wells, William. *Authorship of Julius Caesar.* London: Routledge, 1923.

White, Richard Grant. *Essay on the authorship of the three parts of 'Henry VI.'* Cambridge, Mass.: H. O. Houghton and company, 1859.

Williams, Maud Leon. *Shakespeare's contribution to chronicle history; a comparison of Marlowe's Edward II and Shakespeare's Richard II.* Utah M.A. Thesis, 1909. [MS.]

Wilson, J[ohn] Dover. "Marlowe and 'As you like it.'" TLS, 26: 12, 6 Ja 1927.

[Wilson, John Dover, ed.] *As you like it.* Cambridge University Press, 1926, pp. 103–105.

Wölcken, F. "Shakespeares Julius Caesar und Marlowes Massacre at Paris." *Jahrb.* (OS) 63 (NS) 4: 192–194 (1927).

Wolff, Max Josef. *Shakespeare, der dichter und sein werk.* München: H. Beck, 1907–1908. 2 vols. [References to Marlowe *passim.* See index.]

Wynne, Arnold. "Tragedy: Lodge, Kyd, Marlowe, Arden of Feversham." In *Growth of English drama.* Oxford: Clarendon Press, 1914.

Zeigler, Wilbur Gleason. *It was Marlowe. A story of the secret of three centuries.* Chicago: Donoghue, Henneberry & Co., 1898; London: Kegan Paul & Co., ca. 1898. [Satirical review in *Academy,* 54: 41, 9 Jy 1898; *Critic,* 33: 373–376 N 1898. See also *New Shakespeareana,* 6: 14–17 (1907).]

CHAPTER XVII: THE MARLOWE APOCRYPHA

Ainger, Alfred. *See* Chattock, C.

Anon. "Seager a painter. — Marlowe's autograph." N&Q, 1st ser. 1: 469–470, 18 My 1850. [Supposed holograph poems, now lost.]

Anon. *Shakspere Tercentennial Celebration.* [Pamphlet.] University of Chicago, February 25, 1916. [Reproduces the Jig erroneously attributed to Marlowe.]

Baskervill, Charles Read. *Elizabethan jig.* University of Chicago Press, 1929.

Berkenhout, John. *Biographia literaria.* London: J. Dodsley, 1777.

Brereton, J[ohn] Le Gay (ed.). *Lust's dominion; or, the lascivious queen.* Louvain: Librairie Universitaire, 1931. [Materials for the Study of the Old English Drama (NS), no. 5.]

B. R. L. "Marlowe's 'Lust's dominion.'" N&Q, 1st ser. 7: 253–254, 12 Mr 1853.

Brooke, C[harles] F[rederick] Tucker. *Shakespeare apocrypha.* Oxford: Clarendon Press, 1918. [Introduction especially valuable.]

Brooke, C[harles] F[rederick] Tucker. "Marlowe canon." PMLA, 37: 367–417 (1922).

Bullen, A[rthur] H[enry] (ed.). *Arden of Feversham.* London: J. W. Jarvis & Son, 1887, pp. xii–xiv. [BM]

Chattock, C., Grosart, A. B., Ainger, Alfred, *et al.* "Soul's errand." N&Q, 5th ser. 3: 21–22, 72–73, 158, 229–230, 9 Ja–20 Mr 1875.

Collier, J[ohn] Payne. *Alleyn papers.* London: Shakespeare Society, 1843.

Collier, John Payne. *Select collection of old plays.* [3rd ed. of Dodsley.] London: S. Prowett, 1825–27, II. 311, 313.

Crawford, Charles. "Edmund Spenser, 'Locrine,' and 'Selimus.'" N&Q, 9th ser. 7: 61–63, 101–103, 142–144, 203–205, 261–263, 324–325, 384–386, 26 Ja–18 My 1901. [See *Jahrb.* 38: 297–299 (1902); and also Chap. XII.]

Crawford, Charles. *Collectanea.* Stratford: Shakespeare Head Press, 1906.

Cust, Lionel. "Arden of Feversham." *Archaeologia Cantiana,* 34: 101–129 (1920).

Daniel, P. A. "Locrine and Selimus." *Athenaeum,* no. 3677: 512, 16 Ap 1896.

Eckstädt. *See* Vitzthum von Eckstädt.

Fleay, Frederick Gard. *See* General Section, especially the references in his *Shakespeare,* II. 73–82.

Foard, James T. "Joint authorship of Christopher Marlowe and William Shakespeare." *Gentleman's Magazine,* (OS) 288 (NS) 64: 134–154 F 1900.

Gilbert, Hugo. *Robert Greene's Selimus.* Kiel Diss. 1899. Kiel: H. Fiencke, 1899.

Golding, S. R. "Authorship of 'Edward III.'" N&Q, no series number, 154: 313–314, 5 My 1928.

Golding, S. R. "Authorship of 'Lust's dominion.'" N&Q, no series number, 156: 399–402, 8 D 1928. [See *Jahrb.* (OS) 66 (NS) 7: 237 (1930).]

Grosart, A. B. *See* Chattock, C.

Hart, Alfred. *See* Chap. XVI. [*Edward III.*]

Hickson, Samuel. "Marlowe and the old 'Taming of a shrew.'" N&Q, 1st ser. 1: 194, 26 Ja 1850.

Hopkinson, A[rthur] F[rederic]. *Shakespeare's doubtful plays*. London: M. E. Sims & Co., 1900. [NYPL]

Hopkinson, A[rthur] F[rederic]. *Selimus*. London: M. E. Sims & Co., 1916. [CUL]

Hunt, Mary L. *Thomas Dekker*. New York: Columbia University Press, 1911.

Malone, Edmund. *Supplement to the edition of Shakspeare's plays published in 1778*. London: [various booksellers], 1780. [Folger]

Miksch, Walther. *Die verfasserschaft des Arden of Feversham*. Breslau Diss. 1907. Breslau: H. Fleischmann, 1907, pp. 29–32.

Oliphant, E[rnest] H[enry] C[lark]. "Problems of authorship in Elizabethan dramatic literature." MP, 8: 411–419 (1911).

Oliphant, E[rnest] H[enry] C[lark]. "Marlowe's hand in 'Arden of Feversham.'" *New Criterion*, 4: 76–93 Ja 1926.

Oxinden, Henry. *Commonplace Book*. *See* List of MSS.

R. B. I. "Marlowe's 'Lust's dominion.'" N&Q, 1st ser. 7: 253–254, 12 Mr 1853.

Robertson, J[ohn] M[ackinnon]. *See* Chap. XVI.

Rutherford, Vera Randolph. *Play of Edward III: its sources, structure, and possible authorship*. Texas M.A. Thesis, 1927. [MS.]

Sachs, R. "Die Shakespeare zugeschriebenen zweifelhaften stücke." *Jahrb.* 27: 135–199 (1892). [*Fair Em* not Marlowe's, p. 173.]

Shoaff, Edgar Allen. *Problem of the pseudo-Shakespearean Edward III*. Illinois M.A. Thesis, 1930. [MS.]

Simpson, Richard. "Some plays attributed to Shakspere." *New Shakspere Society's Transactions, 1875–6*, pp. 155–180.

Simpson, Richard. *School of Shakespeare*. London: Longmans, 1872. [Especially introduction to *Alarum for London*.]

Smith, Robert Metcalf. *Froissart and the English chronicle play*. New York: Columbia University Press, 1915, pp. 77–81. [Studies in English and Comparative Literature, no. 14.]

Spens, Janet. *See* Chap. XVI.

Swinburne, Algernon Charles. "Notes on the historical play of Edward III." *Gentleman's Magazine*, (OS) 247 (NS) 23: 170–181, 330–339 Ag, S 1879. [Volume wrongly numbered 245 on title.]

Sykes, H. Dugdale. *Sidelights on Shakespeare*. Stratford: Shakespeare Head, 1919.

Sykes, H. Dugdale. *Sidelights on the Elizabethan drama*. Oxford University Press, 1924, pp. 99–107.

Symonds, John Addington. *See* General Section.

Symons, Arthur (ed.). *Venus and Adonis*. London: Griggs, n.d. [Shakspere Quarto Facsimiles, no. 12.] [See Introduction.]

Tannenbaum, Samuel A. *Shakesperian scraps and other fragments*. New York: Columbia University Press, 1933.

Theobald, Bertram G. Francis. *Bacon concealed and revealed*. London: Cecil Palmer, 1930, pp. 83–150.

Theobald, R. M. *Shakespeare studies in Baconian light*. London: S. Low, Marston & Co., 1901. ["Appendix on the authorship of Marlowe" contains parallels useful if carefully checked.]

Tolman, Albert H. *Shakespeare's part in " The Taming of the Shrew."* Strassburg Diss. 1889. Ripon, Wis.: privately printed, n.d. Reprinted in PMLA, vol. V, no. 4 (1890).

Wann, Louis. *See* Chap. VII.

Warnke, K., and Proescholdt, L. *Pseudo-Shakespearian plays*. Halle: Max Niemeyer, 1886.

Vitzthum von Eckstädt, K[arl] F[reidrich graf]. *Shakespeare und Shakspere. Zur genesis der Shakespeare-dramen*. Stuttgart: Cotta, 1888, pp. 38–42. [Marlowe wrote none of his plays.]

INDEX

INDEX

Aaron, I. 374, II. 208, 260
abdication scenes, II. 20–21, 242–243
Abigail, I. 332, II. 208, 218–221
Abu Taulib ul Husseyny, I. 228
academic dress, I. 51 ff.
Academy, I. 197, 214 ff.
Acheson, Arthur, II. 213
Acta Capituli, I. 34
actors: costume, II. 14; English, abroad,
  I. 302, 341; "gags" by, II. 47; poverty
  of, II. 206
Adam, I. 111
Adams, J. Q., II. 94–95, 226, 263
Aden, I. 334
Admirable et prodigieuse mort, II. 88
Admiral's Men, I. 298, II. 89–90
Admission Book, I. 67
Aeneas' Revenge, II. 64
Aeneid, I. 292, II. 56–63, 146, 176–178,
  184
Æschylus, I. 186
Affectionate Shepherd, II. 28, 37, 115,
  131, 159–160
Ailesbury, Thomas, I. 135
Alamanni, Luigi, II. 177
Alarum against Usurers, II. 31
Alarum for London, II. 285
Alderich, Simon, I. 119 ff.
Aldrich, Thomas, I. 122
Alexander and Campaspe, II. 155
Alexander, Peter, II. 217, 226
Alexander, Pope, I. 309
alexandrines, I. 310, II. 183–189
Aleyn, Thomas, I. 65
Ali-i-Yazdi, I. 229
Aljay Tūrkān Aghā, I. 230
Allde, John, I. 358
Allegro, II. 139, 159–160
Allen, John, I. 98 ff.
Allen, Thomas, I. 132
Alleyn, Edward: allusions in "Peele"
  letter, II. 295–296; Barabas, I. 194, 366,
  368; costume, II. 14; Faustus, I. 300–
  301; *Massacre*, II. 90; Tamburlaine, I.
  193–194, II. 17, 182
Alleyn Papers, II. 277
alliteration, II. 184, 200
Allott, Robert, II. 278
All Saints, Canterbury, I. 19
All's Well That Ends Well, II. 189

Almogaver, Juan Boscan, II. 103, 135
Almonry, I. 33, 45
Alphonsus, Emperor of Germany, II. 256
*Alphonsus, King of Aragon: Edward the
  Second*, II. 28, 39; *Jew of Malta*, I. 374;
  Tamburlaine, I. 248–252, II. 4, 242, 255
Amanda, II. 139
Ambassadors, I. 36. *See also* Walsingham,
  Sir Francis
Amintae Gaudia, II. 123
Amores, see Ovid
Amurath II, I. 233–236
Amyntas, I. 313
Anatomy of Melancholy, I. 122, II. 116,
  138
Anderson, Maxwell, I. 325
Andria, I. 353
Anecdotes of Rare Books, II. 275
Angel Inn, I. 166
angels, I. 286
Annals of the Turks, I. 215
Anne, Queen, I. 165, 178, II. 26
Antigone, I. 62
Anti-Machiavel, *see* Gentillet, Innocent
Antonio and Mellida, I. 241
Antony and Cleopatra, II. 181–182, 217,
  II. 255, 283
Antwerp, I. 276
Aplegate, Lawrence, I. 24–25
Apocrypha, *see* New Testament
Apologie for Actors, II. 207
apprentices, I. 23–25, 37
Arabian Nights, I. 358
Arabs, I. 368
Arcadius and Sepha, II. 116, 133–134, 140
Archer, Edward, I. 193
Archer, Francis, I. 151–152
Archer's play list, II. 96
Arden family, I. 11
Arden, Mary, I. 4
Arden of Feversham, I. 369, 374, II. 38, 73,
  269, 285–290
Aretino, Pietro, I. 127
Ariel, I. 286
Ariosto, Ludovico, I. 205, 209
Aristophanes, I. 186, 283, II. 102
Aristotle, I. 70, 133, II. 25, 60, 82, 203
Armada, I. 88
Armitage, Walter, I. 304
Arnim, L. Achim von, I. 320